The Man Who Made Movies: W.K.L. Dickson

The publication of this book has been made possible thanks to the cooperation of
Le Giornate del Cinema Muto (Pordenone, Italy).

William Kennedy Laurie Dickson

The Man Who Made Movies:
W.K.L. Dickson

Paul Spehr

British Library Cataloguing in Publication Data

The Man Who Made Movies: W.K.L. Dickson

A catalogue entry for this book is available from the British Library

ISBN: 9780 86196 695 0 (Hardback)

Published by
John Libbey Publishing Ltd, 3 Leicester Road, New Barnet, Herts EN5 5EW, United Kingdom e-mail: libbeyj@asianet.co.th; web site: www.johnlibbey.com

Orders: **Combined Academic Publishers Ltd.**, 15a Lewin's Yard, East Street, Chesham HP5 1HQ, United Kingdom
direct.orders@marston.co.uk   www.combinedacademic.co.uk

Distributed in North America by **Indiana University Press**, 601 North Morton St, Bloomington, IN 47404, USA. www.iupress.indiana.edu

Distributed in Australasia by **Elsevier Australia**, Elsevier Australia, Tower 1, 475 Victoria Ave, Chatswood NSW 2067, Australia. www.elsevier.com.au

Printed in Malaysia by Vivar Printing Sdn. Bhd., 48000 Rawang, Selangor Darul Ehsan

Contents

Introduction

The Man Who Made Movies

Through much of the twentieth century authors gave only passing attention to the first years of cinema. There were interviews with surviving pioneers, occasional disputes about who "invented" movies and efforts to promote national champions but by mid-century those interests faded. If the early years were talked about, it was often just a brief homage to recognized pioneers whose work seemed to anticipate the development of cinema as a serious "art". There were exceptions, of course, but in-depth coverage was unusual. This has changed. In recent years a global community of scholars has been studying and writing about the history and the social and cultural impact of the early years. They have discovered that what once seemed prosaic and incidental is actually a rich and fertile domain that offers new perspectives on the cultural and artistic forces that made the twentieth century so different from its predecessor.

Cinema was a new art and this is a book about it's beginning; actually, the beginning of the beginning; the emergence and introduction of cinema as we know it today. It examines this period through the work of William Kennedy Laurie Dickson, a central player in creating and shaping moving images as we know them. I have called him "the man who made movies" and while he was not *THE* man who made movies – many people share that credit – during cinema's earliest years few others contributed as much, as comprehensively as Mr. Dickson. He was an inventor, designer of studios, film producer, founder of production companies, journalist, historian, author and adventurer. His story is a perspective on cinema as it became a transforming force and international phenomenon.

My involvement with Dickson can be traced to the late 1950s when I began working with the motion picture collection at the Library of Congress. His films and others from the early years were an important part of the collection and working with them was both enjoyable and fascinating. My interest continued through my thirty-plus years at the Library. The immediate stimulus for this book was a never-realized exhibit to celebrate the centennial of the motion picture which we hoped to mount at the Library of Congress. Dickson's career seemed an interesting window on cinema's origins. The exhibit was tabled for lack of funding but I found the process of research stimulating and the material we gathered was so interesting that after retiring from the Library and completing another project, I returned to Dickson in the late 1990s. After ten years of digging, mulling about and writing, this book is the result.

Resources

Researching the early years is a detective game. The caches of material recording cinema's beginning years are rich and challenging. A surprising number of films from the period survive. Archives around the world have made a point of acquiring, preserving and making them available and the ability to see them has stimulated the revival of interest in the period. The films are short and silent so they demand context – an understanding of who, how, when and why. Providing context is a challenge but there is a wealth of surviving documentation: production records, catalogs of film distributors, articles and advertisements in newspapers and journals, correspondence, interviews with and articles by pioneers. To supplement these there are patent and copyright records, court documents from lawsuits, corporate records, etc. Working through these records requires patience, persistence and judgement – the movies attracted colorful individuals who had very loose notions about the nature of truth and honesty, Mr. Dickson being a conspicuous member of this group.

The records recording Mr. Dickson's career are scattered and uneven. The information about his work for Edison is rich and, indeed, almost too rich. Much of the documentation from Edison's laboratory survives and in recent years it has become readily accessible. But the search for his life before and after Edison required visits to many institutions in many locations and there are voids that I have been unable to fill. During the past decade I have been in Washington, DC, New York City, Boston, Philadelphia, Los Angeles, Richmond, Indiana, Canton, Ohio, Rochester and Canastota, NY, Iowa City, Iowa, Chicago, Dearborn, Michigan as well as West Orange, NJ. Abroad I have visited archives and libraries in London and Brighton, England, Paris and Jersey, in the Channel Islands.

I found precedence for this peripatetic activity in the rich collection of material compiled by Gordon Hendricks whose research for books on Thomas Eakins, Muybridge, Edison and Dickson are kept by the Archives Center, National Museum of American History, Smithsonian Institution, Washington, DC. Hendricks was a thorough and exhaustive researcher and I owe him a huge debt. It may be churlish to tread unkindly into his territory but recent scholarship and the passage of time have given new perspectives so it is time to revise his revisionist history of Edison and Dickson. His first book, *The Edison Motion Picture Myth*, is seriously flawed. It is difficult to read and he had a passionate dislike of Edison which led him to choose evidence selectively and make some unwarranted assumptions. Readers will find my version of Edison's contributions to his invention different from Hendricks –

though I have tried to avoid quarreling with him. Despite his flaws, Hendricks' research was exemplary and the time I spent with his material not only provided valuable documentation of the period but guided me to supplementary resources.

Thomas Edison's papers are better organized and more accessible than they were when Hendricks used them. When I began my research the Thomas A. Edison Papers project at Rutgers, The State University of New Jersey was well underway and during the past decade much of the collection has become readily available, first on microfilm through University Publications of America, then on line at http://edison.rutgers.edu. But the collection is so vast that the project staff is forced to be selective. In West Orange I found valuable supplementary material in documents that had not been processed. Of particular interest were employee pay records. These made it possible to document day-to-day work on the Kinetoscope and other projects. There were also purchase and order records that had not been copied. While I had a detailed record of activities at the lab, a crucial element was missing: Edison and his staff kept notebooks recording and dating their activities but only one of Dickson's notebooks survives and it is for work on ore separation. His notebooks recording work on the Kinetograph are missing, so speculation about some of his activities is unavoidable. Dickson claimed the notebooks were destroyed by staff at the Laboratory, but it is more likely that he took them and they were lost along with much of his other personal documentation. Hopefully they may appear someday and someone can revise my revisions.

Dickson left several first-hand accounts of his work. His sister Antonia was a musician and author who joined him in writing several articles about his work on the Kinetoscope/Kinetograph. The pair also wrote a biography of Edison. Dickson published his diary accounts of filming the Boer War and late in life he wrote an article summarizing his work for the Journal of the Society of Motion Picture Engineers. In common with most first hand accounts, these are self-serving and they are difficult to read because much of the writing is florid, but they provide valuable clues to Dickson's activities.

The record of Dickson's life after he left Edison's lab in April 1895 is inconsistent and scanty. The records of the American Mutoscope Company at the Museum of Modern Art document the establishment of the company, some key business activities and are particularly useful in documenting film production, but there is little about day-to-day activities. Accounts by participants, testimony in legal cases, newspaper and journal articles and research material gathered by predecessors are useful. I have been particularly aided by research, shared information and the generous encouragement of colleagues. Which leads to ...

Acknowledgements

I must begin with the staff of the Motion Picture, Broadcasting and Recorded Sound Division at the Library of Congress. They were and are my partners and co-workers whose friendship, experience, knowledge and enthusiasm have sustained me for years. I would like to list the entire staff but for consideration of space I will limit this to those closely involved in this research. Joseph Balian, Sam Brylawski, Gene DeAnna, David Francis, Rosemary Haines. Barbara Humphrys, Steve Leggett, Jan McKay, Mike Mashon, Madeline Matz, Calvin Morman, David Parker, David Reese, Pat Sheehan, Zoran Sinobad, Christopher Spehr, Ken Weissmann and George Willeman. Elsewhere in the Library I had invaluable help from the staff of the Manuscript Division, especially Mary Wolfskill, the Prints and Photographs Division, especially Maja Keech, the Newspaper Reading Room and the Rare Book Reading Room, with thanks to Clark Evans.

Washington, DC, my home base for many years, has splendid resources. Nicholas Sheetz at Georgetown University's Lauinger Library guided me through their Armat, Quigley and Ramsaye collections. At the National Archives John Butler, Robert Ellis, William Murphy, Les Waffen and Patty Young assisted with films, legal records and patent documents. I spent weeks pouring through the Gordon Hendricks and Eugene Lauste Collections at the Smithsonian's National Museum of American History and benefitted from assistance from David Haberstich, Wendy Shay, John Fleckner and Kay Peterson in the Archives Center and Michelle Delaney and Shannon Perich of Photographic History. John Hiller, now retired from Smithsonian's film production unit has been lovingly caring for the Smithsonian's marvelous collection of early motion picture equipment. John revealed the mysteries of cameras and projectors to this neophyte.

I spent weeks in a room at Edison's laboratory in West Orange, NJ where Edison sometimes worked and where George Tselos and Doug Tarr gave me help and guidance to the collections of the Edison National Historic Site. More recently Leonard DeGraaf gave welcome assistance. I must also acknowledge the work of Harold Anderson and Norman Speiden who were caring for the collections when I visited the lab in the 1960s and 1970s. The Thomas A. Edison Papers Project has been supervised by Reese Jenkins and Paul Israel whose dedicated and capable staff have been responsible for making this remarkable resource so much more accessible. I owe Charles Musser a warm thank you not only for his invaluable research and perceptive writing about Edison and the other pioneers, but for generously supplying illustrations for this book.

The staff of the Film Department of the Museum of Modern Art has been both helpful and supportive. I owe particular thanks to Charles Silver, Ron Magliozzi, Eileen Bowser, Mary Lee Bandy, Steven Higgins, Ann Morra, Peter Williamson and Mary Corliss. I must also acknowledge help from staff at several other institutions: at Baker Library, Harvard University: Barbara Dailey, Laura Linard and Al Bartovics; at the Franklin Institute, Philadelphia: Virginia Ward and Irene Coffey; at the Margaret Herrick Library of the Academy of Motion Picture Arts & Sciences in Beverley Hills: Linda Mayer; Sam Gill and Barbara Hall; at George Eastman House, Rochester, NY: Paolo

Cherchi-Usai, Ed Stratmann and Patrick Loughney; The Henry Ford Musem, Dearborn, Michigan: Carol Ann Missant; Canal Town Museum, Canastota, NY: Rose Raffa and Joe DiGigorgio; The Seaver Center, Los Angeles County Museum of Natural History: John M. Cahoon; University of Iowa Library, Iowa City: Robert McCown; Wayne County Historical Museum, Richmond, Indiana: Michele Bottorff; and at Historic Petersburg (VA) Foundation: Pam Covil.

Rob Gibson, of Gibson's Photographic Gallery in nearby Gettysburg gave me a practical demonstration of collodion photography, a technique he uses to provides to visitors to the Civil War battlefield with authentic photographs reminiscent of the era.

A number of colleagues made it possible for me to make maximum use of very limited time during visits abroad. They generously exchanged information, shared research and gave invaluable guidance to resources. In England Barry Anthony and Richard Brown shared information gained researching their book on the British Mutoscope companies and Barry guided me to documentation on Dickson's life in London; Stephen Bottomore guided me through journals and other periodicals and shared his encyclopedic knowledge of the period including his ground breaking research on war and the cinema; Deac Rossell shared his insights and understanding of early cinema especially the technology of the period; Frank Gray gave me early access to Emile Lauste's papers at the Southeast Film and Video Archive in Brighton and shared his insights and enthusiasm for the period. Others providing help and support are: Tony Fletcher, Luke McKernan, John Barnes, David Robinson and Stephen Herbert. Dr. E.S. Leedham-Green of the University Archives, University of Cambridge provided information on matriculation at the University and N.M. Plumley, Curator and Archivist of Christ's Hospital, Horsham provided details on the education of Dickson's son John Forbes Laurie-Dickson. In France, Jean-Jacques Meusy, my co-author in an article on the French Mutoscope company and Laurent Mannoni, Cinémathèque française have provided priceless help and guidance. At the Bibliothèque du Film, Valdo Kneubühler, Nadine Tenéze and Delphine Warin not only gave generous assistance, they helped me report the theft of a credit card and I am greatly in their debt. M. Françis Heugel generously welcomed me at Manoir St. Buc, Mr. Dickson's birthplace near Le Minihic-sur-Rance and shared information about the house; Pascal Gautier, Mémorialiste près de la Société Archéologique, Pleurtuit, gave additional information on Château St. Buc; Michel Mauger, Services d'Archives, Rennes provided Dickson's registration of birth. In Jersey, Channel Islands, Mary M. Billot and Sally Knight were my helpful assistants at Société Jersiaise, Lord Coutanche Library, Société Jersiaise, St. Helier.

Finally, I must recognize the good hearted consideration and support that I have received from my wife, Susan Dalton who remained encouraging through the many days, weeks and months that Mr. Dickson has demanded my attention.

Part I

Introducing Mr. Dickson

Chapter 1

Family Matters

"I was born Aug. 3rd 1860 of Scotch parents at the old chateau of St Buc, Minihic on the picturesque River Rance near Dinan, France – When old enough we traveled much in many lands absorbing the French, German Italian languages, then returned to England for that part of my Education with instructions in science."[1]

He was William Kennedy Laurie Dickson. The name was important! He was never Bill, Billy or even William, and certainly not Will – or Willy. At work he was William Kennedy Laurie or W.K.L., but usually just "Dickson", or "Mr. D.". His family apparently knew him as Laurie. When Edison wrote notes to him he almost always addressed them to "Dixon" – perhaps to take him down a peg. His fellow Brit, Samuel Insull once referred to him as the "Right Honorable" William Kennedy Laurie Dickson.[2] About 1900 he added a hyphen between the two middle names and became William Kennedy-Laurie. In late life he moved the hyphen and became Laurie-Dickson, the form that appears on his death certificate. But though the hyphen moved, the full roster of names remained.

As all of this attention to names indicates, the family heritage they represent was important to him. "Dickson", of course, came from his father, James Waite Dickson, a painter and lithographer, who, the family claimed, numbered Hogarth and Judge Waite, one of the judges who sentenced King Charles I to death, among his ancestors. "Kennedy" and "Laurie" were the legacy of his mother, Elizabeth Kennedy-Laurie Dickson, who listed among her antecedents the Lauries of Maxwellton, celebrated in the ballad *Annie Laurie*, as well as the Robertsons, of Strowan, related to the Earl of Cassilis, the Duke of Athol, and the Royal Stuarts.[3] Heritage and blue blood made little difference for Dickson in his work for Edison, but may, in fact, have been useful during his years spent producing films in England and on the continent as rank and station aided negotiations with military officers, politicians and representatives of royalty.

As stated above, William Kennedy Laurie was born in France at Château St. Buc near the Breton village of Le Minihic-sur-Rance at 3:00 a.m., 3 August 1860. His birth was registered at Le Minihic by

1   Bibliothèque du Film, Fonds Will Day (hereafter BiFi Fonds Will Day), W.K.L. Dickson to Will Day, 20 June 1933.

2   Edison National Historic Site, West Orange, N. J. (hereafter EHS). A note written 5 July 1888.

3   W.K.L. and Antonia Dickson, *History of the Kinetograph, Kinetoscope and Kineto-Phonograph* ([New York], Albert Bunn, 1895) p. 54. Citing W.E. Woodbury, *American Annual of Photograph*. Undoubtedly the information was supplied by W.K.L Dickson.

*The Château St. Buc near Le Minihic-sur-Rance, Brittany where W.K.L. Dickson was born. James
Dickson was at château St. Buc through Mme. Colin de la Béllière who inherited the estate from her
brother, le Chamoine Françoise Hay, a prominent eclesiastic and an amateur artist who was a close
collaborator of l'abbé Jean-Marie de Lamennais, founder of the Brothers of Plöermel, a teaching
congregation established in Brittany at the beginning of the 20th century. This photo was probably taken
by W.K.L. Dickson in the late 1890s or early 1900s. [NMAH Hendricks.]*

Mayor Gaubert and witnessed by Jean Marie Lecharpentier, a gardener
living at the château and by Julien Lemasson, verger. The registration
listed his father's age as fifty and his mother's as thirty-seven and
referred to both parents as "propriétaire domicilié au château".[4] A
census a year later in 1861 recorded that William Kennedy Laurie was
James Dickson's fifth child and the only male child in the family. The
older sisters were Dora, thirteen, Hanna, twelve, Antonia Eugénie,
seven and Linda, three. Another sister, Eva, was born 3 March 1865, in
Dinan, France. Dickson's mother, Elizabeth, was James' second wife
and, apparently, the two older girls, Dora and Hanna were half sisters
while Antonia, Linda and Eva were full sisters.[5]

Beyond these fairly firm records from the early 1860s, there is only
sketchy information about Dickson's childhood. Although Dickson
said that both of his parents were Scottish, his mother was, apparently,
not born in Scotland. Her burial record gave her birthplace as Chesterfield County, Virginia. There is no apparent record of his father's birth,
but using the information from W.K.L. Dickson's birth registration that
he was 50 years old in August 1860, he would have been born about
1809 or 1810, presumably in Scotland or England. There is a remote
possibility that James Dickson might have been born in the United
States. There were Dicksons living and working in Virginia in the early
19th century, including a John Dickson who was editor of the *Petersburg
Intelligencer*, a newspaper in Petersburg, Virginia. Chesterfield County,
where Elizabeth Kennedy-Laurie was apparently born c. 1823, is the

4   A copy of the
registration was
provided by Michel
Mauger, Directions
des Services
d'Archives, Conseil
Général d'Ille et
Vilaine, 20, Ave. Jules
Ferry, 35700 Rennes,
France.

5   Per census
records (A.D.I.V. 6 M
336) for the year
1861, also from
Service d'Archives,
Rennes. Robert M.
Pleasants, the son of
Eva Dickson
Pleasants, told
historian Gordon
Hendricks that his
Grandfather Dickson
was married twice
and that his
Grandmother
Elizabeth was the
second wife.

These portraits are from a collection of photographs belonging to W. K. L. Dickson that were given to Gordon Hendricks by Ms. Kathleen Polson, a former neighbor of Mr. Dickson's. They were probably made by Dickson' father, James Dickson and Ms. Polson speculated that one might be a portrait of Dickson's mother and the others may be ancestors. [NMAH Hendricks.]

county situated between Petersburg and Richmond, Virginia located 23 miles north of Petersburg. If the Dicksons lived for a while in the area, they might well have been acquainted with a family of fellow Scots. Though it is pure speculation, this might explain how two people who were apparently so widely separated geographically came to marry. As we shall see, William Kennedy Laurie and his two sisters Antonia and Eva were very much attached to this area of Virginia, even though they did not live there until they were young adults.

W.K.L. Dickson said that his father was an artist specializing in miniatures and lithographs who was also interested in astronomy and the study of dead languages. His mother was "... a brilliant scholar, musician, and renowned for her beauty ...".[6] The record of James Dickson's career as an artist is, to say the least, skimpy. In 1842, a J. Dickson, 3 Bentinck Terrace, London, a miniature painter exhibited "Portrait of a Lady, Portrait of a Gentleman; Portrait of a Lady" at the Royal Academy Exhibition and in 1850 J. Dickson exhibited "Italian Peasant Girl" also at the Royal Academy Exhibition. Photographs of paintings that at least match the titles of the three portraits from 1842 were among the photographs belonging to Dickson that historian Gordon Hendricks acquired from a former neighbor of Dickson in Twickenham, England.[7] Beyond this, we must rely on Dickson's information about his father.

Other than these scant references there is little, if any, indication that James Dickson made a lasting impression on the art world, but skill in drawing, perspective and composition were talents he passed on to his son and there is ample evidence of these skills in W.K.L.'s drawings, photographs and films. Dickson also inherited musical talent, apparently from his mother. He played the violin in amateur performances in Virginia and New Jersey and was reported to have a pleasing tenor voice which he occasionally displayed in concert.

6   Dicksons, Op. Cit.

7   I am indebted to Barry Anthony for finding the references to J. Dickson's exhibition. The Dickson photographs are in the Gordon Hendricks Collection, National Museum of American History, Smithsonian Institution. Hereafter, NMAH Hendricks.

This photo was annotated in Dickson's hand: "Market Day/Place du Gucklin". It was taken in Dinan, near Dickson's birthplace and it is likely that the young lad is Dickson. On a visit to Brittany in 2000 I was startled to look out my hotel window and realize that I was looking at the corner in this photo. [NMAH Hendricks.]

Dickson's birthplace, St. Buc, is a handsome manor house located outside the village of Le Minihic-sur-Rance on the north coast of Brittany. It is on the west side of the river Rance about midway between Dinan and Dinard. The estate of St. Buc is inland from the river, but within walking distance of the village's small harbor area. The Rance is very broad and subject to remarkably extreme tides, which are now partially controlled by a dam across the mouth between Dinard and St. Malo. It is not too far from one of France's premiere tourist attractions, Mont St. Michel. Le Minihic is a pleasant village located on a rise above the river and there are splendid vistas along the river and to the west there are prosperous looking farm areas. The town is by-passed by most of the major roads in the area and it has no special qualities to attract tourists so it is quiet and very much off the beaten path, but it is not far to either Dinard, a lively and picturesque market town, or St. Malo, a major sea port and trading center.

It is not clear what the family was doing in Le Minihic or how long they remained there. They were not listed in residence at St. Buc in the census records that survive in Rennes for 1856 or 1866 and the marriage of James and Elizabeth Dickson apparently took place elsewhere because it was not recorded at Le Minihic. Among the photographs that Gordon Hendricks acquired are two made by Dickson that he captioned in his own hand as being his birthplace in St. Buc, one is an attractive picture of the impressive manor house, the other is of a much more modest cottage attached to the main house. It is not clear which house the Dicksons occupied – whether as the principal occupants or as a

A photo of St. Malo, near Château St. Buc, taken by W.K.L. Dickson about 1898.
[NMAH Hendricks.]

secondary residents. The specification on the birth certificate that both his mother and father were "propriétaire" indicates that each of them had property or independent income. The 1861 census entry for Elizabeth Dickson also classified her as "rentière", another indication of independent means – but how much and how independent? As we shall see, in later life, Dickson complained that he was poor and dependent upon others for financial support, yet there are hints that in his youth if his family was not well off, they were at least quite comfortable.

Apparently both of his parents were well educated and Dickson received a very broadly based education, apparently patterned on the Victorian conception of the Renaissance ideal. In addition to training in art, letters and music, he was skilled at languages, an avid amateur photographer and well trained in science. He told film pioneer and historian Will Day that when old enough "... we traveled much in many lands absorbing the French, German Italian languages ...".[8] He probably lived for a while in Germany while his older sister, Antonia, studied at music conservatories in Leipzig and Stuttgart. He seems to have finished his education in England where, in addition to his training in music and art, he added enough skill in science, with a speciality in electricity, to qualify him for work with Edison's electrical specialists.

Beyond this rather general sketch, there is very little specific information about Dickson's childhood. The family vanished during most of the 1870s, emerging from the shadow in February, 1879, when

8   BiFi Fonds Will Day. Dickson to Will Day, 20 June 1933.

18 year old William Kennedy Laurie wrote a letter to "Mr. Eddison [sic]" asking for employment for "... a friendless and fatherless boy". He said that he did not have Edison's talents and was willing to start at the bottom of the ladder. He had "... patience, perseverance, an ardent love of science, and above all a firm reliance on God".

"I ... have had a good English education, can speak French and German, being born on the Continent, have a fair knowledge of accounts, and draw well. For all these things, I have certificates from the Cambridge Examiner ... I am neat handed and inventive, and have already constructed, or attempted to construct ... [an] electric bell, worked by two Bunsens, two Micro Telephone transmitters, a couple of switches, four Leclanches, etc. I also gained a prize for the best model of the Tabernacle in the Wilderness at school last year."[9]

There is no record in the University Archives at Cambridge that W.K.L. Dickson or W.K. Laurie-Dickson passed the Cambridge Examinations in the late 1870s, so this may be an untruth told to impress Edison. However, the roll of students examined and approved in the Michaelmas Term 1877 and the Easter Term of 1877 include a "Dixon", listed without a first name and with no college affiliation. Dr. E.S. Leedham-Green, Assistant Keeper of the Archives told me that this might indicate a student not enrolled full time but taking the examination anyway. The family name was important and Dickson was fussy about his heritage and identity, but it is possible that an error was made by the University records turning Dickson into Dixon. This happened frequently during his life. If this is the case, the University would have examined Dickson in Greek. In 1877 it was Mark's Gospel in Greek and Greek classic, a selection from Lucian; and a Latin classic, Terence: *Heauton timoroumenos*, as well as a paper in Greek and Latin Grammar. This was for Part I, the Michaelmas Term. For Part II, the Easter term, it was Paley, Euclid, Arithmetic and Algebra. A rather full plate for a lad of 16 or 17, but quite impressive if he did pass it.[10]

The family's view of a liberal education defied the stereotype of Victorian sexism. His sisters were also well educated. Dickson's older sister, Antonia was a child prodigy, a pianist who reportedly performed with an orchestra in Leipzig at the age of 12, playing from memory and after completing studies at the conservatories in Leipzig and Stuttgart she performed in concert in France, Scotland and at the Crystal Palace. She completed her musical education at the music conservatory at Trinity College, London. In January 1879 she was made an associate of the College of Organists, the only woman to pass the examination and only the third woman to be made an associate. The family claimed that her performance was praised by Sir Julius Benedict, conductor of the Liverpool Philharmonic who also conducted at Covent Garden and Drury Lane. Antonia was particularly close to William Kennedy Laurie and their life-long relationship and her intense devotion to the cultural life had a strong influence on him. She never married and lived with "Laurie" throughout her life. In addition to performing skills, she composed music, lectured on musical history and theory, wrote essays

9 EHS. The letter is reproduced in its entirety in Gordon Hendricks' *The Edison Motion Picture Myth*, pp. 144–145 (hereafter Hendricks ... *Myth*).

10 Letter, Dr. E.S. Leedham-Green, 4 November, 1996.

and poetry and collected rare manuscripts. At seventeen her first published work appeared in *Chamber's Journal* and she became a frequent contributor.[11] She was co-author with William Kennedy Laurie of a biography of Edison and a small book on the invention of the Kinetoscope-Kinetograph.

By February 1879, when he wrote to Mr. "Eddison" the family had shrunk to four: W.K.L., his mother, Antonia and Eva. Dickson's father was dead, but it is not clear when he died, though he had probably been dead for a year or more. The two older half-sisters, Dora and Hanna probably remained in England. Hanna was living in Chester, England in 1913 when she appeared on the list of stockholders for a company Dickson formed. She apparently never married because she was listed as Hannah Dickson, "Spinster". At least one sister apparently married because Dickson made references to nieces and a nephew in Australia at various times in later life. The third sister, Linda, died though the date is not clear. In the nineteenth century the death of young children was a tragedy suffered by many families. Her name never appears in Dickson's comments about his life but it was mentioned in Antonia's obituary.[12]

While it may seem like a foolish, boyish error for Dickson to address his application for employment to Mr. Eddison, his mistake was probably an honest one. It is likely that he had read an article, "Cet étonnant Eddison" (This astonishing Edison) which appeared in the Paris newspaper, *Figaro* in 1878. It reported that the Paris Exhibition had the celebrated "Eddison's" latest invention, the stupendous aerophone, "It is a steam machine which carries the voice a distance of eight kilometres. You speak in the jet of vapor "a friend previously warned understands readily words at a distance of two leagues. Let us add that the friend can answer you by the same method ...". Dickson mentioned this article in a biographical piece about Edison which he co-wrote with his sister in *Cassier's Magazine*, March 1893. Edison biographer, Frank Dyer, was particularly incensed about *Figaro's* article which he cited as an example of the work of "yellow Journalists" who were creating the "Edison myth". He quoted the article: "'It should be understood', said this journal, 'that Mr. Eddison does not belong to himself. He is the property of the telegraph company which lodges him in New York at a superb hotel; keeps him on a luxurious footing, and pays him a formidable salary so as to be the one to know of and profit by his discoveries. The company has, in the dwelling of Eddison, men in its employ who do not quit him for a moment, at the table, on the street, in the laboratory. So that this wretched man, watched more closely than ever was any malefactor, cannot even give a moment's thought to his own private affairs without one of his guards asking him what he is thinking about.'"[13] Despite, or perhaps because of, this ominous implication of luxurious captivity Dickson pushed ahead with his application.

Edison responded promptly – and negatively – on 4 March 1879. It was a letter that Dickson later called as a "cold douche".[14] The four Dicksons sailed to the U.S. anyway, arriving in Virginia at the end of

11 *Chamber's Journal*, 1901, pp. 55–56. An obituary tribute written by the editor. "Miss Antonia Dickson, who possessed a versatile literary gift, besides being an old contributor to our columns, was a friend of the present Editor and of his father and predecessor in the editorial chair. We do not hesitate to say that as a pianist, the subject of this sketch was one of the most amazing and brilliant of the many whom it has been our privilege to listen to ...". I am indebted to Luke McKernan who found this article and forwarded it to me.

12 Ibid.

13 *Cassier's Magazine*, March, 1893, pp. 375–376; Frank Dyer, *Edison: His Life and Inventions*, pp. 211–212.

14 BiFi Fonds Will Day. Dickson to Day, 20 June 1933; W.K.L. Dickson, "A Brief History of the Kinetograph, the Kinetoscope and the Kineto-phonograph" *Journal of the SMPE*, Vol. 21, December 1933, p. 9.

This pastel of a young girl is the only surviving original art work by James Dickson. It was acquired by Gordon Hendricks from Ms. Polson who got it from Dickson's adopted son. Hendricks believed that it was a portrait of Antonia made in June, 1865. However, the pencil marking on the drawing could be January or June, 1860. The age of the young girl would make 1860 more likely since Antonia was born c. 1854 and her sister Eva would have been too young in 1865. [NMAH Hendricks.]

May on the Old Dominion Steamship Line after traveling by way of New York in what Dickson called a stormy crossing. Although Dickson claimed he persuaded his mother and two sisters to come to the U.S. in spite of Edison's discouraging letter, it is unlikely that the family's decision really hinged on Edison's response. The Dicksons arrived in the Richmond area 28 June 1879, and stayed at a hotel in Manchester, Virginia, a community on the south side of the James River, across from Richmond. Manchester has now been incorporated into the city of Richmond. About four weeks after their arrival, Dickson's mother died of "gastric fever" in nearby Petersburg, Virginia. The state of his mother's health seems a much more probable reason that the family

This photo of a young man with a violin may be a picture of Dickson. The violin was a companion in his later life. (NMAH Hendricks)

moved to Virginia. Her death notice in the *Richmond Daily Dispatch,* 1 July 1879, said she died after a long illness. As we have seen, despite conflicting information, Virginia seems to have been Mrs. Dickson's birthplace and apparently there was family and, perhaps, some property in Virginia.

The three Dicksons seemed to like Virginia. Dickson referred to Virginians as "Gods [sic] own people" in a letter to Will Day outlining these early years.[15] After their mother's death, the three Dicksons remained in Virginia. At the time of their mother's death they were living just south of Manchester at Chesterfield Courthouse. By 1882 they were in Petersburg living at a house known as Strawberry Hill.[16]

Petersburg was a prosperous commercial city of about 18,000 on the Appomattox River, near the junction with the James River. During the 19th century it was a port city, shipping tobacco and cotton. It was also an important transportation hub with several rail lines and highways intersecting the city. It was the site of a prolonged, epic siege during the Civil War. The Confederate Army of Northern Virginia under the command of General Robert E. Lee defended the city with a perimeter of fortifications that surrounded the city against a steady assault by the Army of the Potomac commanded by General Ulysses S. Grant. The siege, which lasted from June 1864 until April 1865, was the last major defense of the Confederacy. It was a nasty campaign of

15 Ibid.

16 Ibid., Dickson to Day, 20 June 1933; Gordon Hendricks, *Myth ...*, pp. 146–147. Hendricks cites an article in the "Manchester and Vicinity" section of *Richmond Daily Dispatch*, 30 May 1879 which reported "A family from England arrived at the Chesterfield Hotel yesterday and will spend the summer at that place". We are indebted to Hendricks for most of the information about the Dickson's life in Virginia.

attrition and trench warfare that seemed to predict the brutal warfare of the twentieth century. The fall of Petersburg led directly to General Lee's surrender at Appomattox on 9 April 1865, the end of the war and the death of the dream of an independent Southern Confederacy.

Although the war was fifteen years in the past at the time of the Dicksons' arrival, mementos of the conflict would have been very evident. The city was rebuilt, commerce revived and social life active, but the residents who survived the siege would have had strong memories of their experiences. There is little information about the activities of the three Dicksons from 1879 until 1882, but newspaper reports from 1882 tell of an active social life, though they give no hint that William Kennedy Laurie was employed or how the "orphaned" trio subsisted. On 28 April 1882 Antonia played and Eva sang at concert in Petersburg. On 7 June 1882, the *Petersburg Daily-Index* reported a social gathering hosted by the Dicksons: "Tableaux Vivants. The friends of the Misses Dickson and their brother, enjoyed a very delightful little entertainment last evening, at their residence, Strawberry Hill ... The evening was in every way a delightful one". In August they vacationed at Mountain Lake in Giles County, Virginia. The report in the *Daily-Index* commented "The Misses Dickson and brother are here from Scotland, though natives of France. The senior sister, only twenty-six years old, has given piano concerts in Great Britain, Germany and France, and has received honors from celebrated musical institutions of Europe. Miss Eva, eighteen years old, has a superb voice, and expects soon to make her *début* in New York. The brother accompanies his sisters with a fine tenor, and is also given to the pencil art."

But life in Virginia was more than performance and salon entertainment. Although his interest in music and "the pencil art" implies a pallid existence, Dickson also enjoyed the outdoors and the vigor and challenge of what Teddy Roosevelt would later call the "strenuous life". At some time during their stay in Virginia, Dickson visited the Natural Bridge where he claimed that he discovered three large caverns. While exploring one of them he was trapped in by a cave-in. Rock debris fell all around him and he survived for three days before he was rescued. He would later claim that he was elected a Fellow of the Royal Geographic Society for this accomplishment, though I was assured by the Society that one could become a fellow without being recognized for some exploit of discovery.[17]

Eva Dickson was not the only one hoping for a debut in New York City. Late in 1882 or very early in 1883 the three Dicksons moved to New York City where W. Kennedy Laurie applied again for work with Thomas Edison. Although their stay in Virginia was relatively short, only about three and a half years, the Dicksons established long-term ties to Virginia. Dickson and his sister Eva both returned to Petersburg a few years later to marry, cementing ties established during this Southern idyl.

17 NMAH Hendricks. The obituary for W.K.L. Dickson, *Thames Valley Times*, 2 October 1935. Dickson is undoubtedly the source of this story and no contemporary accounts confirm it.

Part II

1883–1888
With Edison, Electricity and Iron Ore

Chapter 2

Goerck Street

"We orphened [sic] youngsters made for New York City 1881, as soon as we were settled, I took my book of credentials to show Mr. Edison at H.Q. 65 5th Av. should I be lucky to get this interview which I did – my reception was unique. 'But I told you not to come didnt [sic] I?' I agreed, but told him I couldnt [sic] do otherwise after reading what work he was engaged in – He watched my face while turning my testamonials [sic] over, until I had to remind him to please read them. He only replied 'I reckon they are all right you had better take off your coat and get to work –' I had won." W.K.L. Dickson to Will Day, 20 June 1933[18]

This is a fanciful account, embellished by age, pride and instinct. The interview with Edison – if it took place – happened in 1883. Dickson was careless about dating events, sometimes through error, sometimes deliberately. He found it very easy to stretch the truth – and yes, even to lie. By the 1890s he was already claiming he began work for Edison in 1881, though it is almost certain that he started working for Edison early in 1883, probably in April. Late in March 1883, probably 28 March, Dickson sent a note to Edison's private secretary, Samuel Insull:

"Having called several times & finding you out I take the liberty of writing you to ask you to make an appointment with Mr. Edison for me so that I can present a letter of introduction & have an interview with him some day this week that he may have a few moments of Leisure."[19]

He had a letter of introduction from Raymond Sayer, an artist who had done some work for Edison and was, presumably, acquainted with him. He introduced Dickson as "... a talented young man speaking German and French fluently & and has studied electricity".

This time his application was well timed. Edison was hiring – and it is possible Dickson knew it. In 1879 when Dickson first applied, Edison was planning to close down his laboratory in Menlo Park. In his response, Edison had told him he was not hiring because he expected "... to close my works for at least 2 years, as soon as I have finished experiments with the electric light". In a nutshell, this is what happened. Late in 1879, after achieving success in designing the light bulb, Edison began closing down his experimental work at Menlo Park and he established businesses to profit from his experimentation. By 1883

18 Fonds Will Day, BiFi. A cleaned-up version of this story appears in "A Brief History of the Kinetograph, the Kinetoscope and the Kineto-Phonograph", Dickson's description of his work in *Journal of the SMPE*, Vol. 21, December 1933.

19 EHS, Emp. Appls (1883-03–28).

these businesses were growing and Edison was adding rather than reducing staff. Dickson was hired and sent to the Testing Room of Edison Machine Works located on Goerck St. in New York City. His workplace was almost underneath the almost completed Brooklyn Bridge.

The enterprise that Edison envisioned was a complete system for electric lighting: a generating plant, a system for distributing power and the installation of wires, sockets and bulbs in businesses and homes – though businesses were his first objective. Edison took out patent after patent for various facets of electric lighting – for incandescent lamps and their manufacture, systems for distributing power, dynamos as well as related items such as sockets, switches, meters, underground conductors, parts, etc.[20] From 1880 through 1883 he set up several companies to implement these plans: The Edison Lamp Company to make light bulbs, The Edison Machine Works to manufacture dynamos and The Edison Tube Company for the manufacture of underground distribution equipment. At first, light bulbs were manufactured in Menlo Park but as demand grew Edison moved the operation to a former oil cloth factory in East Newark (now Harrison), New Jersey. He bought the former Roach Iron Works at 104 Goerck Street in New York City and began to make dynamos and other major mechanisms there. Tubes for underground wiring were made at a rented building on Washington Street in New York and he entrusted the making of lamps, brackets, sockets, meters and other related equipment to Bergmann & Company an existing business organized by Sigmund Bergmann, a friend and former employee. Bergmann made sockets, fixtures, meters, safety fuses, and related items in a loft on Wooster Street, New York. By 1883 Edison was spending almost all of his time in New York City and Menlo Park was gradually closed.[21]

To launch these enterprises, Edison sold his lighting patent to a large parent company, The Edison Electric Lighting Company and although he was, for a while, the largest shareholder, he did not hold a controlling interest and he found himself contending with financial movers and shakers whose objectives were quite different from his own.

A separate company, The Edison Electric Illuminating Company, built and operated the Pearl Street facility, the pilot municipal lighting system which introduced electric lighting. It began operation on Monday, 4 September 1882 at 3:00 pm. Only a small part of Manhattan had lights when Dickson started to work.

The parent organization, the Edison Electric Lighting Company did not want to take on the management and expense of making the elements of the lighting system which gave Edison the opportunity to organize the four manufacturing companies. While Edison had to borrow, mortgage and sell assets in order to establish these companies, he was able, for a while at least, to maintain control over them. He placed day-to-day management in the hands of trusted lieutenants who had worked for him. Day-to-day money management was handled by Samuel Insull, who came from England in 1881 to serve as Edison's

20 Frank Dyer, *Edison, His Life and Inventions*, p. 343. Dyer says that Edison took out 375 patents for electric lighting systems between 1880 and 1908.

21 Tate, Op. Cit.

private secretary. This allowed Edison to be involved in business affairs while paying particular attention to producing a marketable product – one that was both efficient and affordable.

One of Edison's particular skills was an ability to rework an invention into an economical product that worked well at a cost that made it practical for general use. Edison used the manufacture of lamps as an example of this principle:

"... The first year the lamps cost us about $1.10 each. We sold them for forty cents; but there were only about twenty or thirty thousand of them. The next year they cost us about seventy cents, and we sold them for forty. There were a good many, and we lost more money the second year than the first. The third year I succeeded in getting up machinery and in changing the processes, until it got down so that they cost somewhere around fifty cents. I still sold them for forty cents, and lost more money that year than any other, because the sales were increasing rapidly. The fourth year I got it down to thirty-seven cents, and I made all the money up in one year that I had lost previously. I finally got it down to twenty-two cents, and sold them for forty cents; and they were made by the million. Whereupon the Wall Street people thought it was a very lucrative business, so they concluded they would like to have it, and bought us out."[22]

By 1883 the Edison Electric Light Company was still setting up operations and was not profitable. When the Pearl Street Station opened in September it supplied about 400 lights. By the end of December there were over 240 customers wired for over 5000 lamps.[23] The four companies that Edison controlled, which supplied Pearl Street and future installations, were expanding and beginning to show a profit.

Goerck Street

"He there & then gave me a note to Mr. Ch. Clarke (Chief Mathematician) and another to Mr. W.S. Andrews Superintendent of the Technical part of the Edison Elec Light works Goerck St – Where under his able & kindly tutilage [sic] I secured a good knowledge of what was wanted – the following year W.S. Andrews gave me his place approved of by Edison while Andrews went throughout the States erecting Elec. Light & power stations – he was a man of extraordinary ability & knowledge –" (Dickson to Will Day, 20 June 1933)[24]

22 Dyer, Op. Cit., pp. 356–357.

23 Dyer, Op. Cit., pp. 403–407 and A.O. Tate, *Edison's Open Door*, p. 47. Prior to the opening of Pearl Street a small lighting system was opened in Appleton, Wisconsin in August, 1882 and some private installations had been sold to companies and wealthy individuals.

24 Fonds Will Day, BiFi.

William Kennedy Laurie Dickson began work in the Testing Room of the Edison Machine Works on Goerck Street. The manager of the Machine Works was Charles Dean and the supervisor of the Testing Room and Dickson's immediate supervisor was William S. Andrews. Andrews was an Englishman who had been Headmaster of Cunzer's Collegiate Academy at Beckington, England, before migrating to Canada in 1875. He joined Edison at Menlo Park where he experimented on armatures and lights under supervision of John Kruesi, one of Edison's most trusted and skilled machinist-experimenters. Andrews helped Edison develop the three wire system which made home wiring practical. When Edison's trusted assistant Francis Jehl went to Europe in February 1882, Andrews was put in charge of the Testing Room at the Machine Works. Charles Dean was a long-time employee whose relationship with Edison apparently went back to Milan, Ohio, Edison's birthplace. Dean had worked for Edison since his days in Newark, NJ before he moved to Menlo Park. A skilled machinist, he was a large imposing man, but he had a reputation for hard drinking. Charles L. Clarke was the chief engineer of the Edison Electric Light Company who made most of the design drawings.[25]

The Brooklyn Bridge, which opened in May, 1883, was the most impressive thing in an otherwise bleak neighborhood. In Dickson's words, the "... shop was grim of aspect, not over clean, and located in an uninviting portion of the great metropolis ...".[26] The streets were lined with old buildings and poor tenements. Sometimes when Edison went there at night he was escorted by Jim Russell, a detective familiar with "... all the denizens of the place". Frank Dyer quoted Edison: "We used to go out at night to a little low place, an all-night house – eight feet wide and twenty-two feet long – where we got a lunch at two or three o'clock in the morning. It was the toughest kind of restaurant ever seen. For the clam chowder they used the same four clams during the whole season, and the average number of flies per pie was seven. This was by actual count." Edison depended on the good graces of the local Tammany leader to help keep the site safe.[27]

The shop produced the heavy equipment needed for lighting installations, chiefly the electric generators, which Edison called dynamos. They were the key element for Edison's system. In March 1883, the shop was producing at least six different dynamos along with the pulleys, armatures and switchboards required for installation. Andrews and his crew were testing dynamos to evaluate and improve them. In addition to checking the shop's finished products from the Testing Room, they occasionally appraised other Edison products.

At the time that Dickson was hired, Edison had become discouraged with the quality of the new "electricians" joining his staff. Most had limited electrical experience such as installing doorbells and burglar alarms or doing elementary work in telegraphy or telephone. Although he had a reputation as a self – or home – educated wizard, Edison decided that he needed to set up a formal training program for his new electricians. He contacted Columbia College, the Cooper Institute in New York City as well as the Stevens Institute in nearby New Jersey. He also considered Cornell University who contacted him when they learned of his plans. After some consideration, he decided to use his own facilities and put E.H. Johnson in charge with additional instruction from Charles Clarke. At first they anticipated teaching at Goerck Street but apparently decided to do it at the headquarters at 65 Fifth Avenue, though some classes may have been held in the Testing Room while Dickson was there.

Dickson never mentioned receiving training from Edison, but he credited Andrews with giving him a secure start "... his executive skill, gently yet forcibly exercised, went far toward smoothing the path of his successor [Dickson]". Despite its grim surroundings and utilitarian atmosphere, Goerck Street had a positive side. Dickson enjoyed the

25 Francis Jehl, *Menlo Park Reminiscences*, Vol. 2, Dearborn, The Edison Institute, 1938, pp. 676–677; Edison Historic Site, card file EHS and Edison Pioneers obit.

26 Antonia & W.K.L. Dickson, "The Life and Inventions of Thomas A. Edison." *Cassier's Magazine*, Vol. 4, no. 21 July 1893, pp. 208– 212.

27 Dyer, *Edison, His Life and Inventions*, pp. 380–381. When the Brooklyn Bridge was opened Edison and members of his staff were invited to be among the first to cross it. It is nice to imagine that Dickson was among them.

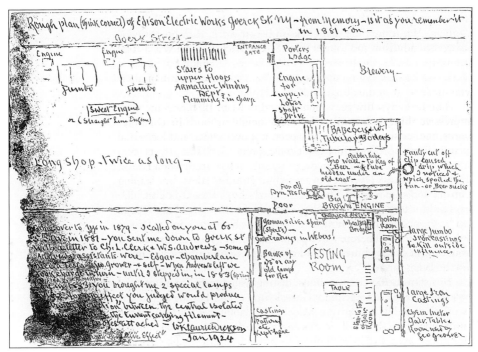

The floor plan for the work shop on Goerck Street made from memory and sent by Dickson to Thomas Edison on 23 January 1924. [EHS.]

association with some exceptional co-workers, among them Charles Edgar who went on to manage the Boston Edison Electric Light Company, Henry N. Marvin, who became Dickson's life-long friend and his associate in the founding of the American Mutoscope Co. and Nicola Tesla "... that effulgent star of the scientific heavens ...". Tesla, who came to the U.S. in 1884, had worked briefly at Edison's recently established lamp factory at Ivry-sur-Seine, France and the position in the Testing Room was his first in the U.S.

"[Nicola Tesla]... even then gave strong evidence of the genius that has made him one of the standard authorities of the day; but like most holders of God's intrinsic gifts, he was unostentatious in the extreme, and ready to assist with counsel or manual help any perplexed member of the craft. Such were the men at Goerk [sic] street, and many a delightful symposium comes to remembrance in which these congenial elements took part. Time was not [sic], and surroundings were not forgotten, as they listened spell-bound to the emanations of Tesla's brilliant intellect, alternately fired with the rapid sketching of his manifold projects, or melted into keenest sympathy by pictures of his Herzogivian home."[28]

Although it was not as popular as the generating plant at Pearl Street, Goerck Street also had its share of celebrity visitors and unusual occurrences. By 1883 Edison's reputation as a popular hero was well established and now that he was accessible in New York City rather than tucked away in the unknown territory of New Jersey, many

28 Dickson, Op. Cit., pp. 208–212; Tate, Op. Cit., pp. 148–149. I credit the florid Victorian prose in Dickson's piece to his sister, Antonia who seems to have composed most of the text for the articles and the resulting book based on information supplied by W.K.L. and Edison's staff. Other writing by Dickson, independent of his sister, is in a simpler, more direct style.

prominent figures asked to be introduced and sample the Wizard's wonders. About the time that Dickson began work, Richard D'Oyley Carte visited Edison and toured Pearl Street. Dickson related a visit by Sitting Bull and several members of his tribe. After the staff spent a hectic two hours cleaning up, the group "... arrived, sitting in all their war paint and grotesque bedizenment on the top of several omnibuses and carriages. Stolidly they surveyed matters from their elevation. Stolidly they descended and stalked through the establishment, betraying by neither work, sign, nor look their appreciation of the unusual surroundings ...". Edison finally elicited a reaction from them by placing them next to a wire which heated so intensely that it caught some cotton cloth on fire. Frank Dyer told of a visit by a group of ladies, one leading a small poodle on a leash. The dog climbed onto a long flat belt which was used for testing the dynamos. The belt was running at high speed and "... the poodle did not notice the difference between it and the floor, and got into the belt before we could do anything. The dog was whirled around forty or fifty times, and a little flat piece of leather came out – and the ladies fainted."[29]

But stimulating conversations, distinguished visitors and memorable incidents were a sideline at Goerck Street. The Testing Room was a workplace and in true Edison style it could be busy at any hour of the day or night. Edison gave little attention to clocks and his ability to work for hours – even days – with little sleep was legendary. The staff that joined Edison in these marathons became his trusted associates. During 1881 and 1882 Edison had given particular attention to perfection of his dynamos and he spent quite a lot of time in the testing room. Francis Jehl, who supervised the Testing Room before Andrews recalled:

"I remember the nights when [Samuel Insull] ... had to come down to the Goerck Street Machine Works, and Edison, sitting in a chair by the Jumbo under test, would go through the correspondence. Edison would jot down a marginal 'yes', 'no', or a note. Insull then would give him a batch of letters to sign. Sometimes Edison would read a few but the greater part was signed without reading. Insull would now and then linger on for a while to watch the test and then start back with the horsecar for [the office at] '65'. He, like the other Edison 'boys', had no special hours, and the time was passed between work and sleep."[30]

Samuel Insull, who joined Edison in March 1881, recalled:

"The first few months I was with Edison he spent most of the time in the office at 65 Fifth Avenue. Then there was a great deal of trouble with the life of the lamps there, and he disappeared from the office and spent his time largely at Menlo Park. At another time there was a great deal of trouble with some of the details of construction of the dynamos, and Edison spent a lot of time at Goerck Street, which had been rapidly equipped with the idea of turning out bi-polar dynamo-electric machines, direct-connected to the engine, the first of which went to Paris and London, while the next were installed in the old Pearl Street Station of the Edison Electric Illuminating Company of New York ...".[31]

During Dickson's tenure at Goerck Street there were, apparently, periods when Edison spent a quite a lot of time in the Testing Room,

29 Dickson, Op. Cit.; Dyer, Op. Cit., pp. 739–740.

30 EHS, Francis Jehl, *Menlo Park Reminiscences*, Vol. 3, p. 987.

31 Dyer, Op. Cit., p. 368.

but during his first months this was not as much as Dickson might have liked. The earliest surviving record of Dickson's employment is a note to Edison written 23 May 1883 enclosing designs Dickson made for lamp brackets. In the note Dickson made a plaintive, but blatant plea for direct attention. "If you only knew how I am heart in soul in all your inventions & all you do you would now & then stoop to assist & better my prospects in life." It is not known whether Edison read this or not, but on 26 May Dickson was sent a curt note from Edison (but initialed by Samuel Insull who had authority to respond to some of Edison's correspondence without his seeing it) saying that designs for brackets and fixtures should be sent to Mr. Bergmann[32] Dickson's fawning, unsubtle appeal could be dismissed as folly of youth, but it was a practice that continued throughout his life, particularly in his relations with Edison – as we shall see.

It is not clear how Edison felt about such flattery, but he did not seem to discourage it. On the other hand, he was impressed by workmen who joined him in his nocturnal marathons and, given the opportunity, Dickson was certainly one of them. He recalled:

"The beds were more original than luxurious, and generally consisted of a table or bench, with galvanometers and resistance boxes for pillows. But revenge was obtained once in a while, upon the author of these miseries. One night, after an exasperating vigil of many hours, one of the boys conceived the brilliant idea of putting the clocks several hours ahead, so as to induce the slumbering chief to quit work a little earlier. On awakening, after one of his cumulative naps, Edison found, to his amazement, that it was 4 a.m. and gave the order to stop for that night. He was puzzled to discover that his watch, usually so reliable, should be a laggard to the tune of six hours, and was still more astonished, on emerging into the streets, to find many of the theatres emptying themselves. Then it was that he realized the nature of the joke perpetrated, and indulged in a hearty and unresentful guffaw."[33]

If Dickson felt discouraged in May about his opportunity to better himself, his chance came soon enough. During the first half of 1883 Edison was preparing to launch an effort to install lighting systems in smaller communities in the U.S., another aspect of business that the larger holding company left for Edison to exploit. The first community selected was Sunbury, Pennsylvania in the Susquehanna River Valley in the north central part of the state. Sunbury was chosen because it was a small community close to coal fields. A local company had been organized which was ready to invest the $20,000 to $30,000 cost that Edison estimated for setting-up a system to support about 400 lights. In May or June they were ready to start and Edison selected Frank J. Sprague and William Andrews, Dickson's supervisor, to work with him supervising the installation. Andrews was in Sunbury for a number of days during June. The plant began operation on July 4, 1883, but only after a frantic day during which Andrews, Sprague and Edison scrambled to solve a number of problems. Twenty-five buildings were wired and it served about 500 lamps, operating only from sunset to sunrise.[34]

Andrews returned to Sunbury four times during July and four

32 EHS

33 Dicksons, Op. Cit., pp. 208–212.

34 EHS; Dyer, Op. Cit., p. 426; Conot, *Thomas A. Edison, A Streak of Luck*, pp. 208–209.

Above and on facing page: In an effort to restore favor with Edison, W.K.L. Dickson sent Edison drawings of the floor plan of the work shop at Goerck Street, a sketch of Edison and Dickson working on the experiment that led to discovery of the Edison Effect and his own caption for the drawings. A photo of an Edison light bulb taken by Dickson is said by him to be the one used in these experiments. However, Mr. Dickson's penchant for exaggeration makes this claim open to question. [EHS.]

times in August in order to solve problems. A few days after the opening Andrews had to calm panicking residents of a hotel that had been struck by lightning during a storm. Sparks were coming from the gas fixtures and lightning was being fed along poorly insulated wires. By August he was working on the installation of a system in Shamoken, Pennsylvania followed by Lawrence, Massachusetts in October, Tiffin, Ohio and Fall River, Massachusetts both in December 1883. Optimistic that the business would continue to grow, Edison created a new organization, the Thomas A. Edison Construction Dept., gave Samuel Insull responsibility for it and on 21 November 1883 notified Andrews that he was now in charge of all electrical work in the various stations with the title Chief Electrical Engineer.

This seemed to end Andrews' responsibility for the Testing Room and he had been away from New York for a great deal of time during the preceding five months. Dickson took his place, but exactly when is not certain. For a while Charles Clarke seems to have been responsible for the Testing Room, but he apparently managed it from the headquarters of the Light Company at 65 Fifth Avenue. In a 1924 letter to Edison, Dickson recalled that for a while the staff of the Testing Room took turns supervising but by June 1884 Dickson was addressed as supervisor and he may have been acting in that capacity for several months previous to this.[35] His relatively rapid rise was abetted by personnel changes that took place at Goerck Street. In October Charles Dean and some of his associates were fired. Samuel Insull suspected Dean of giving contracts to cronies, paying them exorbitant sums and

35 EHS; Dickson's letter to Thomas Edison 23 January 1924 has an interesting drawing of the Testing Room.

> ~ Jan. 1924 ~
>
> Sketch 1 - Shows the main Room of the Edison Testing & Experimental Dept. at Goerck St N.Y. -
>
> End of 1883 you brought me two special lamps for Test - The lamps looked alike Externally but each contained a central isolated wire (presum platinum) - The filaments were of the ordinary carbonized Bamboo type then in use - one a simple loop the other a one turn spiral ⟜ -⊃- 110 V. lamps 75↘
>
> Galv. Tests - Galv. suitably Shunted - Res. etc as usual - First Tests were with Dyn. current - then with Daniel Standard cells for steady readings - shunted down to 200 deflections between A & B - the reading & results were practically the same with the both lamps - straight or spiral carbons -
>
> I was unable for some time to get the same readings until I discovered that on taking off one lamp & putting on the other I had inadvertently reversed things & was only getting 25 to 30 deflections that is between A & C - Accidentally I happened to connect up one of the lamps immediately got the old reading - then I tumbled to the scheme - re. a greatly increased deflection on one side - sorry I cannot say if Anode or Cathode - But I dont think that matters the facts remain - I remem. making a small commutator for reversing & Testing first one side the other - WS/ WKLaurieDickson

receiving kick-backs as well as blackmailing companies who supplied goods to the Works. Insull had Jim Russell, the detective, investigate Dean and although Russell found only a relatively minor problem with the sale of some scrap, it was used as justification for replacing Dean – and canceling a $9,000 bonus committed to by Edison. Dean was replaced by a Mr. Soldan who also seems to have been based at the Edison headquarters at 65 Fifth Avenue.[36]

With some of staff being sent into the field and others being fired, Dickson, although a recent hire, was rapidly rising in seniority while gaining recognition as a skilled employee. In July 1883, Charles Clarke wrote Edison recommending that the staff of the Testing Room be reduced. "... there are now ten men there, three of whom are well trained & expert. They can do work of any class that is required ..." One of these three may have been Dickson because on 18 July 1883, Dickson signed the test sheet for a Type T dynamo, the earliest such document of Dickson's that survives in the Edison archive. The dynamo ran for seven hours during the test. In August the Testing Room

36 EHS; Insull to Charles Batchelor, Paris, France, 5 November 1883. Batchelor, perhaps Edison's closest and most trusted assistant, had been sent to Paris to head Edison's European activities.

Workers standing outside the entrance the Edison's Goerck Street facility in the 1880s. [EHS.]

1 Jim Carr   4 E.J. Berggren.
2 R Lozier   5 W. Scott
3 H. McLean   6 J. R. Campbell
            7 W.M. McDougall

received indirect praise from Edison himself. Edison wrote Clarke asking for additional data in tests of dynamos and commented "... you seem to have plenty of talent down there."[37]

This was a very busy period for the Machine Works and a time of considerable turmoil. In November of 1883, while Andrews was on the road supervising installations, Insull wrote him that the Machine Works was "... straining every nerve to turn machines out ..." but orders were backed-up three to four months. The same month, in a letter to Charles Batchelor, Insull said that they had done a quarter of a million dollars of contract work installing central stations and anticipated brisk business in the spring. By this time, the management of the Machine Works was at the main office at 65 Fifth Ave. and Insull was handling paper work, placing orders and paying bills. Insull told Batchelor "The Superintendent of the Works builds machines at Goerck Street and takes charge of his men and there his functions end".[38]

Although he seems to have benefitted from being in the right place at the right time, Dickson's rapid rise to favor was based more on talent and skill than on chance and chutzpah. He was only one of dozens, even hundreds, of new employees and though Edison despaired of the general lack of skill in the talent pool, there were more than a few new employees who demonstrated real potential. Co-workers like Tesla and

37 EHS. Clarke to Edison, 6 July 1883; Dickson, "Dynamo Test /The Edison Electric Light Co. Testing Room", 18 July 1883; Edison to Clarke, August 1883.

38 EHS, *ibid.*; Insull to Andrews, 19 November 1883.

Marvin were serious competition![39] Despite their talent Tesla and Marvin seem to have been unappreciated. Charles Batchelor, managing the Goerck Works, refused to give Tesla a raise from $18 a week to $25, saying "the woods are full of men like him. I can get any number of them I want for eighteen dollars a week." Dissatisfied, Tesla left, found his way to Edison's rival George Westinghouse's electrical company where he was instrumental in creating a rival generating system that eventually displaced Edison's.[40]

By the beginning of 1884, less than a year after he started, it appears that Dickson was, if not the "head", at least the responsible person in the Testing Room. A letter from A. O. Tate, the Edison Construction Company, 23 January 1884 requesting tests on several dynamos was addressed to Mr. W.K.L. Dickson at Goerck Street and another letter, the same day, written to Bergmann & Co. asked them to send "Mr. Dixon" the information he needed for tests for the standardizing of ampere motors. "We are under the impression that the information Mr. Dixon asks us for (we have never seen his letter) is always given to him by you." The earliest letter addressed to Dickson as Superintendent of the Testing Room is a letter of 4 June 1884 from Edison, but it was initialed by Insull, who was signing for Edison. It requested a test of six safety catches sent to the Testing Room by Bergmann and Company. Dickson responded with results on 6 June 1884, apologizing for the delay in his response. Interestingly, Dickson said that he sent a copy of the test to Mr. Andrews, his former boss, who was in Circleville, Ohio to install a lighting system. The reason is not clear, but Andrews may still have been involved in the work of the Testing Room and Dickson, who had great respect for Andrews may have valued his comments.

An anecdote that Dickson related in a Christmas letter to Edison in 1926 gave a glimpse of work and "play" at Goerck Street in what Dickson referred to as "the olden & golden days".

"You (thro' Ch. Clarke) sent me 'an English Dude to lick into shape' ... He arrived gloves & all – a college graduate & very cocky – to begin with one of my bad boys promptly destroyed the gloves when he could be persuaded to discard same, acid accidently? spread on the side board did the trick.

"My tabulated list of duties for each man – was to sweep the room & keep the stove replenished daily in turn – this was however too much for our friend – but as your orders were to 'lick him into shape' we persuaded him to do his part – I was very young then & with a spirit of mischief connected up the stove with a small coil. When his turn came one of my assistants (Geo Grower) depressed a distant key as the coal scuttle came in contact with the stove, with dire results. Naturally we were interested but got no shock which pointed to the fact that he had acquired the Electric Fever the only cure known was the free use of water drunk in great quantities which he carried out with good results ([the] coil reduced) [the] fever, to his delight, at each trial was abating.

"Sunday intervened – as a church goer he was advised to carry a flask of water to keep up the treatment – which he used surreptitiously every ½ hour. Our victim much excited over this extraordinary phenomina [sic] ... ask me to communicate with you. I sent him to you with a sealed explanatory letter – knowing yr grand appreciation of a joke. We got him to turn

39 Before joining Dickson in establishing the American Mutoscope Co., Henry Marvin invented a drill that was widely used in the mining industry.

40 EHS, Letter, Marvin to Edison, 23 July 1885; A.O. Tate, *Edison's Open Door*, pp. 148–149.

out trumps after a time realizing that 'live wires' were what you wanted to assist in these early pioneer days of research work."[41]

Dynamos and accessories for lighting systems were not the only things tested at Goerck Street. During 1883 Edison resumed tests on what was to become known as the "Edison Effect", an emission of electrons in a vacuum bulb that later became the basis for the vacuum tube. During his experiments developing the light bulb Edison and Francis Upton had observed a blackening at the positive pole of a wire in a vacuum light bulb. Other matters intervened and nothing further had been done with it, but Edison resumed experiments in 1882 and 1883. Presumably Dickson conducted some of these tests and claimed, in a letter written to Edison in December 1923, that he made the first galvanometer tests of the effect. At Edison's request, in January 1924 he sent Edison a description of a test along with a drawing of a man, presumably Edison, casually discussing two light bulbs with a young man, presumably Dickson (see illustration on page 29). Dickson's detailed description of the test seems to have been made from notes that he retained and still had in 1924. Although in his article for SMPE he would claim "... I had the good fortune to help Mr. Edison to determine the meaning of the 'Edison effect', or the first concept of the famous 'valve' used now in radio apparatus", his actual contribution was more modest. Although Edison applied for a patent in the fall of 1883 for a "voltage regulating device using a two-electrode bulb" it only recorded his observations on the effect. Edison never developed these experiments into a commercial application and it would be several years before other scientists explained the "effect" and converted Edison's observations to practical use.[42]

Home life

There is scant information about his private life during the period that the Dicksons lived in the city. His application for employment was sent from 255 West 24th Street, presumably a residence, but there is no clue whether it was temporary or semi-permanent. In a city directory for 1885 his occupation was listed as machinist with residence at 310 E. Broadway. If Dickson's account in the *Journal of the SMPE* is accurate, his sisters Antonia and Eva were in New York with him and apparently they continued their active social and cultural life. It was reported in Dickson's obituary that "... in New York he won considerable distinction as a violinist and orchestra leader. He started a series of subscription concerts at which Madame Patti and other world-famous artists sang and played, one of the concerts being attended by the then President of the United States. He also had a fine tenor voice, and sang in a New York choir."[43] There is nothing to confirm this, and the claims that Patti performed and the President attended could qualify as Dicksonian embellishment passed on by his family after his death. We know more about their activities in Virginia and Orange, New Jersey and these bracketed their stay in New York. In both places they had a lively social

41 EHS, Dickson to Edison 12 December 1926.

42 U.S. Patent No. 307,031. EHS, Dickson to Edison, 23 January 1924; Matthew Josephson, *Edison, a Biograph*, pp. 273–279; Israel, Op. Cit., pp. 469–470.

43 Hendricks Collection; Obituary in *Richmond and Twickenham Times*, 5 October 1935. The President of the U.S. from 1885–1889 was Grover Cleveland.

and cultural life and since they were still young and New York offered possibilities far beyond those available in Petersburg there is every reason to believe that the three Dicksons found expression through performances, lecturing, writing and other social and cultural activities. Eva, the amateur singer, was young, having just turned 18, so it was probably Antonia, the older sister who took the lead. She was an aspiring concert musician with a desire to write who had the time and inclination to lead an active cultural life.

Music and painting were invaluable avocations for Laurie, but he had begun a promising career with a particularly proficient and demanding mentor. If he had ambitions towards a life as an impresario, the rigorous and irregular requirements of his new career would have made it difficult to accomplish much. But however pressed for time he might be, he was able to express himself creatively. Sometime, apparently in 1885, he registered copyright for eight engravings: "Oh Alone in This ...", "Auld Lang Syne", "Softest Pleadings", "Give Oh Give Me Back My Heart", "I Won't Go Home Til Morning", "Who's at the Window", "Why I'm So Plump" and "All Human History Attests". The Library of Congress, which received hundreds of similar applications, chose not to keep these for posterity so we can only speculate about their nature, but they probably resembled the sentimental drawings with similar titles illustrating popular poems and songs that filled popular magazines during this period.[44]

A similar engraving survives in the form of a damaged photograph, apparently made by Dickson. It was found in a collection that Gordon Hendricks acquired from one of Dickson's former neighbors. Although it survives in very poor condition it is an important indicator of their taste and interests. Laurie illustrated his sister Antonia's undated poem "Indian Lullaby to the Pale Faces" with a romantic drawing of an Indian village and the two verses were hand lettered in a rustic, Adirondack-inspired style that Dickson particularly admired and used frequently. The capital letters were drawn as logs or tree branches and the smaller letters were twig-like. Although this particular drawing was probably made during the 1890s the earlier engravings were probably comparable.

In addition to dabbling in culture, Dickson took a stab at an ambitious business deal. In 1885, Dickson, who had apparently moved to 49 West 24th Street, sent a detailed letter to Edison describing experiments on an improved insulation material – apparently, gum balata or gutta percha. He said that he and some associates had been testing the new material for several months and could report it was very cheap and had up to twenty times the resistance of materials being used to insulate electrical wiring. They tested samples coated with the material for 21 days under water with "... constant unchanging resistance ...". His associates had patented the process and expected to sell rights or set up a company to manufacture it. They anticipated asking $300,000 for rights but Dickson said that he felt Edison should have first rights to use it and asked him to make an offer. Three days later he

44 Library of Congress. The exact date of Dickson's application is not certain. The card recording the registration, apparently dated 1 December 1897, had a note on the back that the photographs of these engravings bore no date of receipt but they had been filed among cabinet photos of 1885.

"Indian Lullaby to the Pale Faceas" a poem by Antonia Dickson illustrated by W.K.L. Dickson is probably similar to other art work that Dickson copyrighted in the 1880s. [Condition note: This copy is from a glass plate made by Dickson. The original is badly deteriorated but it is the only surviving example of these efforts.] (NMAH Hendricks)

In Powhatan's Camp, by Antonia Dickson Copyright 1897

Indian Lullaby to the Pale Faces

Rest. Rest. Rest
The south wind sighs in the pine trees crest
The dew drops sleep in the roses breast
The curtains of night are ever the [west]
The beautiful West

Sleep. Sleep. Sleep.
See! To our feet the moon[light] creeps
By the waves of that silver tide caressed
We shall float through [the] gates of the mystic West
The beautiful West.

received a terse letter from Samuel Insull, on behalf of Edison, saying "... that he would not be disposed to purchase the patents which you refer to on any such terms as those stated in your letter".[45]

Robert Conot, in his biography of Edison, interpreted this correspondence as an attempt by Dickson to undercut his associates and personally profit from Edison's search for an improved insulation, but the tone of Dickson's letter does not seem to support this. Specifically, Dickson proposed "... that you make *them* [my emphasis] an offer for the U.S. or U.S. & Foreign (Engl. Germ. France & Italy) ..." rights, saying that foreign and domestic patents had already been taken. Dickson was aware of the problems that Edison was having with materials being used for insulating electrical wire and that concerns about fire and electrocution were being exploited by the well established gas companies to combat Edison's upstart system for municipal and home lighting. Though Edison may not have been willing to invest $300,000 in Dickson's system, he may have given it a test. Dickson mentioned such a test in a letter to Edison 5 April 1928.[46]

Whatever ambitions Dickson and his associates had in the fall of 1885, they apparently never developed. There are no indications of sudden wealth either from the sale of patents or a new insulated electrical wire company. Instead, Dickson remained with Edison for another decade.

These efforts to interest Edison in insulation and lamp designs show Dickson's ambition and willingness to take chances in order to advance himself. Though his methods seem impulsive and even tactless, they seem to have served the useful purpose of making him better known to Edison. Attracting Edison's attention was a challenge. Edison had little patience for the day-to-day details of office management and he used his private secretary as a filter. As Edison's gate keepers, Samuel Insull and, later, A.O. Tate had enormous power. As we have seen, each of Dickson's attempts to reach Edison by correspondence, his application for work, his proposals for lamp designs and insulated wire, were handled by Insull who responded on Edison's behalf. Insull had license to judge whether or not Edison needed to see correspondence and when he did read his mail, he often went through it rapidly. As Insull described his duties:

"... 'I never attempted to systematize Edison's business life. Edison's whole method of work would upset the system of any office. He was just as likely to be at work in his laboratory at midnight as midday. He cared not for the hours of the day or the days of the week. If he was exhausted he might more likely be asleep in the middle of the day than in the middle of the night, as most of his work in the way of inventions was done at night. I used to run his office on as close business methods as my experience admitted; and I would get at him whenever it suited his convenience. Sometimes he would not go over his mail for days at a time; but other times he would go regularly to his office in the morning. At other times my engagements used to be with him to go over his business affairs at Menlo Park at night, if I was occupied in New York during the day. In fact, as a matter of convenience I used more often to get at him at night, as it left my days free to transact his

45 EHS. Dickson to Edison, 28 September 1885. In 1933 Dickson told Will Day that the material they were working with was gum balata, a non-elastic rubber material from South America which was similar to gutta percha, a material frequently used for insolation in the 1880s.

46 EHS. Dickson may have succeeded in persuading Edison to experiment with gum balata because Edison was purchasing samples of it in 1888. It may seem ironic today, but the gas companies were touting gas as much safer to use than electricity.

affairs, and enabled me, probably at a midnight luncheon, to get a few minutes of his time to look over his correspondence and get his directions as to what I should do in some particular negotiations or matter of finance. ..."[47]

In the long run Dickson benefitted more from his position in the Testing Room than from his ambitious projects. In March and April, 1893, when Dickson started, his boss, W.S. Andrews was sending Edison regular test reports on generators. Since Edison occasionally retreated there in order to get back to basics, Dickson got to work hand in hand with him – provided that he was willing to work the irregular hours that Edison found natural. Dickson, who seems to have been something of a workaholic, apparently had no problem with a long, arduous schedule. As we will see, all-night sessions, work days of 14 and 16 hours and Sundays on the job were a regular part of Dickson's work schedule on the Kinetograph and apparently this began very early in his career. Edison chose his close associates from those who accepted his eccentric work habits and those who stuck with him through marathon projects were favorites. Dickson joined this group very early and it was probably because of skill and willingness to work in Edison's pattern.

There is enough documentation of Dickson's first months with Edison to get a picture of his activities, but the surviving record for 1885 and 1886 is scant. By his own account, Dickson said that he was "... chief electrician in the Edison Electric Tube Co., of Brooklyn, and was charged with the office of laying the first telegraphic and telephone wires underground in New York City during Mayor Grant's admini-stration".[48] Dickson's penchant for exaggeration raises doubts about claims that he was in charge, but being moved to the Tube Company could account for the lack of documentation of his work during this period. If that is case, he was probably transferred there in 1884 or early in 1885.

By way of background, the Tube Works moved to Brooklyn in the summer of 1884, but the work of laying underground wiring took place in various locations in the city. The New York State Legislature enacted a law requiring all telephone, telegraph and electric light wiring to be laid underground in cities with a population of 500,000 or more – i.e. New York City. The city was already criss-crossed with miles of overhead telephone and telegraph wires. New York's mayor, Hugh Grant promised enforcement, hence Dickson's reference to him. Al-though the order was ignored by some companies there was an increase in the amount of wire buried underground. Partly because of the law and partly to compete with the underground gas lines, Edison chose to put his wiring underground.[49]

Dickson's tour with the Tube Works was fairly short. Changes were taking place which altered the course of his career. Midway through the 1880s, spurred by problems in his business and personal life, Edison's interest in experimentation and invention revived.

47   Frank Dyer et al., *Edison, His Life and Inventions*, pp. 278–279.

48   Dicksons, *Cassier's Magazine*, 1894 and *History of the Kinetograph, Kinetoscope and Kineto-Phonograph*, 1895. Both of these early articles mention that he was supervisor at the Electric Tube Works. This quote is from a reprint of a biographical article by W.E. Woodbury, "From American Annual of Photograph – By Request" which was reprinted in *History of ...* Although the words are Woodbury's his information was undoubtedly supplied by Dickson and although it is possibly Dicksonian hyperbole, the articles are closer to the events than Dickson's later accounts and because he was still working for Edison he would have been careful about his claims. Though Edison probably did not review the articles before publication he would have read them later and Dickson also would have been subject to comments by fellow workers familiar with the facts.

49   Byron M. Vanderbilt, *Thomas Edison, Chemist*, p. 92.

Chapter 3

The Business of Invention: Electricity, Ore and the Phonograph

A.O. Tate: "... Two other corporations had been formed at this period – vis., The Edison Electric Lighting Company, capitalized at one million dollars in shares of the nominal value of one hundred dollars each, and known briefly as the Parent Company, which owned Edison's United State's Patent covering the art (Edison did not own a controlling interest in this company, but up to a certain period ... was the largest individual shareholder); and The Edison Electric Illuminating Company, which owned the Pearl Street Station and the rights to exploit the industry within the limits of the City of New York ... a war waged for their possession by two Titans, one a giant of finance representing the resources of two great German banks and motivated by cold, calculating industrial prescience, and the other a giant of invention actuated by the ardor of pride in the institutions created by his genius: Henry Villard and Thomas A. Edison ... [Edison,] ... consciously and deliberately, he sacrificed millions to maintain the unalloyed integrity and identities of the institutions erected upon the foundations of his own inventions."[50]

Although recognition of his skills and abilities were important to W.K.L. Dickson's rapid advance in the Edison organization, there were changes in the electrical business and Edison's personal life that also played a role and these will be reviewed in this chapter along with two projects that Edison revived and which continued during the Kineto experiments. These were the phonograph and ore milling. Some background information is in order.

The electrical business

At the beginning of the 1880s Edison launched an ambitious effort to turn his experiments in lighting into a commercial system by building generating plants and installing wiring, lighting systems and the necessary related equipment. It was an expensive scheme that demanded much of his time. He created The Edison Electric Light Company, shifted operations from Menlo Park to Manhattan and to fund his venture he tapped into the Wall Street moguls that had been using his

50 Tate, *Edison's Open Door*, pp. 48–49.

services since he introduced his stock ticker. To attract investors he gave the Light Company rights to his principal lighting patents and loose control over a cluster of related companies created to install systems and manufacture the supporting elements. German-born railroad mogul Henry Villard was a major investor and J. P. Morgan's investment firm, Drexel Morgan and Co. was a conspicuous investor. Villard had his own fortune as well as the backing of several German banks. Edison was a major stock holder and his personal attorney, Sherbourne Eaton, was President. Eaton shared day-to-day management with Villard but it was Morgan who ultimately called the shots.[51]

Dickson came to work for Edison as the company was taking shape and in 1883, when Dickson was hired, Edison was prospering. His companies were expanding but the situation was volatile.

At first the Light Company concentrated on installations in New York, large commercial organizations and other major urban centers. Edison was allowed to manage what they regarded as the peripheral businesses: the companies that manufactured generators, wiring, lamps, bulbs, connectors, etc. and a cluster of companies formed to install lighting systems for smaller communities. As it became apparent that the manufacturing companies were essential to the success of the enterprise – and potentially very profitable – the Lighting Company pressed for control through a reorganization. Edison resisted, but found himself vulnerable. He had overextended himself by subsidizing the construction of local electrical companies. These were small independent companies that were locally financed. Most of them had difficulty raising the funds necessary to get their systems up and running so to get them started, Edison bore most of the heavy initial construction costs as a loan to be paid back once the system was running. Edison found himself troubled by cash flow problems because it took a while for the returns to cover the initial costs and, though he pressed for payment, the locals had trouble raising cash and often paid him in stock.[52]

In April 1884, Edison agreed to a reorganization. This set off a series of intensely difficult negotiations which resulted in an eventual restructuring of the whole lighting business. By fall, the control of all of the companies had been reorganized and the manufacturing companies made subsidiaries of Edison Electric.

On the surface Edison seemed to come out well. He held the major shares in Edison Electric Light, the parent company. Sherbourne Eaton was replaced as president of Edison Electric Light by Edward Johnson, another Edison man. Former Edison assistants were in charge of each of the manufacturing companies: Francis Upton at the Lamp Co.; Charles Batchelor at the Tube Shop and Machine Works and Sigmund Bergmann at Bergmann & Co.[53]

It seemed an ideal situation for Edison, but there was a down side. Growth and reorganization generated a great deal of internal animosity and despite having his compatriots in management he found that the manufacturing companies were now dominated by investors who had

51 The Edison Lamp Company which made light bulbs; Bergmann & Co. which made lighting fixtures; The Edison Tube Company which made the underground distribution equipment and The Edison Machine Works which manufactured generators and related heavy electrical equipment.

52 Building local electrical companies was the job of the Construction Department, the new branch to which Dickson's first boss, William Andrews had been transferred. The Construction Department was the focal point of Edison's money problems.

53 See Israel, Op. Cit., pp. 205–229; Conot, Op. Cit, pp. 210–222; Tate, Op. Cit., p. 47. This is a very simplified account of a complicated series of events. The most detailed account is in Paul Israel's biography.

little understanding of Edison's methods. As long as he controlled the supporting companies Edison was able to experiment in order to upgrade products, improve manufacturing techniques and reduce costs. Edison's method of experimentation involved trying a wide variety of approaches. It was, or seemed to be, a hit-or-miss scheme which ran contrary to the careful planning and systematic approach favored by the scientific community – as well as by his financial associates. Since most of the money that funded Edison's research came from the business community, he found himself increasingly at odds with investors who were impatient for results and critical of spending for experiments that seemed wastefully unprofitable. As long as he controlled the manufacturing companies he was free to act on his own and judge the results himself. Now he faced pressure and criticism which he viewed as interference.

Edison's situation was further complicated by a crisis in his personal life. In the midst of the reorganization, on 9 August 1884, Edison's wife died in Menlo Park, NJ. Mary Stilwell Edison's health had been poor for some time. The Edisons had spent February and March in Florida and she seemed improved but shortly after their return her father died unexpectedly and soon after her health deteriorated rapidly. Edison, who was, at best, a difficult husband and neglectful father, was now a widower with three children, Marion, Thomas Alva, Jr. (whom Edison called Dot and Dash) and William Leslie. While Edison worked in Menlo Park the family was only a short walk away but with his irregular hours and marathon projects, Mary and the children never knew when Tom might appear. With the growth of the electric business and the move to New York, the family's life became even more fractured. After setting up his office at 65 Fifth Avenue, near 14th Street, the family moved to the city. Mary, who came from a modest small-town background, was not particularly happy there. Edison was gone more than ever and she had few friends. The house Edison rented was near up-scale Gramercy Park and Mary found it difficult to adjust to the new neighbors. As her health deteriorated she showed signs of mental disorder and this was a particular worry. Edison's own mother had suffered similarly before her death and Edison seemed concerned that his family might suffer an inherited mental affliction.

Mary's health problems and death forced Edison to become a family man for a while. The children were being cared for by Edison's recently widowed mother-in-law, Margaret Stilwell and, despite his unease about business matters, he apparently made an effort to spend more time with them. It was soon after their return from Florida that he agreed to the reorganization of the electrical companies and the reorganization seemed to convince him that the laboratory suited him better that an office in Manhattan. Though he retained his office in New York, he began spending more time in the lab. But his lab life was also in flux.

Mary's death brought an end to Edison's Menlo Park years. While his wife's health declined, Edison became entangled in financial problems affecting the property at Menlo Park. He was threatened with a lawsuit for refusing to pay a note which he believed was owed by business associates rather than himself. Confronting an order to seize the property in order to satisfy the debt, he transferred the title of the lab to Mary. She already held title to their house and other property and his lawyers assured him that this would leave him without property in New Jersey so the lab could not be seized. Mary's death upset this plan. Edison inherited the property and the sheriff's auction, which had been postponed, was rescheduled for 10 November 1884. Although Charles Batchelor was able to intervene and purchase the property at a reasonable price, keeping the building in Edison's hands, it was closed and it never reopened.

This happened as Edison was reviving interest in experimentation. While shifting operations to New York, he also moved much of the lab work to Bergmann & Co., gradually phasing out operations at Menlo Park. Bergmann's became his principal lab though he occasionally experimented at the Lamp Works in East Newark and at Goerck Street. With Samuel Insull representing him in the reorganized Edison Electric Co., Edison felt that he could devote more time to experimentation, his first love.[54]

The reorganization did not end the turmoil in the electrical business. At the end of 1886 Edison decided to move the Machine Works from Goerck Street to Schenectady, New York. His decision was precipitated by labor troubles. On 1 May 1886 the workers at Goerck Street went on strike demanding a union shop and adjustments in pay.[55] After some negotiations, Charles Batchelor, who was now the Supervisor of the Machine Works, agreed to give ten hours' pay for nine hours work but he would not agree to a union shop. The workers returned in late May, but the turmoil was not over. The company had outgrown the facilities and even before the strike they had been considering relocating. When a large locomotive works in Schenectady came on the market at a bargain price the directors agreed to a purchase and plans were made to move at the end of the 1886.

The move necessitated personnel changes. Edison wanted "Batch" to stay in New York, but, as supervisor, Batchelor felt it was important to go to Schenectady and to take John Kruesi the manager of the Works. Kruesi, a native of Switzerland, was one of Edison's most skilled machinists and a trusted veteran of Menlo Park. Samuel Insull, Edison's Private Secretary, was named Secretary and Treasurer of the Works and was moved as well, though he retained his title as Edison's Private Secretary. Alfred O. Tate, Insull's assistant, stayed in New York to take care of Edison's correspondence and appointments. Tate was in the awkward position of having to handle Edison's appointments, letters and other affairs while also reporting to Insull in Schenectady.[56]

The old guard was dispersing, giving way to a new generation.

Edison's assistant

"Joined Mr. Edison personally as one of his assistants in his laboratories –

54   Conot, Op. Cit., pp. 218–219; Israel, Op.Cit., pp. 230–233.

55   EHS. This was a period of growing labor trouble in the United States. On 6 March 1886 the Knights of Labor began a strike against Jay Gould's Missouri-Pacific railroad and there were several others during the next months. *Almanac of American History*.

56   Conot, Op. Cit., pp. 243–245; Israel, Op. Cit., pp. 253–254.

over Bergmans [sic] and at Edison Lamp Works, Newark, NJ upper floors, where I carried through experiments on magnetic ore separation of ... gold bearing pyrites." (Dickson to Terry Ramsaye)[57]

It was in the context of Edison's reviving interest in experimentation that W.K.L. Dickson became "... one of his assistants in his laboratories." Having moved several of his closest associates into management, he needed new blood and Dickson was among the chosen. The surviving records don't confirm the where or when of his move to the lab, but by 1887 he was working on ore milling in Edison's laboratory in East Newark [see below]. Dickson claimed he became an assistant in 1885, and, if, as he told Terry Ramsaye [above], he worked in the lab when it was at Bergmann and Co., it would have been in 1885 or early in 1886. Bergmann's was Edison's principal lab from the second half of 1884 until the spring of 1886 when he moved the lab to the Lamp Works in East Newark (now Harrison), NJ. The lab remained in East Newark until the new laboratory opened in Orange (now West Orange) at the very end of 1887.

By the early fall of 1886, when Dickson returned from a lengthy honeymoon in Europe [see Chapter 4], he would have found changes taking place. Edison was working on a variety of experiments. Improvements on lights and elements of the lighting system continued to engage him but he had several new projects and revived some that had been tabled during his push to introduce the lighting business. He was testing a method to telegraph from moving trains with his long time associate and friend Ezra Gilliland and he revived work on ore milling and the phonograph.[58]

But Dickson would not have seen much of Edison during the early months of 1887. During the Christmas holidays, while the Machine Works was moving, Edison contracted pneumonia and pleurisy. He was confined to bed in his home at Glenmont for the month of January and there were alarming reports that he was near death. In February he was sent to his new vacation home and laboratory in Fort Myers but suffered another set back when he developed an abscess below his left ear. He remained in Florida in the company of his wife and a male nurse until the end of April and had not fully recovered when he arrived back in Glenmont at the beginning of May.[59]

During his extended recuperation in Florida Edison began planning a new laboratory to be built at the foot of the mountain in Orange, New Jersey less than a mile from his new home in Llewellyn Park. Before returning to New Jersey, preliminary sketches were made, the land purchased and Hudson Holly, who designed his new home, Glenmont, was engaged as architect. Ground was broken on 5 July with a predicted completion in the fall of 1887. It was to be the largest, most complete research laboratory in the world. As it was being built, Edison continued to enlarge his plans. During the summer he decided to add four ancillary buildings to provide additional support and for specialized work in electrical measurement, chemistry and metallurgy. The focal point of the main building was a two story library which was to

57 Ramsaye, GU. Undated chronology.

58 Israel, Op. Cit., p. 256.

59 EHS, Conot, Op. Cit., pp. 247–248; Israel, Op. Cit., p. 257.

have reference books on every conceivable subject, scientific journals, published patents and other documentation that would support the work of his experimenters. The Library would serve as Edison's office but he also had a private research room tucked away on the second floor. There were to be two machine shops. A general shop with the most up to date equipment and a specialized shop for precision work. A large supply room was to be stocked with every imaginable type of material so that an experimenter could find what he needed on site and not have to wait. The advance publicity claimed that the lab would be capable of making anything from a lady's watch to a locomotive and that the stock room would have everything from screws, nuts and bolts to walrus hide, swan's down and porcupine quills. There would be a carpentry shop, a blacksmith and glass blowers. On the third floor there was a large room for meetings that became a music room and occasional recording studio. There was a room for photography on the second floor.

At the beginning of 1887 this was still in the future and Dickson was not involved in the new laboratory until the end of the year. But Goerck Street was closed and he was probably working in the laboratory in the Lamp Works in East Newark. We don't know what he worked on while Edison was recuperating in Florida, but by June, after Edison's return, he was working on the magnetic ore separator, one of the projects that Edison revived in his return to active research.

Magnets and mining: ore milling

"The object of our invention is to remove magnetic particles from an inclosing mass of foreign matter – as, for example, the gangue in magnetic iron ore – and while the method is applicable to all grades of ore and to all mixed magnetic and non-magnetic materials, it is especially adapted to those ores in which the iron is in exceedingly fine particles separated or surrounded by a large proportion of gangue." (U.S. Patent, No. 434,588, issued to Thomas A. Edison and William K.L. Dickson on 19 August 1890)

Edison's interest in mining and minerals dated back to the 1870s and was possibly derived from his research into various metallic materials to use in telephones, telegraph, wiring, insulation and as filaments in light bulbs. He liked to tell a story of seeing black material mixed with sand on a beach at Quogue, Long Island and discovering that it was iron and that it could be separated from the sand by attracting it to a magnet. Magnets were familiar as basic components of his generating system and he devised a machine to separate iron from sand, created a company and set up an operation at Quonochontaug Beach, Rhode Island. The company, Edison Magnetic Ore Milling Co., was organized in December, 1879 and a patent for an magnetic ore milling device was granted 1 June 1880.[60] There were a number of problems that prevented the company from succeeding, not the least of which was that the ore was too fine to be processed in the existing iron furnaces. There were questions about the purity of the ore and it proved to be difficult to ship such finely granulated ore in the open rail cars usually used for ore. In the early 1880s, as Edison devoted more of his time to commercializing

60   Conot, Op. Cit., appendix; Dyer, *Edison ...*, appendix XVI, p. 941. U.S. patent no. 228,329, 1 June 1889, Edison, for Ore milling device. A magnet to attract iron particles into a separate hopper from the residue.

the lighting system, the Rhode Island plant was shut down and magnetic ore separation was one of several projects set aside.

Edison was not the first to experiment with magnetism as a means to separate iron deposited in rock, sand and other "low grade" sources. A paper, "The Concentration of Iron-Ore" by John Birkinbine and Edison, read before the American Institute of Mining Engineers February 1889, described experiments made in the U. S., Bohemia, Sweden and New Zealand which were contemporary or previous to Edison's. Birkinbine, who wrote the article, was a prominent expert on mining and an advisor to Edison. He credited Edison's process with simplicity of construction and operation.[61]

Edison's interest was revived in the mid-1880s. Edison spent part of August 1885 visiting the Lewis Miller family at Chautauqua, NY He was courting Miller's daughter, Mina, but the opportunities to pursue his interest in Mina were limited and he had a good deal of time to visit with the rest of her family. Mina's brother, Ira Miller introduced him to a family friend, Walter Mallory, an iron manufacturer from Chicago, and ore processing was one of the topics they discussed. Edison's renewed interest probably dates from this time. In March, 1887, while recuperating from his serious illness, Edison resumed experiments with separating iron ore at his small laboratory in Ft. Myers and on return to Orange at the end of May, he assigned Dickson to the project.

The stimulus for Edison's interest in iron was a shortage of good quality iron ore in the eastern part of the U.S. Through most of the 19th century steel processing had been centered in the East but now the mills were having difficulty finding an adequate supply of ore for processing. There were deposits of iron in the Appalachian range extending from Canada to North Carolina, but much of it was unusable because it was trapped in rock or mixed with undesirable minerals. While some unwanted material could be removed at the mills, the cost of shipping and disposing of tons of waste material made it uneconomical to process the ore. The rich deposits of iron in the upper Great Lakes region were still being developed and it was expensive to ship to the existing plants in the East. Ore was shipped from the Upper Peninsula of Michigan, but the locks at Sault St. Marie were too narrow for ore boats. It would be another decade before the problems were resolved and ore from Lake Superior was added to the national steel mix. Edison hoped to relieve the shortage by removing most of the waste at the mine so that almost all ore shipped to the mill would be usable.

During the last half of the 19th century iron was the key to wealth. Edison was well aware that directly or indirectly, most of the richest American businessmen built their fortunes on iron and steel or products made of iron and steel: railroads, bridges, girders for new and larger buildings, ocean going greyhounds, machine tools, large and small, etc. Edison saw acres and acres of ore lying idle. The person who tapped this resource might join the ranks of the wealthy and powerful – and

61 EHS. As we shall see, Birkinbine was a consultant to Edison at the time this paper was written.

function independently, free from reliance on the Morgans, Vanderbilts and other moguls.

The company Edison set up for his earlier experiments in magnetic
ore separation, The Ore Milling Company, was still in existence in
1887. In its annual report, 19 January 1887, it reported "... The assets
of the Company consist of 430 shares of its own stock in the Treasury
of the Company, Letters patent and contracts and machinery of the
value of about $[1]000. The existing debts of the Company do not
exceed $5000 for money expended for its use and for labor performed
and for machinery supplied ...". A correspondent inquiring about
purchase of stock was told "The affairs of the Company are at present
in a wholly experimental state and the value of the stock will of course
depend upon the results attained."[62] Although Edison reorganized the
company in the fall of 1887, increasing its capital, he funded most of
the research from his own assets.

In his earlier experimentation Edison had designed a machine in
which ore that had been ground to relatively small granules would be
dropped from a hopper past powerful magnets. The magnets would
attract charged particles, i.e. iron, away from uncharged particles – sand
and other minerals, etc. The iron would fall on one side of a dividing
wall, the residue of unwanted material on the other. A prototype
machine had been installed at Quonochontaug Beach, Rhode Island in
the early 1880s. Though the results were not satisfactory, Edison was
satisfied with the general design but felt that it needed refinement. He
was also interested in extending the experiments to see if other metals
could be separated using the technique. Dickson was set to work on a
series of experiments to separate iron and gold.

W.K.L. Dickson and ore milling

A month after Edison's return from Florida, on 5 June 1887, W.K.L.
Dickson began a notebook recording his tests using a version of the
earlier machine that had been built at the East Newark laboratory. This
is the only one of Dickson's notebooks that survives and because it
shows the nature of Dickson's assignments and casts a light on his
interaction with Edison, it is worth some attention.

It was headed "Magnetic Ore Separator Experiments – Gold and
Iron ... *Problem* – To Separate Mettalic [sic] Gold from Pyrites etc.
Magnetically". There was a drawing of the recently constructed separator.[63] For the first test he made a sieve of coarse mesh; pulverized the
material to be tested – the first was iron pyrites (FeS_2, commonly called
fool's gold) – and fed it by hand into a v-shaped hopper which directed
the material past an electromagnet "of considerable strength". He
observed the effectiveness of the magnetic pull on the charged particles.
In this case these were iron pyrites, the gold was non-magnetic. The
two streams fell past a divider into separate containers. Ideally the
desired material would be in one box, the undesirable in the second.
The tests continued for several weeks.

His notes recorded changes made to improve the separator as the

62 EHS, Edison to
J.M. Sears, Boston,
Mass., 21 March
1887.

63 Although the
notes do not specify
it, Dickson may have
been involved in the
construction since the
experiment is dated as
beginning 5 June
1887 the tests dated
from 10 June.

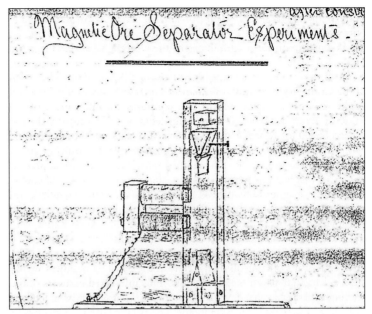

A drawing of the magnetic ore separator in Dickson's notebook made on 10 June 1887. [EHS.]

tests progressed. The sieves were altered and he redesigned the hopper. He reported that "... very fair results were attained with these improvements ...". He also decided it was "... desirable to use a much larger and more powerful magnetic field ...". He was trying to overcome an undesirable separation of particles happening before they reached the magnets, the point where separation was supposed to begin.

The tests involved a variety of mineral combinations. Edison was surveying available Eastern ores and soliciting some from other locales. In addition to iron pyrites, Dickson tested oxide of iron mixed with sand, copper dust, copper dust with sand, copper dust and iron sulphide; oxide of iron; oxide of iron and whiting, arsenopyrite, hematite, micacious hematite, chalcopyrite, pferruginous quartz, galenite – among others.

By 22 June, they were using "much stronger magnets" and they improved the movement of the sifter by using a pulley. After several experiments they decided that the problem of the particles spreading before reaching the magnet was caused by the distance between the hopper and the magnets being too great. In late June they experimented for several days with iron ore (hematite) and white sand with Dickson changing the distance between the hopper and the magnet and between the magnet and the stream of falling minerals. After testing distances from ¼ inch to 3 inches, it was determined that the best distance was ½ inch. They were also troubled by clogging in the hopper.

On 27 June a shipment of gold in quartz arrived from California and was tested during the five days that followed. As noted, the process of separating gold differed from iron and the Edison separator was only effective with gold that was mixed with magnetic iron in sand. Processing this gold required multiple passes through the sieves and past the magnets.[64]

In late July Dickson changed the design of the magnet. It had been U-shaped with the column of ore directed past the open end. The two parallel magnetic rods were tapered into a horse-shoe shape, bringing the rods closer together. He hoped this would improve the strength of the magnet at the point of attraction. He also hoped that other modifications to the separator would bring good results: "The whole apparatus was improved considerably, finer adjustments, slide table, rubber edged openings making the machine practically air tight". The slide table allowed the magnet to be moved nearer or farther away from column of falling minerals. His optimism was in vain. The tests with the California gold were disappointing: "Numberless experiments were tried with the new machine with no better results".

He found that heating the gold ore brought better results. He also devised a means of controlling the flow of the particles by adjusting the angle of the slide towards the magnets. This initiated a redesign of the feeding apparatus. On 12 August he reported that Mr. Edison advised that a longer tube would accelerate the speed of the fall so a much higher apparatus was built and a tower built to hold the apparatus. This was being constructed on the 15th and a few days later, on the 19th, Dickson returned to experiments with heating the ore. Roasting increased the magnetism of the unwanted materials improving the fall on the side away from the magnets. Most of these tests involved roasting and re-roasting the particles so he was also looking for a technique to reduce roasting time. A new gold separator was completed by 26 August and "... several experiments were tried with good results – all plate side". He drew the new machine, but it needed improvements which were completed by 12 September.

In his final report he listed 12 improvements that had been made in the device. He had learned that magnetism was increased by carefully controlling the time of the roast and that over roasting reduced the magnetism. He also concluded that the density of the dust affected the angle at which it should be fed past the magnets; almost perpendicular for light dusts but at a greater angle for heavier material.[65]

It was a significant period for Dickson and this surviving notebook is important evidence of the meticulous care and orderly manner with which Dickson approached research. He was given an important assignment and his performance established credibility with Edison when he was planning his new lab. The quality of his work led to his assignment as head of the ore milling department, a position that became all the more important as ore milling evolved into Edison's most favored venture. Although Dickson was not involved in all aspects of Edison's mining and mineral prospecting, the research and testing in Dickson's ore milling department was an important component of one of the Wizard's more remarkable ventures. It absorbed the lion's share

64 EHS, a letter from Samuel Insull, signed by A.O. Tate, to Grace Co., New York, NY, 21 June 1887 explained this.

65 EHS.

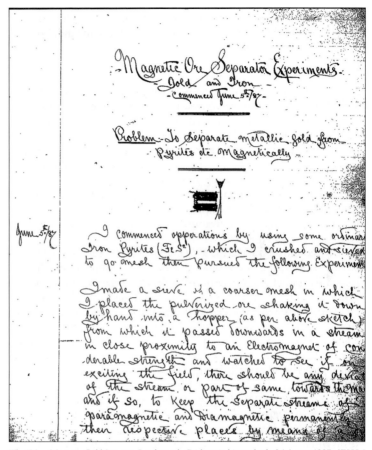

The "New Magnetic Gold Separator" as drawn by Dickson in his notebook, 26 August 1887. [EHS.]

of Dickson's time during the next five or six years, the period when he also led the Kinetoscope experiments.

The phonograph, the Wizard's magic

Thomas A. Edison: "... I was working on the telephone, developing the carbon button transmitter. My hearing wasn't too good and I couldn't get the sounds as clearly as I wanted to, so I fixed a short needle on the diaphragm of the receiver. When I let my finger rest lightly on this needle the pricks would show me its amplitude and that's what I wanted to find out.

"One day when I was testing this way it occurred to me that if I could indent a yielding substance with these vibrations I could reverse the process and reproduce the sounds. I sat down and made a sketch of a machine that I thought would do the trick.

"Then I called in John Kruesi, my chief mechanic. I explained the mechanism and asked him what he would charge me for making it. He said he would make it for thirty dollars, and I told him to go ahead. Then he asked me what it was for, and I told him it was going to talk. He thought I was joking and went away laughing.

"When he finished the machine and brought it back to me I put the tinfoil on, started her up, and recited 'Mary had a little lamb'. When I reversed and the words began to come back, Kruesi nearly fell over.

"'That was the only one of my inventions,' he added, 'that was perfect from the start. When we began to manufacture it we didn't have to alter a single detail.'"[66]

It was the phonograph that established Thomas Edison as a "Wizard". Most of Edison's inventions were things that had been predicted by others and discussed in the scientific and popular press. This is true of electric lighting and moving pictures, devices that other inventors were working on at the same time as Edison. Many of his record number of patents were for improvements on existing devices like the telegraph and telephone, innovations that the public knew or cared little about. But the phonograph was unique and completely unexpected. When it was introduced in 1878 – a machine that could talk and repeat sounds made earlier – the whole world was astounded and Edison became a national and international celebrity – the Wizard of Menlo Park.

Not surprisingly, it was Edison's favorite invention. More than any other, it was his own and he was quite possessive of it. But regardless of Edison's feelings about it, after a brief attempt to commercialize it, the phonograph was among the inventions that Edison set aside while he developed the electric light and commercial lighting systems during the early 1880s.

The revival of Edison's interest in the phonograph was stimulated by an old rival, America's other hero-inventor, Alexander Graham Bell. In 1881, one of Bell's assistants, Charles Tainter, a technician and skilled machinist who was interested in the phonograph, began experimenting with it at Bell's Volta Laboratory in Washington, DC. He was joined by Alexander Graham Bell's cousin Chichester Bell, a chemist. To improve on Edison's machine, Tainter began experimenting with wax applied on a cardboard cylinder as a recording medium to replace the tinfoil used by Edison. By 1885 they had developed a spring driven machine in which the recording was made by cutting or incising rather than by indenting as Edison had done. In June they applied for five patents for the Graphophone, a name derived from inverting Edison's term, phonograph. The patents were awarded in May 1886. Bell's prosperous father-in-law, Gardner Greene Hubbard, was an investor in the Edison Speaking Phonograph Company and through him Bell approached Edward Johnson and Uriah Painter, other major investors, with a proposal that Bell and Edison join forces and share the market. After months of fruitless negotiation, Bell formed his own company, the Volta Graphophone Company. In May 1887, Bell and Tainter brought their Graphophone, a model powered by a sewing machine treadle, to New York for a demonstration at the St. James Hotel. Afterwards they visited Edison, proposing a fifty-fifty commercial ar-

66 Tate, ...*Open Door*, pp. 114–115.

rangement. Edison offered them a smaller share which they rejected and the negotiations came to an end.

Edison and Bell were frequent rivals, often dove-tailing each other's inventions. They were quite different in appearance and background, but they also had a good deal in common. They were the same age, born a few weeks apart in 1847, Edison on 11 February and Bell on 3 March. They each began serious work as inventors while living in Boston; both specialized in electricity and communications; each captured the public's imagination as the personification of Yankee know-how (though Bell was born in Scotland) and they shared a common interest in deafness, Edison, because of his personal affliction and Bell through his mother's deafness and his own training as a teacher of elocution specializing in teaching the deaf. But their common interest resulted in common rivalries. They worked on similar projects in telegraphy and Edison made improvements to Bell's telephone that made it commercially viable. Before Edison discovered that the human voice could be successfully captured, Bell had been working in the same direction. Like Edison he had been developing a device to capture and relay the human voice so that it could be transmitted more clearly over long distances.[67]

Although he often disparaged rivals, Edison found competition stimulating. It was not unusual for him to react to news of a rival by starting a crash project to catch and pass the challenger. After learning of Bell's advances, Edison charged his closest associate Charles Batchelor and his friend Ezra Gilliland with upgrading the phonograph. Edison had Batchelor test various substances to improve on the wax being used in the graphophone while Edison worked on improving the reproducer so that it would not wear down the recorded groove. The work went slowly. Batchelor took the month of July for a long vacation and Gilliland was troubled with illness. Edison intended to work on the machine himself but had little time during the summer and fall of 1887 when his attentions were diverted to building and equipping his laboratory.

In August Edison's London associate Col. George Gouraud reported that he had been invited to head a British agency for the Graphophone Company and asked if Edison agreed. Edison cabled: "Have nothing to do with them. They are bunch of pirates ... Have started improving phonograph. Edison."[68]

But by August Edison's construction of the new lab was in full swing. The building demanded so much of his time that Batchelor was asked to help. The improvement of the phonograph was delayed but Edison felt that enough progress had been made that he could plan production and marketing. Possibly influenced by the prominence of Bell associates among the investors, he decided to by-pass the Edison Speaking Phonograph Company which had been created in the 1870s. In October he organized the Edison Phonograph Company and offered Gouraud foreign rights to the improved machine. Uriah Painter, Gardner Greene Hubbard, Charles Cheever and other stockholders in the

67 Conot, Op. Cit., p. 246; Josephson, Op. Cit., p. 317 ; Milllard, Op. Cit., pp. 64–65; Israel, Op. Cit., pp. 277–281. Gardiner Greene Hubbard was a patent attorney with a strong interest in innovative technology. Bell met Hubbard through his daughter, Mabel Hubbard, who Bell was tutoring, and later married. Hubbard backed Bell's early research in telegraphy which eventually led to the development of the phonograph. Edwin S. Grosvenor and Morgan Wesson, *Alexander Graham Bell*, pp. 47–49.

68 EHS; Josephson, Op. Cit., p. 318; Conot, Op. Cit., p. 261.

older company were offered a minority interest in the new company in exchange for their stock in the older company. They declined. A building was leased in Bloomfield, NJ with Gilliland in charge of manufacture. He offered Gilliland marketing rights in the U.S.

The "improved" Edison phonograph continued to have problems. Ezra Gilliland was not satisfied with the prototype he received and began to work on improvements. Edison was upset when Gilliland told him that improvements were necessary if it was to compete with the Graphophone, but he reluctantly accepted the criticism. At that time, mid-December 1887, Edison was just beginning to move into the new laboratory building. The phonograph would be a priority for the staff that was beginning to occupy the new facilities.[69]

69   Conot, Op. Cit., pp. 264–265; Israel, Op. Cit., pp. 281–283.

Chapter 4

Personal Matters

"I had received frequent invitations from himself and his wife to visit them at their home ... After dinner, though there were several [other] persons present ... Mrs. Dickson invited my son and myself to come with her and Mr. Dickson to another room. She then said that she desired to talk and to have Mr. Dickson talk in my presence ... about the matters that my sons and Mr. Dickson had so long been discussing. My recollection is the conversation was prolonged till near twelve o'clock ..."[70] (Woodville Latham, 19 October 1897)

"... Sometime in October, 1894, Mr. Woodville Latham and his two sons, Messrs. Otway and Gray Latham, accepted an invitation to dine at my house, at 166 Cleveland Street, Orange, NJ and after the guests had all left, Mr. Woodville Latham and his two sons made a proposition to me, in the presence of my wife, which was untenable, which, however, was modified and to which I agreed heartily, namely, that, as Mr. Woodville Latham was desirous of going into public exhibitions of the Kinetoscope, using same for projecting purposes, if on trial, it proved satisfactory, I should use my best endeavor to persuade Mr. Edison to give them the exclusive right for this special branch of the business, and that if I succeeded, I should have a substantial interest, subject of course, to Mr. Edison's approval. I signed such a letter, which was approved of by my wife, whose sense of right and wrong naturally was of the highest order."[71] (W.K.L. Dickson, 11 April 1911)

1886 was a year for marriages in the Edison and Dickson families. There were three weddings that year: Edison's second, Dickson's first and Dickson's sister Eva's.

Edison

Edison's came first. He married Mina Miller on 24 February 1886 in Akron, Ohio. She was the daughter of Lewis Miller, a prosperous manufacturer of agricultural machinery, a prominent Methodist layman and a founder of the Chautauqua movement. The seventh in a family of eleven children, she was twenty at the time of her marriage. Edison, who was now thirty-eight, met Mina through the good offices of Ezra Gilliland and his wife. Gilliland, who we met working on Edison's phonograph, had been Edison's friend since they were telegraphers working in the Mid-West during the Civil War. Gilliland's wife

70 NARA. Patent Interference No. 18, 461.

71 EHS, Dickson testimony, IMP 1911.

was a friend of the Miller family and Edison was introduced to Mina during the winter of 1884–1885 either at Gilliland's home in Boston or while attending the World Industrial and Cotton Centennial Exposition in New Orleans. We found Edison pursuing his suit while vacationing at Chautauqua – though with seemingly middling success. He did succeed in teaching Mina Morse code so that he could communicate with her privately. During the winter of 1885–1886 he wrote to Mr. Miller asking for her hand and received consent. They were married at the First Methodist Episcopal Church in Akron and left for a honeymoon at Ft. Myers, Florida, where Edison and Gilliland had built adjoining vacation homes. The newlyweds returned to "Glenmont", a substantial Victorian estate that Edison purchased for his new bride in Llewellyn Park, a suburban development on the fringes of Orange, New Jersey. It was after his move to Llewellyn Park that Edison moved his laboratory operations to East Newark, a location more convenient than Bergmann's in New York City. The marriage and return to New Jersey symbolize the shift in Edison's life and a recognition that he was better suited to life in the laboratory than among the bulls and bears of Wall Street.

W.K.L. Dickson

W.K.L. Dickson's wedding was two months after Edison's. He married Lucie Agnes Archer in Petersburg, Virginia on 21 April 1886. Lucie (sometimes Lucy) was the daughter of Allen L. and S. R. Archer of Petersburg.[72] We know less about their courtship than we know about Edison's. Lucie's father was the bookkeeper for A. Rosenstock & Co., a dry goods store in Petersburg, a prosaic sounding position, but it probably entailed management of the store's financial affairs and, in fact, the Archer family was prominent in Petersburg. Fletcher H. Archer, Lucy's uncle, had been mayor and played an important role in defense of the city during the Civil War when Petersburg was the site of an epic siege, the penultimate battle in the bloody struggle. The Dicksons became friendly with the Archers during their stay in Petersburg but there are no clues as to when Dickson proposed or how long their engagement lasted. Dickson was in Petersburg on 18 April when A.L. Archer wrote a letter of permission allowing his daughter to marry "Wm. K. Laurie Dickson". The letter was witnessed by John T. Pleasants. The couple got their Marriage License the next day and two days later were married at Grace Episcopal Church.[73]

Following the wedding the newlyweds left for an extended honeymoon, a "grand tour" of Europe. They landed in Cobh, Ireland 6 May 1886, and were in Europe until the end of summer. They were in London in mid-summer and missed a concert by Anton Rubinstein in London and later, 27 August 1886, visited Rubinstein at Peterhof, outside St. Petersburg. In between they visited a number of European countries, including Italy where W.K.L. visited the sculptor Longworth Powers at Villino Powers in Tuscany.[74] By the early fall they were back in New York City and Dickson returned to his job with Edison.

72 Hendricks Collection and General Register Office, London. Her name was recorded as Lucy on their marriage license dated 19 April 1886; but her father, A. L. Archer spelled it Lucie on a written permission of marriage dated 18 April 1886. It was recorded as Lucie on her death certificate, 12 February 1908. Dickson's two middle names were hyphenated on the marriage certificate, William Kennedy-Laurie, a form that he used at the turn of the century, but not during his years with Edison. This is the earliest that I have seen the hyphenated form for his names.

73 NMAH Hendricks.

74 EHS, Doc. File Ser. – 1887. Longworth Powers was the son of Hiram Powers, a popular American sculptor who had settled in Florence. Longworth Powers was working on a bust of Edison at the time. Powers sent Edison a photograph of it 16 January 1887 and in the accompanying letter he mentioned visiting with Dickson. "I had, only a short time ago, a very pleasant conversation about you with Mr. Dickson who spent an evening with us. He saw the bust & was pleased with it."

Was he gay?

There is speculation that Dickson was homosexual though there is no substantiating evidence confirming his sexual orientation. The suspicion that he might have been gay is based upon a number of his films that have a strongly homoerotic overtone, particularly the several films of the nearly buff muscle man, Sandow, and boxer Jim Corbett in equally revealing briefs. His childless marriage to an older woman and his life-long close relationship with his sister Antonia might seem further evidence. A possible cover of legitimacy for a lesbian relationship between Antonia and Lucie.

As was usual in the Victorian era, Dickson did not discuss his sex life. The only clues we have are a comment from Billy Bitzer that Dickson was a lady's man and dutiful letters to his wife from Dickson's associate William Cox during the Boer campaign, commenting about Dickson's writing to his wife, and Dickson's own comments in his book recording the campaign in which he mentions missing his wife. Dickson's second wife was a younger woman and they seem to have had a loyal relationship.

Edison's lab was a male enclave that few women breeched and Dickson often befriended young male employees, fostering their careers.

The all-male state of Edison's lab was not unusual in the late 19th century and Dickson's interest in promising young people may have been entirely altruistic, perhaps related to his not having children of his own. The films are the most intriguing clue, but he was recording Sandow's act and Corbett's customary boxing attire. His films offer an interesting conundrum, open to interpretation as seen by the viewer.

Perhaps that is true of his life as well.

If Edison's was a May–December marriage, Dickson's was December–May – and unusual for the convention-prone Victorian era. Although their marriage license recorded that they were both 26 years old and single, Lucie seems to have been a dozen years older than William Kennedy Laurie. Her death certificate in 1908 gave her age as 60, indicating that she was born about 1848. There is little information about her youth and no clue as to why she had not followed the usual path and married in her twenties as most of her contemporaries did. Nor is it clear why she lied about her age on the marriage certificate. Perhaps a clerical error since it is unlikely that Dickson was being deceived and probably not for the benefit of folks in Petersburg, a town small enough that most of the locals would know she was marring a younger man. Nor do we have a hint why Dickson chose to marry a woman older than himself in an era when it was more common for a man to marry a younger woman. Edison, whose new bride was 18 years younger and only recently a school girl, followed the more common practice of the period.

At twenty-six, Dickson was entering his prime and was probably a very good catch. If not drop dead handsome, he was a person with a flare for appearance and a vibrant, energetic demeanor which masked any flaws. He was lean and fit, standing 5 feet 10 inches and four years later at age 30 he weighed 137 ½ lbs.[75] He chose his clothes with care

75 EHS. A table of physical records of the lab staff done for an experiment in 1890.

and groomed himself meticulously – hair neatly cut and in place with an ever changing pattern of facial hair, usually a small beard and moustache that he altered according to whim and style. *All* of the surviving photographs show him as a person of elegance, exceptional style and pizzazz, one who could, and *did*, stand out in any crowd. Although he left no record of personal conquests, Billy Bitzer referred to him as something of a ladies man: "He was a magnificent dashing figure of a man, with an eye for the ladies and a manner I admired and hoped someday to achieve".[76] With his rising prospects in the domain of one of America's most noted celebrities he would qualify as a very eligible bachelor, so it seems remarkable that he would elect to marry an older woman .

Lucie

Lucie was neither beautiful nor plain. The two or three surviving pictures of her show a pleasant but not specially striking face and a trim figure dressed in modestly conservative, well made clothes. Even if she was not a spectacular beauty, Lucie Archer had cultural qualities that would have appealed to Dickson. She was well educated and though she did not seem to take part in the Dickson's concertizing, she appreciated music and had a literary bent. She knew German well enough that her translation of "Rosa von Tannenberg" stories from German to English had been published (though possibly in a vanity press edition). In short, she was well suited to the cultural climate that the Dicksons favored and may have been the principal organizer of the soirees and other cultural social gatherings that the Dickson household seemed to enjoy.

A letter from one of Dickson's young protégées gives a glimpse of the Dickson's cultural activities:

"... I do not see why, but Mr. & Mrs. Dickson seem to take a great interest in me. ... In the afternoon they asked me to go to New York with them as they were going to the Theatre there, but I declined, as I was not dressed well enough to go in a box with a man as prominent to the world as Mr. D.[77]

As the quotation at the beginning of this chapter indicates, Lucie took an active interest in Dickson's affairs and he respected her opinion. Woodville Latham, who was a Southerner of the old school, seems to have been a bit put off that Mrs. Dickson was asked to consult on a "gentleman's agreement", but Mrs. D. was a necessary component that had to be dealt with.

Visiting Anton Rubinstein

In March 1895, *Leslie's Weekly* published "A Reminiscence of Anton Rubinstein" by Mrs. W.K.L. Dickson. This florid and rather sensuous

76 G.W. Bitzer, *Billy Bitzer, His Story*, p. 12.

77 EHS, M135-273-274, letter, E.E. Cowherd to his father, 7 October 1894.

Lucie Archer Dickson. The photo on the left is from the set of Dickson's photographs Gordon Hendricks acquired from Mss. Polson and though it is unidentified it is probable that it is Dickson's first wife, Lucie Archer. The picture on the right is an enlargement from a portrait made c. 1897 (see page 477). [NMAH Hendricks.]

account of the Dickson's meeting with Rubinstein is the best surviving example of her literary efforts:

"It was in the year 1886 that I met Rubinstein, and by reason of one of those seeming *contretemps* which often yield a richer harvest than our most carefully planned undertakings. He was playing in London at the time, and had succeeded in completely revolutionizing the metropolis. Rubinstein – Rubinstein! was on every lip. It was a genuine sensation, something apart from the obligatory ceremonies of the Row and the conventional art of the picture galleries. The spontaneous and untrammeled genius of the great maestro had torn away the incrustations of society, and laid bare the fountains of national being, the Norman culture, the Scandinavian fire."

But the Dicksons missed the concert because of confusion about the time, but Mr. D contacted Rubinstein.

"... It was the last appearance of the imperial virtuoso, and we also were birds of passage, winging our flight from one Continental city to another. Necessity is the mother of courage as well as of invention, however, so after hurried consultation my husband sought Rubinstein's hotel, secured an interview and detailed our pitiful case. Rubinstein received him with exquisite cordiality, laughed at his despair and enjoined upon him to bring his wife to see him the next morning, an invitation to which I promptly acceded. ... His manner was completely opposed to the opinion I had conceived of him, and which his leonine appearance seemed to guarantee. It was simple and gentle, with a certain caressing tinge, exquisitely fresh and spontaneous, with that mellow boyhood which we ascribe to the larger children of the golden age."

320   *A REMINISCENCE OF ANTON RUBINSTEIN.*

rest of the building and completely isolated from outside sounds. The room, although unostentatious, was handsomely and tastefully furnished, and presented an essentially homelike aspect. It was supplied with a sonorous and sweet-toned Baby Grand, and was literally walled around with manuscripts, the originals of those inspired compositions with which the stage and concert platform have familiarized us. The windows looked out upon the waters of the gulf. These waters were still now, with the glassy serenity of midsummer; but it was not difficult to image them quickened with turbulent anguish and yielding their burden of inspiration to this storm-tossed and Titanic musician-soul.

After a few introductory words Rubinstein took his seat at the instrument, and while we listened, scarcely allowing our breath to stir the silence, the broken cadences of the improvisation shaped themselves into a melody of ineffable loveliness, tinged at first with sadness and a half-entreating inquiry, but rising through successive modulations and mutations to a strain of such seraphic joy, and purity, and triumph, that my soul parted with its last conventional fetter, and I found myself on my

RUBINSTEIN.

knees before him, covering his hands with tears and kisses, and murmuring, brokenly: "Master, master, you have played us into heaven!" He stroked my hair gently, while his eyes remained for awhile in some deep region of thought unknown to our cruder philosophy. Suddenly, with one of those swift transitions which are so essentially mirrored in his compositions, he threw back his massive head and said: "In heaven? Well, now, my child, I will play you into hell!" And then began the wildest, most demoniacal performance that it ever entered into the heart of man to conceive—a desperate fuga, or flight, interwoven with mad cachinnations of mirth; short, sharp outbursts of pain and despair, as of an impotent soul in the grasp of an inexorable destiny; clanging

dissonances, tantalizing suggestions of unfinished themes, weird and unsatisfactory harmonies; then a broken fragment of melody, an unresolved discord and—silence, throbbing with ghostly chaotic echoes.

After a long while I ventured to look up. Rubinstein's face was tense and ghastly, his brows were clammy, his fingers locked and unlocked themselves nervously. Presently, but still without speaking, he took a cigarette, offered me one, lighted his own, and leaning back wearily in his chair, closed his eyes. In a little while his features had resumed their usual sunny and benignant expression, and as we rose to go he tucked me impulsively under his arm and bore us off to the garden. There he rifled the floral sweets unmercifully for my benefit, crowning the gift by his own picture and autograph.

"Where and when shall we hear you again, Herr Rubinstein?" I said, wistfully, as we bade him adieu. An expression of extreme sadness crept over Rubinstein's mobile face. "I shall play no more," he answered, quietly. Then, in answer to our shocked exclamation, "I may lead orchestral concerts at the Gevandhaus, but I shall never play again in public. I shall devote myself to composition." "Then we shall never hear you in America?" I said, sorrowfully. "No," he replied; "I can never cross the ocean; my playing days are over."

The words were prophetic, as after events proved, but they came strangely at the time from one who seemed to be in the full tide of artistic activity.

And so ended my glimpse of the great maestro. It came at an eventful period of my life, and was necessarily brief. Since then I have passed through many experiences, have met diverse peoples in diverse lands, but no strain in the Great Psalm of Life has had power to displace those magic measures with which my soul was flooded in the Russian home of Anton Rubinstein.

An article by Lucie Dickson relating a visit with Anton Rubinstein during the Dicksons' honeymoon. It was published soon after Rubinstein's death. [NMAH Hendricks.]

His crowded schedule allowed only a short visit in London but he invited the Dicksons to come to his home outside St. Petersburg where he would play for them. They were in Russia at the end of August and visited Rubinstein in Peterhof:

"After a few introductory words Rubinstein took his seat at the instrument, and while we listened, scarcely allowing our breath to stir the silence, the broken cadences of the improvisation shaped themselves into a melody of ineffable loveliness, tinged at first with sadness and a half-entreating inquiry, but rising through successive modulations and mutations to the strain of such seraphic joy, and purity, and triumph that my soul parted with its last conventional fetter, and I found myself on my knees before him, covering his hands with tears and kisses, and murmuring, brokenly: 'Master, master, you have played us into heaven!' He stroked my hair gently, while his eyes remained for awhile in some deep region of thought unknown to our cruder philosophy. Suddenly, with one of those swift transitions which are so essentially mirrored in his compositions, he threw back his massive head and said: 'In heaven? Well, now, my child, I will play you into hell!' And then began the wildest, most demoniacal performance that it ever entered into the heart of man to conceive – a desperate fuga, or flight, interwoven with mad cachinnations of mirth; short, sharp outbursts of pain and despair, as of an impotent soul in the grasp of an inexorable destiny; changing dissonances, tantalizing suggestions of unfinished themes, weird and unsatisfactory harmonies; then a broken fragment of melody, and unresolved discord and – silence, throbbing with ghostly chaotic echoes.

"After a long while I ventured to look up. Rubinstein's face was tense and ghastly, his brows were clammy, his fingers locked and unlocked themselves nervously ... In a little while his features had resumed their usual sunny and begnignant expression, and as we rose to go he tucked me impulsively under his arm and bore us off to the garden. There he rifled the floral sweets unmercifully for my benefit, crowning the gift by his own picture and autograph."

On asking Rubinstein when they would hear him again:

"... An expression of extreme sadness crept over Rubinstein's mobile face. 'I shall play no more.' he answered, quietly. Then, in answer to our shocked exclamation, 'I may lead orchestral concerts at the Gevandhouse, but I shall never play again in public. I shall devote myself to composition.' ...

"The words were prophetic, as after events proved, but they came strangely at the time from one who seemed to be in the full tide of artistic activity.

"..."78

Antonia, who would live with Dickson and his bride for the remainder of her life, seems to have been a particular friend of Lucie's. Although Lucie didn't join them in performances she apparently shared their strong interest in literature, art and music. As we shall see, Lucie's article for *Leslie's* closely resembles Antonia's writing style and may have been strongly influenced by her.

Eva

Dickson's youngest sister, Eva, married John Thomas Pleasants of Petersburg, Va. on 24 December 1886. Since she will play only a marginal role in the rest of this story she deserves some attention here. She was a singer and housewife, born 3 March 1865 in Dinan, France. Her husband was a newspaperman who worked for the *Baltimore Sun*. According to Eva's son, Robert M. Pleasants he was "... one of the chief editors ...". The Pleasants were friends of the Archers and were also prominent in affairs in Petersburg. John T. Pleasants' grandfather, had been a mayor of Petersburg and a state senator. He was a medical doctor, a graduate of Johns Hopkins but he did not practice. John and Eva Pleasants had three sons but two died in childhood and only Robert M. Pleasants survived. Eva's husband died in 1911 but she lived until February, 1953, one month before her 88th birthday.[79]

78 NMAH Hendricks Collection. This unexpected encounter with popular pianist-composer may have been made possible because of an earlier meeting between Dickson and Rubinstein. It may be that Dickson's sister Antonia played for Rubinstein while she was in conservatory in Germany. If he remembered such an earlier encounter it could have smoothed the way and made Rubinstein more receptive.

79 NMAH Hendricks Collection. Most of this information is from correspondence in 1963 and 1964 between Gordon Hendricks and Robert M. Pleasants who was living in Kansas City.

AAlthough he lived in England from 1897 until his death, Mr. D. visited Eva and her family whenever he was back in the U.S.

Who pays?

Dickson's marriage came at the time that his career was on the rise and his decision to marry may indicate that he felt optimistic about his future. If he was already experimenting at the laboratory above Bergmann's, his optimism was probably justified and Edison seems to have given him encouragement. Although Edison's own marriage may have made him sympathetic to Dickson's request to be away for more than four months, his return to work after such a long absence shows that Dickson had gained favor with his boss. Paid vacations were not usual in Victorian America and Edison's employees usually had only a week or two and they went without pay while they were gone, although Edison occasionally paid a portion of the vacation for some of his veteran experimenters.[80]

Dickson had not been with Edison long enough, nor was his position important enough to have earned any vacation pay so he bore the all the cost himself – or it was paid for by someone else. He may have saved some expense by staying with relatives in England – at least one of his half-sisters, an aunt and several cousins lived there, but this would have been only a minor saving. At any rate it was a far more expensive trip than he could afford on his salary. He probably earned no more than $18.00 a week, i.e. more or less $1000 a year[81] The cost of ocean passage, ferry and rail tickets, meals and hotels for four months of touring in Europe were well beyond his wages. It is possible that their extended honeymoon was a gift from the Archers. (A cynic might speculate that it was a sort of dowery, a reward from a family happy to be relieved of the burden of a spinster daughter.) Although it might have been a romantic fling financed on a shoestring, it is possible that Dickson was able to pay for it from his own inheritance.

The state of Dickson's finances is one of the mysteries surrounding his life. Was he rich or poor? A grand tour of Europe certainly implies that he was "comfortably well off" or, perhaps, even wealthy and there are persistent hints that he was at least prosperous if not well to do, yet he frequently complained about money problems. He was born at a manor house in a charming, comfortable region of France, but we do not know if the family lived in the main house or occupied one of the servant's quarters attached to the manor. We know it was owned by Mme. Colin de la Bélière and did not belong to Dickson's father, but was James Dickson an employee, a renter or an artist being supported by a rich patron? Dickson's birth record and the local census from 1861 say that Dickson's father and mother both were persons of property – but not how much, how large or small; and where and what sort of property? The young Dicksons stayed almost four years in Virginia with no evidence that William Kennedy Laurie was gainfully employed. His job with Edison is the first that we know of. The three young Dicksons found a comfortable niche in local society, something that outsiders

80   EHS. This is based on a review of the pay slips for the laboratory from 1888–1893. The pay slips for the earlier period do not exist.

81   No pay records survive for this period, but in January 1888, he was paid $24.00 a week as an experimenter. According to A. O. Tate Nicola Tesla was being paid $18.00 when he was in the Testing Room. Tate, ... *Open Door*, pp. 148–149.

moving into small towns usually find very difficult. Petersburg, like other Virginia communities of the period, probably had a fixed, rather inflexible social strata. Petersburg natives also shared the unique memory of the extended siege of the city that placed an unusual burden on its citizens. That Dickson and his sisters, three young orphans, were able to penetrate it and gain acceptance indicates that Dickson's mother's family had strong roots and some status in the community before the younger Dicksons arrived.

As we shall see, Dickson's complaints about impoverishment were often made while he lived in relatively comfortable, sometimes luxurious surroundings in prosperous well to do communities. The state of Dickson's finances is an enigma, a mystery that will we will continue to follow as we chart Dickson's more tangible fortunes.

A Dickson vacation as a preview of coming attractions

In the summer of 1887, while experimenting with gold at the lab in Newark and before the new lab opened, Dickson took a week's vacation. On 10 August he registered at the Sanitarium in Clifton Springs, NY. It was just a break from the routine of work but, in retrospect, it was a harbinger of important components of his later life.

Clifton Springs was, and still is, a European-type health spa featuring hot sulphur springs for cure, rehabilitation and relaxation; the sort of place that his family might have visited during his youth. There were hotels, a health center and a pleasant park for strolling. It is a few miles and at that time, probably, an easy train ride away, from Rochester, home of George Eastman's Dry Plate and Film Company, a focal point of interest for Dickson's work on the Kinetoscope. There is no record that he visited there on this trip, but we will find Dickson returning to Clifton Springs.[82]

The day after he arrived, Dickson's friend and former co-worker, Harry Marvin joined him and the two stayed for the week.[83] Marvin, a native of upstate New York, probably introduced Dickson to Clifton Springs. They met in 1883 or 1884 while working in the Testing Room at Goerck Street. After leaving Edison, Marvin, an 1883 graduate of Syracuse University, returned to Syracuse in 1885 and the following year he received an AM degree from the University. A month before meeting Dickson in Clifton Springs, on 13 July 1887, Marvin applied for a patent for an Electric Magnetic Drill for use in mining and excavations. The patent was awarded 1 January 1889, U.S. 395,575 and was the basis for a successful machine-tool business which Marvin established in Canastota, New York, a small commercial town on the Erie Canal a few miles east of Syracuse and the home of his wife Oramella Tackabury, another Syracuse University graduate and the daughter of a local banker.[84]

This was the first of a number of vacations in upstate New York that Dickson shared with Marvin. The two had a number of common interests: electrical engineering, camping and, as we shall see, creating

82 Clifton Springs is one of those places that has changed relatively little over the years. Streets are paved and there are automobiles, but many of the 19th century buildings remain and it is still possible to take the cure there.

83 Gordon Hendricks, *The Edison Motion Picture Myth*, pp. 153–154.

84 EHS & NMAH Hendricks Collection. There is no indication that Dickson contributed to Marvin's design of the mining drill, but the meeting in Clifton Springs shows that they were corresponding.

novelties for popular entertainment. Their wives were usually along but there is no record that the women, or Marvin's son Robert, were along on this trip – though they certainly might have been. In a few years, Herman Casler, who had family in Syracuse, would join this group. Marvin may have met Casler while they both worked at the Edison works in Schenectady. The roots of the syndicate that established the Biograph Company, the subject of several later chapters, can be traced to this getaway in Clifton Springs in August 1887.

After his week in upstate New York, Dickson returned to Newark and ore milling, but his life was about to take a significant change. Edison's new lab was being built and he would soon be moving to Orange.

Chapter 5

From a Ladies' Watch to a Locomotive: The New Laboratory

Edison to Al Tate, [1887]: "'Tate! See that valley?'
"'Yes,' I replied, It's a beautiful valley.'
"'Well,' he responded, 'I'm going to make it more beautiful. I'm going to dot it with factories.[85]

Edison to J. Hood Wright (a partner of J. Pierpont Morgan): "... I will have the best equipped & largest Laboratory extant, and the facilities incomparably superior to any other for rapid & cheap development of an invention, & working it up into commercial shape with models patterns & special machinery – In fact there is no similar institution in existence we do our own castings, forgings can build anything from a lady's watch to a Locomotive.

"The machine shop is sufficiently large to employ 50 men & 30 men can be worked in the other parts of the works – Inventions that formerly took months & cost a large sum can now be done 2 or 3 days with only small expense, as I shall carry a stock of almost every conceivable material of every size and with the latest machinery a man will produce 10 times as much as in a laboratory which has but little material not of a size, delays of days waiting for castings and machinery not universal or modern ...

"... My ambition is to build up a great industrial works in the Orange Valley starting in a small way & gradually working up –. The Laboratory supplying the perfected invention models pattern & fitting up necessary special machinery in the factory for each invention My plan contemplates to working of only that class of inventions which require but small investments for each and of a highly profitable nature & also of that character that the articles are only sold to jobbers, dealers, etc. – No cumbersome inventions like the Electric Light. Such a works in time would be running on 30 or 40 special things of so diversified nature that the average profit would scarcely ever be varied by competition etc."[86]

The new lab was supposed to be completed in November but it ran late and over cost. Before construction started *The Orange Journal* described it as the "... largest and most complete electrical and experimental laboratory in the United States ..." and reported that it would cost about $50,000.[87] By September the paper reported the

85 Tate, Op. Cit., p. 139

86 EHS, lab notebook N-87-11-15, pp. 671–680. Edison's draft of a letter apparently sent August, 1889 seeking money from Morgan who declined to give Edison the support he requested.

87 *The Orange Journal*, 18 June 1887.

The Edison laboratory in Orange, NJ taken about 1888, but the lack of a signature indicates it was probably not taken by W.K.L. Dickson. [EHS.]

estimated cost to construct and equip the lab had risen to $180,000. "Largest and most complete" was the Edison mantra and he stinted nowhere. The original plan called for a single three-storied building, but four subsidiary buildings were added and nothing was spared to equip and supply the place. A.O. Tate and Samuel Insull who handled Edison's finances, were scrambling to meet the rising costs. At the beginning of July, when ground was broken, Tate wrote to Insull, who was based in Schenectady, that Edison had about $10,000 to meet anticipated bills of more than $20,000. He warned Insull that Edison would be contacting him to arrange payment of a loan Edison had made to Insull. There were signs of rising tension among Edison's supporting staff and Insull complained that his position was very difficult because there was no one in New Jersey to tell Edison he should be more prudent in his spending.

At the time the laboratory was built Edison was a wealthy man. Not on the scale of the Vanderbilts and Morgans, but he had a diverse portfolio of investments with Drexel, Morgan and a reserve in accounts at a bank in Newark. Although he could be very shrewd in dealing with commerce and was in the "business of inventing", he could be careless about managing funds on a day-to-day basis. Money could be moved to cover the costs of completing the lab but cash flow was a problem that continuously plagued him.

Beyond the cost of building and equipping there was the cost of day-to-day operations. He anticipated a staff of about 80 persons, much larger than worked in the labs in Menlo Park or Newark. In August he approached William Lloyd Garrison Jr., a Boston investment banker and son of the abolitionist, and J. Hood Wright, a partner in Drexel

Morgan with the description of his plan to fill the valley at Orange with factories quoted above. He proposed an arrangement where investors would support a company that would pay the laboratory up to $25,000 a year to conduct experiments. The investor's company would spin-off manufacturing companies to exploit his inventions. Edison would be paid half of the profits after the earnings reached 10 per cent. Wright and Garrison declined so Edison turned elsewhere. He negotiated with railroad baron Henry Villard, proposing that Villard pay all laboratory costs above those being funded by contracts with the telephone, telegraph and with A.B. Dick who had developed Edison's electric pen into a growing mimeograph industry. As Edison's estimate of the total costs of experiments grew, Villard also bowed out.

Edison decided to concentrate on several areas where he could count on money to cover costs of research: contracts for lighting, telephone and telegraph. He negotiated agreements with each of the manufacturing branches of the light company to conduct experiments to improve existing products and create new ones. A.B. Dick agreed to pay for research on mimeograph-related materials. Although Western Union did not agree, he was successful in getting an agreement with Bell Telephone Company to conduct experiments to improve the telephone. To these he added contracts with companies he organized to commercialize the phonograph and ore milling. He had prepared a long list of other research he proposed but he had to pare it down because the costs of experimentation would have to come from his own funds.

Edison began moving into the new laboratory at the end of November or beginning of December, 1887. The main building was a three story structure 250 feet long by 50 feet wide. Its feature, the two-story high library which also served as Edison's public office, was wood paneled with a marble fire place. It was stocked with 10,000 volumes of scientific and technical books, journals, published patents, etc., on many subjects and in several languages. New publications were added on a regular basis. Also on the first floor was a machine shop with the most modern equipment. It was large enough to accommodate a staff of fifty. In between was the stock room. Its legendary inventory was assembled comprehensively in order that no worker should be delayed while waiting for material to be shipped in. On the second floor was Edison's private office and work room, offices, experimenter's space and a precision machine shop for complex and sophisticated machine work. On the third floor above the library was the assembly room, later the recording studio. Attached to the main building was a power plant which provided power for the laboratory as well as Edison's home and some other residences in nearby Llewellyn Park.

The four one story auxiliary buildings, each 100 feet long by 25 feet wide, were aligned in a row, each building running perpendicular to the main building. The first, fronting on Main Street, was the galvanometer room, for fine measurements of electricity. It was built on a substantial foundation to reduce potential vibrations and no iron was used in construction. A small court yard separated it from the second which was the chemistry laboratory; the third was for carpentry, glass blowing, etc. The fourth, farthest from Main Street, was for metallurgy – it was to be Dickson's ore milling domain.

According to Edison historian Paul Israel, W.K.L. Dickson was one of four experimenters brought to Orange from the Newark laboratory. The others were Arthur Payne, H. De Coursey Hamilton and Patrick Kenny. Edison veteran John Ott was the principal machinist in charge of the Precision Room and his brother, Fred Ott was in the general machine shop along with A.K. Keller. Additional staff had to be hired. Edison was looking for a skilled chemist, a mathematician, someone with an understanding of physical measurement, etc.

Although they began moving in December, most of the staff seems to have started in January and new staff was still being added during February and March. Many of these new hands spent part of their time "fitting-up" since the working areas needed preparation before serious work could be begin. Among those "fitting-up" was Eugene Lauste, who was brought down from Schenectady. Paris born Lauste would become Dickson's close friend and associate.

A system to track work was begun so expenses could be charged back to the various contracting companies. Each experiment was assigned a unique number. Workers filled out a weekly time sheet, listing the time spent each day on various tasks, and supplies and materials were also charged by experiment number. Pay records were kept by John Randolph. The administrative staff, Edison, Alfred O. Tate, Edison's Personal Secretary, Tate's assistant, Thomas Maguire and John Randolph, were not included in these records. The records survive for the entire period that Dickson worked in Orange, making it possible to track his work and that of his assistants with remarkable specificity.

For this first pay period the total pay roll was $376.04. W.K.L. Dickson, who was paid weekly, received $24.00 and his time was charged to ore milling experiments. Another employee, A.E. Colgate, was also charged to a full week on ore milling and he was paid $8.00. During this period Dickson continued to work regularly on ore milling, but in the new laboratory, Dickson had a new project: on the second floor of the laboratory. Edison had set aside one room, room 5, for photography and placed Dickson in charge.

"Keen on photography"

"In 1887 Mr. Edison, who knew that I was keen on photography, disclosed his favorite scheme of joining his phonograph to pictures taken photo-graphically with a device like the *Zoetrope*."[88]

The information files at the Edison Historic Site in West Orange, New Jersey, say that Dickson became Edison's photographer in 1884. This biographical note was probably made in the 1950s or 1960s by staff at the Historic Site and it seems to be based on a letter that Samuel Insull sent 15 September 1884 to an inquirer which said that Edison "... has a man in his Laboratory who does all the photographing that he requires".

88 *Journal of the SMPE*, Vol. 21, December 1933, p. 9.

Since Dickson is the one and, probably, only staff member from this period who is known to have had skills and interest in photography, it is not unreasonable to assume that this was a reference to Dickson.

Dickson apparently learned photography during his youth and while there is no specific information about when he became Edison's photographer, it could have been as early as 1884. Almost all of the surviving photographs that Dickson made for Edison were made at the new laboratory. There is no reliable information about how much and what kind of photography Dickson might have done before the lab moved to Orange, but he was involved enough that Edison relied on his advice in planning for photography in the new lab.

Edison's interest in photography predates Dickson's involvement. Photography had been a part of Edison's record keeping in Newark, NJ in the early 1870s when he was just beginning the business of invention. Pictures were taken of the staff, the exteriors of the laboratory buildings in Newark and Menlo Park, the working areas and his inventions. To satisfy a growing demand from the press and general public, Edison sat for portraits, usually taken by commercial photographers. It is certainly possible that Dickson was taking routine photographs of equipment, buildings, etc. prior to 1887.[89]

Since he did not work at photography as a primary profession, Dickson would probably have been considered an amateur by his contemporaries, but in the 1880s the term "amateur photographer" was not necessarily deprecatory. Many of the most daring and creative photographers of this period were amateurs – Alfred Stieglitz was a director of the Society of Amateur Photographers of New York, whose meetings Dickson claimed to attend.[90] Because photography was still a complicated system involving a variety of equipment and chemicals, its practitioners, including amateurs, were serious people who invested time and money to learn the mysteries of lenses, exposure time, emulsions, sensitometry and the chemistry of developing, fixing and copying photographs. A lively and extensive national and international trade literature kept track of the rapidly changing technology, reporting new developments, advising about up-to-date methods, and new equipment, and offering an opportunity to exchange information. Among the relatively recent innovations were faster emulsions and dry plates which allowed the photographer to take an exposure – even several exposures – and develop it later, freeing the photographer from bulky and awkward paraphernalia necessary to prepare and develop photographs on the spot. Despite these changes, many photographers still used wet collodion, a cumbersome process which required mixing a sensitive photographic emulsion, applying it evenly on glass, exposing and then developing it – all in rapid succession. Point, shoot and send it to the drug store was the photography of the future, though, as we shall see, George Eastman was struggling to create it. In the meantime, photography, professional or amateur, remained the province of the dedicated – though the number of committed practitioners was surprisingly large.

Though an amateur, Dickson was in the ranks of the very skilled.

89 There are a number of photographs of Edison's inventions signed or initialed by Dickson in the biography of Edison which he co-authored with his sister Antonia Dickson. These are not dated so it is impossible to tell if they were made specifically for the biographic articles or were shot earlier. The earliest of these articles appeared in *Cassier's Magazine* in November 1892.

90 Beaumont Newhall, *The History of Photography*, p. 153. Steiglitz was in Europe in the late 1880s, returning to New York in the early 1890s. Dickson might have met him at meetings, but not at those that he mentions in his memoirs.

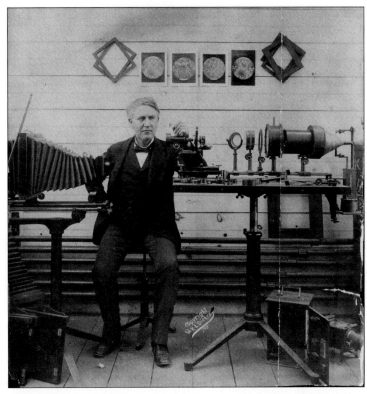

These three pictures of Mr. Edison are the only surviving examples that demonstrate how Dickson worked. They were probably taken on two different days as indicated by the change in Edison's tie. They are captioned as showing Edison taking microscopic photographs, but the camera is not in position to take images. [EHS.]

His inherited artistic skills and youthful training in the arts are most evident in his photography. He possessed a strong sense of composition, used light to advantage, chose the placement of his camera very carefully and was able to time his exposure so that he captured what seemed the essence of his subject. This was often the result of taking several negatives in order to get the desired image. At least three separate takes of Edison posing with a microscopic photographic device survive at West Orange and these allow us a rare view of his photographic techniques. After selecting a desired take, he created prints from his negatives with great care, enhancing them by masking unwanted images, occasionally high lighting them by hand and sometimes decorating the mounted photograph with hand drawn embellishments.

During his years at the lab he produced some of the most memorable photographs recording Edison and his work – images that are beyond the realm of industrial record. Perhaps the best known is a portrait of Edison with his improved model of the phonograph taken at 5 a.m. June 16, 1888 after a seventy-two hour session. It has become known as the "Napoleon of invention" picture. Edison, slumped in a

This photograph, called "The Napoleon of Invention", is, if not the best known of Dickson's photos, certainly the most reproduced. It was taken 16 June 1888 following a marathon session revising the Edison phonograph. [EHS.]

chair is listening to a phonograph through ear tubes with wisps of hair on his brow after the style of the emperor. His aspect conveys fatigue, concentration and, perhaps, triumph accompanied by a distant expression implying that his mind might be on the future.

With space for photography in the plans, as the new laboratory neared completion, Dickson began ordering equipment. A shipment of unspecified photographic goods was received on 24 November from Scovill Mfg. Co., NYC., one of America's leading suppliers of photographic materials and several shipments followed. In April 1888 Scovill billed Edison $918.63 covering 10 shipments made between 29 November 1887 and 6 March 1888. In January 1888, Dickson was in Philadelphia seeing W.H. Walmsley, a leading supplier of optical and photographic goods. He ordered several large microscopes, a quantity of extra eye pieces and three first class 1½ inch lenses.[91] The microscopes were probably for working with minerals but the 1½ inch lenses were probably for photography. Edison was ordering quantities of microscopes because they were used throughout the lab, but this order from Walmsley is the only instance where Dickson ordered one for himself and it is of particular interest because microscopes were important in the early Kinetoscope experiments.

The correspondence from Scovill and Walmsley mentioned that Dickson visited their offices in New York and Philadelphia, the earliest examples of his free-wheeling, unfettered approach to work. Rather than rely on catalogs and time-consuming exchanges of correspon-

91 EHS & Hendricks Collection.

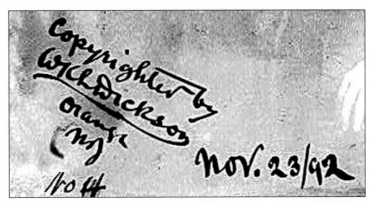

Dickson's unique signature is easy to identify and it usually appeared prominently on photographs that he liked. [EHS.]

dence, if he needed something Dickson would go and get it. This earned him a well-deserved reputation for being impulsive and unpredictable. It may have annoyed some co-workers, but apparently appealed to Edison who admired initiative and was equally unbound by convention.

There is no list of the equipment Dickson ordered from Scovill but, like the rest of the laboratory, the Photographic Room was well equipped. It caught the attention of journalist Horace Townsend who did an article on the recently opened lab for *Cosmopolitan Magazine*:

"... Not the least interesting of these little scientific headquarters is the photographic studio, under the superintendence of a good-looking young artist, who, like every one else about the place, is refreshingly enthusiastic about his own specialty. He has an establishment which a leading professional 'knight of the camera' might envy, for he has one lens which enables him to use plates about the size of an ordinary newspaper, and so prevents the necessity of enlarging. Some of his exterior views betray the skilled artist in their picturesqueness and the cleverness with which the point of view which is the right one has been taken advantage of. Hanging on the walls are pictures of inventions and machines in their various stages of development, and this little gallery forms a fitting complement to the scrap-books we looked over down-stairs; for here is the old 'barrel-organ' phonograph of ten years ago side by side with the perfect little instrument of to-day, while the electric-light lamp is shown in its infancy as well as in its maturity."[92]

It would be useful to know what model camera or cameras was used and what supplementary equipment was chosen, but the only item specified in this early correspondence was one ferrotype plate. But this is interesting because ferrotype is a process similar to tintype and a technique from an earlier generation. It was no longer in vogue and was different from the more contemporary photo materials he commonly ordered. It indicates that Dickson was trying to familiarize himself with some of the less commonly used photo techniques.

There are many orders for supply, however, and they show that Dickson favored dry plate photography for conventional photography.

92 EHS, unbound clippings. "Edison, His Work and His Work-Shop" in *Cosmopolitan Magazine*, April 1889, pp. 598–607.

In the early years he usually ordered Harvard Plates to make negatives. These were manufactured by the Harvard Dry Plate Company of Cambridge, Massachusetts and purchased from Scovill Manufacturing Co. (later Scovill and Adams). Prints were made on photographic paper also purchased from Scovill. Negative plates were ordered in sizes ranging from 4 by 5 inches to 11 x 14 inches. The frequency that 11 x 14 inch plates were reordered indicates that he favored the large negatives as mentioned in Townsend's article. Smaller plates, 5 x 8 and 4 x 5 inches, were ordered in quantity, but irregularly and seemingly for specific projects. Although he used 8 x 10 plates more commonly in later years, he used them sparingly during the first three years at Orange. Although the negatives were in large format, prints were commonly made on 8 x 10 or 5 x 8 paper during these years.[93] This indicates that he favored the large format for work requiring a sharp, clear image and the smaller formats for more conventional jobs. The size and clarity of images were critical concerns during the Kinetoscope experiments.

The largest assembly of Dickson's photographs from this period are those that he used to illustrations in *The Life and Inventions of Thomas A. Edison*, the biography of Edison which he co-wrote with his sister Antonia [see Chapter 22]. It is easy to identify his best photos because if he was proud of the picture he signed them in a corner either as W.K.L Dickson or W.K.L.D. – usually underlined with a flourish. Among these are a number of photographs of Edison's inventions made prior to 1888.

There was a steady demand for portraits of Edison and applicants usually received a formal portrait, usually made by a professional in New York. The surviving portraits of Edison taken by Dickson were made at the Orange laboratory and were often taken in a working environment such as the library, the chemistry room, the ore milling department or with inventions such as versions of the phonograph. This provided a context, a moment of rest in the midst of activity. They illustrate the work and accomplishments of the laboratory – and Mr. Edison. They are taken with a variety of angles and lighting. Some are full figure, others closer showing a partial figure. Although clearly posed, the informal – or at least, less than formal style of the poses – creates an impression similar to a candid shot.

Edison gave Dickson unusual control over his photographs. During the 1890s Dickson registered copyright in his own name for a dozen of so of the photographs he made at the lab. Most of them were illustrations from the Dicksons' biography of Edison and among them are photographs of Edison at the age of 14, Edison's mother and pages from his *Grand Trunk Railway* newspaper, pictures that Dickson could not have taken himself. These photographs were among a group of more that 60 of Dickson's photographs offered for sale by *Phonogram* magazine in the fall and winter of 1892–1893, a date that coincides with the publication of the Dickson's biographical articles in *Cassier's Magazine*. The magazine offered 8 x 10 photographs mounted on 10 x 12 cards for $1.25 each or $14.00 per dozen. It was an independent activity – a private business. It was done openly and must have had Edison's

93   This is based on orders received at the laboratory. During the period 1888–1890 the lab received 156 ea. 11 x 14 plates; 12 ea. 10 x 12 plates; 24 ea. 8 x 10 plates; 72 ea. 5 x 8 plates (all in 1888) and 72 ea. 4 x 5 plates (also all in 1888). During the same period they received 12 ea. 11 x 14 papers; 60 ea. 8 x 10 (plus "1 package"); and 72 ea. 5 x 8 (plus "one package"). 48 papers of unspecified size were also received.

Edison
at Work in Chemical Dept
Orange Cal.

This picture of Edison experimenting in the chemical lab demonstrates the care that Dickson took to create the impression of reality in carefully posesd pictures. Chemistry was one of Edison's passions and he would spend hours working on formulas, sometimes for business, sometimes for pleasure. Dickson was familiar with Edison's style of work and was able to pose him convincingly even though the limitations of the film made taking interior shots in natural light difficult. [EHS.]

94 A modified version of the "Napoleon of Invention" photo was used on the cover of the magazine.

consent. Edison did not own *Phonogram* but it was a magazine catering to the phonograph industry and he was a dominant force in the market. He probably saw each issue and it was read by his staff, some of whom contributed to the publication.[94]

Room number 5, on the second floor in the center of the building near the elevator, was Dickson's realm. It was an unusual work area. Most of Edison's experimenters shared spaces with others and in some rooms, like the machine shops, a number of people worked together. The photographic room was exclusively for Dickson, an assistant and occasional helpers. Others were excluded. The door was often locked and supplies, messages, food, etc. were passed through a smaller portal. This reclusiveness was prescribed in part by the need to keep photo sensitive materials from unexpected exposure to light but also because Dickson was entrusted with an experiment that was confidential, requiring a degree of secrecy.

Part III

1888–1893
The Quest for the Kinetoscope-Kinetograph

Chapter 6

The Germ of an Idea

"In the year 1887, the idea occurred to me that it was possible to devise an instrument which should do for the eye what the phonograph does for the ear, and that by a combination of the two, all motion and sound could be recorded and reproduced simultaneously. This idea, the germ of which came from the little toy called the Zoetrope, and the work of Muybridge, Marié [sic], and others has now been accomplished, so that every change of facial expression can be recorded and reproduced life size." (Thomas A. Edison's introduction to "Edison's Invention of the Kineto-Phonograph" by Antonia and W.K.L. Dickson, 1894)[95]

On Saturday, 3 March 1888, the *Orange Journal* published a letter from a reader, A.N. Tinude, who commented on a lecture at the New England Society on the previous Saturday. He (or she) questioned "... the propriety of exhibiting semi-nude human figures to a promiscuous assembly ...". The protest was directed to an illustrated lecture on "Animal Locomotion" presented a week earlier by Eadweard Muybridge, the prominent chronophotographer. While the principal subject of the lecture was Muybridge's pioneering study of the trotting horse, he also included recent photographs from his work at the University of Pennsylvania. It was the latter, with studies of athletes and dancers as well as dogs, horses and zoo animals that incurred the wrath of Mr. (or Ms.) Tinude. Among those in the "promiscuous assembly" gathered at the New England Society on 25 February 1888 was Thomas Edison and, it is assumed, William Kennedy Laurie Dickson

Muybridge was the pioneer – the father – of a new field of research, chronophotography, which used rapid photography to analyze the movements of humans, animals and other creatures. In 1877 and 1878 Muybridge successfully captured the motion of several of Leland Stanford's prized horses using a battery of still cameras. Legend has it that Stanford hired Muybridge to settle a bet that a running horse lifted all four hooves off the ground – or had one foot on the ground and three lifted off – the versions vary. Bet or no bet, Muybridge's photographs were a sensation because they showed that common conceptions of how horses moved were incorrect. Zoologists, medical researchers, artists and others were drawn to Muybridge's images and he began a

95 *Century Magazine*, Vol. XLVIII, No. 2, June 1894, p. 206.

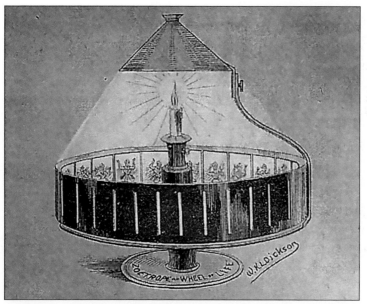

By 1888 devices existed to view moving images, though the images were brief and drawn rather then photographed. Muybridge demonstrated his photographs of motion by projecting drawings made from his images with his Zoopraxiscope (facing page) which he had adapted from the Zootrope, a popular children's amusement. The drawing of a Zootrope on the left was made by W.K.L. Dickson for the publication History of the Kinetograph, Kinetoscope and Kineto-Phonograph which he wrote with his sister Antonia Dickson. It was probably made from one he owned. [LC.]

series of publications and lectures. After touring Europe he was hired by the University of Pennsylvania to continue his work. When he came to Orange he had completed most of his research and was preparing a new publication of his recent photographs.

Although the purpose of Muybridge's research was the analysis of human and animal movement by capturing phases of motion with still photographs, his lectures usually included a reversal of the process with the projection of briefly reconstructed movements. Muybridge had adapted a child's entertainment device, the Zoetrope and he called his creation the Zoopraxiscope. A series of images showing a complete cycle of motion were drawn on a glass disk from his original photographs. The disks were projected by a magic lantern and when rotated they created an impression of movement on the screen. He had a number of disks which enabled him to show his audiences a variety of different subjects in action. The Zoopraxiscope was the closest approximation of genuine moving pictures yet achieved.

Two days after his show, on Monday, 27 February 1888 Muybridge visited Edison at the recently opened laboratory. According to Muybridge they discussed the practicability of joining Muybridge's Zoopraxiscope with the Edison's phonograph. Although Edison would later deny that the combination was discussed, subsequent events support Muybridge's claim.[96] Dickson, who was certainly aware of Muybridge's

96 Muybridge's claim appears in the forward to *Animals in Motion* in 1899. Edison's denial was made in 1921 to Terry Ramsaye when Edison reviewed the draft of Ramsaye's chapter on Edison's early motion picture work. Edison: "no, Muybridge came to [the] Lab to show me pictures of a horse in motion he took in California nothing was said about phonogh [sic]." See Hendricks, *Myth...*, p. 12 and Terry Ramsaye Collection, V. I, Mss: 692; Baker Library, Harvard Business School, Cambridge, Mass.

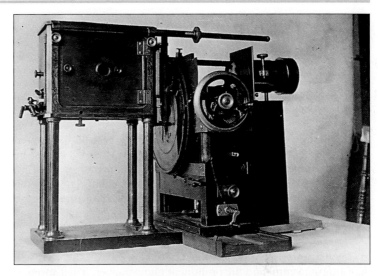

work and undoubtedly curious about the presentation probably attended the lecture and may have been at the meeting at the Lab – though there is no evidence confirming his presence.

Two months later, on 4 May 1888, Muybridge was back in Orange this time to lecture at the Music Hall for the benefit of the Free Library.[97] This visit set off an exchange between Edison and Muybridge. Edison asked Muybridge for plates from his most recent publication, *Animal Locomotion*. On 12 May Muybridge wrote to tell Edison that he had sent a catalog and invited him to make a selection. He added that if Edison was too busy Muybridge would make a selection based on information about the subjects that interested Edison. "... I think my judgment in the matter will meet your approval ...". Muybridge added a suggestion that Edison might create a piano particularly adapted for phonograph recording, "... which will serve your purposes more effectively than one in which the necessity exists for conveying the sound by means of a wire connected with the frame work ...".[98]

Edison ignored the pianistic proposal, but took him up on the offer of plates, made a selection and the plates arrived about six months later, 15 November 1888.

It was apparently Muybridge who reported their meetings to the press. The *New York World*, 3 June 1888, reported that they discussed a possible marriage of Muybridge's photos with the phonograph. The *Electrical Review* said that Muybridge was working on a device to take sixty or seventy photographs of a speaker or performer and if combined with the phonograph it would be possible to see and hear Edwin Booth or Lillian Russell. There was a similar report in the *Photographic Times* on 22 June 1888.[99]

Muybridge visited Edison at the time that he was implementing the shopping list of research projects for the recently opened laboratory and it stimulated his growing enthusiasm for pictorial material. When

97 Hendricks Collection. Reported by *East Orange Gazette*, 10 May 1888.

98 EHS.

99 Hendricks Collection. The article in *Electrical Review* appeared 9 June 1888.

the plates from *Animal Locomotion* arrived they were put on display around the Library. Writing in 1939, Walter Mallory recalled:

"I have a distinct recollection that in the spring of 1889 someone sent Mr. Edison a set of photographs of running horses which were taken by Meyerbridge [sic]. The pictures were mounted on boards and set up in the library for Mr. Edison's inspection and they were there for some months. It was these pictures which again started him working on the development of the moving picture machine ...".[100]

Mallory's visit to the laboratory would have been in connection with an ore milling machine for an iron mine in Michigan owned by Mallory. Edison and Mallory were organizing a company to process ore from Mallory's mine with Edison's separating machine. The machine was being built for Mallory in the fall of 1888 and he visited the lab several times. Modifying the design of Mallory's separating machine occupied much of Dickson's during this period.[101]

Edison made his first announcement of work on motion pictures in October, a few months after the well publicized exchange between the famous inventor and the prominent photographer. Their meeting is usually cited as the starting point for the Kineto, and Dickson himself is among those acknowledging the importance of the Muybridge-Edison meetings. In 1898 he wrote to his friend Eugene Lauste "... Mr. T. Edison saw Mr. Muybridge in 1887 and told me to make a machine for taking and seeing, that is to say, in connection with his phonograph ..." and in a hand written manuscript sent to Edison in 1921:

"... Mr. Edison disclosed his scheme to me in 1886 having received from prof. Muybridge in 1885 or 6 a large number of motion charts produced by a battery of cameras as now well known – which urged Mr. Edison to endeavor to produce an apparatus wh' w<u>d</u> be of practical use – & sh<u>d</u> we succeed he proposed to join the new motion picture machine to his phonograph – secure the effect of sight & sound".[102]

As was frequently the case, Dickson's dates are inaccurate – as are some of the details – but in substance he accepted Muybridge's role in arousing Edison's interest in moving pictures.

Edison and images

Muybridge may have supplied stimulus, but the idea of adding something visual to the phonograph lurked in the back of Edison's mind before their meeting. A decade earlier a cartoon, "Edison's Telephonoscope (Transmits Light as Well as Sound)" was published in *Punch's Almanack for 1879*. Drawn by the prominent English cartoonist George du Maurier, it pictured English grandparents conversing with their children and grandchildren in the Antipodes through a television-like screen on the wall above their fireplace.[103] His fanciful image was a reflection of the public's astonishment at the recent news of Edison's phonograph. A machine that talked and retained bits of the past was an unanticipated wonder and it set-off rumors that the Wizard was working on some sort of "far seeing" device, speculations that cropped up from time-to-time, especially in England.

100 NMAH Hendricks & EHS. A letter from Edison's friend, sometimes business partner and employee, W.S. Mallory, 1 February 1939. The plates from *Animal Locomotion* were received 15 November 1888 from Photo Gravure Co.

101 EHS; Israel, Op. Cit., p. 344. The company organized by Mallory and Edison, The Edison Iron Concentrating Company, was a family owned business with Edward Mallory, Walter's father and Edison's father-in-law Lewis Miller and his brother-in-law, Ira Miller as principal share holders. It was formed in the late spring of 1888 and the plant in Humboldt, Michigan was completed December.

102 Merritt Crawford Collection, MoMA. Letter W. K.-L. Dickson to Eugene Lauste, 4 February 1898 and EHS, W.K.L. Dickson to Thomas Edison, 7 May 1921, " Some Facts Relating to the Founders of Moving Photography; Pioneer *Thos Alva Edison*" by W.K. Laurie Dickson – Wolsey House, Montpelier Rd. Twickenham – England.

103 *Punch's Almanack for 1879*, 9 December 1878.

PUNCH'S ALMANACK FOR 1879.

EDISON'S TELEPHONOSCOPE (TRANSMITS LIGHT AS WELL AS SOUND).

This charming cartoon speculating that Edison would invent a television-like device appeared in Punch's Almanack for 1879. It reflects the amazement that much of the world felt when the introduction of the phonograph showed that the human voice could be captured and reproduced. It was drawn by the popular illustrator George du Maurier who gained fame later as the author of Trilby. Edison was familiar with the cartoon and the memory of it may have lingered in the back of his mind. The phonograph created the impression that Edison, the Wizard, was capable of working wonders and rumors that he was working on a "far sight machine" or something to make images move cropped up from time to time. [LC.]

While Edison generally ignored science-fictional speculation, from time-to-time he fed the rumor mills by providing overly zealous reporters tales of experiments that existed only in the imagination. One of his favorites was the "far seeing" device – images sent through the air à la du Maurier. His comments were often vague, imprecise and, occasionally, off the wall but they recurred so often and over such a span of years, that he must have had serious thoughts about it – though the Kinetoscope is the closest he came to acting upon his conjectures.

But not all of Edison's speculations were fodder for journalists. In November 1887, while preparing for the new lab, he scribbled a list of potential experiments and the names of assistants to work on them. For "Dixon" there were three involving photography: first, "Photograph through metals & other thin plates opaque to light"; second, "Idea for photoghg red or heat end of spectrum Coat a plate with material which at ordinary temperature decompose but do not below Zero – now absorbtion of hcat rays will raise temperature on certain points up to combining point & thus photogh lines of spectra Etc." and third, "Photograph Scintillations". The first two were ignored or forgotten, but the third, seems an intention to use high speed photography to photograph a spark or something similar.[104] This seems an interesting suggestion that Edison and Dickson may have discussed high-speed photography before meeting Muybridge.

104 Scintillation n. 1. The action of scintillating. 2. A spark; flash. ... (*The American Heritage Dictionary of the English Language*, New York, American Heritage Publishing Co., Inc. & Houghton Mifflin Co. 1969).

It has been assumed that Edison had little interest in and no skill with photography. Pictures of Edison with cameras, often movie cameras, tend to support this view, since he usually looks as if he had no idea how to operate it. While there is little evidence that he ever used a camera with any regularity, that does not mean that he lacked curiosity about – or knowledge of – photography. In addition to using photography to record his activities, there is one interesting instance where he may have made more personal use of a camera. In the fall of 1886 a sizable shipment of "photographic goods" was ordered from E. and H. T. Anthony and delivered to Edison's Florida home, arriving about the time of his extended period of recuperation during which he planned his new lab. There is no hint as to the purpose or who might have used it, but a letter asking for a replacement for a thumb screw that held a camera to the tripod, indicates that it was being used.[105] It was paid for by the lab and Edison had a small lab at Ft. Myers so it may have been for research but it is also possible it was for less serious business. Ft. Myers was an undeveloped, unspoiled area and potentially photographic. Edison and his friend Ezra Gilliland were among the earliest to build vacation retreats there. Fishing was good, the Everglades were not far away, wildlife was abundant and opportunities for photography were almost unlimited. We can only speculate about the camera's use but it was during this interval that Edison decided that photography would be a tool for research – and an object of experimentation.

This is one of several instances that show that Edison's interest in images was thriving at the time that the lab was being planned. In April 1888, a bit more than a month after Muybridge's first lecture and while the lab was still being staffed and equipped, a magic lantern was purchased. The price, $200, indicates it was a professional-quality machine.[106] In November a magic lantern sheet, i.e. a screen, was purchased and apparently installed in the Library. A very large number of lantern slides were ordered and, rather surprisingly, Arthur E. Kennelly, one of the most skilled of the recently hired experimenters, was the principal in contacting suppliers. In October, a month before the screen was purchased and co-incident with the beginning of the Kineto experiments, he wrote to T.H. McAllister, 49 Nassau St., NYC for prices of slides from York and Son, a leading English magic lantern company. He asked if special prices would be given for orders of $1000 or $1500. At the beginning of November Kennelly, Theodore Lehmann and F.P. Bergh, all recently hired experimenters, began reporting time spent on a new project, no. 233, Magic Lantern. Kennelly's correspondence with McAllister continued through the end of the year and Edison viewed and selected some of the slides. McAllister sent several large shipments and brought samples to the Lab for Mr. Edison to view. The purpose of the Magic Lantern project is unclear, leaving room for speculation. Kennelly was experimenting with methods to conquer Yellow Fever by killing insects and bacteria by various means – among them gasoline – and this project may have been the initial purpose, but the quantity and variety of subjects indicates a more general objective

105 EHS. The equipment was ordered 21 November 1886, delivered c. February 1887 and the bill for $123.37, dated 31 January 1887, was paid for from laboratory funds.

106 EHS. It was purchased from Richardson and Metzger and the set included an extra lens, a focusing lense, two slide bars and a condenser.

than the study of microbes and insects – a thousand dollars would have bought a lot of bugs in 1888![107]

Arthur Kennelly was one of the most eminent of Edison's employees. He was about the same age as Dickson and like Dickson, he was British and born abroad, but in India rather than the continent. He was an electrical engineer and a skilled mathematician with a strong background in telegraphy. He was educated in England, Scotland, France and Belgium. After working for Edison he had his own consulting firm then taught at Harvard where he was named an honorary professor and Massachusetts Institute of Technology where he served as Chairman of the Faculty. During his distinguished career he won numerous awards. Edison hired him at the beginning of 1888 to head his new Galvanometer Room which conducted electrical tests on motors, lamps, wiring and other elements of experiments being conducted by others.

Kennelly's involvement suggests another possible purpose for experimenting with magic lanterns. He was an expert electrical engineer, particularly skilled in the analysis of motors, testing of wires, wiring systems and lamps. It is possible that Edison asked him to test for a cheaper and more powerful light source for projection.

Although not all of the lantern slides were microbe-related, Edison's interest in health was very real. He greatly admired Louis Pasteur and was genuinely interested in efforts to improve medical practice. He understood that enlarged and projected microscopic images had great potential as a tool for research and took steps to join the field. On 25 September 1888 – another date close to the beginning of the Kineto experiment – Edison's purchasing agent, John. C. English requested a price quote for microscopes and for slides of bacteria of diseases from two suppliers, J.M. Queen and Walmsley. Two weeks later Edison's book dealer, D. Van Nostrand & Co. sent copies of *Bacteria Investigation* by Joubert and *Relations of Micro Organisms to Disease* by Belfield and Edison's interest in finding a cure for Yellow Fever was reported in an article in the *New York World* on 7 October 1888.[108] The article described and illustrated a micro-photographic outfit being used by a number of doctors engaged in research with microbes. Edison had already negotiated for a similar device and about this time pressed J.W. Queen to order the micro-photographic outfit from Zeiss. It was very much like the one pictured in the article.[109]

The convergence of Edison's interests in magic lanterns, microscopic images and Muybridge's pictures of movement in the fall of 1887 is significant. Although the purposes seemed diverse, they occurred in parallel with his growing interest in photography and at the time the experiments to record and reproduce movement were started.

[107] EHS, Order Books. Douglas Tarr, Archivist at the Edison National Historic Site told me that according to the building records for the Historic Site the screen in the Library was installed at a very early date.

[108] EHS. The books were received 5 October 1888. A copy of the article was put in a scrapbook at the laboratory.

[109] EHS. The micro-photographic unit may have been ordered in the fall of 1887, but the order was forwarded to Zeiss about the time that the lantern slides were arriving and the work on the Kinetograph was beginning. The outfit arrived in the spring of 1889.

Chapter 7

The Beginning of a Quest: The Kineto-Phonograph

Daniel H. Chamberlain to Edison's lawyer Sherbourne Eaton: "... The Greek verb for *move* is kivew and the word for *motion* is kivnsis – hence a word formed ... like *photograph* and *phonograph* to express a picture of *motion* would be *kivnsigraf* or *anglicized* Kinesigraph ..."[110]

"I call the apparatus a Kinetoscope. ... in recording motions it may be called a Kinetograph, but when used for subsequent reproduction, which will be its most common use to the public, it is properly called a Kinetoscope. The principal feature of the invention consists in continuously photographing a series of pictures at slight intervals, not less than eight per second." These pictures are photographed in a continuous spiral line on a cylinder or plate in the same way that sound is recorded on the phonograph.[111] (Edison's first motion picture caveat, October 1888)

"There is scarcely an invention of importance made within the last generation which has not been disputed upon frivolous grounds ... I am an inventor and not a lawyer, and I hate litigation ... one of my objects in building my present laboratory is to search for trade secrets that require no patents ...".[112] (Edison, 1888)

Despite having reservations about the patent system, Edison persistently used it to protect his creative work. The draft for his first motion picture caveat, written in his own hand, was sent to his patent attorneys, the firm of Dyer and Seely, on 8 October 1888. He added a note to H.W. Seely: "Rush this I am getting good results. Edison". Seely's firm transcribed the draft into legal format, returned it to Edison for signature on 12 October and sent it to the U.S. Patent Office where it was accepted as Caveat 110 for Improvement in Photography and placed in the confidential archives of the Patent Office on 17 October 1888. A caveat was a formal notice that a person or company was working on a potentially patentable device or procedure. Although no longer sanctioned, at that time 4in the 1880s, if accepted by the Patent Office, a caveat established short-term priority by preventing competing applications from being accepted for one year. This gave inventors protection while they continued experimentation. Over the next thirteen months Edison modified his claims for the Kine-

110 EHS. Daniel H. Chamberlain to Sherbourne Eaton, 10 October 1888. Eaton recommended to Edison that it be spelled Kinesigraph to ensure correct pronunciation. Previously they had discussed "Motograph" but rejected it because it improperly combined roots from Latin and Greek. Edison didn't like either term.

111 EHS. Edison Caveat 110, filed 17 October 1888. The files at West Orange have Edison's hand written draft with rough drawings, a typed version and a certified copy of the Caveat which was printed in Complainant's Exhibits for Equity 6928, Edison v. American Mutoscope Co. and Benjamin Keith.

112 Hendricks Collection. From an article in *NY Evening Post* was quoted in, "Mr. Edison on the Patent Law" in *The Electrical Engineer*, February 1888 p. 65.

toscope-Kinetograph with three supplementary caveats. The four caveats record the changing character of Edison's and Dickson's experiments.

When the Kinetoscope-Kinetograph project was launched, lantern slides were being delivered, a sophisticated micro-photographic outfit was being ordered and a set of photographs by Muybridge was expected shortly. To prepare the caveat Dickson and Edison had done background research into magic lanterns, various persistence of image devices such as the Zoetrope and chronophotography. Edison's remark that he was "... getting good results" indicates that some actual testing had taken place. Caveat 110 described a machine which, in effect, was a modification of the phonograph – and could even be considered a version of the phonograph. A cylinder for the capture of images was attached to a cylinder phonograph by a common drive shaft. The Kinetograph cylinder was similar in size and shape to the phonograph cylinder. Minute images, 1/32nd of an inch wide would be recorded in a continuous spiraling line by a microscope-like camera. The images would be synchronized with the phonograph which would record sound while the images were being taken. By changing the camera to a binocular microscope and using ear tubes, the device was supposed to play the sound and images in synchronization.

Several important decisions were made before the caveat was drafted. Most significantly, the photographs would be taken by *one camera* rather than by several lenses or cameras, as used by Muybridge. It would be necessary to stop the photographic cylinder so that it would be still as each exposure was made, i.e. it had to have *an intermittent movement*, and the advance of the cylinder to the next exposure area had to take place while the lens of the camera was closed by means of *a shutter*. "... there is a practically continuous rotation of the cylinder but it takes place step by step and at such times as no photographic effect takes place ...". *A minimum of 8 exposures per second* would be necessary to create an effect of motion but it specified that *25 per second would be preferable*. At 25 per second, images 1/32nd of an inch wide would result in 42,000 images on a cylinder which would give 28 minutes of running time. Edison scrawled the mathematics calculating this running time on a draft drawing of the Kinetograph made for the Caveat.

The Caveat was less definite about the recording process and here Edison hedged his bets. They had made a realistic appraisal of the limitations of available photo materials – and, quite possibly they were hoping to cover the processes of potential rivals as well their own. Edison expressed preference for using a *cylinder*, but he said that a *plate* or a *continuous strip* could be used. The possibility of using a plate or strip was followed by the phrase "... but there are many mechanical difficulties in the way ...". The cylinder would be a hollow shell made of a substance such as plaster of Paris which could be molded to support the photographic surface. The cylinder would be tapered so that it fit the taper of the shaft. The photosensitive material would be *collodion* or "*other photographic film*" which might be flowed over the cylinder in the

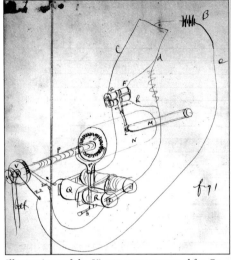

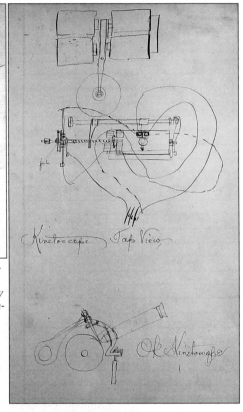

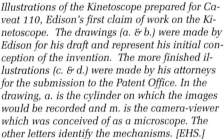

Illustrations of the Kinetoscope prepared for Caveat 110, Edison's first claim of work on the Kinetoscope. The drawings (a. & b.) were made by Edison for his draft and represent his initial conception of the invention. The more finished illustrations (c. & d.) were made by his attorneys for the submission to the Patent Office. In the drawing, a. is the cylinder on which the images would be recorded and m. is the camera-viewer which was conceived of as a microscope. The other letters identify the mechanisms. [EHS.]

same manner as photo plates. The resulting image would be a positive but a negative could be taken. "... but if it is desired to produce a negative series of photographs a glass cylinder is used, [the] surface of the cylinder or shell is flowed & the records taken, the cylinder of shell being exceedingly thin say of mica is slipped over the regular cylinder ... whose surface is sensitized & printed from the negative by light in straight lines without reflection from side surfaces". This could be used to produce another cylinder. It would be possible to produce additional prints from the original "... just as one photograph may be taken from another".

Kineto-this, Kineto-that, What's in a Name?
Kinetograph? Kinetoscope? Kinetophonograph?

Edison and Dickson were working on a system of devices. A camera (the Kinetograph), a viewing apparatus (the Kinetoscope) and a viewing-listening apparatus (the Kinetophonograph). The Victorian era favored long, difficult Greek-based names for their novel inventions. Edison had rejected motograph and kinesigraph, but settled on the series of Kineto graphs and scopes.

These long names can be confusing – the staff at the lab sometimes

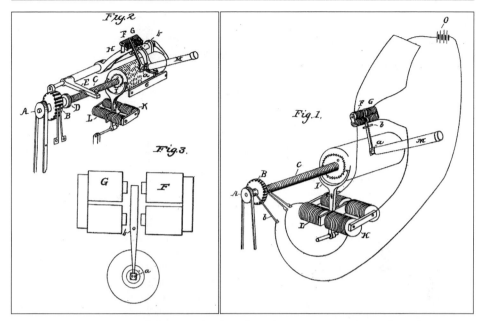

mixed them and referred to the camera as a "scope" or the viewing machine as a "graph". But we are stuck with them and it will be difficult to be clear as to which device we are talking about. As we proceed through the future experiments, I will try to simplify things by using the compromise term, "Kineto" when is seems appropriate. It is shorter, simpler and covers camera, viewer and projector.

Although specifying that the images would be *viewed* through a microscope, projection was a possiblity. By using very large transparent shells "... as is done in the enlargement of micro-photographs" images might be thrown on a screen with the light source placed inside the cylinder. In his draft Edison prophesied that "... by insertion of the listening tubes of the phonograph into the ear the illusion is complete and we may see & hear a whole opera as perfectly as if actually present although the actual performance may have taken place years before". Edison's attorneys removed this optimistic speculation from the version sent to the Patent Office but Edison knew the value of a catchy phrase, and repeated his operatic prophecy in later Kineto publicity.

An enormous number of pictures

Edison, commenting about Muybridge's Zoöpraxiscope: "... [the images] were very jerky, and only a few pictures in a single movement, and they produced no illusion except they merely illustrated motion".[113]

Although Muybridge's initiative gave them impetus, Edison and Dickson were critical of his methods. First, they rejected the limited number of images that Muybridge – and the other chronophotographers – were taking.

113 EHS. Edison's testimony, January 29, 1900 in Equity 6928, Edison v. American Mutoscope, p. 108.

The quotes in the text above taken from the text of Edison's draft as sent to Dyer and Seely who modified Edison's statements and made them more clinical: "Thus there is a practically continuous rotation of the cylinder but it takes place step by step ..." became "The movement of the cylinder or plate is thus a step by step movement ..."; "many mechanical difficulties" became "mechanical difficulties" without the modifier; "other photographic film" became "soft film" and the romantic reference to viewing complete operas was eliminated completely. The most radical change made by Dyer and Seely was in the description of taking positives or negatives. This was changed to a confusing statement: "In this way a positive is taken, but it produces a negative series of photographs. I use a transparent cylinder, the surface of which is flowed with the chemical material. This thin cylinder is then slipped over the cylinder which is to be used in practice and which will have a sensitized surface, and this is printed from the negative by light in straight lines ...".

The objective of chronophotography was the study of motion by using rapid exposure photography to capture and freeze aspects of motion. The most prominent chonophotographers, Muybridge, Étienne-Jules Marey and Ottomar Anschütz were usually taking from 12 to 24 exposures using rapid emulsion dry plates. In his earliest work, 1878–1879, Muybridge made 12 exposures and increased this to 24. During the 1880s, working at the University of Pennsylvania, he had the capability of taking between 12 and 24 exposures of a subject and photographed some from more than one angle. Marey's experiments involved a greater variety of subjects some, like birds, that could not be relied on to activate the shutter of a camera by their motion. This led him to develop several cameras capable of capturing specific types of movement. Although he was taking different numbers of exposures as dictated by the nature of his subjects, the range was usually from 12 to 20. Anschütz was taking a similar number and his exhibition of the Schnellseher displayed from 20 to 25 images.

A dozen or two dozen images were sufficient to examine the phases of motion but Edison was not interested in freezing and analyzing movement. Others were doing that and the premise of the Kineto experiment was to create an extended reproduction of motion. It would only be limited by the size and scope of the available materials. A dozen or two dozen images were far too few for the results they had in mind. Edison started with a calculation that 28 minutes of action and sound could be recorded and theoretically, there were no limits to the potential length of recording. Dickson said that Edison always intended to produce long scenes: "From ... the very earliest day, Mr. Edison's idea was to reproduce long entertainments, such as operas, to build such an apparatus that would be capable of taking necessarily an enormous number of pictures ...".[114]

Muybridge's use of a bank of twelve to twenty-four cameras was also rejected. They, Edison and Dickson, were bothered by the slight change of aspect from camera to camera that was inevitable in Muybridge's system. Instead, they decided to use a single lens because it

[114] EHS, Legal Box 173, M116-288-289. Dickson testimony, 6 May 1910 in Equity No. 28,605, Patents Co. v. Chicago Film Exchange.

limited distortion from image to image. As Dickson explained, "... I think it has been satisfactorily proven that for many subjects the results would be more or less incorrect or unsatisfactory, if taken from a battery of lenses. But if taken from a single viewpoint the absolute super-position of each phase [frame] is microscopically registered."[115]

The decision to take a large number of images and photograph them in continual sequence from a single point of view is the most important made during this stage of experimentation. Although most of the other elements of design would change radically over the subsequent years, they continued to use one lens to take an extended, continuous line of successive images. Although the cylinder experiments were destined for failure, several other elements of this design were carried over to subsequent revisions: intermittent exposure, the use of a shutter and taking a large number of images per second.

Scientific reasoning may not be the only explanation for Edison's critical reaction to Muybridge. In his statements to the press, Muybridge relegated Edison to perfecting the phonograph while he, Muybridge, would create the photo image – he claimed that he had already "perfected" a device that could take sixty or seventy images of a famous person like James G. Blaine, Edwin Booth or Lillian Russell.[116] In all likelihood Edison sensed that he had a secondary role in this scenario and Edison did not like second place. He usually viewed proposals from other inventors with scorn, but sometimes regarded them as a challenge. For years he refused to share experimentation on the telephone and phonograph with Alexander Graham Bell and in 1887 when Bell's cousin Chichester Bell offered a deal to share phonograph patents Edison refused and launched a concerted effort to improve his version.[117] He did not scorn Muybridge's offer, which was more amicable, but this Caveat effectively put an end to any notion that Edison and Muybridge would produce a cooperative moving image-sound device. Edison maintained a cordial but intermittent correspondence with Muybridge and stubbornly resisted cooperating with others experimenting with moving images.

Edison claimed that use of a single camera was an original innovation but others had reached a similar conclusion before him, notably the eminent French physiologist Étienne-Jules Marey. A chronophotographer inspired by Muybridge but more dedicated to pure science and more flexible in his experimentation, Marey had used a single lens camera since the early 1880s and by 1888 had developed several single-lens cameras. This would have been apparent to Edison or Dickson from articles in *Scientific American* describing Marey's work. Dickson acknowledged this while reminiscing about their experiments in a letter to Edison written in 1921: "Later we received a still further impetus by reading about Prof E.J. Marey & Demenÿ's work in Paris published by the Academy of Sciences on 12 September 1887 – revolving disc pictures & the like highly scientific & exact work".[118]

The determination that more than 8 frames per second were needed to create the illusion of motion was reached by studying Marey

115 Ibid.

116 NMAH, Hendricks Collection, from *Electrical Review*, 9 June 1888.

117 EHS; Conot, Op. Cit., p. 260

118 EHS, Dickson to Edison, 21 May 1921. His date for the article is not accurate and he seems to lump together information from a number of articles about Marey. It is possible that he referred to the *Scientific American* Supplements No. 579 and 580, 5 and 12 February 1887. This paper made no mention of Georges Demenÿ although he was working for Marey in 1886. Demenÿ came to prominence during the 1890s.

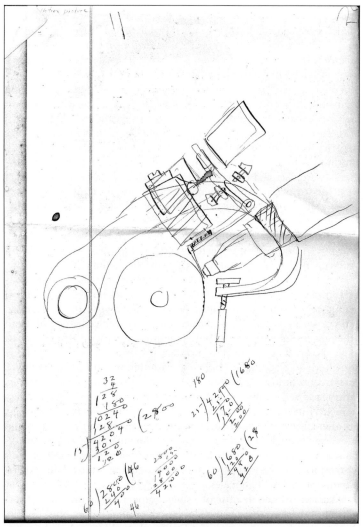

Edison's two sketches for Caveat 110, 8 October 1888. Before submitting his first caveat for the Kinetoscope, Edison made these sketches of how the device might function. The left one, his concept of viewing, is dated 8 October 1888, the other, probably made about the same time, is preliminary to the drawings for the caveat. [EHS.]

and Muybridge who were photographing at about that speed, but the choice of 25 images per second seems more speculative. As yet, Dickson had little or no experience with rapid photography so the numbers must have come from articles about the chronophotography. In a paper read for the French Association for the Advancement of Science in 1886 and reported in *Scientific American* in 1887, Marey speculated that 50 frames per second would be best to obtain an accurate record of human movement and this may have influenced Edison and Dickson. Fifty

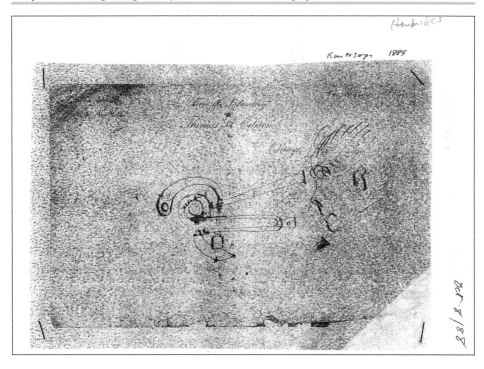

frames per second would have been an ambitious goal so 25 may have
been a compromise. As we shall see, Edison would decide later that 25
images per second were not enough and both Dickson and Edison
ultimately decided that recording 40 to 45 frames per second would
overcome the problem of flickering that plagued early cinema. Ironically, even though Edison, probably on the advice of Dickson, changed
his mind, this initial estimate is almost identical with the standard used
by the movie industry when sound pictures were adopted in the late
1920s – 24 frames per second. This is still the standard projection rate
for theatrical motion pictures.[119]

    The decision to record an unlimited number of images in a con-
tinuous line reversed the emphasis of chronophotography whose os-
tensible purpose was to freeze motion in order to analyze it. They
photographed brief phases of motion – a few steps, a quick run, a jump,
climbing a few stairs, swinging Indian clubs, using a broom, etc. The
brief action was usually broken down into single photographs – each a
phase of the movement. Dickson adopted the term and throughout his
life referred to single frames of a film as a "phase". While the original
purpose was frozen motion, the chronophotographers often recreated
motion from their images by printing them on disks or strips to be
viewed as continuous movement in Phenakistiscopes or Zoetropes.
Marey, the scientist, did this to check the accuracy of his research
material but Muybridge and Anschütz, who were primarily photographers, found that the public was fascinated by the recreated movement

119 The
chronophotographers
were taking
sequences 20 to 24
frames long, and
these ran about one
and a half seconds
when projected
which may also have
influenced Edison's
decision. These
numbers were also
mentioned in articles
about
chronophotography.

and developed them into public exhibitions. But their shows were limited – a dozen or two dozen phases, usually arranged to be cyclical in nature, i.e. they ended as they started so that the series of "phases" could run on indefinitely – or be shown in reverse. A horse trotting, a man jumping, a boy juggling endlessly, on and on and on until the wheel stopped spinning or the eye moved from the viewing device. It was Edison's objective to break this endless cycle and free the subject to show more variety of movement. Although the goal of 28 minutes of running time or opera with "people long since dead" proved elusive, Edison and Dickson stuck with their objective to record a quantity of images successively in a continuous line.

The Caveat also specified that images would be recorded intermittently by the camera, i.e. the sensitive photographic surface would be stopped for exposure, advanced to the next position, stopped again and exposed, then advanced again, stopped, etc. In Muybridge's battery of cameras the sensitive surface did not move, but if a single camera with a single lens was used the photosensitive surface had to move to the next exposure position. There were two choices: intermittent, i.e. stopping the photographic surface for exposure or continuous, or allowing it to keep moving but admitting a brief amount of light to various places on the photographic surface through narrow slots on a disk revolving between the lens and the photo surface. The solid part of the disk would keep the light from the sensitive film as it advanced to exposure position. Marey had used both techniques. This was a decision for a photographer, so it would have been Dickson's call. He selected an intermittent movement because if the sensitive surface was still while the exposure was made it was more likely to be sharp. He needed as much exposure as he could get given the limited sensitivity of the photo material available to him. He would continue to use intermittent movements in the camera but would opt for a continuous movement for the viewing device. Proper, i.e. effective, intermittence was one of the most difficult technical problems he had to solve so the question of intermittence will appear again as Dickson's work progresses.

The phonograph was very much on Edison's mind so it was natural for him to think of moving images in terms of a modification of the phonograph. He spent much of 1888 improving the mechanism, testing new materials for recordable cylinders, negotiating contracts to market the machines and setting-up manufacturing facilities. Although the Caveat justified using a cylinder because it made it possible to record longer scenes, that was not the main reason it was chosen. Phonographs and cylinders had his attention and with much of his staff helping him the resources to work on the mechanics of a cylinder Kineto were at hand.

Although cylinder devices were mechanisms *du jour* at the lab, the format was completely foreign to photography. The most commonly used photo format was the glass plate which was either coated with photo sensitive material just before exposure (wet plate) or purchased with photo sensitive emulsion already applied by the manufacturer (dry plates). The Caveat mentioned the possibility of using a plate with a "volute spiral" of images but said the cylinder was preferred. No explanation was made except that the cylinder would require a simpler mechanism. The mechanical problems were not spelled out, but the weight and fragility of the plate were considerations. To record a large number of images they would have wanted the largest sheet of dry plate available, which would have been 11 by 14 inches. Designing a camera to take very small images on such a plate would have been difficult. To get steady images using an intermittent movement, the plate would have to move and stop eight or more times in a second and if minutes of action were photographed there would be hundreds, even thousands of stops and starts. It would be difficult to keep the glass steady and prevent breakage. The alternatives were to use a shutter while the glass moved steadily or hold the glass steady and move the camera. Both of these choices were rejected.

The mention of "a continuous strip" may seem rather startling since they are not usually associated with photography of the 1880s, but the Eastman Dry Plate Co. had introduced strips of photo-sensitize paper in the mid-1880s. The paper was mounted on roll holders designed to fit conventional cameras. The roll holders found very limited acceptance in the photo community but George Eastman had another market in mind. In June, 1888, he introduced a small camera that was pre-loaded with paper film. It was comparatively simple and for $25 a novice could take one hundred photos. Although the Kodak No. 1 camera was destined to revolutionize photography, serious photographers were skeptical about it. The new "film" was very complicated to use. The Kodak camera and the roll holders Eastman had introduced earlier used "stripping film", a sensitive photographic surface mounted on paper. After the roll was exposed it was sent to Rochester where Eastman developed it, dissolved the binder that held the "film" to the paper and transferred the photographic image to glass and then made a positive print on paper. It was possible for professional photographers to develop the film themselves, but most shunned this as too complicated.[120] Dickson and Edison discussed the paper strips and decided that there were "many mechanical difficulties in the way ...".

Though transparent photographic materials using celluloid as a base were being introduced in 1887 and 1888, they were in sheet form, not strips, and a variety of problems discouraged wide-spread use by photographers. Images were sometimes distorted because of graininess or uneven thickness of the celluloid and there were complaints about brittleness, stiffness, tackiness during developing and a propensity to curl tightly after being developed. These problems were highly publicized and photographic specialists experimented to improve the material. In Philadelphia John Carbutt was working with Newark's Celluloid Manufacturing Company on transparent sheet film base and in Rochester, NY, George Eastman was experimenting with substitut-

120 Reese Jenkins, Op. Cit., pp. 96–117.

ing transparent base for paper in his roll holders. Though both would eventually be successful, in October 1888 Carbutt was just introducing his celluloid and Eastman was still experimenting.

The wording of the Caveat hints that Edison and Dickson had read enough about the rapidly changing photo market that they anticipated future improvements but until celluloid and strips improved they were stuck with older, flawed products. Dickson would struggle with collodion, wet plates and miniature images.

The size of the image, 1/32nd of an inch, was determined by the decision to record on a cylinder while sound was being simultaneously recorded. This was Edison's call. It was logical too that the two cylinders should be the same size and if this was the case and a large number of images were wanted, they would have to be small, very small. Mathematical calculations by Edison on a drawing for the Caveat show that he worked backwards from the size of the cylinder to calculate the size of the image. As stated in the Caveat, "The cylinders may for instance be about the same size as those of the phonograph, the number of threads to the inch on the feed screw being about thirty-two. This will give photographic images of about one thirty-second of an inch ...". Edison later commented "... we did not try very large pictures, because it would require a cylinder so enormously large in diameter and length that we could not make it practicable ...".[121] At any rate, as we have seen, in the fall of 1888 Edison was thinking small, even microscopically. Dickson was probably less than delighted with the prospect of recording minuscule images on the curved surface of a cylinder, but he accepted the challenge and probably did not object too strongly. Edison liked to challenge his experimenters and he urged them to attempt the difficult or impossible because it could lead to unexpected results. This was certainly the case during the fall and winter of 1888–1889 when Dickson struggled with impossible expectations and inadequate material.

121 EHS. Edison Caveat no. 110, 17 October 1888 and testimony, 29 January 1900 in Equity 6928, Edison v. American Mutoscope, p. 112.

Chapter 8

Trials, Errors, Mergers, Shenanigans and Speculation: Cylinders, Electricity, Phonographs and Iron

122 Dickson, *SMPE*, p. 10.

123 This is the same Walter Mallory whose comment about seeing Muybridge's photographs was noted previously. Walter Mallory, a wealthy Chicago based iron manufacturer, was a friend of Edison's brother-in-law Ira Miller. Edison met Mallory in 1885 at Chautauqua when he was courting Mina Miller. During 1888 Edison and Mallory became business partners in a company, the Edison Iron Concentrating Company, which also included Ira Miller and other members of the Miller family.

124 EHS, LB-027. Tate, Dickson and other Edison employees often bragged that a device was "perfected and left nothing to be desired" but it rarely meant that no more work would be done and the claim was frequently followed by additional intense redesign. This was certainly true in the case of the ore separator.

W.K.L. Dickson: "I pointed out to him that in the first place I knew of no medium that was sensitive enough to take micro-photographs at so rapid a rate while running continuously on the same shaft.

"'Well, try it; it will lead to other things,' was Edison's reply. I did ...'"[122]

By September, 1888 Edison felt that Dickson could take on a new project. The ore milling experiments had progressed to a degree that Edison was entertaining proposals to put separators in pilot locations. A machine to be installed at Walter Mallory's mine in Michigan's Upper Peninsula was being built and a version of the separator was being sent to England where an Edison associate, Osgood S. Wiley, was to make a confidential demonstration for a British engineer, James Dredge and some associates in the British mining community.[123] In December, 1888 A.O. Tate, now Edison's private secretary, wrote W. H.. Meadowcroft, at Edison's New York Office "... his new separator [is] perfected and leaves nothing further to be desired". Dickson was still responsible for tests and modifications of the machines but he was not directly involved in constructing or installing new machines. Much of his time was spent supervising tests of ore samples sent to the lab and adjusting the separator to suit the composition of different mineral mixtures. The work was becoming more routine and some could be handled by staff assistants.[124]

Edison chose Dickson for the Kineto project because of his interest in photography. Although he knew and understood electricity and mechanics, photography was Dickson's unique skill and it continued to be his major responsibility in the Kineto experiments. The lab had a stable of skilled machinists, among them several who had spent years working on the phonograph, but no one else was qualified to deal with the challenges of high speed photography. Almost all of the early drawings of the Kinetoscope were made by Edison who had John Ott his most experienced machinist examine and witness them. This suggests that during the initial experiments the mechanical aspects – design and construction – were supervised by Edison and Ott,. There is logic to this as it would have left Dickson free to concentrate on the photographic tests. The principal mechanical work was done in one of the lab's two machine shops. Specialized work was handled by John Ott in his Precision Room which was on the Second Floor, down the hall from Room 5, Dickson's Photographic Room. More general machine work was done in the big shop on the first floor, a flight of stairs away from Room 5. The only mechanical work done in the Photo Room would have been adjustments required for tests. Although he certainly made suggestions and recommendations, it is quite possible that Dickson was not directly involved in making the first cylinders. The concept was Edison's and he and John Ott had more experience with phonographs and were working with them on a daily basis so it makes sense that they supervised the preliminary construction of the Kinetoscope.[125]

Dickson had his hands full testing photographic materials. The objective was to capture an accurate image – in sharp focus and without flaws or distortion – and determine how rapidly this could be done. As Dickson explained it: "These drum experiments were invaluable to us to determine if such pictures could be taken, and what the effect would be when viewed. It was also necessary to see how fast the pictures could be taken, for definition, if such pictures could be properly enlarged, etc." Edison had given Dickson a very thorny charge!

At the end of September, 1888, about the time the Kineto experiments began, Charles Brown, who had been working on lamps, was assigned to work with Dickson on ore milling. Brown said he requested the assignment because he did not have enough work in the Lamp Department. Since he started ten days before Edison drafted the text of the first Caveat it appears that the assignment was related to the changing nature of Dickson's assignment. During his first days he worked on ore milling but on 9 October, the day after Edison's motion picture caveat was drafted, Brown's time was charged to "Room 5", the photographic room. For the next five weeks, with the exception of two

---

Charles A. Brown

Charles Brown, a machinist, was hired shortly after the Orange lab was opened. He said he came to Orange at the time of the legendary blizzard of March 1888. He worked as Dickson's assistant from Friday, 28 September 1888 until the work week that ended 16 January 1890. He worked for a short time as an experimenter on lamps, then left to set up a workshop in Springfield, NJ where he experimented on lamps for Edison. He returned to the lab briefly in 1896. In 1900 when he testified in Equity 6928, Edison v. American Mutoscope Co., he was unemployed. In 1908, testifying in Edison v. Kleine, he had a stock farm near Maplewood, NJ.

---

125 4 EHS, Edison made drawings for Caveat No. 110, the first motion picture Caveat, and additional drawings of the Kinetoscope made January 11, 1889 which were submitted as evidence in Equity 6928, Edison v. Amer. Mutoscope. Some drawings of the Kinetoscope are in Edison's notebook N-87-09-02. In Dickson's testimony in Equity 28,605, Patents Co. v. Chicago Film Exchange, May, 1910, he commented: "The mechanical parts were nearly all made in the upper Edison machine shop under my directions and that of Mr. Edison, ...with the exception of some small parts necessary for tentative experiments, which were made in the photographic department. ...Mr John Ott, who assisted in designing any of the more complex work."

days on other assignments, he was in the photo room and did not return to ore milling until 17 November. Brown's tour as Dickson's assistant encompassed the initial work on the Kinetograph, all of the cylinder experiments and the beginning work on a strip machine.[126] His assignment as Dickson's assistant coincided with the start of serious work on the Kinetograph and Brown's time sheets are the most accurate record of the time spent on the project. As a supervising experimenter, Dickson was paid by the week and his weekly time sheet only recorded the project or projects worked on during the week. Brown was paid by the hour and his time was charged against a specific project so it was recorded by the number of hours worked on a specific project during each day of the work week

During these first experiments all of Dickson's and Brown's time was charged either to ore milling or the Photographic Room. There was no budget for the Kineto at this stage. The time Dickson spent on the Kineto was extra duty. "... Mr. Edison when disclosing his idea or ideas, regarding the [Kineto] ..., told me that this must not interfere with the big work at hand [ore milling], but that I must do it in my spare time."[127]

Brown was an experienced machinist with a reputation for hard work, but he had no experience with photography. He had to be taught the basics of photography: chemistry, darkroom, lenses, exposure, etc. During October and November Dickson was both experimenter and teacher.

Dickson had a photographic assignment that was an ideal training

126 EHS, payroll records. Though he had worked primarily on lamps, Brown had also worked on the phonograph. He was photographed 16 June 1888 with the group who had worked all night and most of the previous five days "perfecting" the improved version of the phonograph. Brown is the only journeyman machinist in the group. The others are John and Fred Ott. The rest of the group, Dickson, Chas. Batchelor, A.T.E. Wangemann, Edison and Col. Gouraud are executives. His acquaintance with Dickson dates at least from this time.

127 EHS, Legal Box 173, m116-290. Dickson's testimony in Equity No. 28,605.

Keeping track of time

A system of numbering experiments began when the new lab opened. It was a way to document expenses so contractors could be charged for laboratory services and to estimate the cost of a product when the invention was perfected. Edison explained his purpose to A.O. Tate who was responsible for designing and managing the system: "I want a better time sheet used for the Experimenters. Something which describes [the] nature [of an] experiment, time consumed & Roughness [sic] of amount material used so in charging up we know somewhere the amount material used ...".

The weekly time sheets for the employees at Edison's lab survive mostly intact. The work week was six days, with Sunday off and, in 1888, each work day was 10 hours. It began Friday and ended the following Thursday. With the exception of experimenters most of the staff was paid by the hour. The employees or their supervisor recorded the number of hours worked each day and broke it down by project that they worked on. Each project had a budget number which was recorded. If they worked on more than one project in a day, the number of hours for each project was recorded. Charles Brown was paid $0.25 per hour, so he normally earned $2.50 per day or $15.00 per week. If he worked more than 10 hours it was recorded but he was paid at his regular rate of $0.25. Dickson was a salaried experimenter and paid $24.00 for a week's work. His time sheet was not usually broken down by hours and only rarely annotated with specific days spent on a project although his salary was reduced if he worked less than 60 hours in the week.

course for his new helper. He was preparing pictures for Edison's exhibit at the international exposition scheduled to open in Paris the following summer. Edison had ambitious plans and asked William Hammer, who had done several previous exhibits, to design this one. The arrangements were being handled by Francis Upton head of the Edison Lamp Company based in Newark. Upton and Hammer apparently asked for photographs of Edison's inventions, the laboratory and manufacturing buildings. Brown apparently helped Dickson with the project. Brown described his early experiences as "... [taking] pictures of the different buildings around, and then of all the phonographs and things that he got up".[128]

The earliest photographic tests for the Kineto project were made in the late fall of 1888. At this beginning stage no attempt was made to record movement for reproduction, instead they were still photographs taken in search of "... a medium that was sensitive enough to take micro-photographs at so rapid a rate ...". A lantern slide of Sir Edwin Henry Landseer's very popular painting of a stag was used as a test image. The images were recorded on the curved surface of a drum with a camera that Dickson built from one of his microscopes "... using various objectives ..." as lenses.[129] Although Edison's Caveat specified images 1/32nd of an inch, there is no record that Dickson made any that tiny. The smallest size mentioned in his most accurate account of the early experiments, his 1933 article for the *Journal of SMPE*, was 1/8 inch and Edison's annotations on Kinetoscope sketches made on 11 January 1889 also mentions 1/8 inch as the image size, an indication that the "microscopic pin-point photographs" were abandoned early on.[130]

Since they had rejected glass and Eastman's paper strips, Dickson was saddled with the photographic materials available in the 1880s and his options were limited. He had to learn how to improve exposure time which was invariably too slow. Oddly, the first material he is known to have tested was daguerreotype, a notoriously slow process. A "Hand Book [of] Daguerreotype" was received from Scovill on 22 November – just before Thanksgiving. A few days later he went into New York to get supplies from Scovill. He explained his impulsive actions in a note to a report to Edison: "Having waited unnecessarily long for the silver plates I thought it the best plan to go over first thing Wed. morning to NY & see what I could get all ready for the Daguerreotype Exp. hoping this may meet with your approval I remain etc." This seems an odd diversion from the intent to improve speed and clarity, but it seems to fit with Dickson's desire to explore all avenues of photography.

Edison expected his experimenters to balance priorities and make full use of their time and this sojourn to New York demonstrates that Dickson's free-wheeling methods were not out of place. At the time of the trip Edison had raised his requirements for ore milling, but Dickson met the increased work load, found time to experiment on the Kineto and for a trip into New York City in order to apply a little heat to a supplier. The day before going to New York Dickson demonstrated his commitment to ore milling by means of a report detailing experiments

128 EHS, Charles Brown, testifying 31 January 1900 in Equity No. 6928, Edison v. Amer. Mutoscope. On 2 November 1888 a note scribbled on a piece of correspondence was to Dickson: "Dickson / We have promised Mr. Hammer and Mr. Upton photos of the Grand Trunk Herald ..." The *Grand Trunk Herald* was the newspaper that Edison published as a youth working on the Grand Trunk railroad in Michigan. Dickson published this photo in his biography of Edison.

129 Dickson, Journal of the SMPE, p. 10.

130 Dickson used this phrase in the article he wrote with his sister in 1894 for *Century Magazine*.

on a modified ore milling machine[131] and two days earlier he reported revisions he made to work procedures in room 22 "the ore milling outhouse". Ore milling was demanding most of his time, but he had the leeway to pressure a supplier. It was the type of initiative that Edison appreciated – as long as the job got done![132]

The daguerreotype experiment was short lived. Exposure times for most Daguerreotypes were measured in seconds, even minutes and Dickson's test exposure, made on a piece of highly polished silver, took three-quarters of a minute.[133] It was a process that was already considered *passé* but it seems to have been a way to test a process that used metal rather than glass or paper as a base for the photo sensitive emulsion. They had not decided what material to use for the photo cylinders.

They had rejected pre-coated processes, i.e. dry plates, usually glass or paper such as Eastman's stripping film. This meant that the photo-sensitive material had to be coated on the cylinder. There were two coating processes that had been around for a generation or more, albumen (prepared egg whites) and collodion (a solution of nitrocellulose in alcohol and ether). Dickson experimented with both. Albumen was most commonly used in the preparation of printing paper but it could also be used to make negatives and as a support for the photo-sensitive agent. Collodion, better known as wet plate, was widely favored by professional photographers. Because both were liquids, they could be coated fairly easily, but both had a serious drawback: exposure times were slow, too slow to record movement accurately. Dickson warned Edison about the problem and was told to experiment to improve the speed. In addition to modifications to albumen and collodion, they tried making their own emulsions with those used in dry plate photography as a model.

Gelatin, albumen, camphor and collodion, the components commonly used in photography, were probably available in the lab's stockroom which claimed to have "...a quantity of every known substance on the face of the globe".[134] This was particularly true in the fall of 1888 because the laboratory was testing an assortment of substances, including those listed, in an effort to improve the quality of phonograph cylinders. Edison's notebooks from this period show that they experimented with albumen as a softening ingredient in cylinders. Gelatin, mixed with albumen, camphor as a base and collodion as a flexible binder were among the items listed as possible materials to use for a cylinder that could be mailed.[135] So, during the winter of 1888–1889 and the spring that followed, Dickson had resources at hand to experiment with a variety of substances as he tested exposure speed and image registration.

The receiving records of the laboratory show that supplies for these tests were most plentiful during this period. Seven shipments of collodion were received between October 1888 and January 1889 and there were no more until March 1891, two years later. The only shipment of

131 EHS, "Report of Progress made in Displacement Exp."

132 EHS. Dickson to Edison, 27 November 1888. Dickson's note was appended to a report he made about his progress on the ore milling experiments.

133 W.K.L. Dickson & Antonia Dickson, *Century* ..., p. 207.

134 *Scientific American*, 57:184. "Edison's New Laboratory"

135 EHS, notes Edison made 17 October 1888 for a phonograph caveat. notebooks, N-88-10-01, M99 –764–765 & 819-820.

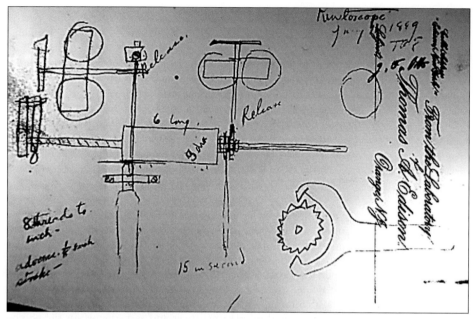

During the early stages of research Edison and John Ott worked on the mechanism for the Kinetoscope-Kinetograph. This drawing, and several others were dated 11 January 1889. [EHS.]

albumen was received in October 1888, though Dickson would have had little trouble finding egg whites.[136]

Dickson described one of these early tests in his 1933 article: "Next I tried silver nitrate on wet collodion, using an exposure of 10 seconds, which was finally shortened to 5 seconds", and in their 1894 article the general results were described in Antonia's flowery prose: "The photographic portion of the undertaking was seriously hampered by the materials at hand, which, however excellent in themselves, offered no substance sufficiently sensitive. How to secure clear-cut outlines, or indeed any outlines at all, together with phenomenal speed, was the problem which puzzled the experimenters. The Daguerre, albumen and kindred processes met the first requirements, but failed when subjected to the latter test. These methods were therefore regretfully abandoned, a certain precipitate of knowledge being retained."[137]

Dickson tried in vain to accelerate exposure time and the experiments of 1888 could be dismissed as failures – at least as far as motion picture work is concerned. But, as Antonia put it, he gained "...a certain precipitate of knowledge ...". His problems were inevitable given the material that was available at the time. Images 1/32nd – or 1/8th – of an inch were too small to be recorded accurately. Even at relatively slow exposure time the curvature of the cylinder caused distortions which were evident even though the images were microscopic. Dickson was a perfectionist and this was unacceptable. The correction was obvious, enlarge the image and flatten the surface. Glass strips coated with photo

136 EHS, receiving ledgers, 1888. Four shipments were received in October and one each in November, December 1888 and January 1889.

137 Dickson, *Journal of the SMPE*, p. 10; Dicksons, *Century Magazine*, p. 207.

sensitive material and mounted on the cylinder might provide speedier exposure time. This new design was proposed in the second motion picture caveat drafted on 3 February 1889 and filed with the Patent Office on 25 March 1899. The change was decided earlier than that, perhaps early in January. It was described and illustrated by Edison in notes made before the caveat was written. These were dated 11 January 1889 and witnessed by John Ott. The date may have been added later for use in one of the court cases, but they were made before the draft of the caveat. He drew two cylinder-like circles and above them wrote: "If 1/8 photo taken on 3 inch cylinder then there should be 72 parallel flattened places longitudinally along Cylinder so that all parts of photo be in focus". In a second note he wrote: "glass strip could be [pasted] along side each other but this is perhaps [unnecessary] a varnish might be used Collodion etc. [enamel] etc." [138]

These notes are an interesting evidence that at this stage Edison was very much involved in designing the mechanism and that John Ott was assisting. They also show that the problems that Dickson had with image size and curvature of the cylinder found a sympathetic audience with Edison.

There is also evidence that Dickson may have tried the design and showed it to Edison before he revised the caveat. There was a very unusual set of photo plates in a shipment of photo items received just before Christmas, 1888. In addition to the conventional dry plates of the sort Dickson used for still photography there were six dozen gelatin plates: ¾ inches x 4 inches. They were completely different from anything received before or after. It is possible they were for microscopic work – Edison's hopes for conquering Yellow fever were still running high – but they would not fit a conventional camera which raises the possibility that Dickson had something different in mind. They probably had a faster exposure rate than the collodion and albumen he had been using and thus would have been suitable for a demonstration of alternate possibilities. Edison was spending the holidays with his in-laws in Akron so there was a lull in activity at the lab, giving Dickson a chance to experiment – and, perhaps, prepare a show for the boss.[139] Edison changed the design the following month, possibly because Dickson shown him a new direction.

But this is speculation and whether there was a demo or not, the design of the Kineto changed several times during the new year. In part this was because of changes outside the lab, but the experiments were also influenced by changes in Edison's fortunes and objectives. The Kineto experiments did not take place in a vacuum so this is a good place to pause and catch up on some events and changes that affected Edison's business and lab activities.

Electricity, phonograph and iron ore in 1889 – mergers, shenanigans and speculation

Edison's creative output was reaching a peak in 1889. The lab was staffed, equipped and he had funds to support his activities. Not as

138 EHS. Edison notebook, N-87-09-02. Edison's Caveat No. 114, which was Motion Picture Caveat II combined Edison's revisions of a number of different experiments.

139 EHS. The shipment was received 21 December 1888 Scovill Mfg Co.

much as he might have liked, but enough to keep a miscellany of endeavors active simultaneously. During the year Edison applied for sixty patents, more than half related to incandescent lamps (32) but others for electrical distributing systems, motors, sockets, dynamos, electric railways, telegraph relays, signaling apparatus and ore separators. His biographer Frank Dyer ranked this year, along with the years 1881, 1882 and 1883 as Edison's most productive.[140] He prepared a major exhibit for Paris and chose to attend. His visit was a trial and a triumph [see Chapter 11]. In general things looked rosy but there were clouds on the horizon. Some ominous, some stormy and others seemingly benign.

General Electric: merger

"A new corporation called the 'Edison General Electric Company,' with Mr. H. Villard and his friends at its head has been organized, with a capital of twelve million dollars, to take over the Edison Electric Light Company, and the three shops, which of course includes the United Company. A lot of fresh capital is to be put into the business, and Edison electric lighting interests are to be vigorously pushed. I think that the plan of operation is, to go into the large cities of the United States, and instead of soliciting local capital for the purpose of erecting Central Stations, the Edison General Electric Company will put the Stations up with its own capital. This will give them an immense advantage over their competitors ...".[141] (A.O. Tate to Frank McGowan 31 January 1889).

The changes began at the beginning of the year. On 2 January 1889 the stock holders of Edison's several electric service companies approved a merger which combined the Edison Isolated Lighting Co., Edison Lamp Co., Edison Machine Works and Bergmann & Co. to form the Edison General Electric Company. The merger was engineered by Henry Villard with the backing of financial interests from Villard's native Germany. Edison and his associates surrendered their interests in the manufacturing companies for stock in the new company. Edison's close associates Charles Batchelor and Samuel Insull stayed with Edison General Electric, though Batchelor continued to do some work with the lab. Edison's old friend Sigmund Bergmann left the company. Edison was on the board of EGE and was consulted about business matters, but he lost immediate control of the manufacturing companies. Though he continued to be interested in the electrical business and conducting research for EGE was the largest single activity at the lab, he gradually removed himself from active involvement. A welcome change, he said, because it promised him more time for the business of invention.[142] His name was still on the masthead, but only for a time.

The merger did not directly affect the Phonograph Works or ore milling – or the Kineto. But it was a profound change of relations that ultimately affected the entire lab.

140 Dyer, *Edison: His Life and Inventions*, p. 341.

141 EHS. Frank McGowan was Edison's agent in South America charged with searching for improved examples of bamboo and other fibers for use as filaments in light bulbs. Tate was giving McGowan a run-down on current activities of the company.

142 EHS; Israel, Op. Cit., pp. 321–324.

The Phonograph: shenanigans

During 1889 the Phonograph Works, built next to the Laboratory in 1888, was in full operation and the recently formed North American Phonograph Company was handling the sale of phonographs in North America. George Gouraud was marketing the phonograph in Europe where Edison planned to show the phonograph as a feature of his exhibit at the upcoming Paris Exposition. On the surface the business looked very promising but Edison had been badly burned in the process of negotiating the contract that created North American Phonograph and Edison and Al Tate were nervous about the way Gouraud was handling the business in Europe.

The North American Phonograph Company was the result of a series of negotiations that took place during 1888. Jesse Lippincott, a wealthy manufacturer of tumblers and other glass products, had negotiated an agreement to distribute Bell's Graphophone and after some reluctance, Edison was persuaded to join. He consented so long as he was able to control manufacture of both machines. The agreement was negotiated during the summer of 1888 by Edison's lawyer, John Tomlinson and Edison's long-time friend and business associate, Ezra Gilliland. After the agreement with Lippincott was signed, Edison was stunned to learn that Gilliland and Tomlinson had negotiated a secret payment to themselves of $250,000 worth of stock in the new company. The stock was the purchase price for Gilliland's controlling interest in the company that had marketed Edison's earlier version of the phonograph and Edison was not aware that it was to be part of the agreement with Lippincott. The deal included a cash payment of at least $50,000 to Gilliland and other monies to Tomlinson. Immediately after concluding the deal and before Edison learned about it, the pair sailed for Europe to market the phonograph there.

Edison was shocked, dismayed and furious that a seemingly faithful friend had double crossed him. He severed relations, never spoke to him again and refused to go to Ft. Myers as long as Gilliland owned the adjacent property. Tomlinson and Gilliland were called back from Europe and a law suit against them was initiated. Edison had trusted Gilliland with management of the phonograph manufacture so he had to re-staff the operation. He increasingly relied on Al Tate, who replaced Insull as his personal secretary, to oversee much of the phonograph business.

The troubles with the North American Phonograph Company were only part of the problem. Edison and Tate were worried about marketing the phonograph in Europe and their concern stemmed from George Gouraud's flamboyant and unpredictable methods. Gouraud, an American who had settled in London, had a long involvement with Edison. Previously he handled some of his telegraph and telephone innovations in England as well as on the continent. Somewhere along life's way he had become a colonel, a title he liked to use, and his home in London, called "Little Menlo", celebrated a special relationship he curried with the famous inventor.

Col. Gouraud had an agreement to commercialize the 1888 updated version of the phonograph and was eager to launch a high profile sales campaign by involving voice recordings of prominent persons. If the recordings could be made before the public and the press in popular locations like the Crystal Palace, all the better and he planned to generate publicity by distributing photographs of Edison posing with the phonograph. This was quite different from the more reserved and dignified campaign that Edison preferred. Edison regarded the business community as the legitimate market and in April 1889 he wrote to Gouraud:

"Under cover of exciting public interest in the phonograph you have adopted a plan which retards the progress of real business and keeps the instrument before people as a curiosity ... and so long as this preliminary system continues to pay, it appears to be your intention to sustain it. Nothing of the kind was contemplated by me when I consented to your handling the business. I ... never dreamed that you would side-track the whole enterprise for the purpose of gaining time to indulge in a series of picayune side-shows ...".

As Edison prepared for exhibiting the phonograph in Paris much of his focus, and Tate's as well, was directed toward keeping Gouraud in check.[143]

The Edison phonograph was marketed as an aid to stenographers, a substitute for written correspondence or a means of capturing and preserving important information, particularly legal and legislative proceedings, etc. The machines were expensive and were only available through lease from the North American Company or its agents. They were not offered for sale. Gouraud made Edison uncomfortable because he raised a subject that Edison preferred to ignore: commercializing the phonograph as a device for popular diversion and amusement. Despite the rather uncompromising tone of his admonition to Gouraud, Edison was conflicted about the future of the phonograph market. Edison was aware of the entertainment potential of the phonograph and took delight in predicting the value of recordings of Adelina Patti and other well known singers or famous actors like Edwin Booth. During 1888 he had his staff working on a miniature phonograph which could be used to make a talking doll. (Not co-incidentally he had started a new family.) But a critical technical obstacle had to be overcome before the phonograph could reach the public: only a very limited number of recordings could be made at a time. Lacking a duplicating device, a performer had to be recorded by several machines or repeat the performance over and over. All through 1888 and 1889 he and the staff experimented with methods to duplicate recordings but the problem had not been solved. Even so, in preparation for the Paris Exhibit Theodore Wangemann, dubbed "the professor" by the staff, was creating a library of recorded performances which could be played there. It would be the European debut of the improved phonograph.[144]

Edison's attitude towards popularizing the phonograph remained schizophrenic throughout this period. While publicizing its potential,

143 EHS. Edison to Gouraud, 12 April 1889. Gouraud wanted to charge the public for listening but Edison was adamant that he want no charges for his exhibit.

144 EHS; Israel, Op. Cit., pp. 277–291; Conot, Op. Cit., pp. 260–270.

he resisted the inevitable drift towards developing it as an entertainment device. Edison's private secretary, Al Tate, increasingly responsible for much of the business related to the phonograph, commented about this:

"... His attitude indicates that he regarded the exploitation of this field as undignified and disharmonious with the more serious objectives of his ambition. He dedicated his life to the production of useful invention. Devices designed for entertainment or amusement did not in his judgment fall within this classification. ...".[145]

Edison shared this attitude with much of the business community who regarded the entertainment world as a poor investment – some for moral reasons, others because it lacked the certainty that manufacturing and transportation held in the post-Civil War era. It would be a while before Edison resolved his conflicted views about producing entertainment and the evolution of Edison's attitude played an important role in creating the Kineto.

Although troubled by Gouraud's methods, Edison and Tate had a more immediate and pragmatic worry. The agreement with Gouraud gave him partial responsibility for patent devices in European countries and in a number of countries the term for patents was much shorter than the seventeen years allowed by U.S. law. They were specifically worried about a patent in Portugal where the term was only seven years. With some justification they were afraid that these short term patents might override the longer periods of U.S. and other European patents. While it was convenient to have Gouraud cover costs and the bother of patenting devices in Europe, they felt it was necessary to limit what he could do, so a letter defining his limits was sent in December, 1888. Worries about methods to protect his innovations at home and abroad plagued Mr. Edison throughout his life.

Ore milling: speculation

As Edison's role in lighting faded, his enthusiasm for iron blossomed. After testing the market for milling machines, as 1888 came to an end he was poised to to enter the mining and concentrating field himself. He believed that his method for processing low-grade ore could perform efficiently and economically enough to supply steel plants in the Eastern U.S. The machine built for Walter Mallory was shipped to Michigan in December, where it was to be operated by the Edison Iron Concentrating Company, a concern owned by Edison, Mallory and Edison's in-laws, the Miller family of Akron, Ohio. About the same time he launched a new concern, the New Jersey and Pennsylvania Concentrating Works, to handle the mining and concentrating of ore in the East. The company's outside investors were carefully selected so that they would give him room to operate as he wished and not interfere like the Wall Street powers who usurped the electrical industry. After a search for a suitable source of ore, he settled on the Gilbert Mine in Bechtelsville, Pennsylvania and began making an ore separator to install there. He also launched a study of undeveloped ore deposits in the Eastern United States. A magnetic ore detector was designed for use by

145 Tate, ...*Open Door*, pp. 307–308. Historian Paul Israel, managing editor of the Thomas Edison Papers project, emphasizes that Edison was a pioneer of modern popular entertainment in Chapter 15, "Inventing Entertainment" in his *Edison, A Life of Invention*, pp. 277–302.

a team of investigators he dispatched to survey mining locations. Sample ores from these and locations beyond the eastern seaboard were sent to Orange for evaluation.

Historically the iron industry had been based in the East but what with the mines being depleted and with the existing furnaces searching for ore Edison saw an opportunity. There were still acres and acres of ore in the East, but it was too expensive to extract serviceable ore by conventional methods. He formulated a plan to control all – or at least, most – of the low grade ore in the Eastern United States, anticipating that with a near monopoly he could supply the older, more developed part of the iron industry. If he succeeded – and retained control of his companies – he would have the financial independence he sought.

As head of Edison's metallurgy department, Dickson had a key role in Edison's ambitious mining scheme and his prospects were looking up. On 10 January 1889 Dickson's pay was raised from $24.00 to $30.00 a week and this put him at the upper level of the lab's payroll.[146] By spring the Dicksons moved from a modest duplex at 189 High Street to a larger single family house at 166 Cleveland Street in Orange.[147] The houses were within walking distance of the laboratory. In February the Kineto project was made an officially budgeted experiment, though the demands of ore milling took precedence. 1889 was a critical year for the project and an eventful year for Dickson as well. Success, controversy and hard work lay ahead.

146 EHS. A combined pay roll sheet for 9 October 1890 shows only George Attwood, Superintendent at $36.00 and John Ott, Superintendent at $30.77 paid more than Dickson. Other experimenters were paid less: Arthur Kennelly at $28.85 and Dr. F. Schulze Berge also at $28.85.

147 Hendricks, Op. Cit., p. 154. Hendricks found the address change in the *Orange City Directory* published on 1 May 1889, p. 43. Dickson apparently owned the house on Cleveland Street. He said that when he went to England in 1897 he left it in the hands of a caretaker and only sold it after his sister and wife died in London.

Chapter 9

Competition!

W.K.L. Dickson to Thomas Edison, 7 May 1921: "... "It seems too bad that the whole credit should be given to Friese-Greene as Pioneer & inventor of moving photography – He died here as you have doubtless read rather tragically & a great national funeral is to be organized – a 2 minute silence for prayer imposed, etc. etc. –

"If you chose you could have supported me in my battle over here for you as the Pioneer. ... By allowing this to take root – History will so have it for all time – & your work & my humble contribution to same – by reflection – goes untold, & will never be recognized – Surely as I have so often shown precedence for it than it is now being put to, such as giving moving when he wrote you in 1890, (you showed me the letter) described what he was doing & you had to write that you had already secured the whole thing in 1888 – best hunt up A.O. Tates letter he wrote at yr dictation –

"Who therefore is the pioneer of practical moving photography?"[148]

Adolphe Le Prince, son of Augustin Le Prince, to Richard Wilson of Leeds, 1898: "They have made a lot of money here with his invention and also in France, and it is becoming exceedingly popular here. My father had much higher aims for it than it is now being put to, such as giving moving panoramas and operas. He had a contract with the Paris Opera House which he would have fulfilled had he not disappeared; and he intended exhibiting in America in 1890. He told me he would be over in a few weeks."[149]

Edison could not have known in late June 1889 when a marathon of work on the Kineto started, that four days earlier William Friese-Greene and Mortimer Evans applied for a British patent for a moving image camera.[150] He would learn about it soon enough and the date of the Friese-Greene patent, 21 June 1889 would haunt both Edison and Dickson.

If they didn't know about his patent, they must have been aware that Friese-Greene was working on a device similar to their Kineto. In March 1889, the popular American journal *Cassell's Family Magazine* reported briefly that Friese-Greene had built a camera and combined it with a magic lantern "... to produce an image on the screen which has all the movements of life". It said that the camera produced transparencies that were mounted "... on a long strip wound on rollers ..." and

148 EHS, Dickson enclosed an article "Great Silence in the Cinemas" from the *Sunday Express*, 8 and 21 May describing the death of Wm. Friese-Greene who collapsed and died during film industry banquet.

149 MoMA Crawford. A hand transcribed copy in the Merritt Crawford Collection. Richard Wilson was a prominent banker in Leeds, England and a friend who was on tour in France with Augustin Le Prince and parted from Le Prince just before he disappeared.

150 National Archives and Records Service. British Patent no. 10,131, Improved Apparatus for Taking Photographs in Rapid Series, applied 21 June 1889, awarded 10 May 1890. British patent practice uses the date of application as the date of the patent.

the lantern displayed "... transparent photographs after the manner of
the 'Zoetrope ...".[151] There is no record that Edison read this article but
if he did it would have contributed to his decision to let Dickson
concentrate on the Kineto for a while. Edison was often stirred to action
by word that others were pursuing one of his goals

Friese-Greene was not his only competitor. In fact, Edison was a
rather late entrant in a somewhat crowded field. The exhibition of
chronophotographs by Muybridge and others inspired a number of
photo enthusiasts to try and capture movement. Most of these chal-
lengers worked in obscurity and never emerged, but a few caught the
attention of the press and some obtained patents that anticipated
Edison's. It was these conflicting claims that precipitated the patent
disputes that marred much of the first decade of the twentieth century.
This seemingly endless series of court cases stimulated subsequent
quarrels about the founding of cinema which became a feature of Mr.
Dickson's later life. Because of this, it is important to know the major
players and their work.

We have met the chronophotographers Muybridge and Marey, and
been introduced to Ottomar Anschütz. Anschütz was a skilled Prussian
photographer whose studies of movement gained international recognition. The work of the chronophotographers generally did not concern Edison whose objective was more open-ended. The
chronophotographers typically took only a dozen or two pictures of
their subjects and Edison planned to take many more images. But
chronophotography was the initial stimulus for the Kineto and both
Edison and Dickson monitored the work of its practitioners for inspiration. Anschütz's viewing device, the Tachyscope, which used a Giesler tube for illumination caught the attention of Edison and Dickson.
Rapid light sources – Giesler tubes and Leyden jars – were tried both
for illuminating subjects for photography and for viewing test images.

But there were others who shared Edison's objective of producing
longer sequences of action and several were close to solving the problems. In addition to Friese-Greene and Le Prince, we will look briefly
at Wordsworth Donisthorpe, an English barrister with a strong interest
in photography. In June, 1889 when the intense work on the Kineto
began, all three were probably closer to reproducing movement than
Edison and Dickson.

William Friese-Greene

William Friese-Greene (1855–1921) was a well regarded English photographer who had experimented with the illusion of movement for
several years. After operating photo shops in Bristol and Plymouth he
moved to London about 1885, eventually opening several shops there.
For many years he was regarded as England's leading candidate for the
title of father of cinema, but in recent years his role has been reconsidered. Questions have been raised about the accuracy of his claims and
the degree of success his experiments achieved. But from the end of the
19th and through most of the 20th centuries it was his claims rather

151 NMAH
Hendricks. *Cassell's
Family Magazine* ,
March 1889.

William Friese-Greene (1855–1921), a professional photographer with shops in several English cities, became interested in capturing and reproducing moving images. His experiments led to British patent no. 10,131, 21 June 1889. The date plagued Dickson because, even though Friese-Greene had no success with his device, it predated any success that Edison could legitimately claim.

than his achievements that cast doubts over Edison's claims of priority in the paternity battles. What follows is a summary of Friese-Greene's activities as compiled from his own accounts and early articles about his work.

He seems to have begun working on devices to simulate motion during the 1880s. During this period he worked with John Arthur Roebuck Rudge a scientific instrument maker and a specialist in Magic Lanterns who was based in Bath. This was an affiliation much like that of Dickson and Edison, Friese-Greene handled photographic aspects while Rudge took care of the mechanism. By 1887 Friese-Greene was in London and had begun more serious experimenting on his camera. He now had Mortimer Evans, a civil engineer, to aid him in non-photographic matters. When Eastman introduced the Kodak camera in 1888, it became a model for a version of his camera that used rolls of Eastman's stripping film. Perhaps following Eastman's recommendation, he tried to make the stripping film transparent by soaking it in castor oil. He abandoned paper because the results were unsatisfactory. It lacked transparency and its "... tendency to tear or break placed an insurmountable handicap upon high speed".[152] This led him to experiment with celluloid and since the sheets available to him were very small, he tried to make his own. Aided by Alfred Parker they devised a method of producing the base using crude celluloid purchased from Frederick Mayne of Birmingham. With advice from a Mr. Vargarra [Vergara of the Vergara company?], he claimed that by the end of 1888 he was able to produce strips of celluloid up to sixty feet long and piece them together into longer lengths. Using this film he claimed that he was able to take motion pictures:

"... While Mr. Parker was engaged in the production and development of the celluloid transparent film, I was also engaged in the further improvement of my camera, adapting it to take pictures at a more rapid rate, and toward the end of the year 1888 I had completed these improvements and had constructed an improved camera, and with this camera, in the month of January, 1889, I first was able to use my camera with the celluloid film in the taking of motion pictures at the rate of ten per second. This 1888 camera was built to take a much larger picture than the 1887 camera, and did take a negative about three inches square. This was a stereoscopic camera, taking two pictures, side by side, at the same time upon the same film, at each exposure. I used it both as a single camera and as a stereoscopic camera, the change being made simply by closing up one lens aperture. Due to the size of the picture the film in this camera had to travel three inches at each step, and at ten exposures per second, the film traveled thirty inches per second ...".[153]

This camera used a great deal of film so a third camera was built. Friese-Greene credited Lord Kelvin with recommending that he stabilize the movement of the film by means of sprockets. He also claimed that he made a projector in 1889 and was experimenting to combine the projector with a phonograph. In this version, his first films were taken in early October 1889, with subsequent scenes taken in 1890. According to Will Day, his first film was taken in 1889 and subsequent scenes were taken in 1890. Day said Greene's first film was shown by projection at the Photographic Convention in Chester early in 1890.[154]

While these claims are confusing, by June of 1889 Friese-Greene had enough confidence in his design that he applied for a patent.[155] This patent was cited most often by examiners and the courts to disallow a number of Edison's claims to primacy in the invention of the moving image camera. In fact, it anticipated almost everything Edison would claim as original in his inventions. As a result, Dickson spent much of his late life trying to invalidate Friese-Greene's work and affirm Edison's claim (and, by extension, his own). Regardless of whether it

152 *The Moving Picture News*, 3 December 1910. Testimony in Motion Picture Patents Co. vs. Yankee Film Co. et. al., 1 December 1910.

153 Ibid.

154 This account of Friese-Greene's work is primarily constructed from his testimony in Patents Company v. Yankee Film Co., 1910 and Will Day's paper, "Claims to Motion-Picture Invention. Great Britain: William Friese-Greene" presented 16 February 1926 at the meeting of The Royal Photographic Society and published in *The Photographic Journal*, July 1926, pp. 359-[363]. My copy of Day's paper came from the Theisen Collection at the Library of the Academy of Motion Picture Arts & Sciences..

155 *Who's Who of Victorian Cinema*, pp. 53–54, article by Peter Carpenter and Stephen Herbert. During the 1920s and 1930s a number of film historians, notably Will Day, credited Friese-Greene with successfully filming at a higher rate during 1889 and successfully projecting images in 1889 or 1890. Recent scholarship has cast doubt on these claims and most of the specifics mentioned here are from the claims in his patent and in articles from the period.

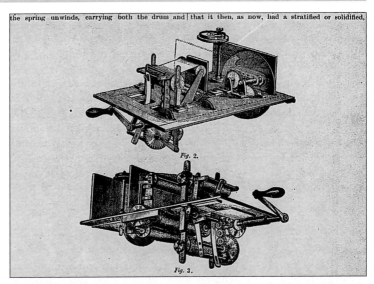

This illustration of the mechanism of Friese Greene's 'Machine Camera for Taking Ten Photographs a Second' appeared in the Scientific American Supplement, No. 746, 19 April 1890, p. 11921. *[NMAH Hendricks.]*

156 EHS & NMAH Hendricks. *Photographic News* had an article on 28 February 1890 and there was one in *The Optical Magic Lantern Journal and Photographer Enlarger* on 1 April 1890. The article in *Photographic News* was reprinted in *Scientific American Supplement, No. 746,* p. 11921, 11 April 1890.

157 EHS. There is a copy of this article, as well as the reprint in *Scientific American Supplement, No. 746* in the files of the Edison Historic Site.

worked or not, by June 1889, when Dickson was still struggling with cylinders, Friese-Greene had patented a single lens camera, moving "film" from one roller to another and stopping it for exposure. 21 June 1889 was a date that plagued Edison and Dickson for much of their lives.

Although Edison may not have been familiar with most of his competitors, he knew about Friese-Greene – and what he knew probably troubled him. In addition to a brief mention in the March 1889 issue of *Cassells*, Friese-Greene's camera was the subject of articles in British and American photographic journals in the fall of 1889. Several more articles appeared not long after Edison's first announcement of the Kineto in February 1890. In early April 1890 soon after Edison returned to Orange from vacation in North Carolina, he received a letter from Friese-Greene enclosing a paper describing his "... machine camera for taking 10 a second which may be of interest to you". It is not hard to imagine that Friese-Greene was reacting to articles about the Kinetoscope which appeared in London papers in February. An interesting exchange, since Edison's announcement of the Kineto may have been a reaction to news of Friese-Greene's work.[156]

The paper that Friese-Greene sent was probably the article from *Photographic News* which was titled "A Machine Camera Taking Ten Photographs a Second".[157] It described his camera in detail. A little larger than a "Kodak", it could take "... a hundred consecutive pictures by the turning of a handle". A strip of "film" coiled on a shaft was fed to a position where exposure took place. At the point of exposure the film was stopped for the duration of the exposure, then advanced to a take-up shaft where it was again rolled into a coil. The two shafts ran continuously and while the film moved a device played-out a loop of film the size of the exposure area. It could be stopped without breaking the continuous movement. A pair of shutters admitted light while the film was at rest in the exposure area. The article did not specify the rate at which exposures were made, but the title stated ten per second. It mentioned film, but not the type of film being used. In early 1890 the term "film" did not necessarily mean photo material on celluloid base.

The camera described by *Photographic News* was a revised version of cameras Friese-Greene designed in 1888–1889. His partner Mortimer Evans applied for a patent for the improved, simplified version on 8 March 1890.[158]

On the surface, this description of Friese-Greene's work, drawn largely from his own accounts, gives the impression that he had achieved a great deal, but Friese-Greene's claims have been as controversial as Edison's. Some film historians, mostly in Great Britain, credited him with being the father of the motion picture, but others dismissed him as a non-achiever who talked a good game, but was unable to produce. W.K.L. Dickson was among the latter.

Friese-Greene was specific that he had made celluloid strips by 1889 but he was not specific about the success of his experiments. But if he made celluloid, it is doubtful that he could use it successfully. The trade press of the day was filled with comments about the problems celluloid users encountered, some of which would have been particularly troublesome when filming movement at a rapid rate. There were complaints about the stiffness and brittleness of the celluloid and Friese-Greene needed maximum flexibility. As it dried after developing celluloid curled into a tight roll. This could be controlled by keeping it taut, but this made processing difficult. Among the problems that Dickson encountered were frilling on the edges, cockling and the separation of the emulsion from the base during processing. Eastman was troubled with spots, electrical discharges that showed on the film as lightening-like streaks, emulsions that faded and problems with increasing sensitivity so rapid exposures could be taken. Despite these problems, Eastman was the most successful producer of celluloid. If Friese-Greene was able to overcome these problems he should have gone into the business of making celluloid.

One of Friese-Greene's films survives, a scene taken in Hyde Park, London. He claimed it was taken in October, 1889 and exhibited at the Photographic Convention in Chester in 1890.[159] But this date is subject to question. What is supposed to be the original was acquired by Will day, the British film historian, collector and ardent champion of Friese-Greene. It is now at the Archive du film du CNC in Bois d'Arcy outside Paris. It is possible that this is a strip of celluloid of Friese-Greene's own manufacture but it looks suspiciously like a strip of Eastman's celluloid roll film. As a prominent photographic merchant, Friese-Greene would have had early access to Eastman's product but none was for sale in

158 British patent no. 3730, Mortimer Evans, applied 8 March 1890, accepted 10 January 1891. It was for improvements to the intermittent drive mechanism.

159 Will Day, Op. Cit., p. 361.

Strips of celluloid film exposed by Friese-Greene survive in the Will Day Collection which was acquired by Cinémathèque Française and are kept by the Archives du film du Centre National de la Cinématographie at Bois d'Arcy, France. These photographs were taken in 2000. Friese-Greene claimed they were taken very early but the date is difficult to confirm. These strips look very much like Eastman's film which was not available in Europe until after January 1890. [Photos by the author.]

England before early 1890. It seems likely that he used Eastman's film so it is doubtful that this strip was made before 1890.

Whatever achievements Friese-Greene made, he was never able to commercialize his invention. In fact, his success was short lived. Although he was prominent in British photographic circles and the proprietor of several photo shops, he seems to have been a poor money-manager. The expense of his animated picture experiments may have proved too much – he claimed to have spent about £1000 of his own money on them.[160] A few months after he wrote to Edison he was forced into bankruptcy and in the spring of 1891 many of his possessions were sold at auction and he was apparently jailed for a time.

This set-back was serious enough that in order to recover he sought a new start. In May, 1892 he wrote Edison applying for a position and inquiring about work in connection with the Fair in Chicago. The reply was written by Al Tate who answered on Edison's behalf, saying there were no positions available and that Edison had nothing to do with arrangements for the Fair. Although he worked on a projector later on and experimented with color photography, Friese-Greene was never again a major factor in the introduction of motion pictures.

Louis Aimé Augustin Le Prince

Friese-Greene may have been approaching success, but Louis Aimé Augustin Le Prince (1842–1890?) may have been even closer and his story is one of the most intriguing from cinema's genesis. Like Dickson,

[160] MoMA Crawford, Friese-Greene to the Editor of *The British Journal of Photography*, 6 July 1896. Printed in their issue of 10 July 1896.

Louis Aimé Augustin Le Prince (1842–1890?) may have come closest to succeeding in making a practical motion picture device but his career was cut short when he mysteriously disappeared after boarding a train from Dijon to Paris in 1890. [NMAH.]

he had roots in three countries: England, the United States and France. The son of an artillery officer in the French army, he was educated in Bourges and Paris and studied chemistry in Leipzig. His interest in science was coupled with skill and training in painting in oil and pastel. In the 1860s he took a job with Whitley Partners, a brass foundry in Leeds and married the daughter of Joseph Whitley, a partner in the firm. With his wife he established a school of applied art in Leeds. He was interested in photography and developed a process to reproduce photographs in color on metal and china which he turned into a business. He came to the United States in 1881 to introduce his process. He sold the process to an American firm and stayed in the U.S. to manage "The Merrimac and Monitor Naval Engagement Illustrated", one of the popular post civil-war panoramic paintings. This one was done by

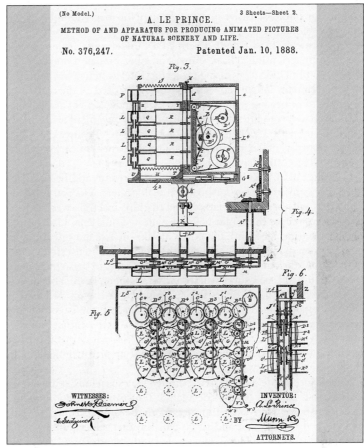

Le Prince's camera-projector was a complicated device. This is the drawing of the mechanism for Le Prince's 16 lens camera-projector which he patented in January 1888 while living in New York City. His son and other champions insist that at the time of his disappearance he had created a simpler, single lens device. [NARA.]

161 This account of Le Prince's experiments is drawn from E. Kilburn Scott, "Career of L.A.A. Le Prince", *Journal of the SMPE*, July 1931, pp. 76–83, reprinted from *Photographic Journal*, May 1931; Christopher Rawlence, *The Missing Reel* (London & New York, Penguin Books, 1992); and MoMA, Merritt Crawford Collection. Le Prince's most vociferous champions were his son Adolphe Le Prince and E. Kilburn Scott, a consulting Engineer and amateur historian from Leeds who worked in the 1930s. Christopher Rawlence tells Le Prince's story with an interesting mixture of history and drama.

Théophile Poilpot and it was mounted in a circular building at the corner of Madison Avenue and Fifty-Ninth Streets in New York City. His wife taught art at a school for the deaf in Washington Heights, New York.

Apparently inspired by the photographs of Eadweard Muybridge, he began work on a device to capture and reproduce movement and in 1886 he applied for a patent for a device "... for Producing Animated Pictures of Natural Scenery and Life". The U.S. patent for his combination camera and viewing device was granted on January 10, 1888. By this time Le Prince had returned to Leeds where he continued work on the camera and started work on a projector using his father-in-law's machine shop and rented workshop.[161]

The first machine, made in New York, was a very complicated device which had sixteen lenses backed by a complicated mechanism to move the photo-sensitive material through the machine and keep the images in sequence.

Le Prince's 1888 patent described a camera with 16 lenses that recorded images using "Glass, Canvas or other Prepared Surfaces ...". It was a combination camera and projector. Intermittence was achieved by using shutters and it used "sensitive films ... stored on the two lower drums ...". For negatives these could be "... an endless sheet of insoluble gelatine coated with bromide emulsion, or any convenient ready-made quick-acting paper, such as Eastman's paper film". Positives "... must be on a transparent flexible material – such as gelatine, mica, horn, &c." A small Glass could also be used.[162]

By the fall of 1888 he had a two lens version and modified it to use the paper strips made for Eastman's Kodak camera. His son Adolphe Le Prince, who assisted his father, said that this machine was made to take stereo images but could be used with just one lens. Using Eastman's paper film, Le Prince filmed his mother-in-law and son, Adolphe in the garden of his father-in-law's house. He also filmed a street scene of traffic on a bridge in Leeds. Adolphe Le Prince said these films were taken at 10 to 12 exposures per second in October 1888. This date is supported by the death of Le Prince's mother-in-law on 24 October 1888. A modern reconstruction of two of these films is convincing evidence supporting claims that Le Prince made the earliest motion pictures.[163] Adolphe said that by 1890 Le Prince had made further modifications to use Eastman's celluloid and opened negotiations to exhibit moving images at the Paris Opera.

Le Prince's wife was still in the United States teaching at the school for the deaf. Early in 1890 he decided to return, apparently intending to demonstrate his invention in New York. Before returning he went to France for a vacation and to visit his brother Albert, an architect working for the city of Dijon. He traveled with friends from Leeds, Mr. and Mrs. Wilson, and after parting with them he took the train to Dijon on 12 September 1890, spent the weekend with his brother and boarded the train to Paris on Tuesday, 16 September. He intended an immediate return to New York. He never arrived in Paris and was never seen again.

It took a while for his family to miss him. He had not given them his sailing schedule and consequently they did not know when he would arrive. Several weeks passed before they were certain he was not coming which delayed the search until later that fall. An investigation by the police and searches by private investigators found no trace of him and no hint of what happened after he boarded the train.

There are a number of theories about his disappearance and speculation has ranged from foul play to suicide. There is even a hint of fratricide. Though both Le Prince and his wife seem to have been comfortably well off he apparently encountered financial problems and his visit to his brother was not just social. His mother died in 1887 and her will was still being settled. Le Prince thought he was owed a thousand pounds from the estate and it is possible that the brothers quarreled about the settlement. Although there may have been other

162 NARA. U.S. Patent, No. 376,247, Method of and Apparatus for Producing Animated Pictures of Natural Scenery and Life, Augustin Le Prince, 10 January 1888, applied 2 November 1886. Le Prince's son claimed that the Patent Office disallowed claims for a two lens, stereo version of this camera. Le Prince's foreign patents include the two lens version.

163 Rawlence, Op. Cit. Copies of these two films are in the collection of the National Museum of Photography, Film and Television, Bradford, England. At the time this is being written they can be viewed at their website.

financial drains, the cost of his moving image experiments could have been a factor.

Random violence? Running off to start a new life? Suicide or fratricide? An accident? His family rejected all of these possibilities and convinced themselves that his disappearance was engineered by Thomas Edison. Le Prince's widow, Sarah Elizabeth (Lizzie) and son Adolphe were the main proponents of this idea and they passed it on to succeeding generations of their family.[164] Mrs. Le Prince apparently could not accept the possibility that her husband was dead and when Edison publicized the Kinetoscope in 1891, she conjectured that Edison had appropriated or stolen her husband's invention. As the family clung to this theory it evolved into a belief that Edison's agents kidnaped Le Prince and were holding him captive. They believed that this plot that went back to 1888 and involved using the Patent Office to steal information from Le Prince's application. As late as 1898 Adolphe Le Prince still clung to the hope that his father was being held captive some where.[165]

The disappearance of Le Prince removed one of Edison's principal competitors and to that extent, Edison gained something from it, but the belief that Edison instigated it is pure fantasy. It is uncertain how much Edison knew of Le Prince's work but probably very little. He may have been aware of his U.S. patent and perhaps his foreign patents as well. There were publications that summarized patents and Edison, his staff and his patent attorneys reviewed them regularly. There was a complete set of French patents in his library and he probably had British patents as well. But unlike the many film pioneers who actively sought publicity, Le Prince did not promote himself. There was a brief notice about him in *Scientific American* June 28, 1888, but few other articles.

The family's belief that Edison was involved in Le Prince's disappearance would not require any further comment except that it raises the issue of Edison's ruthless, even villainous side. Because many – no, most film historians – have accepted that Edison was one of the darkest figures in film's early years, it deserves some clarification. After 1897, Edison's company used almost every available device to monopolize the motion picture business in the U.S. This campaign, which certainly had its ruthless moments, was initiated by Edison's business manager William Gilmore, and continued by Frank Dyer, one of Edison's patent attorneys who succeeded Gilmore as business manager. Dyer was later head of the Motion Picture Patents Company which continued the Edison company's monopolistic efforts into the Teens. While Gilmore and Dyer fronted the campaign, it was conducted with Edison's full knowledge and approval – Edison was never out of touch with what was going on in his companies.

But this started at a later time and was a modeled on business practices that were far from unusual during Edison's time. In 1890, Le Prince was just one of many rivals working on an interesting project, but one with an uncertain future, especially as a commercial rival. Edison tended to ignore rival inventors and he usually regarded them

164 MoMA Crawford; Christopher Rawlence, *The Missing Reel* (New York & London, Penguin Books, 1990). The information about Le Prince's belief he was owed money from his mother's will comes from "notes given to Prefecture of Police in Paris" in the Merritt Crawford Collection. Christopher Rawlence found evidence that Le Prince was being pressed for payment of a large, long standing debt during the spring and summer of 1890 (Op. Cit., pp. 250–251).

165 MoMA, Crawford. Copy of a letter from Adolphe Le Prince to Richard Wilson, Leeds, 1898.

with a certain contempt. Although he may have been aware of Le Prince's patents, it is doubtful that he knew that Le Prince had been experimenting in Leeds and it is unlikely that he knew he was in France – or would have been interested if he did know. Attacking rival inventors was not part of Edison's scheme, at least, not in 1890. If he were so inclined, he would probably have gone after Charles Tainter, Bell's associate who improved Bell's Graphophone or Emile Berliner, a young experimenter connected with the Columbia Phonograph Co. in Washington, DC, who was on the verge of revolutionizing the design of the graphophone by replacing cylinders with disks. Though he was not inclined to attack fellow inventors, he was quicker to react when their inventions threatened the money making prospects of one of his inventions. At this stage the business prospects of the Kineto were doubtful. Edison's rivals were safe.[166]

Emile Berliner

German born Emile Berliner worked with Bell on the telephone and then on the graphophone. He pioneered recording on a flat disk rather than a cylinder and developed a method of recording that was different from Edison's. Edison's stylus cut smooth sidewalls and recorded the sound at the bottom. Berliner's stylus cut a smooth bottom and recorded the sound on the side walls, a patented difference that Edison never challenged. By 1895 he had developed an electrolytic process producing a metallic matrix which could be used to produce a large number of duplicate records on a durable recording media. Recognizing the potential of the entertainment world, he hired quality talent and produced and sold phonographs and recordings at prices the general public could afford. His home phonograph was simple to operate and driven by a hand cranked spring drive that required no electricity. He also introduced a contract system with royalties that assured his talent of continuing income from the recordings made for his company. His innovations played a significant role in creating the modern recording industry.

The mysterious disappearance of Le Prince left an interesting void. He appeared tantalizingly close to success – and yet may not have been close enough. We will never know for sure. Le Prince had access to the same photographic materials as Dickson and others and confronted the same limitations. The materials mentioned in his 1886 patent, "... gelatine, mica, horn, &c. ..." shows how tenuous his situation was. Eastman's paper strips appeared after he applied for the patent and he tried them with apparent success. He was able to expose a negative, but preparing positive images for exhibition proved difficult. The paper negatives had to be cut apart, put in water to dissolve the binder and the emulsion was then transferred to a transparent surface for printing. The resulting prints had to be attached to another transparent support and mounted on a flexible metal belt that transported them through the camera-projector. Glass was transparent but too fragile and heavy for this stage. His son Adolphe said he tried celluloid but it was expensive and difficult to develop because it curled into a tight roll when it dried. The heat from the projection lamp caused the film to cockle and blister

166 Tate, Op. Cit., pp. 275–276.
Chambers Biographical Dictionary, sixth ed., New York, Larousse Kingfisher Chambers Inc., 1997.

so that it could not be focused. Eastman's celluloid might have improved the situation but it was not available until shortly before Le Prince disappeared.

Le Prince's supporters did not serve his reputation very well. Auguste, followed by E. Kilburn Scott who took up Le Prince's cause in the 1920s and 1930s, were energetic and collected documents and testimony to support their accounts, but they pressed his case too vigorously. They made a substantial case for his success in capturing moving images very early and detailed his problems with projection, but they assumed that the introduction of Eastman's celluloid film in 1889 ended his troubles and that he was ready to introduce a completed motion picture system in 1890. Their optimism has not been shared by others who have questioned their generally rosy account. Eastman's new film was an improvement but not the wonder material that they assumed it was. Le Prince would have confronted the same problems others faced with the new film.

Wordsworth Donisthorpe

Wordsworth Donisthorpe, an English barrister, was another who had experimented with moving images for a number of years. Though his patent was less troublesome to Edison, it was occasionally cited in patent cases and his work should be mentioned. In 1876, before Muybridge was successful, he patented a camera for taking a series of images of moving objects and he devised a method of printing the images and viewing them intermittently. He revived his interest in 1888 and by 1889 he was working with his cousin, William C. Crofts on a camera-projector which used a roll of paper film to expose a series of images. It had a complicated interaction between the lens and the film in which they moved in opposite directions in a timed sequence which allowed a brief moment of exposure. They applied for a patent for this device 15 August 1889 and it was accepted 15 November 1890. While a film they made in Trafalgar Square in 1890 indicates that their system worked, Donisthorpe was never able to develop it commercially.[167]

Edison and competitors

It is not certain how much Edison and Dickson knew about the work of competitors. By the end of 1889 they knew about Friese-Greene, but Donisthorpe and Le Prince had attracted little attention from the press. Although Le Prince worked across the river in New York City for several years, there is no indication that Dickson or Edison knew him or of his experiments.

But if he lacked specific information, Edison probably understood that others were conducting similar experiments. He knew from experience that the factors that roused his curiosity and made experimentation possible were available to others. The Kineto project was kept under wraps. His meeting with Muybridge was well publicized and he had discussed his interest in combining the phonograph with instant photography with reporters, but the door to Room 5 was kept locked

167 *Ibid*, pp. 42–43. Article by Brian Coe. Stephen Herbert, *Industry, Liberty, and a Vision, Wordsworth Donisthorpe's Kinesigraph*, London, The Projection Box, 1998.

and only those directly involved in the experiments were allowed in. This would have been Dickson, Charles Brown, Edison and an occasional machinist, carpenter or pattern maker but only when their assignment required work in the photography room. Supplies and other necessities were passed into the room through the small communications shutter and much of the machine work was done in one of the two machine rooms. Though Edison would occasionally tell a reporter he was working on a way of seeing the person you talked to on the telephone or a means of sending pictures through the ether, there was no further publicity about the Kinetoscope until 1890.[168]

Even though the competing experimenters had little contact with each other, each of them were approaching success in the late spring of 1889. This was no coincidence. Nor was it a coincidence that, despite being close to their goal, none of them could quite make it. Mechanical aspects were solvable, but, like Dickson, all of them were "... seriously hampered by the defects of the materials at hand".[169] Although Dickson rejected Eastman's stripping film, it encouraged Le Prince, Friese-Greene and Marey to modify their designs. The Kodak paper could produce images, but getting those images into a form that could be viewed proved difficult. As long as they were stuck with metal, glass, collodion or Eastman's paper they were so limited in what they could achieve that they were stymied from reaching the breakthrough they all hoped for.

Although subsequent events made this competition important, in 1890, Edison was not very concerned about competition and this may well have been true of his "competitors". The chronophotographers had already captured movement and reproduced it but on a limited scale. Edison, Le Prince, Friese-Greene, Donisthorpe and others were attempting to extend the limited range inherent in the study of movement, but it was uncertain what lay in the future if they succeeded. There was a novelty value which would capture the public's imagination – Edison and others understood that, but what lay beyond novelty? How long would it last? What would the public continue to pay for?

Le Prince, Friese-Greene, Muybridge, Marey and Donisthorpe applied for patents for their various devices. As yet, Edison had only registered intent through his caveats in 1888 and 1889. When he finally applied for patents in 1891 their previously registered claims and those of others anticipated some of his own. Although Le Prince and Friese-Greene were no longer threats to commercialization, their patents proved troublesome as Edison tried to create a dominant position in the business of movies.

168 EHS. Testimony by Fred Ott and Charles A. Brown in Equity 6928, 30 and 31 January 1900, pp. 138–139 & 156 & 158.

169 A. & W.K.L. Dickson, *Century Magazine*

Chapter 10

A Certain Precipitate of Knowledge: The Kinetograph, Spring 1889

Dr. Henry Morton: "... at the time when Mr. Edison began his experiments ... and even while he was constructing the apparatus ... there was not ... any material which was adequate and fit for successful use and application for the production of the results aimed at by him. ... Especially it was lacking in ... sensitiveness and ... fineness of grain ...".[170] (Testimony for Edison in Equity No. 6928, Edison v. Amer. Mutoscope et al.)

Dickson: "... the results were more or less encouraging and a special department was created for the more serious development of this problem."[171]

170 EHS, M116-117, p. 201. Morton, the President of Stevens Institute, testified on 26 February 1900 for Edison in Equity No. 6928, Edison v. Amer. Mutoscope et al. He said that to produce more rapid emulsions the "Bromide emulsion" was heated a relatively long time which resulted in larger particles, i.e. visible graininess.

171 EHS, Legal Box No. 173. Dickson's testimony in Equity No. 28,605, 6 June 1910.

172 EHS, Employee time sheets.

173 Israel, *Edison ...*, p. 344,

It *is* possible that some of Dickson's Kineto tests were "more or less encouraging", but to all appearances, the "problems" outweighed any and all "encouragements". From January to late June Dickson, ever the perfectionist, struggled with the image problem, confronted unacceptable quality and had results far short of expectations. The pictures were not sharp. They were marred by grain and distortions. With these problems unsolved, it was not possible to record enough to give the illusion of motion – at least, not the illusion he wanted and Edison expected. Despite these problems Edison felt optimistic enough to give the Kinetoscope project official status by giving it an accounting number. Effective 1 February 1889 the bookkeepers could track the work done for experiment number 262, Kinetoscope. The first work charged to the account was by J.G. East, a pattern maker who worked fifteen hours during February's first week.[172]

Ironically, the account was opened at a time when Dickson and his assistant, Charles Brown were especially busy with ore milling and had less time to spend on the Kineto than earlier in the year. Even though the ore separator had been declared ready for operation and one had been put to work in Michigan, problems continued to crop up. In Michigan the workers complained about fine dust – too much iron ore was displaced by the blowers and too much collected on the face of the magnets.[173] While working on these problems, more and more ore

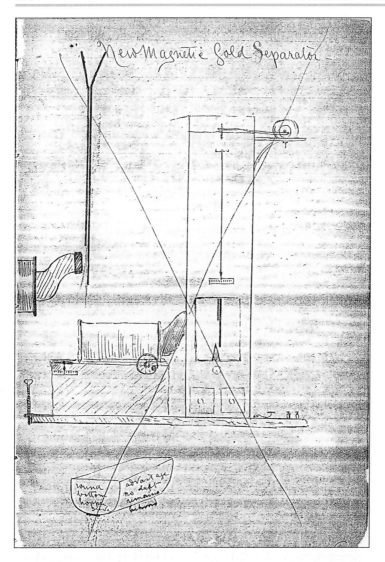

samples arrived for testing. They came from various locations and
evaluating them was complicated because the mix of minerals differed
from location to location.

Ore milling made other demands. On 20 February representatives
of the American Institute of Mining Engineers visited the lab and one
of the highlights of the tour was a demonstration of the separating
machine in Dickson's work shop. He had to hustle to prepare for the
visitors because he had been sick and returned to work just before the
delegates arrived. A second highlight was the reading of a paper, *The
Concentration of Iron-Ore*, by John Birkinbine and Thomas A. Edison.
Birkinbine, who delivered the paper, was a leading specialist on mines

`14`   THE CONCENTRATION OF IRON-ORE.

The Edison unipolar non-contact electric separator differs from the forms described in that it has no moving parts.   Except such facilities for altering the relative position of the parts as are essential for adjustment in treating different ores, or are required to secure certain results, all parts of the apparatus are fixed.   The separator, which is illustrated by Fig. 4, consists simply of a hopper, a magnet and a partition to separate the concentrates and tailings into different receptacles.   The illustration shows but one hopper, but in practice the ore can pass on each side of the magnet, thus doubling the capacity.   The simplicity of the construction, which is the

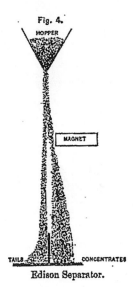

Edison Separator.

result of patient and thorough investigation of many different designs and methods, will commend itself.

The ore after being properly crushed and sized is placed in hoppers, from which its discharge is controlled by bars closing slots which extend the length of the hopper. These slots are made adjustable so as to suit the size to which the ore has been reduced. The hoppers are adjusted to appropriate heights above the magnet. The magnet in the apparatus exhibited at the Edison Laboratory, Llewellyn, N. J., is a mass of soft iron 6 feet long by 30 inches wide and 10 inches thick, weighing 3400 pounds, and wound with 450 pounds of copper wire, the coil being connected with a dynamo

Dickson's sketches of the ore separation machine (left) may have been the source of illustrations for a paper The Concentration of Iron Ore *that John Birkinbine and Edison presented to the American Institute of Mining Engineers in February, 1889.*

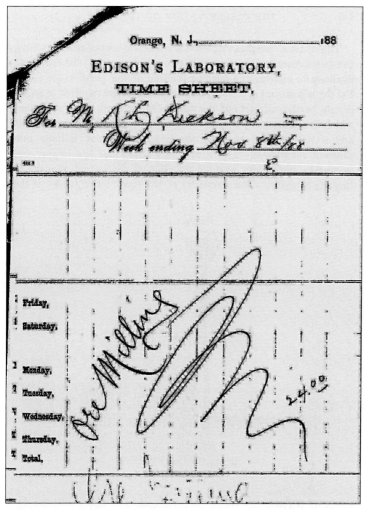

Dickson's time sheet for the week that ended 8 November 1888. Prior to June 1889 most of his time was charged to the ore milling account and since he was paid by the week, he did not itemize his time. He usually signed with a flourish and did not seem to give much attention details of his work week. [EHS.]

and minerals who had been hired by Edison to advise on ore milling. The paper was almost certainly written by Birkinbine since Edison was not inclined to write professional articles, but Edison and Dickson certainly contributed to it. The results of tests Dickson had been conducting were featured and a drawing illustrating Edison's separator appears to have been based on sketches from Dickson's notebooks. Needless to say, Birkinbine reported favorably on Edison's process.[174] So far as we know this was Dickson's first exposure to professionals in his field – and it was prime exposure. Birkinbine and Edison's partner Walter Mallory were spending more and more time in Orange and

174 EHS. Tate to Dickson, 2 February 1889.

while they were with Edison most of the time, Dickson was at their beck and call as well.

Because of the sketchiness of the lab's records and the growing demands of ore milling, it is difficult to gauge how much Dickson worked on the Kineto during the first six months of 1889. Although no time was charged to the Kineto account until the end of June, the evolving design changes incorporated in two caveats that Edison wrote during this period show that Dickson was at work in Room 5. The number of staff members charged to the 262 account during this period was impressive but they were all hourly wage workers: machinists, pattern makers and blacksmiths. Machinists accounted for most of the charges, and one, E. Neubert worked almost full time on the project, 490½ hours, between 2 March and 30 May. He worked a full 60 hour week four times in April and May and on March 7th his work day was 20 hours long – usually an indication that a major effort was underway![175] That week Neubert was joined by four other machinists and a pattern maker. Something was going on. But what? There is no clear evidence, but the time sheets, supply orders and Edison's two revised caveats provide provocative clues, so we will try and clarify the activities during this time of mystery.

Time sheets

175 EHS. Pay records. After Brown and East worked at the beginning of the month, Reuben Hepworth, the staff blacksmith and his assistant worked five hours on 11 February then there was a lull until 20 February, the day the mining engineers visited the lab. A machinist, R. Grabicksky started a five day stint working 10 hrs on 20 February; 4 hrs the 21st,10 hrs. the 22nd, 5 ½ hrs on Saturday the 24th and 7 ½ hrs on Tuesday, the 26th. This was followed by Neubert's nearly regular assignment to the project.
176 EHS. Brown testified 31 January 1900 in Equity No. 6928, Edison v. American Mutoscope & Biograph Co. He was questioned by Edison's lawyer, Frank Dyer.

Dickson was salaried and usually filled out his weekly time sheet at the end of the week rather than daily as the hourly workers were supposed to do. His was usually completed as succinctly as possible (see illustration on page 122) and signed (or initialed) with a flourish. Charles Brown was paid by the hour so was his time was supposed to be entered daily but he (or Mr. D., who sometimes made the entries) was careless about recording his time. From February until 25 June 1889 Brown's time on the Kineto was entered as work in Room 5, the Photo Room. This covered work on the Kineto as well as various photo projects. When Brown was questioned about this during the patent hearings he replied: "Well, you will find it on my time sheets that I put my time down to three different rooms that I worked in. If I worked in the lamp room, I put it down as lamp room; if I worked in the ore milling room, I put it down as ore milling, or when I worked in the photographing room, I charged it as photographing. Of course, I don't know how Mr. Randolph fixed it on his books, but that is the way I always made my time sheets out ... My time sheets will show that I put a great deal more time in the photographing room during that period than I did before."[176] Mr. Randolph, the office manager, charged Brown's time in Room 5 to "indirect labor".

Prior to June 1889 Dickson's Kineto expenses were lumped with his ore milling time. This may have been acceptable accounting because Edison was bearing the costs of ore milling and the Kineto. He expected that he could charge expenses back to the ore milling company when the venture began returning income. Although he had no specific plan in mind for the Kineto, he was covering all indirect labor costs, ore milling and the irregular and comparatively small Kineto charges, so it may have made no particular difference how they were accounted for. The situation began to change at the beginning of 1889 when Edison General Electric became the lab's principal customer. At that time it became prudent to make the record keeping at least appear to be more regular. EGE and other clients paid an administrative cost which Edison probably used to fund pet projects like ore milling and the Kineto. By the beginning of February when the Kineto account was set up, funds would have begun flowing from EGE.

Though they may not be 100 per cent accurate, Brown's time sheets are an indication of times when Dickson, who supervised activities, was behind the closed door of Room 5. As might be anticipated, the pattern was irregular. There would be no charges to Room 5 for several weeks, then there would be a spurt of charges, often for several consecutive days of work, followed by stretch when all charges were for ore milling. With the significant exception of an intense period of work in the summer, this pattern continued through most of 1889 and early 1890. After spending several days in Room 5 during October and November, 1888, Brown worked four days in December, two days in January (which tied to the end of the holidays), four in February, eight days in March, and half a week at the beginning of April. From 11 April until 25 June none of Brown's time was charged to Room 5, a period of intense activity in the ore milling "outhouse" while Edison was preparing operations at his Bechtelsville mine.[177]

An interesting exchange of letters illustrates how tight scheduling was during this period. Horace Townsend, a popular journalist, requested photos to illustrate the extensive and detailed article about the lab he wrote for *Cosmopolitan Magazine* (see Chapter 5, page 69). He was told by Al Tate that "... Mr Dickson, in addition to his work as Laboratory Photographer, runs our ore milling department, in connection with which he is very busily engaged at the present time, and I cannot take him off his work long enough to make the missing views ...". This was early February when Dickson had returned from his sick spell and was preparing for the visiting mining engineers. Townsend's article, which included the description of Dickson's photo room [see above] gave the lab excellent publicity in a popular family magazine so it was not a casual request. Dickson found time to make proof prints which Tate sent to Townsend so he could make a selection.[178]

A few weeks later the lab received a similar request from William H. Wiley who wanted photos for an article he was writing for *Engineering* magazine. He was told that none were available and the photographer could not make them for a week or two because he was busy with other work. Like Townsend's, this was no offhand turn down. Wiley was well connected in engineering circles and had a personal involvement with Edison. His brother, Osgood, had worked on ore milling for Edison and it was he who was sent to England in the fall of 1888 to demonstrate the ore milling machine. William Wiley had suggested the demonstration and made the necessary arrangements with English mining spe-

177 EHS. Time sheets. Brown worked 4, 13, 15 & 17 December 1888; 2 & 3 January; 1, 2, 4 & 5 February; 13, 14, 15, 16, 21, 23, 25 & 28 March; and 5–11 April 1889.

178 EHS. Tate to Townsend, 9 February 1889. Dickson was ill and away from the lab 5–14 February 1889, when he returned he made blue prints which were sent 23 February 1889 and Townsend was told on the 28th that the photographer would prepare the ones he selected. Townsend's article appeared in April 1889.

cialist James Dredge. The demo had not gone as expected. Osgood Wiley was entranced with London and had to be recalled because of his excessive spending and unwelcome involvement with the impetuous Col. Gouraud. His brother's request for photos was a touchy thing for Tate to handle because Edison was still trying to recover money from Osgood Wiley and would probably not have wanted to offend William Wiley. Under ordinary circumstances Dickson would have been asked to make the photos but he and Brown were too busy to do routine photographic printing.[179] Tate solved the problem by supplying Wiley with photos that had been loaned to Townsend for his article in *Cosmopolitan*. That Tate was declining orders for photos which would normally have been accepted may be an indication that charges for time in Room 5 during this period were the Kineto rather than studio photo work.

Dry plate, gelatin and celluloid

Dickson preferred to use dry plates for studio photography but they had been rejected for the Kineto because of their weight, fragility and because the available sizes were not suitable for the project. Dickson's early experiments with "wet" methods confirmed that images could be recorded much faster with the "dry" system and lacking plates suitable to the project, they had to make their own by applying gelatin mixed with photo sensitive material to the surface of the cylinder – though the first tests were probably made on a flat surface. These tests were probably started near the end of 1888 and continued during the mysterious months of early 1889.

Writing in 1894, Antonia Dickson described the endeavor:

"... Gelatine is the most sensitive material in the range of photographic appliances, lending itself, when compounded with bromide of silver, with inconceivable swiftness and pliability to the desired results. Dr. Maddox became convinced of the latent possibilities of the compound by one of those homely combinations of circumstances which relieve the awful majesty of science. He had noticed the delicate plasticity of the gold and ruby molds of jelly which embellished his festive board, and the idea struck him that this substance, in combination with certain chemicals, could be successfully impressed into photography – which stood then in dire need of just such an appliance. After many experiments he succeeded in producing a plate so abnormally sensitive to the action of light as to admit of an impression being taken in a fraction of a second, whereas previously, with Daguerre, Niépce and others, about one minute to twenty seconds per impression was the limit consistent with the attainment of detail – an important stride in the direction of instantaneous photography. Not yet, however, was the goal achieved. Despite the improved facilities the speed was still defective; numbers of intermediate positions were unrecorded, and the gaps between the fractions of attitude militated hopelessly against continuity and realism."[180] (Antonia Dickson, *Leslie's Monthly*, January 1895)

There are only two shipments of gelatin recorded in the lab's records during the period of the Kineto experiments – though the ever resourceful Dickson may have bought some on his own. The first was

[179] EHS. Tate to Wiley, 4 & 23 March 1889. Col. Gouraud proposed demonstrating Edison's ore milling machine at the Crystal Palace. Edison and Tate were very upset and wrote Osgood Wiley a pointed letter objecting to his involvement with Gouraud who represented Edison in the phonograph business and was involved with lighting, but not with the ore separator. They wrote Gouraud that the machine was not to be demonstrated to the public but only to James Dredge and his associates. Osgood Wiley was recalled because of writing an unauthorized check for fifty pounds against Edison's account in England.

[180] Antonia Dickson, Op. Cit., p. 248. Maddox introduced his system in 1871.

received in November, 1888 a month after the first caveat. This was probably for general use as it came from Lehn & Fink one of the lab's regular suppliers of chemicals and related materials. Gelatin was one of a number of substances being tested in the effort to improve phonograph cylinders and this was probably the primary purpose of the order, but it was probably available to Dickson in the supply room. The second shipment was received on 2 February 1889, the day after the start of accounting for the Kineto experiments and a few days before the second Kineto caveat was submitted. This shipment came from Scovill Mfg. Co., the lab's regular photo supplier and was probably for the Kineto since Dickson rarely, if ever, used gelatin for still photography

While Dickson spent much of his time on ore milling, he found enough time to experiment with a variety of photo methods and the resulting design changes caused Edison to modify his Kinetoscope caveat twice. The shipment of gelatin in early February seems to connect with the spate of work by the machine shop that began at the end of February and continued through March and into April with Neubert continuing on the project into May.

In addition to this spate of mechanical work and experiments with gelatin, there are hints that they were beginning to look more seriously at celluloid as a substitute for glass and metal. On 12 March, the lab received samples of "Kristaline" from the Celluloid Varnish Co. of nearby Newark. Two weeks later the lab was told that the material inquired about was not on the market "... as we have not the room for producing it in a commercial way. Sheets have been made 30 ft. long and 12 inches wide made of various thicknesses from 1/2000 to 1/3000 of an inch thick". They added that they could supply it "... if [a] demand arises". These thicknesses would be suitable for photography and the Celluloid Varnish Co., a licensee of the Celluloid Co. of Newark, was supplying Carbutt with the celluloid used for his recently introduced photographic sheets. They had also supplied George Eastman with sample sheets.

Though celluloid was low on their list of potential photo products, there are other indications that the lab was examining its potential. The ingredients to make celluloid were available and Dickson mentioned experimenting with Edison to make their own emulsions [see Chapter 12]. Gun cotton was purchased from Charles Cooper & Co. in December 1888 and a bale of cotton batting was bought in February. Nitric acid was an item normally stocked by the supply room. On 2 March the *New York Tribune* reported that the previous Saturday evening Edison had escaped serious injury when chemicals exploded. "... The flames flashed up in his face, singeing his eyebrows and scorching his hair. Some of the acid struck him on the face and eyes and caused severe painful burns." They reported that he washed his face immediately and escaped serious injury. Edison enjoyed chemistry – experimenting was recreation for him – and there are any number of chemicals he could have been experimenting with, but the description of the flash burning is similar to the way nitrocellulose burns. Since this report came two weeks before the samples of celluloid from the Celluloid Varnish Co., it is clear that celluloid was an item of interest. But, if they toyed with making their own celluloid, it was an unproductive effort.

By itself, Edison's accident would be incidental to the Kineto experiments, but the negotiations with the Celluloid Varnish Co. that followed soon after show that celluloid was being considered for experiments being conducted during February and March of 1889. The celluloid may have been for further work with phonograph cylinders, but sheets as thin as 1/3000 of an inch and as long as thirty feet were very suitable for the Kineto. They would have fit with Dickson's attempts to find a material that he could coat with gelatin. Celluloid would become central to the Kineto project, but in the spring of 1889 it was still incidental. Edison's modifications to his Kineto caveat offer clues to where the experiments stood during this period.

The second motion picture Caveat

"The cylinder is not round, but parallel with its length are a number of flat places about one thirty-seconds of an inch wide. This gives a flat face for the photographic record from the microscope and the picture is not thrown out of focus as it would be if the cylindrical surface was round, especially on very small cylinders which it is necessary to use on a commercial apparatus."[181] (Edison's Caveat No. 114, Motion Picture Caveat II, filed on 25 March 1889)

Caveat, no. 114, was actually a collection of miscellaneous claims on a variety of potential inventions lumped together by Edison. The passage modifying the Kineto was one of a long list that Edison had put together – the drawing illustrating the new Kineto was item No. 54 in the document. The brief description put on record a change from a round cylinder to one with flat strips. This was discussed in the previous chapter (see Chapter 8, pages 98–99). The caveat was filed with the Patent Office on 25 March 1889 and in preparing it Edison told George Dyer, his attorney, "I am putting several inventions in this ... to get it in patent office for dating purposes". The Patent Office objected to his practice of grouping a number of items in a single document, but Edison continued to pass such shopping lists on to the Patent Office. He was quizzed about this when testifying for the patent suits and he explained: "They were notes taken at various times, and when I got a number of them I used to write them up and send them in as a caveat".[182] It seems quite possible that the idea for this modification sat on his desk for some time before being passed on.

The text describing the revision was a single long paragraph accompanied by the drawing. Much of it was an explanation of how the motor, pulleys, belts, escapement, etc. worked, but as with the first Caveat there are clues about the status of the Kineto. It concluded:

"... The action is as follows: The cylinder stands still; the shutter advances and opens the shutter while the cylinder is still; the photographic effect takes place on the flat of the cylinder; the shutter closes, then the cylinder advances another notch, but such advance only takes place while the shutter

181 EHS.

182 EHS. Edison to Dyer, 3 February 1889 and Edison's testimony in Equity 6928, Edison v. American Mutoscope Co., 29 January 1900, pp. 104–105. He was examined by Dyer's son Frank Dyer.

closes off the light. These actions take place continuously at the rate of fifteen or twenty times per second."

Besides flattening the surface of the cylinder, Edison reduced the rate of exposure from 25 per second to 15–20 per second. Apparently Edison was still thinking in terms of very small images because the flat strips were to be 1/32nd of an inch wide instead of 1/8th of an inch which was the size that Dickson later said he had been using – and that Edison annotated on his drawing of 11 January 1889. There was no mention of being connected to a phonograph, though this may have been implied. It was certainly intended because Edison and Dickson never abandoned plans to connect the Kineto to a phonograph. There is an interesting use of the term "continuously". Today's cinema specialists would understand this as meaning that the cylinder was not stopped during exposure but ran "continuously" with the necessary intermittence provided by breaking the light which was usually done with a shutter. While there was a shutter in the new design, the description of the action and the inclusion of an escapement among the parts indicates that this

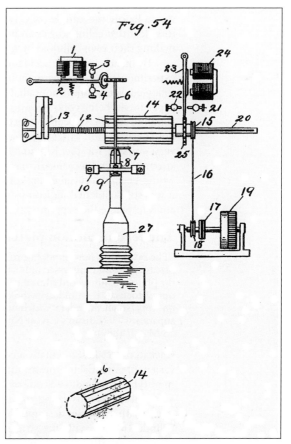

The illustration for Edison's second motion picture caveat (number 114, 25 March 1889) shows a cylinder with faceted flat surfaces, a change made to correct the distortion encountered trying to record tiny images on a curved surface. The number of exposures per second was reduced from 25 to 15 or 20, an indication that tests at the faster rate were unsuccessful. [EHS.]

mechanism was intended to work intermittently and that instead of meaning that the cylinder moved "continuously" (i.e. without stopping for the exposure) they meant that the action continued from one exposed image to the next.

Although it was not specified in the description, the drawing shows a camera that is more complicated than in the first caveat. The earlier camera was a slender tube tapered near the cylinder and with a nob-like cap at the other end where the lens capturing the image would be. One of Edison's sketches for the first caveat showed a slightly fatter tube with a more complex tapering near the cylinder, i.e. the lens transmitting the image to the photo sensitive surface. This was very like the first camera as described by Dickson in his SMPE article: "... I made a small micro camera, using various objectives or lenses taken from one of my microscopes ...". As pictured in the second caveat, two drums of different dimensions were joined by a tapered connection. The smaller drum, which held the lens transmitting the image to the surface of the cylinder, was connected to a larger drum by a tapered area and that drum was connected to what appears to be bellows (or screw-threads) attached to a rectangular box-like ending. This appears to have held the image capturing lens but might have been a shield to keep out ambient light. It bears some resemblance to modern reflex cameras and looks a bit like a rocket on a launch pad. Dickson's accounts offer little information about this modification, but it is a more sophisticated device than was anticipated the previous fall and shows the considerable effort he had put into the photo tests.

The modified camera and reduced number of exposures per second are evidence that Dickson continued his struggle with exposure. In his article for SMPE he described problems he encountered making images on a cylinder using slow exposure:

"Then I had a light drum made and produced a few spirals of pictures on a dead slow shaft. These, even with ammonia acceleration, proved a failure. So I increased the size of the aluminum drum and of the pictures, and coated the drum with a bromide of silver gelatin emulsion; and would have obtained a fairly good reaction but for some chemical action which took place between the aluminum and the emulsion. That made me try a glass drum and a one-opening rapid shutter."[183]

The device described in the second Caveat is not mentioned in Dickson's article for SMPE, but the glass drum is described in the third Caveat and since his description seems to be sequential it is an indication that these tests took place during the first half of 1889 and they involved a number of variations which did not make it into Edison's caveats. In mid-March Brown spent four full days on photography, followed by two days in each of the two weeks that followed. Dickson was also in Room 5 during this period. On 18 March the Zeiss micro-photographic machine was received from Queen & Co. Dickson was asked to check it and found problems which he reported to Tate: "... the plate holders, table &c. of same must have been made of green wood, as they are warped and cracked and all out of shape. This is really a very serious defect ...". He recommended that they ask for a reduction on the bill. It was several months before a settlement was reached with Queen.[184]

In May, while Dickson and Brown were busy with ore milling, Edison put the glass drum into a draft for a third Caveat. It was their most unusual concept.

The third motion picture Caveat

"... P is a break wheel which closes and opens the circuit of an induction coil g with Leyden jar H; a reflector X throws the light of the spark on the moving object A A1. The break wheels are so arranged that there will be say 15 breaks per second allowing 1/8 of an inch of space on the cylinder for each photograph; owing to the instantaneous character and high actinic power of each spark a shutter cutting off and on the lenses from the cylinder as in my first devices is unnecessary. At every spark a photograph is taken

183 Dickson, *Journal of the SMPE.*, p. 10.
184 EHS. The micro-photo device was ordered the previous fall from James W. Queen & Co. of Philadelphia who imported optical equipment from Zeiss. Zeiss denied that there could be defects and blamed the warping on peculiarities of the North American climate. Several letters were exchanged and ultimately John Ott made repairs.

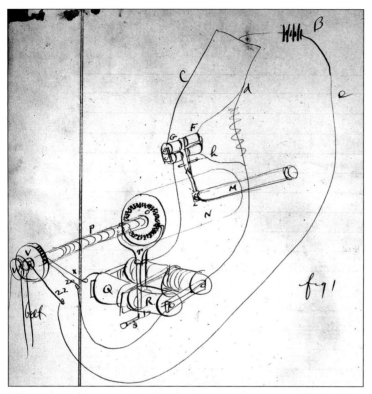

always at definite intervals and as the spark is infinitely quick the continuous movement even of the cylinder does not blur the photograph; of course a shutter through which a powerful arc light beam or sunlight passes to the object may be controlled positively by a lever worked by the machine and thus instead of continuously illuminating the subject to be photographed and the use of a vibrating shutter the light itself is intermitted." (Caveat no. 116, 5 August 1889)

In May, 1889 Edison drafted a motion picture caveat for a device similar to that described by Dickson in his SMPE article, and the change was more radical than Dickson's rather casual description implies. The images, still recorded in sequence, were to be registered on a glass cylinder coated with emulsion. The cylinder would move continuously, a break wheel would generate 15 flashes of light a second from a Leyden jar, this would illuminate the moving subject and register an exposure every 1/8th of an inch on the photosensitive surface of the glass cylinder. The Leyden jar was connected to a reflector which illuminated the subject being photographed as the spark was generated. There would be no shutter since the electrical circuit to the Leyden jar would close and open 15 times a second in sync with the movement of the cylinder. A similar sparking light inside the glass cylinder would illuminate the images through a magnifying lens so they could be projected for viewing.

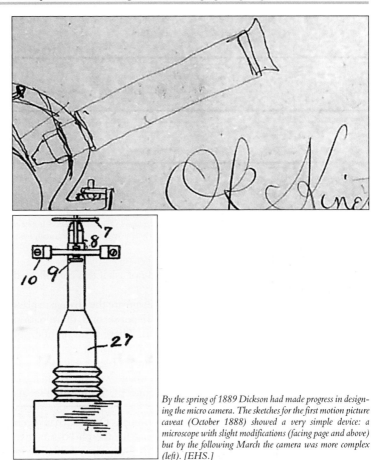

By the spring of 1889 Dickson had made progress in design-ing the micro camera. The sketches for the first motion picture caveat (October 1888) showed a very simple device: a microscope with slight modifications (facing page and above) but by the following March the camera was more complex (left). [EHS.]

185 EHS. The draft was dated 20 May 1889, the drawings of the Kineto, 19 June 1889, Edison signed it 29 July 1889, it was mailed 3 August 1889 (the day he sailed to Europe) and it was received by the Patent Office on August 5, 1889. The Patent Office objected to this bundling of projects. On August 8, 1889 they wrote to him saying: "Before applicant can receive the protection provided by law for this Caveat, he must confine the specification and drawings to a single subject of invention."

This is the most unusual of Edison's concepts and it has an air of mystery about it. It was a detour from the previous line of research and the most complicated concept proposed for the cylinder Kineto. There are questions about when it was formulated, why, and if, in fact, it was actually made. The caveat had a long gestation. It was incorporated in a shopping cart of projects that Edison jotted down during April and May 1889. The draft was dated 20 May 1889, the sketches of the Kineto were dated 19 June and the finalized version was sent to the Patent Office on 5 August, two days after Edison sailed for his visit to Paris. The filing date is noteworthy because Edison, Dickson and a number of lab staff claimed – even testified in court – that cylinders had been abandoned by that time and that would make this caveat an anomaly. (But more about that later!) The draft was a long, rambling document consisting of some seventy pages of notes and drawings. A large number of phonograph, ore milling and other projects were swept together into a single document. The Kinetoscope (viewer) was item number 51 and the Kinetograph (camera) was number 52.[185] In 1900 when Frank Dyer

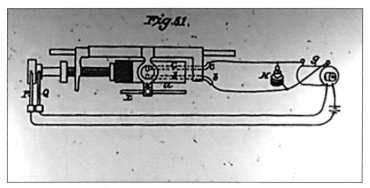

Edison's third motion picture Caveat was the most unusual change in design. When used as a camera, sparks from a Leyden jar would illuminate the subject being photographed and to view the images, the sparks would illuminate the images from the interior of the glass cylinder. The concept, which is similar to Ottomar Anschütz's Tachyscope, was short-lived and there is little evidence that it was actually built. [EHS.]

questioned Edison about his Caveats, he did not ask if this complicated apparatus was made.[186]

The most significant elements of this design are the change to glass base, reduction of the number of images to 15 per second, illumination by sparks of light and mention of projection. There is no mention of flat surfaces or a connection to the Phonograph (though, again, it may be implied). As in the previous Caveat, the problems Dickson was having with exposure are apparent here: the image was finally enlarged to 1/8th of an inch. Although an interesting concept, this solution seems almost desperate.

The switch to glass seems obvious enough. Dickson had been struggling with using solid material as the base for the photo-sensitive emulsions and transparent materials which facilitate the penetration of light through the emulsion were much more effective. Glass was the base preferred by most photographers but they had rejected it as unsuitable for the cylinder. The disappointing results of tests with metal bases made the change to glass an obvious one, but the change was complicated because the cylinder format was not abandoned. Since no photo manufacturer produced cylindrical dry plates, they would have to be made at the lab and this was tricky business. The glass used in photography had to be free from streaks, grains and other defects. Small impurities in the glass could become large impurities in a photograph, and even more so when the photographs were micro. Glass was readily available at the lab where experimenting with light bulbs was ongoing. A glass blower, J.J. Force, was on the staff and Dickson's assistant Charles Brown worked with lamps before his assignment with Dickson and was occasionally detailed to the lamp room. Coating the emulsion evenly on the cylinder would have been a challenge but they apparently felt it could be done.

The apparent inspiration for this experiment was the Electric Tachyscope of Ottomar Anschütz, the German photographer whose

186 EHS. Edison's testimony in Equity 6928, Edison v. American Mutoscope Co. et. al., 29 January 1900, p. 103.

187 EHS, NMAH
Hendricks Collection
and Deac Rossell,
*Ottomar Anschütz and
His Electrical Wonder*,
London, The
Projection Box, 1997.
A typewritten,
undated copy of the
article "Anschütz's
Motion Pictures and
the Stroboscopic
Disk" translated from
*Photographische
Wochenblatt*, and
published in *The
Philadelphia
Photographer* is in the
collections of the
Edison Historic Site.
Ottomar Anschütz
was born in Lissa,
Posen (East Prussia)
the son of a well
regarded painter of
house decorations
who had turned to
photography late in
life. His father sent
him to Berlin to
study in the portrait
studio of Ferdinand
Beyrich and then to
the photolithographer
and artist Franz
Hanfstaengl in
Munich and finally to
Vienna to the court
photographer Ludwig
Angerer. By 1889
Anschütz had moved
to Berlin.

188 Dicksons,
Century Magazine, p.
208.

189 Encyclopaedia
Britannica. The
Leyden jar is a device
for storing static
electricity and the
Geissler tube was a
vapor lamp which
was illuminated by
static electricity. The
Leyden jar is not
necessarily used for
illumination, though
it was to be used this
way in this experi-
ment. The Geissler
tube is an ancestor of
neon lamps and
mercury and sodium
vapor lamps.

work as a chronophotographer had attracted international attention. After photographing phases of motion after the manner of Muybridge and Marey, Anschütz found that the public marveled at the recreation of motion. With the help of an organ builder named Schneider in his hometown of Lissa, Prussia, he built a device that allowed groups of people to see images move. Twenty-four photographs mounted around the edge of a large disk were illuminated by a Geissler tube which gave intermittent light as the disk was wound by a hand crank. He demonstrated his Tachyscope in Berlin in 1887 and the event was reported in the United States by *The Philadelphia Photographer* and *The Journal of the Franklin Institute*. In March 1889 *Cassell's Family Magazine*, a popular journal which would have been readily available to Dickson, had an article about William Friese-Greene which compared Friese-Greene's device with Anschütz's.[187]

The Dicksons described making a Tachyscope-type device in their *Century Magazine* article:

"Each accession of size augmented the difficulty, and it was resolved to abandon that line of experiment, and to revolutionize the whole nature of the proceedings by discarding these small photographs, and substituting a series of very much larger impressions affixed to the outer edge of a swiftly rotating wheel or disk, and supplied with a number of pins, so arranged as to project under the center of each picture. On the rear of the disk, upon a stand, was placed a Geissler tube, connected with an induction coil, the primary wire of which, operated by the pins, produced a rupture of the primary current, which, in its turn, through the medium of the secondary current, lighted up the Geissler tube at the precise moment when a picture crossed its range of view. This electrical discharge was performed in such an inappreciable fraction of time, the succession of pictures was so rapid, and the whole mechanism so nearly perfect, that the goal of the inventor seemed almost reached."[188]

This could be a description of Anschütz's machine. If Dickson built this in 1889 he must have based his work on descriptions he read, since it is doubtful that he had seen the device. This is a viewing machine, not a camera, and the comment that the small photographs were discarded and "very much larger impressions" substituted indicates that it was made separately from the experiments with micro-photographs and was intended to test the use of a Geissler tube or Leyden jar as a light source for viewing.[189] It would have been a challenge to make a system of contacts that would turn the light on and off in synch with the images and do it many times a second. A large mechanism might have been a preliminary step to working on a smaller one.

There are questions about when these devices were built and if the camera described in the third caveat was ever built. Charles Brown testified in the American Mutoscope case that they built a glass cylinder viewing machine as described in the third caveat: "Yes sir; we had a transparent drum with a light inside of it, and then we put these on that drum and looked at them through a microscope". Brown also testified that a viewing machine was used before August when Edison sailed for Europe. Dickson said that the images taken on the final version of the cylinder machine were viewed on a glass cylinder lighted inside by a "sparking device".[190] If this was the case, this viewing device would have been built prior to August 1889 – as we will soon see.

The Dicksons' account in *Century Magazine*, which seems to be sequential, places the Geissler tube – Tachyscope-like device before the final phase of cylinder experiments and since it was written in 1894, the events would have been comparatively fresh in Dickson's mind. Dickson's statement in 1910 was specifically about an experiment with Carbutt's sensitized celluloid sheets. The single piece of evidence that gives a hint about the time of this Tachyscope-type experiment is a shipment of four dozen 3½ x 4 crystal albumen transparency plates received from Scovill and Adams Company on 10 May 1889. This was an unusual size, one not usually used by Dickson for regular photography and though they may have been used for some other special purpose, they might have been suitable for an imitation Tachyscope. As we shall see, it is also possible that Dickson worked on this later.

It is not the elements of the camera version which cause doubts about whether it was ever made or used – the lab had plenty of experience in working with electricity, batteries, sparking, magnetism and amplification of light. Arthur Kennelly was a specialist in measuring electricity and his galvanometer room would have been capable of designing the device. The question is whether the spark generated by the Leyden jar could have given enough light to make it possible to capture fifteen images in one second. It seems doubtful since adequate lighting of his subjects remained a critical focus of Dickson's work throughout his experimentation. By late spring he was having more success with rapid exposures so questions of illumination were becoming more important. Room 5 had not been designed as a photographic studio and natural light came through the same kind of windows that served the rest of the lab building. As he experimented with rapid exposure, he would have been experimenting with artificial light to supplement his insufficient natural light. Leyden jars would have been one possibility. Interestingly, the Caveat mentions "... using a powerful arc light beam or sunlight passe[d] to the subject ... controlled positively by a lever worked by the machine ...". Arc lights were never adequate, but sunlight became ever more important as the experiments progressed.

The focus on lighting is the most significant facet of this most unusual of Edison's Caveats. It shows that the experiments had moved beyond the slower, more traditional photographic methods, but Dickson was still struggling with photo materials that were incapable of producing the desired results. That was about to change. The introduction of new, improved photo products stimulated a flurry of activity in Orange and changed the entire focus of the Kineto experiments.

190 EHS. Charles A. Brown testimony 31 January 1900 in Equity No. 6928, Edison v. Amer. Mutoscope et al., pp. 143–147. Dickson's testimony 6 May 1910 in Equity No. 28,605, Patents Co. v. Chicago Film Exchange, p. 145.

Chapter 11

Edison Triumphs in Europe and Dickson has a Busy Summer

"The scientific men abroad were greatly surprised that I was not more of a scientist, in the higher sense of the phrase. They could not understand that I am between the scientific man and the public."[191] (Thomas Edison's comment after returning from the Paris Exposition, 6 October 1889)

"As soon as the impracticability of the pin point photographs on the earliest drum was demonstrated, Mr. Edison commenced to talk again about trying to get pictures on very long bands, but as there was nothing on which we could work at the time, this was laid aside for the moment ...".[192] (Dickson's Testimony, 6 May 1910)

191 EHS. An article, "Edison at Home Again" *Newark [N. J.]News*, 7 October 1889

192 EHS, Dickson, Equity No. 28,605, pp. 147–148.

193 Outcault, creator of the "Yellow Kid" and often credited as the father of the comic strip, was hired by William Hammer to assist him in decorating an Edison exhibit in Cincinnati in 1888 and was engaged again to help prepare the exhibit for the Universal Exposition. While in Paris he was allowed to spend half of his time studying in the Latin Quarter. He acknowledged the role that Hammer and Edison played in launching his career.

Edison's visit to the Universal Exposition of 1889 in Paris was one of the high points in his remarkable career. His trip was also a defining moment in the genesis of the Kineto. Even incidental workers on the Kineto used Edison's journey abroad as the defining event that measured their contribution to the project. In Paris Edison was received as an international celebrity and was introduced to many prestigious figures in society, the arts, politics and the French scientific community. During his absence the character of the Kineto changed dramatically.

Edison had planned an elaborate exhibit for the Expo and while it was being prepared he decided to attend. He would stay for several weeks, then visit Germany and wind-up the tour in England. He sailed on 3 August accompanied by Mina. Al Tate, his private secretary had preceded him and stayed with him during the visit to handle official matters. The exhibit was designed by William Hammer who had done several previous exhibits. Hammer and his assistant, Richard Outcault also preceded Edison to Paris.[193] He wanted major alterations made to the laboratory while he was away so most experiments were wound up or tabled and the work force was substantially reduced. Charles Batchelor came from Syracuse to supervise the lab during his absence and Samuel Insull also came from Syracuse to resume his role as Edison's secretary.

Before his departure Edison was absorbed by ore milling projects.

Walter Mallory's Michigan ore separator continued to have problems and in April Edison advised him to shut it down and send some ore for testing. Several staff members worked on modifications to the Mallory device and a couple of experimenters, among them future radio pioneer Reginald Fessenden, experimented with separating copper and nickel. Edison spent more and more time at Bechtelsville installing his separator. He was there for most of July, returning just before he sailed for Paris.

The demands of ore milling slowed work but the Kineto remained a work in progress with machinist E. Neubert on the project until late May. But no work was charged to the account during the first three weeks of June, a period when Dickson and Brown were, presumably, dedicated to the Bechtelsville project.

On 25 June Dickson and Charles Brown ended their work on ore milling and launched a period of uninterrupted work on the Kineto. Fred Ott, a topnotch machinist, was assigned to the project and a significant support staff of other machinists, carpenters and pattern makers were available as needed. Ott's assignment lasted through mid-August. He worked full time during July and part time during early August. This gave Dickson his first opportunity to experiment without interruption and with the assistance of the cream of the lab's staff. With Edison in Pennsylvania, other experiments shut-down and the staff reduced, normal activity was at a stand-still, but Dickson and his crew were busy – very busy. This was the most intense period of work during the Kineto's prolonged gestation.

It was a rather abrupt shift of focus and the timing is interesting. Ore milling was becoming Edison's primary interest and the separator had reached the stage where it was being tested in the real world. As it moved from experimentation to implementation and he became more involved, Edison apparently felt that Dickson could devote more time to the Kineto. Dickson's primary duty was perfecting the experimental machine but as the separator was put to work, his duties changed to solving problems with the working versions, testing ore samples and experiments with other metals. In theory this gave Dickson more time for the Kineto – though it did not quite work out that way.

Other factors may have contributed to Edison's decision. Recent articles about Ottomar Anschütz and William Friese-Greene may have made him more aware there were others working on moving images [see Chapter 15]. It is also possible – even likely – that Dickson had either demonstrated substantial progress or given him hope that a break-through was possible. The latter is certainly possible because by that June there were celluloid photo plates that were more readily available and a growing number of photographers were using them. Celluloid held great promise and the lab had ordered some.

Celluloid

Dry plates using sheet celluloid rather than glass began appearing in 1887, sold by Vergara in England and Balagny in France. The Vergara

Film Co. of London sold them under a patent from Francis A. Friedman of Dublin. Georges Balagny of Paris had an agreement with Lumière Frères of Lyon. Although celluloid sheets were less fragile and offered the benefits of flexibility and light weight, neither product gained widespread acceptance. They were pricey and plagued with technical problems that made them unacceptable to most photographers. As John Carbutt explained in November, 1888: "The objection to this film [Vergara] is its extreme limpness when wet, and propensity to assume any shape but a flat one on drying".[194] Late in 1888 – about the time of Edison's first caveat – Carbutt, a photographer and manufacturer of photographic products, introduced his own celluloid, an improved product which gained wider acceptance. He bought celluloid sheets from The Celluloid Company of Newark, NJ and coated them under a license from the Rev. Hannibal Goodwin, an Episcopal minister also from Newark. *The Photographic Times and American Photographer* declared that Carbutt's film was "... as transparent as glass, very tough and flexible, develops easily and its weight is almost unappreciable. ...".[195] But celluloid was not for everyone. Photographers who worked in the field, away from their studios, appreciated its light weight, flexibility and lack of fragility, but many professionals regarded the new product as inferior. As put by the editor of *Philadelphia Photographer*: "... in the name of all that is beautiful ...", he mused, why would anyone make photographs on celluloid.[196] It would be another two or three years before celluloid gained widespread acceptance and several more before the manufacturers solved the problems that caused so many photographers to reject it.

Film? What is film?

For moviegoers "film" is what you see in the theaters and some even use the term for the product of their video cameras. For photographers, film is what you buy for your camera. For others it is what forms on tomato soup.

Dickson claimed that Edison was the first to call celluloid photo material "film". But he was wrong. Photographers were using the term before celluloid "film" appeared on the market. It goes back at least as far as 1887 and maybe earlier. It seems to have first been used to describe the emulsion. Wet collodion flowed on glass does look like the film on tomato soup and as it dries resemblance continues. As celluloid gained a place in the photo market it came to be applied primarily to transparent celluloid "film".

But this didn't happen until the 1890s. In 1889 and 1891 the term could apply either to the emulsion or a base coated with emulsion.

This has caused confusion for film historians (and others). When one of the pioneers uses the term "film" it has usually been interpreted as meaning celluloid but this is not necessarily the case, particularly in these pre-invention years. Champions of Friese-Greene and Le Prince have claimed they used "film" early, and indeed they may have, but the use of the term by the inventor is not necessarily evidence that they

194 NMAH Hendricks. John Carbutt, "A Perfect Substitute for Glass ..." A paper read before the Franklin Institute, 21 November 1888, and published in the *Journal of the Franklin Institute*, December 1888. I have less information about the limitations of Balagny's product, but Georges Balagny was upset when the Lumières purchased Blair film to test their Cinématographe and then contracted with another French manufacturer to make their film for their camera. The Lumières' evidently found Balagny's celluloid unacceptable for moving image work.

195 NMAH Hendricks. *The Photographic Times and American Photographer*, 7 December 1888. Carbutt's paper delivered at the Franklin Institute was reprinted in this edition along with an evaluation of Carbutt's film.

196 NMAH Hendricks, *Philadelphia Photographer*, 6 October 1888.

used *celluloid* film. There is a similar confusion with the equivalent French term "pellicule" which was first used for the emulsion and then came to be used for celluloid based photographic material.

But celluloid must have seemed a panacea for experimenters struggling to make photographs move. Years later Dickson, Friese-Greene and the champions of Le Prince all claimed that they began using celluloid during the spring or early summer of 1889 – and even as early as 1888. But their success with the new material is questionable. Celluloid was an elusive cure-all and their enthusiasm must have been dampened as they encountered its limitations. First there was the problem of size. It came in sheets suitable for still photo work – the largest offered by Carbutt, was 11 by 14 inches. The sheets had to be cut and reformatted in a darkroom to work in a camera designed to take a series of rapid exposures. The composition of the celluloid caused problems. It was flexible, but not particularly pliable. Carbutt's celluloid was heavy and stiff, making it difficult to handle and resistant of being bent or rolled into a coil. In addition, there were complaints that some was of uneven thickness resulting in distortions that were particularly evident when taking small images.

Marey, Friese-Greene, Donisthorp and Le Prince had built cameras designed to use Eastman's stripping paper so they were better equipped to test celluloid than Edison. The Kodak camera used paper strips that were about three inches wide and took circular images 2 5/8th inches in diameter so several of these cameras took images of comparable size. Formatting celluloid sheets to fit their existing cameras was complicated. To cut the sheets and join the pieces together into longer strips was a time consuming and risky business – a lot of cutting and pasting in a darkroom. The reformatted strips were no stronger than their weakest joint and poorly made joints would catch, tear or break as they moved rapidly through the camera. As the speed of exposure increased, so did the strain on the strips. The ideal strip would have been one that was very long and made in one piece. Until one appeared, everyone experimenting on moving images was a shade short of genuine success. It was these limitations that caused Edison to reject strips in favor of micro photos on a cylinder – doubtless on Mr. Dickson's advice.

We have seen that Friese-Greene claimed to make his own. Later on, Birt Acres and the Lumières launched businesses.

Edison and celluloid

On 25 June 1889 the Edison Laboratory received a shipment of celluloid photo material. Scovill Adams & Co. sent two different brands of celluloid, one dozen of John Carbutt's emulsion no. 1298, size, 11 x 14 and one dozen of Allen & Rowell's Ivory film, size 8 x 10 along with a package of Hydrachinon developer. Both were charged to the Kineto account and because they arrived the day Dickson and Brown began their intense work on the Kineto, the shipment seems the start of a new phase of the project, a shift to celluloid.

As we have seen, while this was the first charged to the Kineto account, it was not the first celluloid received at the lab. Celluloid was readily available and a familiar product to Edison whose long-time home base, Newark, New Jersey, was also the home of the Celluloid Manufacturing Co., the largest producer of raw celluloid. In the fall of 1888 celluloid was tested as a material for phonograph cylinders and the tests may have continued into 1889.[197] The unsuccessful negotiations with the Celluloid Varnish Co., the purchase of sheets of Zylonite from Scovill and possible attempts to make celluloid predate this purchase. There is no evidence that any of these were used in tests for the Kineto, but Dickson's later statement that he used Carbutt's celluloid and the flurry of activity that followed immediately after the receipt of celluloid from Carbutt and Allen and Rowell is grounds for assuming that tests with sheet celluloid took place during July 1889.

If Dickson, Brown, Edison and Fred Ott can be believed, the final work on the cylinder project was done during this period and a version of the Kineto using strips of film was started, probably just before Edison left for the Paris Exposition. Since many historians have challenged this, a careful look at the claims and the surviving evidence of activity during this controversial period is necessary.

Testimony

Fred Ott, Charles A. Brown and Edison all gave depositions in 1900 for Equity 6928, Edison v. American Mutoscope Co. et al., much of which focused on the events immediately preceding and during Edison's trip to Paris. Dickson testified about it in Equity No. 28,605, 6 and 7 May 1910 and was subsequently questioned by several film historians to confirm these events, among them Terry Ramsaye, Merritt Crawford, Earl Theisen, Glen Matthews and Will Day. Edison's lawyers and Dickson were very concerned about establishing that Edison's work preceded Friese-Greene's patent which has caused some subsequent historians, particularly Gordon Hendricks, to question the validity of this testimony. Dickson's accounts almost always dated the events earlier than they actually happened, but the testimony by Edison, Fred Ott and Brown places these events in the summer of 1889 and is, despite some minor inconsistencies, remarkably accurate. Hendricks, who was searching for ways to disprove every shred of Edison's testimony, went to great lengths to discredit all three, but a careful examination of the surviving evidence casts serious doubt on Hendricks's conclusions which strongly influenced subsequent writing about this period [EHS. Testimony in Equity 6928].

[197] EHS Doc. File – 1887. Edison corresponded with J. M. Cook, Celluloid Manufacturing Co., 295 Ferry Street, Newark, NJ, 6 and 12 December 1888 about the availability of transparent celluloid in sheets and rods and asked them to fill an order, charging it to himself rather than to the phonograph account. There is no other indication of what this was intended for.

Fred Ott's tour started two days before the celluloid was received, in apparent anticipation of starting the new phase. In 1900 Ott testified that he worked on several versions of the Kinetograph (camera), but only on one of the various cylinder machines. From those presented in evidence at that time, he identified "Cylinder No. 3" which was also identified by Edison and Brown as the one made for the final cylinder experiment and the one on which a strips of images were taken. It had a larger diameter than earlier versions, a row of pins around the circumference at one end, gear teeth at the other and a slot in it to secure sheets of photo material. Ott said he worked on two variations of this

This photograph of cylinder no. 3 was submitted as evidence in Edison's protracted suit with the American Mutoscope & Biograph Co. This was the final and most successful of the cylinder experiments. Images that reproduced motion were captured on celluloid strips cut from larger camera sheets. The spikes on the left are not "sprockets" used to guide and steady the film, they are contacts to cause the sparks from a Leyden Jar or Geissler Tube which illuminated the subject. The dating of this device is uncertain, but it was probably built and used during June or July of 1889. [EHS.]

machine, one that was lighted by "… just the bright light, and then there was another one made with a flash light". He indicated that the model exhibited in 1900 was the version using the flash light – a Geissler tube or Leyden jar. It was the first in which successive images of motion were captured and Ott said that he was one of the staff members who posed for films made on this device. Three versions of this subject, a film that has come to be known as *Monkeyshines*, were sent to the Patent Office to supplement Edison's application for a patent on the camera and presented as evidence in the suit against the American Mutoscope Co. Ott also testified that though he had seen an earlier version of the cylinder which had flat surfaces, he had not worked on it.[198]

Dickson's description of cylinder no. 3, made during his 1910 testimony, agrees with Ott's account:

"… we adapted some of the cut film as used by John Carbutt. A sheet of this material was wrapped around the drum, the two ends pressed into a slot cut across the drum. An improved stopping and starting device was made to actuate the drum and shutter. The pictures were, therefore, increased in size and taken in rapid succession or as fast as the mechanism would allow, being greatly hampered as well by the momentum or re-bound of the more or less heavy drum. This was later substituted by a much lighter shell. Pictures taken in this way did not reach more than eight or ten per second. Another difficulty which arose, the size of the picture was limited by the curvature of the drum."[199]

If the final version of the cylinder machine was built during Ott's

198 Ibid.

199 EHS. Dickson's testimony, 6 May 1910 in Equity 28,605, pp. 144–145.

tour, it was probably made during the last week of June or the first three weeks of July. Ott said that he made much of the device and he specifically mentioned the screw thread and part of the drum.

The time sheets recording the work during this period provide a clue to the progress and intensity of the experiment. At the beginning, the last week of June, work progressed at a normal pace. Dickson, Brown and Ott were the only ones charged to the Kineto account and they recorded a regular six-day stint of 10 hours each day. After the first of July another machinist was added and a carpenter worked ½ hour each day on the 3rd and 5th. Ott took three days off after the 4 July holiday, but additional machinists, carpenters and pattern makers were assigned to the project. After 15 July the pace of work became more intense. Ott put in 71 hours during the week ending 18 July and 72 hours the following week. From Monday the 29th through Wednesday the 31st, there was a three-day marathon: Ott worked 14 hours Monday, 15 hours Tuesday and all night Wednesday the 31st. As supervisor of the project, Dickson probably put in similar hours and although Brown reported a regular schedule during this period it is possible he also spent extra time.[200]

After 1 August, as Edison prepared to leave for Paris, the pace slowed. During the first week of August, Dickson returned to ore milling for half of the week, Brown remained full time on the Kineto until August 23rd and Ott continued to work with Dickson until August 15th, but he no longer worked every day and when he did work it was from two to five hours rather than the full 10 hour day.

The intense activity in late July was characteristic of the crash efforts that Edison used to bring promising projects to a conclusion. The final all-night marathon, Wednesday, 31 July, took place two days before Edison sailed for Paris and almost certainly anticipated an opportunity to show Edison the results from six-weeks of special effort. Dickson, Ott and Brown all claimed that before he left, they showed Edison a promising new device – the prototype of a machine for recording images on strips of film. Edison confirmed that he saw an early version of the strip Kinetograph before he left for Paris and that "a number of strips were taken". Dickson said Edison was encouraged and urged him to continue this new direction. These claims have been widely challenged in court and in histories describing the period.[201]

Exactly what Edison saw, how "finished" the Kineto was at this stage and how he reacted is certainly open to question. The skeptics have reason to question these claims. Dickson and Edison needed to prove they were ahead of Friese-Greene and Le Prince. Edison's reasons were primarily commercial but Dickson was motivated by pride. The witnesses in the patent and court cases were chosen by Edison's attorneys because they would confirm Edison's claims and were probably coached before testifying. Even when they were not in court, Edison, Dickson and other lab staff were prone to hyperbole and exaggeration but not all of their claims were untrue so they deserve to be examined and evaluated carefully. Something significant was taking place in

200 EHS. Pay records. Fred Ott worked 15 hours on the 15th and 17th, 13 hours on the 18th; a regular 10 hour day on the 16th, 19th Saturday the 20th and Tuesday the 23rd; 14 hours on the 22nd, 15 on the 24th and 13 on the 25th. There were two days normal schedule on Friday the 26th and Saturday the 27th and then the marathon began.

201 EHS. Edison, Brown and Fred Ott's testimony in Equity 6928, 1900. Dickson made this claim in his 1910 testimony and in several articles and letters and though he was inconsistent in dating the experiments, sometimes claiming that the strip machine was developed as early as 1888, he remained consistent in claiming it was finished before Edison sailed to Europe.

Dickson claimed that he cut some of the Carbutt celluloid into narrow strips and cut notches cut in the top to advance the strips through the camera. He said this technique was demonstrated for Edison in 1889 before he left for Paris. This sketch was made for Edison in 1928. [EHS.]

Orange during July, 1889 and the juxtaposition of the receipt of celluloid and the period of intense work on the Kineto is potent evidence. There is more evidence, as we shall see. But first, it's time for a trip to Paris.

Edison in Paris

Charles Batchelor to Edison, 21 August 1889: "I need not tell you that no one is more pleased than myself at your magnificent reception on that side of the water. I knew what the feeling was there in regard to you & there is no one who knows better than I how well you deserve it. 'Monsieur le Compte d'Edison' you have the heartfelt congratulations of yours very truly 'Batch'".

Tate to Insull: "People here [in Paris] say that nothing has ever equaled the reception which has been given Mr. Edison by representative bodies of the French nation. On 4 September the Ministry of Commerce &c. Mons. Tiraud [President of the Council of Ministers] gives him a dinner and on the 9th he is to be entertained in the same way by the City of Paris."[202]

Edison: "Oh, they don't have inventors, in the American sense of the word, in Paris at all. They haven't any professional inventors here as we have on the other side – that is to say, men who will go into a factory, sit down and solve any problem that may be put before them. That is a profession which they seem to know nothing about over here. In America we have hundreds of such men." ("Edison Talks About Paris" *New York World* September 9, 1889, datelined Paris, 7 September)

Edison's European excursion was a bell-weather event; a watershed in Edison's affairs. Edison's associates remembered the occasion well and often used it as a measure of their activities during the period.

There was an air of euphoria in Orange on the eve of his departure. On 30 July Samuel Insull, in from Schenectady to help manage affairs, wrote to Al Tate, who was already in France in anticipation of the visit, that things were relatively quiet in the lab. "... Mr. Edison is giving little or no attention to experimental work. The order of the day now is 'I will take that in hand when I return from Europe.' Insull felt that the status of the Edison General Electric Company could not have been better from Edison's standpoint and more than that, he was bubbling

202 EHS, Doc. File Ser. – 1889.

over with enthusiasm over the mine at Bechtelsville which seemed a success, "... There is no doubt but that we are going to make a great deal of money in concentrating iron ores. [Harry] Livor [manager of Bechtelsville] and Edison are practically intoxicated by the business ...".[203] Edison was off to Europe on a high note for what was to be one of the most memorable interludes in his remarkable career.

Edison was received in Paris as a celebrity among celebrities. Tate reported that crowds of would-be inventors lined up for advice or encouragement, many with models in their arms "... and usually these were flying machines". As he appeared on the streets the crowds would yell *"Vive A-de-sohn! Vive A-de-sohn!"*.[204] Tate juggled a busy social schedule and took on a French stenographer to answer a flood of correspondence. Edison, who sailed on 3 August, landed at Le Havre on 10 August and went directly to Paris where he stayed at the Hotel du Rhin in Place Vendôme. Two days after his arrival King Humbert of Italy made Edison a Grand Officer of the Crown of Italy. It was the first of a series of honors, fetes, banquets, tours and visits which lasted until he left for Berlin on 11 September 1889. He met crowned heads, government officials, renowned celebrities and a who's-who of the French scientific community. In the article quoted above, the *New York World* reported that Edison was sick from banquets. In late September, when he arrived in England after a brief, but equally strenuous visit to Germany, he retired to the countryside and, complaining of a cold, canceled all appointments.

Frank Dyer quoted Edison's description of his trip:

"At the Universal Exposition at Paris, in 1889, I made a personal exhibit covering about an acre. As I had no intention of offering to sell anything I was showing, and was pushing no companies, the whole exhibition was made for honor and without any hope of profit. ...

"... I visited the Opera-House. The President of France lent me his private box. The Opera-House was one of the first to be lighted by incandescent lamps.

"The city of Paris gave me a dinner at the new Hôtel de Ville, which was also lighted with the Edison system. ... As I could not understand or speak a word of French, I went to see our minister, Mr. Whitelaw Reid, and got him to send a deputy to answer for me ... Then the telephone company gave me a dinner, and the engineers of France; and I attended the dinner celebrating the fiftieth anniversary of the discovery of photography.

"I visited the Eiffel Tower at the invitation of Eiffel ... Gounod sang and played for us. We spent a day at Meudon, an old palace given by the government to Jansen [sic], the astronomer. He occupied three rooms, and there were 300 He had the grand dining-room for his laboratory. He showed me a gyroscope he had got up which made the incredible number of 4000 revolutions in a second.

"Pasteur invited me to come down to the Institute, and I went and had quite a chat with him.

"Of course I visited the Louvre and saw the Old Masters, which I could not enjoy. And I attended the Luxembourg, with modern masters, which I enjoyed greatly. To my mind, the Old Masters are not art, and I suspect

203 EHS. Letterbook Series, Insull to Tate, 30 July 1889. Insull was primarily looking after Edison's general business. Charles Batchelor was to manage the laboratory in Edison's absence, though Insull reported that Batchelor had been away much of July. Both Insull and Tate owned stock in Edison's ore milling operations.

204 Tate, Op. Cit., pp. 233–235.

many others are of the same opinion; and their value is in their scarcity and in the variety of men with lots of money."[205]

It is the dinner celebrating the fiftieth anniversary of photography that holds particular interest for us. This was held at the Hotel Continental on the evening of 19 August 1889 and was organized by Société française de Photographie. It came at the end of the Congrès international de Photographie and celebrated the discoveries of Niépce and Daguerre. Edison was the guest of honor and it was attended by many of the most prominent persons in the photographic field in France and elsewhere in Europe. Edison was at the head table with the President of the Société, M. Jules Janssen of the Institut and Director of l'observatoire d'Astronomie physique de Meudon and M. Gylden, director of the observatory of Stockholm. Among the attendees were Prince Bonaparte, Georges Balagny, Albert Londe, Étienne-Jules Marey, Antoine, Auguste and Louis Lumière, J. Maes (Belgium), Marco Mendoza, Paul Nadar, Louis Pasteur, Albert and Gaston Tissandier (Editor of *La Nature*) and Léon Vidal. In Edison's party were his British phonograph representative Col. George Gouraud and A.O. Tate. Janssen was the principal speaker and Gustave Larroumet, Directeur des Beaux-Arts also spoke.[206] The bringing together of Edison and two pioneers of chronophotography, Janssen and Marey and adding the Lumières to the mix gives unusual interest to this possibly overlooked event.

In the midst of his social whirl, Edison visited several centers of scientific research in an around Paris. He was most impressed by a visit to Pasteur's laboratory. He admired Pasteur as a scientist, particularly for his accomplishments in the improving the human condition. Edison remarked about his visit to Janssen's observatory in Meudon – Edison's had an interest in astronomy, though it was not as intense as his interest in health. But a meeting with Marey has direct interest to our story.

He probably met Étienne-Jules Marey at the banquet and it is assumed that at some time during his stay he visited Marey's Physiological Station in the Bois de Boulogne where Marey showed Edison his most recent chronographic camera, a device that used strips of photo-sensitive material mounted on rolls (or bobines) and moved successively past the lens of the camera to record sequences of motion. Edison had seen Marey's exhibit at the Universal Exposition in which positive strips of his photographs could be viewed in reconstructed motion in a large Zoetrope-type device.

Following Gordon Hendrick's lead, a number of film historians have credited Marey with introducing Edison to the use of strips in a camera and inspiring him to revise his design for the Kinetoscope from cylinder to strips. The origins of Hendrick's premise were an interview with a former associate, M. Pierre Nogues, an 1892 paper by Marey and a gossipy account of this visit, purportedly based on Edison's own words, in Albert Smith's *Two Reels and a Crank*. The article that Hendricks quoted, "Nouveaux Developpement de la chronophotographique" was published *Revue des travaux scientifiques*, 1902. In it

205 Dyer, Op. Cit., pp. 741–745.

206 *Bulletin de la Société française de Photographie, 1889*, pp. 261–288.

Marey said that the demonstration at the Exposition in 1889 "... s'en inspira sans doute pour créer son Kinetoscope ...".[207] Since the fourth and final Edison motion picture caveat was prepared by Edison in November, a month after his return shows this change, it is cited as proof that Marey's camera inspired Edison. Marey has also been credited with introducing Edison to "film", i.e. celluloid, so the meeting between Edison and Marey has been regarded as a pivotal point in Edison's experiments.

Marey and Edison both confirm that they met at the Exposition where Marey showed him through his exhibit and demonstrated his Zoetropic viewing device. Edison confirmed the meeting in his testimony in 1900 and said he also saw Anschütz's Tachyscope at the Exposition, but made no mention of visiting Marey at the Physiological Station. Edison may have visited the station but the accounts that have been used by subsequent historians were written after the fact and lack evidence confirming the visit. Edison's activities in Paris were well documented, but I have found nothing specific about visiting the photographic station. The members of the Congrès international de Photographie who were meeting in Paris, visited Marey a few days before the banquet, but it is doubtful that Edison was in that group.

Albert Smith said that Edison saw a motion picture camera which took pictures in sequence, "... one under the other as they are today. 'I knew instantly that Marey had the right idea', Edison told me. On the return trip aboard ship, he said, he pencilled out a mechanical draft of a machine and immediately upon his arrival at Orange he ordered a halt on all work on the cylinder idea and the new project was launched. Out of that brief visit with Marey came the famous Kinetoscope." This was written with the help of a professional writer, Phil A. Koury. Like similar ghosted autobiographies, Smith's book is an interesting account that has been spiced-up to make it more palatable for the mass audience. Without footnotes, we are left to guess how accurate the information is. Some of the stories are misleading and others are incorrect. The story about Edison is followed by an erroneous assertion that Raff and Gammon suggested the coin operated phonograph to Edison – Edison had been in the coin phonograph business for more than two years when he met Norman Raff and Frank Gammon. Smith's account of the meeting is probably based on comments by Edison that he saw Marey's machine and liked the design, but the assertion that it inspired a radical change in design does not agree with Edison's other accounts and seems at odds with what was happening at the laboratory.

In his 1900 account of the meeting, Marey did not claim that Edison was an imitator who copied or stole ideas from him: "The ingenious American announced a few years later that he had constructed an instrument, called the Kinetoscope, in which one saw all sorts of scenes in motion reproduced with perfect fidelity. We saw in 1894 at Paris this interesting instrument functioning, in which a continuous band, covered with pictures, passed in front of a lens and received intermittent lighting reproduced each time that the a new

207 Hendricks, ...*Myth*, pp. 171–172. *Two Reels and a Crank* (Garden City, N. Y., Doubleday & Co., Inc., 1952), pp. 80–81.

picture was presented to the eye of the observer. These periods of lighting were so brief that the pictures, in spite of their continuous motion, appeared stationary. In order to guide the film in a uniform manner, Edison had conceived the idea of perforating it and having it drawn through a notched cylinder which turned with a regular motion."[208]

The problem with the premise that Marey inspired the change in Edison's design is that it assumes that Edison never considered using a strip and that he clung stubbornly to the cylinder as the only way to record images. It is based on a premise that a self-trained amateur inevitably learned from an experienced scientist. The first two are misleading assumptions and the last is only partly true. Edison probably learned something from Marey and benefitted from the meeting. Although he criticized the quality of the reproductions of Marey's chronographic images that he saw in Paris, Edison had great respect for Marey and the French scientific community. Edison was a pragmatist rather than a theoretician as his statement "They haven't any professional inventors here ..." indicates (see above). Marey seemingly understood and appreciated this difference – as indicated by his description in *Revue Scientifique*. Although they were on similar paths, they were headed in different directions. The "rivalry" between the two pioneers that some have suggested was less dramatic than supposed.

Though the documentation is lacking, there is little reason to doubt that Edison visited Marey's studio. He would have welcomed the opportunity to see Marey's facilities and examine his devices. He would have had only moderate interest in the Zoetropic machine that Marey was exhibiting, but the chance to see Marey's camera and method of using photographic strips would have been particularly inviting. But he did not experience the revelation of new and unfamiliar technology that Hendricks and others have postulated. The image of Edison slapping his forehead and saying 'why couldn't I have thought of that' is absurd. Edison was very familiar with machines that manipulated strips. His earliest inventions, the stock ticker and improved telegraph machines, used strips of paper – in fact, he had built his early career on manipulating such strips. The notion that Edison learned about the potential of celluloid from Marey is also misleading. As we have seen, Edison experimented with it for the phonograph, Dickson was using it before Edison left and Newark, Edison's home base, and the home of the Celluloid Manufacturing Co., was a leading manufacturing center of raw celluloid. Edison, the avid amateur chemist, probably knew more about it than Marey did.

Marey was working on a new version of his camera and was ready to introduce it. It used strips of photographic material and Edison may have picked up details of design from Marey's machine. Marey's strip camera, the one which would have interested Edison, was designed to use Eastman's paper-based stripping film which came mounted on rollers for use in Eastman's Kodak camera. The revolutionary camera that Eastman introduced in the summer of 1888 stimulated Marey as it

208 MoMA, Crawford Collection. "Physiologie: Nouveaux developpements de la Methode graphique par la chronophotographie." in *Revue Scientifique (Revue Rose)* No. 9, 4th Series, Tom XIV, 1 September 1900.

had stimulated Le Prince, Friese-Greene and Donisthorpe.[209] Marey could, and certainly did, purchase celluloid sheets from Paris-based Georges Balagny who had marketed a variety of sizes under license from Lumière Frères of Lyon. Marey probably experimented with celluloid, but because the sheet film available in 1889 was difficult to work with he was apparently not using it regularly. Whatever Marey told Edison about using celluloid would have interested him and may have confirmed the enthusiasm that Dickson felt for the material.[210]

Marey and Edison seem to have parted on amicable terms. After his return to Orange in November, Marey sent Edison a copy of his book *Le Vol des Oiseax*, which Edison acknowledged with courtesy. This seemed to end direct contacts between the two.

Although Paris may not have been the source of startling new revelations, Edison had images on his mind while he was there. In the presence of reporters he once again mused about television and on 1 September 1889, the *Levant Herald* quoted him: "I am ... at work at an invention which will enable a man in Wall-street not only to telephone to a friend near Central Park, say, but to actually see that friend while speaking to him. That would be a practical and useful invention, and I see no reason why it may not soon become a reality; One of the first things I shall do on my return to America will be to establish such an apparatus between my laboratory and the phonograph works. I have already had satisfactory results in reproducing images at that distance, which is only about one thousand feet. Of course, it is ridiculous to talk about seeing between New York and Paris; the rotundity of the earth, if nothing else, would render that impossible." Apparently the story was well received because on when he arrived in New York on 6 October, he repeated it to a reporter for the *Newark News* and the story was picked-up by *Scientific American* later in the month.[211] It would be a while before television filled the air in New Jersey, but Dickson was preparing a controversial surprise for him on his return!

209 Stripping film seems a difficult product now, but when introduced in 1886 it answered the needs of certain photographers. Users of Kodak cameras sent their exposed rolls to Eastman who processed and returned the developed photographs but Marey processed his own photographs.

210 Marta Braun, *Picturing Time, The Work of Étienne-Jules Marey (1830–1904)* (Chicago & London, University of Chicago Press, 1992), 150–191; MoMA Crawford. Marey may have suggested the possibility of exploiting the Kinetoscope as a coin-operated machine. He told Eugene Lauste, who met him c. 1898, that he had made such a suggestion to Edison in 1889. A number of coin-operated machines were introduced at the Paris Exposition among them coin machines where you could have your photo taken.

211 EHS, unbound clippings; NMAH Hendricks.

Chapter 12

"Good Morning, Mr. Edison": The Strip Kinetograph

W.K.L. Dickson (1933): "Mr. Edison's return to his laboratory took place 6 October 1889. Within the hour I had him by the arm and led him to the new studio and Kinetophone exhibit, on which we had been working day and night. On seeing the studio, Mr. Edison asked, 'What's that building?' I explained its necessity. 'Well, you've got cheek; let's see what you've got.' We went in. Gradually his face lit up, the clouds of disapproval were dissipated and finally dispelled. I had placed him in a chair in the upper projecting room to witness his first 'talkie,' or exhibit, of the Kinetophone. For a wonder, the exhibition was good. No breakdown of the film occurred nor did the Zeiss arc lamp sputter. There was much rejoicing. Edison sat with the eartubes to the phonograph. My assistant started the arc lamp and removed the metal sheet interposed between the arc and the film. The phonograph motor controlled the projecting Kinetograph.

"I was seen to advance and address Mr. Edison from the small 4-foot screen; small, because of the restricted size of the room. I raised my hat, smiled, and said, 'Good morning, Mr. Edison, glad to see you back. Hope you like the Kinetophone. To show the synchronization I will lift my hand and count up to ten.' I then raised and lowered my hands as I counted to ten. There was no hitch, and a pretty steady picture. If the pictures were steady in the taking, why not in the reproduction on the screen."[212] (*SMPE Journal*, 1933)

Eugene Lauste (1933): "My conclusion is that Mr. D. has told this story to so many people that he think now was a fact."[213]

E ugene Lauste was neither the first nor the last person to express skepticism about Dickson's tale of projecting synchronized sound for Edison on the day he returned to the lab from Paris. Edison himself was ambivalent about it – except when trying to establish the priority of his patents in court. Contemporary scholars have dismissed the claim as an exaggeration – a case of bravura or an outrageous lie. Yet, though Dickson told many tales, he was most consistent in the details of this one and for all his inconsistency in dating other events, he was most consistent about when this happened. The account appeared first in *A History of the Kinetograph ...*, the booklet that W.K.L. and Antonia wrote in 1894–1895 for Raff and Gammon to use

212 Dickson, *Journal of the SMPE*, p. 13.

213 MoMA, Crawford. Lauste to Will Day, 30 May 1933.

to promote the Kinetoscope. At that time the story was simple and concise: "The crowning point of realism was attained on the occasion of Mr. Edison's return from the Paris Exposition of 1889, when Mr. Dickson himself stepped out on the screen, raised his hand and smiled, while uttering the words of greeting, 'Good morning, Mr. Edison, glad to see you back. I hope you are satisfied with the Kineto-phono-graph.'"[214] It became more elaborate as the years went by and Dickson had to defend himself against those who doubted his story.

There is little question that Dickson prepared something to show Edison on his return from Paris. Most of the skeptics grant him that and there is evidence of preparation in the surviving lab documents. After maintaining a normal schedule of work on the Kineto during September, the pace stepped up during first week in October. Two machinists, Hugo Kayser and a man named Westering , were added to the project. On Thursday, 3 October, Fred Ott returned and stayed until the 5th. Westering continued to work Monday and Tuesday, the 7th and 8th, then on the 9th work returned to normal (although Eugene Lauste spent the day "fitting-up" in a new photographic building that was built during Edison's absence). Cylinders of oxygen and hydrogen were charged to the Kineto account and received on 5 October. Then on the 9th Dickson sent an order to the Phonograph Works for one 4 cell battery, one speaking tube, one "earing" tube and an unidentified apparatus (see page 165).[215] They were received the same day. Two days later, on Friday the 11th, Dickson and Brown returned to ore milling and for the rest of the year all of their time was charged to ore milling.

This was only a mini-burst of activity – intense, but not as intense as the one at the end of July. There was no all night session, but there were late night sessions on October 1st, 2nd and 3rd. Fred Ott worked 11 hours on Saturday and half a day on Sunday, the day that Edison returned. Once again, this seems directed towards some sort of dem-onstration for the boss. Exactly what is open to speculation – and there has been a deal of speculation about it!

Whatever it was, his eagerness and the emphasis he placed on it throughout his life shows that Dickson felt it was a significant advance. As has been mentioned, subsequent statements by Edison and his staff – and Dickson as well – claim that it was a Kinetograph, a camera modified to project strips of Kodak's new film. Some even said it was built during July and in use before Edison sailed for Europe. Since these claims have been widely challenged, the information that might – or might not – support them merits review.

A review of Kineto experiments

At the end of June, Dickson and Brown were continuing their experi-ments with cylinders – and with limited, rather modest success. Several designs had been tried with the modifications made in response to problems confronted while testing a variety of photographic media – daguerreotype, albumen, wet plate collodion, dry-plate bromide. After trying traditional photo methods, Dickson tried various modifications

214 Dickson and Dickson, Op. Cit., p. 19.
215 The exact date is uncertain, see pp. 164–168.

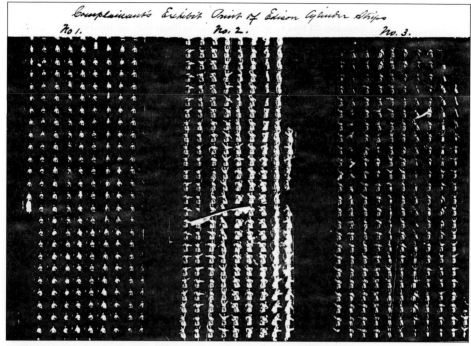

Monkeyshines nos. 1, 2 & 3 presented as evidence in the suit with American Mutoscope & Biograph Co. These were the first successful moving images: they were made during the final cylinder experiments. This is a print made from negatives on celluloid made during the cylinder experiments. [EHS.]

in an effort to improve speed and clarity of registration. Images were recorded, but only single images in the early tests; then a few at a time but at speeds too slow to reproduce movement. A device to advance a cylinder slowly and record a succession of images had been built which "... produced a few spirals of pictures on a dead slow shaft". They had begun with micro-images and gradually increased the size because those captured were far from satisfactory. The very small images lacked definition because of excessive grain and distortion. To compensate for these deficiencies the size was gradually increased, though they contin-ued to test micro images throughout the early experiments. As Charles Brown explained: "... we made a great many experiments during that time in trying to see how small pictures we could get". and Edison, himself, described the results:

"We had difficulty in getting the details in a small picture on account of the coarse character of the emulsion, and the parties who were making the film material experimented on producing a finer emulsion so that the figures photographed would be sharper and we found that in very small pictures the results were quite unsatisfactory on account of the coarseness of the emulsion. The larger the pictures the less this coarseness of the emulsion would affect the definition. From time to time the parties furnished us with improved emulsions, and we got finer details, but we had to abandon the small microscopic pictures on account of the makers not being able to furnish the emulsion fine enough."[216]

216 Dickson, *Journal of the SMPE*, p. 10; EHS, Equity 6928, pp. 84 (Edison) and 141 (Brown).

The tests using sheet celluloid, which started at the end of June, brought an end to the efforts to record images on cylinders. The sheets of Carbutt and Allen & Rowell celluloid with emulsions that were "faster" made it possible to reproduce movement for first time but with disappointing results. In the first successful tests, the image was 1/8th of an inch in diameter. Not satisfied, they increased the size to ¼ inch for the final tests. The exposures were made intermittently at a rate of eight or ten per second on negative which was treated with bi-chloride of mercury after developing to give a positive appearance for viewing. Since it was hard to view them on the metal drum, a transparent glass drum was used and the images were illuminated from inside the glass with a sparking device. The viewing device ran continuously with intermittence created by the sparks illuminating the images. If these images were not the three *Monkeyshine* sheets exhibited in the court cases (see illustration on page 150), they were very similar. The images are a circle and those on *Monkeyshines no. 1* are 1/8 inch in diameter, the other two are ¼ inch.[217]

Although they had finally made pictures that moved, the quality did not match the standard Dickson hoped to achieve. They were unsteady and not sharp. He blamed this on a combination of inadequate film speed, the slow rate of exposure and the mechanical limitation of the cylinder. Once again he wanted to increase the size of the image, but the cylinder was an obstacle. To accommodate larger images the number of images had to be reduced or a much larger cylinder would be needed. They were at an impasse. The distortion caused by the curvature would still be evident and at some point the cylinder would become too bulky. As Edison put it: "Well, we did not try very large pictures, because it would require a cylinder so enormously large in diameter and length that we could not make it practicable ...".[218]

This quandary seems to have persuaded Edison to abandon the cylinder. Enlarging the image to ½ inch made the shift to strips an acceptable alternative. *And*, it became feasible when Dickson learned that Eastman was planning to market celluloid in long rolls!

While tradition has it that Edison clung stubbornly to the cylinder, if Dickson is to be believed, it was not difficult to persuade Edison to make the change. In fact, he indicated that Edison may have encouraged it. From the very beginning Edison talked about producing scenes that ran for a relatively long time and according to Dickson, he talked about recording complete operas or scenes from operas before the first caveat was written . In his 1910 testimony Dickson said that they considered using strips at the beginning but rejected them in favor of the cylinder because there was no suitable material in strips. "... I have a distinct recollection as to Edison speaking to me of taking such pictures [on long bands] , still sticking however, to small pictures on bands. Mr. Edison doubtless, conceived the whole idea from having in mind, his large narrow reels of tape, which he used in his telegraphic tape machines, which were lying around the laboratory at different stages of work. Naturally, it could be but a passing idea, owing to the fact that

217 EHS. Dickson's testimony in Equity No. 28,605, pp. 144–146.

218 EHS, Equity 6928, p. 112.

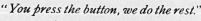
George Eastman's Kodak camera revolutionized photography by making it possible for anyone to take photos. This ad appeared in Cassier's Magazine in 1893, but the campaign "You press the button – we do the rest" started almost immediately after the camera was introduced in 1888. [LC.]

we had no material on which to work." He also said that Edison raised the possibility of using strips again when Dickson's early tests demonstrated the difficulty of getting good images on cylinders. "... there was absolutely nothing on the market at the time in the way of photographic bands or strips of any appreciable length that would at all answer the purpose ...".[219]

As discussed, Eastman's stripping film was introduced a few weeks before Edison's experiments began and had been considered for the Kineto project but was rejected because of "... mechanical difficulties in the way". While the paper-based stripping film wasn't suitable for the early experiments, a transparent strip of celluloid was a different matter. As soon as he learned that the Eastman Dry Plate & Film Company planned to market such a film, Dickson tried to get samples.[220]

Eastman's celluloid

Celluloid roll film was a new phase in the larger revolution that Eastman launched a year earlier. Its roots can be traced to 1885 when Eastman introduced roll holders that allowed paper strips to be advanced exposure by exposure through professional cameras. They allowed a number of exposures to be taken without reloading the camera for each exposure. They were a convenient tool that appealed to a small group of

219 EHS. Dickson, testimony on 6 May 1910, in Equity No. 28,605, Patents Co. v. Chicago Film Exchange, pp. 147–148.

220 EHS. Equity 28,605, pp. 147–157.

professional photographers. The Kodak camera, introduced in July 1888, combined the roll holders and narrower rolls of stripping film in a simple mechanism that anyone could use. Ads with their slogan "You press the button – we do the rest" appeared in national magazines. All the amateur had to do was expose the 100 shots, send the camera to Rochester and the pictures were developed and returned along with the camera reloaded with a fresh roll ready for exposure. Everybody could shoot pictures with a Kodak. It was relatively inexpensive and was immediately successful. Eastman's revolution changed the nature of photography and ended the era when photography was the exclusive province of professionals and skilled amateurs versed in the mysteries of photochemistry.

George Eastman was aware of the limitations of his stripping film and recognized that it would be more effective with a celluloid base. As soon as the Kodak was introduced he began experiments to produce celluloid and in the spring of 1889 he applied for patents for a method for producing celluloid and a system for flowing the base and coating it on long glass tables.[221] A new factory building was put-up on Court St., in Rochester. Eastman told Scovill & Adams about it in mid-May. "This is confidentially to inform you that we perfected a new transparent flexible (non-stripping) film for roll holders and that it will be ready for market about 1 July ...". Eastman's ads appeared at the beginning of July and during July the photographic press was filled with discussion of the pros and cons of the new product. At the end of the month Eastman sent representatives to introduce the film at regional camera clubs and at a national photographic meeting in Boston. With a promise that regular manufacture would begin in September or October, the first rolls were sold on 27 August 1889. Because of glitches in the manufacturing process, the product was slow to reach the market. Some film was sold in the U.S. in the fall of 1889, but Eastman did not ship any celluloid to Europe for general sale until 1890.[222]

Edison and Eastman's celluloid

Although it was not designed for moving image use, Eastman's celluloid was the product Dickson had been waiting for. He probably learned about it when it was announced in early July, 1889, though it is possible that he learned about it earlier – as he claimed. At that time he was in the midst of the final cylinder experiments. Before the end of July Dickson had gone on his own to Rochester to see if he could get some.[223]

Among the many fanciful tales spun by Mr. D., his claim of a special relationship with George Eastman and his company seems particularly far fetched – at least at first glance. Late in his life, he said he helped Eastman develop and improve the method of making celluloid film and in the most elaborate version of the story he claimed that the relationship began in 1888 before celluloid was marketed. In this version he said that he saw his first piece of celluloid in 1888 at a demonstration by an Eastman representative, went immediately to Rochester where

221 U.S. Patents no. 417,202, Henry M. Reichenbach, Rochester, NY, Manufacture of Flexible Photographic Film. Awarded 10 December 1889 and assigned to Eastman Dry Plate and no. 441,831, George Eastman, Photographic Film. Awarded 2 December 1890.

222 Braun, Op. Cit., pp. 150–159; GHE, Eastman Papers.

223 GEH. George Eastman to W. [I.] Adams, 17 May 1889; EHS, Equity no. 28,605, pp. 173–174.

he met George Eastman who gave him short strips to experiment with. His tale was further embellished with claims that he made a number of trips in 1888 and 1889; recommended improvements that helped Eastman perfect his celluloid and that these trips enabled him to standardized the modern 35mm format with four perforations per frame that year or the following one. This account was told in outline to Merritt Crawford in 1930 and early in 1932 he repeated it in more detail to Earl Theisen, Glenn E. Matthews and John Crabtree of the Historical Committee of the Society of Motion Picture Engineers, modifying the claims slightly to say he received the first film from George Eastman at the end of 1888. By December 1932 the story of his dealings with Eastman was elaborated again in a long letter, complete with drawings, which he wrote to Oscar Solbert of Eastman Kodak.[224]

Dickson gave George Eastman credit as an essential contributor to the development of the motion picture. After reviewing his claims, Matthews, Crabtree and Theisen accepted much of Dickson's account. Since Mathews and Crabtree were Eastman employees, they vetted Dickson's claims very carefully and discussed them with veteran Eastman employees, so their acceptance gives some credibility to Dickson's account.

The claims that he worked in Rochester in 1888 and designed the modern 35mm film format in 1889 are fiction – at least there is no evidence to support them – but with the date changed to 1889 – and after – much of the rest is apparently true. A few weeks after Dickson testified in 1910 in the Patents Co. v. Chicago Film Exchange case, George Eastman testified and supported important parts of Dickson's claims. Asked if he knew Dickson he said "Yes; I met him for the first time in Rochester in the year 1889. We had announced our intention of putting a transparent film on the market and he came to see me about it." He added that Dickson wrote repeatedly asking when the film would be available and supplied copies of six letters Dickson wrote to Eastman in 1889 and eight that Eastman wrote to him. Apparently Dickson wrote from home since there are no copies in the Edison Papers. At least four were written before the first of September 1889. An annotation on one of the letters recorded that a roll of Kodak film was sent to Dickson on 24 August 1889. It was a roll about 50 feet long, designed to fit in Kodak camera no. 1 and on 2 September Dickson sent a post office order for $2.50 to pay for it. This was one of the first rolls delivered to anyone outside of Eastman's company and the first strip of celluloid in the hands of any of the moving image experimenters.[225]

Dickson corresponded and met with Eastman and with representatives of his and other companies in a persistent effort to get film suitable for his needs. Frustrated by poor registration, he seems to have been pestering his suppliers for improvements even before he went to Rochester. He was capable of being difficult in matters he considered crucial and he was particularly concerned about getting better sensitometry. Charles Brown said that product representatives came to the laboratory and brought samples of improved emulsions. "Well, Mr.

224 The correspondence of Theisen, Matthews and Crabtree is in a number of places. The Natural History Museum of Los Angeles has Earl Theisen's papers which include a number of Glenn E. Matthew's letters as well as documents that he forwarded to Theisen, including Dickson's draft of the article for the *Journal of the SMPE*. There is a collection of Matthews and Theisen papers in the Margaret Herrick Library at the Academy of Motion Picture Arts and Sciences in Beverley Hills but some of their correspondence is elsewhere. I found letters in Fonds Will Day at Bibliothèque du Film, Paris, the Merritt Crawford Collection at the Museum of Modern Art and in the Terry Ramsaye Collection at Georgetown University Library in Washington, DC. At the time that Matthews and Theisen were trying to clarify Dickson's claims, Matthews was also corresponding with people in Richmond, Indiana in an unsuccessful effort to uncover more accurate information about C. Francis Jenkins' claim that he projected film in Richmond in 1894. Since Matthews and his associate on the Historical Committee, John I. Crabtree, worked for Eastman Kodak, they would have examined Dickson's claims very carefully.

Dickson went ... saw the Scoville [sic] people and the Eastman people and they sent their representatives out here and had a talk with him about it and then they sent us samples, and kept making samples and sending them to us to try ... I know there was quite a strife here between the Scoville [sic] people and the Eastman people to see which could get the best strips for us."[226] While Brown may have dramatized matters, his testimony makes it clear that Dickson dealt directly with his suppliers to solve problems and sometimes put pressure on them. Brown was specific that these meetings happened in the Photographic Room which implies that were occurring as early as July, well before moving to the new studio which was ready in October. "... these men were out here while we were in Room 5; they kept coming out here to see us about them." Since Brown's tour with Dickson ended in mid-January, 1890, the events he described happened in 1889.[227]

The prospect of having celluloid in strips made it possible to abandon cylinders and radically change the design. The earliest version of a machine using strips was very crude. The available celluloid was 11 x 14 plates of Carbutt's and these were cut into narrow bands which were then notched along the top edge to guide the film (see illustration on page 142). "My next attempt, after abandoning drums and the like ... was to proceed with narrow strips of Carbutt celluloid, 18 inches long, notched on the top, and impelled intermittently by a clock escapement movement. A rotating shutter and a 1½-inch focus lens were used. The pictures were ¼ inch square. ... On trying to join these strips, the usual trouble was that the joints stuck in the frame or open guide, which, however, we made as springy as possible." To join the strips, about 1/8 inch of emulsion was removed and acetone used to cement the splice. Carbutt's film was too stiff to wind onto a reel so the strip was enclosed in a box and moved horizontally past the lens from beginning to end. Images were lost because the film peeled at the joint and sometimes the film tore when caught at the join. Dickson also commented that "... the coarseness of the grain forbade too great magnification". Dickson drew a picture of the arrangement in a letter to Will Day and labeled it "a very early crazy experiment" he also noted that Carbutt's was "stout substance celluloid" indicating that Eastman's was more pliable.[228]

It *was* a crazy experiment! The crude mechanism would have been difficult to work with and the notches were an inefficient way to advance the film. With film catching in the drive wheel, tearing and riding off track, it would have been difficult – almost impossible – to film anything. It is easy to imagine that a re-design would have been on the agenda very quickly. Notches were replaced by perforations and a sprocket wheel with teeth that fit the perforations. The first version of this design had a single row of perforations along the top of the film which moved horizontally through the camera. This was tested on a piece of paper before it was tried on film. Because it made the film steadier, the perforations were moved to the bottom (see illustration on page 157).

225 EHS. *Ibid*. pp. 172–174. Dickson's letter sending $2.50 to Eastman on 2 September 1889 is reproduced at p. 70 of Terry Ramsaye's *A Million and One Nights*.

226 EHS, Equity 6928, pp. 151-152.

227 *Ibid.*, p. 155.

228 Dickson, *Journal of the SMPE*, pp. 10–11; BiFi, Will Day, Dickson to Day, 17 February 1933. EHS, Equity 6928, pp. 146–147. A drawing of the experiment with Carbutt's film also appears in the SMPE article. For the SMPE article Dickson dated this experiment as happening in 1888 and for Will Day he dated it 1887, clearly exaggerations.

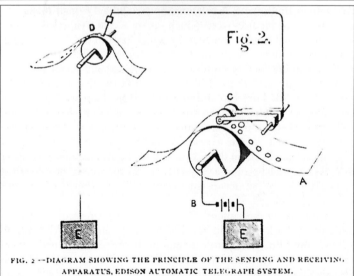

FIG. 2 —DIAGRAM SHOWING THE PRINCIPLE OF THE SENDING AND RECEIVING
APPARATUS, EDISON AUTOMATIC TELEGRAPH SYSTEM.

The shift to strips and redesigning the mechanism was not as overwhelming a problem as it might seem. Dickson did not have to start from scratch. The sprockets and perforations that are features of the Kinetograph were borrowed from Edison's earlier machines. As mentioned, Edison had been designing machines to move strips of paper intermittently – and rapidly – through telegraph machines since the

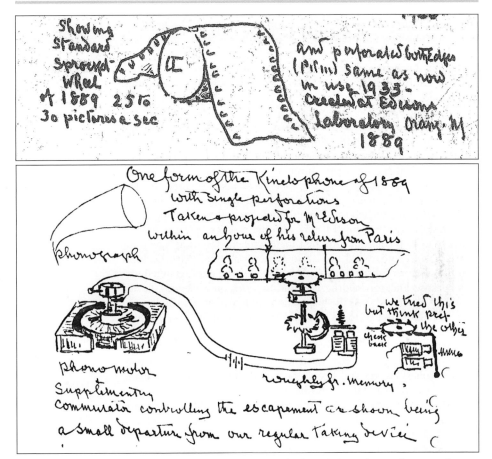

Both pages: *The staff of Edison's lab were familiar with devices that moved strips, usually paper, through various mechanisms so the change from cylinders to guided strips of celluloid was quite easy. Edison's earliest success as an inventor was his stock recorder (above) and paper recording strips were used in several telegraph devices such as his automatic telegraph system (below right). Dickson's drawing of the celluloid transport (above) shows the influence of the earlier devices. Dickson misdated the drawing. The 35mm prototype which is shown, was not adopted until late 1891 or early 1892. The drawing on the right is Dickson's illustration of an early adaptation of the strip telegraph devices. [EHS & NHMLA & MoMA.]*

1870s and the paper used in these devices was often fed from rolls – as Dickson commented, examples were lying around the laboratory. He also said that the use of perforations to align and steady the film for exposure, was inspired by the "... sight of [Edison's] perforated automatic telegraph".[229] Edison's machinists were experienced in working with these devices and the staff in the lab's two machine shops, particularly the two Otts, John and Fred, were familiar with the transport systems which moved the paper strips through machines. In an account of his experiences with Edison written in 1919, John Ott said that one of the first things he worked on when he started with Edison in 1869 was a "... perforator to prepare paper strips, for automatic chemical

229 *Ibid.*, pp. 10–11. Again the dating is skewed by his identifying William Heise as the assistant working on this. Heise did not work on the Kineto until late in 1890 and this perforator punch was made earlier, as we will see.

telegraph ..." and for stock and private line printers.[230] Though these were not photographic devices, the mechanisms were similar and adaptable. Edison's automatic telegraph and a Wheatstone telegraph are credited by Dickson as ascendants of the strip Kinetograph.

The court testimony about these events gives the impression that the changes happened quickly, but that is certainly not the case. Progress depended on experience, experimentation and the availability of material. During June, July and August Dickson's experiments were limited to using the celluloid from Carbutt and Allen and Rowell. Although he knew about Eastman's rolls of celluloid as early as July, none were available until late summer so if, as claimed, he showed Edison a strip device before he left for Paris it was the "crazy" version using strips cut from pieces of celluloid and was probably the early version with the notched top. Even though Dickson was having problems with it, Edison seemed happy with the progress because he told John Ott to help Dickson with the Kineto while he was away; and John Bachelor, who supervised the lab in Edison's absence, gave Dickson unusual support. Edison apparently had seen some photographed images because Dickson said he was told to work on a viewing device during his absence. "... As the boat glided out I saw Mr. Edison leaning over the railing, his fists to his eyes to imitate the viewing of the pictures in our experimental Kinetoscope. I understood the pantomime to mean that I was to have the Kinetoscope completed before his return. A rough model of the instrument was constructed."[231] Although this story may be apocryphal, Edison and Brown both said this machine was made while he was away and used after his return.

Edison may have seen a sample of Eastman's celluloid before his departure. Dickson said he got a sample from an Eastman representative following a demonstration in New York, showed it to Edison whose "... smile was seraphic: 'Good,' he said, 'we can now do the trick – just work like hell'." With his usual hyperbole, Dickson dated this in 1888, but Eastman was not ready to demonstrate celluloid in 1888. But there were two demonstrations in New York during the summer of 1889. One was made during the presentation of the new Kodak camera number 2 at an informal meeting of the Society of Amateur Photographers of New York on 21 August 1889 and it is assumed that Dickson attended this meeting. But there was an earlier presentation also for the Society of Amateur Photographers of New York. This one, on 30 July, was specifically to introduce the new celluloid and if Dickson attended this one and if Eastman's representative, Gus Milburn gave him a sample, he would have been able to show it to Edison before he left. So it might be true that Edison told him to "... work like hell".[232]

Regardless of when he got the film sample, Dickson seems to have been corresponding with Eastman during July and Eastman's testimony implies that Dickson visited Rochester during July – and, perhaps earlier. In his 1910 testimony Dickson said he went to Rochester to buy a lens from Bausch & Lomb and visited Eastman twice before getting the sample from Milburn. There is no record that Edison ordered a lens

230 EHS, Biographical files. John Ott, "My Experience with Mr. Edison in 49 years ..." 29 April 1919. Ott said "... I took great intrest [sic] in perfecting ...[the motion picture]."

231 Dickson, ...SMPE, p. 12; EHS, Equity 6928, pp. 97 & 150. Dickson insisted that Eastman gave him samples of celluloid to experiment with before supplying him with the first roll but there is nothing to substantiate his claims except the comments that Brown made about photo dealers supplying him with test samples.

232 Dickson, Op. Cit., pp. 11–12; NMAH Hendricks.

in 1889 and Dickson may have confused this with a visit in 1891 when he did order lenses. Eastman's testimony indicates that he met Dickson in Rochester before film was sent to him at the end of August so Dickson may have gone to Rochester once or twice before Edison sailed. If he met George Eastman in July, it would have been early in the month because Eastman went to Europe in July to visit the Paris Exposition and conduct business. He returned to Rochester in September which could have been the occasion of their first meeting. Dickson was on vacation from 8 September through to the 15th and it is possible that he spent it in the Rochester area. He was fond of Clifton Springs, the spa not far from Rochester and if he was there it was convenient for drop-in visits to near-by Rochester.[233]

Regardless of who he met with and when, Dickson was persistent in his attempts to get film. As an example, here is his description of a later meeting with Mr. Eastman: "... I received nothing then from him, but on the second visit ... I again interviewed Mr. Eastman emphasizing the great importance of producing such a film and he promised me that I should have the very first sample produced, and that if I would wait he expected [it] shortly when they had got through a few difficulties of adhesion ... the sticking of the gelatine emulsion to the base ... so I waited ...".[234]

On Monday, 2 September Dickson sent the Eastman Dry Plate & Film Co. his payment for the roll of film received the previous week. "Enclosed please find sum of $2.50 P.O.O. due you for one roll Kodak film for which please accept thanks – I shall try same to-day & report – it looks splendid – I never succeeded in getting this substance in such straight & long pieces – [signed & added:] Can you coat me some rolls of your highest sensitometer – please answer."[235] On 7 September Eastman wrote that they had no film of greater sensitivity. Though pleased, Dickson encountered problems with Eastman's celluloid. "... We were very much troubled with peeling off, so that when we did get as sharp a picture as possible, we had very little left to try and project with even by single picture projection. When we discovered that the image appeared when projected extremely coarse, due in a great measure to combined difficulties of imperfections in the base or comparative coarseness of the bromide of silver emulsion, which was very perceptible when enlarged on a screen."[236]

These problems were real and not confined to the earliest tests. Eastman had delayed release for good reason. They were having manufacturing problems and had only limited quantities of the new film for the general market. In fact, Dickson was fortunate to have received film ahead of general distribution – an indication that he had, indeed, established a special relationship with Eastman and his company. An article in *Philadelphia Photographer*, 5 October 1889, reported that Eastman was not yet supplying roll film and on 26 October 1889 George Eastman wrote Henry Strong, president of the company, that they shipped $3000 of transparent film during October and hoped for $6000. "I have not dared to commence shipping Walker [Eastman's English

233 NMAH Hendricks. The *Rochester Post-Express* and *Rochester Morning Herald* reported Eastman's trip on 7 & 8 July 1889. See also. Brayer, Op. Cit., pp. 74–75. Because the newspapers sometimes listed out of town hotel registrants, Gordon Hendricks searched newspapers to find reference to Dickson's visit to Rochester or Clifton Springs but found no indication that he was in either place in September 1889.

234 EHS. Dickson's testimony in 1910 in Equity No. 28,605, Patents Co. v. Chicago Film Exchange. Dickson said that this preceded the demonstration in New York City and that he was given the one and only sample after the demonstration. He said it was this sample that he showed Edison.

235 A copy of this letter, in Dickson's hand, is reproduced in Terry Ramsaye's, *A Million and One Nights*, p. 70. It is also referred to in Carl W. Ackerman, *George Eastman*.

236 EHS. Dickson's testimony in Equity No. 28,605, Patents Co. v. Chicago Film Exchange, 6 May 1910, p. 149.

manager] any of it yet because we have had so much trouble with it ... ".[237]

Dickson seems to have stepped into the midst of Eastman's efforts to make the product marketable – apparently with welcome effect. Dickson said he made several visits to discuss the peeling emulsion and other problems and that he made recommendations to correct some of them. A lively exchange seems to have developed. He described working with Eastman in a letter to Oscar Solbert of the Eastman Co.:

" ... [I] tried it, developed, hypo fixed & then washed off most of the film ... I returned to Rochester rather glum. We tried washing the base in weak caustic soda sol.[ution] washed, dried & coated ... I fancied an improvement in regard to the adhesion to the base ...

"I went straight back & got out at the wrong station while cogitating on the subject of the peeling after hypo washing & glycerine – It then occurred to me, not to try & coat a dead dry base, but coat when fresh or perhaps slightly tacky – Anyway I went back to Rochester & this was done & I returned with the sample –

"Doubtless you will find among your old records my telegram to Mr. Eastman early in 1889 reading "Eureka" signed Dickson".[238]

While this account may be embellished, it seems to have a factual basis. Dickson and Edison had been experimenting with making their own emulsions and modifying existing ones. They had even toyed with making their own celluloid. Dickson said the tests were on-going and continued even after receiving Eastman's film. "While this work was going on, Mr. Edison and I devoted considerable time in pulverizing bromide of silver, but need not say we were not very successful ...". But they gave him more than a passing knowledge of photo chemistry. He said their experiments were abandoned when Eastman improved their product enough to make it usable.[239] It took quite a while for Eastman to resolve all his problems so Dickson's interaction with Eastman's company extended over several years.

The new photo studio

When Edison returned from Paris, Dickson led him to a new photo studio which had been put up during his absence. With the possible exception of Marey's physiological station, it was the world's first motion picture studio. "On my return from the boat, I persuaded my friend Mr. Charles Batchelor, who was in charge of the laboratory, to build an outside studio to my specifications, combining a sliding glass roof to let in the sunlight unobstructed, for photographing before a black or suitable background."

According to Brown, Edison had turned down Dickson's previous request for a purpose-built photo building, but as construction supervisor in Edison's absence Batchelor had some leeway. The modifications to be made while Edison was away were quite extensive: a new water system, re-wiring a portion of the electrical system and laying tracks for an on-going experiment with electric locomotives. The new water system was a major disruption. A tank was built on the roof of

237 NMAH Hendricks; George Eastman House, George Eastman's Papers. Henry Strong, President of Eastman Dry Plate & Film Co., lived in Tacoma, Washington where he was president of a bank. Eastman, who was Treasurer of the company, and Strong had been friends for a number of years and Eastman was quite frank in describing activities in Rochester to Strong.

238 NMAH Hendricks. Dickson to Oscar N. Solbert, 10 December 1932.

239 EHS. Dickson's testimony in Equity 28,605.

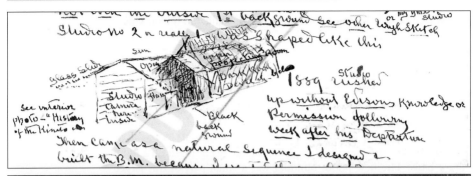

Two photographic facilities were built in 1889. The first was a shed attached to the sunny side of the ore milling building. The second was a purpose-built photo studio. Dickson's drawings illustrate the plan of the photo studio (top) and the location of the shed (bottom). They were made for Will Day in 1933. The photo in the center shows the interior of the photographic area of the studio. [BiFi & LC.]

the main laboratory building, new pipes were installed in the buildings and grounds and, because of a rash of recent fires, a sprinkler system was installed. Plans were drawn up for a phonograph duplicating building at nearby Silver Lake, New Jersey. As if this were not enough, there were modifications to Glenmont, Edison's home, and electrical wiring was extended to some additional houses in Llewellyn Park. (A number of Edison's neighbors were powered by the generator at the lab.) In anticipation of these disruptions, experiments were curtailed and staff laid off. All of this work was done by lab staff rather than contractors, so carpenters, tinkers, laborers, etc. were hired on a temporary basis. The new photo building was a small part of this larger construction project.

Dickson had complained that vibrations from an elevator next to the Photo Room were spoiling images and this was given as the reason that Batchelor allowed construction of the studio. The vibration problem was not the only reason Dickson wanted new quarters. Room 5 lacked the illumination needed for rapid photography. But vibration was also a problem. The lab building's wood frame was capable of transmitting the considerable whir that the two machine shops created when at work. The main shop was almost under the photo room on the first floor and the mechanism that drove the equipment was installed in the ceiling. John Ott's precision shop, on the second floor just down the hall from Room 5 set off its own tremors. Dickson had lived with these interferences since the building was occupied, but Batchelor probably surrendered when Dickson asked that the elevator be shut down while pictures were being taken.

The progress Dickson was making may have influenced Batchelor and once convinced, he had enough independence to approve the construction without specific consent from the boss. Construction began near the end of August, very near to the time that the first roll of Eastman's film arrived. It continued through September. It was a project with a work order number: carpenters, laborers, glazers, tinsmiths, tinkers, electricians, etc. were charged to the account so it is possible to track the pace of the work. Most of it was finished by the end of September (They knew how to get work done in those days!) and Dickson began using it immediately prior to Edison's return and before it was fully operational. Several steam fitters were at work during the week following Edison's return and various laborers continued to work on the building through the remainder of October. Among them was Dickson's friend, Eugene Lauste who said he was working on wiring in the building the day that Dickson demonstrated the Kineto to Edison.[240]

Dickson's design for the building anticipated the glass studios built during the first decades of movie production. It was constructed in two parts. On the lower floor there was a single story greenhouse-like structure with sliding glass windows on the front and back walls and a roof mostly of glass. The other part was two stories with two darkrooms on the first floor and an upper room for general use – Dickson called it

240 EHS, pay records & expenses, Equity 6928, Kineto work to date. It was order no. 342. Lumber began arriving on the 23rd and construction materials continued to arrive through much of September. Lauste's time was never charged to the account for constructing the photo building, but he was charged to "fitting up" on 9 October 1889.

a projection room. The greenhouse structure was the studio and one wall, the one closest to the darkrooms, had a recessed area with black walls and ceiling to provide a contrasting background for subjects photographed. The camera was positioned at the wall opposite the darkened recess with the subject to be photographed in front, bathed in natural light and contrasted against the light-absorbing black wall. (This design utilizing natural light to contrast the subject against a darkened background was featured later in the second studio, the Black Maria.) The new studio was near the ore milling building so it was convenient to activities in both of his projects. It was Dickson's main work area for the next three years, though he continued to use Room 5 as well.[241]

But not all of the films were shot in the new studio. An outdoor filming area was built on a sunny side of the ore milling building. There is no documentation to date the facility, but Dickson said the cylinder strips and earliest celluloid strips were photographed in the outdoor shed so it was probably completed before the studio – but it could have been built as late as 1890. Carpenters and pattern makers were available and charged to the Kineto account from time-to-time. There would have been reason to build it before the photo studio because there was barely enough light in Room 5 for timed exposures let alone rapid ones. Room 5 had the same windows as the rest of the lab and direct sunlight was hard to come-by. As Dickson told Will Day "... [I] could not do much taking in Room 5 ...". The alternative was artificial light and the staff at the lab, led by Arthur Kennely, were testing ways to improve arc lamps and other kinds of lighting. There were attempts to film with artificial light – but with only limited success. Fred Ott said that a version of "monkeyshines" was lighted by sparks from a Geissler tube or Leyden jar. The outdoor site also provided an alternative when the light in the new studio was unsatisfactory. Like the studio, the outdoor site was designed to film in sunlight against a recessed blackened area.

Although Dickson used imagination and his own experience to design these and a series of later studios, he had examples to adapt from. Professional photo studios made generous use of glass and illustrated articles discussing design solutions for various photo problems had appeared in the photographic press, so it would not have been difficult for him to find designs to suit his needs. His inspiration for the dark background was probably the descriptions of the darkened, light absorbent area used by Marey at his Photographic Station. Dickson could have read a fairly detailed description of this installation in an article by Marey in an 1887 issue of *Scientific American*:

"The condition most difficult of fulfillment is the absolute darkness of the screen before which we operate. Little light as this screen may reflect upon the sensitive plate during a single exposure, these small quantities of light, accumulating their effect over the whole surface of the plate, end by fogging it completely. A wall painted with any black pigment, velvet even, exposed to the sun, reflects too much light for a plate to withstand, that is of sufficient sensibility to receive at different points a long series of successive images.

241 This led to some confusion because the staff was apparently used to identifying photo activities as work in "Room 5" and this designation seems to have been applied to both photo locations.

Thus the term black screen is used metaphorically. The work is done before a dark cavity."[242]

Although Dickson may have found the vibration of the elevator a convenient justification for a new building, the continuing difficulty he had in getting images that were as sharp and well defined was a more plausible reason As he began making multiple exposures each second, the problem became more severe and it harried him for the next four or five years. The range of emulsions available to him was very limited so he needed a flood of light to capture the dozen or more images per second required to give the illusion of motion. The new glass photo-graphic studio with its darkened background, visits to Rochester and negotiations with other film dealers were efforts to resolve this persist-ent difficulty. The search for a sharp image with ideal contrast is the consistent theme of the years of experimentation and testing that followed the "breakthrough" in the summer of 1889. Dickson was a perfectionist and he was not satisfied with "almost good enough". It was a determined quest and his persistence, as much as any other factor, accounts for the years that passed before the public saw moving images.

What did Edison see and when did he see it?

Edison returned from his European trip on Sunday, 6 October and after talking to reporters at the dock, he apparently went to the lab for a brief visit. Dickson, who had a flair for the dramatic, had some sort of demonstration prepared to surprise the boss. There was the new build-ing, of course, but the flurry of activity just before the 6th, indicates that he had something else prepared. As Dickson described it to Will Day, "... I never worked so hard in all my life – day & most of the night struggling to accomplish things by the time E. returned – many days & weeks I slepped [sic] on the floor when exhausted my only companions the stoker & watchman!".[243] Dickson said that within an hour of Edison's return he led him to the new photo building. But did he?

Edison had been away for a long time – two months. He had been engulfed by a seemingly endless series of public events and social activities that he found disquieting. The familiar surroundings of the lab would have been welcome and comforting. He was not an observer of the Sabbath; and, since his wife had been with him, his family obligations were minimal. But the Kineto would not necessarily have been his first interest. Mining and the phonograph were immediate priorities and after returning he immersed himself in both of those projects. But regardless of other priorities, Edison would have wanted to know everything that went on in the lab during his absence – progress on the water and electrical systems, the electric railway as well as Dickson's work on the Kineto. The new photo building would have been hard to miss! So Dickson's Kineto show had a lot of first day competition. Rather than "within the hour" as Dickson claimed it probably happened when things were quieter. Wednesday, 9 October, or the following day, Thursday the 10th, look like more likely dates for

242 EHS. *Scientific American Supplement, No. 579*, 5 February 1887, p. 9245. "Photography of Moving Objects, and The Study of Animal Movement by Chrono-Photography." A reprint of a paper Marey presented to the French Association for the Advancement of Science, at Nancy, 1886. The second part appeared in the 12 February 1887, issue. Copies of both articles are in a collection of papers on moving image photography at the Edison Historic Site. They were evidently assembled for the patent lawsuits but may well have been in the library in 1889.

243 BiFi Fonds Will Day. Dickson to Will Day 12 March 1933.

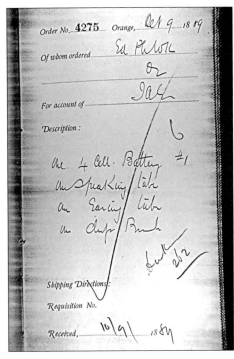

On 9 October 1889 the laboratory send a requisition for one 4-cell battery, one speaking tube and one "earing" tube to the Edison Phonograph Works. When received it was signed for by Dickson who charged it to no. 262, the Kinetoscope account.

This is evidence that Dickson was working on something related to the phonograph in the days after Edison's return from Paris (6 October 1889). [EHS.]

Dickson's show. On the 9th the Phono Works sent Dickson the "speaking" and "earing" tubes he ordered – the one indication that Dickson tried to join image with sound.

Dickson insisted that he showed Edison a strip machine – in fact, *the* strip machine – and his claim is supported by testimony given by his assistant Charles Brown, other Edison employees who worked on the Kineto and Edison himself – though the boss' several accounts are ambiguous. In 1900 Edison said: "I recall the fact that the moment I got back I went to see the Kinetoscope where they had worked it up to reproduce the films taken on the Kinetograph, and that they had it practically perfect, but there was no screen as Mr. Dickson says". Since the Kinetoscope is the name for the peep show machine, this has been interpreted as denying that Dickson projected a film. But it could be interpreted as supporting Dickson's claim since the question posed to Edison included a quote from the Dicksons' account in *The History of the Kinetograph* ... "The crowning point of realism was attained on the occasion of Mr. Edison's return from the Paris Exposition of 1889, when Mr. Dickson himself stepped out on the screen ...". "... there was no screen ..." could mean just that; no screen in the modern sense, but perhaps a sheet as Dickson said in at least one of his many accounts. But Dickson's critics have a point. Edison said he left instructions to make a prototype Kinetoscope viewer during his absence and there could have been a demo of a new version of that device. Or, possibly he saw both devices?

Although it is plausible that Dickson demonstrated something, the various accounts vary so much that it's impossible to conclusively establish what took place. Dickson's accounts are consistent in some details. In particular – that the arc lamp from the micro-photographic outfit was used with the camera to project; that the camera was modified in order to project the slightly shrunken film; and that Edison saw a scene in which Dickson, as the performer, "... raised my hat, smiled, and said, 'Good morning, Mr. Edison, glad to see you back. Hope you like the Kinetophone. To show the synchronization I will lift my hand and count up to ten."[244] This claim of synchronized counting clouds the issue. We have only Dickson's word and the inability of Edison to produce a marketable sound system for the next two decades makes Dickson's claim seem farfetched. Furthermore, the scene he describes would run about twenty-five to thirty seconds which is quite long considering the limited amount of film he had and his own description of the problems he encountered with first examples. But there is no question that the scene he describes was filmed at some point. Fragments of a similar scene, exhibited in 1891, survive. They show Dickson greeting the camera by tipping his hat to it and seemingly saying "good morning", but the scene was almost certainly filmed that in 1891 rather than 1889. Since it fit what he wanted to say he showed Edison, he may have changed the date of this later film to suit his story of events in 1889. But it is also possible that the same action was filmed two times. As the three surviving versions of "Monkeyshines" indicates, there were instances where almost duplicate scenes were taken, particularly during this test period. The existence of the later version clouds the claim that he showed something similar for Mr. Edison.

In Dickson's favor, it would have been in character for him to appear in his demo and without the attempt to count to ten, his claim is more plausible. Critics have speculated that he created some sort of impressionistic effect – a slide show, an Anschütz-type device or something similar, but there is evidence that he was able to film motion and had moved beyond creating effects and impressions. Greeting Mr. Edison would only take a few seconds of film time. Combining the two machines was a critical objective so it is possible that a recording with Dickson speaking accompanied his demonstration. Ear tubes were commonly use at that time so the requisition for an "earing tube" indicates that an attempt to create an impression of the two devices working together is possible.

Dickson said the demonstration was successful: "... There was no hitch, and a pretty steady picture".[245] But "success" is a relative term and, like beauty, depends on the beholder – and hearer. At this early stage, and after a succession of missteps, almost any image – and any sound – would have been accepted as an accomplishment. Around Edison's lab "perfect", "perfected" and "leaves little to be desired" were frequently used descriptives. They were often applied to new inventions that were far from perfect and required much reworking. The phonograph and ore milling machine had been "perfected" several

244 Dickson,
...*SMPE*, p. 13.
245 *Ibid.*

times, but were still being worked on and the work of "perfecting" lamps and electrical systems kept Edison's lab in business. The Kineto had a long way to go and others were not as enthusiastic about this early demo as Dickson.

There are other accounts of the event. Charles A. Brown said Edison saw the first image on the day he returned from Paris, but saw it on the prototype of the Kinetoscope: "While Mr. Edison was in Paris we built a machine for exhibiting the positives of the strip negatives. We built this according to Mr. Edison's directions which he had left when he went away, and it was a rough box made of pine with a peep-hole to look through and the films were run over wheels and there was a lamp beneath the film. This was exhibited to Mr. Edison on his return from Paris, with positives printed from negatives taken on the strip Kinetograph." According to his account, the projection was made two or three days later in the upstairs room of the new photo building and a curtain was put up to use as a screen.[246]

Dissenting testimony came from Dickson's friend Eugene Lauste who told Merritt Crawford that Dickson's projection was a failure. Lauste repeated his story in a subsequent letter to Will Day. He said he was in the photo building installing the screen when Edison arrived and that he hid because he was not supposed to be there. Dickson ran one of the few pictures he had on the Kinetograph camera, adapted for projection. "... unfortunately the pictures was blur and out of focus, also the film jump from the sprocket". Lauste explained that this was positive film which wouldn't fit the negative sprocket on the camera because it had shrunk during developing. "... conseqantly [sic] the show was a failure, and Mr. Edison leave the room with dissatisfaction." He denied that there was any attempt to synchronize sound and commented "My conclusion is that Mr. D. has told this story to so many people that he think now was a fact".[247]

Lauste is by no means the only person skeptical about Dickson's glowing account of successful synchronized projection. Although few have objected to Dickson's claim that he made a demonstration for Edison, film historians from Terry Ramsaye to Charles Musser have expressed skepticism about its success and many have doubted that it indicated an advance in the experiments. Lauste's assertion came in the midst of a debate between Merritt Crawford, Lauste, Will Day and Dickson. Crawford's comments to Day are typical:

"... I am inclined to concede that Dickson may have shown Edison on or soon after his return from Paris, a 'small picture' of himself on a glass cylinder synchronized with his greeting on a phonograph, or perhaps I should say *accompanied*, for that is far as I think they had progressed at that time. But as to there being any such thing as a 'projection' of the pictures, I cannot find a single bit of evidence, except Laurie Dickson's assertion and he has so frequently contradicted himself in the past, so often been shown to be inaccurate as to dates and other devalued of fact, that something more really is needed to convince me that any projection took place."

And went on to comment:

246 EHS. "Memorandum for Charles A. Brown. Film Suit." Prepared for Edison Mfg. Co. vs. Kleine Optical Co., et. al., 1908–1909. Brown was questioned 22 July 1908. Edison, Brown and Fred Ott gave similar testimony in 1900 in Equity 6928. Though Brown testified for Edison, he was not employed by Edison in 1900 nor in 1908.

247 MoMA, Crawford Collection. Lauste to Will Day, 30 May 1933. Dickson was incensed by Lauste's statement which Crawford included in an article. He told Day that Lauste did not see the successful demonstration but probably saw a later test that was a failure. BiFi Fonds Will Day, Dickson to Day, 8 May 1933. Though Lauste denied that the demo was successful, he is one of several who mentioned using the revised version of the strip Kinetograph.

"Bear this in mind. Laurie Dickson is an artist and a dreamer, as well as a brilliant engineer and inventor. What he can see in his mind he can draw upon paper. Later he may even believe that he saw the actual thing."[248]

A generation later, in 1961, Gordon Hendricks devalued Dickson's efforts even further: "... He [Edison] did not see ... a motion picture projection, although he may have seen a small device built by Dickson for viewing the microscopic pictures taken by Dickson on the cylinder machine. ..."[249]

But for Dickson this was a significant event and, though time and pride may have caused him to embellish it, it was not a flight of fancy. The prominent role it plays in his chronicles shows that he believed that it was important; a demonstration of progress that was a watershed in the experiments.

With his flair for drama, something audacious like projection with sound would have appealed to Dickson and would have pleased Edison who enjoyed a good show. There had been some test projection of single cylinder images, but moving images were a different matter. The obstacles were formidable. To create the illusion of movement the images had to be recorded at high speed – the caveats said at least eight to ten per second. Projected images had to run at the same speed and a strong, focused light was necessary. Each image had to be interrupted as it passed the lens either by stopping it or breaking the scene with a revolving shutter, otherwise the images would be blurred. They had only negative film and while it could be projected it required more light and is difficult to view since the light values are reversed – black is white, white is black and many areas are confusing blends of grey. Dickson had no print stock other than the stiff sheets of celluloid and so he created the effect of a positive by chemically altering negative film.

According to Dickson the strip machine was used for the projection. The arc lamp from the Zeiss micro-photographic outfit was the light source. To convert the Kineto for projection the sprockets were changed to fit the projection copy which shrank and was enough smaller than the negative film that it would tear or ride off the sprockets used in taking images. Viewing copies were essential to test results, but was the strip machine ready to be used for projection? Edison's critics and many historians claim that the strip machine was built later and could not have been used in the fall of 1889. An impressive number of those who worked on it say that it was, but they testified at a later time and in support of Edison in his court cases. But there is evidence that argues for Dickson's claim. Some has already been introduced and there will be more. Since the date of the shift to film strips is a contentious issue that has often been misstated and misconstrued, it will be necessary to keep it in focus.

Beginning in late November 1889 the lab began ordering film custom cut to ¾ inches by 54 feet, a size tailored for the strip Kineto. This came during a period when the amount of work charged to the Kineto account dwindled perceptibly. The intense pace of the summer and early fall slackened after Edison's return. Dickson had an important ore milling assignment that took priority and except for the week

248 BiFi Fonds Will Day. Crawford to Will Day, 31 May 1933.

249 Hendricks, *The Edison Motion Picture Myth*, p. 80.

between Christmas and New Years, all of Dickson and Brown's time was charged to ore milling and the only work charged to the Kineto account was for an occasional machinist or pattern maker. This more leisurely pace continued during most of 1890. There were no all night sessions and little or no overtime, lending support to the claims that the basic structure of the strip machine was finished before Edison's return.

But if the strip machine was used, the images that were projected must have been very primitive and certainly not as perfect as Dickson claimed. Also, if Eastman's new film was used, Dickson worked very efficiently because he had little margin for error since there was not much to work with. He had only one roll of 48 exposure film, 3¼ inches wide perhaps supplemented by some short samples given by Eastman. The second roll was not received until 14 October, a week after Edison's return. Given the problems with the emulsion encountered on early rolls of Eastman film, he would have been very limited in his options. The stiff celluloid sheets which they cut and joined into lengths with primitive splices could not have been projected on the strip machine.

Whatever Edison saw must have been short – a brief wave and tip of Dickson's hat – and the count to ten seems unlikely. The emulsions were slow so it would have been possible to take only a few exposures per second – barely enough to show movement. The image was probably dark, possibly blurred and the slow rate of exposure would have caused flicker. Imperfect and unacceptable by today's standards, but any image that moved would have delighted Edison and even if it was indistinct it would have been an accomplishment with promise for the future. Dickson said that Edison was pleased with what he saw, but pleased or not, he curtailed work on the Kinetoscope because Dickson was needed to for additional work on the ore separator. The Kineto was far from perfect and there was a great deal of work to be done, but the busy, eventful summer was over, fall was in the air and Edison was launching one of his most ambitious projects. He planned a huge plant for concentrating iron ore at a mine in Northern New Jersey. For the next year and a bit more the Kineto was the step child of ore milling.

Chapter 13

Caveat, Film, an Announcement and a Conundrum: The Kineto After Paris

"... The sensitive film is in the form of a long band passing from one reel to another in front of a square slit ... on each side of the band are rows of holes exactly opposite each other and into which double toothed wheels pass on [as] in the wheatstone automatic telegraph instrument. This ensures a positive motion of the band. (Caveat no. 117, 16 December 1889)

... The experiments were perfectly successful and are now concluded, the next stage being the development of the commercial side of the invention and the creation for a demand for the new process."[250] (*The Orange Chronicle*, 1 February 1890)

Although Dickson returned to devoting most of his time to the ore separator and tests of various ore samples, he still found time to improve the Kineto and though Edison was increasingly distracted by his iron ore ventures, he sent the fourth and final caveat for the Kinetoscope to the Patent Office and made the first public announcement of work on the device.

Caveat No. 117

Edison drafted the caveat in early November and it was submitted to the Patent Office on 16 December 1889. Like the two previous caveats, No. 117 was combination of claims covering a number of projects that Edison was overseeing. The Kinetoscope was items number 46 and 47 which were sandwiched between a device to make use of waste chimney heat and a recording and reproducing diaphragm for a phonograph. It was a radical revision. It was a camera and a projector which used a long strip of sensitive film which passed from one reel to another. The film was advanced by a "toothed wheel" (i.e. a sprocket) which engaged two parallel rows of holes on either side of the film. As a camera the strip ran in front of a micro-photographic apparatus and was stopped for

250 NMAH
Hendricks.

exposure by an escapement connected to a polarized relay. This was timed so that the film was at rest 9/10ths of the time for exposure and in motion 1/10th of the time to advance the film to the next unexposed portion. The relay was run by a motor, preferably an electric motor. The caveat stated that this formula would produce "perfect results" if ten exposures were taken each second, though it indicated that more might be made. Ten exposures per second eliminated the need for a shutter. For projecting, the film could be illuminated by a Leyden jar or by a continuous light. The Leyden jar would be timed to illuminate the film while it was at rest but if continuous light was used, a revolving shutter would be necessary for intermittence. The system could be connected to a phonograph and it mentioned using a cylinder as well, but neither of these alternatives were illustrated or described in detail. There was no mention of viewing in a peep-show device.

The shift from cylinders to strip film is the caveat's most obvious innovation, but there are other equally interesting features. The formula for film exposure is especially noteworthy. The quest for improved light and better image convinced Dickson that for optimum quality the film should be stopped as long as possible and the period for advancing the film kept at a minimum. His conclusion was that the film should be stationary 9/10ths of the time and in motion 1/10th. It is not clear how this formula was reached but it became a fixture for describing the requirements for taking moving images that was accepted by both Edison and Dickson. It was specified in Edison's patent application for the Kinetograph and used by his lawyers in the subsequent patent suits. In 1891, Dickson used it to explain his exposure problems to George Eastman. While it is not clear that it was put into practice, it is a reminder of the key role that exposure played in designing the Kineto.

Caveat 117 also introduced Edison's unique and enduring contribution to film technology, the use of holes in the film (perforations) which were engaged by sprockets to advance the film. We will discuss this more detail later, but it is important and its debut should not be overlooked. Although Edison had first crack at it, Eastman's strip film was soon available to others, but it was Edison who introduced the perfs and sprockets that facilitated the movement of film through cameras and viewing machines. Interestingly, the caveat specified two rows of perforations, one on each side of the image (actually on the top and bottom of the film strip because it ran horizontally). This was at variance with the strip Kinetograph, which used only one row of perfs. In the first design these were at the top but were moved to the bottom to improve stability. The use of a double row came later when a camera using larger film was designed and this may be another indication that the camera using a single row of perfs had already been built when the caveat was drafted.

The drawings that accompanied the caveat show that Edison's Kineto was similar to Marey's strip camera – but it was also very much like Eastman's Kodak camera. All three cameras had very simple mechanisms. A strip of film moved from a feed roller to the lens via a guide.

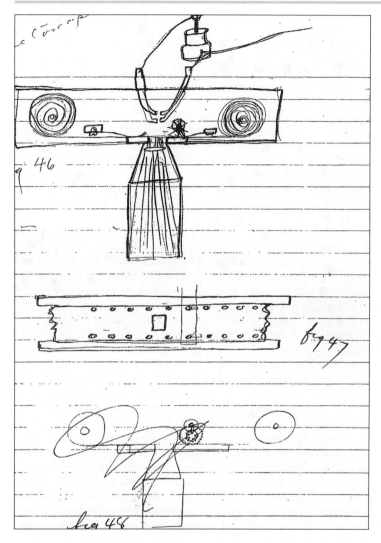

The film stopped during exposure then advanced to a take-up reel. There were no additional roller-guides or devices to reduce tension as the film started and stopped. The difference between the three cameras was the speed of movement and the continuing exposure in Marey and Edison's cameras. Edison's was the only one that used sprockets engaging with holes to guide the film and keep it from slipping. Marey's roll film camera was only one of a number that he designed for the study of human and animal movement and used several different methods of providing intermittence depending on what sort of action he wished to analyze.

Marey and Edison owed something to George Eastman's associate William Walker who designed Eastman's roll holder in 1885. It was

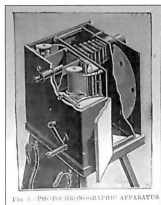

Fig. 5. PHOTOCHRONOGRAPHIC APPARATUS.

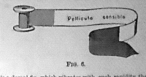

the beart, and which produce also the expansion of liquid. Ten images per second suffice to obtain (as Fig. I) a pretty complete series of the phases of the motion. My photographs were obtained under the following conditions.

The back of the aquarium was dark, and the animal brightly illuminated from above, stood out in a light color. These images, like all those that correspond to periodical motions, gain much by being examined in the zoetrope, wherein they reproduce, with absolute perfection, the aspect of the animal in motion.

Motion of the Hyppocampus. — The principal propeller of this animal (which is vulgarly known as the sea horse)

Fɪɢ. 6.

is a dorsal fin, which vibrates with such rapidity that it is almost invisible, and has an appearance analogous to that of the branches of a tuning fork in motion. With twenty images per second, it is seen (Fig. 6) that this vibration is undulatory, and we have before us the successive deviations of the lower, middle, and upper rays of the fin. In the present case, the undulation takes place from the bottom upward. These images are too small and too few to permit of grasping all the detail of the motions, but it would be easy to increase the number of them, and to make them larger

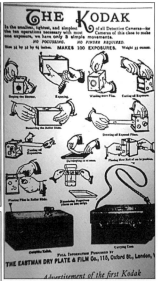

Advertisement of the first Kodak

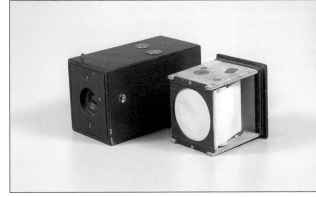

Both pages: *Marey and Edison owed a debt to Eastman whose roll system advanced photographic material through a camera. Marey's 1889 camera is above and below it is a photo of the Kodak no. 1 camera in the collection of George Eastman House (courtesy of Todd Gustafson, Curator Technology Collection). On the right is a contemporary ad for the camera. Edison's sketch for Caveat No. 117 is opposite.* [LC & GEH.]

Eastman's roll holder and the subsequent Kodak camera that demonstrated the basic method for feeding a strip past a lens.

While the laboratory had not bought a Kodak camera, the Phonograph Works, which was next door, ordered one at the end of May 1889. Edison had undoubtedly seen this camera – and presumably, Dickson as well – for among the many things bundled with the strip Kineto into Caveat 117, was an interesting innovation: "For determining the position of the sun and horizon at sea use a kodak instantaneous photograph apparatus and afterwards measure the distance on the photograph. This would render artificial horizons unnecessary, and probably the photo by proper glasses for screening could get position even in a fog ...". While it is not very clear what was intended by this inovation, it indicates that Edison had handled a Kodak camera in more than a cursory fashion. In late October the Lab ordered "One [medium sized] Portable Kodak Camera [Complete]" which was charged to the account of Thomas Edison. It was received on 23 November 1889, after the Caveat was drafted, but before his lawyers sent it to Washington.[251]

The caveat described a device that was similar to, but not identical with, the strip machine that was later shown and testified about in the court cases. The drive mechanism shown in the Caveat version was

251 EHS. The Phonograph Works ordered the Kodak Camera 30 May 1889. It was apparently received in June 1889 just before the intense work on the Kineto began. The camera received from Scovill and Adams in November 1889 was apparently a Kodak no. 1, though Kodak was just introducing their number 2 model.

simpler than the version that was built. In their testimony, Brown and Kayser said the mechanism was modified during the winter of 1889–1890, after the Caveat was submitted. The strip machine was driven by two motors, rather than one.

Edison's "far-sight" machine

In Paris, and on his return, Edison revived his story of working on a "far-sight machine", and it is difficult to understand why. The Kineto was in a rudimentary state and he never seriously experimented with sending images or sound through the ether. Perhaps his memory was jogged the previous June when A. Dalgleish of Edison & Swan United Electric Light, London wrote that London papers were reporting that Edison was working on a "far-sight machine" for electrical transmission of visual images which was to be ready by 1892. Dalglcish complained that since he had represented Edison for eight or nine years he should have been informed if the reports were true. "A 'Telechroscope' ... would without doubt find a vast field of practical usefulness ...".[252] Dickson's progress may also have encouraged Edison but the Kineto was still veiled in secrecy. Perhaps the far-sight story kept moving images in the public mind while diverting attention away from what he was really going on. On the other hand, it is possible that he actually believed he might move on to something like television. Not yet, however. The siren lure of the Ogden mine – and the potential wealth that iron and steel promised – drew his attention away from images and ether.

Although the Kineto was not able to send images through the air, it was still a work in progress. But with mines, ores and separation consuming much of Dickson's time the work on it continued at a noticeably slower pace. Improvements were made during the fall and winter. In November and December a machinist, Herman Wolke, worked on it almost every day. Another machinist, Hugo Kayser worked three full days and parts of two other days during November and in 1900 Kayser testified that he made changes to the intermittent movement. Dickson and Brown returned to the project at the end of December, but only part time. In mid-January Brown's tour came to an end. He was not replaced, but he helped Dickson with a photographic project during the last week of the month. During that week Sam Allen, a carpenter, worked in the photo room for several hours.

Marrying film and Kineto

Sometime during the fall or winter they designed and built a device to prepare film for the Kineto. The first two rolls Dickson received were Kodak camera film, designed to take 48 exposures that were 3 ¼ inches in diameter. In November Dickson ordered six rolls and requested they be cut to a width of ¾ inch, the size that fit the strip machine. He had established his working relationship with Eastman and they agreed to cut the rolls to his specified size. He sent a clarifying letter on 20 November 1889: "... I should like if possible to get you to see that it is   252 EHS.

clear ¾" (full) – no less. I shall require a considerable number of these rolls should my experiments turn out O.K. I am specially anxious to secure from you a non frilling film which I don't doubt but that your present film proves to be." He went on to congratulate them on the product. "I have often thought that colodion [sic] would be a perfect substitute for glass etc. except for the shrinking in drying, etc. Now that acetate of amyl is used by you for a solvent and [you] have so perfectly succeeded in getting up a process for procuring these long sheets I consider you have a magnificent thing. Have used this material but in a small scale and hoped that someone would put such an affair on the market. I see my enthusiasm has run away with my pen which I hope you will excuse."[253]

These letters were addressed from his home, 166 Cleveland Street in Orange. Dickson was negotiating with Eastman outside the normal Edison purchasing procedures but apparently with tacit approval because the six rolls were delivered to the lab in December. The tone of his letter makes it clear that his enthusiasm for Eastman's long, flexible strips was genuine. His comment that Eastman used amyl acetate to make the celluloid base shows that he was familiar with Eastman's manufacturing process.

He had problems with these strips as indicated in the next order which was sent on 19 February 1890. This one specified film one inch wide. The previous film, "¾ (full) – no less", was either not cut evenly or there was not enough room for the image and a row of sprocket holes. At any rate, the order was now for film a little wider than needed. It would be trimmed to fit the camera at the lab. Sometime during this period a combination film-trimmer and perforator was designed and built, presumably by February when the one-inch film was received.

The perforator was adapted from one designed earlier for a telegraph machine and it was combined with two parallel metal wheels whose sharpened edges trimmed the excess off the film. The device was driven by a sewing machine treadle which advanced the film from a feeding reel into the trimmer–perforator then onto a second take-up reel. It was a delicate operation which had to be done in the dark or the unexposed film would be spoiled.

The trimming-perforating device mounted on its sewing machine treadle appears in a photograph of the strip Kinetograph submitted as evidence in the Edison-American Mutoscope case. In his testimony Hugo Kayser identified himself and described both the strip Kinetograph and the perforator. It was taken in the spring of 1890, he said.

"Well, that is myself ... at the machine. After a test I took it apart or took the cover off, and Mr. Dickson happened to want to test a camera and was looking around for something to take, and I said 'Take me with the machine,' and he did. ... [Question by Edison's attorney, Mr. Dyer:] On your right in the picture I see something on a table which looks like a sewing machine table; what is that machine on the table? [Answer by Kayser:] That is the punching machine that we used for punching the strips by foot power ..."[254]

253 GEH; NMAH Hendricks Collection. Hendricks obtained these letters from Eastman Kodak and his copies are typescripts.

254 EHS. Equity 6928, pp. 126–127. Testimony of Charles H. Kayser, 30 January 1900.

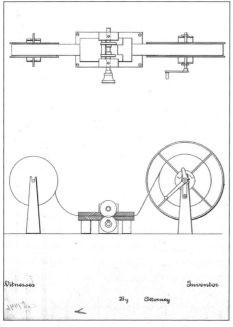
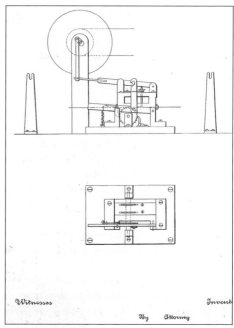

To prepare film for exposure it had to be trimmed to the correct width and perforated. Dickson designed separate devices and proposed patenting them. In practice the two devices were combined into a single mechanism driven by a sewing machine treadle. The work was done by an assistant working in the dark. [EHS.]

This photo was almost certainly taken between 1 October 1889 and 8 May 1890 and it is the most convincing evidence that the strip Kinetograph was completed in 1889, or, at the very latest, early in 1890. Kayser, one of the better paid machinists on the staff, worked briefly on the Kineto during the fall of 1889 and as a sort of temporary assistant for seven weeks in April–May, 1890.[255] Kayser had two other brief assignments with the Kineto, three days in May, 1893 and he was assigned to secretly work in New York City on a projector in the fall of 1894. His tour in April 1890 seems the most likely time that this photograph was taken, though it could have been earlier. The distinctive round image is characteristic of the Kodak No. 1 camera and the lab purchased one which was received Saturday, 23 November 1889. Kayser worked the following Monday, the 25th and if Dickson wanted to test the new camera, it could have been taken then. However, since the photo shows the Kineto and the perforator-trimmer in virtually complete condition, it seems likely that April is more probable.[256]

Kayser's testimony about the Kineto is quite specific. He said that it was virtually complete when he first worked on it and that he made improvements to the stop mechanism, i.e. the intermittent movement. "I tried to improve it, yes sir. Sometimes it worked satisfactory and sometimes it did not, so we wanted to get something positive, but it was

255 EHS. Kayser did his first work on the Kineto on 1 October 1889. He worked five days during the period when Dickson was preparing for Edison's return, another five days in November 1889, 18–21 November and 25 November. His full-time stretch was from 26 March 1890 until 8 May 1890.

256 The strip machine can be seen at the Edison Historic Site in West Orange, New Jersey. It is virtually the same as the camera in the photograph of Kayser except that the camera in the photo does not have a revolving shutter and the canisters containing film are missing. They would be on either side of the lens.

positive in one way, only you could not depend on it entirely, because sometimes it was a little hitch in the machinery on account of being a experimental machine."

Kayser's testimony fits with the on-going pursuit of a reliable method for exposing the film. Dickson credited Edison with the design of an intermittent movement which improved reliability: "... a slotted circular plate on which a tooth attached to a wheel was made to rest, sliding along the surface ... and on reaching the slot tooth ... being at rest the period in which it was sliding ...". Edison's device was included in his application for the patent and was eventually patented separately.[257] It's not clear that Edison made his contribution this early, but his contribution is one more indication of the important place that stopping the film for exposure held.

There were other modifications during this period. Charles Brown mentioned that after he left in January extra pulley wheels were added to help guide longer lengths of film. He called these small changes.

257 This device was patented in 1893, U.S. Patent No. 491,993, Stop Device, 21 February 1893, Original application filed 24 August 1891, Serial No. 403,535 was divided and this application filed on 11 April 1892, Serial No. 423,614.

The earliest photograph of the strip Kinetograph was probably taken prior to May 1890. Charles Kayser is posed with the machine and the sewing machine treadle-operated trimmer-perforator can be seen in the background at the left. The Kinetograph is supported by cases used for the batteries that drove the motors. Kayser said that Dickson had a new camera he wanted to test and took this "snap" of the Kinetograph. This is consistent with size of the image and its circular shape which conform to the image produced by the Kodak No. 1 camera. May 1890 is the last month that Kayser worked with Dickson (not to scale). [EHS.]

The pace of work was regular during this period with no spurts of intense activity like those before and after Edison's trip to Paris. During January there were intermittent periods when two, and sometimes three machinists worked on the Kineto, but the pace slowed during February and March. Dickson charged a week in January to the Kineto account, then spent half-weeks during the last two weeks in February and first three weeks in March. Kayser began his tour at the end of March and stayed as a sort of temporary assistant until the first week in May and during April Dickson worked half weeks with him. On 9 May, all work on the Kineto stopped and was not resumed until the following October. The ore-mill at Ogdensburg needed Dickson's attention and Edison had already told the public that the Kineto was ready.

"To catch a speaker's gestures"
Introducing the Kineto

At the beginning of February Edison allowed the press to report the Kineto project for the first time. On 1 February 1890 the *Orange Journal*, the local weekly, ran an article "Another of Edison's Wonders". It began "For many months past Mr. Edison has been at work on a series of experiments in instantaneous photography which have been at last successfully concluded". It went on to say that it would be possible to photograph "... a public speaker ... eight or twelve times a second throughout his entire speech, the subject matter being at the same time recorded by the telephone", and the images and sound could be reproduced on a screen.

This launched the first wave of publicity about the Kineto. The next day a similar article, "To Catch a Speaker's Gestures", perhaps written by the same person, appeared in *New York Herald*. The story was picked up by two papers in nearby Newark, the *Morning Advertiser* in London and *Nachrichten*, Hamburg, Germany. Not everybody was impressed. The *Morning Advertiser* spoke glowingly of the possibility of preserving the words and images of famous people for future generations, but warned that it would capture flaws as well and could "... add a new terror to [the] life" of public figures. The *Pall Mall Gazette*, London, commented that "Mr. Edison has added a new horror to existence. ... the oration can be re-delivered *ad infinitum*".[258]

This first foray of publicity was brief and isolated. Although there was interest, it was hardly a sensation. Edison's recent and more sensational claim of sending voices and images through the air may have made this less appealing. There is no hint of why Edison let the story be published. He may have been testing public interest because he told the reporters he was uncertain about its commercial future. The report was generated by a local resident, a newspaperman, who learned something about the experiments and approached Edison who let him publish the story – with some Edisonian embellishment. Orange was a small town and most of the lab staff lived there. The reporter for the

258 EHS Clippings Files; NMAH Hendricks. *Morning Advertiser*, London, on 4 February 1890.*Pall Mall Gazette*, London, 3 February 1890 and *Nachrichten*, Hamburg, 5 February 1890.

Herald, who may also have written the article in the *Orange Journal*, mentioned in his story that he lived near the lab and talked to experimenters who "... are continually hearing of wonderful things that he [Edison] has done or is doing ... It was only by accident the other day that I got a clew to a series of remarkable experiments which have been silently going on for nearly a year past and which have been brought to a successful conclusion and – dropped". He then described in detail, experiments to photograph a bullet in flight (the only account anywhere of such experiments). He followed this with a more general account of recording a public speaker, preacher or lecturer and reproducing the speech with images and sound.

Edison cautioned the reporter that he was skeptical about how practical the Kineto would be. "What the commercial value of the invention may be is yet to be decided. It cannot fail to be intensely interesting as an exhibition feature, but whether it will fill a useful niche in the everyday life of the world is another question entirely." He added that "Mr. Edison is not pushing the matter at present, being absorbed in his experiments on electrical traction for street cars. When that problem is decided he may bring this new invention prominently before the public." The article in the *Orange Journal* reported that "The experiments were perfectly successful and are now concluded, the next stage being the development of the commercial side of the invention and the creation for a demand for the new process".[259] Even though the experiments were called "perfectly successful" Edison was not ready to show the Kineto. There was no demonstration for the press or the public. It would be more than a year before it was exhibited to outsiders and another four before commercial release.

Edison may also have been motivated by publicity about the experiments of Anschütz, Marey and Friese-Greene. During 1889 and 1890 there were a number of articles about and exhibits of Ottomar Anschütz's Electric Tachyscope. Articles about Anschütz and his Tachyscope appeared in *Report of the Society of Amateur Photographers*, *The American Annual of Photography*, *Philadelphia Photographer* and *Science*. In November *Scientific American* reported that the Tachyscope was being exhibited by C.B. Richards & Co., 3 East 14th St., NYC. Edison saw a Tachyscope in Paris, met Marey, saw Marey's devices and received a copy of *Les Vol des Oiseax*, Marey's book on the flight of birds. Edison or Dickson may have seen an article about Friese-Greene which appeared in *The Optical and Magic Lantern Journal* in November and it is possible they examined his patent. Friese-Greene claimed he sent a copy to Edison in June, immediately after filing it. Dickson denied ever seeing it and there is no communication from Friese-Greene in the surviving Edison correspondence before March, 1890. Even if they had not received the copy from Friese-Greene, the texts of patents were published and staff at the lab probably kept as current on new patents as they could considering their busy schedules.[260] It would have been difficult for them to be unaware of the growing public interest in moving pictures.

259 NMAH Hendricks.

260 EHS, NMAH Hendricks, Deac Rossell, *Ottomar Anschütz and His Electrical Wonder*.

"... actual performances of living beings."
The Lenox Lyceum Show

The interest in Anschütz's Tachyscope may have stimulated work at Edison's lab. Dickson may have worked on a similar device in January 1890, either as a new project, or an update of the Anschütz-inspired cylinder experiment. Early in the December 1889 the lab received two dozen 3¼ in. x 4 in. transparency plates and two dozen glasses for lantern slides, also 3¼ x 4, along with mats and borders for lantern slides. During the last week of January Charles Brown and Dickson had a half week of their time charged to the photo room. This is the same time that carpenter Sam Allen worked several days in the photo room.

Gordon Hendricks believed Dickson was building a Tachyscope or a similar device which was used later in an exhibit which opened in April 1890 at the Lenox Lyceum in New York. An article by David Curtis in the Chicago *News* on 1 April 1890, described the exhibit which was an opportunity for New Yorkers to see the exhibit Edison presented at the Paris Exposition. The central feature was a tower eight feet in diameter and twenty-five feet high dressed in natural flowers and greens with fourteen streamers of green running to points in the hall. Edison's inventions were displayed in aisles radiating from the tower which was illuminated with five thousand colored electric lights. "... the tower is a thing of almost indescribable beauty. When these performances begin, however, the audiences can readily imagine themselves in fairy-land, for a magic lantern of almost unimaginable power casts upon the ceiling from the top of the tower such pictures as seem to be actual performances of living beings."[261]

Arrangements for the exhibit were made at the request of Henry Villard, the financier behind the Edison General Electric Co. Villard's wife was the member of a New York benevolent society which wanted to mount the exhibit as a fund raising activity. Edison was not particularly enthusiastic about this as his relations with Edison General Electric were souring, but he agreed to go ahead with it. In January he asked W. J. Hammer, his exhibit specialist, to take charge of it. Hammer agreed and designed some modifications for the New York site. Something related to moving images seems to have been part of this modification but what it was is an intriguing mystery.

Dickson may have been asked to prepare something for the Lenox Lyceum. He made photographs for the show in Paris and the photo work at the end of January might have been for New York. Hendricks theorized that the two dozen 3¼ x 4 transparency plates and glasses for lantern slides received in December were suited for an Anschütz-type device and that this initiated Dickson's Tachyscope experiments. Since the plates were received a month before Edison charged Hammer with handling the exhibit, they were not specifically for the New York show. While it is possible that Dickson was experimenting with a Tachyscope, he may also have been making magic lantern slides for some other purpose. Edison was using microscopic and magic lantern slides to gather information about prospective ore deposits and Dickson was

261 EHS; Hendricks, Op. Cit. and NMAH Hendricks. Hendricks used an article describing the exhibit which appeared in *Western Electrician*, April 12, 1890 as indication that a Tachyscope device was shown at the Lenox Lyceum. The article in *Western Electrician* is a reprint of the article from the Chicago *News*.

now using the Zeiss micro-photographic device to photograph insects and germs. A Tachyscope device is one of several possibilities.[262]

Whatever was planned for the Lenox Lyceum, it apparently opened without any spectacular images on the ceiling. The effect as described by Chicago *News* is one that might have been made by Anschütz's device, but it is a description of what was intended, not what was seen by the public. The article was datelined New York, 25 March 1890, two weeks before the opening and it was published in Chicago on 1 April, a week before the exhibit's opening on 7 April. Since the exhibit was still being set up when it was written, it was based on a press release or an interview with Hammer. Other than an article in *Western Electrician* which was based on Curtis' article, there are no other newspaper accounts of projections on the ceiling. After closing in New York, the exhibit moved to Minneapolis in late August and there was no mention of living pictures by newspapers in the Twin Cities.

There seems to have been a plan for some sort of spectacular movie-like device which was either cancelled or modified. Richard Outcault's description of the exhibit casts an interesting light on the question. The famous illustrator was Hammer's assistant in designing the exhibit for Paris and setting-up in New York. He was interviewed in the 1920s by *New York World* for an article "Creator of Yellow Kid Once Served Edison":

"... Then, early in 1890, an electrical exposition was held at the Lenox Lyceum in New York, to reproduce some of Edison's display at Paris, the proceeds going to charity. I was still on the job, as I had worked two expositions before that.

"We had a miniature theatre, showing what this world would be in a hundred years. One switch turned on condensed sunlight, another gave you moving pictures while you dined, the opera was brought to you by phonograph and movie. Much of this was anticipatory of what has subsequently become reality; but reality has far out-distanced our wildest imagination."[263]

In Outcault's description the movies were in a theater and not on the ceiling , but unfortunately, he shed no light on how the illusion of life in the 1990s was created. It might have been done by a Tachyscope but it is also possible that it was some sort of rapidly changing magic lantern. Hammer and Outcault undoubtedly saw the exhibit of Anschütz's device in Paris and might have tried to acquire one in Europe or even in the U.S. since it was being demonstrated in New York. There is even a possibility that in planning the show they considered using the Kinetoscope. In May 1891, when the Kinetoscope was demonstrated, *The Morning Journal* (New York) said "It was intended to exhibit it at the display of electrical inventions made at the Lenox Lyceum a year ago, but although a screen for the reproduction was even made, a hitch in the apparatus itself prevented it at the last moment".[264]

If Dickson designed something for the Lenox Lyceum it did not take a great deal of his time. This was a very busy period for him. Edison's growing interest in ore milling made heavy demands on his time and it is doubtful that he had time to design a new machine. An

262 EHS. The Zeiss micro-photographic outfit was received through James W. Queen & Co., Philadelphia, 18 March 1889 but the wood was warped and the lab complained to Queen. After several letters were exchanged, John Ott was asked to repair the device in June. It was apparently operational sometime during the summer of 1889.

263 EHS, unbound clippings; M146 – 588–589. Edison's exhibit opened at the Minneapolis Industrial Exposition, 21 August 1890. The copy of the article from the *New York World* in the Edison papers was undated, but from the 1920s. It also appeared in *The G.E. Monogram*, November 1928. Outcault was an Edison pioneer who got his first work as an illustrator in 1888 when he was hired by E.W. Hammer to assist with an exhibit of Edison devices in Cincinnati, Ohio. He helped design the exhibit in Paris and was allowed to study art while he stayed through the run of the exhibit. Drawings by Outcault illustrate the Dicksons' biography of Edison.

264 NMAH Hendricks. *The Morning Journal*, 29 May 1891 "Pictured on the Run." "Wizard Edison's Latest and Most Curious Invention."

exhibit of the Kinetoscope or another of his devices would have required preparation and installation but there was no concentrated
special effort by Dickson or the staff assigned to him during the weeks
before exhibit opened on 7 April. Neither Dickson nor anyone connected with the Kineto went to New York to install or train operators.[265]

Although there was no special effort on the Kineto before the
exhibit, there was one a month later. During the first week of May,
Hugo Kayser worked all night on Friday, 2 May: a ten hour day on
Saturday for a two day total of 36 hours and there was another all night
session Thursday, 8 May. This dove-tailed with some work in the Photo
Room because Eugene Lauste worked two hours on Saturday and an
unusual seven hours on Sunday. There is no clue what the objective
was but apparently they were tying-up loose ends. After 8 May Hugo
Kayser was shifted to work on a toy phonograph and, with the exception
of a quarter of the week of 16–22 May, in the Photo Room, Dickson
returned to full time work on ore milling.

This brought an end to the first phase of the Kineto experiment.
The budget account number 262 was closed and there were no further
charges for the Kineto until 10 October 1890. This five month suspension of activity, which coincided with the opening of the plant at Ogden,
was the longest interruption of the Kineto experiment.

We may never know what the audience at the Lenox Lyceum saw.
It seems destined to remain a mystery, but Richard Outcault's account
shows that at the beginning of the last decade of the 19th century the
public's interest in recordings of sound and moving images was strong
enough to make it a feature in a program speculating about the wonders
of the next century. Despite this bow to popular curiosity, Edison had
more immediate concerns. The Kineto experiments were postponed
while the wizard turned his attention to converting iron into gold.

265 EHS. Several
phonograph
specialists from the
lab were detailed to
the Lenox Lyceum to
make sure the
equipment operated
properly. Among
them were Edison's
most experienced
experts in
performance, Walter
Miller and Prof. A.
Theodore
Wangemann.
Canisters for
limelight were
ordered from T.H.
McCallister and
carbon for arcs from
E.S. Greeley & Co.
may have been for a
magic lantern used in
the exhibit.

Chapter 14

"We Had a Hell of a Good Time ...". Ore Milling and Electricity: Dreams and Reality

"We then started in a small way and continued making changes in the mills to meet conditions which arose from testing and have continued since that time to the present – The mills now being almost finished & tested."[266] (Thomas Edison, undated note, probably made during the summer or fall, 1890)

"When the General Electric Company was formed in 1892 Edison received stock in payment for his interest in the former concern. This stock was gradually sold out at the market by Edison to provide funds for carrying on his ore milling work. That you know was a failure owing to the discovery of the Mesaba [sic] mines After that failure, when Edison and Mallory were riding back on the train to West Orange, the former asked what the stock would be worth if he had hung on to it, and Mallory after finding the morning quotation said, "$5,000,000". Edison simply smiled and said, "That is a lot of money, but we had a hell of a good time spending it!"[267] (Frank L. Dyer to Francis Jehl, 29 August 1936)

Edison's conversation with Walter Mallory may be a parable, but if it took place, it would have been late in the 1890s or early in 1900. During the decade of the nineties Edison poured much of his energy and wealth in a vain effort to extract profitable iron ore from the rocks on a mountainside in northern New Jersey. This huge facility for mining and processing low grade iron ore at Ogden, New Jersey became Edison's obsession and is the most spectacular failure of his career. Although his losses may not have reached $5,000,000, his close associates placed the figure in the vicinity $2,000,000 – and this in 1890–1900 dollars. Considering that Dickson was regarded as well paid with a salary of $1,500 per year and workers at Edison's plants could survive on $15.00 per week, Edison's losses were huge, consuming his

266 EHS, Doc. Film Ser.: 1890: (D-90-49) – Mining – NJ & Pa. Conc. Wks.

267 Henry Ford Museum, Box 31–17. Dyer, Frank L. Correspondence. Dyer to Francis Jehl, Edison Institute, 29 August 1936.

wealth, time and energy. In retrospect it seems the height of folly – perhaps tinged with madness. Nevertheless, he had a "hell of a good time".

The Ogden project did not seem foolish when it began. Although he complained about the endless round of banquets and speeches, Edison was apparently buoyed up by his Paris experience. He launched a busy and intense period of work for himself and his staff. Dickson described the months after Edison's return as one of his busiest. In addition to the contract experiments for Edison General Electric there were a number of special projects. The phonograph had been "perfected", but problems arose during the exhibition in Paris and a crash project was started to revise the design. The electric powered locomotive remained a priority and a toy version of the phonograph was in the works, but the new mining and ore separating complex demanded more and more of his time.[268]

Encouraged by the test project in Bechtelsville, Pennsylvania, Edison turned his interest to a property near Ogden in northern New Jersey. Negotiations for mining rights started before he left for Paris and were completed after his return. For several months he had been surveying potential properties up and down the East coast and while negotiating for the Ogden property he intensified this search, ordering geological surveys from various places as far north as Canada and extending down into the Carolinas and Georgia. He was particularly interested in lands that had measurable quantities of magnetite. This iron ore, often trapped in rock, could be located with a compass so he set experimenters to work on improved surveying equipment which could locate magnetic deposits and provide estimates of the intensity of the field. Several specialists were sent on surveying trips and chief among them was Theodore Lehmann. A young German-born experimenter, he joined the staff in 1888, working with Jonas Aylsworth and Reginald Fessenden in the chemistry room. Lehmann was a skilled cellist who performed in concerts with Dickson and his sister. They became close friends and for a while he lived with the Dicksons.

It was Edison's ambition to exploit most, if not all of the low grade ore in the Eastern United States. His preliminary surveys indicated that there were huge deposits. Frank Dyer says Edison estimated that there were over 200,000,000 tons around the New Jersey property alone. He took out options on several properties that he felt were promising. The installation at Ogden was to be the prototype and once functioning, similar facilities would be set up at other locations. Edison was confident that he could produce quality ore, suitable to the needs of furnaces in the Eastern U.S. at a price that would compete with iron ore coming from mines being opened in Michigan and Minnesota. Ore from Lake Superior was relatively expensive because the limited capacity of the locks at Sault Ste. Marie made it costly and difficult to ship. When larger locks opened later in the '90s, Edison's prospects soured, but until then he was optimistic about the future.

The goal was to make money – lots of it. Samuel Insull's giddy

268 Tate, Op. Cit., pp. 270–272. A. O. Tate said "... at that time Edison was plunged in perhaps the heaviest work of his whole career ...".

comment in July, "... There is no doubt but that we are going to make a great deal of money in concentrating iron ores" typified the post-Paris mood among Edison and his close associates.

Although money was Edison's objective, it was not for comfort or power. He was not a greedy person. Even though he was wealthy, lived in a mansion in an exclusive suburb and wanted for very little in life, Edison was remarkably indifferent to money. The mansion, servants, carriages and other aspects of prosperity were for his wife. She came from a wealthy family and was accustomed to such things. A.O. Tate, who handled Edison's accounts at this time, said that Edison rarely carried money and if he went into New York City, Tate had to be sure he remembered to bring some along. He paid little attention to the way he dressed, wore the same outfit for days on end and was known to brag that he hadn't bathed for days and days. His tailor had his measurements and if he needed a new suit or shirt it was Tate, or Mrs. Edison who ordered it.[269]

Edison's urge for money was driven by a need to keep his experiments going and, more importantly, to gain independence from big money interests – the powerful investors who controlled the stock market as well as the telegraph, telephone and electrical industries that engaged the lab for research. Edison had served all of them and watched them increase their wealth, aided and abetted by his innovations. While he had prospered too, he resented the way they had muscled him out of the top echelons and criticized or interfered with the way he experimented on their behalf. The more unfettered wealth he had, the more independent experimenting he could do. Projects like ore milling and reproducing motion depended on a reserve of independent cash.

Financing the lab was a nagging problem that never quite went away. At the beginning of 1890 he jotted down notes about how to improve his cash flow – to improve his income while not reducing the funds available for experiments. From Edison's viewpoint, two of his most important supporters, Edison General Electric and North American Phonograph were behind on their payments for research. But money was not his only concern. He was worried about his long-term relations with Edison General Electric and the direction that the electrical business was going . The market for the phonograph was not developing the way he had hoped. To add to his business problems, in early January he received news that Marion, the daughter he called "Dot", was critically ill with smallpox in Dresden, Germany where she lived. Her illness was a serious worry because smallpox was often fatal or crippling. A few years earlier a favorite nephew, Charles, who had been his assistant, died suddenly while in Paris. Marion recovered, but the news came after several weeks of serious worry. Soon after receiving this welcome news Edison, who seems to have been susceptible to winter illness, came down with a bronchial infection.[270] In early February, shortly after the press announcement of the Kineto, he decided to go to North Carolina to combine rest with an exploration of potential ore sites.

269 EHS, Israel, Op. Cit., pp. 344–362; Tate, Op. Cit. pp. 124–127

270 Conot, Op. Cit., pp. 155–156, 290–291.

Electrical troubles

Before leaving for Carolina he wrote Henry Villard, who controlled Edison General Electric, a long, dismal letter complaining about finances and the prospect of having to borrow money from Villard's company.

"... I lose confidence in this kind of financing. I have been under a desperate strain for money for 23 years, and when I sold out [at the formation of EGE], one of the greatest inducements was the sum of cash received, which I thought I could always have on hand, so as to free my mind from financial stress, and thus enable me to go ahead in the [technical] field. ... I had an income of $250,000 per year, from which I paid easily my laboratory expenses. This income by the consolidation was reduced to $85,000, which is just sufficient to run the Laboratory. I do about $20,000 worth of work for the General and local Companies of such a nature that I can't charge for it, and devote about half my time to the same work. ... I feel that it is about time to retire from the light business and devote myself to things more pleasant, where the strain and worry is not so great."[271]

Even though worries about paying for experiments were on-going, Edison resisted limiting the money spent on experiments. Regardless of his financial condition, if he felt that the potential results justified it he would spend large sums. But when things got really bad there were periods of retrenchment and the size of the staff was reduced and experiments were discontinued. But experimenting only stopped if the results did not justify continuing. At the beginning of 1890 he was not in bad shape personally. A note to Drexel Morgan, 6 January 1890, asked to confirm the previous balance in his account which was $465,440.25 on 14 November 1889.

The lab was negotiating with Edison General Electric for new arrangements to fund experiments. The discussions were protracted, stretching-on almost a year from the fall of 1889 until October 1890. Edison's relations with the growing electrical giant was further complicated by disagreements within EGE about how to deal with the increasingly vigorous competition from their rivals, Westinghouse and the firm of Thomson-Houston. An element of the disagreement was the debate over the relative merits of alternating vs. direct current. Westinghouse and Thomson-Houston were installing generating stations using alternating current. Citing safety considerations, Edison was opposed to alternating current in urban installations, but other executives in Edison GE felt that they should be flexible and consider also using alternating current. There was talk of merging with one or both of the competitors. Internal management squabbles and the threat of mergers raised the specter of refinancing the parent company and the potential return of dominance by the Morgan interests. When EGE was created, Villard had secured principle investment from friends in his native Germany and had managed to keep Drexel Morgan in a minor role. This pleased Edison, but he was nervous about any potential change. Edison's long letter to Villard in February, 1890 was triggered by a request from Villard that Edison give up 1,000 shares of EGE so the Vanderbilt interests could enter the company. Edison was disturbed

271 EHS, Edison to Villard, 8 February 1890. This letter was written at the time that Charles Brown was laid off.

by the suggestion because he felt that Vanderbilt and Morgan had close ties.[272]

In October 1890 Edison General Electric and the lab signed a contract supporting Edison's research for five years. Edison agreed to devote half of his research time and three-quarters of his laboratory staff to research for EGE. In return they would pay about $1200 per week to the lab and Edison would receive a royalty for profits from his inventions. EGE also paid $33,000 for work done during the previous year and a half. Even though this firmed up the lab's relations with the electrical company, Edison was winding down his involvement in company affairs. He had suggested that he might end his involvement with the electrical industry in his letter to Villard and he apparently was quite sincere. As his interest in iron grew, his active participation in the affairs of the electrical companies diminished. Edison complied with the agreement and continued to experiment in electricity, but his energy was directed towards making the ore-mill a success.

Ogden, leveling a mountain

Construction of the ore separator in Ogden was underway by late December, 1889 and in January, 1890 more than 100 carpenters, masons and laborers were employed.[273] Before Edison left for Carolina, he put Harry Livor in charge of construction, relieving Livor of responsibility for the plant at Bechtelsville, Pennsylvania. Edison said he wanted to oversee the Pennsylvania plant so that he could learn more about the operation. "… in view of the extent to which I am going into mining … I want to learn the business from actual experience." Problems were developing at the Pennsylvania plant that soon caused him to shut the facility down, but these did not deter Edison who liked to learn from mistakes.[274]

The size and complexity of ore separating facility at Ogden, NJc an be judged from this picture Dickson made in the summer of 1894. [EHS.]

272 EHS & Israel, Op. Cit., pp. 321–337. Critics considered Edison particularly stubborn in opposing alternating current, accusing him of being close-minded. Recent scholarship seems to take the more moderate view that in the early years Edison had sincere doubts about the safety and practicality of alternating current and that he did experiment to see if safe and economic systems could be devised. The complicated relations between Edison and the electric companies is beyond the scope of this book. I found Paul Israel's summary the most useful.

273 EHS, G.W. Ruckold told Harry Livor he had 104 men at work on 3 January 1890. Ruckold wanted some small change so that he could take money for lodging out of the pay envelopes of employees whose names were "X".

274 EHS, Edison to Livor, 27 January 1890. Livor was general manager of the New Jersey and Pennsylvania Concentrating Works, the parent company operating the facilities at Bechtelsville and Ogden. Livor was based in New York City at 19 Dey Street.

The Ogden plant was much larger and more ambitious than the one in Pennsylvania or Mallory's in Michigan. Edison had detected iron ore extending deep into the earth, much of it imbedded in rock. He planned to strip mine, eventually leveling a mountain. Once it was operational, huge steam shovels loaded massive rocks, some as large as five or six tons, on narrow gauge railway cars which carried them to a mill where they were put through a series of iron rollers which gradually crushed the rock to the fine powder. The biggest pair of rollers were solid iron, six feet wide, five feet in diameter and weighing 167,000 pounds. After crushing, the powder was put through a large dryer, conveyed to the top of the separator and dropped past a succession of magnets which drew the powdered iron away from non-magnetic waste. Edison hoped to process six thousand tons of ore per day.

Explosions, huge rocks flying through the air, car-splitting noise, lung choking dust: it was an ecologist's nightmare and a prime example of unrestrained exploitation of the environment! In addition it was crammed with safety hazards. This predated the general awareness of life-threatening working conditions and protests against the plundering of the environment. Edison was oblivious to such considerations. It is doubtful that he had read Thoreau and it was another decade before Teddy Roosevelt and Gifford Pinchot aroused public awareness of the importance of conserving and protecting resources. For Edison, who hoped to beautify Orange and its environs by filling its valley with factories, iron locked in soil and rock was an underused resource and a challenge to his imagination – and persistence.

And he faced serious challenges at Ogden. To solve them he introduced interesting innovations. He was fearful that the operation would be labor intensive and he knew that some steps in the processing were potentially dangerous, so, with Dickson's assistance, he designed a system of conveyers to move the rock through the crushing and separating using a minimum of human labor. Belts transported the resulting powder to the top of the separator. It was a pioneering system of automation. As Edison described it: "... The separating machine is but a small part of the apparatus, as the whole process, from start to finish, is designed to work automatically, whereby the very smallest amount of labor is necessitated".[275]

Mr. D and Ogden

Dickson played a key role in designing and installing the facility at Ogden. After spending most of July 1889 on the Kineto, in August he returned to concurrent work on ore separators. During August and September machinists and lower level experimenters worked on at least three versions of the separating machine and the testing of shipments of sample ores continued. Much of the staff was on a water concentrating machine (experiment number 304); others on an earlier version (experiment number 275) and one or two on a small water concentrating machine (experiment number 328). Chemist-experimenter Reginald Fessenden and experimenters Dorr and Brightman were working

275 EHS, LB-039, p. 353, M140 – 954, Edison to D. W. Dunn, Hughes and Gawthrop, Pittsburgh, 7 April 1890.

with copper and nickel ore (number 276). During August and September, 1889 most of Dickson's time was charged to the Kineto account (number 262) and only a small amount of his time was charged to ore milling.[276] As supervisor he must have monitored work done by the ore milling and metallurgy staff though he seems to have had help from his friend Charles Batchelor who was supervising the lab in Edison's absence. Batchelor was interested in the ore milling venture and had asked about investing in the New Jersey and Pennsylvania Concentrating Co.[277]

In October, after Edison's return, Dickson focused on ore milling – he concentrated on concentration. Though others worked on the Kineto and he ordered Eastman's film from his home, all of his time from 10 October through to mid-December was charged to ore milling. Normally Dickson's pay records, often filled in by his own hand, did not specify a specific experiment, but his pay record for 7 November 1889 was annotated "Started Monday, Mallory ore milling machine, dry". His time, and Brown's, was charged to the Mallory project for the next three weeks. A number of machinists, pattern makers, carpenters and lower-level experimenters were also on the Mallory project. After 27 November Dickson returned to signing his pay roll sheet without specifying a project number and Charles Brown filled his in the way Dickson did (sometimes Brown's entry was in Dickson's hand).

The "Mallory ore milling machine, dry" was at least the third version of the separator designed for his mine in Michigan. The 1888 machine had been shut down in the spring because the very fine powder clogged the magnets or blew away in uncontrolled streams. A "Water Contact Machine" worked on during August and September seems to have been for the Michigan installation with the apparent intent of controlling the powder by dampening it. It was finished just before Edison's return and tested during October. Mallory was not happy with it. He was particularly concerned about having wet ore to work with during the Upper Peninsula's cold winter weather so the project was dropped. The "dry" machine used belts and a series of magnets to control the particles; blowers directed unwanted particles to receptacles. It was a while before the machine was declared satisfactory so it was not delivered until the spring of 1890. By this time a larger separator, modeled after the Mallory device was being built for Ogden.

In mid-January, 1890 Thomas Edison and William K. L. Dickson applied for patent on a Magnetic Ore Separator. The document said that they "... have jointly invented a new and useful Method of and Apparatus for Magnetic Separation ...". The application was filed on 20 January 1890 and accepted on 19 August 1890, U.S. Patent Number 434,588. It described an apparatus with a pair of large cylinder rollers which drove a wide belt made of leather, rubber or other non-magnetic material. Powerful magnets mounted on fixed bars were grouped between the two cylinders. A conveyer device directed crushed ore against the lower line of magnets where the iron was attracted to the magnet while the non-magnetic "gangue" began to fall away. The

276 EHS. Pay records. Reginald Fessenden was another distinguished alumnus of Edison's laboratory. He joined the lab staff late in 1887 and during 1889 conducted a number of experiments on various ores, probably under Dickson's supervision. Fessenden left Edison and joined Westinghouse later in 1890. He began his experiments with radio and radio waves after the turn of the century .

277 EHS. Batchelor to Edison, 21 August 1889.

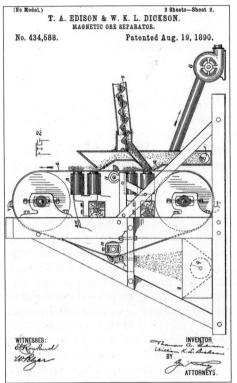
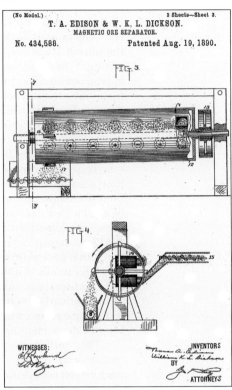

The drawings illustrating the mechanism of the Edison-Dickson ore separator from U.S. Patent 434,588, 19 August 1890. [EHS.]

powerful attraction of the magnets and movement of the belt pulled the iron up and across the belt while agitation caused by the combination of magnets and a moving belt loosened more of the gangue. Pockets on the belt scooped excess iron off the magnets and dumped it in a receptacle. Blowers were employed to help move gangue away from the iron and conveyers moved both the gangue and iron powder away from the machine. The specification said it could be used with ore that was wet or dry.

This patent is unique and a special honor for Dickson because it is the only shared patent among the 1,093 patents that Edison took out during his lifetime. Edison allowed staff members to patent some inventions in their own name – John Ott applied for a patent for device to operate a phonograph with a coin in the spring of 1890 – but this is the only one where Edison shared credit a member of his staff. Of course, as was expected of an employee, Dickson assigned his rights to Edison, but it was recognition of Dickson's achievements and his singular contributions to Edison's work.

The specifications for the separating machines were ready by late January and by that time the staff was constructing at least one of the six machines to be installed in Ogden.[278] During February Dickson and

278 EHS, Dickson's pay slip for the week ending 16 January 1890 has an entry "Large Ore Milling" in his hand which is scratched out, with account numbers for two earlier ore milling accounts entered along with 1/3rd of the week for 262, the Kinetoscope. On 23 January 1890, Harry Livor asked for the specs and drawings and Edison asked Batchelor to send the specs to Livor.

Mallory exchanged correspondence discussing details of Mallory's machine and by March 1890 the lab was working on machines for Mallory and Ogden. Dickson divided his time among several projects and gave some of his time to the Kineto – this is the period when Hugo Kayser worked with him. Edison returned from his trip to Carolina in mid-March and by June they were ready to begin setting up separating machines in a new building at Ogden. On 8 May the Kineto project was shut down and Dickson devoted full time to ore milling. In June he ordered rubber paint to coat belts for the dust separating machine which were being fabricated in Orange.

On 30 June Dickson went to Ogden to set up, tune and test the separating machines. He was accompanied by James Duncan, one of his young protégés. Duncan had come to the lab as a "boy", moved on to become a laborer and was now a lower level experimenter – a promotion apparently fostered by Dickson. Apparently Duncan had an interest in photography and had hung around the photo studio. Though he floated about the lab, both as laborer and experimenter, he was often under Dickson's supervision. He later gained a degree of immortality by performing in several of the first film tests.[279]

They were installing all six separators. Numbers one, two and three were the primary separators for ore; four, five and six processed the tailings, apparently to remove any iron not separated during the first pass. The mine was expected to supply 1,200 tons of iron-bearing material every twenty four hours. Each of the three main separators were expected to concentrate 530 tons a day, with the tailings supplied to the other three separators. By August Edison was ordering machinery and constructing facilities to add a refining mill and negotiating with the Central Railroad of New Jersey to build a branch line from nearby Lake Hopatcong.

Edison was in Orange during the last week of July when the first test of the separators was made. The results were disappointing. Harry Livor, who came from New York for the test, told Edison that the concentrates from the tailings were "abominably ... bad" and Dickson described them as "n.g. with a vengeance ...". In an exchange of letters, phone calls and telegrams, Livor urged Edison to come to Ogden, but Edison was reluctant since his wife was expected to go into labor very soon. Charles Edison was born on 3 August 1890 which was Dickson's thirtieth birthday. Edison told Livor that he would give instructions to Dickson who was responsible for adjusting the machines. When they were ready to test the machines again he would try to come up for a few hours. Dickson wrote to John Randolph, the lab's bookkeeper asking for an additional $50 expense money saying that he "... thot to leave here Sat [26 July] but find that out of the question".[280] The problems persisted and Dickson extended his stay into August.

He was in Ogden until 11 August, repositioning the magnets on the separators and making other adjustments. He was in Orange from the 11th to the 23rd supervising the analysis of shipments of ore coming from agents scouring the Eastern U.S. for prospective sites. This was

279 EHS. Dickson may have been ambivalent about his relationship with Duncan. In a letter to William Meadowcroft, 1 May 1921 he commented: "... that cut throat ore milling assistant or cleaner who used to know a good bit about the camera doings – Wasn't his name Duncan?"

280 EHS. Doc. File Ser.: 1890 (D-90-49) Mining – NJ & PA. Conc. Wks. These tests were made on 23 July and the exchanges took place on 23 and 24 July 1890.

interrupted only briefly by a photo assignment. Since the separators continued to perform below expectations he returned to Ogden on 25 August and began a series of tests to record and analyze the process to find out why.

Edison monitored this activity but he was diverted by other projects. Representatives of the phonograph and electric industries were meeting in Chicago and Minneapolis. The lab was busy with projects for Edison General Electric and a new phonograph enterprise was being launched – more about that subsequently. At the end of August Edison went to Schenectady to work on experiments at the EGE's main plant. At the beginning of September Tate sent the company a list of forty-five experiments between 1 January and 1 September 1890 which were being charged to them. On 20 August Edison and Dickson were interviewed by James Clancy, of the *New York Herald* for a long article that appeared on 24 August. In early August Tate wrote Dr. C. Klug of the Eden Musee "... Mr. Edison has been at home very little during the past two months and his movements for several weeks to come are so uncertain that it is impossible for us to make an appointment ... to visit the Laboratory with your Microscope".[281] Despite this busy schedule, he may have found time for a brief vacation in Akron timed to show his new son to his in-laws.

When Dickson returned to Ogden on 25 August he began making daily reports for Edison with measurements of the percentage of ore separated and comments on working conditions. His reports give an impressionistic glimpse of the situation. In his first, he reported that the 'Stream shorteners" on the machines "... (of which you did not inform me) aparently [sic] work OK". He found doors and windows open that should have been closed, had a carpenter fix one and posted notices *"Keep shut, important"*. There was a drawing showing ore that he found stuck in the middle of number three separator and another showing bolts, nails, wood shards and rocks that were found in the hoppers. Because of rainy weather he began tracking information on the behavior of damp versus dry ore. On 27 August he sent a table of statistics that showed "... The record is always much lower on rainy days ...". The weather was dryer at the end of the month and he raised the voltage on the magnets which improved separation but still was not satisfactory. He complained about changes made without instructions. In order to verify and improve his statistics, he began to analyze the ore before going through the separators and he found some differences that accounted for part of the fluctuations in the rate of separation.

On 6 September Dickson apparently went to Orange for an evening meeting. The next day he sent a longer, more general report to Edison. "I regret not getting an opportunity to get in a word edgeways last night so encrusted were you with people & business I only had time to say that all was well." While he was in Orange he tested belting because he was concerned that the belts at Ogden were wearing out too fast. He was particularly concerned about the clogging of the sieves "I found after the most careful & watchful experiment that ½ of our

281 EHS, EHS, LB-043 p. 114. "Edison's Latest Work, Inventions and Improvement" appeared 24 August 1890 in the *New York Herald*. Dickson was not mentioned in the article but a letter from A.O. Tate to James Clancy of the *Herald* mentions that Clancy spent time with Dickson as well as Edison.

trouble lay in the sieves ..." and he was taking steps to clean and brush them.

After this meeting he sent only three more reports, one on Wednesday the 10th, one Friday the 12th and a final report on Tuesday, September 16th. New fans were installed, but after three days of rain, he reported the results were still unsatisfactory and specified changes he was going to make. Edison responded with a recommendation to apply several thick costs of shellac varnish to the canvass and magnets with each coat applied after the previous one dried. In his final report on the 16th Dickson reported a "grand success". He sent four boxes of samples. The table listing the results showed percentages significantly improved, 68.8 per cent to 72.4 per cent, while previous results had been in the 40 to 50 per cent range. Dickson remained in Ogden for two more weeks, returning to Orange on Thursday, 25 September 1890. On Friday, 3 October, when delegates from the International Convention of Iron & Steel Manufacturers visited the lab, Dickson met them at the Llewellyn station in Orange. Though he did some occasional work for the concentrating works, he did not return to Ogden until March 1891. For the balance of 1890 most of his time charged to ore milling seems to have been for analysis of the ore samples arriving at the lab.[282]

Safety at the separating mill

Dickson mentioned two accidents, both involving the conveyer belts. On 29 August he reported that Delaney, who was apparently a supervisor, caught his arm in the belt and twisted it severely before the belt could be stopped by "... a quick witted fellow ...". His hand and arm were swollen and lacked feeling but he said he would be OK in "some weeks". On 3 September he reported that a carpenter had caught his hand in a belt "... hand torn horribly – ligaments laid bare – thumb, first joint may have to be amputated". Although he reported the accidents, he made no recommendations about plant safety which was probably the responsibility of Livor and his on-site supervisor. Livor was working from his office in New York City.

Although his summer at Ogden ended on an optimistic note, most of Dickson's time had been spent uncovering and verifying problems that delayed operations. He was able to establish that the separating machines had to be adjusted to suit changing conditions. The machines were affected by the mixture of elements in the ore being fed to the separator and its moisture content. For efficiency, as conditions changed, the angle that the ore moved had to be altered and the position of the magnets changed and there was now a minimum voltage for operation of the magnets. He concluded that wet ore clogged the sieves making it almost impossible to separate and this caused Edison to order a heating system to dry the ore before processing. The design and installation of the drying system delayed the opening of the Ogden facility until the spring of 1891 and apparently was the reason that Dickson returned to Orange.

282 EHS & NMAH, Hendricks.

Despite an arduous work schedule, discouraging test results and occasional accidents, Dickson probably enjoyed his excursion at Ogden. He stayed at Nolan's Point Villa at Lake Hopatcong, a convenient location at a railroad stop on the Central Railroad of New Jersey with a telegraph, express station and apparently easy access to the plant. The hotel offered rooms with views of the lake, a steamboat dock, a bowling alley and "sanitary closets both inside and outside of [the] house" as well as baths – all for $2.00 per day. In an era when home air conditioning was unheard of this was the sort of summer retreat offering city dwellers relief from the oppressive heat. The Dicksons enjoyed summer vacations at rural spas where there was scenery and outdoor activities and while there is no record to confirm it, it seems likely that his wife and sister probably shared part of his stay. But when summer turned to fall, Dickson returned to the lab, acquired a new assistant and resumed work on ore milling. During the second week of October he resumed work on the Kineto.

As Edison explored ways to market the Kineto he used the phonograph as a guide. Although the Kineto was no longer a cylinder, it was still the phonograph's cousin and the market for the phonograph was in flux. As the phonograph evolved, the Kineto changed as well.

Chapter 15

The Nickel-in-the-Slot Phonograph

"...[Edison] dedicated his life to the production of useful invention. Devices designed for entertainment or amusement did not in his judgment fall within this classification. ... Spurred by his resentment at the loss and alienation of this great industry [lighting and electrical power], he poured his energies and his wealth into his iron ore milling enterprise in the belief that this would expand to the dimensions encompassed by his mind. But there the Fates opposed him and forced him to develop an ephemeral though profitable industry into which his heart never entered. It is a remarkable circumstance that the field which he always viewed with such pronounced aversion, which he so earnestly tried to avoid, the amusement or entertainment field, was the one in which through two of his inventions, the Phonograph and the Kinetoscope, he recouped his fortunes and accumulated the greater part of the wealth which he left behind him ...".[283] (A.O. Tate, *Edison's Open Door*)

Before venturing into iron, Edison looked to the phonograph as the most reliable source of independent, unfettered income to support the lab. The creation of the North American Phonograph Company in 1888 seemed to put the phonograph on track – this despite the treachery of his one-time friend Ezra Gilliland. By the end of 1889, the Phonograph Works, built the fall of 1888, produced a steady flow of new machines. North American Phonograph bought machines from Edison and leased them to customers through a network of regional companies. Although Edison produced some voice recordings for the Paris Exposition, the Phonograph was marketed as a business machine useful to record legislation, legal statements, dictation and even as a substitute for mail – send a voice recording instead of a letter. But this market developed very, very slowly. The business community was reluctant to adopt the new technology and too many first-time users failed to renew their leases. Edison continued to produce Phonographs at a steady pace, but the North American company was struggling. Jesse Lippincott, the founder of the company, fell behind on the balance of payments owed Edison under the original contract and he was unable

283 Tate, Op. Cit., pp. 301–302 & 307–308.

to pay for the numerous improvements Edison had to make to solve various defects discovered in the machines.

Lippincott's North American Phonograph Co. had commercial rights in the U.S. and Canada for Edison's phonograph as well as Bell's graphophone and both machines were manufactured by the Edison phono works. After buying them from Edison, North American sold them to thirty-odd licensees who then offered them to clients on a rental basis. The machines were expensive – about $250.00 each. One of the reasons for Edison's trip to Europe was to introduce the machine throughout Europe. The exuberant Col. Gouraud had been marketing it, but primarily in England. Edison and Gouraud were negotiating with a syndicate of German bankers to manufacture the phonograph in Germany, but the Graphophone company was also negotiating for distribution in Europe. After his return, Edison's attention was on these negotiations and he was worried about Lippincott's problems meeting his payments and the charges for experiments to improve the phonograph.

A new wrinkle appeared at the beginning of 1890. Several of North American Phonograph's local concessionaires banded together to organize a company to offer coin-operated phonographs for popular amusement. The Automatic Phonograph Exhibition Company was headed by Charles Cheever, but Louis Glass, head of the Pacific Phonograph Company in San Francisco and Felix Gottschalk of the Metropolitan Phonograph Company in New York were the movers behind the company. They proposed making phonographs with multiple ear tubes so recorded music could be heard after dropping a coin in a slot. They envisioned placing machines in hotel lobbies, railroad stations and other places where people might want some brief diversion or amusement. There was mention of parlors and several participants were already recording popular music. To Edison's great annoyance, one of the members of the group was the brother of Ezra Gilliland. In fact, Jim Gilliland designed the coin slot device they planned to use.

Edison's secretary, Al Tate, got wind of it in February, 1890 while Edison was in North Carolina resting and exploring mining prospects. Tate's secretarial responsibilities extended well beyond correspondence and office records. He acted as Edison's financial manager and his duties included monitoring Edison's phonograph business. Edison stayed in Carolina, but gave Tate the go-ahead to intervene and keep the alliance from becoming too independent. Tate met with representatives of the Automatic Company and North American Phonograph Company. He had clout not only because Edison's name had important market value but also because his phonographs were crucial to their plan. The Edison phonograph was generally regarded as superior in quality to the Graphophone and it sold better. The negotiations went on through March and into April.

Acceptance of popular entertainment was a major turn around. Although Edison was happy to speculate about people listening to grand opera sung by people long dead, he was reluctant – Tate said adamantly opposed – to using the phonograph for something as frivolous as amusing the public.

"One morning ... I found an envelope on my desk in my New York office containing a penciled note from Edison reading, 'Tate – I don't want the phonograph sold for amusement purposes. It is not a toy. I want it sold for business purposes only.'

"It was the old story. I knew it perfectly. He was unable to visualize the potentialities of the amusement field. Either that or he had made up his mind to combat it – I could not determine which, but I decided to make a renewed effort to gratify his wishes. It was impossible to control the use of the instruments after they had been sold, and if it had been possible to eliminate the entertainment branch the whole industry would have been wrecked."[284]

Edison's attitude towards the public use of the phonograph was complex. Historian-biographer Paul Israel, who credits Edison with being the father of – and fostering – America's most popular leisure activities, points out that even though he developed the phonograph for the business community, he began recording singers and public figures very early and was working on a talking doll as early as 1888. In 1890, when Tate was alarmed by the proposal for a coin-operated phonograph, Edison had staff working on the doll and a toy version of the phonograph.[285]

As both Tate and Israel point out, Edison was familiar and comfortable with the business community. He had been serving it for more than twenty years and almost all of his inventions were directed to practical use in a business environment first and the general public after that. He regarded the telegraph and telephone as communication devices for government and commerce. The first lighting installations were in business districts. Residential areas came later. It was natural that he would try the phonograph in the business market first. Popular amusement was foreign territory and he was uncomfortable with it. But he did not ignore it. Recordings of singers and famous public figures were a feature of his exhibit at the Paris Exposition, but he was adamantly opposed to a proposal by Col. Gouraud to charge for listening. He sent Gouraud insistent letters and cables telling him that there would be no fees. After the exhibit William Hammer and his recording specialist A.T.E. Wangemann remained in Europe demonstrating the phonograph. Among those fascinated by it were the Emperor of Germany and the Tsar. A very young Josef Hofmann was intrigued with the possibility of recording his performances and a specially constructed machine was shipped to him in February 1890, about the same time that Tate was expressing alarm at the threat of coin operated phonographs.

Whatever doubts Edison had about the amusement business, they did not prevent him from giving Tate the go-ahead to negotiate an agreement with the Automatic Phonograph Exhibiting (Co.) Edison insisted that Gilliland's brother could not be a party to the agreement. By this time Thomas Lombard, Vice President of North American

284 Tate, Op. Cit., pp. [248–250]
285 Israel, Op. Cit., pp. 277–302. A chapter titled "Inventing Entertainment."

Coin operated phonographs were an innovation in 1891. This illustration from Phonogram magazine taken about that time shows a bank of them set up for a demonstration at a trade fair. [LC.]

Phonograph had developed a better coin device. Never one for second place, Edison set John Ott to work on designing one. Gilliland's name disappeared from the list of organizers and a contract for coin devices was signed 25 April 1890.

The amusement market created new challenges for the struggling phonograph business. The phonograph of 1890, designed for office use, was made for recording voice and playing the recording back and it was not anticipated that the recordings would be played repeatedly. Edison's improvements had been directed towards better and easier recording and clearer play back. Although there had been some experiments in methods for duplicating recordings, there was no way to produce a large number of the same recording. If several copies were wanted, the performance was repeated several times or several phonographs were used to simultaneously record a performance. Or both. These were costly and inefficient methods which were not very effective. Edison was experimenting with methods to reproduce records from a master recording but it would be a while before he was successful. Repeated playing of the same recording also required that the composition of the wax be changed to improve durability. Edison decided not to produce recordings for the coin machines. He felt that the profits would come from making machines and blank cylinders that could be used by others. As Edison put it: "... I do not want to make original cylinders, and have no objection to the local companies making them. What I want is the manufacturing of duplicates, which are very different things from records made by musicians direct. The moment duplicates are to be had, the direct production of records will cease, as the former will be better and cheaper."[286]

286 EHS, Edison to Maj. Eaton, 11 December 1890, LB-046, pp. 97 & 99–100.

He would change his mind about the amusement business as it grew more profitable, but in 1890 and 1891 the phonograph business was struggling and debts loomed larger than profits.

Miners and stenos

On the surface mining speculators and stenographers seem to have little in common, but the roster of pioneers in the phonograph business is dotted with men who made some money in mining, usually in the West, and others who gained prominence as stenographers. Since these men were among the pioneers who first invested in American movies it is worthwhile to take note of this strange congruence.

Among the former miners were Louis Glass, Ezra Benson, Thomas Lombard and Norman Raff, all of whom speculated in mines in the West, apparently with enough success to enter the less risky field of banking. Benson and Lombard were partners in the phonograph business. Benson apparently met Norman Raff through his brother, Edward who worked for a while at banks in Omaha where Ezra Benson was in the banking business. Louis Glass mined successfully in California and settled in San Francisco. Tate said that he was colorful and personable.

In the 1880s and 90s stenography was a man's profession and, as is evident from the complicated duties of Edison's stenographers, Samuel Insull and A.O. Tate, they did not restrict their work to taking and transcribing dictation – though they knew and used shorthand. Since the phonograph was being touted as an aid in taking dictation, it is not surprising that stenographers were prominent in the group investing in the phonograph business. In addition to Insull and Tate, other stenographers were the Holland brothers of Ottawa, former reporters for the Canadian Parliament; E.D. Easton, W.H. Smith and R.F. Cromelin, all officers of the Columbia Phonograph Co. of Washington, DC, the most successful and aggressive of the pioneer phonograph companies. Columbia Phonograph was the parent organization of Columbia Records and Columbia Broadcasting System. In Washington, another young stenographer and budding inventor, C. Francis Jenkins allied himself with Columbia Phonograph Co.

Strange bed fellows, but they fathered two hugely successful American entertainment industries.

Even though it took a few more years for the phonograph to establish itself as a viable part of America's entertainment world, the potential of cheap, convenient popular entertainment seems to have taken root in Edison's lab. Edison became increasingly convinced that coin operated machines which required little maintenance and earned money twenty-four hours a day seven days a week had great potential. During the winter and spring of 1890–1891, Dickson and his new assistant were experimenting with taking pictures and working on a device for viewing them – the prototype of the coin-operated Kinetoscope.[287]

287 EHS; Israel, Op. Cit., pp. 289–292; Andre Millard, *Edison and the Business of Invention*, pp. 78–87 & 160–165.

Chapter 16

"See the Germ Work ...
Edison 'Out-Edison's Edison"

1891: Problems, success, revisions

"'But', he explained, 'this invention will not have any particular commercial value. It will be rather of a sentimental worth. What is it? We – el' – he hesitated as if loth to part with his secret, then seeing the look of expectancy in the faces of his listeners released a diminutive laugh and said:

"'It is not yet completed. But when it is it will surprise you. I hope to be able by the invention to throw upon a canvas a perfect picture of anybody and reproduce his words. Thus, should Patti be singing somewhere, this invention will put her full length picture upon the canvas so perfectly as to enable her to distinguish every feature and expression of her face and see all her actions and listen to the entrancing melody of her peerless voice. The invention will do for the eye what the phonograph has done for the voice ... I have already perfected the invention so far as to be able to picture a prize fight – the two men, the ring, the intensely interested faces of those surrounding it – and you can hear the sound of the blows, the cheers of encouragement and the yells of disappointment. ... 'And when this invention shall have been perfected ... 'a man will be able to sit in his library at home and having electrical connection with the theatre, see reproduced on his wall or a piece of canvas the actors and hear anything they say. The only thing the invention wants is that finesse to reproduce the most delicate features and expressions.' ..."[288] Thomas Edison, interview, published by *The Chicago Evening Post*, 12 May 1891.

In the spring of 1891, Edison appeared very confident of his success with the Kineto. The "germ of an idea" had become the "germ" of an invention. A week after the boastful interview quoted above, on 20 May 1891, Mrs. Edison entertained the presidents of the Women's Clubs of America at Glenmont, the Edisons' home in nearby Llewellyn Park. Following a luncheon the 147 ladies went down the hill for a tour of Edison's famous laboratory and to see his most recent invention, the Kinetoscope. One by one they peeked through a hole in the top of a wooden crate and saw an image of W.K.L. Dickson doffing a straw boater and nodded in greeting. Mrs. Edison's guests were the first people outside of the lab to view this ancestor of the modern motion picture. Edison's comments and this public exhibit were widely reported in the press. Reporters from *The New York Sun* and *The New York Herald* came to see the Kinetoscope a week later and the *Herald* proclaimed that the Kinetoscope "... out-Edison's Edison". Edison talked of introducing his new invention at the World's Columbian Exposition in Chicago in 1893. In August 1891 Edison applied for patents for the Kinetoscope, the Kinetograph and a system tying them together.[289]

Ironically, this burst of optimistic hoopla and the patent applications came at a time when Dickson and Edison had decided that major changes were needed before the camera and viewing devices were ready. Dickson was about to begin another period of intense work revising the design of both machines. But before that, we will review the critical period when work on the Kineto advanced to a point where Edison felt he could publicize it.

Winter and spring, 1890–1891

After spending the summer at Edison's mine, Dickson resumed work on the Kineto in the fall. On 13 October William Heise was detailed to work with him as machinist-assistant. It was the beginning of a long involvement with the Kineto for Heise. He remained as Dickson's right-hand through the remainder of Dickson's career with Edison, and he continued as Edison's principle camera operator after Dickson left. Heise was a veteran machinist who had been working in at the laboratory since it opened in January, 1888. Dickson described him as a "capable mechanic" who "was always proud of his mechanical work".[290] Just prior to his assignment with Dickson, Heise worked on several phonograph projects and for the balance of the year he split his time between the Kineto and the phonograph. Unlike his predecessor, Charles Brown, with the exception of occasional details to photograph projects, Heise worked only on the Kineto and was almost never assigned to ore milling. There is no evidence that he had previous experience with photography, so he had to learn how to set up and operate the still and motion cameras, prepare the film and develop and print film after exposure. His intermittent work on the Kineto during October was probably his training period.

From the time he started, Heise's time was charged to a new Kineto account, number 462. For the first couple of weeks in October, Dickson charged his time to the old account 262, but then switched to 462. It is not clear whether this was a mistake or he was clearing up unfinished work chargeable to the old account. Most likely it was a mistake. He did not always fill the time sheets himself, but when he did his writing often seems hasty, even impatient – as though done at the last moment. His sheet for the first week of October had "photographing" written in another persons hand, then scratched out and below it, in Dickson's hand "Kinetoscope ½" and also scratched out, with "5 ½" substituted, meaning it was work charged to the photograph room.

289 Hendricks, ... *Myth*, p. 111. Mrs. Edison's luncheon was held on Wednesday, 20 May 1891. Articles appeared in *The New York Herald* and *The New York Sun*, 28 May 1891; *The New York Morning Journal*, 29 May 1891 and *The Orange Journal* and *Orange Chronicle*, 30 May 1891, *The New York Herald*, 1 June 1891. Several journals also reported the Kinetoscope: *Phonogram*, May 1891, pp. 122–123; *Electrical Engineer*, 20 May 1891, *Photographic Times*, 22 May 1891, and *Western Electrician*, 23 May 1891, *The Photographic News*, and *Electrical Engineer*, 5 June 1891, *Harper's Weekly*, 13 June 1891 and *Scientific American*, 20 June 1891.

290 Dickson, *Journal of the SMPE*, p. 11 and EHS, Dickson to Meadowcroft, 1 May 1921.

Confusion about how to charge time may have been the result of a change in funding for the lab. On October 1, 1891, Edison signed his agreement with Edison General Electric Co. that EGE would pay the labs expenses as long as Edison devoted at least half his time to making improvements in electric lighting. The charges were to be broken down into cost of labor, cost of material and general expenses. It may have taken a while for the system to be adjusted to the new arrangements. Dickson would have known about the new contract but may not have understood how time for photography (room 5) and the Kineto accounts should be charged.

It is not clear why there was a new account number for the Kineto. Perhaps it was because of the new agreement, but the Kineto was not funded by Edison General Electric and other accounts were not changed. For example, the original ore milling account number remained number 43. The Kineto was funded from Edison's own funds as it had been before, probably from the overhead that Edison was charging EGE. So EGE's contribution was indirect rather than direct. In Edison's bookkeeping, new account numbers were almost always started for new projects or an important new phase of a larger project. The surviving paper work for both the new (462) and old account (262) referred to them by the simple designation "Kinetoscope". Most, but not all, account names indicated the intent or purpose of the experiment, so this was somewhat unusual.[291]

The explanation may be as simple as needing a new number because the old account was closed, but there was no indication that the project ended when work stopped in May. A better guess is that the objective was changed from creating a new device to exploring its commercial potential. Prior to May 1890 Dickson experimented to capture motion and reproduce it – find the right mechanism, the best material and the means to join the mechanism to material. In February, 1890, in his statement to the *Orange Journal* Edison declared this stage a success. A comment he made at that time may explain the new direction for the research: "... The experiments were perfectly successful and are now concluded, the next stage being the development of the commercial side of the invention and the creation [of] a demand for the new process".[292]

"Screen machines" or "direct observation"

There was a change of emphasis in the Kineto experiments about this time. During the first half of 1891 Dickson experimented with shooting films and concurrently worked on a viewer. During 1889 and 1890 the camera had priority and viewing was a secondary objective. Now that there was a workable prototype camera, improving the viewing device became more important – if only to check the quality of what was being filmed. The first cylinder cameras were conceived as dual purpose machines, primarily a camera, but convertible to viewing machines or projectors. The strip machine was also convertible and if Dickson is to be believed, it was used as a projector. But converting the strip machine

[291] A sample of contemporary accounts in the fall of 1890 illustrate this: "New Model for all size cylinders", "New Phono Model with sprocket belt", etc.

[292] Orange Public Library, *Orange Journal*, 1 February 1890. Edison's statement to the *New York Herald* the next day said that the search for the commercial side would be delayed while Edison worked on other projects.

to a projector had drawbacks. A light source had to be added – Dickson used the lamp from the Zeiss micro-photographic outfit. This was a minor inconvenience, but there was a more serious problem. Film shrank during developing and the positive and negative film shrank at different rates. The positive film shrank a bit more than the negative and the sprocket holes in the positive film would not engage accurately with the sprockets that fit the film used in the camera. In order to prevent damage to the holes and tears to the film Dickson had a second set of sprockets made that fit the positive film. Although the camera lens could be used for projection, a better image would be made by a custom made lens. So by the time these changes were made, it was virtually a different machine which was a lot of bother to check a short piece of film. A viewing device was better.

As we have seen, a crude peep-show device may have been made as early as August 1889.[293] The early version must have been crude. It was probably cobbled together from available parts using whatever lenses were available – microscopes were plentiful and there were other glasses around the lab. There are no purchase records for special lenses. But as the camera became more efficient, evaluation had to improve because accurate viewing was important to Dickson. He wanted the best quality, i.e. images with clarity, sharpness, correct contrast in the grey scale, etc.

As work on the viewing device progressed, it evolved from a convenient research tool into the preferred version for viewing by the public.

At the beginning of the experiments projection shared a place with individual viewing – at least as stated in Edison's pronouncements. As late as June, 1891 Edison was still talking about projection [see above]. As a master of what we now call the sound bite, he returned again and again to his favorite: "... [to] do for the eye what the phonograph does for the ear ..." which he regularly embellished it with predictions that opera with legendary performers like Adelina Patti would be seen "... full length picture upon the canvas ...". A synchronized recording would complete the illusion.

He seemed serious about developing a projector for a while, but by the spring of 1891 this was just talk. There was no serious effort to design a projector. There were occasional tests with the modified Kinetograph but nothing else. When Edison applied for a patent for the Kinetoscope in August there was no description of a method for projection – only a mention of an optical system to project a stereo image. Since the drawings for the patents were made in early June it is clear that the commitment to the peep show machine had been made before Edison's public posturing about projected opera.[294]

In fact, Edison became so firmly committed to the peep-show that he would not listen to recommendations from Dickson and others that he also develop a projector. This was a serious, nearly fatal mistake. Later, while trying to secure his monopoly in the "patent wars" he had to rely on his camera patent because he had no patent for a projector.

293 EHS & Dickson, SMPE, p. 12. A silvered reflector, costing $2.00, received 15 August 1889 from Josephine D. Smith, [Newark] and charged to Mr. Dickson.

294 EHS, accounts, 1891. Dyer and Seely's bill for 30 June 1891 included expenses for a draughtsman and Charles Catlin who went to Orange "on Kinetograph case" 8 June 1891. A draughtsman returned on 10 and 24 June, also for the Kinetograph case.

He was unable to combat the flood of projectors, most designed to use the "Edison format" and his protracted, disruptive and ultimately unsuccessful lawsuits sullied his image. This, combined with the tiny image and short life of the Kinetoscope, caused many historians to downgrade or ignore the genuine contributions he made to the beginnings of the American motion picture industry.

If this decision seems short sighted, it was not arbitrary. The laboratory was only a stage in Edison's business strategy. He expected the laboratory to generate factories where machines would be manufactured. In this schema the Kinetoscope was a gamble. There was no proven market for viewing moving images and though Edison understood that it would be a novelty, he was skeptical about how extensive and lasting the public's interest would be. But in his view, one machine for each viewer was better than one machine exhibiting to fifteen, twenty, maybe a hundred, or more viewers – especially true if the novelty had a short life. At this time, in 1891, there was no understanding that producing films for the machines was important and might be a more profitable business. Experimental filmmaking had just begun and it would be another year before producing them for public consumption had to be given serious consideration. Edison was a hardware person and he came very reluctantly to the software market. Though he manufactured phonographs and blank phonograph cylinders, he had recently decided against making pre-recorded cylinders. Making movies for anything other than testing the mechanism was not yet a consideration.

Edison's decision was influenced by the recent introduction of the coin-operated phonograph. In 1925 Edison had this to say:

"The most fruitful field immediately before me was the exhibition of the pictures by direct observation rather than by projection, because in the year 1890 and for some time afterwards a very popular form of entertainment in this country was the so called slot parlor where phonographs were installed, arranged to be operated by the coin-controlled mechanism. It therefore occurred to me to start out with a device by which the motion picture could be made use of in the many hundreds of slot parlors which were then doing a flourishing business in the United States ...".[295]

295 *Journal of the SMPE*, September 1925, a letter from Thomas A. Edison to F.H. Richardson, 24 January 1925, reproduced in an article "What Happened in the Beginning" by Richardson. The article is reproduced in Raymond Fielding, ed., *A Technological History of Motion Pictures and Television*, Berkeley & Los Angeles, Univ. of California Press, 1967, pp. 23–41.

Well, Edison exaggerated the success of the coin operated phonographs, but by 1891 he had modified his earlier reservations. When proposals to market coin-operated phonographs first came up, Edison was distrustful but his resistance was temperate. He persisted in promoting the phonograph primarily as an office machine but that business was not going as well as he hoped so the additional income the coin machines generated was welcome. Actually, the automatic phonograph business developed rather gradually. By November 1890 twelve companies were operating 743 machines with most of the machines in the East. But public enjoyment of the phonograph was becoming more important. With apparent backing from Edison, a trade magazine, *The Phonogram*, was being published in New York City with V.H. (Miss Virginia) McRae as Editor and Business Manager. It was described as

"... the official organ of the U S. Phonograph Companies ...".[296] The phonograph business as we know it was beginning to take shape.

Nickel-in-the-slot devices
Coin machine troubles: a dissenting voice and business problems

Not everyone was enthralled with coin-operated machines. When he heard that there were problems with automatic phonographs in the exhibit of Edison's achievements, Francis Upton, General Manager of the lamp factory in Harrison, New Jersey complained to the manager of the Minneapolis Industrial Exposition: "I understand that the automatic phonographs ... are practically a cheat upon the public. I consider that it is an outrage to allow any catch penny affair to be shown in your exposition, especially, such as cheat in so many instances ...". Upton's branch of Edison General Electric funded much of Edison's exhibit in Paris which moved to Minneapolis after being exhibited at the Lenox Lyceum.

Upton's complaint touched off a spirited exchange. Felix Gottschalk of the Automatic Phonograph Exhibition Co. protested against Upton's remarks, saying that he should have taken steps to see that the problems were corrected before complaining about them. Eventually Upton apologized.

Not everyone grew rich off of coin machines. *The Year-Book of Photography, and Photographic News Almanac, 1892* commented: "The year 1891 has witnessed the collapse of the penny-in-the-slot principle applied to photography. The automatic machines were cleverly designed, and replete with ingenious arrangements, and experienced photographers are apt to wonder not at their failure, but at the possibilities of getting any results at all by such means."

Although they were a recent development, coin-operated devices were an attractive marketing ploy that was catching on in Europe and North America. Boxes dispensing things the public needed or wanted were appearing in hotel lobbies, stores, railway stations, ferry boats, bars and other places where the public gathered. The profit-making potential of a machine that consumed coins and required no live attendant and that could be used twenty-four hours a day was especially attractive. No on-the-spot clerk, just someone to service the machine from time-to-time; no closing at five or six to go home; no demand for a vacation and the box would not ask for a raise (though it might quit unexpectedly). Edison was not the first to be intrigued by their money making possibilities

In 1889, vending machines for gum and candy were introduced at stations on New York's elevated railways. At the Paris Exposition there were coin-operated machines for taking photographs and some for viewing photographs and other images. Edison probably saw these and other coin machines and this might have occurred near the time that he viewed Marey's exhibit. Eugene Lauste said that when he visited Marey's laboratory in the late 1890s, Marey said he recommended that

296 EHS, Tate to Luther Stieringer, Edison General Electric Co. LB-045, p. 359. The largest were New York Phonograph Co. (140 machines), Old Dominion Phonograph Co. (139 machines), and Columbia Phonograph Co. (136 machines).

Edison might make money with a coin machine to view moving images. The idea may have stuck in Edison's mind even though it was still a new, evolving business. It was anybody's guess what the future held, but by 1891 Edison was ready to chance it.[297]

Despite his later insistence that he favored projection, Dickson may not have been adverse to this decision. He liked to tell inquirers that he pioneered and championed projection, but throughout his life he was fascinated with gimmicks, novelties and amusement items and as we will see, developing novelties for amusement was a characteristic interest. He probably found designing a peep-show viewer appealing.

Improving the Kineto
Dickson the free-wheeling experimenter

Dickson's reputation for independent, sometimes impetuous action was well earned and is illustrated by an incident in January 1890.

On 30 January 1890 Al Tate wrote Henry C. Ware, Edison Phono Works, Orange, about an order for link belting dies placed verbally rather than by written order. Tate couldn't identify who did it and said he deplored the practice. "... I understood that you had instructed your people not to accept verbal orders, but it appears that in these two cases they have done so. It is impossible for me to keep track of each individual connected with the Laboratory, and in the present instance we cannot ascertain who it was gave instructions for experimental work on the new ore separator. In all probability it was Mr. Dickson ..." (Dickson was working on a new model dust separator for Walter Mallory).

On 2 February 1891 he sent a correction. It was Mr. Edison who had arranged for the work with Mr. Ballou of the Phono Works. "... Mr. Edison's time is too valuable for us to expect him to arrange personally for written requisitions ...". Tate asked the Phono Works to request a requisition from the laboratory when Mr. Edison gave verbal instructions for work but not to accept a verbal order from other lab employees either in their own or Mr. Edison's name.

When William Heise joined the project, work on the Kineto was sporadic and he split his time between the Kineto and a "new model phono w. sprockets", but he worked a full schedule on the Kineto during the week of 17 November and put in a 13 hour day on Monday the 24th. During this period Dickson spent time on several ore milling projects. But in January, after the holidays were over, the pace picked-up and remained intense through the end of February. Dickson continued to split time between the Kineto and ore milling, but Heise worked full time on the Kineto. In fact, with the exception of a few sporadic assignments, after 5 January 1891 Heise worked exclusively on the Kineto for the rest of his four year stint as Dickson's assistant. During January Heise worked overtime six days and then fourteen days in February. As with previous spurts, a mix of machinists, carpenters and pattern makers were assigned to the project. Most worked a day or

297 Encyclopaedia Britanica; MoMA, Crawford. Lauste to Merritt Crawford, [1928]. Lauste visited Marey in 1898 and introduced Dickson to Marey very soon after his visit.

two, but one machinist, Tony Duppler, worked two consecutive weeks at the end of February and into March.[298]

The purpose of this spurt is unclear but since there was no similar burst of work before May when it was exhibited, a prototype of the new Kinetoscope seems likely.

Preparations for serious filming were also underway. As the systems for producing and viewing film improved, the facilities for processing the film had to be upgraded. Without usable tanks for developing, drying devices and a machine for printing positives from negatives there would be nothing to view.

The two existing darkrooms, one in Room 5, the other in the Photo Building, were designed for still photography. The short pieces used in the early Kineto tests could be developed in the existing facilities, but longer strips needed different techniques. Revisions to the darkrooms were begun the previous January. Dickson ordered tanks, cylinders and had a wooden frame built to wind the film around for drying. These facilities evolved slowly over a year or more.[299]

Dickson described and illustrated the developing equipment and printer in his SMPE article:

"[In the photo building there] were two darkrooms – one for punching, trimming, joining the films, and printing the positives; the other for developing, fixing, washing, and 'glycerining' the films. These operations were done by using large, black, enameled drums adjustably suspended at each end when immersed in long, shallow troughs.

"The films were spirally wound around these drums and the ends clamped to hold the film in place. When deemed to be throughly developed, the drum was carried to a similar trough to revolve in water coming from a spray over the length of the film or drum. The used water was carried away by an overflow from the trough. The film was then carried to the fixing trough and back to the washing arrangement, thence to the glycerine trough, and dried before a fan while revolving on the motor driven drum.

"... As to our method of printing negatives, I had a large 8 or 10 inch sprocketed drum made, geared to run slowly, over which the films came in contact, the unexposed film being under the negative and the pins engaging both films. A small pea-lamp and reflector were placed above the negative. A square of ground glass was interposed between the light and the film, and the light was regulated by a small slide resistance to give the right exposure. Two spools on each side were used, geared to pick-up the negative and positive films."[300]

Dickson's SMPE article implies that this was done while Edison was in Paris, but realistically the method of developing evolved over an extended period. Dickson was still working on devices for developing and printing as late as the fall of 1893.

The process for printing the film may not have been completed in May when Mrs. Edison's guests from the women's clubs saw the Kinetoscope. Some of the articles from this period suggest that the film they viewed was negative rather than positive. But they were written

298 EHS pay records and time sheets.

299 EHS. In January 1890, Dickson ordered two cylinders, 7¾ inches by 24 inches from Milne & Platt, Orange, NJ and had them Japanned. In mid-February 1891 John Ott sent an order to the Phono Works to have a trough and roller Japanned. Japanning was a process of applying a lacquer varnish to an item to protect it and give it an attractive, durable finish, so these orders indicate that the various parts were expected to be used frequently and possibly be seen by others

300 Dickson, Op. Cit., pp. 11–12. Dickson explained that a bath of glycerine and water was used to make the film more flexible.

301 The reporter for the *New York Herald* whose article appeared 28 May 1891 seems to have seen the film. He said he viewed a negative. The reporter for the *New York Sun* also writing on the 28th, was not specific, but reported seeing a man who smiled and waved his hands – smiling would have been difficult to determine from a negative. George Parsons Lathrop, writing in *Harper's Weekly*, 13 June 1891, said it was negative, but he had not been in Orange and was sent a sample strip of the film. The staff at West Orange regarded Lathrop's article as the most authoritative and referred a number of subsequent inquirers to it.

after the women viewed the film and only two were by reporters who seem to have viewed the film themselves.[301]

During this period only one kind of celluloid was available from Eastman, negative, and Dickson ordered it with emulsion as rapid as possible. Since it is difficult to read details in negative, a positive version had to be made to judge accuracy and clarity. In still camera work the negative would usually be printed as a positive on paper. Paper could be used to evaluate an individual frame but it was impossible to see any movement, so as soon as there were multimple images, the positive image had to be transparent. There were techniques to produce a positive-type image and Dickson used a method of making a negative film enough like a positive that he could see the image. In his early experiments negative celluloid was turned "... into a positive effect with

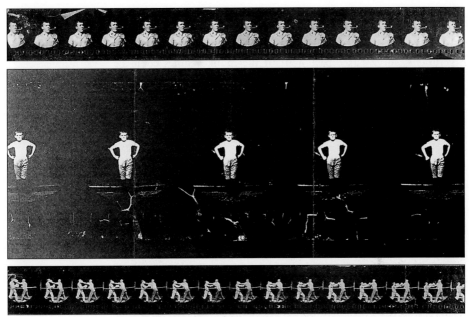

Both pages: *During 1891 a number of test films were made with the strip Kineto and several examples survive. The film of Dickson tipping his hat was shown to the representatives from the Women's Clubs on 20 May 1891. The others are: Duncan Smoking; Newark Athlete (aka Indian Club Swinger) and Men Boxing. Although these films captured movement, Dickson was not satisfied with the quality so further revisions followed. [NARA and Musser.]*

302 Dickson, Op. Cit., pp. 11–12.

303 EHS, receiving records. Eastman had sent the lab a total of 20 rolls of film and the last shipment was received 12 March 1890. To be specific: Dickson bought two rolls of film for Kodak cameras in September and October 1889. These would have been 3¼ inches wide by about 50 feet, each. In December he received 6 rolls, ¾ inch wide by 50 feet; 19 February 1890, 4 rolls, 1 inch by 50 feet and the final shipment was for 8 rolls, 1 inch by 50 ft. Dickson said these were supplemented by strips of film given by Eastman.

bichloride of mercury". In later tests with Eastman film he said "... we had to use this rapid negative for our positive prints; and although they lacked pluckiness, we partly overcame it by using potassium bromide in our developing bath to reduce its sensitiveness ...".[302]

More monkey shines

As the facilities for processing film improved, it was possible to put the Kinetograph through more purposeful testing. Early in 1890 Edison pronounced the Kineto a success. But, realistically it was still a work in progress and little changed during the remainder of the year. Movement was recorded but, if the purchasing records are any indication, they had not produced enough images to confirm their quality. About 1200 feet of film had been purchased from Eastman and even though Dickson was adept at supplementing his supply with gifts and purchases not recorded on Edison's books, the amount of film consumed so far was surprisingly small and the total was significantly reduced by accidents in the darkroom, damage in the camera and troubling flaws in what was a far-from-perfect product.[303]

Serious experiments to improve the images and test techniques of filmmaking began during the first half of 1891. The previous tests were attempts to evaluate how well movement was registered. A person, usually a staff member, danced about, waving his arms and changing position enough to confirm how well the changes were captured. *Monkey Shines* was the generic name used by Dickson and his associates to identify these tests and three of the them made during the cylinder experiments survive (see page 150]. If the monkeyshines could be followed in a viewer, the camera was effective. Dickson, the perfectionist, probably examined each frame for blurring, graininess, unsteadiness and other flaws. He was satisfied with the speed and the ability to register motion, but not with the quality of the images. The size of the image was increased but experimentation was suspended before more sophisticated tests could be made. The Kineto was at this stage when the experiments resumed in the fall of 1890.

Serious filming began after the New Year but before that there were training sessions and what was an apparent review, apparently including another *Monkey Shines* test. In late November Heise put in his first full week on the Kineto and during that week G. Sacco Albanèse, a recently hired machinist, worked two half days November 25th or on the 26th that were charged to the Kineto. Dickson later identified Albanèse, who he described as "A bright sunny-natured Greek" as one of those who posed for *Monkey Shines*. This test of the camera does not survive, but it was probably made at this time.[304]

Dickson resumed ordering film at the end of the year. Four rolls arrived 29 December, and in February, apparently preparing for more extensive tests, Dickson ordered a dozen rolls.

In his filmography of Edison's films made prior to 1901, Charles Musser identifies seven films made during this period. Although they did not have titles, the names they have come to be known by are: "Dickson Greeting" (the one shown to Mrs. Edison's guests on 20 May 1891); "Duncan and Another, Blacksmith Shop", "Monkey and Another, Boxing"; "Duncan or Devonald with Muslin Cloud"; "Duncan Smoking"; "Newark Athlete" (also called "Indian Club Swinger"), and "Men Boxing". Sample frames, in the form of short strips, exist for four of these films [and are reproduced here]. Two of these, "Dickson Greeting" and "Men Boxing" were found in a notebook kept by Charles Batchelor. All of these strips are ¾ inch wide with the image in a circular aperture and small oval perforations along the lower side of each strip. In this version of the camera, the film moved horizontally rather than vertically.[305]

These were certainly not the only films made during this period, but the accord that Edison and his staff gave them shows that they represent successes. There were probably many failures, but, not surprisingly, those were not recorded.

Charles Batchelor dated the samples he put in his notebook as being shot it in June, but they were made earlier than that, some possibly as early as January.

Dickson kept his eye out for staff members with a playful side and used them as performers in test films. Fred Ott was a favorite and posed for two or three tests – Charles Brown called him a comic genius. Dickson was a colorful figure who performed with his sisters in musical

304 EHS, payroll; Dickson, Op. Cit., p. 12; Hendricks, *...Myth*, pp. 45, 100–102. Although Gordon Hendricks felt Albanèse's *Monkey Shines* film confirmed that Dickson was still working on the cylinder, nothing else in the surviving records indicates that there was work on a cylinder in November 1890. It is much more probable that what G. Sacco Albanèse posed for was filmed with the strip Kineto. G. Sacco Albanèse was a trained engineer and machinist from Malta who joined Edison in the summer of 1890 and left in March or April 1891. He worked for several firms in the U.S., Venezuela and Europe, eventually settling in Paris where he had his own firm, G.S. Albanèse, Ingénieur. He may have posed for some other photographs for Dickson before he left Edison's employ, since he spent four half-days in March working in the Photo Room.

305 Charles Musser, Op. Cit., pp. 73–75; EHS & NMAH Hendricks. Batchelor's notebook had three strips, two were from the boxing film and one from Dickson's greeting. Four frames of Dickson's greeting were later sent to the Patent Office as evidence for Edison's claim. These are now at the National Archives. A strip with fifteen frames from Dickson's greeting was reproduced in

presentations and parlor entertainments. He appears in at least three of his own films. The older staff members were probably somewhat stodgy, but energetic youngsters on the lab staff were ideal subjects. They were less set in their ways and their duties were not as crucial to the lab's schedule. Sacco Albanèse was 19, Jimmy Duncan and Fred Devonald were about the same age, though Duncan might have been a bit older. Albanèse was new to the staff, but Dickson had known the other two for a while. Both Duncan and Devonald were probably anxious to be part of Dickson's tests as a break from the routine of their not always exciting day-to-day work. Another youngster on the staff who may have also been filmed was Nick Cronin who was on the payroll as "Boy in Room 11". Three hours of his time were charged to the Kineto on 2 March 1891.

Duncan and Devonald

James Duncan was hired as a laborer in May 1888. In the fall of 1888 he began working under Dickson frequently, but irregularly. He handled various ore milling assignments and seems to have become Dickson's protégée. By the spring of 1890 Duncan had risen to the status of "experimenter", apparently through Dickson's good offices. At 17¢ an hour he was really a low-paid assistant rather than a full fledged, work-on-your-own experimenter. Dickson seems to have used him primarily in testing the many ore samples that arrived with regularity during 1889 and 1890. When Dickson went to Ogden in July 1890, Duncan went along with him.

Fred Devonald also worked occasionally with Dickson but was not often under his supervision. Like Duncan, Devonald was hired in 1888 as "boy on the second floor". This was where Room 5 was and Devonald undoubtedly ran errands for Dickson. By 1889 he had become a laborer and later was promoted to head of Edison's stock room. As a laborer he worked briefly for Dickson and probably was well acquainted with him from his days on the second floor. As head of the stock room he would have been responsible for ordering and receiving the supplies Dickson needed for both ore milling and Kineto.

Jimmy Duncan, Dickson's frequent assistant in the ore milling department, was filmed in two or three of the films that we know about. Duncan's time was charged to the Kineto for three days in January and then five days in early June,[306] These seem likely dates for "Duncan and Another ...", "Duncan or Devonald with Muslin Cloud" and "Duncan Smoking". If it was Fred Devonald who did something with a muslin cloud, his time was not charged to the Kineto account.

For these tests, Dickson relied on familiar subject matter and followed examples already established by the chronophotographers. In their studies of movement, Muybridge and Marey filmed people, birds and many kinds of animals. Dickson concentrated on filming humans – except for a "Monkey and Another Boxing", there are no other animals in these early tests. Movement was the essential, indispensable element

George Parsons Lathrop's article in *Harper's Weekly*, 13 June 1891.

306 EHS payroll & time records. Friday, 9 January, Saturday the 10th and Monday the 12th; June the 2nd, 3rd, 4th, 8th and 9th.

and most of these films involve vigorous activity: boxing, club swinging and blacksmithing. Some subjects seem to have been made more than once during various stages of the invention. There were three or four "Monkeyshines", and perhaps more. "Dickson's Greeting" which was shown to the ladies from the women's clubs was probably made in the spring of 1891 but it matches Dickson's description of what he showed to Edison his return from Paris – though some will argue that the earlier version was never made. Edison and his staff liked boxing and several boxing scenes were made, probably anticipating a potential audience for fight films. Finally, at least three blacksmith subjects were made, one in 1891, a second in 1892? and the final one in 1893. The blacksmith shop was in the same building as ore milling and though the blacksmith, "Rube" Hepworth and his assistant, George Gilmore had been trans-ferred to the Phonograph Works in March, 1890, the equipment may have been handy to use as prop in the outdoor film site which was attached to the building.[307]

While motion was essential, the tests were not limited to vigorous activity. Some involved subtler movement. These were particularly important to Dickson who wanted even minor details to be visible. "Dickson's Greeting" has a vaudeville quality and although his feet are not visible, it is almost like a soft shoe dance routine. He wore a straw boater, removed it and greeted the camera-audience. The reporter from *The Sun* who viewed it at the laboratory, mentioned the broad move-ments of tipping the hat and waving arms but also more subtle effects of smiling and shaking his hand. No images from the muslin cloud film survive, but it is easy to imagine the waving and trailing of a piece of cloth, possibly while turning and twisting in the fashion of the butterfly dances which later proved to be so popular. The movement of the cloth would have given Dickson an opportunity to judge subtle changes of tone, as well as details of folds in the cloth, etc. Duncan Smoking may be particularly important since it featured very little obvious motion. It was a medium close-up showing head and shoulders and the action would have been limited to a shift of the head, facial changes, movement of the pipe and, perhaps, wisps of smoke. If these fine details were visible in motion, Dickson was doing very well, indeed.

There are some common elements in the staging. Each is shot against a black background with overhead illumination for the subject. Significantly, the position of the camera was changed for each film. Dickson's Greeting was shot from a middle position, showing him from the waist up. The camera is aligned so that his head appears high in the frame. For Indian club swinger, the camera was positioned so that the full figure is shown and there is room at the top to show the clubs moving around above the boy's head. The camera moved a bit closer for Men Boxing. The boxers are shown full figure, but their feet are not always visible. As noted before, Duncan Smoking is a close-up. The changes of camera positions confirmed the sharpness of registration at various distances, but they also anticipate the variety of set-ups Dickson would use when he began regular production. It is clear that from the

307 Hepworth probably did not pose for the last two films since he could not get along with the superintendent of the Phono Works and was let go in October 1891.

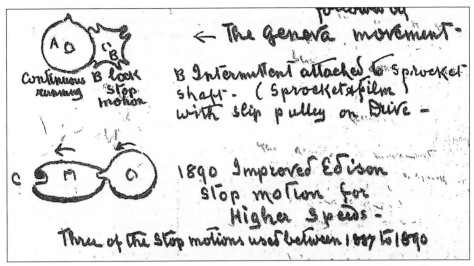

To successfully capture movement the film had to stop for a fraction of a second for exposure, then be rapidly advanced for the next exposure. For this to happen up to forty times in a second it was necessary to have a reliable "stop" or intermittent movement. At first Dickson said that he used a Geneva (or Maltese cross) movement, so called because it was the type of movement used in a clock or watch (top). He credited Edison with designing an improved movement (bottom). These drawings were made by Dickson for Earl Thiesen in January 1932. [AMPAS.]

beginning he sought visual variety while producing images with clarity and sharpness.

This was not easy to achieve. He was using film with relatively slow emulsion and trying to expose it at a very high rate of speed. This necessitated a lot of light. In 1890 he was taking eight to ten frames per second, barely enough to capture movement and reproduce it. The early tests showed that at 20 frames per second there would be flicker and jerkiness. This convinced Dickson – who convinced Edison – that the images would be smoother and more natural if taken and viewed at a faster rate. They set an objective of 46 frames per second. This did not allow much time for exposure. The tests also established that it was essential to have an intermittent rather than continuous movement of the film in the camera, i.e. the film had to be stopped during exposure. According to Dickson, the earliest version of the strip Kinetograph used a maltese cross to provide intermittent movement and the best they could achieve was 20 frames per second. He said that a new intermittent movement that Edison designed in 1890 or 1891 improved the exposure rate to 40 to 46 per second. In their scheme, the film was stopped and at rest for 9/10ths of the time and advanced for the next exposure in the remaining 1/10th. At forty-six times every second Dickson estimated the exposure time was 1/100th of a second which was supposed to be in the range of exposure using "ordinary good light".[308]

In practice, "ordinary good light" was not good enough. A sharp, precise image required a lot of light. To compensate for the minimal exposure time, Dickson borrowed the black background used by

308 EHS, Dickson to Edison 7 May 1921; Dickson, *Century Magazine*, p. 208; *SMPE*, pp. 11–12; *History of the Kinetograph ...*, p. 13. Without intermittent movement Dickson calculated the exposure time to be 1/27 20th of a second. The "ordinary good light" quote is from *Century Magazine*. Photo: Dickson's drawing of maltese cross and Edison's intermittent movements (letter to Theisen, 1 January 1932)

Étienne-Jules Marey. A recessed area coated with a deep, light-absorbent black provided contrast – and clarity – for the subject bathed in light. The filming area in the studio had a glass roof to admit maximum light and the stage was backed by a black wall. The outdoor filming area on the side of the ore milling building also had a black, light absorbing background and was often used as a backup. The need for ample light meant that the opportunities for filming were limited to the bright light of mid-day on sunny days. Experiments with artificial light were unsatisfactory so Dickson relied on the sun, a preference he followed throughout his career.[309]

The Kinetograph was large and heavy, hence, not very mobile. The camera position was changed before filming and once the scene was set up, the camera had to stay in place. It had two motors and was weighted to reduce vibration, but the slightest jiggle could spoil the film. The performers were restricted to a small area immediately in front of the camera and the area photographed was further restricted because the ¾ inch image was circular limiting the action to the center of the frame.

The speed of exposure and adequate light were only a few of the problems encountered. There were a number of things that could and did spoil the film. Some were machine problems, others were problems in the manufacture of the film. The list of problems photographers encountered with celluloid was long and disheartening and Dickson encountered most of them. Dickson was using Eastman's film for an entirely different purpose than it was intended. Eastman was making a product intended for amateurs which Dickson was adapting for a highly sophisticated and technically complicated apparatus. Matching the design of the camera to the idiosyncracies of the film was Dickson's major concern during this period. It was a hard struggle that persisted throughout the experiments. In the summer of 1891 he went to Rochester to discuss his problems with Mr. Eastman and his associates.

309 EHS, Dicksons, Op. Cit.. Ten Sperry arc lamps charged to the Kineto account were received from Sperry Electric Co. 3 February 1891. Marey described his light absorbing black photographic area in a paper read before the French Association for the Advancement of Science, at Nancy, 1886 which was reprinted in the U.S. in *Scientific American Suplement, No. 579.* pp. 9243–9245 & *No. 580*, pp. 9258–9260. Dickson seems to have been familiar with the technique and Edison may have seen Marey's facility in 1889. *Century Magazine*. The Dicksons mention four parabolic magnesium lamps and twenty arc-lamps in their article.

Chapter 17

Edison's Agent

"Enclosed is a small fragment of film furnished Edison for his phonograph arrangement. He perforates it on both edges and delivers it by means of cog wheels. The film has to move 40 times a second and the movement has to be made in 1/10 of that time. It is then quiet for 9/10 of the period while the picture is being taken. The trouble with the film we have sent him is that the cogs tear the film slightly, as you will see by the enclosed, and gives blurred images. I gave the Edison representative a sample of the double coated film made last August and told him if heavy enough we could furnish him that if he would take a whole table at a time in 41 in. strips. His idea is to have us slit it 8 in. wide and then make a slitter of his own and cut it up narrower. Edison now has an order in for some narrow strips of film of our regular make. Please fill this and use the thickest skin that you can find. Edison's agent will let me know about the double coated film in a few days."[310] (George Eastman to his chief chemist Henry Reichenbach, 23 July 1891)

"... I quite agree re Eastman – whom I always classed as jointly with Edison the pioneers of Kinematography he was awfully nice to me & at each visit to Rochester always tried to satisfy me in my exacting requirements – I got lots of scrap lenths [sic] gratis for experimental purposes – yes we were very good friends & knowing my difficulty with E. I had all his sympathy – for he was a just man.[311] (Dickson to Will Day, 12 March 1933)

On the morning of 23 July 1891 W.K.L. Dickson visited George Eastman, showed him a sample strip of film from the Kinetograph, and after discussing his problems, Eastman wrote the note quoted above and sent the sample to his chief chemist, Henry Reichenbach. The note was signed by Eastman's secretary, Alice K. Whitney because Eastman left immediately after to catch a train to Chicago. Dickson, who also had appointments with lens makers, remained in the Rochester area for two weeks. Half of his stay was vacation time, a mix of pleasure with business.

While Dickson's earlier visits seem to have been made on his own, this visit was official business and it initiated a period of close interaction with Eastman's company. Dickson apparently visited Eastman's factories during his two weeks stay and over the next six months he carried on an lively, sometimes heated correspondence. Ultimately it benefit-

310 GEH, Eastman papers.

311 BiFi, Will Day.

ted Eastman as well as Edison. The end result was the creation of modern motion picture film and the 35mm format which became the standard for an international motion picture industry. The format also influenced Eastman's camera film business for much of the following century.[312]

Eastman's note is the most concise statement of where the Kineto experiments stood half-way through 1891. The mention that the film was perforated on both sides is startling. All the surviving samples from the spring were perforated on one side which indicates that the decision to change had already been made and was the reason for Dickson's trip.

In fact, the decision to enlarge the image dates from about the time of the demonstration of the Kinetoscope the previous May. In an article written shortly after the demo, George Parsons Lathrop reported that the Kinetograph "... is regarded only as the basis for still further development ... The regular size to be used hereafter will be one inch in diameter ...".[313]

Lathrop had gained special favor with Edison and Tate, and he had access to information not available to other reporters and Edison and his staff regarded it as the most authoritative. Several correspondents asking for information about the Kineto were referred to it.

Of the several articles written about the demo, Lathrop's is the most revealing. Even though he was apparently not at the lab during the demo he had unusual access to Edison and the staff. He described the demonstration device as an interim step; that operas would be projected but, he added, a cylinder phonograph combination was in the works. The photographs would be recorded on glass and would be "... only one twenty-thousandth of an inch square each – i.e. invisible to the naked eye except as very small dark spots". A drawing illustrated this ensemble. The Kinetograph enclosed in a large box and the cylinder Kinetoscope were shown on a table with the phonograph connected to the Kinetoscope sitting between them. A funnel attached to the cylinder Kinetoscope carried the sound and a lens (not shown) projected the greatly magnified image from the cylinder to a screen. It would also be possible to view the images through a microscope.

This fanciful reversion to the original caveat seems a product of one of Edison's excursions into speculation. But it is an indication that Edison maintained his fascination with miniaturization and had not given up on linking the phonograph and the Kineto.

Edison and Lathrop had been speculating about the future for the past year. In 1890 Edison agreed to co-author a futuristic novel with Lathrop. There had been several meetings and Edison had jotted some speculative notes, but as the months went by and Edison became more immersed in ore milling and fulfilling his contract with EGE, the project, entitled "Progress", began floundering. About the time of the Kineto article Lathrop complained that despite spending a month in New York City and Orange, he only talked to Edison for fifteen minutes.[314]

312 35mm still photo film feeds horizontally and is sprocketed differently, but the width clearly owes origin to the Cine film that Eastman was manufacturing, based upon the format that Dickson devised in this period.

313 *Harper's Magazine*, 13 June 1891.

314 EHS, Doc. File Ser. – 1891 (D-91-02) Edison General. Lathrop's frustration grew as the summer proceeded. On August 10, 1891 he sent Edison a nine page letter filled with bitter complaints about his inability to meet with Edison and the difficulty of even getting a reply from him. "... the net result of the month was about fifteen minutes conversation with you regarding the book which did not help me forward a particle. ...all effort to go forward with the book would have been paralyzed by the discouragement with which I met at Orange." Edison's interest in the project faded as he became more involved in trying to correct problems at Ogden and "Progress" never saw the light of day.

Edison looks into the future

In 1890, journalist George Parsons Lathrop, persuaded Thomas Edison to co-author a science fiction novel about life in the future. Lathrop was a journalist and aspiring novelist who was a prominent contributor to *Harper's Weekly* and *Monthly* magazines. He had done several articles about Edison and work at the lab. Edison admired his work and he was very popular with the lab's staff. He and his wife Rose, the daughter of Nathaniel Hawthorne, were occasional guests at Glenmont and at Al Tate's home in Orange.

In October 1890 Edison sent Lathrop his first contribution, three pages of notes, his ideas of inventions which would change life in the future. Several involved photographs, reflecting Edison's continuing interest in photography as a tool of research. At the head of the list was "Photography of the bottom of the sea" it was followed by the related topic, "Photographs ... taken of objects in absolute darkness by means of radiant heat ...", possibly based on information from Dickson. Also on the list: 'Phonogh newspapers – opera – Kinetoscopic opera with phono every family wealthy, ... Photography colors – photoghy of surface sun by iron salts in a alternating field only ultra waves due to high temperatures, ... phono publishing houses Kept star Cos of actors & stage and produced for family use Kinetographic phonograms of whole Dramas & Operas – no theatres with actors in vogue ...". The list included predictions of artificial teeth, open hats to prevent baldness, artificial silk and leather, sun engines to produce electricity, artificial wood from compressed chloro-cellulose, etc.

Although Edison sent another speculative list a couple of months later, as he became more involved with problems in Ogden he gave less attention to his novel. Unable to pry Edison away from his projects long enough to complete the novel, Lathrop eventually gave up. But brief though they are, Edison's ideas are an interesting window on his imagination as well as the focus of his mind at the time the Kinetoscope was in development.

This is one of the last mentions of plans for a cylinder and rather surprising since there is little question that the cylinder project had been abandoned months earlier. The micro images 1/32nd of an inch described in the original Edison caveat were impractical and for two years Dickson pressed Edison to improve clarity by continuing to enlarge the image. Sketches of the Kineto that accompanied articles about the demo in the *New York Sun*, *New York Herald* and *New York* Journal were similar to the one in Lathrop's article but showed only a phonograph, no connecting cylinder machine and there was no mention of a cylinder.[315] At the end of August, 1891 a correspondent in Texas was told that a glass cylinder was not practical "... on account of the great difficulty of stopping and starting 40 times in a second, which is necessary in order to take a complete picture. Mr. Edison uses simply a thin band of film ...".[316]

It is possible that Edison planted this fanciful concept to divert

315 NMAH Hendricks. The articles in the *Sun* and *Herald* appeared 28 May 1891, the *Journal* on 29 May 1891 .

316 NMAH Hendricks; EHS, [Edison] to Mr. Jennings, Dallas, Tex. 31 August 1891. This was the second letter to Mr. Jennings. The cylinder is mentioned as a possibility in Edison's patent application filed in August 1891.

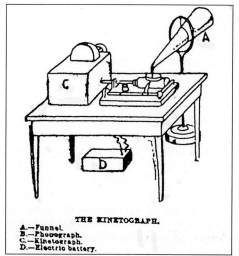
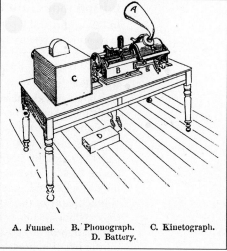

THE KINETOGRAPH.
A.—Funnel.
B.—Phonograph.
C.—Kinetograph.
D.—Electric battery.

A. Funnel.   B. Phonograph.   C. Kinetograph.
D. Battery.

These drawings, the only images showing the version of the Kinetograph from the spring of 1891, were apparently made from images given to reporters covering the event. The illustration from The New York Sun of 28 May 1891 (left) is a rather crude illustration but according to the reporter it was made from a drawing by Edison that was given to him. The source of the more detailed drawing in Harper's Weekly, 13 June 1891 (right) was not specified. The device shown is connected to a phonograph but although Edison was committed to joining image and sound it is doubtful that the two functioned together at this stage. [NMAH Hendricks.]

attention from what was really planned. The newspapers describe Edison's future plans rather than the present reality, though they describe the "Dickson Greeting" film in detail. The drawing of the Kinetograph was apparently supplied by Edison and is unique because it does not resemble any known version of the machine. The description of the viewing device is quite different. It was described as a small pine box with a viewing hole about an inch in diameter.[317]

The reporter for *The Sun* said that the drawing was based on one made by Edison and given to him. Neither Lathrop or the reporter for *The Herald* identified the source, but it appears that some sort of sketch was prepared at the lab and given to reporters and the variations occurred as the newspaper's artists modified the sketches for publication.

Redesigning the Kinetograph

Regardless of what was shown to the ladies and the reporters, the Kinetograph and Kinetoscope were very much in flux. Edison gave Dickson a go-ahead to enlarge the image and stabilize it by adding a second row of perforations on the other side of the image, but no decision had been made about the exact size and shape of the image – except that it would be increased to about one inch. In Lathrop's article the artist's conception of the new image was round and one inch in diameter, simply a larger version of the ½ inch round image from the ¾ inch wide Kineto strips.[318] But Dickson had not decided on the shape of the image and would not make his mind up till later in the year.

317 NMAH Hendricks. *NY Sun*, 28 May 1891.

318 Several of the journal articles describe the "Dickson Greeting" as having a square image, but the surviving frames are a circle as are the other strips from this period. The lenses that Dickson used were round and he seems not to have masked them into any other shape.

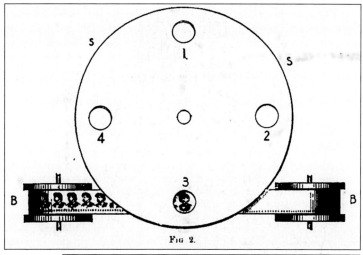

FIG 2.

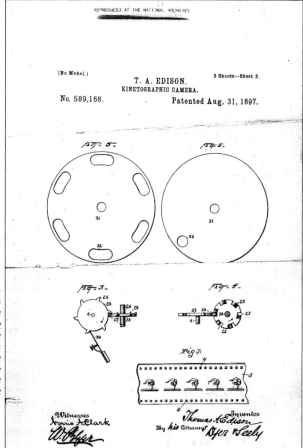

When Edison applied for patents for the Kinetograph and Kinetoscope the design was still in flux. The size, shape and orientation of the images had not been determined. A drawing that appeared in Harper's Weekly, 13 June 1891 (above) showed an image in a circle on the horizontal plane of the strip and only one line of sprocket holes. It is very similar to the drawings of the mechanism sent with the patent applications the following August, but by that time the drawing of the film was ambiguous, apparently to suit prospective changes of size, shape and orientation. (See also, illustration 1 in Chapter 18.)
[NMAH & NARA.]

The version of the Kinetoscope shown to the ladies and the reporters from *The Sun* and *The Herald* was also a work in progress. The wooden box was crude, perhaps finished just before the demonstration. At the end of April Dickson was corresponding with a supplier in New York for thin pieces of opal glass, "Clear white milk glass & not less than 1 inch square". This may have been for the viewing slot on the Kinetoscope. A week later six miniature lamp sockets and rings were delivered from the Lamp Works in Harrison, NJ.[319]

Here is the description of the Kinetoscope by the reporter from *The Sun*:

"... To outward appearance the 'germ' is nothing but a pine box, which looks very much as if it might have been originally intended as a packing case for shoes or boots. It stood on end in front of a lathe, and the open top was nearest to the lathe. In the upper end was cut a hole about an inch in diameter, and in this hole was set a lens. On the bottom of the box was arranged a series of wheels and spindles. A role of gelatine film was placed on a spindle on one side of the bottom. The end of the gelatine strip was then carried over one of the wheels and past the lens in the hole in the top of the box to another spindle on the other side of the box bottom and fastened. A small bolt ran from the lathe to the shaft, on which was set the spindle, to which the end of the gelatine film was fastened. When the motor was turned on the roll of gelatine strip was transferred from the first spindle to the second, and in the transfer passed under the lens. The photographs on the slip came out perfectly ...".[320]

Dickson described how it worked:

"... The band ran continuously as an endless band over velvet covered rollers & carried forward by a sprocket wheel – the film moving under a single slotted 10" shutter through which slot the image was seen illuminated by a small incandescent bulb – The focussing [sic] reflector at back of lamp illuminated the picture – the rays crossing at a focus where the 1/8" slot of the shutter was situated – & the images magnified by a suitable lens."[321]

Ore milling and the Kineto

By mid-July, with a design change in mind, Dickson had received a go-ahead to concentrate on the Kineto and for the next three years it was his primary activity. From July 1891 through April 1892, more of his time was charged to the Kineto than to ore milling. In fact, after April 1892, except for a brief time analyzing ore during 1893, he was finished with ores and mining. A final trip to Ogden in the summer of 1894 to photograph the facilities and staff was his last assignment.[322]

His revised work schedule reflects the evolution of the ore milling project. Dickson's primary assignment was basic research and the planning and designing of separation machines for Mallory and Edison's installations with additional responsibility for analyzing ore samples and matching machines to dissimilar ores. By 1891, with processing ore changing into a business venture, Edison assumed more and more of the design and adaptation work. Analysis of ore became Dickson's major responsibility. Edison's frequent trips and long stays at his ore processing facilities gave Dickson more time to work on the

319 NMAH Hendricks; EHS. The order for glass was to Seman Bach, NY, 30 April 1891, for samples of single & double thick opal glass not be thinner than 10/1000 "... & not thicker than 30/1000".

320 NMAH Hendricks, *The New York Sun*, 28 May 1891, p. 1

321 NMAH Hendricks; EHS. Dickson, "A Brief Record of the early days of Moving photography" Prepared for Thomas Edison, 1928.

322 EHS, time and payroll records. Between July 1891 and April 1892 less than half his time was charged to Ore Milling and there was an assignment for analysis ore which began 2 July 1893 lasted through mid-October 1893. The last charge was one quarter of the week ending 12 October 1893. He may have supervised the work analyzing Cornwall ore which James Duncan charged to the ore milling account on Friday and Saturday of the following week. Through this period Dickson continued to work on the Kineto as well as some other photo projects.

Kineto project. In fact, it might be possible to track the periods that Edison was away from the laboratory by charting the frequency that Dickson worked on the Kineto because when Edison was at the lab Dickson spent more time on ore milling. The intense period of Kineto work in July and August, 1889 came when Edison was at the mine in Bechtelsville and on his European trip.

This should not be interpreted as an indication that Dickson worked on the Kineto when Edison's back was turned. Edison tracked what Dickson and his other experimenters were working on. When he was at the lab, Edison met and talked with the major experimenters to review their progress. He made tours to see projects first hand and when he was out of town, received written reports. As Edison's interest in ore milling grew and the process was in the experimental stage it was inevitable that ore milling dominated Dickson's work schedule. When the separators were ready for installation at Ogden, Dickson had to be there, but once running, he was theoretically done. Dickson's involvement should have declined after the summer of 1891, but it did not. Ogden did not function as expected and Edison needed Dickson's help.

Dickson's final major involvement with ore milling came at the end of 1890 and early1891. In October, 1891, Edison closed operations at Ogden because he was frustrated by poor results. He wanted to rebuild the separators and during the winter Dickson's work on the Kineto was shared with assisting the redesign, working on another dust separator for Mallory and analyzing a steady flow of ore samples. There were other demands on his time. At the beginning of March the Kineto and ore milling were put aside so he could work for five days installing a magic lantern in Edison's home – one of his most unusual assignments. It seems to have been a complicated assignment since his assistant, Heise, spent two weeks on it. Late in March the new separators were ready for installation. By spring he was able to give more time to the Kineto, but Ogden continued to need his help. He went to Ogden on 27 March and stayed for two weeks and returned later in April, twice in May, five days in June and six in July.

Though his priorities were changing, Dickson was probably happy to remain involved with the Ogden project. He had invested some of his own money in Edison's ore business and in February, Edison gave Dickson a $300 bonus, but with a proviso. His note read: "This $300 is given Dixon for his Labors on belt machine. This is to be paid by NJ Conctg. Co. when the Ogden mill is a financial success". Presumably he received the payment even though the Ogden mill was never really successful. In the spring of 1891 Dickson had motivation to make Ogden work.[323]

Things looked good when the plant began running in April but it soon turned sour. Edison's patience wore thin – and thinner. Although he sold some ore to Bethlehem Steel, the problems persisted. On 29 June he sent Samuel Insull a telegram: "I am going to Ogden tonight and stay" – and he did. Shortly after Edison's arrival his manager and long-time employee, Harry Livor quit and soon after that Edison fired

323 EHS. In a note to Al Tate, 11 September 1893, Dickson said that Edison gave him 100 shares of Edison Ore Milling stock when he signed over the rights to his share of their joint patent. He said these shares were different from those lost when McGowan disappeared. Those were shares given him for work on separation of gold from iron pyrites, probably given him in 1888 or 1889. On 7 March 1894 Dickson received $1500 in ore milling stock, 100 shares at $15.00 ea. in addition to his salary, Certificate #1092, dated 16 May 1889, "... given to Mr. W.K.L. Dickson for his services on the old belt machine and for other services in connection with the iron concentrating business".

P.F. Gildea. his mining engineer. For the next year or more he spent most of his work week in Ogden, returning only on weekends, sometimes visiting the lab on a Monday to catch up with affairs. Eventually he persuaded his business associate Walter Mallory to join him in managing the Ogden operation.[324]

With Edison in Ogden amd his ore milling duties declining and Dickson had more freedom to cultivate the "germ".

This suited Edison's changing priorities because the Kineto had gained a spot on his long-term agenda. In June, while in Chicago, Edison met with the planning committee for the World's Columbian Exposition and made a tentative commitment to mount a major exhibit similar to the one at the Paris Exposition. He also announced that the public unveiling of the Kinetoscope would be part of his exhibit. From this time on he frequently repeated this pledge to reporters and to the many correspondents inquiring about his latest wonder. So the opening of the Fair set Dickson's timetable. A working version of the Kinetoscope, complete with films, would be ready by 1 May 1893. The first step would be to redesign and rebuild the camera to the new one inch image with sprockets on each side of the image. Then the supporting equipment, the trimming device, perforator, developing tanks and drying racks would have to be modified and the peepshow machine refitted to handle the new film format.

Rochester, summer 1891

Dickson's trip to Rochester came at this turning point in the evolution of the Kineto. In addition to prodding Kodak for improvements in the film, Dickson needed professional lenses for the camera and the viewing machine. In addition to meeting Eastman, Dickson had appointments with Bausch & Lomb and Gundlach, optical firms based in Rochester and he may have also met with the American branch of the German optical firm Zeiss, which was also in Rochester.

On the evening of 22 July he took the overnight sleeper from New York and checked into the Livingston Hotel in Rochester the next morning. He stayed through the 29th, then took a week's vacation, apparently at nearby Clifton Springs where he had vacationed previously.[325] This was a working vacation, an opportunity to reconfirm his special working relationship with Eastman and establish relations with the optical companies. Eastman's note to Reichenbach (quoted above) indicated that Dickson planned to get in touch with him when he got back from Chicago. He returned on Thursday, 30 July 1891, the day that Dickson's vacation started.

Re-enforcing relations with Eastman was critical. After two years of testing, Dickson had established that he needed tougher film coated with emulsion that was faster and more sensitive. This was the topic of his first meeting with Eastman. Following their discussion Eastman instructed Reichenbach to fill Dickson's order for four rolls of film with "... the thickest skin that you can find", He also showed Dickson an old test sample of a "double coated" film, i.e. one made with a double

324 EHS. Harry Livor had been associated with Edison since Menlo Park days and had held several managerial positions with Edison's various concerns. P. F. Gildea had been the mining engineer in charge of operations at Bechtelsville in the summer of 1889.

325 NMAH Hendricks; Hendricks, ... *Myth* p. 123. Hendricks cited Ed. accts. p. 261; Letter book E1717; and *Rochester Union & Advertiser*.

coating of celluloid. But Edison would have to order a "table" before they could make it. This was a difficult proposition for both parties. Eastman had tested double coated film, but had not developed a manufacturing process and was not really sure they could produce it – or how it would perform. A "table" was more film than Dickson had been using – much more. He had been ordering a few rolls at a time and it would be weeks before the new camera was ready to use film. Eastman did not want to get stuck with a product he couldn't sell. His process involved pouring base on glass-topped tables that were 41 inches wide and 200 feet long, treating it then coating it with emulsion. Since this was a custom order. And Edison was the only potential customer. Dickson postponed his decision, but he was not through with his negotiations.

Dickson was familiar with Eastman's manufacturing techniques. He probably toured the facilities in 1889, but he may have seen them again during this visit, though he probably was not shown the recently opened buildings in Kodak Park. They were still in a shake-down phase. Drawings of the coating rooms made years later show that he knew the facilities in some detail. In 1932 he gave a description of the plant that was vivid enough to persuade veteran Eastman employees that he had been there. "The central table was covered with long sheets of plate glass, carefully fitted together in lengths. The atmosphere was pregnant with the fumes of amyl acetate, and I was glad to get out of it ...". Although there is no sign of intimate relations – no "Dear Tom" or "W.K.L." – in George Eastman's correspondence, the evidence that Dickson received special treatment from Eastman is clear, doubtless because of his status as Edison's agent. Film was cut to specifications and the best available stock with the highest sensitometer was usually supplied. Dickson's letters were often demanding, but he established his credibility well enough that his requests

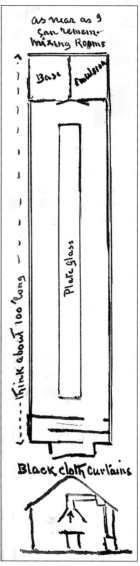

This drawing shows Dickson's familiarity with Eastman's process for manufacturing celluloid. It was made in December 1932 for Oscar Solbert, who was president of Eastman Kodak following George Eastman's death. [GEH.]

were understood and accepted. This was crucial during the next several months while the final versions of the Kinetograph and Kinetoscope were being worked out.[326]

When Dickson returned to Orange on 7 August the four rolls of film he ordered in Rochester were waiting for him. Two lenses from Bausch & Lomb were received on 10 August. At the end of the month a lens for the Kinetograph came from Gundlach Optical Co. and six more rolls from Kodak arrived. The change was underway. He was working on the camera, but at the end of August the modification was in flux and important decisions had to be made. While the size of the image had been decided, the shape had not. The film received in August was in the old format, suitable for the old strip machine, but too small for the new version. He lacked a suitable lens. He asked Gundlach for one that gave a one inch image but the one received at the end of August made a three inch circle. He immediately rejected it and sent a letter clarifying his requirements. He was now able to specify that he wanted to photograph a thirty foot object, thirty feet away and concentrate the most light possible in that one inch image. But what shape? His letter specified a one inch square in the text but he drew a sample that was rectangular. The experiments over the next few months would settle issues of size, shape and orientation of the image, but the final form of the Kinetograph and Kinetoscope was up in the air at the end of August. Nevertheless, Edison finally decided to apply for patents.

326 EHS; NMAH Hendricks; GEH; Dickson, ...*SMPE*, p. 11. Dickson to Oscar Solbert, 10 December 1932. Dickson's visit coincided with a period when Edison seemed to occupy Eastman's attention. Eastman had just bought stock in the local Edison electric company and on 31 July he played pool with Harry Brewster of the Edison Co. Brewster was a Rochester banker and at a later date a Congressman and director of the Eastman Co. He apparently had stock in the local electric company. Dickson's description of Eastman's plant was accurate enough to convince Eastman employees reading his text that he had been there in 1888.

Chapter 18

"A Method of Taking and Using Photographs". Patenting the Kineto

"The present invention relates to a method of taking and using photographs in such manner as to give a visual impression as of an object in actual motion. The invention consists in a method having two unexpected steps, first, taking a number of pictures, one after another on a suitable film or surface at a rapid rate, and second, bringing said pictures before the eye of a beholder in the same order, and at the same or approximately the same speed, as they were taken, whereby they are seen as a single picture, the object represented being in motion ...".[327] (Edison patent application number 503,534)

"... the original Edison patent covered not only the modern camera but also the product of that camera, a film having photographs thereon of a moving object."[328] (Frank Dyer to Earl Theisen, 8 June 1932)

On 24 August 1891 Edison's attorneys sent the U.S. Patent Office three applications; one for the Kinetograph, one for the Kinetoscope and the third for a system to combine camera, film processing and viewing into a unified system. The Kinetoscope moved through the system relatively soothly but the application for the Kinetograph ran into problems and its tangled progress first through the Patent Office and then the U.S. courts affected the American industry profoundly. It began the tortured legal process that engaged the American motion picture industry for much of its first two decades and severely tarnished Edison's reputation with film scholars. Although Mr. Dickson was a secondary participant in the patents, the outcome of Edison's legal battles was of both personal and professional concern to him. His vexation continued long after the turmoil had abated.

Applying for patent

327 NARA.
328 AMPAS Library, Theisen Papers.

As submitted in 1891, the patents were hierarchical. The basic patent was for the Kinetograph (camera) and the Kinetoscope (viewer) was described as a "sub-method". The second of the applications described

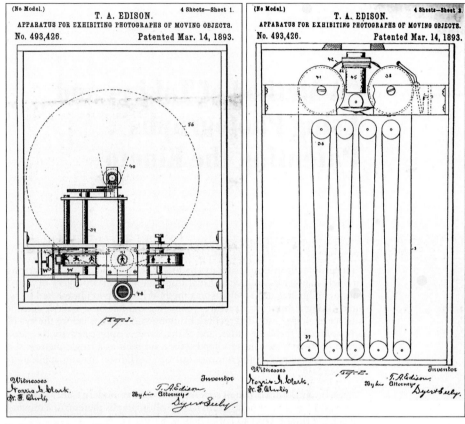

Both pages: *In August 1891, when the patent application for the Kinetoscope was submitted the device was only a prototype and aspects of the design were still being worked out but the mechanism changed very little. Sheet 1 shows the top of the Kinetoscope and Sheet 2 a side view with the threading of the film. Illustrations from an article in* The Literary Digest, Vol X, No. 4, 24 November 1894 *show the interior and workings of the finished product. [NARA & NMAH Hendricks.]*

the method of taking and preparing the film for the Kinetoscope. The application for the camera included a description of the Kinetoscope. This description was repeated in the application for the viewer but with the addition of specified items for which patent was claimed. The Patent Office would not accept this linkage, rejecting it on the grounds that it linked devices that had to be patented separately and included methods which could not be patented. "... it is held that there is no combination between the steps of taking the picture and of exhibiting it. The steps are not consecutive acts, as the film has to be removed from the machine, developed, fixed, and printed, between the taking of the picture and the exhibition of it. The exhibiting of the finished picture has nothing to do with the taking of the negatives, and the claims covering aggregations, and will be rejected on that ground ...".[329] Edison chose not to press his separate claim and divided the application in April 1892. He abandoned the attempt to link the machines and revised the

329 NARA. U.S. Patent Office to Thomas A. Edison c/o Dyer & Seely, 17 January 1894. Although this letter is directed towards claims in the application for the Kinetograph it expresses the position of the Patent Office rather clearly.

Vol. X., No. 4]   THE LITERARY DIGEST.   (105) 15

SCIENCE.

DEPARTMENT EDITOR, · · · ARTHUR E. BOSTWICK, PH.D.

MECHANISM OF THE KINETO-PHONOGRAPH.

THE results of the kineto-phonograph have been familiar to the public by many newspaper articles and illustrations. The general working of the instrument was described in our columns July 21 (Vol. IX., No. 12), as well as that of an accompanying phonograph which heightens the effect of the successive pictures by reproducing the voices of the mimic actors. The mechanism of the instrument is described, with diagrams, in *La Nature*, Paris, October 20, from which we extract the following :

"The kinetoscope, by which the illusion is produced, is shown in Fig. 1. It is enclosed in a wooden box furnished on top with a lens. The eyes being placed to this lens, one sees a transparent photograph not larger than one-sixteenth of a carte-de visite, with all the personages in movement, the picture presenting a marvelous scene of successive, life-like movements.

"How is this apparatus operated? Turning to Fig. 1 in which the mechanism is exhibited, it will be seen that there are two compartments, one above the other. The mechanism is contained in half the depth of the case, the other half being reserved for the ribbon of photographs, of which we have already spoken, and which is shown in Fig. 2.

"At the foot of Fig. 1 in the lower compartment is shown the electric motor C, which sets all the mechanism in movement. It is an Edison dynamo of eight volts, operated by four accumulators, with a capacity of eighty ampere-hours. The current passes across a resistance which is varied to augment or diminish the light of the incandescent lamp. This renders the ribbon of celluloid more or less transparent, according to its thickness and transparency, which are very variable. Opposite the motor C, Fig. 1, is another apparatus, A B, one aspect of which we confine

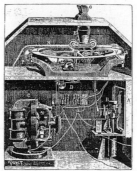

FIG. 1.—MOTOR-MECHANISM OF THE KINETOSCOPE.

ourselves to giving. It is in some sort independent of the kinetoscope, and operates a money-box, which, when a piece of money is dropped into it, sets the whole scene in motion.

"In the upper compartment of Fig. 1 there is a metal disk F, which forms a screen before the pellicle of ribbon R. The little incandescent lamp, which lights up the ribbon and renders it transparent, is shown at L. The lense O, where the observer places his eyes, is mounted on a conical tube E, and serves to lift

the electric motor is set in motion. By means of a mechanism of toothed wheels ingeniously combined, the motor turns the circular metal disk F; this is furnished with a slit F which enables the observer to see the photographic figures on the pellicle of ribbon at R, every time the slit passes under the eyes, but practically the disk rotates so rapidly that the pictures are seen all the time as if through a screen.

"The photographic ribbon is attached to the metallic disk, to which it is secured by the wheels. It revolves at the same speed,

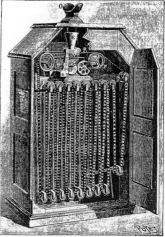

FIG. 2.—CELLULOID RIBBON CARRYING PICTURES.

and glides over the pulleys, P S. The speed is such that forty-two photographs per second pass in review.

"The length of the ribbon is about 15 meters [fifty feet] ; it is an endless ribbon, mounted on the front part of the case of the kinetoscope, as shown in Fig. 2. The ribbon traverses the pulleys, which are about 60 cm. [two feet] apart. One may count 750 chronophotographic proofs on the length of this pellicle of celluloid ribbon.

"To give an idea of the results achieved by Edison's kinetoscope, we would say that in one of these photographs which is shown to visitors, one sees a monkey, dancing on an organ. The jump, which appears to be accomplished in an instant, requires 53 photographic proofs passing successively, for its exhibition. In a kinetoscopic scene which represents an American barber plying his trade, there are not less than 1,700 poses."—*Translated for* THE LITERARY DIGEST.

Electrical Purification of Drinking-Water.—Oppe man , a German chemist (*Elektrochemische Zeitung*, September), has patented a process of this kind. The current acts, according to the inventor's statement, not by directly destroying organisms but by decomposing the mineral salts that are found in small quantities in all drinking water. Under certain circumstances, ozone and peroxid of hydrogen are thus produced, both of which destroy the organisms by oxidation, and thus exert a cleansing

---

330 NARA. The original application, filed on 24 August 1891, was for "Improvement in Method & Apparatus for Taking the Pictures," Serial No. 403,535. It attempted to tie the camera and viewing device into a system, describing a method for photographing an object in motion. It was Dyer & Seely's Case No. 929. After rejection, it was divided and filed 11 April 1892, Stop Devise, February 21, 1893, Serial No. 423,614, which became U.S. Patent No. 491,993, 21 February 1893. The Patent Office did not keep the documents from the original patent after it was divided and there are no copies in the surviving records at the Edison Historic Site so exactly what was claimed in the original application can only be surmised from the related description in the application for the Kinetograph .

application as a patent for an improved stop mechanism. This was accepted and patent granted on 21 February 1893.[330]

The specifications in the application for the Kinetoscope are significant because they described the device in a formative state: after the film was developed and printed the positive copy, several hundred or even a thousand feet, was mounted on a series of rollers and an endless belt was created by connecting the ends together. The film could then be moved back and forth at a speed that was governed by a reel mounted on a shaft and connected to a suitable motor by a belt. At the top of the mechanism, the film passed under a lens which had a light below it. The illumination was furnished by an incandescent bulb and a reflector below the lamp which concentrated and directed the light to the film. Intermittence was provided by a shutter with one opening. The unopened portion covered the film then opened as the frame passed the lens. The film and shutter ran continuously and were timed to expose the picture at about the speed it was taken, though the speed could be varied to run as desired. The image was enlarged by a magnifying lens at the top of the box that enclosed the mechanism.

The application included a claim for an apparatus in which an electric spark illuminated pictures on the surface of a drum – a holdover from earlier experiments – but this was canceled 25 November 1891 and is not in the final version of the patent. However, the final version does have a claim for reproducing picture stereoscopically as well as a provision that a tinted plate could be used to give the impression of color. It claimed that the stereo images could be projected on a screen and the screen could be painted to give a colored effect. But this is the only mention of projection and no mechanism for projection was described or illustrated. There was a description and illustration of the optics for reproducing the stereo images but no description of a method for taking stereo images in this application or the one for the Kinetograph. A method taking stereos was described in the application linking the two.

Several provisions in the application for the Kinetoscope were rejected by the Patent Office and had to be changed, but the patent moved through the system in a rather normal manner and was approved on 14 March 1893 as U.S. Patent No. 493,426.[331]

Although the Patent Office ruled that a description of the Kinetoscope could not be included in the application for the Kinetograph and the Kinetograph could not be described in the application for the Kinetoscope Edison did not abandon that description in the camera application until late in the process.

The application for the camera was submitted as "Improvement in Kinetoscope" illustrating the confounding of terms that confused the participants and those who followed. It described "... a method of taking and using photographs in such a manner as to give a visual impression as of an object in actual motion". It would use "... a long gelatine tape film ..." with a sensitive surface, coiled on reels, taking a picture one inch in diameter between rows of holes at regular intervals on the two edges. The film could be "... several hundreds or even thousands of feet long ...". The holes engaged teeth on wheels (sprockets) which advanced the film. A plate was forced against the film by a spring to hold it steady when it stopped for exposure. It specified that the film was "... at rest for nine-tenths of the time in order to give as long exposures as practicable, and is moving forward one-tenth of the time, ... thirty or more times per second, preferably at least as high as forty-six times per second, ...". The speed could be regulated to give satisfactory results. No specific speed was called for, but it cautioned that if taken too slowly the images would produce a "... trembling or jerky appearance in the reproduced picture". The camera had a shutter in the form of a revolving disk with as many as six holes which blocked light as the film moved for the next exposure. The camera's lens could be adjusted back and forth.

331 NARA. U.S. Patent No. 493,426, Apparatus for Exhibiting Photographs of Moving Objects, 14 March 1893. Application filed 24 August 1891. Serial No. 403,536. Originally filed by Dyer & Seely as Case No. 930.

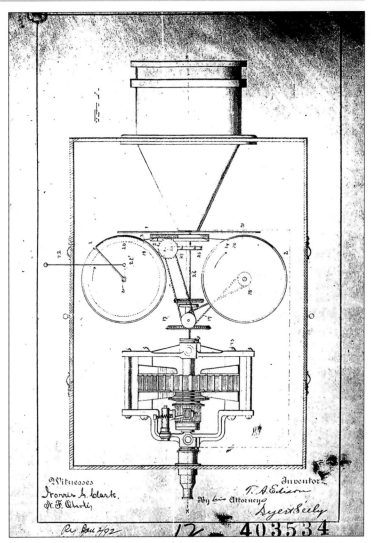

The Kinetograph as illustrated in Edison's application for the patent in August 1891. [NARA.]

There were some additional claims which may have been put in by Dyer & Seely to anticipate and prevent subsequent conflicting patent claims. Although it described taking images with intermittent movement, it said that the camera could be used continuously with the light interrupted by a shutter as the film continued to move. It specified a one inch image with a double row of perforations but said that narrower film with one row of perforations could be used. After describing both devices, the application made specific claims which only applied to the Kinetograph camera.

On 2 January 1892, William H. Blodgett, an Examiner in the Patent

Office sent Dyer & Seely a letter rejecting the claims in Edison's application for the Kinetograph: "The claims are anticipated by patents to Le Prince, 376,247, 10 January 1888; Donisthorpe, 452,966, 26 May 1891, and British patents to Greene, 10131, 21 June 1889 & Dumont, 1457, 9 June 1861 (Cameras) they are therefore rejected". This launched a series of revisions, but it was not finalized, and Edison decided to delay completion. In December 1892 Dyer & Driscoll advised him that he could "... let it soak ..." until 20 May 1894.[332] It soaked well past that date and the Patent Office finally threatened to close the application as incomplete, but in 1896 as the international market for motion picture devices began to develop, Edison revived the application. Since this was beyond the normal three year period allowed for completion this was a controversial move, but Edison's attorneys managed to plead successfully and the application was reopened. Despite a challenge from the American Mutoscope Company, the patent was approved on 31 August 1897.[333] It was Edison then that launched his series of lawsuits against rival American film companies, launching the so-called "patent wars".

The key case was the hotly contested suit, Edison v. The American Mutoscope Co., a legendary legal battle that dragged on from 1898 until 1908[334]. During the protracted course of this lawsuit there were several decisions, each followed by an appeal. Following an early ruling that American Mutoscope had infringed Edison's patent, an appeal resulted in a decision on 10 March 1902 by the U.S. Circuit Court, third district, which dismissed Edison's claim. The court famously ruled that Edison invented nothing new, that his claims lacked novelty or invention in view of prior art and invalidated four of the six claims in his patent.

"... The photographic reproductions of moving objects, the production from the negatives of a series of pictures, representing the successive stages of motion, and the representation of them by an exhibiting apparatus to the eye of the spectator in such rapid sequence as to blend them together and give the effect of a single picture in which the objects are moving, had been accomplished long before Mr. Edison entered the field ...".[335]

Edison's attorneys rewrote the claims and submitted a revised version of the patent on 17 April 1902 which became reissue patent no. 12,037, on 30 September 1902, covering four claims for the motion picture camera. They also filed additional claims for motion picture film which became reissue patent no. 12,038, also 30 September 1902.[336] The decision was appealed and the suit dragged on, finally ending in February 1908 with the creation, out-of-court, of the Film Service Association, a forerunner of the Motion Picture Patents Company. This ended the case with American Mutoscope Co. but the lawsuits were not finished. Once the Patents Company was formed they continued suing competitors using their patents, including the Edison camera patent. In 1911 reissue Patent no. 12,037 was invalidated in an adverse decision in the case of Motion Picture Patents Co. v. Imp. The patent was revised one more time and became re-issue Patent No. 13,329, 5 December 1911.[337] Although the court cases continued, their impact

332 EHS. Dyer & Seely to Edison, 1 December 1892.

333 NARA. U.S. Patent 589,168, Kinetographic Camera. Application filed 24 August 1891. Serial No. 403,534. Dyer & Seely Case No. 928.

334 NARA, United States Circuit Court, Southern District, New York, Thomas A. Edison v. The American Mutoscope Co. And Benjamin F. Keith, in Equity No. 6928. Bill of Complaint filed 14 February 1898.

335 EHS. 137 F. Rep. 262; 128 C. R. 6928 U.S. Circuit Court of Southern District, New York; 131 C. R. 6928, 10 March 1902.

336 NARA. Reissue Patent No. 12,037, Kinetoscope, 30 September 1902. Original No. 539,168, dated 31 August 1897. Application for reissue filed 10 June 1902. Serial No. 110,937. And U.S. Patent No. 772,647,647, Photographic Film for Moving-Picture Machines, 18 October 1904. Application filed 5 March 1903. Serial No. 146,343.

337 U.S. Patent No. 13,329, Kinetoscope, Reissue 5 December 1911. Original No. 539,168, dated 31 August 1897. Original Reissue No. 12,037, dated 30 September 1902, Serial No. 110,937. Application for this reissue filed 24 May 1911. Serial No. 629,240.

on the industry was fading as was the influence of Edison's company and the Patents Company which Edison dominated.[338]

Questions?

The timing and content of these applications raise questions. If the Kinetograph was in working order by the spring of 1890 (or earlier?), why wait so long to apply for patent? Why apply for patent when the design was being revised? And the question that has been asked most frequently: why didn't Edison block foreign competitors by applying for foreign patents?

There are no clear-cut answers to these questions. The best explanation for the delay seems to be that Edison wanted to have the effective date of the patent as close as possible to the time when the Kinetoscope was ready as a viable commercial entity. The term of patent is relatively short, only seventeen years, and Edison was looking for the possibility of controlling the business, not for the glory of patenting an interesting but unproductive invention. Recent patents by Friese-Greene and Marey may also have motivated him. Edison was ambivalent about the patent system and though he was the most active user of patents, he was also a frequent and vocal critic.[339] He complained that the system favored infringers because the courts required the person holding the patent to prove ownership and infringement, and also that the resulting legal disputes were protracted and expensive and allowed infringers to profit while the term of patent continued to run down. Despite these complaints Edison's lawyers prospered because he was constantly in court in cases relating to lighting, the phonograph as well as the Kinetograph.[340]

Apparently Dyer and Seely advised Edison that he could go ahead with his patent applications even though the designs of the Kinetograph and Kinetoscope were being revised. The three patents were written in very general terms. The applications were not intended to describe a specific version of an invention, but to describe the basic elements – Edison's "germ" – in phrases broad enough to cover variations of the invention, minor changes and, hopefully, block potential rival applications by anticipating elements that others might try to patent. This was tricky business and the stuff that fostered the careers of well-heeled patent lawyers – Dyer & Seely profited handsomely from Edison's business. The examiners in the Patent Office were on the lookout for these broad, sweeping claims. The wording of the patent and the nature of the accompanying drawings were crucial to getting it accepted and preventing competitors from taking advantage of loopholes. Submitting the three applications for the Kineto while it was in transition was probably all right so long as Edison's "germ" was accurate enough to cover the improved version. Significant changes could be covered by additional applications. This practice had been followed in patents for various versions of the phonograph, the lamp, ore milling and a number of other items the "wizard" patented.

Edison steered away from trying to cover himself with foreign

338 NARA; EHS; NMAH Hendricks; *Moving Picture World*, 1907, pp. 21 & 1911, p. 1001.

339 During his lifetime Edison obtained 1039 U.S. patents, more than any other individual. According to the *Report of the Commissioner of Patents for the Year 1895* Edison had received 711 patents. The runner-up, Elihu Thompson had 394; George Westinghouse, 217; Hiram Maxim, 131. (NMAH Hendricks)

340 EHS. During the winter-spring 1891–1892 Edison was involved in a Patent Interference involving conflicting applications for the installation of electrical lighting systems. One of the conflicting patents was filed by Charles Chinnock a former Edison employee. Dickson testified in the case the following spring.

patents, not because of the cost of registration, but because of the complications and expenses involved in international litigation. Occasionally he permitted his European licensees to take out patents in his name if they would pay any legal expenses that arose. He encountered problems with at least one such foreign registration. Col. Gouraud patented a version of the phonograph in Portugal where the term was only seven years and at the end of the seven years a court ruled that all of his patents had expired with this short term registration. Edison was not happy and this contributed to his very cautious attitude towards European and other foreign patents.

Dickson: copyrights and patents

Dickson insisted that he urged Edison to apply for patents before 1891. His artistic skills and scientific interests made Dickson sensitive to creativity and the laws that protected the rights of artists and inventors. Since Edison was regularly involved with patents Dickson and others on the laboratory staff were familiar with patent procedures, but Dickson also made use of the protection offered by the copyright law. As early as 1885 he registered original engravings for copyright and in 1889 he began registering versions of the photographs he made at the laboratory. A "Durer" of Edison was registered in 1889 and two photos were registered in 1890, "T.A. Edison listening to phonograph" and "T.A. Edison at work in Chem Lab". As early as 1890 he seems to have prepared patent information and drawings for the processes related to the Kinetograph that he was developing: trimming and perforating the film and printing and developing it. He said that he pressed Edison to apply for patents before the 1891 registrations. "... I never failed to remind Mr. Edison of his risk in not patenting all these 'movie' devices. I think it was Mr. Frank L. Dyer who at last persuaded him to move in the matter, after I had talked it over with him."[341]

Dickson's interest in patents went beyond urging Edison to act and discussing details of devices with Edison's patent attorneys. He hoped to register his own claims and may have begun preparing patent claims as early as January 1890. During 1890 or 1891 an application for a patent for the perforating-trimming mechanism was prepared, professional drawings were made and Dickson wrote the text.[342] Edison's patent attorneys Dyer & Seely, prepared a draft of the petition in Edison's name for "Improvement in Methods of an apparatus for obtaining positive Pictures from Negatives" but it was never sent to the Patent Office. A copy of the application is in the files at the Edison Historic Site.

This was not the only patent application that was prepared and never filed. On 8 October 1891 Dickson signed over rights to a patent application for "certain new and useful improvements in the art of photography" to Edison. The application was already in the hands of the Patent Office which had assigned it application no. 408,340. This was one of two cases that Dyer & Seely worked on in August 1891 that were never completed. One was Dickson's application, the other, prepared in Edison's name, was for the machine for printing positives

341 Dickson, ... *SMPE*, p. 14. It was probably not Frank Dyer who urged Edison to apply for patents. Frank Dyer was the son of Col. George Dyer the partner in Dyer & Seely. Frank was just graduating from law school in Washington, D. C. He eventually succeeded his older brother Richard Dyer as head of the firm, but in the early 1890s Frank Dyer was based in Washington to take care of patent business for the firm. Though Frank Dyer dominated Edison's patent affairs for the phonograph and Kinetoscope during most of the 1890s and eventually became head of Edison's business affairs, he had not reached that prominence in the summer of 1891.

342 EHS. On 31 January 1890 the Kineto account was charged with time spent by George Mayer, a draftsman, who apparently worked on this application during the previous week.

from negatives (which Dyer & Seely numbered case no. 940). Edison instructed Dyer & Seely to withdraw case no. 940, the printing machine, and it was probably Edison who caused Dickson's application to be withdrawn.

It is not clear what "new and useful improvements in the art of photography" were described in Dickson's application. After registering the assignment with the Patent Office, the case was dropped without going to completion. The Patent Office did not keep documents on cases that were not completed and there is nothing in Edison's records that describes the application. The other two aborted applications had

---

© Wm. Kennedy Laurie Dickson

The records of the Copyright Office, Library of Congress list thirty-six works registered by W.K.L. Dickson, two published works written with his sister and the photos, forms and engravings listed.

The earliest were eight engravings: "Oh Alone in this [night]", "Auld Lang Syne", "Softest Pleadings", "Give Oh give me back my heart", "I won't go home till morning", "Who's at the window", "Why I'm so plump" and "All human history attests". They are dated from a note on the back of the card "(Photo) of these engravings bearing no date of receipt has been filed among cabinet Photos of 1885" the entry was stamped "2nd copy del. To art gal. 1 December 1897". Unfortunately it appears that the Library did not keep these for the permanent collection – unless by some chance they are in an as yet unprocessed backlog. Thousands of similar decorative engravings illustrating popular songs or poems were copyrighted during the Victorian era and only samples were retained. It is possible that these illustrated original poetry by W.K.L. or one or both of his sisters.

The other registrations:

1889:	"Durer" of Edison.
	Photographs
1890:	Edison listening to the phonograph Edison at work in the chemistry lab. 1892
	Edison's Den Glenmont
	Library Edison Laboratory
	Thomas A. Edison profile
	Thomas A. Edison Autograph
	Edison Phonograph Exper Dept
	Corner Edison's Library
	Edison & Assistants at phonograph
	Edison talking to his phonograph
1893:	Edison experimenting with microphotography
	Edison in ore milling dept.
	Edison with organ cabinet phonograph
	Edison with most of laboratory staff
	Thomas A. Edison [no.] 1
	Thomas A. Edison [no.] 2
	Grand Trunk Herald
	Nancy Elliot
	Thos. Alva Edison 17 yrs
	[Forty] dollar bill signed by Edison
	Edison Kinetoscopic record
1894:	Edison Kinetographic Record of a Sneeze Edison
	Kinetoscope Records
	Souvenir Strip of Edison Kinetoscope
	Edison at his home, Glenmont
	Cobett & Courtney before the Kineto ... Kinetograph

to do with preparing and printing the film, so this one was probably another device or method to make the film ready for the camera or for viewing. Developing the film was not included in the two cases for which there are descriptions so that may have been what this was about, but it is also possible that it tied all of these ancillary, but very necessary activities together.

All three of these applications died because Edison did not want to push them through the Patent Office. We are left to speculate about his reluctance, but his uncertainty about the future profitability of Kineto devices made him cautious. It proved to be a very unwise decision. If these patents had been completed it would have strengthened his hand in the patent suits. Dickson's innovations in preparing, developing and printing were forerunners of modern techniques that became standards for the motion picture laboratories that were essential supports of the commercial movie business. The devices that Dickson was using in 1891 and 1892 in his prototype laboratory would be quite familiar to professionals who worked in the field later. Edison's failure to register these innovations made it possible for his competitors to prepare, process and print film without fear of pursuit by Edison's batteries of detectives and lawyers.

Whatever the terminated application was for, it is clear that Dickson hoped to have one or more patents in his own name. This was not an unreasonable expectation. Edison permitted some employees to patent devices they designed, but had them sign the rights over to him. At the time Dickson's application was being readied, Dyer & Seely were preparing an application for a Coin Controlled Kinetoscope apparatus which was registered in the name of John Ott. Ott had earlier received a patent for a coin control apparatus for the phonograph.

While this patent activity was going on, Dickson found himself in hot water because of his copyrights. In the mid-August J.I.C. Clarke of the *Morning Journal* wrote complaining about a letter he received from Dickson asking for a royalty payment for a photograph the paper planned to use in an article about Edison. Tate forwarded the letter to Ogden, commenting to Edison: "It strikes me Mr. Dickson's letter is the essence of gall. What shall I say to Clarke?" Edison returned it with the annotation: "... say to Mr. Dixon that without he withdraws his letter that there will be trouble E". Dickson was instructed to write Clarke withdrawing his demand. Tate expanded on Edison's comment "... Mr. Edison desires me to direct your attention to the fact that this photograph was made in his Laboratory, with his instruments, and by one of his own salaried employees, namely, yourself, and that you have no more right to claim copyright upon it than any other member of the Laboratory staff".[343]

This would seem to have closed the issue and put Dickson in his place for overstepping his bounds, but the issue did not die with Tate's letter. Apparently Dickson discussed this further with Edison, perhaps making the case that his skill added artistic value to the photographs. At any rate, a year or so later Edison allowed Dickson to create a personal

343 Ibid. Dickson's letter was written August 11, 1891; Tate's to Edison was August 19, 1891 and Tate's to Dickson, August 27, 1891.

business selling versions of photographs taken by him. Dickson expanded his library with sample frames from successful Kinetoscope films and some photographs from Edison's earlier years which he copied so that they could be reproduced. During the surge of publicity following the demonstration of the Kinetograph in May 1891 he saw that newspapers wanted photographic copies of Kinetoscope strips. Anticipating that this interest in examples of Kinetograph films would continue, from this time on Dickson made still photographs of many of the subjects that he filmed and selected frames from his films which he arranged in strips imitating the film strips. He made them available to journalists, apparently charging a fee that Edison evidently allowed him to keep. It was a practice he continued throughout his career as a filmmaker.

He did not copyright any of these sample frames until 1893 when Edison was ready to commercialize the Kinetoscope. He sent his first application for a motion picture on 16 August 1893, an application to register *Edison Kinetoscopic Records*. It was in his own name and it was the first attempt to register a motion picture for copyright. The Copyright Office apparently didn't know how to handle it because the registration was delayed and not issued until 6 October 1893. Dickson's practice of copyrighting frames from motion pictures, which was based on his experience registering his still photographs, set a precedent for the registration of motion picture copyrights in the United States. The sample frames that he deposited established that a motion picture could be registered as a series of photographs and from that, the practice of depositing paper prints in the Library of Congress evolved. This began at the very start of the commercial motion picture business, many years before the copyright procedures were amended to accept motion pictures as copyright-able items.

In addition to his photographic activity, Dickson continued to be involved in a number of other extra-curricular activities. In February *Phonogram* reported that Dickson made the slides for a lecture about Edison "from his extensive collection of private photographs". In June some carpentry tools – a saw, planes and bits – were ordered for by the lab, marked as ordered by Dickson and Sam Allen with the charge marked "personal". Allen, a staff carpenter often assigned to Dickson, was doing some work on the Kineto, so this may have been related to that, but later in the month the Phono Works did a casting that was also charged to Dickson "personal".[344] While not regular, there are enough of these "personal" charges that appear to indicate that Dickson had some other projects on-going that were sanctioned by Edison.

Personal projects did not distract Dickson from regular work and the next several months were very productive. Beginning in August, 1891 he was deeply involved in the Kineto project although there were brief periods when ore milling demanded his attention. During this period the design of the Kinetograph was completed and Dickson created the film format that served the motion picture industry for the next century and beyond.

344 NMAH Hendricks; EHS.

Chapter 19

"... Unaltered to Date". Creating the Modern Motion Picture

"... I increased the width of the picture from ½ inch to ¾ inch, then, to 1 in. by ¾ in. high. The actual width of the film was 1 3/8in. to allow for the perforations now punched on both edges, four holes to the phase or picture, which perforations were a shade smaller than those now in use. This standardized film size ... has remained, with only minor variations unaltered to date."[345] (W.K.L. Dickson, *Journal of the SMPE*)

"... You will however agree to making it [the lens] as much after the 'fixed focus' as possible. I mean in other words of as great a depth of focus as possible – for what use could I make of a lens that would have to be changed during 'a taking' – the subject approaching & receeding [sic] from lens would make it in focus & then out of focus. Our first machine is ready & have been depending on you to furnish the lenses ...".[346] (Dickson to Gundlach Optical Co., 7 December 1891)

Dickson claimed that he created modern 35mm film in 1889. This was one of his many exaggerations, but only the date is wrong. He really did createthe modern film format, and in 1933 when he wrote the passage quoted above, he probably believed it was true. While 1889 is too early, very early in 1892 he was using film in the modern format. He did not realize it at the time, but it was his most enduring achievement. In 1933 almost every movie theater used the 35mm format and Dickson would be happy to know that despite a number of competing formats, this is still true. There have been "minor variations", but his claim that it is "unaltered to date" is still valid seventy-five years later. In the intervening years the shape of the frame has been altered, the image sometimes squeezed by special lenses and the size and shape of the perforations modified, but the width of the film and number of perforations has remained the same. Although challenged today by digital projection, this format has survived from 1892 into the twenty-first century and it is still the consistent, basic format for the commercial movie industry. The format Dickson created made it possible for motion pictures to be shown world wide, in cities

345 Op. Cit., p. 14.
346 EHS; Letterbook 91.

and small towns. It launched a world-wide industry before the 19th century ended and has sustained it for more than a century.

Dickson and Edison did not call it "35mm". That came later when the format was adopted by the French and other metric system countries. 35mm is the measure of the film from one side to the other and that was not the determining factor in 1891. The key measurement for Dickson was "one inch" which was the desired size of the image to be produced by the camera. It became 35mm wide when rows of perforations were added on either side of the image. The image, as established in 1891–1892 was ¾ of an inch high and there were four perforations on each side and the resulting width was 1 3/8 inches.

The new Kinetograph

Work on the new version began in earnest after Dickson returned from vacation. The camera had priority, but time was also spent improving the optics for the Kinetoscope. There were also some final tests with the ¾ inch machine. The film he ordered in Rochester was still one inch wide, the width used on the ¾ inch machine and a rush order later in August for six more similar rolls indicates that he was still testing the old machine, though it is possible that some tests of a one inch image were made with these unperforated one inch strips.[347]

Although redesigning the viewing device would wait until the new camera was ready, they apparently decided that they needed an improved lens for viewing. While in Rochester Dickson shopped for lenses for both devices with Gundlach Optical Company and Bausch & Lomb Optical Company. It made sense to shop for both machines while examining what was available. In late August Gundlach sent a sample lens for the Kinetograph and Bausch & Lomb sent a selection of samples for the Kinetoscope.[348]

Dickson had developed quite specific requirements for lenses. He had learned something about how they behaved while adapting lenses from microscopes and other devices for the experiments. He spelled this out in letters to his suppliers. Gundlach was told that he wanted a lens that could capture a maximum amount of light and produce a sharp, clear image one inch in diameter. It should be capable of filming an area as wide as thirty feet from a distance of twenty-five to thirty feet and keep objects moving toward the camera or away from it in focus. For the Kinetoscope he told Bausch & Lomb that the lens should enlarge the image and make it sharp and clear when viewed by a casual spectator. The viewing experience had to be comfortable and convenient and Edison wanted the cost held down so the machines would not become too expensive.

Increasing the size of the image to one inch seems about as far as they had gotten. The new format raised issues that had to be resolved before the redesign could be completed. While selecting a lens Dickson had to determine the shape of the image and before the mechanism could be built, decide how image would fit on the film and how the film would move through the camera. There were several options.

347 EHS. Dickson returned from vacation on 7 August 1891. Two film shipments were received in August 1891, the four rolls ordered in Rochester arrived on the 15th, and on the 21st a telegram ordering six rolls was sent to Eastman and the film was received on 25 August 1891. Both orders were for film one inch by fifty feet.

348 EHS. The selection of lenses for the Kinetoscope came from Bausch & Lomb on 10 August and one for the Kinetograph was received from Gundlach on 31 August.

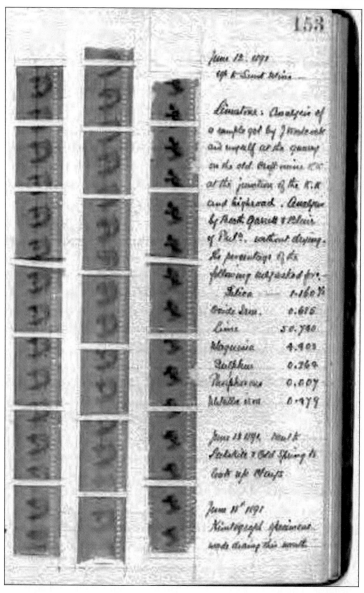

Would the image be round, square or rectangular? Landscape or portrait? In the ¾ inch machine the film moved horizontally from one side to the other and took a circular image. The image was round because that was the shape of the lens. Was that OK, or should it change?

Early on it was assumed that the image would be circular. An illustration in George Parsons Lathrop's article in *Harper's Weekly*, written about the time the change was decided on, showed a one inch circle. The drawings for the patent application were made about that

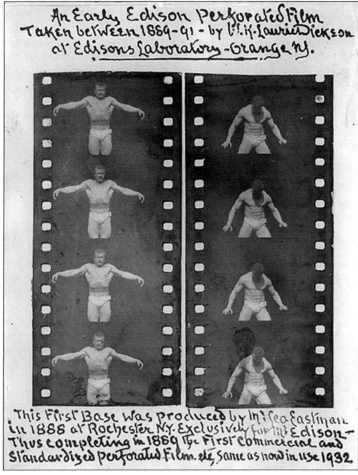

Both images: *The decisions that Dickson made while revising the design of the Kinetograph had a profound effect. At the left are sample films from the strip Kinetograph that Charles Batchelor put in a notebook in June 1891. The image is circular and the strip runs horizontally guided by a single row of sprocket holes. On the right are two pieces of film with Eugene Sandow in the format as revised by Dickson during the fall and winter of 1891–1892. The image is an inch wide and three-quarters of an inch high with four perforations on each side. His format became known as the Edison format and was later called 35mm. With some minor modifications it is still used today and modern audiences can see this film of Sandow which was made in 1894. The film of Sandow was made in March 1894, not 1888-1889 as Dickson claims. (LC & GEH)*

349 NMAH
Hendricks & EHS.
Harper's Weekly, 13
June 1891, p. 440.
The drawings for the
patents show strips of
film but no frame
lines. The figure
drawn to show
movement could be
viewed from several
angles.

time and they are ambiguous (see page 219).[349] Dickson's correspondence from August and September 1891 suggests that his mind was not made up. The words "diameter" and "square" appear and at least one of his illustrations is a rectangle. The decision was his and in making it he would have been influenced by his experience as a photographer and illustrator. Rectangular images were common, but round ones were not unusual. The very popular Kodak no. 1 camera took a round image and photo albums were being filled with the resulting 2 ¼ inch circles. Most serious photographers preferred rectangular pictures and it was a shape that Dickson was used to. But if a rectangle was used should it be horizontal or vertical? Photographers could change between landscape and portrait formats but this option would not be available for the Kineto. He decided on a rectangular image, one inch wide by ¾ inch high.

Dickson never discussed his reasons for choosing the landscape format even though it was one of his most important and influential decisions. None of the experts who interviewed him in later years questioned how or why he made the choice. Perhaps we are so accustomed to it that it seems normal and natural. This may have been how Dickson felt about it at the time. Nevertheless, his choice of the size and shape of the image set a standard that was followed by successive generations – and his decision ultimately influenced the shape of television and computer screens.

He changed the path the film took through the camera from horizontal to vertical. This may have been dictated by economics. If a landscape image was used and it was rectangular there would be fewer images per foot if the film ran horizontally. Eastman charged by the foot so by running the film vertically there would be more images per foot and money would be saved.

These decisions, made in the early fall of 1891, set the standard for modern film. The one inch by three-quarter inch image with four perforations on each side made the film about 1 3/8 inches, close to 35mm. Modern film was born – though nobody was aware of it at the time.

It was a while before Dickson could use it.

Building a mechanism

This was a decisive period in the creation of the Kineto but the pace of work was not hectic. While Dickson was making decisions about optics and image format, the mechanism for the new camera was being designed and assembled, but it was not a crash project. There were no all night sessions and no thirteen or fifteen hour days. During September and October the pace of work was steady rather than feverish. There was a gradual increase in the number of machinists, pattern makers, carpenters and lower level experimenters assigned to the project.[350] In early October the two Ott brothers worked on the project. Fred worked three hours on 1 October and ten hours on the 5th, then John worked four full days beginning 7 October. The involvement of the lab's top mechanics is an indication that specialized work was taking place – possibly the mechanism to advance the film through the gate. John Ott placed orders with the Phonograph Works to cast a variety of parts charged to the Kineto account and nickle plating was ordered for a number of them, probably to improve durability and make them appear more attractive and professional. The mechanism may have been almost finished by the end of October. The number of machinists assigned to the project decreased noticeably after the first week of

350 EHS. Duncan worked six days during early September, a low level experimenter named Le Pontois worked two days in September and eight days during October and a machinist named Spitzel worked full time during September.

November; Dickson was negotiating with Eastman for a large order of film and he stepped-up his efforts to get a suitable camera lens.[351]

Lens warfare

Dickson was not satisfied with the sample lenses he received in August and returned them almost immediately. Heated correspondence with both of his suppliers followed. He had a clear idea of what he wanted and his standards were difficult to meet. He tested and returned a variety of lenses for both machines during the next four months and at the end of 1891 he was still searching.[352]

He returned the lens Gundlach sent the day after it was received because it gave a three inch circle instead of the desired one inch. In a terse letter he told them it was "entirely unfitted for our work" and asked them to correct it. He specified that the image produced should be one inch square then drew a rectangular image in a note he scribbled along the side of the page. In this note he said that he could allow a ¼ inch over one inch "but not much more".[353]

The negotiations with Gundlach did not go well. Gundlach said they could not produce a lens that would give a one inch image as he described it and a prolonged and heated exchange followed. Dickson kept restating his requirements while Gundlach objected and explained why his demands could not be met.

A letter in September describing a microscope lens that produced a one inch circle shows Dickson's impatience. He drew a picture of the lens and said "... I would say that I have your theory contradicted by a projecting microscope lense of which this is an actual size ... [it] gives a flood of light sharp with about an inch circle (I wanting 1 ¼) – focus 1[inch] ... this lense is a flat contradiction to your theories. ... it takes & is supposed to throw a thirty foot picture perhaps of a one inch subject – if it is intended for that why cannot one be made a little larger & do the same work practically giving me the 1¼". He asked them to use it as a model.[354]

Gundlach acknowledged that they had not fulfilled their agreement and Dickson modified his conditions slightly, reducing the width of the angle of exposure and accepting a slightly larger (but focused) image. He illustrated his revised instructions with another drawing: "... The following are the conditions – A lens of as large Diameter as possible Say 1½" to 2½", to be exceedingly sharp in detail to give a one inch square picture *converging* a 25 foot subject @ 40 [feet] distance to said one inch square & with as little loss in other auxiliary light-rays, that is to keep within ... the heart of the 2" circle ...". He repeated his request for as much light and sharpness as possible. Gundlach's calculations for a new lens did not satisfy Dickson. He asked them to modify their two inch circle by making the lens larger. "... Cannot you extend your focal distance & so greatly increase the Diam lens, consequently giving us very much more light."[355]

Unhappy with the way this was going, Dickson wrote Joseph Zentmayer asking for an estimated price for a lens for the Kinetograph.

351 EHS. During the remainder of October three or more machinists worked on the Kineto each day and on Saturday, 17 October six machinists were assigned to the project doing a total of 47 hours of work. During the first week of November two machinists worked on the Kineto but they put in only a partial day on Tuesday. After Friday. 6 November machinists were only assigned sporadically to the project.

352 EHS. Most, if not all of Dickson's correspondence for this period survives and it gives a clear picture of his work during this period. When combined with the surviving pay records it is almost possible to recreate a day-by-day record of his progress.

353 EHS. Dickson to Gundlach Optical Co., 31 August 1891.

354 EHS. Dickson to Gundlach, 3 & 9 September 1891.

355 EHS. Gundlach to Dickson 22 September 1891; Dickson to Gundlach 25 September & 14 October 1891.

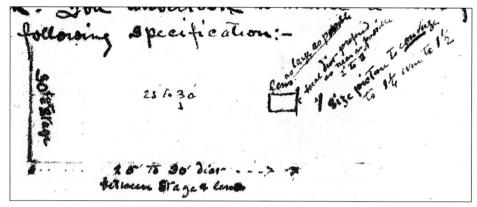

Finding a suitable lens for the camera proved difficult and in the process Dickson was considering problems he might confront while making films. In a letter to Gundlach Optical Company on 16 September 1891, Dickson sketched some requirements. He wanted a large lens with a focal length of 2 to 3 inches and capable of producing an image 1¼ by 1½ inches from a stage 30 feet wide at a distance of 25 to 30 feet. (The image would be cropped to 1 inch by ¾ inches by a frame in the camera.) It was months before Gundlach produced an acceptable lens and by that time Dickson's specifications changed. (EHS)

He sketched a filming area much like one sent to Gundlach. On 23 October he told Zentmayer that he tried the front lens of his lantern objective and the "... result [was] not sharp in definition, circle very large & altogether unsatisfactory – please proceed to construct lens agreed in my last letter ... we are now in need of same".[356] On 1 December he told Zentmayer their lens was disappointing. "... there is not a ¼ of an inch in focus at a time ...". He wrote Gundlach that same day, telling them to make the lens the way they wanted, a two inch circle focusing to a one inch rectangle, but he insisted that they make the image as sharp as possible and design the lens to admit as much light a possible. He urged them to "... make all speed ..." to finish it. In this and subsequent correspondence he repeated the requirement that the lens have depth of focus so that subjects that moved while being photographed would stay in focus. "... for what use could I make of a lens that would have to be changed during a taking – the subject approaching & receding from lens would make it in focus & then out of focus ...".[357] Gundlach reacted slowly so on 29 December he wrote to William Zeiss Opticians, sending them a detailed description of what he needed for his camera and sent additional information on 4 January 1892.

By March of 1892, Dickson was becoming desperate. He had cast his net wide searching for the right "taking" lens. Zentmayer and Zeiss had not come through and now he added Bausch & Lomb. But he continued to hope that Gundlach would come through. The same day that he wrote Bausch & Lomb, he pleaded with Gundlach to send a new version. "... Many months have come & gone & yet the Gundlach optical have not sent us our lens – we should like to have the pleasure of opening an express packet from you immediately in reply." Appar-

356 EHS. Dickson to Zentmayer 19 & 23 October 1891.

357 EHS, Dickson to Gundlach Optical Co., 7 December 1891.

By December 1891 they were testing lenses for viewing. On 16 December Dickson wrote to Bausch & Lomb that Edison had tried the five lenses illustrated in this sketch and none were acceptable. The lens on the left was closest to what they wanted. Viewing to be done by both eyes (the dots above the lens are eyes) so the two monocular lenses were rejected. The large binocular lens on the right was too complicated for use by people unfamiliar with it and the second from the left was a condensing lens. [Quality note: The text and images are blurred because the originals were made by ink on tissue paper.] [EHS.]

ently this pushed the right button because it arrived on 16 March. This one seems to have been satisfactory. Dickson wrote that he would keep it and Gundlach was paid the following July.[358]

Although the lens for the Kinetoscope was not as critical as the camera lens, Dickson was having problems finding the right one. In August Bausch & Lomb sent several microscope objectives and one binocular lens and Dickson returned the binocular lens immediately. While in Rochester he asked Edward Bausch for a simple glass that would enlarge the image three or four times. They had not sent one so he tested the binocular microscope. It was a professional instrument that was costly and complicated to use. Dickson spelled out his objections in a three page letter using illustrations to compare what he received with what he hoped to use. The tubes were too long and didn't magnify enough. "The latitude or distance between center of eye piece [is] not enough. They need to be brot nearer, tube shortened in other words ... eye piece lenses to be as large as possible – so that the adjuster need not be used except in extraordinary cases ...". He complained: "I wrote for a *short* tube binocular microscope of low power enlarging 3 times". A second binocular lens sent a few days later was also rejected At the end of September he returned several more lenses including a binocular lens that Mr. Bausch delivered in person.[359]

Through the next several weeks Bausch & Lomb sent a variety of samples, but none that were suitable. Most were binocular microscopes, apparently with altered optics. They were designed for exacting scientific work and therefore inconvenient for the casual user. Most required manual adjustment and the eyes had to be in the right place in order to see the image. Dickson was aware of these drawbacks, but continued to test them. In December, after rejecting a number of them he asked

358 EHS. Dickson to Gundlach, 11 & 16 March 1892; Dickson to Bausch & Lomb, 11 March 1892; Gundlach to Edison, 8 July 892.

359 EHS. Dickson to Bausch & Lomb, 3, 8 & 27 September 1891. The first lenses were received from B&L 10 August 1891.

for six different lenses and set them up for Edison to try. After testing
them he rejected binocular microscopes in favor of a single magnifying
lens. An individual could see the image easily with both eyes without
needing to make adjustments. Dickson returned three of the examples
and asked Bausch & Lomb if the magnification could be increased from
two times to four times and if it could be made cheaply. In mid-January,
1892, Dickson asked Bausch & Lomb to send another, larger sample
lens which seemed satisfactory – at least for now. There was no more
correspondence with until 11 March 1892 when Dickson wrote asking
a price for buying the lenses in quantity. "... say per doz or per 100 –
they want to be cheap & specially mounted as all will be [hidden behind]
black tube ...".[360]

"Ready to chew up film"

At the end of October, with the mechanical work on the camera nearing
completion, Dickson wrote Eastman about placing a large order for
film. "We are about to place the trial order ... which will require the
specially heavy film 5/1000" thick, sample of which you gave me – but
feel somewhat stunned with the expense ... by careful calculation we
cannot see how it will pay us. We should require the 41" – 100 feet long
cut to 1½ " as we have no facilities for such risky work ...". Eastman had
quoted a price of $140.00 to make a table of film 40 inches wide and
one hundred feet long. Dickson wanted half of it very high sensitometer
for negatives and half of normal sensitometer for making prints – the
first time that making prints for viewing was mentioned in an order.
Eastman responded favorably on the 30th and a trial order for double
coated film was placed on 2 November. This was by far the largest order
the lab had made for film: 54 strips, 27 strips of the highest sensitometer,
the other 27 to be of "... lantern plate type emulsion – about 10 sen. To
be as *Tough, clear & exactly cut* to 1 ½ – wide – this we would most
earnestly request – we are also very anxious to get as close an adherence
of gelatin to backing as possible ... with avoidance of frilling – He added
that it would be all right if it was a bit thicker. "... Kindly pack very
securely with directions how best to keep it well ...". Eastman agreed to
cut to the new size, one that would accommodate the one inch image.[361]

Negotiations for an improved celluloid reached a crucial point
during the next few weeks. Dickson was tenacious and sometimes
difficult, but in the long run his persistence benefitted Eastman as well
as Edison. Despite some rocky moments, Eastman continued to treat
Dickson very well. The personal relationship he had established with
Eastman and his company proved invaluable!

Eastman had trouble making the heavier film. It was an experimental product which they had worked on for more than a year and what
Dickson saw during his visit was a sample. It was not ready for manufacture and his order was accepted as a test of a potential product. Before
filling it, they wrote that they were not certain the thickness would be
exactly 5/1000th of an inch or that they could cut it accurately. Dickson
favored "... material somewhat tougher ..." and preferred that they err

360 EHS. Dickson to
Bausch & Lomb, 5 &
16 December 1891.
One 2½" diam.
achromatic lens was
received from Bausch
& Lomb 21 January
1892.

361 EHS. Dickson to
Eastman Dry Plate &
Film Co., 22 October
1891 & 2 November
1891.

on the thicker side. He said that previous orders had been cut satisfactorily. "... As to slitting, it will be absolutely necessary to get it cut exactly – 9 times out of 10 the film you sent was cut right."[362]

It took two weeks to prepare and the shipment arrived Saturday 5 December. Instead of 54 rolls, they sent 21 of fast emulsion. On Monday Dickson wrote: "We were pleased to receive the first consignment of films (rapid emulsion) today ... but greatly astonished on opening the little roll ... to find that ... the film does not adhere to the emulsion – what is to be done? We cannot of course use it ...". Eastman was aware of the problem and had sent this sample shipment to let Dickson know what was happening. Dickson pleaded with them to continue their tests. "... We shall require a large quantity if we intend to make this a success – as we undoubtedly do ... The machine is ready to chew up film & should like to make our first trial of the film 1½" wide. We sincerely hope the slower emulsion will be OK." Nine spools of "transparent support" were received two days later and were apparently satisfactory.

Without a satisfactory lens for the camera, he was not ready to shoot films so this small shipment seems to have satisfied the immediate needs. It was another month – and a new year – before he troubled Eastman again. On 13 January 1892 he asked how they were "getting on" with the order for heavier film and asked if it was possible to cut the strips a little wider than 1½ inches. "... please add a 32d of an inch ... we shd prefer a 16th more (1/16th) but fear you cannot do it economically, so that if when you are cutting up the sheet and can make it 1 9/18th economically please do so". Apparently tests made with the reels received in December showed that there was not quite enough of a margin for trimming the film accurately. With Eastman's agreement, Dickson placed an order for six rolls of film on 8 February 1892 but they weren't received until 5 March. From this time on, film orders specified a width of 1 9/18th inches wide; 3/16th of an inch was trimmed off.

But Eastman's problems were not confined to producing the experimental thick film. On 1 January 1892, the day The Eastman Co. became The Eastman Kodak Co., George Eastman sent a terse note to Henry Reichenbach: "Your services are no longer required by this Company". Identical notes were sent to Reichenbach's brother Homer, Gustav Milburn and Dr. S. Carl Passant. George Eastman had learned of plans to form a competitive company and he accused them of conspiring with a competitor, the Celluloid Co., and of sabotage which resulted in the spoiling of 1,417 gallons of emulsion ruining $50,000 worth of materials. It was a crippling blow. Henry Reichenbach and Carl Passant were his principle chemists and Milburn was his best sales representative. Film manufacture came to a halt and Eastman brought in George Monroe to revive it. A photographer and emulsion specialist, Monroe had been Eastman's first instructor in photography. Monroe introduced a new formula which produced a thinner film base and emulsion. It reduced costs because it used less silver and there was an

362 EHS. Dickson to Eastman, 20 November 1891, responding to Eastman's letter 13 November 1891. The film was trimmed after it was received. Dickson's order had an allowance of 1/8th inch which would be trimmed off before camera use.

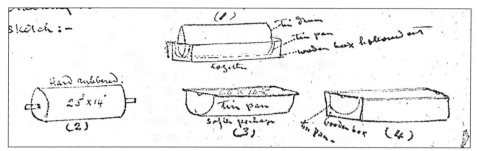

In addition to the specifications for the camera and viewing device, Dickson had to design facilities for processing film. These drawings of a tank to develop the film were made in November 1891 for Columbia Rubber Works Co. The exposed strips would be wound around the drum and revolved through the developer. Similar tanks were made for the other solutions and reels were built to dry the film. [EHS.]

impressive increase in sensitivity. This seemed to solve the problems and George Eastman was happy, but his pleasure was short-lived. By spring there were reports of spots, streaks, hair lines and spoiled emulsions. Eastman fired Monroe in June.[363]

Surprisingly, Dickson was not affected by these problems – at least not at the beginning of 1892. He continued to receive usable film from Eastman through most of 1892. After the spoiled sample sent him in December he continued to order film from Eastman and since there were no further complaints from the sometimes prickly Dickson, apparently Eastman sent film from their most satisfactory lots.

Final preparations

There were details that had to be taken care before testing the camera. Even mundane activities were important because the camera and viewer could not function without them. Even though the Patent Office made no allowance for a system, a system was necessary to make the Kineto functional. While much was borrowed from practices used in related disciplines, it all had to be adapted to suit the specific needs of the Kinetograph and Kinetoscope. Some of the modifications were simple, others required continuous reevaluation and change.

On 23 November Dickson bought a four cell Gibson storage battery, apparently a power source for the camera. On the same day the Phonograph Works were told to let him have a dozen musical records – an indication they were continuing experiments to joining image and sound.

The facilities to develop and print film had to be revised. While based on the darkroom techniques used for still photo work, they had changed considerably as the machines changed. Short strips could be developed and printed like stills, but the longer strips needed special equipment. Here Dickson may have used Eastman's facilities as models. By 1891 the darkrooms had developing tanks, drums to mount the films and reels to dry them. These had to be modified for the wider film.[364] On 7 November, the lab contacted Columbia Rubber Works Co. asking if they could coat a tin drum and pan with rubber and specifications

363 GEH; Eastman corresp., ltr. bk. 1; Brayer, Op. Cit., pp. 82–100; Reese Jenkins, Op. Cit.. Pp. 152–156.

364 The method he devised was described by Dickson in his article for *SMPE ...*, p. 12 and quoted on p. 207.

and drawings of the developing tank were sent a few days later so they could prepare an estimate. He wanted the drum, which was 25 inches by 14 inches, coated with hard rubber and the interior of the tin pan with softer vulcanized rubber. The tin pan went inside a wooden box and the drum was made to immerse inside the tin pan. A rod ran through the drum, protruding at the end to fit into slots in the tin pan. It took several letters to get estimates and place the order. Two rubberized drums and three troughs were received two months later on 8 January 1892.[365]

After developing, the negative film was wound around a wooden reel to dry. Dickson also designed a printing machine to make positive prints from negatives. It was a contact printer, meaning that the unexposed positive film was put in direct contact with the developed negative in a gate where the image was exposed by an electric light. It was a simple device, but one that professional laboratory personnel working today would recognize. Once the positive film was exposed, it was developed and dried using separate tanks and reels.[366]

The photo building was also modified. Work on an addition began just before Christmas. It must have been a modest addition. Most of the work was done by William Craig, a staff carpenter. Dickson also charged some time to the project as did several other lab employees. Craig continued to work more or less steadily until early March when the project seemed to have been finished. Craig's time was charged to an account number called "Addition to Photograph Building".[367] It is possible that the darkrooms were modified to accommodate the new equipment.

Meanwhile ...

It has been a while since we looked at Mr. Dickson's other activities. The Kinetograph was not the only thing occupying his time and some of his activities reveal interesting aspects of his character. At the lab he continued his ore milling duties, though the Kineto was now his primary project. He and his staff continued to test samples of various ores from Ogden, other potential mine sites and from mines owned by Walter Mallory. Since Harry Livor's departure in July, Edison was in Ogden more than in Orange. He was usually there during the week, returning to Orange on the weekends. The problems at Ogden were neverending. Dickson remained on call but did not have to go very often. Near the end of March 1892, during a period when he was back in Orange, Edison received a request from Ogden asking that Dickson be sent to deal with problems. Edison penned a testy reply: "I cannot send Dixon up every time the Separator gives bad results. Why should Dixon know any more [than] the electrician ... I am getting tired of electricians ...".[368] But he sent Dickson anyway. He stayed less than a week.

He had several photographic assignments and the one that attracted the most attention from the lab staff was a request to photograph Edison's awards and medals. Most of these were at Edison's home,

365 EHS. Columbia Rubber Works Co. to Edison, 9 November 1891; Dickson to Columbia, 12 November 1891; Edison order to Columbia, 19 December 1891; F.C. Devonald to Columbia, 30 December 1891. The work was done at Columbia's factory in Akron, Ohio.

366 Dickson described and illustrated this system in his 1933 article for the *Journal of the SMPE*.

367 EHS. Payroll records. Le Pointois and Duncan charged time to the project as did a pattern maker and Peter Solomon, a cabinet maker.

368 EHS & NMAH Hendricks. Dickson was in Ogden 25 March and 29–31 March 1892

Glenmont, so Dickson had to make the arrangements with Mrs. Edison to locate them and take the photographs. The project dragged on for several weeks before he was able to finish it. During the fall, when the machinists were busily working on the Kinetograph, the mysterious patent application for "new and useful improvements in the art of photography" was assigned to Edison and then cancelled.

From time-to-time Dickson was called on for advice and comments and he was capable of caustic responses. D.B. Keeler, 767–9 Broadway, NY, wrote a recommendation that a camera lens be made like the human eye in order to reproduce color and Dickson scribbled a comment on the letter: "Keeler must have just got over a bad case of D.T. I fancy to write such stuff". A Wall Street correspondent was told that a paper on magnetic concentration of ore had been read by a staff member, probably Dickson, who said that the statements "... would make Baron Munchausen green with envy".[369]

Not all of Dickson's research and advice was so light heartedly cynical. In January 1892, C.J. Reed, a former employee of the lab, wrote Edison informing him that he purchased an 1879 patent of Cyrenus Wheeler, Jr. Reed wanted to meet with Edison to discuss Edison's infringement of his new ore milling patent. Sherbourne Eaton, Edison's attorney advised him that it was expensive to have it searched in Washington and recommended that someone familiar with the separation process examine Wheeler's patent. Edison asked Dickson to check the patent. Dickson and Léon J. Le Pontois spent several days searching patents in the Astor Library in New York. Dickson sent Edison a report on 28 January reviewing Wheeler's patent, Reed's employment at the laboratory and factors that were novel in Edison's patent. Dickson accused Reed of stealing Edison's ideas and trying to patent them himself. On the basis of Dickson's report Edison told Eaton that he did not want to take any further action and asked if a letter should be sent to Reed saying that "... owing to the facts revealed by the research of our experts in the state of the art we have decided to stand [fast]".[370]

The late winter of 1892 was apparently a relatively slack period for Dickson. Much of the work on the Kinetograph was done and he was waiting for lenses that would allow work to go ahead. During the last week of February, 1892 Dickson took a group of men to Menlo Park to collect information to resolve a patent interference on electric street railways – a continuing Edison research project, but one that Dickson had not been directly involved in. When he returned he reported to Al Tate that they had not been able to secure all of the apparatus used at Edison's former lab. Tate wrote Eaton that on the basis of Dickson's report it was "...Mr. Edison's desire that you arrange with Mr. Hughes to have all the material at Menlo collected together and placed in the office building there for safe keeping ...". This was the beginning of the end of Edison's connection with the laboratory where he became a wizard.[371]

The winter of 1891–1892 was a period when Dickson was involved in Edison's legal matters. Late in April Dickson went to New York City

369 NMAH Hendricks; EHS, LB-052.

370 EHS. Reed to Edison, 18 January 1892. Wheeler's patent was No. 213,895, 25 March 1879. Eaton to Edison 25 January 1892; Dickson report, 28 January 1892; Edison to Eaton, 29 January 1892.

371 EHS, Tate to Eaton, 29 February 1892.

to testify in a patent interference: Edison v. Wheeler v. Chinnock.[372] At issue was an ampere indicator connected to the wiring for electric generators. The patents involved went back to the 1880s. Edison's was filed 12 December 1883, Schuyler Wheeler's October 1885 and Charles Chinnock's, December, 1886. Edison was well acquainted with Charles Chinnock who had a long involvement with Edison. He was a pioneer of Edison' electric lighting venture and a stockholder in Edison companies. Edison had selected him as superintendent of the Pearl Street Station in the 1880s and he credited Chinnock with turning the Pearl Street Station around, making it profitable after a faltering, money-losing outset. Wheeler was a former Edison employee who apparently worked at Goerck Street at the same time as Dickson. Edison claimed Wheeler's patent was based on observing the tests made there.

Dickson's testimony was crucial to Edison's case. In his testimony he presented drawings from a laboratory book he kept at Goerck Street. The drawings were not dated and he said they were made between 25 and 29 March 1883. The notebook had other drawings and details of tests of dynamos made that were made prior to 1 June 1883. The case was decided for Edison in March 1893.[373] Gordon Hendricks pointed out that the dates Dickson gave for his drawing are earlier than the date when he apparently began working for Edison – Dickson applied for work at the end of March, and had a letter of recommendation dated 28 March 1883. Early April seems the most likely date that he began work at Goerck Street. It seems that Hendricks was not the only one to question the validity of these dates. The Patent Office's decision indicates that Dickson was questioned about the date of the drawings when he testified. According to the decision, the drawings were not dated so Dickson probably dated them during his verbal testimony. Whether he deliberately misdated them or couldn't remember accurately is hard to determine. The entries were apparently made by Dickson in the spring of 1883 and Edison's attorneys, Dyer & Seely used them to prepare Edison's affidavit. They advised Edison to review the notebook before he testified. They told Edison "The facts stated in the affidavit we have carefully arrived at after considerable investigation, and we believe you will readily recall them, especially after consideration of the note-books and sketches referred to. These note-books are in the possession of Mr. Dickson ... ." In his decision, the examiner specifically discounted the dating since it was not written on the drawings. And March was not the critical date. The examiner's decision concluded: "... the sketches by themselves do not impress us as evidence, and a date upon them would not add to their impressiveness. It is the positive testimony of the expert Dickson concerning them and what they indicate and when they were produced that impresses us, and we do not see our way to a conclusion in the face of it that Edison was not the inventor of this matter in controversy in the early summer of 1883 as he claims ... ".[374]

Hendricks accused Dickson of deliberately lying in dating these drawings. He had reason to be suspicious because he was aware that Dickson was notoriously careless about dates and had few scruples

372 EHS, ; Payroll. Dickson testified one day during the week of 15–21 April 1892.

373 EHS, Doc. File Ser.–1893; Hendricks ...*Myth*, pp. 155–156.

374 EHS. Doc. File Ser.–1893: (D-93-36) Patents. U.S. Patent Office, 28 March 1893.

about his many inaccuracies. Questionable dates appear so often in Dickson's writings and statements that it almost seems compulsive. Hendricks was also aware of other flaws in Dickson's character. He knew about his unsubtle efforts to curry favor with Edison such as the fawning letter from 1883 in which he pleaded "... If you only knew how I am heart in soul in all your inventions ..." and unsolicited gifts such as a wooden box secretly made in February, 1892, to store Edison's personal and family photographs. He felt it showed Dickson's inclination to fake things and dissemble.[375]

There are many examples of misdating by Dickson and while he was occasionally careless, some were deliberate. The date he started to work changed from 1883 to 1881; the date that work started on the Kineto became 1887 rather than 1888; and he suggested that Edison was thinking about it as early as 1886. His motives are obvious. He wanted to be counted among Edison's pioneers so it looked better to start earlier. Misdating work on the Kinetoscope was a misguided attempt to "prove" that Edison pre-dated Friese-Greene and other experimenters. Others would call this lying but Dickson had no such qualms. Nevertheless, Gordon Hendricks is not the only one bothered by Dickson's misstatements and exaggerations.

Regardless of whether or not Dickson deliberately lied in testifying about his drawings, it was not crucial to the decision in Edison's case – as ruled by the examiner. What was important was that Dickson was at Goerck Street in the spring of 1883 and was familiar with the issue in question. It was this that swung the decision in Edison's favor. Whether or not he was at the lab in March was not at issue. Wheeler's patent was submitted after Edison's and Dickson's testimony and drawings supported Edison's claim that Wheeler saw enough of Edison's dynamo while working at Goerck Street that spring to use it as the basis of his patent.

Dickson's career as an expert for legal matters ended in April, 1892 with a brief appearance in a Newark court on 19 May 1892 where he testified in what the pay records called the "Lehmann – Newark dog trial."[376]

The McGowan case

"... Frank McGowan walked down Liberty Street at twenty minutes past two o'clock on a bright day in early spring and walked clean out of life."[377]

On the ides of March 1890, an Edison employee, Frank McGowan was reported to have vanished after having lunch with friends in a New York City restaurant. His mysterious disappearance is a curious story worth relating because it casts perspective on Dickson's character.

McGowan was a colorful figure. He was a former seaman, whaler, violinist and an explorer of jungle wilds. At the beginning of the 1890s the public was fascinated by adventures in distant lands and the romance of exploration. The stories of the exploits of Richard Burton, Henry

375 Hendricks, *Myth* ..., pp. 163–168. Appendix C., Fifty Representative Dickson Errors. Lists some of Hendricks' complaints. He was also bothered by a photo that Dickson sent Edison at Christmas 1892, which was doctored to show Edison at the control of the experimental locomotive at Menlo Park.

376 EHS, pay records. This was probably Dickson's friend Theodore Lehmann.

377 Tate, Op. Cit., pp. 201–209.

Stanley and David Livingstone were very popular – Stanley's *In Darkest Africa* was published in 1890 and it was the year of Burton's death. While McGowan was never a celebrity, his trip to the wilds of the Amazon for America's most popular inventor was the stuff that journalists loved and McGowan's career is a fascinating and rather improbable story.

In the 1880s McGowan was Private Secretary to Major Sherbourne Eaton, who the President of the Edison Electric Light Company and Edison's personal lawyer. Al Tate described McGowan as stocky, black-haired and of Irish descent. "... I never learned how he came to graduate from this strenuous life of the harpoon into the comparative inactivity of a shorthand writer with notebook and pencil ...". Ultimately the strenuous life prevailed. Edison hired him to search for bamboo in the jungles of the Amazon, a quest inspired by the explorations of Alexander von Humboldt who reported that there were unusual stands of bamboo in the Amazon valley. Bamboo was the significant material used for filaments in Edison lamp bulbs. McGowan traveled to Paraguay, Uruguay, Argentina and Equador. He crossed the Andes and before returning to Orange in 1889 he had been out of touch for many months while exploring in the Amazon and Southern Brazil. According to New York's *Evening Sun* he defied fevers, beasts, reptiles and deadly insects. "No hero of mythology or fable ever dared such dragons to rescue some captive goddess as did this dauntless champion of civilization. Theseus, or Siegfried, or any knight of the fairy books might envy the victories of Edison's irresistible lieutenant."[378]

Tate said that he arrived in Orange with "... his vigorous frame reduced almost to a skeleton and shaking with jungle fever ...". Since he had been away for months Edison owed him a very sizeable back salary which was paid to him by check, but after finding the check lying around the lab several times, it was decided to send him to a bank. He went but instead of depositing the money as advised, he returned with cash. The amount was more than $2600 – a very tidy sum in 1890. The day before this happened, W.K.L. Dickson had approached Tate asking to borrow $500 from Edison for an unexplained private matter. Tate was concerned about the amount of cash that McGowan was carrying and to solve two problems he advised McGowan to lend Dickson the $500. As security, Dickson agreed to give McGowan stock certificates for 150 shares of stock in Edison Ore Milling Co., Ltd., certificates No. 1122 (100 shares) and No. 123 (50 shares). Tate described the transaction:

"Still grinning, he detached bills for five hundred dollars and handed them to me. I then explained the transaction with Dickson. 'And,' I concluded, 'Dickson will pay you interest at the rate of six per cent annually for the loan."

"Again those Irish eyes blazed. 'What the hell do you mean?' he shouted indignantly. 'D' ye think I'd charge a friend interest on the loan of a bit of money?"

"'Well, Mac,' I replied, 'this really is a business deal. But I see your point. We'll cut out the interest.'

378 Dyer, Op. Cit., pp. 303–306. Dyer quotes the *Evening Sun*, May 2, 1889.

"The rate of interest had not been written in the note signed by Dickson, so I wrote in 'without interest,' which satisfied McGowan and I knew would satisfy Dickson. Then I attached the note to the collateral, put them in an envelope with McGowan's name written on it and handed it to Mac. 'Now,' I said, 'take this envelope to Johnny Randolph' – Johnny was our book-keeper and cashier – 'and ask him to put it in the safe. ...'".[379]

Accounts of this affair by Tate and Frank Dyer imply that McGowan left immediately for New York City without putting his cash in a bank or in Randolph's safe. In New York McGowan enjoyed a long lunch with friends and after lunch left, ostensibly to return to Orange where he had a room. Tate and Dyer disagree on where the lunch was, Tate said he ate at Café Savarin with an Edison employee named Hannington, Dyer said it was at a well known French restaurant, Mouquin's and he ate with Luther Stieringer and another Edison employee, probably William Meadowcroft. Despite this difference, both agree that after parting with his friends, McGowan was never seen again. Tate said that after McGowan failed to come to the lab the next morning he sent someone to his room and he was not there so he called the police who could not find him. McGowan, his cash and Dickson's stock certificates vanished and were never seen again.

Edison hired William J. Burns' well known detective agency to search for him. McGowan had spoken nostalgically of an alluring senorita he met in South America so a search was made there in the hope that he had returned there unannounced. The searches were in vain. As Dyer put it "... The trail of the explorer was more instantly lost in New York than in the vast recesses of the Amazon swamps".

Settling McGowan's affairs took several years. Because he had vanished without a trace, he could not immediately be declared dead. Tate had the contents of his room inventoried and among his relatively meager possessions were three violins, two bows and two books of violin lessons. Immediately after McGowan's disappearance Tate, who apparently discussed this with legal advisors, recommended that Dickson hold off repaying the loan. The case quieted down, but Dickson was not finished with it. In September 1891, Dickson applied to the Edison Ore Milling Company to have the stock reissued to him and in October 1891, Tate told Dickson that it was possible that the trustee of McGowan's estate, William Wilder, might sue to recover the $500, but again advised him not to repay the amount unless ordered by the court.

Dickson followed Tate's advice. In May of 1894, Frank McGowan's administrator, William A. Wilder complained to Edison that he had "repeatedly of late" asked Dickson for payment of the $500. "I cannot understand Mr. Dickson's silence if he is still in the land of the living and an honest man." Edison replied "Mr. Dickson is still in my employ but I know nothing of the transaction you mention". Dickson *was* in the land of the living, but there is no record that he ever repaid the loan. While he may have been following legal advice, Dickson seems to have been loath to settle what must certainly have been an annoying problem.[380]

379 Tate, Op. Cit., pp. 201–209; Dickson gave specifics about the shares he held in a letter to Edison Ore Milling Co. 30 September 1891 requesting the stock be reissued to him, EHS, M135–75. The Edison Ore Milling Co. was the company formed to operate the separator at Walter Mallory's mine in Northern Michigan.

380 EHS; NMAH, Hendricks; Dyer, Op. Cit., p. 306 and Tate, Op. Cit. pp. 201–209. Tate's account

The fall of 1891 had been a stressful time for Dickson. The critical part of the McGowan case occurred while Dickson was struggling with lens suppliers and monitoring the design of the new camera. It was also the period when his proposed patent applications were reconsidered and canceled. At the end of the year those issues were over – or in remission – but problems with film added to his troubles. But as the new year evolved those issues calmed. The lenses that had eluded him through the fall and winter of 1891–1892 finally arrived, the mechanical work on the Kinetograph was finished and the addition to the photo studio was complete. He had film from Eastman and was ready to move on to revising the Kinetoscope to use the new films. It was also time to prepare for film production. Despite the delays, they were on target to present the Kinetoscope at the fair in Chicago in 1893.

Chapter 20

The Kinetoscope and Black Maria

"... It obeys no architectural rules, embraces no accepted scheme of color. Its shape is an irregular oblong, rising abruptly in the center, at which point a movable roof is attached which is easily raised or lowered at the will of a single manipulator. Its color is a grim and forbidding black, enlivened by the dull luster of many hundred metallic points; its material is paper, covered with pitch and profusely studded with tin nails. With its flapping sail-like roof and ebon hue, it has a weird and semi-nautical appearance, and the uncanny effect is not lessened when, at an imperceptible signal, the great building swings slowly around upon a graphited center, presenting any given angle to the rays of the sun, and rendering the operators independent of dirunal variations. ... This building is known as the Kinetographic Theater, otherwise the 'Black Maria'."[381] (W.K.L. and Antonia Dickson)

By the end of March, 1892, with an acceptable lens in hand, the modification of the camera was finished – except for some fine-tuning. It had to be tested with film and it was time to updated the Kinetoscope. It had to be reconfigured to accommodate the larger image and made more attractive for the commercial market. By May this work was underway. His involvement with ore milling was winding down. Dickson spent four days in Ogden in late March, and had two short stints of ore milling work in April, but except for a short assignment in the summer and fall of 1893, these were his last ore milling projects. By May both Dickson and Heise were working full time on the Kineto. Much of the work on the Kinetoscope was done by machinists and after getting the overall design from Dickson, John Ott supervised the work. In June three of Ott's workdays were charged to a new account, number 626, "New Model Kinetoscope Nickel-in-Slot". Ott put Paul Spitzel, one of his machinists, on it full time. On 25 June Ott sent an order to John Valentine of Newark to "Make one Cabinet to Drawing as per verbal instructions of our Mr Dickson at price as agreed viz $20.00". This left Dickson free to devote time to getting the Kineto ready for the Fair which was to open in the spring of 1893.

381 *Century Magazine*, p. 212

The new Kinetoscope

This was also not a crash project. There were no all-night sessions and no overtime. If anything, the pace of work was even more routine and methodical than it was the previous fall when Ott's crew worked on the Kinetograph. Changes had to be made but they were not radical. The design for the prototype could be used as a pattern. The wider film now ran vertically rather than horizontally so the size and orientation of the parts had to be altered. There now were two sprockets and the sprocket holes were large and shaped differently, and apparently some alteration was made to absorb heat from the light bulb used to illuminate the image. Oh, and Dickson – and Edison – were still deciding on the viewing lens.

The prototype had been a box likened to a shipping crate and this wouldn't do for public display so the exterior had to be improved in appearance, but it also had to be designed so that viewing would not be too difficult. Parts had to be more permanent and decorated to make those that were visible more attractive. The commercial model would start with the drop of a coin, run a complete cycle and stop when the strip had run once. The automatic phonograph worked the same way, using a coin device John Ott designed and patented. Ott applied for a patent for a similar mechanism for the Kinetoscope in the fall of 1891. The most important change was in the optics and this was Dickson's charge.

Ott's machinists did most of their work during May, June and July. During June and July Paul Spitzel the primary machinist on the project, worked full time. At various times during July Herman Wolke and Joseph Martin joined him. Spitzel's tour ended on 26 July when he was assigned to other projects, but Martin stayed on until 8 August at which time the machine work seems to have been finished. To support their work Ott ordered various castings and other services from the Phonograph Works, but some brass and aluminum parts were ordered from outside suppliers.[382]

Although there was no sense of urgency, the project moved along briskly. The order for the cabinet went to John Valentine of Newark on Saturday, 25 June. Early in July Valentine wrote Dickson apologizing that it wasn't finished. It was delayed because his workers took off for the Fourth of July holiday. "... My men have bin [sic] off for two or three days & i am mutch [sic] put out with them that I have to disapoint [sic] you & others by not getting the work out ...". The finished cabinet was delivered on Bastille Day – 14 July. A carpenter from the Phono Works worked on 26 July and 3 August and Ott's order on 1 August to the Phono Works to have a reflector polished and silvered seems to indicate that the machine shop was nearly finished preparing the guts. It would be up to Dickson and Heise to get it into working order and ready to be used as a model for production.

During June and July Dickson and Heise had been working on the Kineto but had not charged time to the new model. Dickson took a two

382 EHS, Order Books. Orders for brass and aluminum work went to Barlow Condit & Morris, 28 Orange St., Newark, N J on 18 June 1892; cast aluminum to Aluminum Co., 53 Chambers St, NY on 21 June 1892

week vacation at the beginning of August. After he returned, on 17 August he wrote again to Bausch & Lomb: "Please send us a cheap magnifying glass of as high magnification as possible Diam about 3" to 3½" our new machine has 1" pictures – The final model is finished & we will soon build our machines – The compound lens [7.50] would be too expensive & does not greatly magnify for the extra cost – a plain well curved reading glass ... I am desirous of trying before ordering the lot." He added, apologetically, "This has been a long winded affair for all parties -"[383]

The Kinetoscope was out of the machine shop and was now Dickson's to finish. Optics and the synchronized movement of the images were his bailiwick. Starting 4 August Heise charged his time to "New Model Kinetoscope ..." and the last week of August Dickson also charged his time to 626. Heise's order on 21 August to the Phono Works for "Two (2) yds 1/8" round twisted leather belting" charged to 626 indicates that the drive mechanism was being readied.

Although the new version of the Kinetoscope seems to have been assembled by late August or early September, Dickson was apparently not ready to declare it finished. Edison wanted Dickson's OK before starting to manufacture machines but he had to wait until the spring of 1893. Some fine tuning was required.

Camera tests

The viewer took up only part of Dickson's time. During the spring and summer he experimented with the new version of the camera. On 5 March Eastman sent him six rolls of film cut to the new dimensions: 1 9/16ths inches by 50 feet and the next week, on 11 March Gundlach finally sent him two lenses. One was a three inch lens, the other a two inch lens. Dickson tested them and returned the two inch lens but he kept the three inch one. This apparently made the Kinetograph complete and "ready to chew up film".

Eastman continued to give Dickson special attention. He was still asking for the double coated film, but Eastman couldn't produce it and had to give up on it. But they sent him some of the first of their new, faster emulsion stock. The double coated film was among the unsolved problems that were tabled after the "Reichenbach gang" was fired at the beginning of 1892. Reichenbach's replacement, George Monroe had made the base thinner, reduced the amount of silver in the emulsion and significantly improved the speed of the film. The sensitometer was raised to 30 and even got as high as 40. Monroe started work in mid-February so the six rolls Dickson received in early March were among the first produced.[384] While Dickson may have been disappointed that it wasn't the tougher film, he was probably pleased to have faster emulsion. The film arrived on Saturday, the new lens came the following Friday. By this time the modification of the photo building was almost finished. With faster film, a lens that admitted more light and an improved filming area, Dickson was ready to test the camera.

Although Dickson and George Eastman were both pleased, East-

383 EHS, M109–92.

384 GEH. Eastman Correspondence. On 5 March, the day Dickson received his shipment, George Eastman wrote Wm. H. Walker, who was in charge of Kodak, London, that they had been making emulsion since 1 February, but had trouble with film. They were not using the previous formula, but Monroe's own formula which was turning out film of 30 to 40 sensitometer. "It is not so harsh as the peerless. The quality is very fine. [It used less silver and the "skins" were thinner] ...½ to 2/2000 thick, which is plenty heavy enough and there is an immense saving in material ... There is every advantage in thin films and thin coating, providing the emulsion coating is not too thin to make an image ...".

man's pleasure was short lived. A few weeks later, in April, there were reports that spots, streaks and buckling were spoiling film and the joints from the tables were showing. In late June George Monroe was fired. Manufacture of celluloid was suspended for a while in September and in early November *The Chicago Tribune* published an article about the worthless film Eastman was selling for its popular cameras. George Eastman was stung by the article. He wrote a not-for-publication letter to the *Tribune* telling them that "The manufacture of transparent film is yet in its infancy and it is impossible to foresee the exact effect of any slight change of conditions upon a material that is subjected in every day use to tests that are the most delicate known to chemical science". That same day he wrote a confidential letter to his friend and associate Henry Strong: "We have not been able to make any good films yet. ... I believe that we are on the track of the trouble but it may take some time to get around it".[385] Shortly after this they discontinued sale of their celluloid roll films and did not return to the market until late in 1894.

Eastman's problems did not affect Dickson's work until late in 1892. As he experimented with the new camera he continued to order film and made no complaints about – at least no letters of complaint survive. Twelve rolls were received from Eastman in early May and on 19 July he ordered a dozen more which arrived in August. Eastman was still being generous, they sent him a baker's dozen, 13 rolls. All of these were regular Eastman film with high sensitometer for use as negatives, and with each order Dickson asked for the thickest available stock and specified that they be cut to the 1 9/16th inch width that suited the new camera.

This was the last film received from Eastman and the last received from any source until spring 1893. Dickson's source of film was cut off at a crucial moment. Plans were being pushed forward to begin commercial distribution of the Kinetoscopes and it would be essential to have a stock of films to supply the machines. For most of the year he had been unaffected by the Eastman's problems and it was not until late in 1892 that Dickson learned that he had to find a new source of film.

There was enough film on hand for Dickson to conduct his tests. When he place his final order for film on 19 July he added optimistically: "...We are still experimenting you see – but soon hope to get through".

385 GEH, Eastman Correspondence; Brayer, Op. Cit., p. 95. Eastman to *Chicago Tribute*, 7 November 1892; Eastman to Strong, 7 November 1892. Henry Strong was President of Eastman Kodak Co., but he was based in Tacoma, Washington where he owned a bank. George Eastman was the company's Treasurer.

Filmmaking, 1892 style

We know of only four films that were made during the 1892 tests. Images from these films were published in *The Phonogram* magazine in October, 1892. A selection of twenty four frames from each of the films were illustrations for an article "The Kinetograph, A New Industry Heralded". The frames were arranged in three vertical rows and each row was a segment of eight consecutive frames of action, a short except of the longer film. Three of these, *Boxing*, *Fencing* and *Wrestling*, were sporting scenes, each of them a contest between a pair of athletes The three films were apparently made during a single filming session at the

These frames from three test films Boxing *(page 258)*, Fencing *(page 259) and* Wrestling *(page 260) appeared in the trade magazine* Phonogram *in October 1892 and are examples of the earliest films made in the modern motion picture format. Dickson arranged them this way to make them suitable for publication and the arrangement and choice of subject invited comparison with published versions of motion studies by the chronophotographers Muybridge, Marey and Anschütz.* [Musser & LC.]

end of June, 1892. The arrangements for the filming session were made with Mr. G. Seikel, 158 Court Street, Newark. The athletes were paid, but not until after the films were made. Apparently there had been no discussion of a payment because on 14 July Seikel wrote to Dickson: "I am not only very sorry, but also greatly provoked about the idea that the men whom I took along for to execute a few exercises for your experiment, now demand a compensation for lost time. I may assure you that this does not find my approval, as I think intirely [sic] different of the matter ...". He asked payment of $10.00 to settle the matter, which Dickson OK'd. The payment was charged to Kinetoscope expenses for the month of June, making these anonymous athletes some of the first persons paid to perform in films. And the almost anonymous Mr. Seikel may qualify as the movie's first known agent.[386]

These films were a straight-forward test of the new camera. Unlike the films made with the strip Kineto where he tried a variety of camera set-ups, the camera set up is virtually the same for each film – perhaps because he had to film them during the short time that he had enough sunlight. The choice of subject and the action filmed is very similar to chronographic photographs. Dickson was familiar with the published photos of Muybridge and Marey. The camera is far enough back to allow some side to side movement within the frame and to show the full figure of both contestants. The background is black and the athletes wore light clothes to contrast with the dark background. A balustrade along the back defined the area where the action could be filmed.[387]

The fourth set of images published in *The Phonogram* is the most interesting. It is *A Handshake*, a symbolic celebration of the completion of the Kinetograph. It is easy to imagine that this was made in March or perhaps April, once the lenses, studio, developing tanks and film were all in place. Dickson was not camera shy. Anticipating Alfred Hitchcock, this is the second or third time he appeared in his own film. The left strip shows Heise by himself, in the middle strip Dickson joins him in a handshake and in the right strip they have finished but both are on camera. The camera is close enough to show both men from the hips up. Their clothing only partly contrasted with the black background behind them. Both wore white shirts, Heise dark trousers and Dickson dark trousers and a vest – his watch chain visible. The action is clearly a self-congratulatory exercise – partners celebrating. We don't know if this was their first successful film, but it will do.

It is interesting that both of the experienced camera operators are on the wrong side of the camera! Someone else was operating the camera. Who? There's no hint in the payroll records for 1892. The other person who might have able to operate the camera is Jimmy Duncan, Dickson's sometime-assistant who, as Dickson once remarked "... used to know a good bit about the camera doings".[388] Duncan was assigned to the photo building several times during February and March when the remodeling was being done. He was laid off at the end of March when Edison made a general reduction of the staff, but re-hired a month later as a laborer. After he was re-hired he had no assignments with

386 EHS, accounts, 1892.

387 *The Phonogram*, October, 1892, pp. 217–220. Strips from *Fencing*, titled *The Fencers*, were reproduced in the Dicksons' article in *Century Magazine* (p. 210) and in *History of the Kinetograph ...* (p. 37). In both publications only two strips were shown, but in *Century* there were 10 frames per strip and in *History...* there were nine. They matched the two strips on the right side of the reproduction in *Phonogram*.

388 EHS. Dickson to Meadowcroft, 1 May 1921.

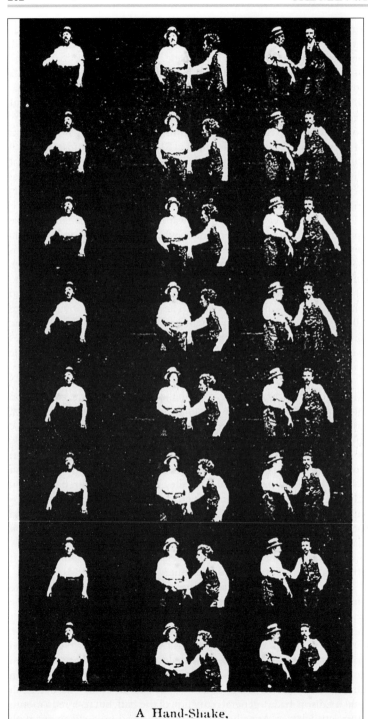

A Hand-Shake.

This image,
A Handshake, *ap-
peared in the same issue
of* Phonogram. *It is
unique because it shows
Dickson and his assistant
William Heise in a con-
gratulatory moment that
seems to symbolize the
success of their experi-
ments. But despite their
evident pride in accom-
plishment, it was almost
two years before the pub-
lic saw the results of their
efforts. [LC.]*

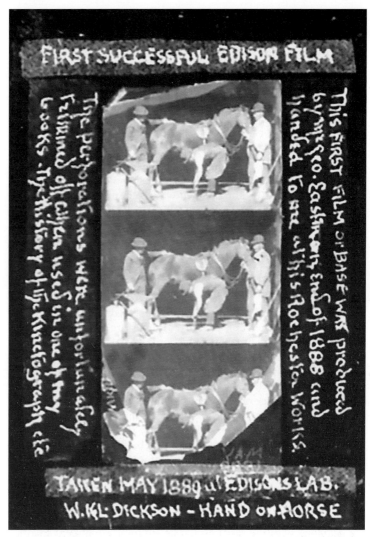

Dickson also appeared in this homespun scene labeled Horse Shoeing. *He was very familiar with blacksmiths and their work and the shed occasionally used for filming was near the blacksmith shop. This film bears no other date than the misleading dates Dickson applied when he sent it to Eastman's Oscar Solbert in 1932, but it may have been made in June 1893 when another blacksmith scene was filmed. [GEH.]*

Dickson. During the spring, summer and fall there was no one assigned to the Kineto or to "room 5" that worked frequently enough to have learned to operate it.

On the other hand, it might not have been necessary to have an experienced operator. "Operating" the camera consisted in starting and stopping it. The crucial work – loading it, placing it properly, focusing and setting the lens opening – was done before the shot was taken.

Dickson was off camera at the beginning and may have started the camera and then walked into the shot. We don't know how it ended, but Dickson or Heise may have left the shot to turn the camera off. It would have been possible to do this. The Kinetograph was designed to be stable and it was motor driven. It was a heavy mechanism, deliberately weighted to keep it from shaking. It was motor operated and probably had a timer so as long as the film didn't catch or go out of frame, once started, the operator would not need to stand by and knew when to return.

There is one other surviving film that could be from this period, a "scene" set in a blacksmith shop and usually called *Horse Shoeing*. It is hard to confirm when this film was taken. It could have been one of the 1892 tests but it is more likely it was taken in the spring of 1893. Dickson added to the confusion by telling Earl Theisen and Will Day that it was taken May 1889, then modified his claim to say it was taken on Eastman film of 1890–1891. Since the samples he sent them are 35mm, it was taken after March 1892 but apparently before 9 May 1893 when this and a second blacksmith scene were shown to a gathering at the Brooklyn Institute. Newspaper accounts of the Brooklyn program described both films.[389]

This is another film where Dickson appeared on camera and it is one of the first where props and costumes are used to create an atmosphere of reality. Dickson stands at the rear of a saddled horse that was having a horseshoe nailed on one of its fore hooves. A man with a leather apron is shoeing the horse while another man holds the horses reins. The blacksmith's anvil is immediately in front of Dickson. The balustrade at the back of the set in the films reproduced in *Phonogram* is not apparent in these frames so it does not appear to have been taken in the photo studio. Dickson told Will Day that it was staged in the outdoor studio on the side of the ore milling building. Even though this film is surrounded with Dicksonian misinformation, this claim may be accurate. The lab's blacksmith shop was in the same building as Dickson's ore milling laboratory. Rube Hepworth, the lab's blacksmith, worked there from 1888 until 1890 when he and the shop were moved to the Phonograph Works, but in 1891 he was laid-off because he could not get along with the supervisor. The smithing equipment that belonged to the lab was returned at the beginning of 1892 and was probably convenient as props for this very early staged scene. Dickson was familiar with the blacksmith's work so it was rather natural for him to use the equipment to create a small scene from what was an aspect of everyday life in the early 1890s, a period when horses were essential to move people and haul things.

As fall approached, the Kinetoscope was on track to be introduced to the public in Chicago when the Fair opened on 1 May 1893, but annoying minor glitches kept cropping up.

There was a problem with the two rubber coated tin drums used in the developing room. The rubber coating cracked and separated from the tin drum. Dickson wrote Columbia Rubber in July asking for an

389 NHMLA, Dickson Collection, Dickson to Theisen, 4 January 1932; BiFi, Dickson to Day, 12 March 1933. Dickson included frames from this film in correspondence with Oscar N. Solbert, 1 December 1932; Earl Theisen in January 1932 and with Will Day in February 1933.

estimate for making two hard rubber drums without a metal base and with a hard rubber shaft "... true – to spin around without 'wobble'. Apparently there was no problem with the rubber lined developing trays because these were not mentioned. Columbia Rubber Co. said they could make the drums but in September they wrote that they could not make them in one piece and had to get special equipment to fill the order which would be included in the price. This seems to have been too expensive because Dickson sent the drums to the Tea Tray Company in Newark to have them japanned. There were problems with this as well. Dickson wrote to them on 15 October, returning one drum and commenting impatiently "... it is worse than useless. We required it perfectly smooth and you send it covered with ridges and heavy lumps (said lumps sticky and not fully baked) ...". Apparently the Tea Tray Co. corrected the problem as this ended the lab's correspondence about the matter. Dickson complaint to the Tea Tray Co. that "We are seriously delayed by this" seems to reflect growing tension as the deadline approached.[390]

Another studio

But nagging problems in the developing room did not delay plans for film production. In the fall Dickson persuaded Edison that even as remodeled he could not get good light in the photo studio and that it would not serve the purpose if films were to be made in any quantity. As Dickson put it, "... to get supplies of subjects – [it was] unsatisfactory – because when the sun didn't come in *straight* our pictures if taken, showed side shadows ...".[391] To solve this problem Dickson drew plans for a studio that revolved on a pivot with a roof that could be opened to admit a maximum amount of sunlight on the shooting stage. The shape was irregular, "... rising abruptly in the center ... it has a weird and semi-nautical appearance ...". Built of wood and covered with black tar paper, it was soon dubbed the "Black Maria" by lab staff who thought it looked like the police wagons that had earned that nickname. The name stuck.

It was a utilitarian building. The peculiar design was dictated by the need for a maximum amount of light. Although Eastman was supplying film with rapid emulsion, the images were clearest when the subjects being filmed were bathed in full sunshine and photographed against a light absorbing black background. And as the rate of exposure increased from eight to ten to twenty or thirty – or even forty per second, sufficient light was all the more critical. The earliest images that reproduced movement were taken at eight to ten per second. The speed increased because both Edison and Dickson were bothered by flicker that occurred at slower speeds. This resulted in their frequently stated objective of filming at 40 to 46 frames per second. In 1891 they were still a long way away from this goal, but by the end of 1892 Dickson may have been taking images at speeds approaching 30 frames per second.[392] This was a problem confronting all moving image experi-

390 EHS. Dickson to Columbia Rubber Works Co., 12 July 1892; 16 August 1892; Columbia Rubber, to Edison, 1 & 8 September 1892. Dickson to Tea Tray Co., 15 October 1892

391 NMAH Hendricks. Dickson to Matthews, 2 October 1933.

392 I have found nothing that indicates the speed at which the films were being taken during 1892, but the films taken in 1894 were taken at speeds around 30 frames per second and the camera was probably capable of speeds approaching this in 1892.

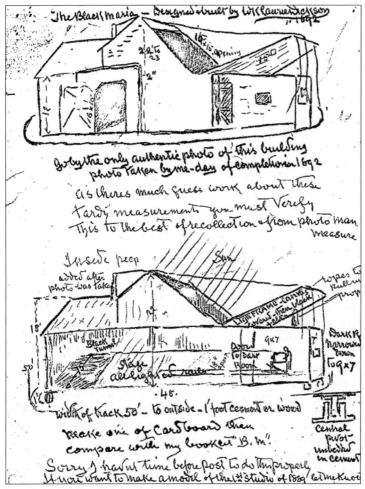

These drawings showing the design of the Black Maria were made by Dickson for Earl Theisen in 1933. He was pleased that Theisen proposed reconstructing the Black Maria and made these drawings to help the process along. [AMPAS.]

menters but Dickson was pushing the limits. The photographic community recognized the problem. In 1891 the trade journal *The Photo-American* predicted that Edison would have a hard time filming with artificial light. They quoted an unidentified English engineering journal: "... With the films at present at the disposal of the photographer it is only possible to get these very rapid pictures in a very brilliant light. Edison will have to content himself with representations of sunlit scenes. When he comes to the magic lantern representation of stage plays he will find that no artificial light at present available will give him detailed photographs at the rate of forty-six per second."[393]

It was an accurate prediction and Dickson's solution was to design the "revolving photo studio" around the performing stage. The ceiling

393 NMAH
Hendricks. *The Photo-American,* November 1891, p. 19.

above the stage was elevated and hinged so it could open to admit sunlight. The building pivoted to allow the sunlight to flood the stage area. The area in back of the stage was blackened with the intent of soaking-up as much light as possible while intensifying the contrast with the subject being filmed. Instead of having a flat wall behind the stage, the blackened area was recessed; a "tunnel" intended to absorb and not reflect light. The design was an elaboration of the stages in the photo building and outside filming area.

As we have noted, this idea was not original with Dickson. He almost certainly borrowed it from the design of Étienne-Jules Marey's Physiological Station.

The rest of the building was also functional. The darkroom for preparing the film and loading the camera was at the end of the building opposite the darkened tunnel. Dickson intended to take his films from a variety of camera positions and the camera could be moved up and down as well as back and forth. The camera area between the darkroom and the stage was elongated allowing the camera to move closer or farther away from the stage. The camera was on a table which could be moved backward or forward on a rail. "... The Kinetograph camera was fixed on an adjustable table which we could wheel out on rails for focusing close-ups or whole stage effects ...".[394] The adjustments had to be made before the take started. Once filming began, the camera had to be stationary.

Construction started early in December 1892. John Ott was in charge and he spent Monday to Wednesday, 5–7 December getting the work underway. Like that for the photo studio, the construction work was done by staff on the payroll of the lab, mostly hired for the purpose. A large shipment of spruce and hemlock boards arrived on 10 December and two carpenters were assigned part-time to the project. The following week, just before Christmas, four carpenters were on the job. The tar paper used to cover the exterior was received in mid-January and most of the work was finished by the end of January 1893 though some carpentry work was done later.

Final preparations and the Kinetophonograph?

The pace of work on the Kineto was unhurried through most of 1892, but it picked-up in November. Several machinists were assigned to the project and during November and December, Charles Wurth, who apparently supervised the main machine shop, worked almost full time on it. Heise began to work overtime again, putting in 12, 14 and even 16 hour days. Work slowed as the Christmas holidays approached and the slackened pace continued into January, but at the end of January, Wurth and one of his machinists, Tony Duppler, started full time work again.

This effort involved a relatively large part of the lab staff. There had been a major reduction in the size of the staff during 1892 so the size of the staff was much smaller than it was during the late 1880s and the beginning of the 1890s. The reductions began in earnest in March,

394 Dickson, ...*SMPE*, p. 14.

1892 and among those terminated was Dickson's friend Eugene Lauste who was fired on 16 March 1892 for "... your not coming to the Laboratory at the time that you should have come and of your trying to put in time for same ...". Some, like Dickson's friend Theodore Lehmann and his former assistant Charles Brown, were transferred to the Concentrating Works in Ogden.[395] In December 1892 there were only six machinists on the staff while in fall of 1891 there had been fourteen. There were now eight experimenters compared with eighteen in 1891. Of the eight experimenters only two were senior experimenters, Dickson and Arthur Kennelly (who specialized in precise electrical measurements). Charles Wurth and Fred Ott who were expert machinists, were on the pay roll as experimenters. Of the eight machinists, William Heise had been working on the Kineto full time for almost two years – and continued full time on it.

Unlike previous bursts of activity, this one does not appear to be work to finish a project or an important stage of a project. Instead, it seems to have been an effort to get both the Kinetograph and Kinetoscope finalized for production along with the support devices like the printer, trimmer-perforator and developing tanks. If the Kinetoscope was to be premiered in Chicago in May, a number of them would have to be produced and films would have to be made. Time was running short. Serious filmmaking would have to start as soon as the new studio was ready. But there were still some problems to solve.

Although the Kinetoscope and Kinetograph were nearly ready, the third member of the trio, the Kinetophone was lagging far behind. Edison had promised scenes from operas; the voices and images of great actors and orators; the sights and sounds of boxing matches and other sporting events. As recently as October, *The Phonogram* talked glowingly of the potential of joining the phonograph to images recorded by the Kinetograph. "Suffice it to say that its capacities are apparently unlimited; especially ... its powers as a source of amusement".[396] As things stood at the beginning of 1893, if the Kinetoscope was presented at the Fair it might have amused the eye, but would have done nothing at all for the ear. The new version of the Kinetoscope had no provision for a linked phonograph and there is no indication that the Kinetograph camera could be used in conjunction with a phonograph.

Although the Kinetophone was out of sight, it was not out of mind. The "... do for the eye ... does for the ear ..." mantra and talk of presenting scenes from opera might seem to be exaggeration and bluster, but the goal of the project was marrying sight and sound and even though it was never achieved, Edison never gave up on it. Dickson understood that the Kinetophone was *the* ultimate goal. He also talked and wrote about it – it was in the title of the pamphlet he wrote in 1894–1895. His later claims that he synchronized sound very early may reflect his frustration that he never successfully recorded synchronous image and sound. Ironically, among the staff that were discharged or left of their own accord were two who later made important contributions to the capture and reproduction of sound, Eugene Lauste and

395 EHS, pay records. Lauste believed that John Ott disliked him and had falsely accused him of working on his own project on Edison's time. However, in view of the general staff reduction going on at the time it seems more likely that falsifying time sheets was more an excuse than cause. Dickson and other staff members seem to have been free to pursue personal projects so long as they worked hard on Edison's projects.

396 *The Phonogram*, October 1892, p. 218.

Reginald Fessenden. Neither of them were involved in the experiments to join sound and image, though Lauste did assist in the photo room and Fessenden worked with Dickson on ore milling.

Experiments to join sound and image seem to have been sporadic and not very systematic. In fact, there is not much evidence that serious testing was taking place, though there are some hints. In November 1891, Tate told the Phono Works to let Dickson have a dozen musical recordings and five months later, on 17 March 1892, the Phono Works provided Dickson with a "6 way hearing tube" and some related apparatus. Dickson apparently had this sent to his attention because the Phono Works' bill was annotated "dl'v'd to Mr. W.K.L. Dickson". The six way hearing tube would have been the sort of listening device used in the coin operated phonographs so it is possible that he was making some tests of how they might work with the Kinetoscope. March, 1892 is just after the new lens for the camera arrived and just before Ott's crew started work on the "new model" Kinetoscope, so this order may have been in anticipation of the redesign. But the trail runs cold at this point. There are no more hints of making or playing recordings along with either of the Kineto devices.

Since there was no advance warning that Edison's newest invention would leave sound to the imagination, work on the much publicized Kinetophone might well have been one of the agenda items during the December-January effort. There was no request for a phonograph or recordings in the several orders sent to the Phono Works, but it would not have been difficult to lay hands on a phonograph or cylinders. The lab worked on them all the time. It is quite possible that Dickson had a phonograph or two and a supply of cylinders in the photo studio to test with the camera and viewing machine. If, as seems likely, there were tests, nothing came of them. The Kinetograph and Kinetoscope remained silent devices and for the next two years the Kinetophone existed only in Edison's – and Dickson's – publicity forays.

An alarming illness

At the beginning of February the renewed activity came to an end. Edison told H.E. Dick, who wanted to market the Kinetoscope at the Fair, that nothing could be done because Dickson had come down with an "alarming illness" and had gone to Florida to recover. Edison sent Dickson to Ft. Myers accompanied by Theodore Lehmann. They left on 4 February 1893, stopped at Savannah and arrived in Ft. Myers on the 13th. They stayed at Edison's house which they shared with Edison's elderly father, Samuel and his companion-care giver James Symington. They stayed until 18 March when they left for North Carolina. Dickson returned to work on 14 April, Lehmann returned a bit earlier.

The exact nature of Dickson's illness is not clear, but it was a serious matter. On 11 February, *The Orange Chronicle* reported he had "... gone to Florida for his health, being much affected by brain exhaustion". In a letter written from Dub's Screven House, Savannah on 6 February,

Dickson told Al Tate "... I am now sitting at an open window with coat off enjoying a tropical climate almost. Palms & the like all round – I feel very sure that I shall very soon begin to improve & return better able to cope with my duties." This is the one hint that job stress had caught up with him and he was overwhelmed by the pressure. In addition to the heavy work load in the laboratory, January had been very cold and unpleasant. *The Orange Chronicle* reported that for 19 days, from the 4th to the 22nd, the mean temperature was only 14–31 degrees and there had been nearly 4 inches of snow.[397]

Edison, who often suffered from mid-winter illnesses, was very generous. In addition to sending Lehmann along as a companion and letting him stay at his home in Ft. Myers, he gave Dickson $225.00, paid for the groceries the pair bought in Ft. Myers and sent Dickson's weekly pay check of $30 to Mrs. Dickson who remained in their home in Orange.

Theodore Lehmann had been Dickson's close friend since joining the lab staff in 1888. He was recommended to Edison by German-born Henry Villard. Lehmann started in the chemical laboratory and Arthur Kennelly's electrical testing room, but for the past two years he had been on the road throughout the Eastern U.S. searching for mining sites and sending samples back to Orange where they were tested by Dickson's staff. Although he was away much of the time, he was living at 166 Cleveland Street in Orange at the time they left for Florida. This was Dickson's home.

In addition to their work with mines and minerals, Lehmann and Dickson shared a mutual interest in music. Lehmann was a cellist and accomplished enough to perform at concerts in Orange and neighboring communities. A year earlier, in February, 1892, Dickson had played violin, his sister Antonia the piano and Lehmann cello in a concert in Orange.[398] They also shared an interest in an active life style. While in Florida they went hunting and explored on horseback.

Ft. Myers, a small town with less than 1000 inhabitants, was still an unspoiled spot. Southern Florida had not been discovered by vacationers and Ft Meyers was situated between the shore and the relatively undeveloped interior, not far from the Everglades. Dickson was a skilled marksman so he probably welcomed the opportunity to hunt and explore the quite exotic surroundings. Dickson asked that a Kodak be sent so he could take photographs. They rented horses on twelve days between 16 February and 14 March. They also ate well. Their grocery bill was $110. Dickson returned in improved health.

Their visit did not sit well with the frugal James Symington. On March 20, 1893, the day after they left for North Carolina, he wrote Edison complaining:

"... They then came and took possession and being sick [Dickson] could not live as we did but hired a negro cook and ran every thing to suit themselves and we became boarders with them – of the bill of groceries and eatables and [delicacies] I have no remarks to make except this –We boarded five weeks with them and for our [board] for 5 weeks with them 15 dollars

397 EHS, Doc. File Ser., 1893; *The Orange Chronicle*, 14 February 1893, p. 4. Dickson's ailment was probably neurasthenia.

398 Hendricks, *...Myth*, p. 156. Reported in *The Orange Chronicle* 16 February 1892.

must be [adjusted] – this is the rate at which we lived before we boarded with them – as a good Samaritan I walked every morning these weeks to get milk for them gratuitously – you will therefore deduct 15 dollars from the account run by them at Parkers during the five weeks they [ran] the place ...".[399]

There is no report on how Edison' father felt about his visitors. Symington's correspondence with Edison indicated that Samuel Edison may have suffered from Alzheimer's. In a letter in April Symington talked of his "... mental loss of fitness or adaptation ...The past is clear the present is in many respects a confusion. He loses himself and his surroundings ...". He also mentioned his father's penchant for wearing ragged shirts, even though he had better. But a visit by the younger men may have been welcomed by the elder Edison. Life with Symington must have been rather grim. He ran a tight ship and what appears to be a joyless home. Symington and Sam Edison had been in Ft Myers since January. They left Port Huron, Michigan two days after Christmas and arrived in Ft. Myers on 2 January. Though Sam wanted to hire a cook, Symington insisted on cooking himself and adhered strictly to a budget of $1.50 a week. In this April letter he bragged modestly about his careful ways and once again complained about the profligate life of his visitors, "... In order to be fashionable and as it did not come out of their own pocket they took the matter into their own hands ...". In April he was still disturbed because they did not want him to cook.

Dickson's illness came at a very inopportune time. The Kinetoscope was nearly finished – but not quite. In his letter to Al Tate on 6 February Dickson said that the viewer was almost ready. "... I left a perfect model – ready for manufacture – It only remains for Mr. Edison to decide on a lamp and motor the machine to be run with gears as of old or with a chain – both tests are at his command – ..." But Edison was engrossed with yet another rebuilding of the plant at Ogden and was too busy to decide about the Kineto. On 17 February he told H.E. Dick that "... it is impossible for me to give it [the Kinetoscope] attention just now." In a very cordial letter written 6 March, Tate told Dickson that "... Mr. Edison's attention is so much absorbed by Ore Milling affairs he cannot devote much time to other matters. Unfortunately, the 'other matters' suffer because of this". Finishing the Kinetoscope was one of the "other matters". It was not OK'd until after Dickson returned in mid-April.

Tate had reason to be concerned about Dickson's recovery. Tate was now wearing two or three hats – perhaps more. Not only was he Edison's private secretary, he was general manager of the Edison Manufacturing Co., Secretary of the Edison Phonograph Works and Vice President of the North American Phonograph Co. Most of the time he was at the Edison Building on Broad Street in Manhattan and he was not in Orange very much. His involvement with the phonograph and his role as the conduit to Mr. Edison made him a key figure in planning Edison's exhibit for the Fair – and the introduction of the Kinetoscope.

399 EHS, Doc. File Ser: 1893.

The fair, the phonograph and a model for the Kinetoscope business

Edison's large exhibit at the Paris Exposition had been a triumph but he seemed to have little enthusiasm for matching it at the much-heralded Fair in Chicago. His attention was now obsessively focused on the plant in Ogden. It had generated little or no profit and produced problem after problem but he was stubbornly determined to turn it into a success. When Frederick Fish, a Boston attorney connected with General Electric, pleaded with him not to reduce the scale of his exhibit Edison explained that he could not neglect the redesign of the milling plant. "... it is an absolute impossibility for me to give the matter of a personal exhibit the attention that would be required to bring it up to the standard which has been elsewhere established". He added that this gave General Electric an opportunity to produce "... a commercial exhibit which will, I am convinced, reflect the highest credit upon the enterprise ...".[400]

Edison's preoccupation meant that Tate had to coordinate the planning. This seems to have begun in earnest in October, six months before the Fair's 1 May opening. Edison had already decided that he could not spend the $60,000 or $75,000 it would cost to match the exhibit in Paris. Instead, he decided that his contribution would be historical – a display of important inventions from the past. Three companies related to Edison's inventions would share the allotted space: General Electric, Bates Manufacturing and North American Phonograph. This was a loose alliance. General Electric had been formed in the spring of 1892 when Edison General Electric merged with their rival electric company Thompson-Houston. Edison was unhappy with the merger, but he was a stock holder and director of the company. Many of Edison's former employees were still with the company, and he was still contracted to conduct experiments, but he distanced himself entirely from active involvement. His name was no longer on their letterhead. Bates was a manufacturer of numbering machines that Edison had recently bought to supplement the Phonograph Works. North American Phonograph Co. would mount the major display of phonographs and – possibly – the Kinetoscope.

Although North American Phonograph was originally an independent company, Edison had acquired control of it by default. Jesse Lippincott who founded the company in 1888 had overextended himself, misjudged the market and found himself unable to pay the large debt he owed Edison under his original agreement. To settle the debt Edison accepted stock in the company, enough to give him a controlling interest. In 1891 Lippincott suffered a massive stroke which incapacitated him. His deputy, Thomas Lombard became the business manager. By the beginning of 1892, Edison had placed Samuel Insull in the Presidency, Lombard was Vice President and Edison, Insull, Tate and Lombard were on the board. In October 1892 Tate replaced Lombard as Vice President.

400 EHS, Gen. Letterbook series, LB-057, Edison to Frederick P. Fish, 27 February 1893.

Tate and Lombard were working on plans for the Fair. Lombard's base of operations was the Chicago Central Phonograph Co., a company licensed under North American Phonograph. The principal investor in Chicago Central Phonograph was Erastus A. Benson, a wealthy banker based in Omaha. Through Chicago Central, Tate and Lombard drew-up ambitious plans to have as many as three hundred coin operated phonographs at the Fair and elsewhere in Chicago. To facilitate this, at the end of October Tate negotiated a loan of $10,000 from Edison. In return for the loan Edison was given 801 shares in the company, half of the stock plus one share. Tate had 400 shares as did Benson, so at this point Chicago Central Phonograph Co. was controlled by Edison, with Tate as his representative. The loan was to be repaid from receipts at the Fair and then Edison's shares would be reduced to 400. Immediately after this agreement was made, on 1 November 1893, Benson, Lombard and Tate signed an agreement giving each of them 1/3rd interest in the earnings the of the Kinetoscopes at the Fair. Although this was a private agreement, it was clearly an off-shoot of the negotiations for the phonograph. Two weeks later, on 14 November, Tate wrote Edison urging that the Kinetoscope be given a priority. "The World's Fair opens on the 1st of May next. In order that there may be no delay in placing Kinetographs [sic], would it not be well to take this matter in hand at once? We will have to have a good many "records" for these machines. I am not familiar enough with the instrument to know whether there is going to be any trouble in getting these; but it seems to me we ought to start at once ...". He recommended filming Christmas pantomimes that were an annual presentation in London.[401] This seems to be the stimulus for building the Black Maria and the attention given the Kineto during December and January.

Thomas Lombard apparently saw a demonstration of the Kinetoscope at the laboratory in September or October, 1892 and was enthusiastic about its earning potential. He began negotiating with the Fair's Ways and Means Committee for concession space and by early December Tate reported to Edison that a decision was expected soon. Construction of the Black Maria started the same week. The negotiations with the committee ran into a snag. The committee wanted one third of the gross. Lombard began negotiations to get this reduced to twenty percent. At year's end, Tate went to Chicago to join the negotiations and told the Committee that they would not exhibit the Kinetoscope if they had to pay 1/3rd of the gross. On his return he reported a further hitch. The power for the Fair would be supplied by Westinghouse and would be alternating current. Edison's equipment, which used direct current, would have to run on batteries. On 18 January Benson wrote Tate asking if any Kinetoscopes had "... been actually built and tested, and show that they will do the work required of them ...". Tate stalled him, but apparently was not ready to give up their ambitious plan.

On 1 February Tate wrote to Edison that they wanted 300 Kinetoscopes for Chicago. Lombard's idea was to accept the 1/3rd fee

401 EHS, Miller File & Doc. File Ser.–1892; NMAH Hendricks.

Thomas R. Lombard. General Manager, North American Phonograph Co.

An 1892 portrait of Thomas Lombard from Phonogram *magazine. After seeing the Kinetoscope demonstrated at Edison's lab, Lombard, the acting head of North American Phonograph Co., led the effort to get a concession for Edison's latest invention at the World's Columbian Exposition scheduled to open in Chicago in 1893. [LC.]*

demanded by the Fair, place one hundred and fifty at the Fair, but put the other one hundred and fifty at locations about Chicago where they could keep all the gross. Edison was more cautious. He responded "I don't want to make too many Kinetographs [sic] – make it 100 in fair & if it pays well the 1st month – we can put 100 or more in city".[402]

This was how things stood when Dickson took ill and left for Florida. Tate was still moving forward with plans for exhibiting the

402 EHS, Doc. File Ser.–1893.

Kinetoscope on a large scale in Chicago, but time was growing short. With three months to go before the opening, the prototype Kinetoscope was almost done – final versions of the viewing lens were received from Bausch & Lomb Monday, 30 January and Thursday, 2 February. Arthur Kennelly was running tests on the motors for the Kinetograph and with the Black Maria nearing completion, Dickson left for Florida the following Saturday.

Dickson's sudden departure did not deter Tate and Lombard. On 8 February Lombard wired Tate that the Committee had approved the concession for 150 Kinetoscopes and agreed to take 25 per cent of the gross. Although Edison knew of Tate's negotiations and had encouraged them, there was no formal agreement for the exhibition. On the 10th Tate wrote a long letter to Edison asking him to define their relationship and it was at this point that he told Edison of the agreement between Lombard, Benson and himself. He told Edison that on the basis of the take from coin operated phonographs, they estimated that each machine would net $10, more or less, per day with a gross income of about $240,000 for the run of the Fair. After paying the percentage to the Fair, their net would be about $180,000 less operating expenses. On a more cautious note, he asked how Dickson's absence would affect their plans and whether it might not be possible to hire a substitute to push matters ahead. Edison responded: "I pay for Cabinets for 150 machines complete except battery – you furnish battery & pay for strips & all other expenses – costs of machines to be repaid from first recepts [sic] – then remaining profits divided equal between E & T & L – This deal only for Chicago & the fair."[403]

Although it was not a contract, Tate was anxious to push this deal ahead because he learned that a third party had entered the picture. The previous week H.B. Dick, visited Edison and discussed a proposal to exhibit the Kinetoscope at the Fair. This was serious competition. H.B. Dick, a Chicago businessman, was the brother of A.B. (Albert) Dick, the Midwest lumber manufacturer who had bought rights to Edison's electric pen and turned it into a profitable business as the mimeograph. Edison was negotiating with A.B. Dick to use his Chicago home during a visit to the Fair in the late summer. When H.B. Dick wrote on 17 February pressing for a formal contract, Edison put him off by saying that Dickson was sick and away for two months: "... the model is about finished but I am afraid that without you come on & hustle things personally about [the] model that nothing can be done as it's impossible for me to give it attention just now".[404]

About this time Lombard wrote Tate that he was skeptical that the Phonograph Works could produce machines in the remaining time.

The negotiations to exhibit the Kinetoscope at the Fair slowed to a halt. On 7 April Edison wrote the Ways and Means Committee of the Fair surrendering the concession for the Kinetoscope. A week later Dickson returned to work. It was the middle of April 1893 and it would be another year before the Kinetoscope was exhibited to the public for the first time.[405]

403 Ibid.

404 Ibid.

405 EHS. Payroll records. Dickson was returned to the payroll on Friday, 14 April 1893, but his time for that day and the next two (Saturday and Monday) were charged to WKLD personal. His first charge to the Kineto account, no. 462, was Tuesday, 18 April 1893.

PART IV

1894–1896
Making Movies and Marketing
the Kinetoscope

Chapter 21

Personal Affairs. Pictures, Words and Inventions

"... Mr. and Miss Dickson have entered into their undertaking *con amore*, but though very properly possessed with a becoming admiration for the man whose life they are depicting, they are not blind adulators. They give what the discriminating public desires and will respond to, not only a vivid picture of the scientific romance of Mr. Edison's life, but also a subtle analysis of his character, together with a scientifically clear description of his great inventions ...". (A review of *The Life and Inventions of Edison* in *The Orange Chronicle*, 20 May 1893, p. 7)

Thomas A. Edison: "The little watch camera, called 'Photoret' is a novel and interesting invention which, aside from the entertainment and edification which it will provide for the young folks and amateur photographers, has merits which will make it of decided value where the use of a large Camera would be inconvenient.

"It deserves success."[406] (Letter of endorsement, 2 January 1894)

The Dickson household must have been a busy place. Although Laurie, as his family liked to call him, worked long hours, six days a week, he involved himself in a series of other projects, some of which were connected with his work in the laboratory, some unrelated. His musician sister, Antonia, who lived with Laurie and his wife, was also very active. Her focus was on culture and the arts – an enthusiasm she shared with Laurie and his wife. Antonia's interest in the arts was as a creator rather than a consumer. She performed, lectured and wrote. Although Lucie, Dickson's wife, was not quite as active, she also had a creative side. Lucie does not seem to have been a performing musician but she was apparently well educated and, like her husband and sister-in-law, was well rounded in the liberal arts. An article she wrote about the Dicksons' visit with Anton Rubinstein was published in *Leslie's Weekly* and the Orange newspapers mentioned translations she made from German.

The Dicksons had no children, but the household was apparently expanded from time to time by live-in boarders who shared some of the Dicksons' interest in the arts and sciences. Laurie's French born

406 NMAH Hendricks. From the collection of Roger Casler, son of Herman Casler.

friend and co-worker, Eugene Lauste apparently lived with the Dicksons for a while before setting-up his own boarding house in the duplex
house on High Street where the Dicksons lived before moving to their
larger home on nearby Cleveland Street. In 1892 Theodore Lehmann
stayed with the Dicksons on the occasions when he was in Orange. The
German-born Lehmann, Edison's principal surveyor of mining properties, was on the road much of the time but he returned to the lab from
time to time and often stayed with the Dicksons. His visits were
probably welcomed because he fit well with the family. He was a skilled
cellist and the Dicksons probably welcomed the opportunity to perform
with him and to speak German, a language Laurie and Antonia learned
while she was at conservatories in Leipzig and Stuttgart. Although
Eugene Lauste does not seem to have been musical, he shared Laurie's
interest in mechanics, electricity and experimentation. Lauste was a
Parisian who never learned to communicate well in English, so his visits
gave the Dicksons an opportunity to use the French they used during
their childhood in Brittany.

At times the Dickson household must have seemed like a music
conservatory. When Lehmann was there, at least three members were
practicing, Antonia on the piano, Laurie on the violin and Lehmann on
cello. There were probably musical evenings when they got together to
play. Antonia and Lehmann performed together in public several times
and Laurie played his violin in at least one of program and sang at
another – he was reputed to have a pleasant tenor voice.

Antonia did not limit her musical contributions to performances.
During the winter of 1894–1895 she gave a series of lectures on the
history of music at her home and these were not light-weight introductions for the novice. The *Orange Chronicle* reported that she traced music
"... from its earliest indications through mythological, legendary and
historical sources and by the results of modern excavations in Egypt,
Chaldea, Assyria, Babylonia, China, India, Scandinavia, Greece, secular
and ecclesiastical Rome, special stress being laid upon the Greek basic
system. ...". The curriculum traced the development of music through
the troubadours of the Middle Ages, the development of polyphony
and harmony and concluded with the works of contemporary compos-
ers. It was illustrated by rare manuscripts from her collection and
musical airs she collected from "... peasants of various lands ...".[407] The
series was apparently successful because the following year she lectured
at the Shepard School of Music in Orange. There her content was even
weightier than in the previous year. Speaking on "The Antiquity of
Music" she claimed that music was the earliest of the arts. She linked
the musical instinct in humans to physical structure and spiritual needs.
She emphasized the role of natural vibrations in human senses and
discussed the structure of the ear in particular. Her lecture examined
the role of music in ancient history and mythology. This lecture was
followed by one on "Ancient Ecclesiastical Music".[408]

Antonia's cultural interests were not limited to music, she was also
an aspiring writer. In December, 1896, the *Orange Chronicle* published

407 NMAH,
Hendricks. *Orange
Chronicle*, 16 March
1895.

408 Ibid. *Orange
Journal Herald*, 7
December 1895.

"Listening to the Voices", a lecture from "Art Leaves", a series of twelve essays selected from more than a hundred she had written based on paintings by "celebrated masters". This one was inspired by an unidentified painting of Joan of Arc. "... Deserted by her king, sold by her country-men, denounced by her church, Joan of Orleans awaits her end. Around her press the dark walls of her dungeon, about her the heavy links of iron chains. Through the window come the hoarse curses of the people, the lewd jests of the soldiery; but Joan is beyond them all. In that fair dream, which God hath laid upon her breast, she has entered into the holy calm of her first estate, and is once more a child upon the hills of Domremy, 'Listening to Voices'."[409]

Laurie was less serious about his music than his sister, but he kept up his interest and continued to work in drawing and photography. A photograph of a tattered illustration for one of Antonia's poems is among the few surviving photographs by Dickson that historian Gordon Hendricks acquired. The poem, "Indian Lullaby to the Pale Face" (see pages 33–34), is illustrated by a romantic drawing of an Indian camp in the woods. Antonia's text is also lettered by Dickson, with the title done in a rustic style that he favored during this period – the lettering made to appear as if it were made from twigs and logs. This is probably similar to the series of engravings that he copyrighted in 1888 (see page 233).[410]

These drawings were probably done with water colors, a medium that Dickson seemed to favor. Relatively few drawings by Dickson from this period survive. One of the most interesting of those that do, is the cover he designed for *History of the Kinetograph, Kinetoscope and Kineto-Phonograph*. The title is prominently centered and done in the rustic style he favored, but the woodsy motif has small embellishments that resemble tiny bolts of lightning – a hint of electricity. The background continues the rustic theme with trees on either side and birds, a squirrel, a bee and a spider web adding visual interest. Surrounding the title are drawings taken from Kinetoscope productions – art emerging from science and nature. Some are from actual productions, some fanciful. Niagara Falls is prominent at the top even though it had not been filmed. At the bottom is an Indian camp with native Americans dancing – the dance was filmed, the camp was a fiction. On the left side are an imaginary horse race, football game and scene of a buffalo hunt, but most of the rest are scenes from productions that Dickson actually filmed.

Painting was a hobby, but photography was part of his livelihood and he seemed to find particular satisfaction in it. He may have had his own darkroom at home, but the photographic facilities at the laboratory would have satisfied most professionals and he seems to have used them for personal as well as professional work. The photographs from this period that have survived are mostly official pictures taken at the laboratory, but he took family pictures and he experimented with trick effects. He joined the Orange Camera Club when it was formed in March 1892 and he exhibited some of his work there. The *Orange*

409 Ibid. *Orange Chronicle*, 19 December 1896.

410 NMAH, Hendricks. Gordon Hendricks acquired this collection of 41 negatives of Dickson's photographs on 11 May 1959 from Kathleen Polson of Twickenham, England.

PHOTOGRAPHY EXTRAORDINARY.

"Photography Extraordinary." Two examples of trick photographs made by Dickson – featuring one of his favorite subjects, himself. These were published in 1895 in the Dicksons' The History of the Kinetograph ... but were made earlier. These, or some nearly identical pictures were described in an account of a presentation for the Orange Camera Club in November 1892. [LC.]

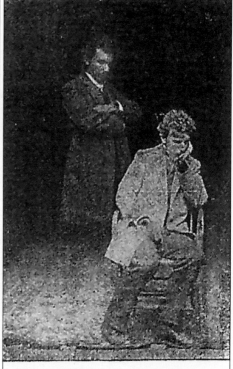

PHOTOGRAPHY EXTRAORDINARY.

Chronicle reported the Club's annual lantern slide exhibit, 18 November 1892: "... some very curious experimental pictures of a man's head on a plate, a man with his head under his arm, one with two heads, and one with a spirit picture in the background ...".[411] The head – and the men – were all Mr. D. who often featured himself in his pictures. Dickson reproduced these, or similar trick photographs in his booklet about the Kinetograph.

Trick photographs were done for his own amusement and to hone his skills, but Dickson saw a more pragmatic potential in the pictures that he took for Edison. The lab received regular requests for pictures of Edison as well as photographs of his inventions, the laboratory building and the staff. Requests for portraits were routinely filled from a supply kept in the office. These were printed from negatives kept by a New York photographer, Falk. Falk would print a dozen or so whenever Tate or his assistant requested a new supply, but the steady stream of journalists visiting the lab wanted pictures that illustrated their stories. In addition, there was a small army of businessmen who wanted something more than formal portraits. They profited by selling the products that evolved from Edison's inventions – phonographs, mimeographs, electric lighting and telegraphic services. Edison's name on their door and letterhead was a plus. His photo on the wall enhanced

411 NMAH, Hendricks. Some photographs of Dickson's family are among the negatives that Hendricks purchased and Dickson mentioned taking photographs of his family, including his nieces in his later correspondence.

their own image and put money in the bank. If one photo was good, a number of them, implying that they had an intimate acquaintance with the Wizard, would be even better.

Dickson sensed this potential market and began assembling and organizing photos that documented the lab and Edison's work. While most were his own photos, he added photos from other sources, including family photos of Edison's parents and pictures taken while he was a boy. We have seen that in the early 1890s Dickson began to register some of these photographs with the Copyright Office. He continued this practice through the first half of the 1890s. In February 1891, *Phonogram* reported that Dickson had made slides for a lecture about Edison "from his extensive collection of private photographs".[412] He continued to add to the collection as he filled photographic assignments. Most of the photographs he copyrighted were his own, but a few were copies from Edison family records. In 1893 he copyrighted photographs of Edison's mother, Edison at the age of fourteen and pages from the *Grand Trunk Herald*, the newspaper Edison published while working on the Grand Trunk Railway.

By 1891 Dickson was trying to earn extra money from his collection. Not everyone approved of this. In August 1891, Al Tate objected to Dickson's attempt to collect a royalty fee from a journalist. Although Edison supported Tate's objections, he knew about Dickson's various extra-curricular activities and ultimately gave at least tacit consent to Dickson's photo business. He allowed Dickson to register copyright in his own name and later, in 1894, when William Gilmore forced Dickson to surrender copyrights for four Kinetoscope subjects, Edison allowed Dickson to keep his copyrights for the still photos. There is no record of why Edison was so lenient, but he may have seen some benefit in Dickson's extracurricular activities. First of all, Dickson was providing a service that Edison's clients wanted and it relieved Edison from having to set up and manage it. Dickson did part of the photo work on his own time and he worked to improve the value of the photo collection by giving it variety, professional quality and order. Dickson prepared the negatives for printing very carefully. He removed unwanted blemishes, altered the framing to improve composition and occasionally made edits to improve the look and, in a few cases, alter the content. He had storage units built to keep the collection and apparently he used a numbering system to identify the negatives which made it easier to respond to requests for specific images – particularly from those willing to pay for the service. The photo business gave Dickson a supplementary income that did not come out of Edison's pockets. In other words, it was a form of bonus that made Dickson happy and cost Edison little or nothing.

Whatever objections Tate and others had to selling photographs, by 1892 they were resolved in Dickson's favor and the issue was not raised again until William Gilmore came to the lab in 1894. In July of 1892 *Phonogram* magazine offered a large selection of photographs of Thomas Edison and the laboratory for sale. These were Dickson's images. In all about fifty different subjects were offered and they were

412 NMAH Hendricks; Conot, Op. Cit., p. 296.

This doctored photo in which Edison's head was substituted for the operator of Edison's experimental locomotive was sent by Dickson to Edison in 1892 as a Christmas greeting. [EHS.]

available in several sizes. The largest assortment of subjects was available as 11 by 14 photographs mounted on 14 by 17 cards. These cost $2.00 each or $22.00 for a dozen. Other subjects were available as 8 by 10s mounted on 10 by 12 cards at $1.25 each or $14.00 a dozen. 5 by 8's on 8 by 10 cards were $1.00 or $11.00 a dozen. Orders for specific pictures were sent to Virginia McRae, manager of the *Phonogram* who apparently forwarded them to a photographer in Orange named Brady (not, apparently, connected to Matthew Brady) who filled the orders from negatives that Dickson had placed with him. Presumably – almost certainly – Dickson received a portion of the money paid for the photographs. Ads for these photos continued to appear in *Phonogram* for the next several months.

One of the photos offered through *Phonogram* was the picture of Edison operating an experimental locomotive in at Menlo Park in 1879 and it is an example of Dickson's practice of doctoring photos. It appears that he took Edison's face from another photograph and substituted it for the operator's to make it appear that Edison was operating the train. Dickson gave this or a similar picture to Edison as a present for Christmas in 1892, perhaps as a light hearted gesture. If this had only been a private joke between friends it would have been innocuous, but this same photo seems to have been the one offered to the readers of *Phonogram*. Since there is no indication that it is not authentic it raises an ethical issue – the one that Gordon Hendricks raised later. Today this would be regarded as an unacceptable, unethical practice, but apparently it did not seem so to Dickson at the time. Altering or "doctoring" photographs was a normal part of processing the picture. He probably would have been uncomfortable with leaving every exposed photo the way it came from the camera.

In the 1890s the public was rather accustomed to seeing edited illustrations and Dickson was not the only illustrator to manipulate the images he produced. While photography gave the impression of producing a more accurate image and an increasing number of photographs were being published in books, magazines and newspapers, most of the illustrations the public saw were drawings made by professional artists, sometimes from photographs. Often these were more impressionistic than accurate. The tools that made photo-journalism possible – high-speed photography and the half-tone process – were still evolving during the 1890s. The printing processes used for books and magazines generally required that photographs be inserted separately rather than printed with the text. As photographs became more common, the expectation that illustrations should be truthful and accurate grew, but in 1892 this was still evolving. We can only speculate about how Dickson felt about this, but he may have believed that if Edison had actually operated the locomotive in 1879 – or even intended to operate it – then the doctored photo recreated an impression of reality. At any rate, he was not bothered by the practice, but the subject will come up again when Dickson devotes more of his time to film production.

A life of Edison

His collection of Edison photographs seems to have initiated one of the Dicksons' most ambitious projects, a biography of Edison. In November 1892, *Cassier's Magazine, Engineering Illustrated,* published the first article in a new series, "The Life and Inventions of Edison", by A. and W.K.L. Dickson. Subsequent articles written by Antonia and her brother appeared monthly over the next fourteen issues with the final article appearing in December 1893. The articles followed Edison's career from his boyhood days in Milan, Ohio and Port Huron, Michigan to recent developments at the laboratory in West Orange, though the Kinetoscope was only mentioned briefly.[413] Since *Cassier's* was an illustrated magazine, there were many photos by Dickson which were supplemented by drawings by L. Bauhan and Richard F. Outcault. Outcault no longer worked for Edison and was now with *Electrical World*. Shortly after these articles appeared he joined the staff of the *New York World* where he made his reputation as the father of the comic strip.

The series had a modest beginning. In June, 1892 Louis Cassier approached Edison for material for a biographical article. Tate told him they were assembling information and added: "I shall arrange with our photographer to furnish such pictures as may be desired".[414] This seems to have opened the door for Dickson with his abundance of pictures – including the slides he had prepared for his lecture on Edison's work. Some time during the summer the article grew into a comprehensive biography. The arrangement between the Dicksons and Louis Cassier was negotiated privately – at least there is no further correspondence

413 *Cassier's Magazine* was published in New York and London by The Cassier Magazine Company. The first article appeared in Vol. 3, No. 13, November 1892, the final article was in Vol. 5, No. 26. December 1893, pp. 131–146.

414 EHS. Tate to *Cassier's Magazine*, 27 June 1892.

about it in the Edison's correspondence for 1892. But the articles were written with Edison's consent and co-operation. The files of the laboratory were available to Dickson and his sister and Edison gave them interviews – though these must have been difficult to arrange since Edison was at Ogden much of the time.

Although *Cassier's Magazine* reached a relatively small audience, its target, the engineering community, was useful to Edison and important for Dickson. They were a dying breed: self-educated professionals. Dickson called himself an electrical engineer but he did not have a university degree in engineering. When he applied for work Dickson told Edison that he had a certificate from the Cambridge Examiners and had done work in electricity but there is no record that he attended Cambridge University, although there is a vague indication that he might have passed the examinations. Shortly after applying to Edison in 1879, he came to the United States and there is no record that he attended university in the U.S. Since he was nineteen when he came to the U.S., unless he was particularly gifted, any schooling he had was at the secondary level. His professional training was largely "on the job." This would have appealed to Edison who was educated at home and started working while in his early 'teens.

Although it was possible for skilled non-professionals to achieve professional standing in late nineteenth century, the professions were organizing and educational standards were one of the priorities of newly formed professional societies. The American Society of Mechanical Engineers was organized in February 1880 and though Edison was admitted as a member, by the 1890s the membership was increasingly populated with PhDs. Even though his situation as a valued experimenter in Edison's lab gave him prestige, Dickson had not yet created enough of a reputation to gain membership. Dickson valued the recognition of his peers and the articles about Edison's work would certainly help his cause!

Although this was a joint project, Antonia did most, if not all of the writing. Laurie provided technical expertise and liaison with Edison and the lab staff. He may have written some of the descriptions of Edison's inventions, but his contributions were probably adapted by Antonia because the writing style is generally consistent throughout. The text is flowery, verbose and laced with classical and mythological references. This is consistent with the examples of Antonia's literary style that survive and quite different from W.K.L.'s surviving prose. Hers was a literary style popular in the Victorian era but shunned in the twentieth century. In the opening paragraphs Edison was identified as "... our hero", establishing a laudatory feeling that persisted. They emphasized Edison's patient, persistent research methods and the professional quality of his laboratory, but they also stressed elements that made Edison a popular hero: self-education, native common sense, disdain for worldly goods and stick-to-itness. The qualities of the common man, but a common man who achieved unexpected accomplishments, something other common people might aspire to. Most of the stories of Edison's youth are here: his mother's role in educating him, going to work in his early 'teens, publishing his own newspaper, chemical experiments with explosions, becoming deaf from having his ears boxed, saving the life of the station master's child, etc.

Edison's reputation as the Wizard of Menlo Park offered an irresistible opportunity for Antonia to play with her love of simile and mythology:

"... A species of glorified mist soon enveloped 'the wizard of Menlo Park', through which loomed, like spectres of the Brocken, the grotesque and exaggerated reports of his powers. By the simple inhabitant of the region he was regarded with a kind of uncanny fascination, somewhat similar to that inspired by Dr. Faustus of old, and no feat, however startling, would have been considered too great for his occult attainments. Had the skies overspreading Menlo Park been suddenly darkened by a flotilla of air-ships from the planet Mars, and had Edison been discovered in affectionate converse with a deputation of Martial scientists, the phenomenon would have been accepted as proper concession to the scientist's genius ...".[415]

Although the passage attributes the Wizard myth to popular fascination, the continuing references to mythology, legend and Greek and Roman gods reinforced the notion that Edison earned special favor from the gods through Spartan (or puritan) behavior and reliance on his god-given natural skills.

The Dicksons inserted a racial element into this mixture of ancient culture and populist idealism. In discussing Edison's parentage, they traced his father to Dutch settlers in New Amsterdam and his mother to Scotch ancestry. "... It will be seen, therefore, that the two national streams which have been most potential in determining the currents of the world's history – the Teutonic and the Celtic – met in the veins of our hero ...".[416] This, of course, linked Edison to the Dicksons who were especially proud of their Anglo-Scotch heritage. While this racial theme does not dominate their text, it is clear that they were describing achievements they felt peculiar to Caucasian, European culture – especially northern Europe.

While the series was praised by the local papers in Orange and by *Phonogram* magazine, at least one unidentified critic took exception to the "... florid language", citing as an example a passage from the June 1893 article:

"The breathings of Marsyas' flute which trenched upon the golden harmonies of Phoebus Apollo, and the glowing fabric of Arachne which outvied the textile intricacies of Pallas Athene; the spell of Arion which smoothed the wrinkled brow of ancient Oceanus, and the magic strains of Orpheus, at which the basaltic gates of Hades rolled suddenly back on their adamantine hinges, all these endangered the attributes of Olympus, and the gods themselves became ashamed of their earthly children."[417]

This leaden prose was interrupted from time to time with useful, sometimes vivid descriptions of Edison's inventions, apparently distilled from Laurie's contributions. These passages were frequently enhanced with Dickson's own pictures or drawings, often based on his

415 *Cassier's Magazine*, Vol. 3, No. 17, March 1893, p. 376.

416 Op. Cit., Vol. 3, No. 13, November 1892, p. 4,

417 NMAH Hendricks. Gordon Hendricks did not identify the source of this review which was apparently from a magazine published in the summer or fall of 1893.

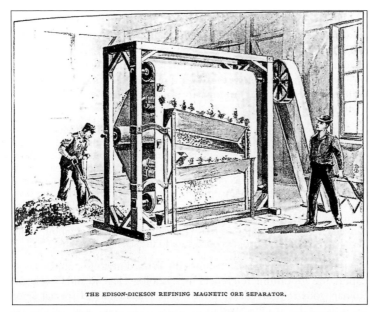

THE EDISON-DICKSON REFINING MAGNETIC ORE SEPARATOR.

This illustration of "The Edison-Dickson Refining Magnetic Ore Separator", which clarified the text, accompanied the Dickson's account of the separation process in Cassier's Magazine, November 1893. *It was probably made from one of Dickson's photographs – a common practice at the time. [LC.]*

photos. Here is the description of the Edison-Dickson ore separator – which was apparently created without the intervention of the Gods:

"... The upper hoppers of the machine, when filled with the ore, are opened below, and a perfect Niagara of particles half an inch wide and thirty feet in length is allowed to rush past the magnets without touching their faces. In this downward progress a large proportion of the ore, being magnetic, is drawn inward, changing the trajectory and bringing two distinct streams into view, whose ultimate destination is secured by means of separate partition boards. The clouds of dust are caught up by fans and whirled away to closed compartments, where specially constructed dust separators are employed to extract the float iron."[418]

Some unusual anecdotes about Edison and interesting descriptions of Edison's associates going back to Menlo Park and Goerck Street seem to be additional contributions from Laurie who apparently collected stories from his compatriots at the lab.

It is hard to avoid the conclusion that the Dicksons' articles were an embarrassingly flagrant effort to butter-up the boss. The text exploited the public's image of Edison and connected his "wizardry" to mythic gods and heroes from classical literature in a transparently self-serving way. Since the series ran for more than a year, Edison had ample opportunity to persuade them to change the emphasis. He enjoyed fame and he accepted and even encouraged their work. Edison would, from time-to-time, feign modesty and claim he was embarrassed by public adulation but, in reality, he was a master of self-promotion. He rarely protested that he was not a "Wizard" and often

418 Op. Cit., November 1893, pp. 16–17.

encouraged the journalists who found this simile irresistible. He made no effort to tone-down the Dicksons' implication that he was a child of the gods, ensconced in the Pantheon and a personification of the best that Western culture could produce. It was a persona he relished.

Laurie Dickson was not shy about using soft soap if he felt it could help him. His attention-getting self-promotion continued through his long relationship with Edison. In the 1920s, years after leaving his position, he sent Christmas greetings to Edison, usually accompanied by flattering accounts of their work and almost always supporting Edison's (and Dickson's) claims for priority in inventing the movies. By that time Edison was paying Dickson an annual pension and these mini-histories were prepared to ensure that the pension was continued. They lacked subtlety, but the annual Christmas effort was successful and his small pension continued.

Antonia's florid literary style apparently suited the editors at *Cassier's*. The first article of the Edison series appeared in the November 1892 issue of *Cassier's* and the same issue had an article about long distance telephone service, "Nine Hundred and Fifty Miles by Telephone" by Miss A. Dickson. (The magazine was reluctant to print her full name, though at least it acknowledged her sex in this article.) She reviewed the development of the telephone, giving Alexander Graham Bell and Edison major credit for perfecting the invention. She then described the extent of telephone service between cities in Europe and the U.S. Although she undoubtedly had help from Dickson in preparing this article, he claimed no credit for it.

Dickson's illness and recuperation in Florida complicated work on the series. It happened at the beginning February, 1892 just as the fourth installment was being published. The burden fell on Antonia to keep it going. Since Edison spent much of his time at Ogden and Al Tate was usually at the office in New York City, she turned to Tate's assistant, Thomas Maguire who was generally in Orange. Shortly after Dickson left for Florida she wrote Maguire asking for accounts of the search for bamboo, particularly the South American trip of Frank McGowan. She also asked for information about the phonograph. She mentioned that she had received a batch of material from Edison. Maguire replied on 15 February, referring her to a couple of newspaper articles about McGowan, an article about the phonograph and advising her to "... consult Miss McRae [of *Phonogram*] , whom I think you know ...". In March Maguire sent her an article from *Electricity* on the origin and development of the electric light. He referred her to Mrs. Edison for information about the degrees and honors that Edison had received. Dickson probably wrote her from Florida, but he did not have direct access to lab records until he returned in mid-April. While he was in Florida he was able to photograph Edison's home and the lab he had there and a number of these appeared in an episode that covered Edison's Florida lab.

Antonia's exchanges with Maguire indicate that she was working about two months ahead of publication. The article on the phonograph appeared in the May 1893 issue and the account of the search for bamboo fibers was in the June, 1893 issue.

By the time Dickson returned from Florida, negotiations were underway to publish the series in book form in both New York and London. In May Dickson wrote Louis Cassier agreeing to accept a contract in which the Dicksons would receive 10 per cent after the sale of 500 copies of the book in Europe. Dickson asked for a similar arrangement for the U.S. He urged that the contract be completed before more written material was sent. "... we must finish the long delayed in a business like manner before sending any more stuff to yr co. I have perfect confidence in you as you know – but, I am dealing with a big firm, & wish to protect my sister as well as myself."[419]

It took another year before the book version was ready. The American edition was published by T.Y. Crowell & Co., Boston in November 1894 and the British edition by Chatto and Windus, London, shortly after. Except for a more detailed account of the Kinetoscope and a new ending titled "L'Envoi", the text had only minor changes from what appeared in *Cassier's*. The new account of the Kinetoscope was based on an article by the Dicksons that *Cassier's* published in their December 1894 edition. This article was, in turn, based on their article in *Century Magazine* which appeared the previous May.

Crowell and Cassier were apparently connected by a business agreement. The December issue of *Cassier's Magazine* carried an ad for the book which said it could be purchased for $4.50 from either company. In February 1895, *Cassier's* offered a package which combined a copy of the book and a one year subscription to the magazine, a $7.50 value for $6.00. The offer was repeated for several months after this.

I have seen nothing that indicates how widely the biography sold, but the Dicksons were apparently optimistic that they would earn the percentage due them after five hundred were sold in Europe and another five hundred in North America.

The Photoret

In December, 1893, Dickson and Herman Casler introduced the Photoret, a small camera housed in a pocket watch case. It was only slightly larger than a standard pocket watch and was offered for sale as a "detective camera". The Magic Introduction Company, New York City made it available for the Christmas gift season and advertised it several issues of *Scientific American* who gave it a favorable review: [it] "... eclipses for compactness and novelty anything of the kind that has come to our note ...". They praised it for being particularly attractive to the young but said that it would be welcomed by experienced photographers as well. It was favorably reviewed in *The Photographic Times* and at a presentation at Société française de Photographie by F.-M. Richard, 4 May 1894. Richard called it "... un merveille de méchanique ..." particularly considering its low cost.[420]

Dickson was introduced to Herman Casler by his old friend Harry

419 EHS. The negotiations may have been started before Dickson's illness. His letter indicates that a draft contract had been offered and was being revised over the issue of the amount of the royalty. Dickson said the question should have been settled before the writing began, but he was not clear about whether it had been decided to publish the series as a book when the series started and he makes no reference to a previous contract.

420 16. *Scientific American*, 23 December 1893; *The Photographic Times*, 19 January 1894; *Bulletin de Société Française Photographie*, 1894, pp. 294–296.

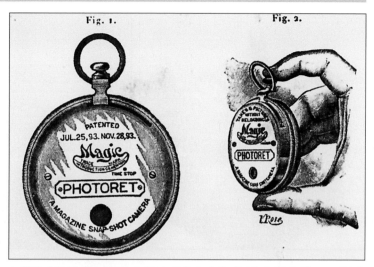

An illustration of the Photoret appeared in the Bulletin de Société française de Photographie *in 1894. It accompanied a favorable review of the "detective" camera designed by Dickson and his friend Herman Casler. Dickson's work with miniature photographs gave him an advantage in creating this well received design. The trade mark "Magic" on the cover is for Elias B. Koopman's Magic Introduction Corporation who marketed the camera. [LC.]*

Marvin. Marvin may have met Casler in 1889 when he had machine work for a mining drill he done at Charles Lipe's shop in Syracuse, NY. Lipe was Casler's cousin and Casler worked there for a while to learn drafting and machine work. Casler and Marvin became friends and in 1891 or 1892, during one of Dickson's summer vacations in New York State, Marvin introduced him to Casler. The trio became life-long friends and their mutual interests led them into joint inventive ventures. They shared a mutual fascination with novelties and this interest sometimes resulted in things of practical value. They had complementary skills and training. Marvin had a degree in electrical engineering from Syracuse University, Casler became a skilled machinist and draftsman. Dickson added his own inventive curiosity which was enhanced by his inherited artistic skills. By the time the three had met, Harry Marvin had married the daughter of a banker in Canastota, a small town on the Erie Canal, a few miles east of Syracuse. This made him comfortably well off and gave him connections in the financial world, a useful asset for aspiring inventors.

In 1893 Casler went to work for General Electric as a draftsman and among the things he worked on for GE was an electric rock drill. But Marvin had already designed a similar drill, and his was a forerunner of the modern rock drill. Marvin's drill was doing well enough to encourage him to set up a business and in 1895 he opened the Marvin Electric Drill Co. in Canastota with Herman Casler as treasurer and superintendent.

The Photoret was probably born during August 1892 when Dickson was on vacation. It was the result of an interest in photography

which Casler and Dickson seemed to share. In March, 1893 Casler applied for two patents, one for a camera shutter, the second for the design of a case. One half interest in the case was assigned to Harry Marvin, probably because of his financial backing. Although Dickson was not mentioned in either of the patent applications, articles in the *Orange Chronicle* and *Newark Call* as well as Edison's letter quoted above, gave Dickson credit.[421]

There was a lot of interest in "detective" cameras in the late 1880s and early 1890s . At first this was a name applied to any camera that was smaller than the bulky commercial models. In fact Eastman's Kodak was called a "detective" camera when it was introduced. Most of these "detectives" were too large to be hidden and few of them could be used surreptitiously. It was their portability that made them suitable for detective work. The Photoret was one of the smallest and one of the few that could possibly be used in secret. It was introduced a full half century before Dick Tracy began using wrist watch radios and cameras.

The design, machine work and paper work for the patent were undoubtedly done in Syracuse but Dickson probably contributed key photographic elements. One of the features of the camera was the short focal distance of the lens, one-fourth inch. It could take a picture from a distance of one foot, could be loaded in daylight and it was possible to take time exposures. These are things that fit with Dickson's experience in photography, work with small images and regular dealings with lens manufacturers. Casler seems to have been responsible for the final design of the shutter and the case – the items that were patented in his name.

The Photoret enjoyed a modest success. The Magic Introduction Company, 321 Broadway which was marketing the camera was owned by Elias B. Koopman and his company specialized in marketing a variety of novelty items. Favorable reviews in *Scientific American* and *Bulletin de Société française de Photographie* brought the novel camera to national and

421 U.S. Patent no. 509,841, Herman Casler, Photographic-Camera Shutter, 28 November 1893. Appl. 1 March 1893, no. 464,161. One-half assigned to Harry N. Marvin, Syracuse, NY U.S. [design] Patent No. 22,649, Camera Case, 25 July 1893. Applied 13 March 1893. The Photoret camera. The application was submitted by Smith & Denison, attorneys. *Orange Chronicle.* 17 December 1893; *Newark Call*, 17 December 1893.

These four mysterious photographs (above) of Dickson and Casler playing about on the roof of a building in New York may be an introductory demonstration of their Photoret.

The fifth photo in the group shows Herman Casler as photographed by the Photoret. Casler's derby and his neckwear seem to tie the Photoret images to the others. [NMAH.]

international attention and Casler and Dickson received small commissions from the sales. The Photoret was and is one of the most interesting novel camera designs from the 1890s. The George Eastman House has one in their collection and has exhibited it in their display showing the evolution of photography.

The introduction of the Photoret seems to have been a cause for celebration. Gordon Hendricks found a set of four photographs of Dickson and Casler together on the roof of a building, apparently in New York City. He could not identify when they were taken, but their actions look like they were celebrating something and in one they seem to be pinning a small object on each other's breasts. The small object is probably a Photoret camera. Hendricks also found a series of photographs of Casler taken with the Photoret and he is wearing the same clothes that he wore in the pictures with Dickson (see previous page).

The Photoret did not make its inventors rich, but it was important because it seems to have brought Koopman, Marvin, Casler and Dickson together. Their association began as a working friendship and it continued for a number of years with profound effect on the development of the motion picture in the United States and Europe. We will meet them again.

Chapter 22

Wizard Edison's Wonderful Instrument: The Kinetoscope

"Thomas A. Edison's modest estimate of his new invention, a nickel-in-the-slot kinetoscope ... scarcely does justice to the instrument. Mr. Edison calls it a mere toy, entertaining, but not the thing he is striving after. The 'toy' is well worth seeing, nevertheless. It is a square box of polished oak, with a slot to receive the nickel that turns on the electric light and starts the marvellously rapid mechanism going. The duration of the show is twenty seconds. The picture is absolutely stable and clear, but the figures in it go about as freely and naturally as though they were alive.". (*The New York Sun*, quoted in *St. Louis and Canadian Photographer*, April 1894, p. 158)

"The kinetoscope is the first instrument ever invented that will reproduce pure motion. There is a toy for children, the Zoetrope, which may be called the prototype ... a very crude device ..." "The advent of the kinetoscope would seem to rob of their application the words of Burns: "Oh, wad some pow'r the giftie gie us, To see oursels as ithers see us!" This power Edison has now given to us.[422] (Thomas Maguire in *Leslie's Weekly*, 4 April 1894)

When Dickson returned from Florida in mid-April, 1893, the Kinetoscope was nearly finished. In February, when he left for Florida he had told Tate that Edison had only to decide which lamp and motor to use and whether it was to run with gears or chain.[423] Although Edison deferred his decision until Dickson's return, he apparently considered it ready. When Dickson reported back to work he learned that Edison had promised George M. Hopkins, president of the Physical Department at the Brooklyn Institute, that the Kinetoscope would be demonstrated in May at the monthly meeting of Department of Physics of the Institute. Hopkins also worked for *Scientific American* so not only would it be seen by a group of technical specialists, it was possible that it would be reviewed in Edison's favorite technical journal.

Whatever his ailment was, Dickson was seemingly fully recovered and immediately launched into a busy work schedule. Preparations for filming were begun, but the Black Maria needed some additional work. A roofing company was called in to put on a new roof, with Charles Wurth supervising. A shade cloth was ordered from New York, the first

422 NMAH Hendricks, and article, "The Kinetoscope", 4 April 1894.

423 EHS. Dickson to Tate, 6 February 1893.

shipment of film was received from Blair Camera Co. and a quantity of developing solution was ordered.

With Eastman no longer making celluloid film, Blair was now the only company supplying suitable film. When he left for Florida Dickson hoped to get film from a new company, the Photo-Materials Co., a company formed by former Eastman employees, including Eastman's chief chemist Henry M. Reichenbach. Dickson probably knew Reichenbach from his visits to Rochester. Following Dickson's instructions, Heise contacted Photo-Materials Co. but without success. Eastman had intervened and prevented Photo-Materials Co. from manufacturing roll film. This left Blair as the only alternative. On 14 April, the day that Dickson returned, the lab received three rolls of Blair's film, 5 inches wide by 50 feet long. Heise had tried a small sample previously and this order specified film of the greatest sensitivity and "... of as great a length as you make". Dickson apparently tested one of the rolls and found it acceptable. On 29 April Blair sent six rolls, 1 and 9/16th inches wide by 50 feet and Dickson returned two of the three 5 inch wide rolls. Based on this test he arranged to have Blair supply film of the same dimension that he had been receiving from Eastman. Like Eastman, Blair did not perforate the film and Dickson ordered it a bit wider than the fit of the Kineto. As before, the film was trimmed and perforated to fit the Kinetograph.[424] Edison continued to buy film from Blair until August, 1896 when they switched back to Eastman.

The first public demonstration

The Kinetoscope was demonstrated at the Brooklyn Institute on 9 May 1893. It was the first showing outside of Edison's lab. and the first time it was seen by a group of specialists. Dickson and Heise accompanied the machine, set it up and ran a scene of a blacksmith shop for an audience of about four hundred. The film, one of the first made in the Black Maria, had apparently been shot in early May, just before the demonstration. After the annual elections of department officers, George Hopkins, the outgoing president, gave a talk describing the Kinetoscope (which he call the Kinetograph). He said that Edison could not send the version he had seen at the laboratory which projected the image with accompanying sound because it was too large, but Edison had sent the smaller version which had no sound. He compared Edison's machine with the previous work of Muybridge, Anschütz and Demenÿ and projected the image of a skeleton from a Zoetrope, using a recently purchased magic lantern. After his talk the audience filed by the Kinetoscope to view the blacksmith film. At the meeting, Wallace Gould Levison, whose experiments with rapid photography had attracted national attention, was elected Vice President of the Department.[425]

The next day there were articles describing the demonstration in *The Brooklyn Eagle*, *The Brooklyn Standard Union* and *New York World*. On 20 May it was described in *Scientific American*. Each of the articles

424 EHS.

425 NMAH Hendricks. George Hopkins' mention of seeing a larger version of the Kinetoscope connected with a phonograph is one of the few hints that there may have been some experimenting with the Kinetophone. There is no other evidence that a larger Kinetoscope with a phonograph attachment existed.

Wallace Gould Levison

Wallace Gould Levison had experimented with a method of measuring the speed of shutters which was reported in *Philadelphia Photographer*, 18 February 1888. On 13 June 1888, shortly after Muybridge proposed working with Edison to produce a combination of moving images and sound, Levison presented his camera for recording rapid motion at a meeting of the Brooklyn Academy of Amateur Photographers. This was described by the *Brooklyn Daily Eagle*, 14 June 1888 which said that the camera took images on glass dry plates 3¼ x 4¼ moving on a polygonal wheel. Although Levison said that twelve plates could be used, he apparently only showed three images of a man tossing a stick in the air and catching it. He claimed it was capable of taking twelve images a second and could be adapted to use Eastman's paper roll film. He also said that it could be used with Edison's phonograph. Earlier in June, on the 1st, Frank La Manna, Vice-President of the Academy of Photography, Brooklyn, N.Y, presented Levison's paper *La vitesse de l'obturateur instantane* at the the General Assembly of Société Française de Photographie, reported by *Bulletin de Société française de Photographie*, Vol. XIV, 1888, p. 141. Levison seems not to have carried his experiments beyond this stage.

426 NMAH Hendricks. There had been a ceremonial opening in October, 1892, but the grounds were opened to the public 1 May 1893. Several newspapers and magazines published before the 1 May opening said the Kinetoscope would be a feature of Edison's exhibit in the Electricity Building,. *World's Columbian Exposition Illustrated*, April 1893 said that the Kinetograph was a camera combined with a phonograph which would project images on the wall. A more accurate description was in an article "The Wonderful Exhibit" by William E. Cameron in *The World's Fair*, pp. 322–323, which quoted Thomas Lombard's description of images shown in a cabinet.

427 EHS, Erastus Benson to Tate, 5 May 1893. Benson was President and Leon F. Douglas was Vice President of Chicago Phonograph Co. Douglas reported that they had not received some parts so not all their phonographs were running at the time of the opening.

quoted Hopkins, mentioned the sizable audience and described the film. They unanimously commented on the steadiness of the image, the amount of detail that could be seen – sparks flying from the blacksmith's hammer – and agreed that it was a great improvement over the exhibitions by Muybridge and Anschütz. They also mentioned that this and other machines would be sent to Chicago for exhibit at the Fair.

Twenty-five Kinetos

The Fair was opened by President Grover Cleveland on 1 May, and although there was advance publicity that the Kinetoscope would be exhibited, the Kinetoscope was not in Edison's exhibit nor in the coin-in-slot phonograph concession operated by Chicago Central Phono Co.[426] None had been shipped and there was no stock of machines ready for shipment. The machine exhibited in Brooklyn seems to have been the only one in working order and as far as we know it remained at Edison's lab.

The opening attracted large crowds to Chicago and this encouraged Tate and Lombard to once again press Edison to begin manufacture of machines but their request was now more modest. On 2 May, the day after the opening, Tate wrote Edison (on laboratory letterhead stationery) asking for authorization to make twenty-five machines. Three days later, Erastus Benson wrote Tate from Omaha with an enthusiastic report from Leon F. Douglas in Chicago about the phonograph business. Despite some technical glitches, they had made money. Douglas said "... the buildings only opened at 2:30 P.M. but out of the fifty that were running, we took in $84. People flocked to them and we could hardly keep them away while we were working on them. The Kinetograph would pay $1000 a day, I believe ...".[427]

Douglas repeated this optimistic prediction on 12 May and on the 15th Tate sent Douglas' letter to Edison saying that the Kinetoscope could now be exhibited without paying the royalty that the Fair had previously demanded. He hoped they would get a few before the Fair closed.

Edison responded cautiously. He annotated Tate's letter of 2 May proposing the purchase of twenty-five Kinetoscopes, with a brief note: "First I want to see the model finished & pronounced OK by Dickson & ourselves. 2nd I want an estimate by [Superintendent of the Phono Works] Ballon as to cost". Presumably Dickson gave his OK before the demonstration in Brooklyn. At the end of May he gave a go ahead for making a Kinetoscope. John Ott, who supervised the construction, charged three days of his time to "New model Kinetoscope nickel in slot" and he began ordering parts the first week of June. The project had a new order number, 626, and a new machinist, James Egan, was assigned to the project.

The parts Ott ordered were for a single machine. This was to be a clone of the existing Kinetoscope and it was probably a pilot meant to measure the requirements for general manufacture of machines by the Phonograph Works. Hence the assignment of Ott, the machinist, rather than Dickson, the experimenter, as supervisor of the work. But Dickson may have had some involvement. On 5 June he asked the Phono Works to silver and buff one reflector. He charged it to 462, the older Kineto number so it may have been a repair or upgrade of the existing machine, but it might also have been for the new one. Dickson was the specialist in optics and would have been consulted about any work done on the Kinetoscope's viewing area.

Dickson had another concern – tension of the film in both machines, the camera and the viewer continued to cause damage to the film. Perforations were damaged and film broke in both machines. The rapid acceleration of the film when both machines started exerted extreme pressure on the film and he had not devised a way to cushion the shock. This was a problem he had encountered in the past and which continued to bother him. It was one of the unresolved issues still facing him as plans for manufacture were being formulated. In May he wrote Blair Camera asking if the twenty-two rolls of film he purchased from them were the less brittle stock that Blair said would be available. In an echo of his previous correspondence with Eastman, he asked if Blair could get the Celluloid Company, who manufactured the celluloid that Blair coated, "... to make a special film of 'leathery consistency ...".[428]

Even though this early effort was a very modest beginning, Edison was considering the larger project. On 8 June he wrote to Cornish Brothers in Washington, NJ, who had made phonograph cabinets, asking if they were ready to bid on making cabinets for 100 machines. To entice them further he added "... we expect to use several thousand a year".[429] Dickson was instructed to photograph the existing cabinet and Charles Wurth was told to mark the photo with appropriate measurements.

428 EHS, Dickson to Blair Camera Co., 21 May 1893. Dickson indicated that Edison would purchase the entire lot of tougher film if the price was not too great. This reflects his previous negotiations for a tougher film from Eastman. The camera fed film directly from the supply reel to the gate with nothing to buffer the strain. I am indebted to Ray Phillips for information about the tension problems in the early Kinetoscopes. Phillips has studied the surviving machines and built new models which are displayed at several cinema museums. He is the author of *Edison's Kinetoscope and Its Films, A History to 1896* (Trowbridge, England, Flicks Books, 1997 & Westport, Conn., Greenwood Press, 1997).

429 EHS.

430 EHS. Ott also ordered sheet brass, steel and sent orders to the Phono Works and foundries in Newark to have parts cast from patterns he supplied.

431 EHS. Tate to Erastus A. Benson, 12 July 1893.

432 EHS, John Randolph to Chas Sturtevant, 23 January 1894. Sturtevant was a Justice of the Peace. Gordon Hendricks mentions Egan's drinking problem in *The Kinetoscope* (New York, The Beginnings of the American Film, 1966), p. 34. He called it a legend and cited Martin Quigley's *Magic Shadows* (Washington, Georgetown University Press, 1948) as a source as well as a mention by a night watchman at the laboratory that Egan wanted to sleep off a drunk at the lab in 1887.

433 EHS, payroll records and Edison to Dr. E. A. Chadbourne, 5 December 1893. Robert Conot, Op. Cit., p. 336 says that Ott fell down an elevator shaft at Bergmanns, apparently in the 1880s, though I have not been able to document this. John Ott remained on Edison's pay roll until Edison's death in 1931. Edison left him $10,000 in his will, but Ott never enjoyed the inheritance. He died the day after Edison.

The same date, Edison wrote Lyman Howe of Wilkes Barre, Pennsylvania that they were making machines for the Fair and that it might be possible that he could buy one after the Fair. This was a different response than had been made to earlier correspondents. Others, and there were quite a number of them, had been told that the Kinetoscope was not ready yet but might be ready in a few months.

By June Edison was apparently satisfied with the way the Kinetoscope was progressing but was not ready to turn manufacture over to the Phonograph Works. On 26 June he made an agreement with machinist James Egan to make twenty-five Kinetoscopes and the work was to be done at the laboratory. Egan was to assemble everything in the case except the motor, mirror, lens and nickel-in-the-slot device. He would be paid $38.00 for each machine in working order. Egan was allowed one week to get the necessary tools and Ott began ordering drills and drill bits.[430]

Edison was being optimistic. He told Tate that the twenty-five would be ready by the end of July and a hundred could be ready within another thirty days. Tate was skeptical. He thought that they might get the twenty-five on time but doubted that they would receive the second batch that soon.[431] As it turned out, he was also optimistic. The twenty-five Kinetoscopes were not ready until the following spring.

Several things conspired to cause the delay. Egan proved incapable of finishing the work, John Ott had to take time off because of health problems and Edison's ever-persistent money problems grew worse.

According to an unconfirmed legend, Egan had a drinking problem and it is clear that he was ultimately dismissed because of troubles, but the specific nature of his problems is unclear. The memo paying him off in March, 1894 simply said that "... Egan did not attend to his work ...". Whether Egan's problems stemmed from the bottle or not, he had run into trouble the previous December when the lab had received an attachment for $35.00 against Egan.[432] At that time Egan had apparently not been reporting for work because he was sent a warning that if he did not return the project would be given to someone else. The project was given to William Heise at the end of December but Egan was not paid off until March.

John Ott's problems were more troubling. He had damaged his back in a serious accident a few years earlier and it apparently affected his spinal cord. During 1893 he was forced to take more and more time off which was quite unusual because his dedication and faithfulness were legendary. His problems began soon after he started to supervise the Twenty-five Kineto project. In December, after he had been away for several weeks, Edison asked a doctor from New York to come to Orange to examine him. Ott's recuperation took several months and when he returned in 1894 he was confined to a wheel chair.[433] John Ott was not only Edison's most reliable employee, by 1893 he was the supervisor for all the experiments at the laboratory so his absence affected the entire laboratory.

THE MAN WHO MADE MOVIES

Money troubles

Edison was no stranger to money problems but those he encountered in 1893 and 1894 were as severe as any he had known. Over the years, Tate and others had struggled with his tendency to spend, spend, spend. Since 1889 he had been pouring money into the hills of northern New Jersey with little return. After another disappointing start, in November 1892 he shut down operations at Ogden and launched another ambitious reconstruction. This was far from complete when the work on the twenty-five Kinetos started. In May, 1893 he and Mina signed an indenture with Mutual Life Insurance borrowing $20,000 with the lab as collateral. In June he borrowed more than $100,000 from Drexel Morgan, using stock in the NY Lackawana & Western railroad and the Northern Pacific railroad as collateral.[434] It was a bad time to increase debt because in May, hard on the heels of the opening of Fair, the American economy took a nosedive. It was one of the worst economic reversals of the post-Civil War era, a depression sometimes compared with the 1930s. On 5 May the stock market dropped suddenly; hundreds of banks failed; several railroads, the backbone of the economy, were bankrupt and many others were in serious trouble; plants closed; workers were laid off; strikes and labor unrest spread. Recovery was several years away.[435]

Although the downturn did not immediately affect events in Orange, by August Edison was pulling in his horns. On 1 August George F. Ballou, the Supervisor of the Phonograph Works resigned. The New York Herald reported it was because some 400 workers were laid off at the plant. Activities at the lab also slowed. After posing for a group photo on 31 July, the staff was told they would be laid off during August for stock taking. At the end of April 1893 the lab had forty men on the payroll and by the end of August it had dropped to thirty. When a trusted former employee, Francis Jehl wrote from Austria inquiring about employment, Tate answered for Edison: "... He directs me to inform you further that the Electric business in this country is perfectly dead, thousands of men being out of employment, owing to the panic which has prevailed here all summer. In Mr. Edison's opinion you had better remain in Europe until the present stringency in the money market is relieved. Just now everything is at a standstill."[436] During the winter of 1893–1894 the "panic" was cited to discourage other applicants.

Edison had always been uncertain about the long-term market for the Kinetoscope. He was sure that there would be enough curiosity about moving images to give the business an early start, but he was skeptical about what would happen after the novelty wore off. His pessimism probably grew as he struggled with problems and changes in the unsettled phonograph business. Edison may have been just as happy that Egan could not complete the twenty-five Kinetos because it gave him a chance to deal with John Ott's illness, his own money troubles and a reorganization of the phonograph business.

434 EHS, EHS, Miller file. On 12 June 1893 he borrowed $65,000 with his Lackawana stock and $50,000 on 19 June 1893 with his Northern Pacific stock.

435 Arthur M. Schlesing, Jr., ed., The Almanac of American History (New York, Barnes & Noble Books, 1993, pp. 375–383; Richard B. Morris, Encyclopedia of American History (New York, Harper & Brothers Publishers, 1953) pp.263–265; Ray Ginger, Age of Excess, The United States from 1877 to 1914 (New York, Macmillan Publishing Co., 1975 & London, Collier Macmillan Publishers, 1975) pp. 163–171.

436 NMAH Hendricks & EHS. The Orange Gazette reported the lay offs at the laboratory, Tate's letter is EHS, LB-058, p. 91; M143 – 387.

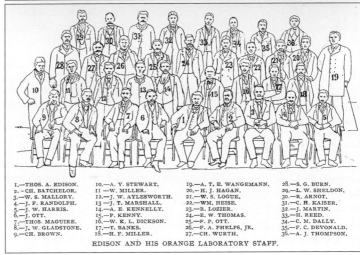

1.—THOS. A. EDISON.	10.—A. Y. STEWART.	19.—A. T. E. WANGEMANN.	28.—S. G. BURN.
2.—CH. BATCHELOR.	11.—W. MILLER.	20.—H. J. HAGAN.	29.—L. W. SHELDON.
3.—W. S. MALLORY.	12.—J. W. AYLESWORTH.	21.—W. S. LOGUE.	30.—R. ARNOT.
4.—J. F. RANDOLPH.	13.—J. T. MARSHALL.	22.—WM. HEISE.	31.—C. H. KAISER.
5.—J. W. HARRIS.	14.—A. E. KENNELLY.	23.—R. LOZIER.	32.—J. MARTIN.
6.—J. OTT.	15.—P. KENNY.	24.—E. W. THOMAS.	33.—H. REED.
7.—THOS. MAGUIRE.	16.—W. K. L. DICKSON.	25.—F. P. OTT.	34.—C. M. DALLY.
8.—J. W. GLADSTONE.	17.—T. BANKS.	26.—F. A. PHELPS, JR.	35.—F. C. DEVONALD.
9.—CH. BROWN.	18.—H. F. MILLER.	27.—CH. WURTH.	36.—A. J. THOMPSON.

EDISON AND HIS ORANGE LABORATORY STAFF.

The staff of Edison's lab taken on 31 July 1893. Edison is in the center with Charles Batchelor and John Ott on either side. Dickson is third from the right in the second row and even though he appears in the picture, he took credit for taking it. He undoubtedly set up the shot but the snap was either done by one of the assistants or remotely by Dickson. The identification page was published with the photo in Cassier's Magazine. Ironically, staff reductions began immediately after this was made. [EHS & LC.]

Phonograph affairs

During 1893 the phonograph business was in considerable chaos. For more than a year Edison had been trying to regain control of the business. The North American Phonograph Company which distributed the phonograph and Bell's graphophone in the U.S. and Canada was in poor financial condition, a situation which was aggravated by the

Even though the stenographic market faltered and the public's interest in having phonographs in their homes grew, Edison continued to offer his phonograph as an expensive prestige item. This picture of Edison posing with cabinet phonograph, modeled after a parlor organ was taken by Dickson in 1893. [EHS.]

prolonged illness of its founder. Jesse Lippincott, who had been incapacitated by a stroke two years earlier. He had paid only part of his original debts and was behind on payments for phonographs and cylinders. In lieu of cash, Edison took stock in the company for part of the unpaid portion which eventually gave him virtual control.

The phonograph market was changing. The company's letterhead proclaimed it "The ideal amanuensis" but the stenographic market was floundering. From its founding in 1888, North American purchased machines from Edison but leased them to clients and never sold them. In 1892 Edison changed this policy and began offering machines for sale, but demand for machines was low. The supply exceeded the demand and a glut of unsold machines developed. As the financial panic worsened, Edison was forced to shut-down production at the Phonograph Works and it was uncertain when manufacture would resume. The coin-operated exhibition business was also in trouble. When the Automatic Phonograph Exhibition Co. was organized in 1891, Edison loaned them money. Their business had not developed as anticipated and he was now prepared to use the loan as a lever to pressure them.

With the stenographic market stagnant, enterprising concession-aires were looking for new business opportunities and the public's interest in recorded voices, particularly music, was the most promising outlet. Some local phonograph companies were considering selling machines to the general public for home use, but the machines were very expensive. Edison's phonograph cost about $200, well beyond the means of most consumers. Also, the only way that multiple copies of a recording could be made was by using several recording machines or recording repeated performances of the same subject. Although he had been reluctant to expand to the home market, by 1893 Edison was ready to produce a phonograph for home use. He had spent years perfecting his phonograph and was reluctant to cut corners on what he considered a superior product so he made a home version of his expensive machine, including one that was in a large wooden cabinet designed to look like a parlor organ. And cost was not the only barrier limiting sales. Edison's phonographs ran on electricity, usually provided by cumbersome and rather messy batteries.

Although Edison was cautious about the home market, since the early 1890s he had been unsuccessfully experimenting with processes to mass produce duplicate recordings. Others were also working on the problem. The most aggressive was the Columbia Phonograph Company, based in Washington, DC an affiliate of the Bell-Tainter grapho-phone interests. By the early 1890s Columbia had produced a number of musical recordings and found a popular recording artist: John Phillip Sousa and the U.S. Marine Corps Band. Another Washingtonian, Emile Berliner was working on technology that would revolutionize the home recording industry. In the early 1890s he introduced disks as a substitute for the cylinder. By 1893 he was working on a prototype for the stamper system to produce recordings in quantity and a heavy duty wind-up spring mechanism to do away with batteries. Berliner's Grammophone was inexpensive and easy to handle. Introduced about the same time as the Kinetoscope, it opened the way for the modern phonograph business.[437]

Edison was reluctant to compromise the quality of his product. He was proud of the superior quality of his phonograph and considered Berliner's innovations inferior. But during 1893 and 1894, when his phonograph business was at a standstill and he was contemplating a reorganization of the phonograph business, he was also keeping his eye on the public's growing interest, a potential new market for his pet invention.

There was also trouble in the international market and the problems were potentially serious. In the early 1890s the Edison United Phonograph Co., a New York based company was established to market the phonograph and graphophone outside the United States and Canada. The United Company followed the American pattern and marketed their machines by buying machines and leasing them through authorized agents in various countries. Despite growing demand to sell phonographs for home use, they resisted selling machines to the public

[437] Though Berliner had connections with the Bell-Tainter group, his company was not a part of Columbia Phonograph.

even after Edison began selling phonographs in the U.S. and Canada. In the spring of 1893 Edison received complaints from the United Company's agents in London that phonographs were being sold illegally. They claimed that machines were being shipped to England by agents of the North American Phonograph Co. The United Company and their English agency, the Edison-Bell Phonograph Corp., Ltd., complained that the illegal machines were ruining their business and begged Edison to do something about it. Edison protested that once a phonograph was sold, they had no control over what happened to it. In the late summer of 1893, the United company stopped ordering machines from the Phono Works and filed a suit against the Edison Phonograph Works and the North American Company, further curtailing the already diminished production at the Phonograph Works.[438]

The problems with the United and North American companies came to a head in the spring of 1894 just as the Kinetoscope was finally ready.

Copyright W.K.L. Dickson

Extracurricular activities kept Dickson busy. The articles in *Cassiers* appeared monthly through 1893 with the last was published in December. The photographs he took to illustrate the articles were sent to the Copyright Office for registration. Among those he sent were the photograph of the lab staff and Mr. Edison with the organ-phonograph. His most important registration was sent on 16 August when he applied for copyright of two different photographs that he titled *Edison Kinetoscopic Records*. Apparently the Copyright Office was not certain what to do with the application as it was never completed. He reapplied, sending a second application on 5 October 1893, also titled *Edison Kinetoscopic Records*. This time it was accepted and registered 6 October 1893 by the Copyright Office. This registration, made in Dickson's name, set a precedent for registering copyright for motion pictures in the U.S. From this time on the Copyright Office accepted registration for motion pictures as long as it was a positive photograph printed on paper. This was the way photographs were registered so it fit the existing system and the Copyright Office did not feel that the law had to be changed. The system remained in place until 1912 when the U.S. Copyright law was amended to allow for motion picture registration. By that time motion pictures had grown into a major business.

Although the two photographs Dickson sent in 1893 represent the first motion pictures copyrighted in the U.S. we do not know what the films were because, unhappily, the photographs were lost. However, most of the photographs Dickson was registering were published in *Cassier's* or sold to journals for publication, it is likely that these were also strips of images intended for publication or already published.[439] During the next several months Dickson registered three more motion picture titles.

438 EHS, LB-058, LB-059, Document File Series–1893. Problems between Edison and the Edison United Phonograph Co. may have existed for a long time. Cables between the New York and London offices of the United Co. were sometimes written in code and in a cable sent from New York on 12 May 1893 their code name for Edison was "Dungyard."

439 In *The Kinetoscope,* Gordon Hendricks speculated that the registration was for a barber shop subject or the images published in *Phonogram* in October 1892 which were Dickson and Heise shaking hands and frames from Newark athletes. It is also possible this was the blacksmith scene which was shown in Brooklyn in May.

Finishing twenty-five Kinetos

The business slow down did not stop work on the Kineto. In the fall of 1893 Dickson and Heise continued to work regular schedules on the Kinetoscope and they made some test films. Heise worked full time, but in July Dickson was testing ore from a mine in Cornwall, Pennsylvania and the project continued part-time for the next three months. This was his last ore milling assignment and although lab staff was being reduced, two of his former helpers, James Duncan and William Craig were hired again to help analyze the ore – but their terms were very short. Dickson finished analyzing the Cornwall ore in early October and returned full-time to the Kineto. It was the end of his ore milling activities.

It is not clear what Dickson and Heise worked on during that fall. The camera and the viewing machine were theoretically complete. But there were still problems. Both needed fine tuning and torn film was a continuing concern. But the major unresolved problem was joining the Kinetoscope to the phonograph. Edison had promised that the two machines would work together and continued to tell reporters that he would do wonderful things for the eyes and ears of the world. While there is no specific evidence of work on the Kinetophone there is at least one hint that Edison wanted it perfected. In September, when George Hopkins asked to have a repeat demonstration of the Kinetoscope for a lecture he was told "Mr. Edison is not yet satisfied with the operation of these instruments in combination, and until certain improvements are effected therein, he would not consent to public exhibition being made ...".[440]

If Dickson and Heise worked on adding sound during the fall it was without success. The Kinetoscope was still mute and when it went to market it was an image machine that left sound to the imagination.

In December, after giving James Egan one last chance, Edison assigned William Heise to finish the twenty-five Kinetos. He started two days after Christmas and apparently supervised the work of Charles Hopflinger, a machinist assigned to the project. Heise was responsible for the mechanism while Dickson looked after the general details. On 30 January 1894, an order to make twenty-five cabinets at $10.00 each was sent to Cornish & Co.: "These cabinets to be of best grade oak as per sample submitted polished and finished as per WKL Dickson ...". The first two arrived on 27 February, the rest were delivered during March, with the last six received 22 March. Twenty-five plano lenses 2 1/16 inch in diameter and with 5¼ inch frames and were received from Bausch & Lomb on 21 February.[441] At the end of March ten machines were ready.

Although months had gone by since they were ordered, these twenty-five machines were still committed to the group that Al Tate had put together at the end of 1892. By this time the group had expanded and with the assembly finally near completion, they were preparing for business. On 18 January 1894 Tate sent Edison a check for $500 which brought the total paid for the Kinetoscopes to $1000.

440 EHS, Edison to George Hopkins, 9 September 1893.

441 EHS, order books. On 8 February Dickson sent the Edison General Electric Co. Lamp Works in Harrison, NJ. An order for twenty five 8 Volt 8 c P, Six ampre spiral lamps "... as per sample sent me".

The payment was a cashier's check from a Chicago bank made payable to F.R. Gammon and endorsed by Gammon to Tate.[442] Frank Gammon, Norman Raff and the Holland Brothers had now joined the syndicate and they brought a new set of check books. Gammon and his brother-in-law, Norman C. Raff had recently invested in the Chicago Phonograph Co. and were now becoming prominent in the company's affairs. Frank Gammon was a member of the Awards Committee for the Columbian Exposition and as such, had been a connection for the Chicago Phonograph Company's concession at the Fair. Norman Raff was the son of a prominent judge and banker in Canton, Ohio. Although he came from a prosperous family, Norman Raff added to his fortune by speculating successfully in mines in New Mexico and oil in the Oklahoma territory. It was apparently his recently won Western riches that Raff invested in the phonograph business. The Holland Brothers, Andrew and George, were stenographers from Ottawa, who had the Canadian rights to the phonograph and graphophone.[443] Working out of the Chicago Phonograph's office in the Masonic Building in Chicago, Raff and Gammon set up a company, The International Novelty Co. which handled part of the early Kinetoscope business.

The addition of Raff, Gammon and the Hollands may have been the consequence of financial problems troubling Erastus Benson. In a letter to Tate the previous June, Thomas Lombard mentioned that a run on one or two banks Benson owned had put him in financial difficulties. He was, however, not out of the picture. Early in February Tate wrote that he had met with Lombard, Benson, Raff and Andrew Holland to discuss the Kinetoscope business. They offered a long-term agreement. Edison would be paid a $10,000 bonus in two $5000 installments, the first on signing the agreement and the second 30 days later. They would pay the expenses of Dickson and his assistants to complete experiments on the Kinetograph. In addition they would pay the salary of Dickson and his assistants as well as Dickson's "... interest in the business". Kinetoscopes would be ordered in lots of 50 each, the first order to be completed in 90 days of signing at a cost not to exceed $60 each. They would pay a royalty of $0.50 per photo strip sold and get rights to the Kinetograph when it was completed. (Tate was probably referring to the Kinetophone rather than the camera.) They guaranteed Edison a minimum of $10,000 per year, paid in quarterly payments. There was no mention of territorial rights but it seemed to imply that they would have exclusive rights. This proposal was written on the letterhead of the North American Phonograph Co.[444]

Edison was not ready for a long term arrangement. He marked the letter "no answer".

Edison's indifference probably irked Tate and his partners, but there was little they could do about it. They had been optimistic about the prospect of exploiting the Kinetoscope during the Chicago Fair and were disappointed that Edison failed to deliver the twenty-five machines during the Fair. Commenting about Edison's slowness to act, Lombard had told Tate "... I thought that in lieu [of having machines

442 EHS, Document File Series-1894 (D-94-25). The check was from the Bankers National Bank of Chicago, drawn on the Chase National Bank of New York. Tate wrote on stationary of the North American Phonograph Co.

443 Terry Ramsaye, Op. Cit., pp. 79–81 and John Danner, ed. & comp., *Old Landmarks of Canton and Stark County, Ohio* (Logansport, Indiana, B.F. Bowen, 1904) p. 1467. *Phonogram*, Vol. I., Nos., 6–7, 1891. I have not been able to confirm that Frank Gammon was Raff's brother-in-law. Ramsaye says he was and he interviewed many of these pioneers, though he did not credit his sources. Danner said that Raff had one brother, Edward and listed no sisters. According to Danner, Norman Raff's wife was Virginia (Duncan) Kingman. I have found very little reliable biographical information on Frank R. Gammon. The Holland brothers were stenographers to the Canadian Parliament. They received the Canadian concession for the phonograph from North American Phonograph in 1891. They also handled the Smith Premier typewriter.

444 EHS, Document File Series –1894. Tate to Edison, 13 February 1894.

at the opening] ... we would be in a position to arrange for a continuing interest in the matter with Mr. Edison when he himself saw how much injustice had he done us by his failure to carry out his part of the contract".[445] But Edison was not feeling contrite about the delay and was growing increasingly unhappy with the way Tate and Lombard were handling the phonograph business. He was leaning towards selling machines rather than leasing them and he was not anxious to be tied down to a single client in a long-term deal. A steady stream of correspondents were told that Kinetoscopes would be sold for $250.00 and at the end of March he told W.F. Brewster of General Electric that he did not intend to organize a company in connection with the Kinetoscope.[446]

The Holland Brother's Kinetoscope Parlor

There was a flurry of activity during March 1894. Dickson had to do some last minute tuning before the machines could be shipped out and at the end of the month several machinists and carpenters were added to the Kinetoscope project. Heise and some of these new workers put in overtime to finish the machines. Dickson was preparing to print films in quantity. He ordered one hundred rolls of the slow emulsion film used to make prints along with a large quantity of developing chemicals. Another drum was Japanned for the developing room. At the beginning of April he ordered five hundred tin boxes to be made from a sample he provided. The cans were designed to store and protect the film rolls which were spliced into a loop before they were sent to the exhibitor. Dickson's order specified that the cover was to fit well. The three pints of cement he ordered were probably used to splice the films.[447]

On 6 April 1894 ten Kinetoscopes were delivered to the Holland Brothers, 1155 Broadway in New York City and on 9 April The Storage Battery Supply Co. of New York delivered twenty-five storage batteries to International Novelty Co. at the same address. Dickson went to New York to set up the machines, get them in working order and, presumably, train the attendants. According to John Randolph, Dickson also delivered a bill for payment due. On Saturday, 14 April the Holland Brother's Kinetoscope parlor opened for business. It stayed in operation for about two more years.[448]

According to A.O. Tate, it was Tate, Lombard and Tate's brother Bertram who set the show in motion. By Tate's account (see below), the Holland brothers, whose name was on the front of the parlor, were evidently at home in Ottawa and did not attend the grand opening. The Canadian brothers were the operators of the concession in New York City and were also connected to the Kinetoscope exhibit in San Francisco. The Kinetoscopes shipped to San Francisco a few weeks later were also addressed to the Holland Brothers though they were exhib-

445 EHS, Document File Series-1893, Lombard to Tate, 27 June 1893.

446 EHS, LB-060, p. 31.

447 EHS, Order books. The cans were ordered from Newark Sheet Metal Ware Co. and the cement came from the Celluloid Co. of Newark. The end of the roll of film was spliced to the head so that it was ready to be threaded in the Kinetoscope.

448 NARA, Patent Interference 18,541, Herman Casler vs. Thomas A. Edison. Theodore D. Bunce, owner and manager of The Storage Battery Supply Co., 239 East 27th St., NYC made a deposition on 17 June 1897; Dickson's deposition was made 4 May 1897. John Randolph testified 3 February 1900 in Equity No. 6928, Edison v. Amer. Mutoscope et al.

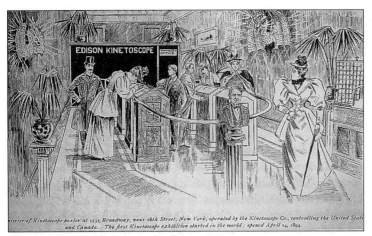

Interior of Kinetoscope parlor at 1155 Broadway, near 28th Street, New York, operated by the Kinetoscope Co., controlling the United State and Canada. The first Kinetoscope exhibition started in the world; opened April 14, 1894.

This idyllic drawing of the Holland Brother's Kinetoscope parlor is the sole image of the site of the first exhibition of Edison's invention. [LC.]

ited at a phonograph parlor that had been operated for several years by San Francisco based Peter Bacigalupi.[449]

1155 Broadway was a former shoe store which was near 27th Street, not far from Madison Square. It had been rented for the occasion by Al Tate. The ten Kinetoscopes were set up in the center back-to-back in two rows of five machines each. The rows had a space between them so the machines could be serviced from behind. The Kinetoscope was designed to be operated with a coin but the plan was to sell customers a ticket instead. The machines had to be modified before delivery because as designed, the drop of a coin in the mechanism completed an electrical circuit that started the machine. A new manual starting mechanism was designed and installed before they were delivered.[450] It was at the rear of the machine and the attendant had to activate it for each customer. The ticket booth was near the entrance. Each machine had a different film and one twenty-five cent ticket allowed viewers to see five films. If they wanted to see all ten they needed two tickets. A metal rail around the Kinetoscopes add a decorative touch and allowed viewers to lean on it while viewing. The room was decorated with potted palms and a plaster bust of Edison that was painted to simulate bronze.

The parlor was supposed to open on Monday, 16 April, but it opened two days early. Al Tate made this rather romantic description of the event in his biography of Edison:

"By noon on Saturday, the 14th day of April 1894, everything was ready for the opening of the exhibit to the public on the following Monday. My brother, the late Bertram M. Tate, was to act as manager, and a mechanic to supervise the machines and an attractive young woman to preside over the ticket booth were to report for duty at nine o'clock in the morning of that day. At one o'clock of this notable Saturday afternoon, after locking the street door, Lombard, my brother and I went to lunch. Returning at two o'clock, I locked the door on the inside and we all retired to the office in

449 The Holland Brothers may have invested in the International Novelty Co. Norman Raff, testifying 23 February 1900 in Equity No. 6928, Edison v. Amer. Mutoscope et al. said that the Holland Brothers were agents of Raff & Gammon. They had the Canadian concession for the Kinetoscope in the fall of 1894 but the nature of the relationship at the time of the opening is not clear. In the fall, when the Raff & Gammon's Kinetoscope Co. took over the concession for the Kinetoscope in North America, the Holland Brothers ran the New York office while Raff & Gammon remained in Chicago. Raff & Gammon moved their office to New York at the end of 1894 or very early in 1895.

450 Ray Phillips says that the machines were started by a rod at the back of the machine and were activated when the attendant received a ticket. He believes that the rod started the motor at full speed and led to film damage. It was soon replaced with a controlling switch that regulated the current and started the motor more gradually.

the rear to smoke and engage in general conversation. We had planned to have an especially elaborate dinner that evening at Delmonico's, then flourishing on the southeast corner of Broadway and Twenty-sixth Street, to celebrate the initiation of the Kinetoscope enterprise. From where I sat I could see the display window and the groups who stopped to gaze at the bust of Edison. And then a brilliant idea occurred to me.

"'Look here', I said, pointing towards the window, 'why shouldn't we make that crowd out there pay for our dinner tonight?'

"They both looked and observed the group before the window as it dissolved and renewed itself.

"'What's your scheme?' asked Lombard with a grin.

"'Bert', I said to my brother, 'you take charge of the machines. I'll sell tickets and', turning to Lombard, 'you stand near the door and act as a reception committee. We can run till six o'clock and by that time we ought to have dinner money.'

"We all though it a good joke. Lombard stationed himself at the head of the row of machines, my brother stood ready to supervise them, and I unlocked and opened the door and then entered the ticket booth where printed tickets like those now in use were ready to be passed out. And then the procession started."

"I wish now that I had recorded the name of the person to whom I sold the first ticket. I cannot recall even a face. I was kept too busy passing out tickets and taking in money. It was a good joke all right, but the joke was on us. If we had wanted to close the place at six o'clock it would have been necessary to engage a squad of policemen. We got no dinner. At one o'clock in the morning I locked the door and we went to an all-night restaurant to regale ourselves on broiled lobsters, enriched by the sum of about one hundred and twenty dollars."[451]

The Kinetoscope was an immediate success. On 1 May 1894 Thomas Edison wrote the Holland Bros., Ottawa: "I am pleased to hear that the first public exhibition of my Kinetoscope has been a success under your management, and hope your firm will continue to be associated with its further exploitation". For several months both Edison and those trying to market the machines could scarcely keep up with the demand.

It must have been a moment of triumph for Tate and his associates. And though Dickson was not there, he must have felt real satisfaction to have the machines he had worked on for such a long time greeted enthusiastically by the public. But this was not the happiest of times and their joy in the success of the Kinetoscope was dampened by other events. A week after the opening Al Tate resigned as head of North American Phonograph and from his other positions well. Although the impact on him was not as immediately drastic, Dickson also began to see dark clouds. Things were changed at the laboratory, and not to his liking.

April fool

451 Tate, Op. Cit. pp. 282–287.

"I sent in my resignation on the first day May in the year 1894, exactly eleven years after I had entered it, I once again passed through Edison's Open Door, But this time it closed behind me.

"The iron bit into the flesh when I broke the link that bound me to a man I loved so sincerely." (A.O. Tate, *Edison's Open Door*, p. 294)

"... There must have been some dirty work going on after I left – swiping things – pity my word was not accepted ... in preference to my arch enemy's word – well he was placed in power – I had to back out."[452] (W.K.L. Dickson to William Meadowcroft, 1 May 1921)

Edison's dissatisfaction with the phonograph business reached a climax that April. During the month that the Kinetoscope made its debut he decided to change the management of not only the phonograph companies, but his whole manufacturing and marketing scheme. On Sunday, 1 April 1894, William E. Gilmore assumed the duty of manager of Edison's interests including the lab, the Phonograph Works and Edison Manufacturing Co. Gilmore came to Orange (and New York City) from General Electric in Schenectady where he had been Samuel Insull's assistant. Apparently Insull recommended Gilmore to Edison. Although, like Tate, he was trained as a stenographer, Gilmore was not Edison's Private Secretary. He took over a number of the business duties that Tate had been handling and was charged with managing the budgets and improving efficiency. Edison gave him license to get results by being hard nosed and Gilmore took this seriously. Changes began almost at once.

Edison took care of dismissing Tate, so it was Dickson who was one of the first to feel the impact of the new order. At the end of April Gilmore asked him to transfer his copyright registrations to Edison and on the fourth of May Dickson and Heise were transferred from the Laboratory to the Edison Manufacturing Co. It ended his career as an experimenter. He was now to concentrate on producing films – and, perhaps, oversee aspects of the production of Kinetoscopes. The Phonograph Works was gearing up to produce a quantity of Kinetoscopes, with the production of the first twenty-five as a model.

On 1 April, the same date that Gilmore began work, a Kinetoscope department (sometimes call the Kinetographic department) was set up in the Edison Manufacturing Co. The shift to commercial manufacture ended the experimental phase of the Kinetoscope project. Some of the lab's machinists and carpenters continued work on the initial twenty-five Kinetos after Dickson and Heise were transferred, but the last payroll charge for the Kinetoscope accounts was made on 10 May 1894, a week after Dickson's transfer. A few miscellaneous charges for photographic material and lamp supplies were made during July and August, otherwise the books were closed on the Kinetoscope experiment.

The curtailment of activity at the lab that began in 1893 reached a climax in 1894. Gilmore's arrival signaled that the cut-backs were accelerating rather than abating. In fact, 1894 was the nadir of Edison's inventive career. Experimentation was at a virtual standstill. The fourteen experimenters on the payroll in June had dwindled to four: Dickson, Charles Wurth, J.W. Harris and Fred Ott (John Ott was still out sick). Wurth and Fred Ott were more often involved with the

452 EHS, staff files.

machine shops than with innovative experimentation. Uncharacteristically, Edison sent no new applications to the Patent Office during 1894 and 1895 and he filed only one in 1896.[453]

The end of his career as an experimenter was a bitter pill for Dickson and he blamed Gilmore for what he felt was an egregious reduction in status. He enjoyed photography and was at the beginning of a distinguished career as an innovative and creative film producer, but it was not his chosen occupation. Though he had considerable success as a filmmaker and became prosperous, gained a degree of public recognition and made important contributions to the movie industry, he continued to regard himself as an electrical engineer and experimenter.

Dickson called Gilmore his "arch enemy" and several times referred to him as his "successor".[454] But Gilmore was not really Dickson's "successor". Dickson never was involved in Edison's business affairs and Gilmore had not been brought in as an experimenter. Clearly Dickson felt that Gilmore displaced him in Edison's favor and while his resentment can be traced to the disagreement that led to Dickson's sudden departure a year later, the enmity may well have begun earlier and may have existed before Gilmore's arrival in Orange. Gilmore had worked as Insull's assistant in the early 1880s and had been based at the Machine Works on Goerck Street at the same time that Dickson worked there. They undoubtedly knew each other and Dickson's dislike of Gilmore might go back to those days – though there is nothing to confirm that this was true.[455]

While it is clear that Dickson disliked Gilmore, it is not evident that Gilmore shared Dickson's antagonism. As a manger charged with improving efficiency, he may have regarded Dickson as running slightly out of control. Dickson's cocky, proud and self-satisfied appearance did not please everyone and Gilmore was probably aware of Dickson's independent attitude and habit of ignoring regulations and routines. Although Dickson was a hard worker, it was not easy to separate his work for Edison from his personal projects. He had at least two outside business activities going: the Photoret camera and selling photographs While the prints he sold were made by a private photographer, most of the photographic work was done at the lab and with equipment and facilities owned by Edison. Dickson was also promoting his own reputation. His name appeared on photographs in newspapers and magazines and in the text of articles publicizing the Kinetoscope. All reason enough to give Dickson a prominent place on Gilmore's list of things that needed to be changed – and changed early. He started with the photo business.

At the end of April Dyer and Seely, who handled Edison's patent affairs, were asked to draw up papers transferring Dickson's copyrights. Dickson was not deterred. He registered one title, *Edison Kinetoscopic Records* on 9 April 1894 and another, *Souvenir Strip of the Edison Kinetoscope*, on 18 May 1894. But Gilmore persisted. In late June Dickson signed a hand written note transferring his copyright in *Edison Kine-*

453 Dyer, Op. Cit., p. 997.

454 EHS, Dickson called Gilmore his arch enemy in a letter to William Meadowcroft, 1 May 1921; and referred to his "successor" in letters to Earl Theisen 1 January 1932 and 5 July 1933 and to Will Day 5 & 12 March 1933 and 27 June 1933.

455 EHS, Edison Pioneers file.

toscopic Records. He thought this took care of the matter because the registration was a compilation of all his "... previous photographic strips on *one* card to make *one* copyright comprehensive". This did not satisfy Gilmore. After consulting with Dyer and Seely, Gilmore pressed to have Dickson transfer the copyrights in his still photographs as well, but Dickson fought back and won part of this round. He persuaded Edison to let him keep the registrations for the stills but he transferred rights in the four Kinetoscope titles. The documents were completed at the end of August and Dickson stopped sending photographs, still or Kinetoscopic, for registration.[456] This put a temporary end to the copyrighting of Edison's motion pictures. Edison did not continue registering film productions and waited until the fall of 1897 to began registering copyrights.[457]

Dickson was probably not aware that he was establishing precedent for copyrighting the films, though Gilmore apparently realized it. Dickson had been registering selected frames which he hoped to sell to newspapers or souvenirs

Copyrights were not the only thing bothering Gilmore. In April and May Dickson was unusually busy making photo prints and Gilmore started pressuring Dickson about the supplies he was ordering. Dickson bought most of his photo materials from the New York firm of Scovill & Adams and it was not unusual for him to combine supplies for his personal business with orders for his official work. He was careless about the accounting for these purchases and Gilmore decided this had to be monitored. In early May Dickson acknowledged that some photo paper he ordered the previous October for had been charged to Edison. Gilmore directed that Dickson's orders be confirmed by Edison or John Randolph who kept the lab's books. The next day a new order to Scovill & Adams for photo paper was annotated that it was placed on the basis of a note from John Randolph that Edison had OK'd the order.

These were minor skirmishes, but they began an enmity that endured through the rest of Dickson's life.

The picture business

The Holland Brother's Kinetoscope parlor attracted more than the curious searching for novelty. At least two early spectators were seriously interested in the commercial potential of Edison's invention. Within a month of the opening Edison received two substantial offers from parties interested in investing in the Kinetoscope. The dollar figures attached to them caught Edison's attention, causing him to reconsider his intent to avoid speculators and sell Kinetoscopes in the open market.

The first proposal came from Col. George Gouraud, Edison's long-time associate in the British phonograph market. Gouraud came from London to New York to join the discussions over the fate of the phonograph business, the talks generated by the crisis of the North American and United companies. Although Gouraud had not come to make an offer for the Kinetoscope he was impressed enough with the

456 EHS, John Randolph wrote to A. [N.] Dyer, 24 April 1894; Gilmore to Dyer & Seely, 9 May 1894 & 22 June 1894; Dyer & Seely to Gilmore, 4 July 1894; Dyer & Seely to Edison, 13 August 1894; Dickson to Randolph, 17 August 1894; Dickson's assignment of copyrights, 31 August 1894.

457 Dickson copyrighted photographs that were apparently intended for reproduction in publications or for sale to the public and it does not seem that he intended to own title to Edison's film productions.

machine and the excitement it was causing to make a bid for a concession. In early May he met with Edison and proposed to purchase 200 machines at $200 each, promising to deposit $20,000.00 with a bank of Edison's choice in an account that allowed Edison to draw from it as the machines were finished and shipped to England. Gouraud apparently discussed the deal with Tate because his proposal included an option for Tate and his associates to also order 200 machines at the same price. Edison put Gouraud's offer in a letter of agreement on 12 May and Gouraud deposited $10,000 with Drexel Morgan on the 18th and ordered the first one hundred machines.

The second order was more modest, but nonetheless substantial. While still considering Gouraud's proposal, Gilmore was visited by Otway Latham, a young man about town who worked for The Tilden Co., a pharmaceutical firm. Latham wanted to buy ten "kenetiscopes" and was prepared to put $1,000 down against a purchase price of $245.00 each. He asked for delivery by 2 July. Ordinarily a relatively obscure young Southerner in his mid-twenties would have had a difficult time persuading Gilmore to take such an offer seriously, but Latham came with some impressive references: Col. Samuel J. Tilden, the nephew and namesake of the former Governor of New York and almost President of the United States, and John Dos Passos, an attorney with offices in the Mills Building. The Mills Building, on Broad Street in Lower Manhattan, was an address which was familiar to Edison and it had an aura of affluence about it. Jesse Seligman, the investment banker who was a principal in the Edison United Phonograph Co. had offices there and Henry Villard, the investor behind the Edison General Electric Co. was once based there. Although the Latham family had no apparent wealth, it looked like there might be money backing the proposal. On 16 May, Latham sent his proposal in a letter. Gilmore accepted the offer on 19 May, but cautioned that the machines would not be ready by 2 July, more likely sometime between 1 and 15 July. A telegram accepting this offer was sent on 21 May and the deposit of $1,000.00 was received on the 25th.[458]

Neither of these agreements had restrictions limiting them to specific territories and they did not specify how the machines could be used, but Gouraud was based in England and involved in European markets. The inclusion of Tate and his associates implied an agreement that they would market elsewhere, probably to the U.S. and Canada. Gouraud and Tate apparently had such an understanding but Edison was not a party to it and nothing prevented him from selling Kinetoscopes to others wanting to show films in North America or Europe. On the surface Latham's proposal conflicted with Tate's, but Latham and his associates wanted to exhibit boxing matches. Even though it was not specified in the preliminary correspondence, this seemingly was understood from the beginning of the negotiations. So the conflict with Tate's syndicate was limited. Ironically, even though Edison said he did not want to divide the turf, his major clients were moving in that direction.

458 EHS, Otway Latham to Gilmore, 16 & 19 May 1894; Gilmore to Otway Latham, 19 & 25 May 1894.

The Latham family

During the mid-1890s Woodville Latham (1837–1911) and two of his
sons, Otway Latham (1868–1906) and Gray Latham (1867–1907) played
a significant role in commercializing moving pictures in the United States.
Woodville Latham was born on a plantation in Mississippi into a family
with roots in Culpeper, Virginia. Educated at the University of Virginia,
he served as an officer in the Confederate Army during the American Civil
War. After the war he lived for brief times in West Virginia, Kentucky,
Missouri and Tennessee. From 1880 to 1885 he was a professor of
Agriculture, Chemistry and Physics at the University of West Virginia and
after resigning, taught at the University of Mississippi for four years. Gray
and Otway, his second and third sons, were born in Shelbyville, Kentucky
and attended the University of West Virginia where their father taught.
(The older brother, Percy, does not figure in the family's motion picture
venture.)

Gray and Otway moved to New York in the 1890s and Otway took a
position with The Tilden Company, a pharmaceutical firm, a position that
he may have gained through meeting Samuel Tilden or Enoch Rector at
the University in West Virginia. The Latham boys had a reputation for
living the fast life and, along with their friends, were enjoying New York
during the "Gay Nineties". This was the era when boxing was very popular
and John L. Sullivan was a national idol. Sullivan had recently lost his
heavyweight title to the picturesque "Gentleman Jim" Corbett (7 September 1892) Interest in boxing was intense, but a strong anti-boxing movement led to banning the matches in most states, including New York.
Corbett had signed with theatrical producer William Brady and was
appearing on Broadway, but most of the public had never seen him in
action. A moving picture of boxers in action might not be considered a
violation of the law and would be a sensation with the sporting world. If
one of the boxers was "Gentleman Jim" it could be a winner.

Latham originally ordered standard Kinetoscopes, but he soon
proposed a modification. He wanted a machine with larger capacity.
On 25 May, the day he sent the deposit, Otway Latham also sent Edison
an authorization to buy film strips of 100 to 150 feet in length. The
standard Kinetoscope film was fifty feet long when loaded in the
camera, but the exposed portion that was used in the Kinetoscope was
forty feet long and ran about thirty seconds. The longer strips that
Otway Latham wanted would record about a minute of action. Latham
wanted to simulate a boxing match of several rounds with longer strips
that would extend each round to a minute. Even though this was shorter
than the three minutes required by the recently adopted Queensberry
rules, each Kinetoscope would present a round and the customers
would hopefully pay to watch several machines. Gilmore agreed to the
proposal and asked Dickson to check with Blair to see if they could
furnish longer strips and what the cost might be.[459] Blair could and on
16 June Dickson and Heise filmed a six round match between Mike
Leonard, a popular boxer from Brooklyn, NY and Jack Cushing, a less
well known challenger.

459 EHS, Latham to Edison, 25 May 1894, annotated by Dickson to Gilmore.

460 EHS, Rector to Edison, 30 July 1894; Gilmore to Phono Works, 7, 15 & 23 August 1894; Gilmore to Otway Latham, 18 August 1894; Otway Latham to Ed. Mfg. Co., 24 Aug 1894; Otway Latham agreement with Kinetoscope Exhibiting Co., 24 August 1894. In his agreement of 24 August 1894, Otway Latham transferred his interest in six machines exhibiting the Leonard-Cushing match at 85 Nassau St., NY to the Kinetoscope Exhibiting Co. and on 26 August 1894 the Latham-Tilden group, now the Kinetoscope Exhibiting Co. deposited $5000 in the German National Bank in Newark as deposit on the 72 Kinetoscopes. Terry Ramsaye credits Enoch Rector with work on expanding the capacity of the Kinetoscope though there is nothing in the Edison records to indicate he worked on it.

461 EHS, order books and Hendricks, *The Kinetoscope*, pp. 56–60. Ten Kinetoscopes were shipped to New York 6 April 1894. On 27 April 1894 Dickson signed an order to ship fifteen Kinetoscopes per instructions in his memo. This was cancelled and then he wrote separate orders to ship five to A. Holland in San Francisco, nine to Norman Rass [sic] in Chicago (eight by fast freight, one by express) and one to

The modification of the Kinetoscope delayed delivery of Latham's order. At the end of July, Enoch Rector, writing on behalf of the Tilden Co. cancelled Otway Latham's earlier order for ten regular machines and placed an order for twelve modified machines. Edison had not decided on a price for the modified machines, but Rector asked that the $1000 be used as a deposit against the first six machines and asked that they be "pushed right through ...". Gilmore forwarded the order to the Phonograph Works and asked them to set a price. The first of the "special" machines were delivered in August. By this time the Tilden Co. had become The Kinetoscope Exhibiting Co. and they increased their order to 72 of the larger capacity machines, which were now priced at $300 each.[460]

After the opening of the Holland Brothers' parlor the syndicate Tate had put together underwent gradual change. After his resignation, Tate announced that he was going to Helena, Montana to take a position with a bank, but he apparently never went West. During most of the summer Raff, Gammon and Lombard were in Chicago and the Holland Brothers were in Canada, leaving Tate as the syndicate's representative in New York. But losing his connection to Edison made his position tenuous and by the end of the summer Norman Raff had become the principal member, though he did not move to New York until fall.

By the end of April the first twenty-five Kinetoscopes were finished. Of the fifteen remaining, nine were shipped to Chicago, one to Omaha and five to San Francisco.[461] But work on the large subsequent orders was delayed while the Phonograph Works was setting-up for regular manufacture. It was July before the Phono Works was tooled-up and ready for serious production.[462]

In June Gilmore met with Tate to discuss his option on the Kinetoscope and on 19 June Gilmore reported to Edison that Tate said that "... Raff's proposition to me [Gilmore] wipes out his [Tate's] option. ...". This modification was not formalized immediately, but on 18 August, the same day that Edison accepted the larger order from Tilden, Raff and Gammon signed an agreement to buy one hundred Kinetoscopes at $200 per machine It was a short-term deal which was renewable. The one hundred machines were to be purchased within two months. Importantly, it gave them a concession for the Kinetoscope in the U.S. and Canada – except for the seventy-two "Special" Kinetoscopes being made. Edison agreed to make only prize fight films for the Latham-Tilden's special machines. After signing the agreement, Raff & Gammon deposited $10,000, half the promised payment, into an account similar to Gouraud's. Edison could draw half of the cost on it as machines were manufactured and Raff & Gammon agreed to pay the other half.[463]

The August agreement was made with Raff & Gammon, but in September Raff & Gammon began doing business as The Kinetoscope Company, a name they chose despite its confusing similarity to The Kinetoscope Exhibiting Co., a name that the Latham and Tilden group had already chosen.[464]

Norman Raff

Norman Raff (1857–1925) was born and raised in Canton, Ohio where
his father was a prominent judge and banker. After graduating from
Wooster (Ohio) University, he took a position with a bank in Albuquer-
que, New Mexico Territory. After a brief sojourn in California, he opened
a bank in Kingston, New Mexico where he had mining interests. Raff's
bank apparently handled a rich strike of gold from a mine owned by
Charles R. Canfield. After selling his mine, Canfield went to California
and along with Edward L. Doheny struck oil and started Sinclair Oil Co.
In 1880 Raff moved from New Mexico to Guthrie in the Oklahoma
Indian Territory and started another bank and speculated in oil. While not
prospering as much as Canfield and Doheny, Raff's combination of
banking and speculating seems to have given him the resources needed to
speculate in phonographs and movies.

Raff's Western ventures ended in the early 1890s when he returned to
Ohio and, along with his brother-in-law, Frank Gammon, apparently
lured by the up-coming Fair, invested in the Chicago Central Phonograph
Co. and set up the International Novelty Co.

Norman Raff's brother Edward was the Cashier of the family's bank, the
Central Savings Bank and one of the bank's trustees was William McKinley, Jr., Governor of Ohio, Congressman and future President of the U.S.
The family had relatives in Omaha, Nebraska and in the 1880s Edward
had worked at banks in Omaha. Norman Raff probably met Omaha
banker and phonograph investor Erastus Benson through his brother.

In an interview published in *New York Evening Journal*, 13 January 1937,
former Edison employee Bill Jamison said that banker and oilman Norman Raff visited Edison's Lab in early 1893 and saw a demonstration of
the Kinetoscope. Apparently he liked what he saw.

Erastus A. Benson in Omaha, Nebraska. Benson's Kinetoscope may have been sent on to Chicago because on 26 May 1894 *Western Electrician* reported that ten Kinetoscopes were on exhibit at 148 State Street, Chicago.

462 Hendricks, *Kinetoscope*, pp. 75. Four Kinetoscopes were made in June 1893; 46 in July; 31 in August; 72 in September; 68 in October and 122 in November.

463 EHS, Gilmore to Edison, 19 June 1894 & Norman C. Raff & Frank R. Gammon, agreement, 18 August 1894.

464 EHS, Norman Raff to Gilmore 24 September 1894. Raff said they would use the name even though they were almost the same and complained that Kinetoscope Exhibiting Co. was harming their business.

465 Hendricks, *The Kinetoscope*, pp. 61–62.

Raff & Gammon bought a number of machines before signing the
agreement in August. During July and August there were reports of
parlors opening in the popular resort locales of Atlantic City and Asbury
Park, NJ. There were two more parlors in Chicago and individual
machines in Philadelphia and Eagle Rock, NJ (very near Orange).[465]
The Kinetoscope was gradually reaching a larger audience.

Although the agreements with Raff & Gammon and Tilden were
made with few hitches, Col. Gouraud had problems.

Gouraud's hefty order accompanied by cash deposited in Edison's
name made it possible to equip the Phonograph Works for production
of Kinetoscopes in quantity, but as we have seem, it took longer than
anticipated to make the output regular. July came and nothing had been
shipped to London. On 18 July 1894, Percy McElrath, of the New York
office for Kinetoscope, Ltd., wrote Edison asking when machines
would be delivered. The next day Gilmore responded that five machines were almost finished and they hoped to have the first order of
ten Kinetoscopes ready next week. They were and Gilmore asked
payment of a balance due before shipping them. This letter was answered by H.N. Powers, Jr. of General Electric Co. who said that

Gouraud had not authorized payment and he asked that the machines be held for a few days. A letter then came from McElrath objecting to a charge for a film repairer which Gouraud thought was excessive. Gilmore reduced the price of the repairer, but no money was forthcoming. On 20 August, two days after closing the deals with Tilden and Raff, Gilmore wrote Powers, now in Washington, DC saying that thirty Kinetoscopes were ready. Edison had taken $100 for each machine from Gouraud's deposit but the other 50 per cent due under the agreement had not been received. Gilmore had received no response to bills that he sent to Gouraud's office and he asked what plans there were for the seventy machines still to be built under the agreement. Because no payment had been received, Gilmore cancelled the part of the agreement that allowed for ordering a second 100 machines. He complained to Powers that "This places [us] in a very embarrassing position, as the machines remain idle here, whereas, we can dispose of them to good advantage, at various points ...".[466]

This began a brief period of turmoil as the various interests vying for the Kinetoscope business sorted themselves out.

Four days after Gilmore wrote to Powers, on 24 August Norman Raff wrote to Gilmore that Maguire & Baucus sent him a telegram announcing that they had taken control of Gouraud's one hundred machines. Raff was not pleased. "... On the strength of Mr. Edison's positive assurance that he would effectively & vigorously dispose of Messrs. Maguire & B if they even attempted to sell any machines in this country as well as my strong belief that you will at once recognize the equities of the case, I am going ahead with my plans on the presumption that you will not only refuse to approve any action of theirs looking to the handling of the Gouraud machines in this country, but that you will *positively prohibit* their doing so *on penalty of losing their agency*. ..." He said he hoped to cooperate with M & B and said he could handle the Gouraud machines.

On the 27th Edison wrote a sharp note to Maguire and Baucus warning them against selling machines in the U.S. and Canada. He asked them to work things out with Raff & Gammon. Edison had received a telegram from Andrew Holland saying that to get control of the machines Norman Raff was ready to pay the amount deposited by Gouraud. Edison cabled Gouraud: "Parties here want to buy some or all of your machines [and] relieve you at cost of whole thing answer". Gouraud responded immediately that he would "cancel everything" if Edison would release the balance of what was deposited with Drexel Morgan. On the 29th Maguire & Baucus telegraphed Edison that they had taken the option on the Gouraud's machines in order to protect Raff from the machines being sold to someone else. They followed up with a letter confirming their telegram. Then, acting on behalf of Norman Raff and the International Novelty Co., Andrew Holland signed a note promising to pay $10,000 to take over Gouraud's option. On 11 September Holland delivered a payment of $6,600 which he made on behalf of Norman Raff to complete the takeover Gouraud's

466 EHS, Gilmore to McElrath, 19, 20 July, 1 August 1894; Gilmore to Powers, 20 August 1894; Powers to Gilmore 24 July 1894 & telegram 20 August 1894.

option. Holland's payment on Raff's behalf was in the form of a check signed by James August. Although this seems confusing, it satisfied Edison who informed Gouraud that his option was cancelled and that Drexel Morgan would refund his deposit less the cost of one machine which had already been delivered to him.[467]

While all this was going on, Maguire and Baucus wrote Edison on 30 August proposing to take over Gouraud's European concession. They said that they understood that Edison was concerned that a territorial concession would restrict his ability to sell machines and assured him that they "... intend to make the selling of machines our chief business ..." and that they had the backing of Irving T. Bush, a young man who was a millionaire several times over.[468] They hoped to establish a permanent business in Europe and handle more than just the Kinetoscope. They offered to put down $20,000 and said they planned agencies in London, Paris, Berlin and Vienna. They proposed meeting with him the following Sunday. This meeting apparently took place and it went well. Edison accepted their offer on 3 September, granting them sole rights to sell and exhibit the Kinetoscope in Europe. They were to place a preliminary order for fifty Kinetoscopes at $200 per machine, to be delivered at the rate of thirteen a week for six months, then at the rate of eight per week. The first check, for $5,000 was received two days later and they ordered one hundred films and asked Edison to select appropriate subjects.

Maguire & Baucus were new players in the Kinetoscope game, but

---

Frank Z. Maguire

In the 1880s Frank Z. Maguire lived in Washington, DC and was friendly with Charles Tainter the inventor working with the Bells on the Graphophone. Despite his friendship with one of Edison's rivals, he ingratiated himself with Edison by writing newspaper articles praising the phonograph as superior to the graphophone. One of these appeared *Harper's Weekly* in 1886. This pleased Edison's friend Ezra Gilliland who gave Maguire, who now had an office supply firm in Philadelphia, a phonograph concession. Maguire continued to be active in the phonograph business but he was never a major player. At the end of 1888 he contacted Col. George Gouraud to get the phonograph concession for South America and he also negotiated with Edison for concessions in China and Japan. Edison advised Gouraud against giving Maguire the Latin American business, apparently because Gilliland had told A.O. Tate that Maguire had misrepresented the terms of his agency to other agents and advised caution in dealing with him. The China-Japan concession fell through because Maguire had never been in the Far East and knew little about those countries or the people who lived there.

During the early 1890s Maguire worked for Edison General Electric and when the company was reorganized in 1892, applied to Edison for a position. By late 1892 he was back in the phonograph business and apparently had repaired whatever damage had been done to his reputation because by the summer of 1894 he seems to have been in Edison's good graces.

---

467 EHS, R&G, Baker Library. Raff to Gilmore 24 August 1894; Edison to Maguire & Baucus 27 August 1894; Edison to Gouraud, [27 August] 1894; Gouraud to Edison, 27 August 1894; Holland to Gilmore, 27 & 30 August 1894; Edison to Gilmore, 29 August & 12 September 1894; Maguire & Baucus, 29 August 1894; Gilmore to James A. August, 11 September 1894; Gilmore to Edison, 18 September 1894; Edison to Drexel, Morgan & Co., 12 September 1894. At the end of August Holland was in New York and Norman Raff was still based in Chicago so Raff authorized Holland to act for him. James A. August who signed the check for $6,600.00 covering the balance of Gouraud's deposit was a stockholder in the Kinetoscope Company. Gordon Hendricks says this was a loan to get Raff started in the business but the Kinetoscope Company records list it as a payment from Norman Raff. (Hendricks, *The Kinetoscope*, p. 132; Raff & Gammon, Baker Collection)

468 *GeneaSearch* online, has a bio of Irving T. Bush from *Men of 1914 Biographical Sketches*. He was the son of an industrialist and secretary of Bush & Denslow Mfg. Co. He does not seem to be related to the Presidents Bush.

Frank Z. Maguire was well known to Edison. Their relationship went back to 1888 when Maguire had a concession for the mimeograph and phonograph in Philadelphia.[469] Joseph D. Baucus, a Wall Street lawyer, was a new name and although he was active in the firm, Maguire was the point man and Baucus played a secondary role dealing with accounts and paper.

Frank Maguire's interest in the Kinetoscope business went back to 12 April 1894 when he wrote asking the cost of a Kinetoscope. By July he had joined forces with Baucus. In July or August they approached Edison with a proposal to market the Kinetoscope in Latin America and on 12 August Edison signed a note authorizing them to exhibit and sell Kinetoscopes in Mexico, the West Indies, South America and Australia. They placed an order for ten machines and a few days later ordered four of the "Special" machines. Four days later, on 16 August, the *Brooklyn Citizen* reported that Maguire & Baucus were showing several Kinetoscope films somewhere in Brooklyn. It was this report and Norman Raff's telegram that triggered Edison's stiff rebuke with the request that they sort-out the territorial issue with Raff & Gammon.

After successfully negotiating for the concession outside North America, Maguire and Baucus organized the Continental Commerce Co. to attract investors and handle the Kinetoscope business. By October Frank Maguire was in London preparing for the Kinetoscope's European premier with Baucus handling affairs in New York City.

This kaleidoscope of persons and companies bidding for the Kinetoscope business was almost as confusing to Edison and Gilmore as it is for those of us trying to sort it out more than a century later. The evolution from Tate, Benson and Lombard to Raff and Gammon is simple enough to follow, as is the substitution of Maguire and Baucus for Col. Gouraud, but the creation of companies immediately after the agreements were signed confused the relationship. The Kinetoscope Company was created 1 September 1894 to attract investors and handle Raff and Gammon's Kinetoscope business in North America. But during September and October Norman Raff, who was still in Chicago, wrote letters on his own stationery and some business was still done through the International Novelty Company. As the business evolved, it was Norman Raff or Frank Gammon who conducted affairs so their company is more often known as Raff & Gammon than the Kinetoscope Company or International Novelty Company. To create further confusion, the Holland Brothers were the representatives of the Kinetoscope Company in New York while Raff & Gammon worked from Chicago.[470]

Similarly, although Continental Commerce Co. was also created in September, 1894 as the business arm of Maguire and Baucus, the names of the partners have overshadowed their commercial company. During the crucial months of September and October 1894, while machines were being manufactured and shipped to Europe and films were being ordered, most of the business was conducted by Maguire & Baucus using their own letterhead.

469 EHS, Maguire to Ezra T. Gilliland, 28 March 1888; Maguire to Edison, 4 August 1888, 9 January 1889, 10 April 1892; Gouraud to Edison, 10 October 1888; Maguire to A.O. Tate, 10 October 1888.

470 EHS & Raff and Gammon Collection, Baker Library, Harvard School of Business. For example, the 30 August 1894 agreement for Raff & Gammon to take over Col. Gouraud's Kinetoscopes was signed by Andrew Holland on behalf of the International Novelty Co. and an agreement to exhibit the Kinetoscope in Washington, DC was made between International Novelty Co. and Columbia Phonograph Co., 6 October 1894.

While Gilmore seems to have had no problem dealing with Raff & Gammon and Maguire & Baucus, he was confused by the changing status of the interests promoting the boxing films. Until August 1894, all of the negotiations for machines and the boxing match between Leonard and Cushing had been handled by Otway Latham. In August when their order was changed from regular to special machines and the number of machines was increased, the negotiations were conducted by Enoch J. Rector on behalf of the Tilden Company. From this time on Rector and Tilden took a more active role although Otway Latham continued to be involved in the fight-film business. In mid-August when the machines and films had to be paid for, Gilmore was told to deal with J.H. Cox who was Secretary of the Tilden Co. The financiers were tightening their control. When the Kinetoscope Exhibiting Company was organized at the end of August, Otway was asked to sign an agreement transferring his rights in the six Kinetoscopes and the films being exhibited at 85 Nassau St., NY to the company.[471]

Gilmore was not aware of this agreement and he continued to assume that Otway Latham was the principal figure in the business. In October, Samuel J. Tilden, who was President of the Kinetoscope Exhibiting Co. wrote Gilmore confirming that E.J. Rector would be the main business contact. His letter to Gilmore began "Understanding that you have been somewhat perplexed by a variety of conflicting instructions in relation to our business with your company, and realizing that this is neither agreeable to you nor for the best interests of all concerned ...". On 30 October, J.H. Cox sent Gilmore a copy of the document made the previous August which transferred the rights of the stockholders to the Kinetoscope Exhibiting Co. Although Otway Latham was Vice President of the company, his negotiating authority was significantly restricted.[472]

By September 1894, businesses were in place to exploit the Kinetoscope world-wide and the commercial future of the Kinetoscope was established. Even though the agreements creating this network were limited to a brief two-month period, they had clauses allowing extension if the business went well and in the fall of 1894 the Kinetoscope business was growing at a rapid pace. Edison had changed his mind about not giving territorial concessions and instead of selling machines to anyone on a first come, first served basis, purchasers now had to contract through Edison's agents. This change of heart by Edison was strongly influenced by William Gilmore who conducted most of the negotiations on Edison's behalf while Edison worried about rebuilding the ore milling plant and re-constructing the phonograph business. The large orders placed by Gouraud, Raff & Gammon and Maguire & Baucus made Gilmore's life much easier. Commitments ensuring payments of thousands of dollars were preferable to dealing with dozens, even hundreds of individual orders for machines.[473] These arrangements were especially welcome because they sustained Edison during an otherwise disastrous period. The battery business was in

471 EHS, Enoch J. Rector to Edison Mfg. Co., 30 July 1894; Otway Latham to Dickson, 11 August 1894; Otway Latham to Edison Mfg. Co., 24 August 1894; Otway Latham to Kinetoscope Exhibiting Co., 24 August 1894.

472 EHS. Samuel J. Tilden to W.E. Gilmore, 15 October 1894; J.H. Cox to W. E. Gilmore, 1894.

473 EHS. The once again rebuilt ore milling plant reopened in July 1894 at what had now become Edison, New Jersey so Edison was away much of the summer. Gilmore kept him informed on his negotiations and the crucial decisions were either made by Edison or cleared with him before action was taken.

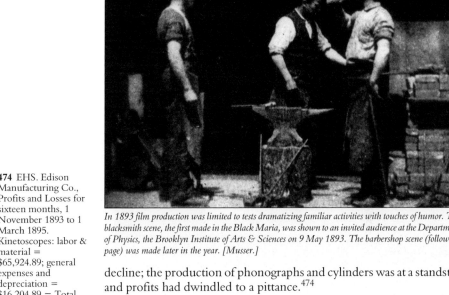

In 1893 film production was limited to tests dramatizing familiar activities with touches of humor. The blacksmith scene, the first made in the Black Maria, was shown to an invited audience at the Department of Physics, the Brooklyn Institute of Arts & Sciences on 9 May 1893. The barbershop scene (following page) was made later in the year. [Musser.]

474 EHS. Edison Manufacturing Co., Profits and Losses for sixteen months, 1 November 1893 to 1 March 1895. Kinetoscopes: labor & material = $65,924.89; general expenses and depreciation = $16,204.89 = Total cost: $82,129.78; Sales = $149,548.64 ; inventory March 1, 1895 = $4,845.00 ; General expenses & depreciation = $1,190.94 = $155,584.58 yielding a profit = $73,454.80. Films: labor & material = $14,294.89; general expenses & deterioration = $3,513.80 = total cost: $17,808.69 ; Sales = $25,882.10; Inventory 1 March 95 = $3,411.69; general expenses & depreciation = $839.62 = Total sales, inventory & expenses: $12,323.72. They reported a loss of $440.69 on Kinetoscope sundries. At the same time the profits for batteries was $545.79; Wax = $2,802.37 and phonographs = $404.40. (EHS, profit & loss, M160 – 115–116)

decline; the production of phonographs and cylinders was at a standstill and profits had dwindled to a pittance.[474]

These affairs would have been incidental to Mr. Dickson's story except that they directly affected his activities during the period and the months that followed. His involvement with them was both professional and personal.

Making movies

Gilmore's agreements committed the Phonograph Works to making several hundred Kinetoscopes but the machines were worthless without films. Edison was skeptical about the entertainment business. He had been very reluctant to produce recordings for his phonographs and left that market to others, but there was no one else who could feed films to the Kinetoscopes. He was the only source and W.K.L. Dickson was the only one qualified to make films. Planning for film production had started in late 1892 with the construction of the Black Maria and design of a laboratory to develop the negatives and make prints.

Serious film production began in March 1894, a month before the Holland Brothers' Kinetoscope parlor opened. Prior to that, Dickson's activities in the Black Maria were experimental and judging from the amount of film he purchased from Blair Camera, some of the experiments were unsuccessful – or, at least, unacceptable. After filming the Blacksmith scene in May 1893 and a similar Horseshoeing scene probably taken about the same time, the next film we know about is a Barber Shop scene, probably filmed in late 1893. The filming was described by the *Albany Telegram* on 7 January 1894 who said that the filming was witnessed by a group of sightseers. These three films are interesting because they use props (furnace, anvil, hammers, a barber pole, barber

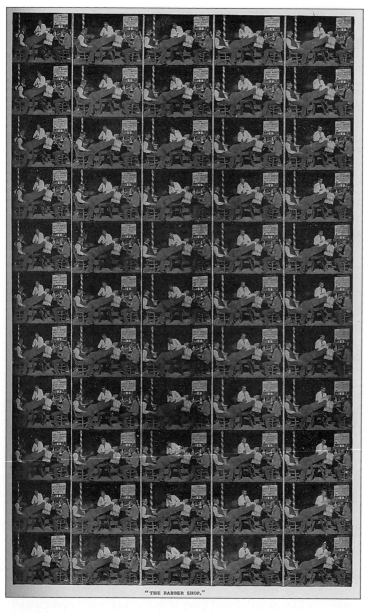

"THE BARBER SHOP."

chair, etc.), and involve several "players" to act out a brief comedy
sketch. They were amateur productions created by Dickson and players
probably recruited from the lab staff. (The *Telegram* said that a real
barber was brought in from a local shop for the Barber Shop film.)
Though very short, the action was intended to be a miniature play. Each
of these films was intended to be comedy. The boys in the blacksmith
shop pass a bottle around as they work; the sign on the barber's wall

reads "The Latest Wonder, Shave and Hair Cut for a nickel" in letters large enough to be read easily. Although crude, these three films were first step towards the story telling tradition that has dominated commercial movie images.

At the beginning of January 1894 Dickson made a film which is probably the best known early film production, *The Sneeze*. It was not made in anticipation of commercial showing but done at the request of a journalist who planned to use it for an article inspired by Edison's new invention. The writer, Barnet Phillips, had toured the lab the previous April and returned in May for a demonstration of the Kinetoscope. In October 1893, he wrote to Edison asking for Kinetoscope pictures "... Might I then ask, if you would not kindly have some nice looking young person perform a sneeze for the Kinetograph? A series of these pictures would be produced in *Harpers Weekly* – and the text would be written by me." There was no response so he wrote again in early January, this time asking that the sneezer be a woman. Edison passed the request on to Dickson, saying "Dixon. Please send the Sneeze to Harpers I wanted it & promised Harpers It will be good add [sic] for kinetrgh".[475] Women were hard to come by at Edison's very masculine lab so Dickson recruited Fred Ott. Ott didn't sneeze the first time, so it was taken again – the first retake. As described by the Dicksons (with some embellishment):

"The victim was requested to assume a seat and favor the audience with that mild convulsion, and to the furtherance of that end, a large pinch of snuff was administered, the operator standing meanwhile in readiness, so as to catch the results in a graded series of one thousand pictures. A breathless silence ensued, the victim's face screwed, puckered and collapsed. There was evidently a hitch somewhere in the anatomical machinery. A second and larger pinch was administered, with no better result; a dose of ground tobacco followed, capped by a generous portion of black pepper. In vain. The wretched youth coughed, choked, sniffed, finally dissolving into tears, and amid shouts of laughter the attempt was abandoned, only to be renewed a few days later when the desired results were secured. Science hath her martyrs as well as religion."[476]

After developing the images, Dickson printed them as strips of photographs and mounted them in rows. He then copied them as a still photo and sent two copies to the Copyright Office to register his claim. Another copy was sent to Phillips by Thomas Maguire, Tate's secretarial assistant.

Dickson had become as publicity conscious as Edison. He was worried about getting proper credit so he sent Maguire a note urging him to insist on a credit line: "Kindly drop a line to the sneeze party & state that as they are not paying for any copyrights of pictures that cld they state under said picture: From "Life & Inventions of Edison by Antonia & W.K.L. Dickson. Photo taken & copyrighted by W.K.L. Dickson. This will be an adv. for our book so please write immediately before its too late." He added: "Please insist upon this".[477]

Phillips' article, "The Record of a Sneeze" appeared in *Harper's Weekly*, 24 March 1894. It was well timed to publicize the Kinetoscope

475 EHS, Phillips to Edison, 27 April 1893; 31 October 1893 & 2 January 1894; Edison to Phillips, 3 May 1893, 9 November 1893; Edison to Dickson, 2 January 1894.

476 W.K.L. & A. Dickson, *History of the Kinetograph...*, pp. 40–41.

477 Dickson to Librarian of Congress, 7 January 1894; EHS, Dickson to Maguire, 12 January 1894. It being early in the year, Dickson dated his letter to the Librarian 7 January 1893.

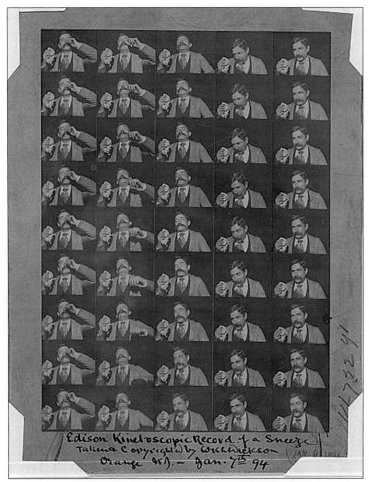

"The Edison Kinetoscopic Record of Sneeze", better known as "Fred Ott's Sneeze" – or just "The Sneeze" is one of the best known early motion pictures. Few people saw it, however, because it was made at the request of Barnet Phillips who used it to illustrate an article about the Kinetoscope that appeared in Harper's Weekly, 24 March 1894. *Phillips used Dickson's lay-out of frames from the picture to illustrate stages of sneezing. [LC.]*

which made its debut a few days later, but too early to publicize the Dicksons' book which did not appear until the following November. Dickson received credit from the "sneeze party", but there was no mention of the Dicksons' book. Eighty-one frames from the film were reproduced as Dickson arranged them. They were in nine rows, with nine frames in each row. The frames were in a grid and Phillips numbered the rows 1 to 9, along the top and put letters from A to I along the side numbered rows to identify each image. His article described the process of sneezing, with a bit about the customs surrounding it. He then characterized the action as shown in specific frames: A-1 (top left) was "... the priming; C 2; the nascent sensation;

G 2, the first distortion; G 3, expectancy; E 4, premeditation; I 5; preparation; C 6, beatitude; A 8, oblivion; A 9, explosion; I 9, recovery".

Although he chose sneezing as a common human weakness that causes us to smile, he predicted that the Kinetoscope would take man higher. He concluded his article: "... Some day, then, the heavens will have star phases Kinetoscopically recorded".[478]

What Phillips could not have predicted was that this sneeze would gain a degree of immortality for Fred Ott, who has been called the first movie star. Ironically, more people today recognize Fred Ott's name than Barnet Phillips. This is partly because for many years "The Sneeze" was regarded as the first movie or the first movie to be copyrighted. While this was disproved years ago, the film continues to be one of the most appealing of the first productions. The subject is an experience that is common to all of us, at once embarrassing and amusing – as Phillips observed. It benefits by Dickson's perceptive filming. It is a close-up, with the camera placed so that Ott's head and hands are clearly visible (Ott's right hand, holding a handkerchief, is always in frame, his left drops out of frame after he takes snuff). Dickson's staging makes Ott's amusing embarrassment easy to see – and remember.

Barnet Phillips' light-hearted article was inspired by the published works of the chronophotographers – photographers and scientists who were analyzing human and animal motion by means of rapid photography. Although Edison did not intend to duplicate their work and directed Dickson to produce a device that would take more pictures at a more rapid speed, it was the published photographs of Muybridge, Marey and Anschütz that established a precedent for the first films taken by the Kinetograph. The public was familiar with chronographic photographs and many of Dickson's first films are modeled on them, showing the movements of animals, athletes, dancers and day-to-day human activity. The first viewers of Kinetoscope films inevitably compared them with chronographic images. As we shall see, one of Dickson's challenges was to find ways to adapt and improve the work of Muybridge, Marey and Anschütz.

A series of these chronographic inspired films was made before regular production started. Athletes from the Newark Turnverein were filmed in various activities: performing with a wand, an unsuccessful somersault, a successful somersault, on parallel bars and boxing. These were similar to, but not the same as the athletic films that were made in the summer of 1892 and Dickson may have chosen to revisit subjects he had previously filmed so the results could be compared. The 1892 films were shot in the old photo studio and this series was made in the Black Maria. Few if any of this group of films were subsequently exhibited to the public, which seems to indicate that they were tests. Even so, they were useful in publicizing the Kinetoscope since frames from several of them, arranged in series similar to published chronographic images, were used to illustrate articles about the Kinetoscope.[479]

I have already remarked that the filming of Eugen Sandow in the Black Maria on 6 March 1894 can be regarded as the beginning of

478 *Harper's Weekly*, 24 March 1894. Instead of the "one thousand pictures" the Dicksons mention in their account, Phillips reproduced 81 pictures and Dickson sent the Library of Congress 45 pictures. In the 1950s Kemp Niver used the 45 frames sent to the Library of Congress to reproduce the action of the picture.

479 Charles Musser *Edison Motion Pictures, 1890–1900*, pp. 89–90. Musser's catalog of Edison productions is arranged as closely as possible in chronological order but the clues as to the date of production are sometimes very slim. He placed these four films between *The Sneeze* and *Sandow*, dating production approximately February–March 1894, but he notes that they might have been filmed earlier. Frames from the "Unsuccessful Somersault" and "Successful Somersault" were reproduced by *The New York World*, 18 March 1894; frames from the "Boxing Match" were in *Electrical World*, 16 June 1894; and frames from "Successful Somersault" were also in *Frank Leslie's Weekly*, 5 April 1894 and *The Photographic Times*, 6 April 1894.

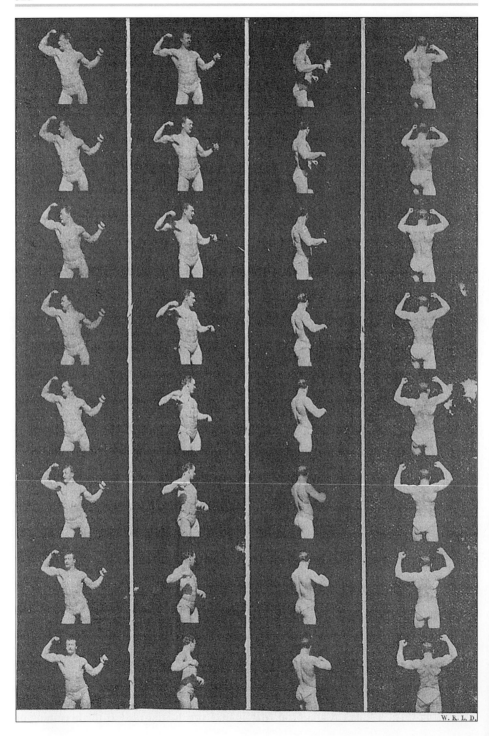

W. K. L. D.

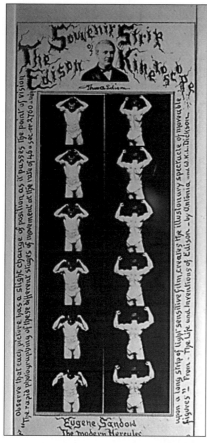

C. B. Cline.   John Koster.   R. T. Haines.
Eugene Sandow.   Thomas E. Edison.

EDISON AND SANDOW WITH A GROUP OF VISITORS.

The filming of Eugene Sandow on 6 March 1894 was the symbolic inauguration of film production in the Black Maria – and the start of the American film industry. The filming was a festive occasion as indicated by the photo of Edison posed with Sandow and his entourage (right). It aroused public interest and Dickson prepared groups of photos for the press (above left) and souvenirs for viewers – or those interested in Sandow's poses (left). [NMAH & LC.]

commercial motion picture production. Sandow (Friedrich Müller) was an German born strong man who was brought to the United States to appear at the Fair in Chicago. Managed by Florenz Ziegfeld, his act featuring demonstrations of physical development, feats of strength and a generous exposure of masculine flesh became something of a sensation. In March 1894 he was appearing in the variety program at Koster and Bial's Music Hall in New York City where the audience admired his well exposed muscularity and was amazed by a variety of feats of strength such as supporting a board topped with a grand piano and six musicians while doing a back bend.

The filming of Sandow was a major event. The local weekly, *Orange Chronicle* described it in a lengthy article and articles also appeared in *Newark Daily Advertiser*, 7 March and *New York World*, 18 March 1894. Accompanied by his manager, C.B. Cline, John Koster of Koster & Bial's and Richard T. Haines of North American Phonograph Co., Sandow arrived at the lab about 11 a.m. and was greeted by Dickson. After resting from a night of experimenting, Edison arrived about an hour later. By this time Sandow had stripped to his brief costume and was ready for the filming which was scheduled to be done when the light was best at mid-day. Dickson shot three films and a number of still photographs, including one of Edison with Sandow, Cline, Koster and Haines. When the filming was finished, the group, without Edison, went to Davis's Restaurant for dinner, cocktails and cigars. After dinner Mr. Davis presented each of them with a box of candy.[480]

Sandow apparently enjoyed his visit. The *Orange Chronicle* reported that he waived his usual fee of $250.00 because of the opportunity to shake hands with Edison. Two days later he returned to Orange accompanied by Mr. Cline. They visited Edison's home, Glenmont, then Dickson took them for a return visit to Davis's restaurant. After dinner they went for a drive then stopped at Dickson's home where Antonia entertained them with several piano pieces. In the evening the party returned to Davis's where Sandow was the honored guest of the Orange Camera Club. As a remembrance of his visits, Sandow later presented Edison with a statuette of himself. This was not the last meeting between Dickson and the German strong man.[481]

There is no information about who made the arrangements to film Sandow, but the likely candidate is Richard Haines who accompanied Sandow's party to Orange. If Haines was the go-between, he was probably acting on behalf of Tate or Norman Raff in preparation for the openings in New York, Chicago and San Francisco. Haines managed the phonograph agency for New York City and he shared his office with the North American Phonograph Company. Since his name appears on a list of stockholders in the Kinetoscope Co. published in March 1895, he may have been a silent investor in the Tate-Raff syndicate. The filming of Sandow seems to have been part of a larger arrangement with Koster and Bial's Music Hall. Two other performers appearing at Koster and Bial's were on the bill when Holland's parlor opened: Carmencita, a very popular Spanish dancer and Ena Bertoldi, a contortionist. This raises an interesting speculation that these films were a form of advertising, promoting interest in popular theater performers. If this was the case, the promotion cut both ways because the appearance of well known performers enhanced interest in the Kinetoscope. By turning the filming into a newsworthy event, the performers and Edison gained added publicity.

But Koster & Bial's did not have an exclusive arrangement. A number of less well known performers trekked to Orange. In preparation for the Kinetoscope's premier Dickson filmed an unidentified trapeze artist, a cock fight, a wrestling match between Petit and Kessler, and a Highland dance performed by an unidentified man and woman.[482] At least one of these filmings took place on a chilly Tuesday, 3 April 1894. That day Dickson sent someone to the Phonograph Works to get 50 pounds of stove coal and a lunch for six was served at the lab. The Kinetoscope account was charged with S. & J. Davis' bill for $9.20 for lunch which was enhanced by 12 beers, 6 whiskies and cigars. There was a similar, but more modest bill on 5 April, this time for lunch for

480 Musser, Op. Cit., pp. 90–94 & EHS, Accounts, 1894. Sandow's party apparently came to Orange the day before but could not be filmed. On 1 April 1894, S. & J. Davis, Druggist Confectioners and Caterers, Music Hall, cor. Main & Day Sts. billed Edison $10.00 for a lunch for twelve, served at laboratory on 5 March 1894. The lunch for five on 5 March cost $7.50, the cigars and cocktails, $1.55 and the candy was $3.75. The latter charge was a surprise, the bill, which was charged to the Kinetoscope account, was annotated: "The boxes of candy were presented as we thot to the party by Mr. Davis as a voluntary act."

481 Dyer, Op. Cit., pp. 644–645.

482 Musser, Op. Cit., pp. 94–98. Musser says it is possible that the trapeze artist was Alcide Capitaine, another performer appearing at Koster & Bial's, but he notes that she was prominent enough that her name would have been used. Alcide Capitaine was filmed 1 November 1894.

This drawing of the interior of the Black Maria with William Heise filming a bar room scene was published in the May 1894 issue of Century Magazine *to illustrate an article by the Dicksons describing the Kinetoscope. [Author's copy.]*

483 EHS, order books and accounts. John Ott's Precision Room Notebook mentions modifying the Kinetoscopes to operate without the coin drop which Ott patented. Ott would not have overseen this work since he was still sick and had not been at work since the fall of 1893. Ray Phillips describes the different starting and stopping devices in Chapter 4, pp. 27–35, and Chapter 11, pp. 98–103. On p. 35 Phillips reproduces operating instructions from the Kinetoscope at George Eastman House, Rochester which Dickson probably helped prepare.

four, an equal number of cocktails and cigars, but no beer – movie making was still a social occasion and Davis' catering service was doing very well by it!

Filming was not all that occupied Dickson and Heise during the first two weeks of April. The negatives they shot in the Black Maria had to be printed, checked and then spliced into a continuous loop of film to fit the Kinetoscope. Film to make prints was ordered from Blair and the first twelve rolls were received on Monday, 9 April, five days before the opening. (The balance of an order for 100 rolls came later in April and May.) The special cans Dickson designed were ordered on 4 April and the first two dozen arrived 13 April, the day before the opening. Since the New York parlor planed to sell tickets for admission, the Kinetoscopes were modified to operate without coins. A number of machinists worked on the modified starting system, a necessary replacement of the coin system which controlled the starting and stopping of the machine. As noted, when the first ten machines were ready, Dickson accompanied them to New York to set them up and train staff in their operation.[483] After the opening, Dickson supervised the packing and shipping of the remaining fifteen machines which were sent to Chicago, Omaha and San Francisco.

The program at the Holland Brother's parlor was a variety show. The feature was Sandow, but the three little comedy-dramas: "Horse Shoeing", "Blacksmiths" and "Barber Shop" were included, as were three acrobatic performances:, "Bertoldi (Mouth Support)", "Bertoldi (Table Contortion)" and "Trapeze." "Highland Dance"; "Wrestling" and "Cock Fight" completed the program.[484] Dickson was one of the performers entertaining the first movie audiences. He was one of the anonymous performers in "Horse Shoeing" so he has the distinction of being the first movie director to appear in his own film.

The varied menu at Holland's was a prototype for future productions. During the months that followed Dickson and Heise filmed a blend of subjects: sports, dances, novelty acts, variety acts and an occasional staged scene, usually with comic overtones. Although props were used in the stages scenes, most were filmed on the bare stage of the Black Maria, shot near mid-day to get the full effect of the sun pouring through the roof to highlight the subject against the black area behind the stage.

Producing a mixture of subjects required a variety of approaches to filming. Dickson was not one to churn out rubber stamp copies of earlier works. Photographs made by the choronophotographers, Muybridge, Marey and Anschütz were the available models and his films of athletes reflect their work, but as Edison liked to point out, Kinetoscope films were longer and therefore recorded more action than the one or two dozen images the chronophotographers usually made.[485] Although very short by today's standards, the thirty to forty seconds was longer than anything previously recorded so Dickson had leeway for more action than his predecessors. But he did not have enough time to include superfluous activity. Blair's film was fifty feet long, but part was used to thread the camera so most of his films were about forty feet long. He had to use footage available to him very scrupulously!

Despite their fragile nature, flammability and reputed chemical instability, a surprising number of these early productions have survived the years and are available for viewing. They are the best evidence of the care Dickson took making them. Borrowing from his experience as a still photographer, he left as little as possible to chance. Planning and preparation were essentials so whenever possible, the shot was set up and rehearsed before film was exposed. The Kinetograph was adjustable in several ways. It was positioned on a table mounted on rails so it could move forward or backward. Apparently it could be adjusted up or down because not all of the subjects were filmed from the same camera height. Although the theoretical rate of exposure was 46 frames per second, it could be adjusted and few, if any, were shot at the maximum speed. Edison and Dickson had concluded that very rapid exposure was important because it reduced the unsteady flicker that occurred at slower speeds, but Dickson got good results at exposures of 30 to 40 frames per second. The camera had a timer which made it possible to rehearse the action and make a decision about when to start and stop the camera before exposure was made. The camera had to be stationary during the take so all of these adjustments were made during the set up.

Dickson had invented more than two machines, the Kinetograph

484 Hendricks, *The Kinetoscope*, p. 56.

485 Kinetoscope films were about 30 to 40 seconds long, shorter than the average take for a modern movie, but it seemed like a major breakthrough in 1894 and most of the journal articles about the Kinetoscope talked about the amazing number of images taken by the camera. Thomas Maguire's article in *Leslie's Weekly*, using 46 images per second as a standard, spoke of making 2760 images a minute or 165,600 per hour. He did not mention that they could not take an hour of film. Edison was more realistic, he told *The Photographic Times* that 900 images would be taken in 20 seconds, but both estimates exaggerated slightly since few, if any films were actually shot at 46 frames per second. Nevertheless, the jump from 24 to 900 frames was an impressive advance.

and Kinetoscope. He had created a system for making and watching moving pictures. Its elements were the camera, studio, darkroom and the viewing machines. Edison had decided that the viewing would be done in a peep show and this influenced the kind of film that Dickson could make. Viewing movies in the Kinetoscope was an intimate, personal experience, quite different from being with an audience in a theater and unlike watching TV. Only one person at a time could see the pictures and the Kinetoscope discouraged long term viewing. Awkwardly bent over and peering down into a wooden box, the viewer saw relatively small images, only slightly magnified from the 1 inch by ¾ inch original. Dickson's first films were tailored to suit this experience. They were brief, intimate and staged to be easily viewed in small format.

Dickson's studio, the Black Maria, was devised to make films for the Kinetoscope and constructed to suit the Kinetograph. All of the films made during 1894 and 1895 were shot there, most, but not all, filmed on the stage. The Black Maria was a utilitarian structure, designed from the inside out. The stage was the focal point and the camera's relationship to the stage governed the rest of the design. The building was enlarged on either side of the stage. An area for the camera was on one side, extended by the track which led into the darkroom. The area behind the stage was enlarged to make room for the "tunnel" lined with dark materials intended to absorb light. The portion of the roof over the stage opened to admit sunlight directly on the stage. Except for the blackening material in the walls of the tunnel, the rest was bare and undecorated, with the wood frame of the building exposed. This gave the building the idiosyncratic appearance that tickled the lab staff in 1893, and still fascinates tourists visiting West Orange today where a reconstructed replica of the original can be seen.

The stage was bare and to keep subjects inside the frame, the limits of the shooting area were defined by crude fences on either side. The exact dimensions of the stage are uncertain, but a newspaper article in June, 1894 said the area was 12 feet square; another in September, 1894 said it was 14 feet square. Both articles described boxing matches staged there, and between the bouts the stage was enlarged.[486] The two surviving photos of the Black Maria, one taken in 1893, the other in late 1894 show that the stage area had been widened, the roof raised a couple of feet, a new door added and the existing side entrance enlarged. Dickson kept trying to improve the facilities he worked with.

Even though it was on wheels and could be raised or lowered, the Kinetograph was difficult to handle and was rarely used outside of the Black Maria. Apparently it was too heavy to be moved about easily. Part of the weight came from the electric motor which drove the camera and determined – and limited – the way it could be used. When he was designing the Kinetograph, Dickson had the choice of three methods of driving the camera: a hand operated crank, a spring driven motor or an electric motor. The electric motor was a natural choice and the other two were probably not given serious consideration. Edison and Dickson worked with electricity and were accustomed to using electric motors.

486 EHS, *New York World*, 16 June 1894 and *New York Sun*, 8 September 1894.

Two surviving photos show the Black Maria during the period when it was in use. The photo above was made in 1893–1894 before it was modified. The photo below was made after the stage area was enlarged. (EHS)

The speed could be adjusted and it could be designed to operated at a steady, consistent rate. Edison was skeptical about using spring driven motors, apparently regarding them as unprofessional and better suited for running toys. A crank was only as steady as the hand that turned it and an electric motor delivered steady, reliable and controllable operating speed. But motors had one very serious drawback: they vibrated

487 I am guessing that the Kinetograph camera had weights to steady it. There are no descriptions, pictures or drawings to confirm this and the only surviving Kinetograph, at Greenfield Village, is possibly a later version. My conclusion is based on the observation that it was seldom taken outside the studio, and the design of the next camera that Dickson used, the American Mutoscope Company's Mutograph was also driven by a very heavy motor and steadied by an iron plate. I discussed this with John Hiller, a professional cinematographer formerly on the staff of the Smithsonian Institution (he is now retired) who has been inventorying their collection of motion picture equipment and he agreed that the camera was probably very heavy and might have had weights to keep it steady. Edison's attitude towards spring driven motors is described by A. O. Tate in his biography of Edison. Emile Berliner introduced a much cheaper version of the Graphophone for home use that was hand cranked then an improved version that was spring driven. The machines undercut Edison's much more expensive home phonograph but he was reluctant to adopt Berliner's innovations (Tate, *Op.Cit.*, pp. 275–278 & 300).

and vibrations could ruin exposure. This would have been a serious consideration for Dickson who was plagued by unsteady images so he probably added more weight in an effort to keep the vibrations from affecting exposure. This seems to have been successful because by 1894 both Edison and Dickson were convinced that the bulky, motor driven Kinetograph operating at exposure speeds of 30 to 40 frames per second gave them a high quality moving image[487]

There was another reason for keeping the Kinetograph in the studio. The motor ran on direct current, the power that the lab used, but direct current was not always available in other places. The electrical market had expanded rapidly but vast areas of the U.S. were still in the dark. Many of the larger cities were only partly wired, electricity had reached but a few small communities and rural areas were yet to be wired. Where electricity existed, it was not always usable. The national electrical grid was actually a patchwork of areas that were wired, unwired, some with direct current and others with alternating current. Edison famously championed direct current, but his rival, Westinghouse was pushing alternating current and so many communities were choosing AC that General Electric was installing both DC and AC systems. The scarcity of reliable direct current made batteries a standard adjunct to the Kinetoscopes which were also run by DC motors. Taking the Kinetograph out of the lab meant taking along the further burden of a stock of heavy batteries. In 1894 and 1895, the Kinetograph stayed at the laboratory and rarely left the Black Maria.

In retrospect the decision to use electricity had serious consequences. A few years later, as competing cameras began to appear like mushrooms after a rainstorm, many were hand cranked, most famously, the Lumières' light-weight, flexible Cinematograph. When it became evident that the public favored scenes filmed outdoors in a variety of locations, light-weight, hand cranked cameras gave their operators a distinct advantage.

In 1896 and 1897 the bulky, awkward Kinetograph was at a disadvantage, but in 1894 it was entirely suitable for the tasks assigned to it. It was custom made to produce Kinetoscopic images and Dickson put it to good use during the spring, summer and fall of 1894.

Movies that move

If a single word could characterize Dickson's film productions, it would be *action*. He was making pictures that moved, and move they did. He was aware that customers would not drop a nickel in the slot to watch something stand still and his films moved from beginning to end. Whether the subject was Sandow flexing muscles, Carmencita twirling in the Spanish style or a smithy and his helpers, they were already in action when the film began and were still moving when it ended. The viewer saw – and still sees – a piece of action that had already started when the film began and that went on after the strip ended. With this in mind, Dickson had to make a choice of what part of the action could be captured and be interesting to the viewer. The film also had to leave the viewers with the impression that they had seen an essential fragment that was the essence of the longer activity. He proved to be a remarkably skilled synthesizer. Over the next few years he captured a *potpourri* of memorable images that recorded an era now passed beyond remembrance.

After the shot was planned, rehearsed and timed, the camera, which had been loaded in the darkroom, was rolled into position (this might have been done beforehand), the lens was focused and the shot was taken on cue. Loading the film, adjusting and operating the camera were tasks assigned to William Heise, Dickson's assistant, who also did most of the routine work in the darkroom. Despite taking every precaution to waste as little film as possible there were failures and occasional retakes, as indicated in the Dicksons' description of the problems filming Fred Ott's sneeze.

Although it was not planned, the change from Eastman to Blair film proved beneficial for Kinetoscope viewing. Blair's film had a dark tone which contrasted with Eastman's clearer film. Blair's darker film seems to have been custom designed to reduce the glare from the light bulb used to illuminate the film in the Kinetoscope, but this was not the case. The dark tone resulted from a difference in the manufacturing processes used by Eastman and Blair – or rather, by the Celluloid Co. which manufactured the film base that Blair coated. The difference was described by James White, who worked for Raff & Gammon and supervised Edison's film production in the late 1890s:

"... the films put out in 1894 were of an opaque or translucent character. ... [which] differed from the clear, inasmuch as it was not as transparent, and arrested a larger percent of the light rays. ... The translucent film is a mat stock, similar to ground glass. ... Ground on one side and polished on the other. ... A clear film is polished on both sides ...",

and by George Eastman, who knew his competition:

[The Celluloid Co. is providing] "... a very fine support for rollable films. It is made 20 in. wide and of any desired length. ... smooth on one side and ground on the other like their sheet film. It is very even in thickness, being about 2½ to 3/1000 of an inch thick."[488]

Even though it was not custom made, Blair's darker toned film did arrest some of the glare and proved to be well suited for Kinetoscope viewing.

While the first viewers were attracted by the novelty of the Kinetoscope and would look at anything that moved, it was understood that this would not continue and that interesting subjects were essential to lure the curious back and build a business that could endure. But what subjects would capture the public's interest? The only precedents were persistence of image devices like the Zoetrope and Muybridge's adaptation, the Zoepraxiscope which showed only a few images in constantly repeated action. They were the devices that Edison hoped to supplant with more varied and interesting fare. In an apparent effort to test the market, a variety of subjects were chosen and they came from several

488 James H. White, testimony in Equity no. 6928, Edison v. Amer. Mutoscope Co. et al., 9 February 1900; GEH, George Eastman to Wm. H. Walker, 27 February 1892.

sources. The stage was an obvious resource, particularly variety theaters like Koster & Bial's Music Hall, Proctor's, Keith's and Tony Pastor's which presented a number of acts and where the performances were relatively short. A number of human and variety acts were filmed during the summer. Sports was another obvious source, but the short length of the film strips and the difficulty of filming outdoors limited the choices to indoor sports like wrestling and fencing or outdoor events that took place in a small area like boxing. As we have seen, the Lathams singled boxing out as being worth a special investment.

By September, when the contracts with Raff & Gammon and Maguire & Baucus were in place and preparations were being made to expand the market in the U.S. and Europe, there were already about three dozen film subjects available. As the Phono Works increased the production of Kinetoscopes, the pace of film production also increased and by mid-winter when the cold and dark weather made filming difficult, the library had grown to more than ninety titles.

The expanding Kinetoscope business created a new, unanticipated problem. As the machines were introduced in new locations, films that had proved popular in previous exhibits were usually on the bill. Popular titles like "Sandow", "Boxing Cats", "Caceido", "Barber-shop", "Anna Belle (Butterfly Dance)", "Blacksmith-shop", "Bartoldi" and "Horse-shoeing Scene" had to be printed over and over to meet the demand and by mid-winter some of the negatives had to be replaced because of wear and tear.

Although technical work of producing prints for viewing was the least glamourous part of Dickson's system, it was crucial to the success of the business. Developing and printing was done in one of two darkrooms in the 1889 photo studio but the studio was not built with production in mind and could not handle the increasing demand for a quantity of prints. The printing machine and developing tanks Dickson designed in 1892 were good models, but they were not intended for large scale duplication. In the fall of 1894 there was a crash program to expand the laboratory facilities. On 18 October Raff & Gammon wrote Edison requesting a renewal of their contract and commented: "We trust that you are making good headway in the matter of increased facilities for turning out films, for we realize with you that the measure of our success must depend largely upon this feature of the work at Orange". Edison assured them that they were enlarging the film department and making new equipment. "... The apparatus necessary to do the work here, has, of necessity, to be very accurate, and some time will be consumed in getting same out ...". They hoped it would be ready in November.[489]

489 EHS, Raff & Gammon to Edison, October 18, 1894; Edison (by John Randolph) to Raff & Gammon, 30 October 1894. This correspondence does not say where the new laboratory was but it was probably in the Phonograph Works.

There is no record of who chose subjects to be filmed, but some of them were chosen by the Kinetoscope companies. In the spring of 1894 Otway Latham proposed films of boxing subjects and after contracts were signed with Raff & Gammon and Maguire & Baucus both organizations paid for specific film subjects. By early October those ordered by Raff & Gammon were identified by a card with the letter

"R" on it placed where it would show on each frame of the film. Subjects ordered by Maguire & Baucus were similarly identified by the letter "C" (for Continental Commerce Co.). Prior to this, some subjects were apparently recommended by someone like Richard T. Haines acting on behalf of Raff and Gammon, or the Holland Brothers who were handling the Kinetoscopes in New York City.

Dickson probably had the most influence of anyone in Edison's employ. Edison was involved with another reconstruction at Ogden and was away almost all spring. After the mill reopened in July he stayed there most of the summer. Gilmore, who came to Orange at the beginning of April, was an "in-charge" administrator and probably wanted to control decisions, but he had been involved with electric lighting in Schenectady for the previous decade. He would not have been well acquainted with the theater scene in New York City. Dickson, on the other hand, enjoyed a good show and apparently went the theaters in New York with some frequency. Another of Dickson's young protégées, E.E. Cowherd described being invited to go to the theater with Mr. and Mrs. Dickson in a letter he wrote to his father in October 1894: "In the afternoon they asked me to go to New York with them as they were going to the Theatre there, but I declined, as I was not dressed well enough to go in a box with a man as prominent to the world as Mr. D". The stream of theater people coming to the Black Maria probably increased the number of theater tickets available to Mr. D.

Although the investors in the Kinetoscope business were keen to have a library of appealing subjects, most of them were novices to the New York theater world. Coming from places like Canton, Ohio, Omaha, Nebraska and Ottawa, Canada, they were more familiar with banking, mining, politics and investments than song, dance, pantomime and stage novelties. While they could attend theater in their home towns, they would not have been up-to-date on the New York scene. In the fall of 1894 most of these speculators had not moved to New York. Norman Raff was in Chicago, Frank Gammon in Washington, DC and the Holland Brothers were running their Canadian business, though Andrew Holland was managing the Kinetoscope parlor and handling Raff & Gammon's affairs in New York. Although Maguire & Baucus were doing business from New York, Frank Maguire sailed for England in September, so Joseph Baucus, a New York attorney, was the only one in the city. While these men probably went to the theater, that would not have helped them book acts, negotiate fees and arrange the logistics of filming. Someone in New York had to do that, this leads to speculation that the contacts for the first filmings were made by Richard Haines, Al Tate or, perhaps, Frank Maguire. It is also possible that Dickson made some of the arrangements himself. Whoever it was, the arrangements had to be finalized with Dickson. He was the only person who knew what could or could not be filmed and his expertise was supplemented by his own sense of showmanship, broad cultural background and more than a passing interest in theater.[490]

490 EHS, letters by C.E. Cowherd, 7 October 1894 and 8 December 1894, mention the Dicksons going to the theater. Cowherd was another of Dickson's young protégées. In December Cowherd said had been to the theater in New York with Mr. D., his nieces and one or two friends. "... tickets & expenses by Mr. D. He can get as many tickets as he wants free, as theatre troupes are out here every day to be photographed for the Kinetoscope."

Although he probably did not choose Sandow as a film subject, Dickson may have gone to Koster & Bial's to see Sandow's performance before filming him. The three films taken on 6 March highlight the subtlest part of his act, muscle contractions, chest expansion and posing – elements that would have been difficult to see from a balcony seat in Koster & Bial's. The more spectacular components such as lifting large bar-bells, tossing people off stage and balancing horses or grand pianos on his chest, were left for viewing in the theater. Dickson's films of dancers, gymnasts and other trained performers shows a similar studied sensitivity to the elements of their performance most advantageously captured by his camera

Not all of the films made in these first months were pleasant fragments of theatrical diversions. Although it has been called an age of innocence and is regarded as a prudish era, audiences of the late nineteenth century had a taste for blood and some of them enjoyed the sadistic abuse of animals. The Society for the Prevention of Cruelty to Animals existed but it did not have the impact that it has today so several films made in the Black Maria are shockingly violent and cruel – unpleasant by today's standards. It would be nice to believe that Dickson had nothing to do with choosing to film boxing cats and monkeys, wrestling dogs, rat killing dogs and cock fights, but there is no indication that he protested against them. In the case of the rat killing dogs, he may have been responsible for setting-up the filming. Although Raff & Gammon paid W.A. Heitler $32.30 to supply rats and a weasel, which Heitler brought from New York City, the *Newark Daily Advertiser* reported that the dogs belonged to the lab.[491] These are among the least successful of Dickson's early films and it is evident that he had problems filming the animals. To capture the action, the camera was moved close and in several of them it is apparent that the animals were carefully manipulated – sometimes abused – by their handlers. Since animals' movements were unpredictable, their keeper-trainers were close at hand to keep them moving and make sure they stayed inside the frame.

Contests between humans were easier to handle, though boxing and fencing matches were confined within the limited stage of the Black Maria and filming could only take place when conditions were right, i.e. when there was good sunlight.

Boxing was one of the most popular sports in the 1890s. Boston's John L. Sullivan had captured the public's imagination during the 1880s, proclaiming that he could lick any man on earth. He could not lick "Gentleman Jim" Corbett, however. He lost his heavyweight title to him in 1892 in a bout held in New Orleans. Though Sullivan and Corbett were sporting idols, very few people were able to see their matches because boxing matches were illegal in most of the states. Sub rosa bouts were held in bars and clubs, but most championship matches were staged at remote locations in the South or West and fans in the populous East and Middle West had to be content with next day newspaper reports or readings from telegraphed descriptions as the bouts went on. The restrictions that the authorities placed on boxing

491 Baker Library, The Kinetoscope Company in acct. with Holland Brothers, NY, 22 September 1894. Musser, *Edison Motion Pictures* ..., pp. 123–124.

made the fans all the more curious and hungry for an opportunity to see something more than a drawing, photo or poster of their heroes.

The Kinetoscope seemed a perfect way to bring boxing to a sports-starved public and it was this craving that led Otway Latham to propose filming prize fights. The first one filmed for his syndicate was a six round match between Mike Leonard, a popular light weight (130 pounds) and Jack Cushing (also 130 pounds) a less well known opponent. It was a six round bout, but it was not a conventional fight. The conditions in the Black Maria only simulated those in a boxing ring. The rounds were one minute each, shorter than the customary three minutes and the 12 foot stage of the Black Maria was smaller than the usual boxing ring. A rope stretched across the front of the stage was the major prop, along with a couple of stools. There was a referee and a couple of seconds. The timing of the rounds was unique. The Kinetograph was the stop watch. The *New York World* called it the "automatic time keeper ... when the minute was ended the Kinetograph man was to announce the fact and the round was to stop." Instead of the usual one minute between rounds, there was a break lasting seven minutes – the time required to change film in the Kinetograph.

Although one minute was a shortened boxing round, it was three times the usual running time of Kinetoscope film. Dickson wrote to Blair at the end of May asking if they could supply 150 foot lengths. They could and apparently sent it almost at once since the bout took place on 14 June 1894, two weeks after Dickson wrote to them. Apparently it was scheduled to take place several days earlier. The *Orange Journal* reported that the filming was delayed four or five days while Dickson and the boxers waited for a sunny morning. During the delay, the fighters stayed in Orange and were awakened early in the morning on the 14th. According to the *World*, Edison was a boxing enthusiast and he, along with some of his staff were the only audience though it was covered by several newspapers.[492]

The *Orange Journal* said that Dickson shared Edison's interest: "... [he] has long had a desire to be able to picture a prize fight". But this was not the first bout that Dickson "pictured". At least two sparring matches were filmed during his tests, one in 1892 and another in early 1894. Frames from the latter were reproduced in an article about the Kinetoscope published by *The Electrical World* on 16 June, two days after the Leonard-Cushing match. Nor was it the first attempt to film a match. In April or early May Dickson filmed a bout with another popular boxer, Jack McAuliffe but the film was not released. The *New York Journal* (which credited Edison with filming it) reported that he was not happy with the results. The Leonard-Cushing bout was satisfactory and in late summer it was the film shown at the opening of the Latham-Rector-Tilden syndicate's parlor at 83 Nassau Street in New York City.

Modified prize fights fit the Kinetoscope rather well, but outdoor scenes were another matter. The Black Maria had been designed to suit the design of Kinetograph and almost all of Dickson's films were made

492 NMAH Hendricks, *Orange Journal*, 21 June 1894; EHS, *New York Journal*, 16 June 1894. Musser reproduces the account of the bout in the *New York World* in *Edison Motion Pictures, 1890–1900*, pp. 103–104.

there and only a handful were shot outdoors. Other than tests, the first production filmed outside seems to have been in April or May 1894 when Dickson filmed a troupe of trained bears. Dickson said that he found the troupe on Main Street in Orange and persuaded their trainer to bring them to the lab. It was an event that tickled Dickson who described it several times:

"... One day ... [I filmed] a troupe of trained bears and their Hungarian leaders. The bears were divided between surly discontent and a comfortable desire to follow the bent of their own inclinations. It was only after much persuasion that they could be induced to subserve the interests of science. One furry monster waddled up a telegraph-pole, to the soliloquy of his own indignant growls; another settled himself comfortably in a deep arm-chair, with the air of a postgraduate in social science; a third rose solemnly on his hind legs and described the measures of some dance, to the weird strains of his keeper's music. Another licked his master's swarthy face, another accepted his keeper's challenge, and engaged with him in a wrestling match, struggling, hugging, and rolling on the ground." (*Century Magazine*)

"You can imagine the Edison Staff & the native's amusement when we arrived *I* marching ahead – (I afterwards wrestled with a bear who soon had me down ...)"[493] (Dickson to Will Day)

In his article for the *Journal of the SMPE* Dickson described how filming out doors was done:

"The outside pictures were taken against a long or very wide grey painted wooden wall so that when the subject moved out of the picture we would still follow it by keeping it centrally framed against an even, gray background ..."

"The camera end of the "Black Maria" used to be swung around and such pictures taken through a small window inside the darkroom ...".[494]

The weight of the Kinetograph limited the ability to keep moving subjects "centrally framed". After taking the bears, Dickson made a test film of a group of Edison employees picnicking, then on 25 July he made two films of Juan A. Caicedo, the self-styled "King of Wire Walkers". There was not room enough in the Black Maria for the full length of Caicedo's wire and his act involved leaps into the air. As the *Orange Chronicle* reported, it was something of an experiment:

"... It is the first time that any Kinetographic pictures have been taken in the open air, and the results were looked forward to with interest. Heretofore, the success of the pictures has depended largely on the intense inky blackness of the tunnel behind the figure or figures, and hence the development of the films was looked forward to with no little interest ...".[495]

In October two cowboys from Buffalo Bill's Wild West show were filmed in the area outside the Black Maria. Lee Martin rode "Sunfish", a bucking broncho, in a small corral which was built to simulate a ranch and keep the horse within camera range. Frank Hammitt, chief of the troupe's cowboys and manager of their horses, sat on a fence and fired his pistol in the air. Hammitt was also supposed to ride but the area was too small for his lively horse "El Diablo". After the Broncho ride, both men were filmed demonstrating their skills with a lasso. The exhibition was watched by an audience of guests invited by Dickson.[496]

493 BiFi, Will Day, Dickson to Day, 12 May 1933 & W.K.L. & Antonia Dickson, *Century Magazine*, p. 213. Dickson told Will Day it was filmed "... *early* very early 1889 if not 1888 ...", clearly an exaggeration.

494 Dickson, *SMPE, 1933*, pp. 14–15.

495 Musser, *Edison Motion Pictures* ... pp. 108–111.

496 Musser, Op. Cit., pp. 140–141. *Orange Journal*, 18 October 1894, p. 5.

Caicedo (with pole)/Caicedo No. 1. Two films of Caicedo performing on the slack wire were among the first filmed outside in natural light (though at least one test was previously made). They were shot on 25 July 1894 and to take the shot, Caicedo's apparatus was set up near the Black Maria so the camera could remain in the studio during filming. [Musser.]

Although the Kinetograph was never taken off the laboratory grounds apparently there were plans to film Niagara Falls. In his letter to his father on 7 October 1894, Dickson's protegee E.E. Cowherd said that he was told he would be taken along on a filming trip to the Falls.[497] A drawing of Niagara Falls is featured prominently at the top and center of a series of drawings taken from actual and imagined Kinetoscope productions that Dickson drew for the cover of *History of the Kinetograph, Kinetoscope and Kineto-Phonograph* which was being prepared for publication in the fall of 1894. If the filming was planned, it never came about and it was several years before the popular falls were "Kinetographed".

With the exception of Ruth St. Dennis, James Corbett, Buffalo Bill, Annie Oakley and, perhaps, Sandow, the names of performers who appeared in Kinetoscope productions are unfamiliar today, but most of them were well known in 1894. Fans of the variety, circus and theatrical world knew Annabelle, Carmencita, Alcide Capitaine, Bertoldi, Armand d'Ary, Caicedo, Walton and Slavin, the Gaiety Girls and others who danced, balanced, contorted and demonstrated expertise for the movie camera. Many of these acts were given high ratings in *New York Clipper, New York Dramatic Mirror, Police Gazette* and other contemporary journals covering the entertainment world.[498]

Most of the acts filmed during spring and summer came from variety stages in New York but in the fall and early winter new sources were tapped. In September and October performers from Buffalo Bill's company were filmed as were scenes from several Broadway shows. They brought variety and added a more exotic and international flavor to films available for the Kinetoscope.

497 EHS. Cowherd to Cowherd, 7 October 1894.

498 See Musser, Op. Cit. I will not list all of Dickson's productions since these are well documented by Charles Musser who not only collected information about the films but also articles from the trade press documenting the work of the performers who appeared in Edison films.

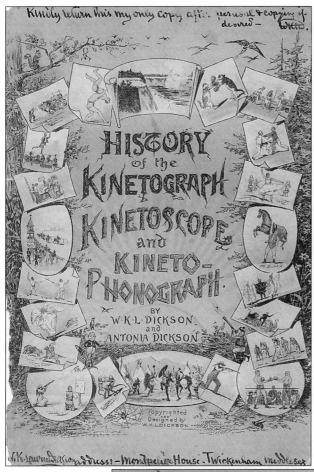

Although all of the films Dickson made for Edison were filmed in, or next to, the Black Maria, he apparently expected to film away the studio at some point. The cover which Dickson designed for The History of the Kinetograph, Kinetoscope and Kineto-Phonograph, the publicity book that he co-wrote with his sister Antonia, is illustrated with images from Kinetoscope films both real and imagined. Prominent in the top center is Niagara Falls (see detail, below) and on the left center is a horse race. There is also a football game (top left), and a lion tamer (bottom right side). Other images are from Black Maria films (clockwise from top center): Niagara Falls; Boxing Cats; Blacksmiths; Mexican knife fight; Carmencita? Sandow (lifting a horse); The Gaiety Girls; a lion tamer; Performing Bears; Corbett & Courtney boxing; Buffalo Bill; Sioux Indian dance; Boxing Monkeys; Annie Oakley; lassoing a buffalo; Annabelle Serpentine Dance; Fencing; a horse race; Barber Shop; a football game and Wrestling. [MoMA.]

Edison had met Col. William F. Cody, a.k.a. Buffalo Bill, in Paris in 1889 and counted a hearty American-style breakfast with Cody and his cowboys and Indians as one of the a highlights of that eventful journey abroad. In 1894, Cody's troupe, performing as Buffalo Bill's Wild West, spent the summer at Ambrose Park in Brooklyn. Although cowboys and Indians from America's West were his stock-in-trade, the show had been broadened to include Mexican knife fights, Japanese acrobats and Arabian acrobats and gun twirlers. Dickson filmed several acts from Cody's troupe including Buffalo Bill and his star attraction Annie Oakley demonstrating their skill with rifles. The day that Buffalo Bill was filmed, Dickson also photographed Indians from the Brule and Oglala Sioux tribes in Ghost Dance, Buffalo Dance and a War Council. These are the earliest filmed record of Native American rituals, albeit in a staged version condensed for the peculiarities of the Black Maria. The filmed records of Buffalo Bill and Annie Oakley give us the earliest glimpses of two legends of 19th century show business. We don't know if Dickson received an "Annie Oakley" for his trouble.

Buffalo Bill and his company had come to Orange on the Ferry, then the Delaware, Lackawana & Western Railroad and finally by the local street car line. With their costumes, drums and rifles they must have made quite a sight! Following the performance Dickson posed the group for still photographs. In the photo were Buffalo Bill, John Shangren, the interpreter; Major John M. Burke, manager of the Wild West company; Edward Madden, the advertising manager; chiefs Last Horse, Parts His Hair and Hair Coat; and Black Cat, Charging Crow, Dull Knife, Holy Bear, Crazy Bull, Strong Talker, Pine Little Eagle Horse and Young Bear. Johnny No Neck Burke, Seven Up and Run About were also along.

Buffalo Bill was filmed on 24 September 1894 and on 6 October Dickson filmed Pedro Esquirel and Dionecio Gonzales in a Mexican Knife Duel; Vincente Ore Passo a champion lasso thrower, Sheik Hadj Tahar an Arabian gun juggler and Hadj Cheriff, an Arabian knife juggler, all from Buffalo Bill's show. Lee Martin, Frank Hammitt and "Sunfish" came on 16 October. On the 18th it was Sie Hassan Ben Ali's troupe of Beni Zoug Zoug Arabs who performed a human pyramid and a sword combat between Saleem Nassar and Najid. Toyou Kichi a Japanese acrobat accompanied them and was also filmed. On 1 November Annie Oakley, "Little Sure Shot", completed the roster of Buffalo Bill's performers. By this time the company had closed their New York run and sailed for Europe. Sie Hassan's troupe had left Buffalo Bill for an appearance at Koster & Bial's and Annie Oakley, who had married Frank Butler, was living in nearby Nutley, New Jersey.[499]

Acts featured in five Broadway musicals were filmed during the fall and early winter: "The Passing Show" a musical review; a pair of musicals commemorating the 400th anniversary of Columbus' voyage, "1492" and "Little Christopher Columbus"; "A Gaiety Girl" an American version of a popular British musical; and "Rob Roy", a romantic musical comedy.

[499] Musser, Op. Cit., pp. 125–129; 135–138; 140–145.

The first African-Americans featured on film were Joe Rastus, Denny Tolliver and Walter Wilkins, dancers who were appearing on Broadway in The Passing Show. *[Musser.]*

"The Passing Show" played at The Casino, Broadway and Thirty-Ninth Street. It was billed as "A Topical Extravaganza in Three Acts" written by Sydney Rosenfeld with original music composed by Ludwig Englander. The second act was a vaudeville entertainment with eight acts, one of which was Lucy Daly, "a bit of dancing sunshine, or words to that effect" performing with The Casino Pickaninnies, Joe Rastus, Denny Tolliver and Walter Wilkins. On 6 October Dickson filmed the "Pickaninnies" dancing a jig and breakdown. Although they were billed as secondary to Lucy Daly, she did not appear in the film. Rastus, Tolliver and Wilkins are the first Black Americans to perform on film.

The 1890s was a low period for Black Americans. Jim Crow laws were being enacted and lynchings were becoming more common. In spite of the growing segregation and open humiliation of Blacks, Americans continued to be fascinated by the songs and dancing of African Americans. The phonograph industry found that "Coon songs" were one of their most popular products – though most of the performers were non-Blacks presenting their versions of African-American music. The popularity of Black American music probably led to the making of this film. It would be nice to report that W.K.L. Dickson was an enlightened person with liberal social attitudes, but this is not the case. Dickson's American ties were in Virginia which was still bitter over the losses incurred during the Civil War. For three years he lived in Petersburg, Virginia, site of the South's final battleground. His wife's family had deep ties to the Confederacy and Dickson's mother, who was apparently born in Virginia, probably instilled her family with Confederate sympathies. We have only hints of his racial attitudes, but what we know of them indicates that at best he was a patronizingly superior Anglo. When he finished the filming he sent Andrew Holland a note: "N ... boys OK. W.K.L.D.".[500]

500 NMAH
Hendricks.

"A Gaiety Girl" came to New York's Daly's Theatre in the summer of 1894 for a short but sensational stay. The New York press was ecstatic, raving about the beauty of the girls, the splendor (and scantiness) of their costumes and the excitement the girls generated among New York's "Johnnies". The *New York Herald* claimed that "... All Dudedom Is in a State of Deliriously Happy Anticipation". Part of the company came to Orange on 1 November 1894 and three of the dancers were filmed: Madge Crossland, Lucy Murray and May Lucas. They were accompanied by Mr. Malone, manager of the company, actors Fred Kaye, Cecil Hope, Decima Moore and Florence Lloyd. One of the show's stars, Cissy Fitzgerald, was ill and did not make the trip. Three films were made. Lucy Murray and May Lucas each danced a solo("Pas Seul, No. 1" and "Pas Seul, No. 2") and they were joined by Madge Crossland in "The Carnival Dance", their high kicking dance from the second act.

It was a busy morning at the Black Maria. This was the day that Annie Oakley was filmed and in addition to the Gaiety Girls, Dickson and Heise filmed the trapeze artist Mlle. Alcide Capitaine (billed as the "perfect woman" and "the female Sandow").

While the Black Maria was designed for filming, the laboratory lacked the support for a handling all these performers, particularly for a group of women. There were no facilities for making or storing props, no make-up or dressing rooms. *The National Police Gazette* reported that the Gaiety Girls had to change costumes in Edison's Library – who knows what excitement this must have stirred among the predominantly male staff at the laboratory. The girls had apparently come prepared to sing as well as dance and were chagrined that no recording could be made. The stage limited the number of performers who could be filmed at a time, hence the solos and single trio. They were additionally disturbed to find that the filming would be less than a minute so they had to severely abbreviate their usual stage routine.

Apparently all this activity was finished by mid-day because the *New York Herald* reported that when it was over Mr. Tate entertained the party at a luncheon at Davis's restaurant. This was probably not Al Tate, but his brother Bertram Tate, a shareholder in Raff & Gammon's Kinetoscope Co. who was working with the Holland Brothers.[501]

The most ambitious day of theatrical filming came later in November when five films were made by members of the cast of Charles Hoyt's musical farce, "The Milk White Flag". Hoyt's farce opened 8 October 1894 and was the first show mounted at Hoyt's Theatre which was formerly the Madison Square Theatre. Hoyt wrote the play and the music was by Percy Gaunt. It satirized small town militia units which vied with each other to have the most elaborate, outlandish uniforms. The show continued its run through February 1895.

Isabelle Coe was filmed in her role of as the "Widow" whose husband may be dead or feigning death (he was laid-out in a casket) and Lew Bloom, a popular tramp, recreated his role as Capt. Dodge Shotwell of the Daly Blues – a part that was added after the play opened. Frank Lawton as the Dancing Master Gideon Foote danced a trio with

501 *The National Police Gazette*, 24 November 1894; *Orange Chronicle*, 3 November 1894, p. 7; *The New York Herald*, 2 November 1894, p. 11 and Musser, Op. Cit., pp. 145–153.

On 24 November 1894 The National Police Gazette *featured the filming of Broadway and London's Gaiety Girls in the Black Maria. It was captioned: "Limbs and Lenses, A Gathering of London Gaiety Girls Invade Wizard Edison's Laboratory at Orange, NJ, and Give an Exposition of Their Dances Before the Kinetoscope". [LC.]*

Etta Williamson and Rosa France. Ten members of the on-stage band performed their band drill, conducted in very tight formation on the stage of the Black Maria. The band was led by Frank Baldwin as Steele Ayers the band master. A summary of the plot in the *New York Herald*, apparently referring to this scene, said that in the play the band was supposed to perform after they had been imbibing heavily at a bar. The most ambitious film of the day was the Finale of the First Act in which thirty-four performers, in costume, were filmed – it was the largest assembly yet photographed.

The dance performed by Frank Lawton, Etta Williamson and Rosa

Roza France.
10602.
13 AND 15 WEST 24TH ST. N.Y.
· MADISON SQUARE ·

Both pages: *During the fall of 1894 excerpts from Broadway dominated the production schedule at the Black Maria.* The Finale of the First Act of Hoyt's Milk White Flag *(upper left) crowded the most performers ever on to the stage area and there was very tight maneuvering for the Band Scene (lower left). Two performers in these scenes were Isabelle Coe who played Aura Luce, the Bereaved and Rosa France who played one of the Vivandieres. [Musser & NMAH.]*

France had a sad aftermath. Rosa France retired from the stage shortly after the filming. The *New York Dramatic Mirror* reported that she had heart trouble and that the dance that she had to perform in "A Milk White Flag" aggravated her condition so she had to give up the role. She died four years later of consumption. She was thirty and had been on stage for thirteen years.[502]

The staged comedies that Dickson filmed using staff from the lab proved to be quite popular. The blacksmith, barber shop and barroom scenes were among the films shown as Kinetoscope parlors opened in the U.S. and abroad. In spite of their popularity, Dickson did not create many other home-grown comedies or dramas, but one of the few he made set a trend that was important to early cinema. In November or December he staged a "Fire Rescue" in the Black Maria. A rude set was constructed to simulate a building, smoke billowed and a uniformed fireman went up a ladder to enact the rescue of a child or small person in a night gown, handing him or her to fire personnel waiting below. It was the first of a popular genre of fire rescue scenes and views of fire equipment that pleased early movie audiences for more than a decade and which remain a theme revisited by today's filmmakers.

The most significant film made during this period was the boxing match between James J. Corbett and Peter Courtney, filmed on 7 September 1894. Arrangements for the bout were made by the Latham-Tilden syndicate, which by that date had become the Kinetoscope Exhibiting Co.

It was Otway Latham who first approached Corbett with a proposal for a bout. On 9 August he wrote Corbett's manager, theatrical producer William A. Brady, proposing to stage a match between Corbett and Peter Jackson. He sent a similar letter to Jackson's manager Parson Davies. He proposed a purse of $15,000.00. The bout would be held in

502 Musser, Op. Cit., pp. 159–162; NMAH Hendricks

a ring ten feet square. If this was too small, he asked what small size would be acceptable. Brady gave a copy of Latham's letter and his own reply to the *New York Journal* who reported it on 10 August 1894 in an article titled "Snap-Shot Gladiators". Brady told Latham that the Olympic Club of New Orleans had bid $25,000 for the match and invited Latham to meet their offer by the following Monday. Brady said that "... Mr. Corbett would be delighted to have his motions and actions in the ring preserved for future generations". The paper contacted Latham who did not raise the offer, but said that their company was still being organized and they had five investors with financial resources to support anything they wanted to undertake. Latham added: "We could settle for all time whether a contest of this kind is really a scientific affair or a brutal fight ...".[503]

While the Kinetoscopic bout between Corbett and Jackson never took place, this apparently opened the way for the Corbett-Courtney match. The article in the *Journal* gave publicity to all three parties and tweaked the public's curiosity about the possibility of seeing the world's champion on Edison's latest invention. Latham's letter also raised the possibility that a filmed bout might evade the laws banning boxing matches because it was a "scientific" examination of boxing skills or a staged fight-drama rather than an competitive match. Evading the legal restraints that hampered the fight game was crucial to Latham and his associates because it opened the way to exploit the markets where boxing was banned.

This first shot of publicity stirred public interest and by the time that Corbett made his trek to the Black Maria, the press was properly aroused. The event was covered by the *Newark Daily Advertiser*, *The Orange Chronicle*, *The New York Herald*, *New York Sun* and *Boston Advertiser*. The reporter from the *New York Sun* met Corbett and his party at the Christopher Street Ferry, the embarkation point for the train connection. As had been the case with the Leonard-Cushing match, poor weather delayed this bout. Corbett's party had come the day before but were turned back at the ferry because the sky was overcast and the filming was postponed. Although it was foggy on the 7th, the sun was breaking it up and the party proceeded. Corbett was bothered because Brady, his manager, was not there yet – he overslept, but Brady arrived in Orange in time for the bout. The *Sun's* reporter gave details of the clothes and jewelry Corbett wore "... a well-fitting suit of light checked cloth, an immaculate white shirt, standing collar, and black necktie in which nestled a cluster of diamonds, while a broad-brimmed straw hat shaded his sunburned features. He carried a massive cane, and on the little finger of his right hand three big gold rings set with diamonds and rubies attracted the attention of onlookers ...".[504]

Corbett's opponent, Peter Courtney, was an unknown quantity but he was proclaimed the heavyweight champion of New Jersey on the basis of the defeat of three relatively obscure fighters and a victory over E. Warren who claimed to be New Jersey's champion. More impressively, he claimed to have gone four rounds with Bob Fitzsim-

503 EHS, Unbound Clippings, *New York Journal*, 11 August 1894. Latham signed his letter on behalf of the Photo-Electric Exhibition Co., O. Latham, President.

504 Musser, Op. Cit.. pp. 114–122. Musser reproduces the complete text of the article in the *New York Sun*.

mons, Corbett's principal heavy weight rival. The *Sun's* reporter did his best to promote Courtney as an suitable match for Corbett. He praised Courtney's physique, fearless attitude and apparent ability to withstand punches. "... the critics sized him up [as] a 'pretty hard-looking nut to crack', one man ventured the opinion that a mallet blow squarely delivered on the top of his head would never phase him ...".[505]

The conditions of the fight were similar to the Leonard-Cushing bout except that the ring size was enlarged to 14 feet and rounds lasted a bit over one minute – perhaps the result of running the camera a bit slower. The time between rounds was reduced to two minutes. A single strand of rope in front of the camera and behind the boxers created an impression of a real boxing ring. The side walls were padded and the floor had been planed smooth and covered with rosin.

Dickson apparently had last minute problems. After the fighters had changed from their street clothes – Corbett in Dickson's Photo room and Courtney in a nearby shanty – they were delayed for a half hour while adjustments were made to the camera. At 11:45 they were ready and before beginning the bout Dickson posed the two fighters for still photos.

The fight was to be six rounds, with a knock-out in the sixth round and it went according to script, though the *Sun's* reporter described it as a regular bout and stressed Courtney's courage and the problems Corbett had in finishing his opponent. When he first stepped into the ring, Corbett was quoted as saying "My, but this is small. There' no chance to bring any foot movement into play here, that's sure. A fellow has got to stand right up and fight for his life."[506]

Corbett was used to staged sparring matches. He was appearing on Broadway in a play, "Gentleman Jack" and one of the scenes was a three round sparring match, the only place where New Yorkers could legitimately see his vaunted boxing skills.

When the filming was over, Corbett and his party returned to New York without being taken to lunch or entertained in Dickson's parlor.

The films of the Corbett bout were shown at the New York parlor soon after the fight, but there were problems. On 24 September Otway Latham asked Gilmore to send someone to New York to adjust their Kinetoscopes. Films were breaking in the machines and the problem was so acute that they closed the parlor. The problem was the motor being used in the machines and over the next several months it continued to plague them, causing them to substitute motors from other companies. In January 1895, Irving T. Bush, President, Continental Commerce Co., paying Edison for six of the 'special' machines commented that it was impossible to keep the motors at a steady speed and that although the Perret motor was more expensive, it was constructed better and required fewer repairs so it was ultimately less costly. Bush said that fluctuations in speed were bothersome on most films but "... absolutely fatal in the prize-fight machines because the blows are struck so slowly as to lose all their force and it makes the fight look like a fake from beginning to end ...".[507]

505 *Ibid.*

506 *Ibid.*

507 By January 1895 Maguire & Baucus who had the modified machines for exhibiting boxing films outside the U.S., were ordering "Perret" motors, apparently on advice of the Kinetoscope Exhibiting Co. and Edison Manufacturing Co. was reducing the price on machines supplied without motors. EHS, Joseph Baucus to William Gilmore, 14 January 1895 and Bush to Edison, 16 January 1895.

Arranging for the Corbett filming precipitated the change in management of the syndicate that Latham had put together. It was an ambitious – and expensive – project. The Kinetoscope Exhibiting Co. had committed to purchasing seventy-two "special" machines at $300 each – sixty in addition to twelve machines ordered earlier in August. To pay for the machines they deposited $5000 in Edison's bank account. Their commitment for machines was $21,600 with an additional amount due for purchase of films. The company also put up a $5000.00 purse for the match with Corbett receiving $4,750.00 and Courtney $250.00. On top of this, Corbett was also to receive a royalty. With the added costs for renting space, setting machines up and hiring staff to man them, their total obligations were in the vicinity of $30,000. This was serious money and well beyond the resources of the Lathams. With the organization of the Kinetoscope Exhibiting Co., Tilden and Rector began to take a more active roll in the business.[508]

The fall of 1894 was the acme of Edison's Kinetoscope business. Maguire & Baucus' Continental Commerce Co. introduced the Kinetoscope in Europe and Mexico. Raff & Gammon's Kinetoscope Co. contracted with local businessmen to market the Kinetoscope in various territories in North America and the Kinetoscope Exhibiting Co. brought their boxing films to Boston and other cities. The Phono Works were manufacturing machines on a regular basis, the laboratory for duplicating films was being expanded and Gilmore was reporting profits to Edison who was otherwise troubled by the faltering phonograph business and continuing problems with his ore milling project.

Dickson was kept busy with regular film production, but he was not happy.

508 EHS, Doc. File Ser.–1894.

Chapter 23

A Discontented Winter

"... Having a large interest in movie work as a compensation for my labours – I was making money & was anxious to avoid competition – so my investigations were *interpreted* as *Disloyalty & Edison who knew what I was doing believed* & gave me *no support* ...

"For years I tried to forgive & forget & ignore the whole sordid thing – too painful for words ..." (W.K.L. Dickson to Will Day, undated, c. 1933)

"... Mr. Dickson's association with the Lathams has been made subject of unpleasant criticism. ... my intimate acquaintance with Mr. Dickson during all that period and the knowledge of his keen sense of honor and of the integrity of all of his thoughts and actions, has convinced me that these criticisms were made unjustly made and without any justification in fact ...".[509] Harry N. Marvin to Glenn E. Matthews, 16 May 1933.

The Kinetoscope was a sensational novelty but despite the early success it enjoyed, Edison's latest wonder had obvious drawbacks. The films were short and the images viewers saw inside the wooden box were small. The public was familiar with spectacles put on by showmen using magic lanterns so the effect larger images could make was obvious to many viewers. As soon as the Kinetoscope appeared there was speculation about how the images would look projected on a screen and new experimenters joined those already working on what Edison called "screen machines". There were also attempts to make competitive variations on the Kinetoscope. By the fall of 1894 Dickson had been approached by two people who were well known to him who had propositions related to the Kinetoscope: Henry Marvin and Otway Latham. Their overtures changed the course of his career.

More scopes and graphs

Henry Marvin, who was living in Syracuse, visited New York shortly after the Holland Brothers Kinetoscope parlor opened. After sampling the machines he met Dickson and they talked about the Kinetoscope. The details of their talk are sketchy, but apparently Marvin felt that the image could be viewed in different ways and quizzed Dickson about possible variations. The focus was not on projection. Apparently they

509 BiFi Will Day, Dickson to Day, "Personal – for Mr WEL Day", undated.; NMAH Hendricks

talked about ways to improve the image, an alternative to the bulky Kinetoscope box and the possibility of freeing the machine from batteries and electrical connections. Dickson suggested a thumb book and demonstrated it by drawings of a series of X's on cards, creating a moving effect by flipping the cards. Marvin took the cards and when he was back in Syracuse, showed them to Herman Casler who was honing his skills at his cousin's machine shop. They decided that photographs reproduced on resilient photo paper could be arranged around a drum and viewed by rotating the drum. A stick or metal rod acting like a finger would keep the cards appearing one after another and create the impression of motion. It could be operated by a turning a crank. Standard Eastman roll film, printed, would give them a larger image. It didn't take long to design the device. It was a simple mechanism, which proved to be versatile and durable. In November 1894 Casler applied for a patent for the apparatus now named the Mutoscope.[510]

Dickson's role in designing the Mutoscope has been debated over the years. Because of his well-known experience with the Kinetoscope it is natural to assume he had the major role in the design, but hid behind Casler because of the obvious conflict with his work for Edison. He admitted playing an important role in the concept, but how much he contributed to the final product is open to question. Since the surviving evidence is very sketchy, speculation is inevitable. The design of the Mutoscope was not the subject of legal battles and lacking court testimony about the work, there is less evidence about it than about the cameras and projectors that were subsequently built. Although a succession of historians questioned Dickson about his work for Edison, few of them asked about his early involvement with the Mutoscope. Dickson was consistent in saying that he gave Marvin the pack of cards and in 1933 he told Earl Theisen that this was the basis of the device – but he also gave credit to Casler and Harry Marvin:

"... I showed him [Marvin] a pack of cards I had devised with consecutive series of crosses showing motion drawn by hand in which he showed considerable interest – & his draughtsman Herman Casler & Mr. Marvin quickly saw it might be a good thing if made circular & turned by hand & held back by a *metal* finger hence the patent taken out forwith [sic]...".[511]

Dickson did not originate the idea of a thumb book. It had been devised years earlier and had taken its place in the toy box along with the Zoetrope and the results of other persistence of vision experiments.[512] This comment implies that Dickson may have already prepared the thumb book before talking with Marvin, perhaps to propose it to Edison as another way of marketing Kinetograph images. It also confirms that the design and machine work was done in Syracuse where Casler was working at C.E. Lipe's machine shop.

While the extent of Dickson's involvement in the Mutoscope is unclear, he was consulted about the project. Casler, Marvin and Elias B. Koopman were his friends and business associates. The Photoret camera which Dickson and Casler designed, was introduced at the

510 U.S. Patent no. 549,309, 5 November 1895, H. Casler, Mutoscope.

511 Academy Library, Earl Theisen Collection, Dickson to Theisen, 18 February 1933.

512 Laurent Mannoni, Donata Pesenti Capagnoni, David Robinson, *Light and Movement* [Gemona, Italy] Le Giornate del Cinema Muto, 1995, p. 355. The authors cite an English patent for a "kineograph" by J. B. Linnett in 1868 as an early example of a "flip", "flick" or "Flicker" book. The names vary from country to country.

beginning of the year and it was still being sold through Koopman's Magic Introduction Company. At this point this was an informal partnership and their relationship was more social than commercial. They were a compatible group who enjoyed each other's company. Their get togethers were often family gatherings which included their wives.

The Mutoscope was a device for viewing images in motion and a prototype was either built or under construction, but there were no images to put on it. According to Dickson, they hoped to use films shot in the Black Maria and he proposed this to Edison who refused to allow it. [513] This was not an off-the-wall proposal. One potential use of the Mutoscope was as an advertising device, a tool to aid business. Koopman was particularly enthusiastic about this. Their concept was a table-top viewer, portable and light enough that a salesman might carry it with him to demonstrate products to prospective clients. Although it had a future in the entertainment world, in this form it would not necessarily compete with the bulky, immobile Kinetoscope and it would open a new market. It was probably this more pragmatic use that Dickson proposed to Edison – but to no avail.

In November, after the patent application for the Mutoscope had been prepared, Marvin and Casler came to New York to discuss future plans with Elias Koopman. By this time Dickson had apparently talked with Edison because it was decided that they would design a camera to take their own pictures. Casler said that he started work on the camera in December 1894. As long as they proposed to work with Edison and supplement the Kinetoscope, Dickson could involve himself in their plans, but the decision to make films was clearly competitive and it put Dickson on the spot. He became careful about his relations with his friends and they were equally cautious. There was a mutual understanding that Dickson would not be visibly involved in their project so he remained behind the scenes and anonymous.

Anonymous, perhaps, but it would have been very uncharacteristic for Dickson to have divorced himself entirely from a moving image project involving some of his closest friends. It is difficult to document his relations with Marvin, Casler and Koopman during the late fall, winter and early spring of 1894–1895. Dickson did not have a great deal of free time to journey to Syracuse where Casler was working. The fall of 1894 was very busy time for him. There was a full schedule of film productions, and he had to supply quantities of film prints for the steady stream of new Kinetoscopes that were now being shipped from the Phonograph Works. To meet this demand, the laboratory facilities were enlarged. To complicate matters further, he was, as we shall see, becoming more involved with the Latham family. Casler was a good machinist and an innovative inventor in his own right, but it is hard to believe that with one of the most experienced specialists in moving images available to him, he would not have tried to pick Dickson's brains. We know of at least one meeting with Casler, and there may have been more. Casler said that they discussed projection during the

513 Academy Library, Earl Theisen Collection, Dickson to Earl Theisen, 18 Febuary 1933.

fall, perhaps at the time that Casler and Marvin met with Koopman.[514] It is possible that they also met earlier.

Since Casler knew mechanics and had access to experienced machinists working at Lipe's shop, he would probably have turned to Dickson for something other than specifics of about the mechanism. Dickson's strong suit was photography. Casler knew something about photography – if he knew little before 1893, he had learned at least the basics while working with Dickson on the Photoret. There are aspects of the Mutoscope's design that show Dickson's influence. The film to be used and the size of the image are matters where Dickson's experience was valuable and the final design seems to reflect his influence. The Mutoscope had an image several times larger than the Kinetoscope: 2¾ x 2 inches compared with 1 x ¾ inches. We have followed Dickson's pattern of increasing the size of the image which began with his micro-image experiments in 1888–1889. The size of the Mutoscope image was determined by a decision to use over-the-counter roll film. The film used in the Kodak No. 1 camera was chosen and it was 2¾ inches wide. Since the patent application sent in November 1894 did not specify the size of the image, this was not necessarily decided during the fall of 1894.

It could have been Dickson who advised them to stay away from motors and batteries. Motors, lights and batteries were basic elements of Edison's work, but Dickson may have felt that a viewing device would be simpler and more flexible without them. But this was not something that only Dickson understood. The disadvantage of depending on expensive, bulky electrical batteries would have been apparent to anyone who looked carefully at the Kinetoscope parlor. By tradition, it is assumed that Dickson advised his friends on design elements that would or would not conflict with Edison's patent and the motor and electric illumination were Edisonian elements in the design of the Kinetoscope. Except for reproducing images of movement, the Mutoscope was a completely different device from the Kinetoscope.

Casler said that he began work on the camera in December 1894, shortly after the visit to New York. He showed sketches of the camera to Harry Marvin and John Pross, a machinist working at C.E. Lipe's machine shop in Syracuse on 12 December. The camera was nearly finished in March 1895 and strips of paper were used to test the film path. In mid-June 1894 they made the first test using celluloid film. It was a boxing match between the diminutive Herman Casler and Harry Marvin who towered well over six feet.[515] The camera operator for this first production was probably W.K.L. Dickson.

Casler's testimony traces progress that appears neat and tidy, but apparently there were problems he did not discuss. Three months elapsed between the time it was nearly completed and the first test with film and another eight months went by before Casler applied for a patent – on 26 February 1896.

The Mutograph camera was quite different from the Kinetograph and, led by Terry Ramsaye, film historians have stressed that Dickson

514 NMAH Hendricks, Casler testimony in Patent Interference No. 18,461, Latham v. Casler v. Armat, 1896. Casler testified that the Mutoscope was completed by 10 November, that he met with Marvin and Koopman about the 12th to the 14th, and he applied for the patent on 21 November.

515 NARA & NMAH Hendricks, Casler testimony, 23 February 1897, in Interference No. 18,460 and January, 1898 in Patent Interference no. 18,461. Testimony about dates was very specific since the decision in awarding priority depended on the earliest conception of the invention (when drawings were made) and when the invention was completed and functional.

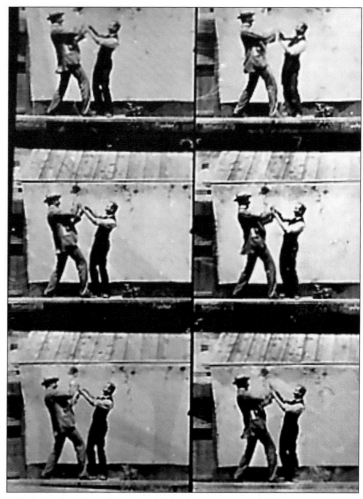

Dickson's friends Harry Marvin and Herman Casler starred in a test of the new Mutoscope camera with Dickson the apparent operator. Marvin is the tall one and Casler is a bit shorter. It was filmed in Syracuse at the machine shop of Herman Casler's cousin Charles E. Lipe. [NMAH.]

advised how the camera could avoid potential infringement of Edison's patent for the Kinetograph (which, in 1895 was still resting incomplete at the U.S. Patent Office). Ramsaye's information was, as always, uncredited, but his source was probably Harry Marvin. Since this was about as close to the horse's mouth as it was possible to get, it can be taken seriously, but it does not clarify the extent of Dickson's contribution.[516] In addition to the important difference in size and the kind of film the Mutograph used, the way the film moved through the camera and was exposed was unlike the Kinetograph. The intermittent movement was completely different from the Kinetograph. Because the Mutograph used regular roll film, it was not a special purchase item and

516 Ramsaye, Op. Cit., pp. 213–215. U.S. Patent no. 629,063, Mutograph, 18 July 1899, applied 26 February 1896.

it did not have to be trimmed to size and perforated before exposure. The film was perforated in the camera after exposure and the perforations did not guide the film, they were used to accurately position the film for printing. The patent claimed a new means of reeling (loading) the film which allowed for use of longer lengths of film.

Even though Dickson never claimed credit for the Mutograph there are signs of his influence. In addition to elements of design that avoid conflict with his Kinetoscope there are other factors that seem drawn from Dickson's expertise. The Mutograph used the larger film that Dickson favored and like the Kinetograph, the Mutograph was designed to operate at 40 frames per second, though the rate of exposure could be altered. Dickson liked 40 fps because he was convinced that rapid exposure reduced or eliminated the annoying flicker. Both had a meter that could be used to time the shot during planning and taking. Both were driven by electric motors which used batteries as the source of power and were mounted on a steel plate to hold the camera steady during filming. The result was a camera that was even larger and more awkward than the Kinetograph. It was almost the size of a small desk and weighed several hundred pounds. With batteries the outfit ran close to a ton. Like the Kinetograph it was better used under controlled conditions in a studio but by the time it came into active use it had to be more versatile than its forebearer.

The Lathams

Almost as soon as the Latham-Tilden-Rector syndicate opened their parlor at 83 Nassau Street in New York City, the Latham family began speculating about projecting their films. As Woodville Latham explained: "... A day or so after they began the exhibitions, one of my sons came to me and asked if I could not devise a machine for projecting the pictures upon a screen. He said that a number of the spectators in his hearing had expressed a wish that something of that sort might be done ...".[517] In September or early October the Lathams approached W.K.L. Dickson about designing a projector.

Dickson's involvement with the Latham family was a complicated affair, complete with elements of drama and mystery. The beginning was cordial, even companionable, but it gradually disintegrated into mistrust and discord. During the summer and early fall of 1894 Dickson had grown to like the Lathams. He had frequent business with Otway and they became friends. For Dickson, social activity enhanced labor, so work days were sometimes followed by social gatherings at the Dicksons' home. During these evenings of food, wine, music and discussion, Dickson came to like and respect the father, Woodville. "I found Mr Latham to be a congenial spirit, owing to his scientific attainments and our friendship grew and throughout such acquaintanceship, we spent many evenings discussing the scientific questions of the day."[518] Besides an interest in science, the Dicksons and Lathams had shared ties to Virginia. Though he was born in Mississippi, Latham's family came from Culpeper, Virginia and Woodville was

517 NARA, Patent Interference No. 18,461, Latham v. Casler v. Armat. Woodville Latham's testimony, 4 December 1897.

518 EHS, Dickson's testimony, 10 April 1911 in Equity 5/167, Motion Picture Patents Co. v. Imp. The principle factor in this case was the Latham's patent for their projector and the so-called "Latham Loop". There was detailed questioning about the invention of the Latham's system so it is one of the main sources of information about the events during the fall, winter and spring of 1894–1895.

educated at Columbia College (now George Washington University) in nearby Washington, DC and at the University of Virginia in Charlottesville.

If science provided a common interest, one aspect of science was supposedly taboo. Dickson said it was understood that they would never discuss moving photography. Although Dickson may have understood this, the Lathams had a different view. According to Dickson, in mid-October, following an evening dinner at the Dicksons' house the topic came up. Dickson said it came as a surprise, but Woodville Latham said it was not a new topic. He claimed that his sons had not only discussed the possibility of projecting film, but had already proposed a business deal in which Dickson would be a partner.[519] They wanted Dickson's help in designing a projector, but they also wanted potential investors to know of his involvement. In return they offered shares in a company they planned to organize and tried to persuade him that the business would make them rich. The Lathams were in the process of financing the project and they asked Dickson to make a written commitment to help them which they could show to prospective investors.

Dickson was interested – but cautious. He asked his wife to join this discussion and insisted that Woodville take part even though he protested that he was not involved because it was his sons who organized the business. Dickson was tempted but he was worried about jeopardizing his relations with Edison but the Lathams assured him they would not ask him "... to do any dishonorable thing ...". He remained on guard, but, with his wife's agreement, he signed a note promising to help them get films for their projector and he also made a verbal agreement to discuss projection with Edison and tell him that the Lathams hoped for the exclusive right to project Edison's films.[520]

The Lathams interpreted this discussion as a tacit commitment to help their project with something more than an approach to his boss. Woodville Latham said that Dickson was dissatisfied with his situation at the lab and that Dickson claimed that he, rather than Edison, had invented the Kinetoscope. Dickson told them that he had been working on a projector at home and had a working model. When questioned about their relationship in December 1897, Woodville Latham said: "My sons and I were under promise to him that if the machinery which he claimed to be able to have constructed at once without experimentation should prove to be efficient we would give to him ... one fourth of the stock of the company which we expected to form ...".[521]

Dickson interpreted the situation differently. In his many testimonials about this affair Dickson usually denied any explicit commitment to the Lathams and claimed there was never any formal agreement, but his subsequent actions show that he had very conflicting feelings about the Lathams' project and continued to give serious consideration to their proposal.

By the end of October he had taken several steps to help the Lathams. He discussed their proposal with Edison, made tests with a

519 NARA, Woodville Latham's testimony, December 8, 1897 in Patent Interference no. 18,461, Latham v. Casler v. Armat. Woodville Latham testified that this discussion took place on 19 October 1894. This interference was called because of four almost simultaneous applications for patent for a motion picture projector by Woodville Latham, Herman Casler, Thomas Armat and Edward Amet. Amet dropped out, but the other three testified in detail about their inventions and called supporting witnesses. This testimony is also a major source of information about these events.

520 EHS, Dickson's & Woodville Latham's testimony, Patent Interference 5/167, Motion Picture Patents Co. v. Imp, 1911.

521 Ibid.

modified Kinetoscope to see if it could be converted to a projector and recommended his friend Eugene Lauste as a machinist and electrician who could help them set up and operate a machine shop.

Edison and the screen machine

Edison was unreceptive to the Latham's project. He reminded Dickson that he had a business arrangement with Raff & Gammon and could not give the Lathams a conflicting concession.

Conflicting business commitments were not the only factors influencing Edison's resistance to projection. He was still uncertain about the commercial future of the Kinetoscope, but for the time being, the business was booming and the Kinetoscope was saving Edison from serious financial trouble. Sales were at a peak during the fall of 1894 and the Phono Works was hard at work meeting the large orders from the clients that Gilmore had lined up. Very welcome checks were being deposited in Edison's accounts at the German National Bank in Newark and Drexel Morgan in New York City. Almost all of Edison's other businesses were stagnant. For the sixteen months between November 1893 and March 1895, the Kinetoscope generated a profit of $73,454.80 and sales of films earned another $12,323.72 in profits. In all the Kinetoscope grossed $185,431. By contrast, during the same sixteen months Edison's battery business earned a paltry $545.79; phonograph profits were worse, a mere $404.40 and though sales of cylinders were a bit better, the profit was only $2,892.37.[522]

Edison was a machine person. In today's terms he was more comfortable with hardware rather than software. His profits came from selling machines to concessionaires and he believed that he could get more dollars for Kinetoscopes than for the films that ran on them. This situation would change, of course, but he and his business associates were just beginning to learn that selling films could be profitable. For Edison one machine that served one viewer was better than one machine serving an audience of fifty, a hundred or five hundred. When he gave in and started manufacturing projectors in 1896 he told Norman Raff that about fifty machines would satisfy the needs of the entire country.[523] Although he was making films for the Kinetoscope, he continued to reject proposals to produce commercial phonograph recordings. Ironically, film production and commercial recordings would rank among his most profitable businesses over the next twenty years. A few machines needed a lot of films to satisfy a growing number of fans. Although the marketing of films would dominate the future motion picture industry, this was not evident in the fall of 1894.

When Dickson approached him with proposals from the Lathams and his Mutoscope friends, Edison was not ready to kill a goose laying such golden eggs, but his skepticism about the future of the Kinetoscope was realistic. The market peaked that fall and by late winter, the demand for machines began to decline.

Dickson was unhappy with Edison's rejection of the Latham's offer. "... my disappointment was intense ...", he said when he testified

522 EHS, Profit & Loss statement for sixteen months, 1 November 1893 to 1 March 1895, 1 March 1895. See footnote on page 321.

523 Academy Library, Theisen. Thomas Armat to Earl Theisen, 24 June 1932.

about the Latham affair in April 1911 and he also said that when he met with Woodville Latham to tell him, he learned that they planned to develop their own machines for taking and projecting based on some design plans that the father had already sketched out.[524]

Sometime during October Dickson brought one of the older Kinetoscopes to Columbia College in New York City for a projection test. Professor Riborg Mann of the college supplied him with a strong arc lamp that could be adjusted for different intensities of light. The Kinetoscope had been modified by enlarging the opening in the shutter slightly to allow more light to pass through. The Kinetoscope had a continuous movement, i.e. the film did not stop to admit light, which was not changed but there may have been some unspecified change to the lens. In one account Dickson mentioned a projection lens and Woodville Latham mentioned an objective lens in his December 1897 testimony.[525] Intermittence was provided by the modified shutter and there was a condenser attached to the arc lamp to change the intensity of the light passing through the shutter. A short piece of film was spliced into a loop so that it could run over and over again, projecting an image about three feet wide. The tests were done in one day and lasted only a couple of hours. Dickson, one or two professors from Columbia and both Woodville and Otway Latham apparently attended.[526]

Dickson's testimony in 1911 implied that this was a continuation of experiments made at the laboratory. In 1924 in a letter to Terry Ramsaye he seemed to confirm this and gave a slightly different version of the dinner party that inaugurated his confusing and conflicted relations with the Latham family:

"I could not get enough light through the 13-inch diameter shutter with a 1/8-inch slot by the use of my Zeiss focus arc lamp and I mentioned this to my good friend, the Rev. C.H. Mann of Orange, NJ, who advised me to go and see his son, Professor Riborg Mann at Columbia College and bring a sample, and he would give me all the light I wanted, ... Professor Latham and his sons were having supper at my house, 166 Cleveland street, Orange, and heard me say what I intended to do. I wasn't sure at the time if I should give way to the Prof's insistent request to be allowed to come – anyway he came ...".[527]

It is not clear when the Kinetoscope was tested at the laboratory, but it is possible that Edison saw one of the tests. In 1924, while working on *A Million and One Nights*, Ramsaye wrote Edison to check Edison's statements to him about watching Dickson's tests of projection. Ramsaye had been corresponding with Dickson who was insistent about projecting for Edison when he returned from Paris. Ramsaye wanted to confirm Edison's 1901 testimony in the American Mutoscope suit when he responded to a question about the demonstration by saying that "There was no screen". Edison's response to Ramsaye was equally unclear. He apparently remembered various projection tests, but either he could not remember the dates or was confused about when things happened. His descriptions seemed to mix the events, but one of his statements seems to describe projection tests that took place before the

524 Dickson, testimony in Equity 5/167.

525 Changing the lens would have been an obvious modification because the Kinetoscope was fitted with a lens that enlarged the image for viewing, not for projection.

526 Dickson, Equity 5/167; Ramsaye, Op. Cit., pp. 118–119; NARA, Patent Interference 18,461; NMAH Hendricks. Gordon Hendricks believed that the tests at Columbia took place about 12 October 1894. He researched passenger records and found that C. Riborg (or Ribery) Mann sailed for Europe 30 October 1894 with the tests taking place before he left. From their testimony about the Columbia College tests it is not clear which members of the Latham family attended but Dickson indicates that Woodville and Otway were there.

527 Ramsaye, Op. Cit., pp. 118–119.

Columbia College test: "I am certain that we projected the picture on a screen before we stopped making the peep machines. One of the peep machines was changed to project a picture about 12 inches square on a large 5 ft. square. The Geneva stop was probably badly made the picture being quite unsteady ...".[528]

This raises an unanswerable question: if there were experiments with converting the Kinetoscope into a projector, when did they take place? Were they stimulated by the Latham's interest in projection or had Dickson experimented earlier and revived the project in response to the obvious interest in projection raised by the public showing of the Kinetoscope? I have found no clues to answer this in the extensive records that survive at the Edison Historic Site.

The images projected at Columbia College were not satisfactory and the test proved that the design of the Kinetoscope would have to be changed before it would work as a projector. Specifically, since the film ran continuously and was not stopped to admit more light the modification of the shutter did not produce effective intermittence and did not allow enough light to reach the screen. It would have been more effective to use an intermittent movement that would start and stop the film but this raised the potential for damaging the film. How to advance the film with a maximum amount of light on the screen and a minimum amount of stress and strain on the film was the major challenge confronting the Lathams and others designing projectors.

Although the images were imperfect, Woodville Latham seemed to feel the demonstration achieved its goal of helping to determine the density of light needed and the kind of condenser that should be used. The Lathams went ahead with their plans to make a projector that used a continuous rather than intermittent movement.[529]

The fact that Dickson would approach Edison with proposals from the Lathams and the Mutoscope group suggests that Edison was not stubbornly committed to peep show machines and may indicate that there were discussions of alternatives to the Kinetoscope. Dickson was not the only one raising the possibility of developing a projector. Edison also heard from Raff and Gammon who were being pestered by their concessionaires.

Lauste and Latham's lab

Dickson's friend Eugene Lauste started working for the Lathams in the fall of 1894. Since being laid off by Edison in March of 1892, Lauste had been through hard times. He tried to set up a machine shop and work independently but could not make a go of it. He worked briefly at Edison's mill in Ogden but found the work distasteful, quit and, according to his account, walked back to Newark in the cold and wet. He was unemployed for a while. Dickson was aware of Lauste's troubles and since he respected Lauste's abilities as an electrician and machinist, when the Lathams asked if he knew of a machinist he recommended Lauste. Dickson contacted Lauste, told him that the Lathams would explain their project and gave him a letter of introduction.

528 EHS. Ramsaye to Edison, 17 June 1924 with Edison's handwritten response for William Meadowcroft to transcribe in his response.

529 NARA. Testimony in Patent Interference 16, 461.

According to Lauste he met with Woodville and Otway in late September or early October to discuss the project. The Lathams told him that they planned to make a projector first to test it with Edison film and after that they would make a camera and a final version of the projector. They asked Lauste what equipment he would need to build the devices and Lauste told them he would need a lathe, a drill press, a grindstone and as many small tools as they could give him. After the meeting, Lauste and Otway looked for a building where they could set up a machine shop. They found one in the Scott Building at 35 Frankfort Street in lower Manhattan.[530]

Lauste had to wait a while to begin work. In order to buy the equipment, supplies and pay Lauste's salary, the Lathams needed capital. They had some income from the boxing films being exhibited on the Kinetoscope and they may have used this to purchase equipment for the machine shop, but it was, apparently, not enough to support the shop they proposed. Woodville went south to look for financing and found enough support to establish a company which he named the Lambda Company, the Greek letter L, as in Latham. The company was organized in December 1894 and headquartered at the law office of Maury & Maury, Richmond, Virginia. Latham claimed it was capitalized at $500,000. Gray Latham was president, Woodville was secretary-treasurer. Among the directors were Mr. Voight and Dr. Prendergast, both from Cincinnati, Ohio, William T. Jenkins from New York City and Valery Trudeau of Nashville, Tenn. Mr. Trudeau was probably a relative of Woodville's late wife, Eliza Trudeau. Most of the stock was held by the Lathams.[531]

With the exception of the Lathams, none of the principals associated with the Kinetoscope Exhibiting Co. were officers of the Lambda Company. The Latham boys were still active in the Kinetoscope operation and during the fall Gray was in Boston supervising the Kinetoscope exhibit there, but the projection project was organized as a separate and apparently unrelated business. The beginning of the Lambda project coincides with the occasion when Samuel Tilden informed Edison that Enoch J. Rector would be business contact for the Kinetoscope Exhibiting Company rather than Otway Latham.[532] This managerial change may have been a way of freeing Otway to supervise the projection experiments, but if that was the case, it would not have been necessary to create a new company. There is no record of animosity between the Lathams and either Tilden or Rector, but their absence from Lambda organization raises the possibility of some friction among the partners in the boxing film organization.

By the end of November equipment had been purchased and Lauste was ready to start work. Accompanied by his teenage son, Emile, he moved into a small room adjacent to the workroom. The first priority was to make a projector that could use Edison's films and the effort moved at a brisk pace. The prototype was completed before Christmas and Lauste started on a version that would use film wider than Edison's, but the Lathams decided to change directions and work on a camera. It

530 According to Woodville Latham's testimony, 14 March 1899 in Patent Interference 18,461, the rent for the Frankfort Street shop started 1 November 1894; Eugene Lauste was on the payroll at $21.00 per week on 2 November 1894. His first salary payment was made 24 November 1894.

531 NARA; NMAH Hendricks. Woodville Latham's testimony in Patent Interference no. 18,461. Woodville Latham married Eliza Trudeau on 5 October 1861 at Hope Estate Parish of East Baton Rouge, Louisiana. She died in St. Louis, Missouri 8 February 1890. The information comes from the Latham family bible.

532 EHS. Samuel J. Tilden to Gilmore, 15 October 1894.

was completed in February and the first tests were made at the end of that month. A projector to use the wider film followed. The first projection, in New York on 20 May 1895, was the first open-to-the public projection of modern motion pictures.

Although this was the Latham's project and as proprietors they owned the machines that were created for the Lambda Company, there have been persistent questions about who designed them – who was the *real* inventor of their camera and projector? It is a mystery that has persisted for more than a century and it is not likely that it will ever be resolved to everyone's satisfaction. There is ample testimony from the participants and pages and pages of documents, records and opinions, but the truth is clouded by conflicting claims, cleverly deceptive testimony and attempts to discredit real or perceived rivals. Nevertheless, it is worth examining the information that survives to see if some of the issues can be clarified.

In the fall of 1894 when the experiments started, the three Lathams and Eugene Lauste had very little experience with photography, limited experience with optics and no experience in capturing and reproducing motion. The person with the expertise needed to expedite the project was William Kennedy Laurie Dickson.

Other than Dickson, the best equipped was Woodville Latham who had a good background in science, administrative experience and a reputation as a skilled teacher. He was trained as a civil engineer having studied at Columbia College and the University of Virginia. He had been executive officer of the Confederate arsenal in Columbus, Georgia during the Civil War and had taught physics, chemistry and agriculture. He was credited with improving the chemistry laboratory at West Virginia University and he published at least one paper on chemistry while at the University of Mississippi. Although he claimed to have studied photography in his youth and may have had knowledge of its general principals, he does not seem to have worked with a camera or in a darkroom. As he described his qualifications in 1897: "Questions concerning the manufacture of photographic and projecting apparatus are questions of mechanics, optics and chemistry, and, to some extent, of physiology, and these are such questions as I have been interested in to a considerable extent from my early boyhood".[533]

Otway and Gray Latham were young and had earned a substantial reputation as gay blades enjoying the pleasures of New York in the 1890s – the Gay Nineties. When they ventured into the Kinetoscope business in 1894 Gray was 28 years old and Otway was 27. There is only scant information about their academic background. Both of were supposed to have studied at West Virginia University when there father was there but unless they were very precocious they would have only begun their college work. Gray was 19 and Otway 18 when they moved from West Virginia to Mississippi. Presumably they attended university there and they may have studied chemistry since both of them worked for drug companies before they speculated in moving images. By their own admission, Otway had better technical skills than Gray. It was

[533] Testimony in Patent Interference 18, 461.

Otway who involved himself in the nuts and bolts of their project while Gray handled business matters.[534] Neither of them seems to have had a strong interest in photography and their involvement with pictures that moved began when they visited the Holland Brothers Kinetoscope parlor in the spring of 1894.

In addition to his abilities as a machinist and electrician, Eugene Lauste was an experimenter with an inquiring mind. He worked on several experiments during the 1890s but was too poor to carry them very far. His retiring nature and inability to express himself well in English made it difficult for him to promote his schemes. He abandoned a gasoline engine he was developing after friends warned him that it had no future in transportation because explosions and noise would keep it off the streets.[535] In later life he claimed that his interest in projecting movement dated to his childhood when he received a small magic lantern, a gift from the owner of a Parisian toyshop where his mother worked. A year later he received a Zoetrope and he tried to combine them.[536] If he harbored a desire to project movement, Lauste had done little or nothing about it before joining the Lathams. During the time he worked at Edison's lab he was not involved in photography and did almost none of the machine work for the Kineto. The closest he came to involvement with the Kinetograph was some wiring in the photography building. He claimed that he was hiding in the room when Dickson unsuccessfully tried to project a film for Edison after his return from Paris. Although he may have discussed the Kineto during visits with his friend W.K.L. Dickson, there is no evidence that he experimented with moving images or that he knew much about photography in 1894.

Because they lacked expertise in photography and particularly moving image photography, it is not surprising that the Lathams turned to Dickson. As Gray Latham put it. "[Otway and I] talked the matter over and came to the conclusion that Dickson might be of service to us should we begin the manufacture of machines for the showing of moving pictures and on one occasion, at least, I remember that my brother and I asked Mr. Dickson whether or not he would be willing to join us in this work. For sometime he hesitated, but finally agreed that he would talk the matter over with his wife ...".[537]

Given the lack of experience among the principals and Dickson's cautious effort to protect his position with Edison, it is natural to suppose that he was the shadow inventor of the Lathams' projector and camera but this is not necessarily the case. Dickson denied having any part in the devices and his claim was supported by the Lathams and Lauste, but this general agreement is suspect since all parties were looking out for their own interests. The truth seems to lie somewhere in the middle, with none of the participants being fully responsible, but each of them, the Lathams, Lauste and Dickson, contributing something.

As for Dickson's contribution, there is agreement among all of the parties that sometime after the test at Columbia College he recom-

534 This is according to their 1897 testimony in Patent Interference 18,461.

535 Merritt Crawford, "Men in the Movie Vanguard II, Eugene Augustin Lauste, Father of Sound Film" *Cinema*, May 1930, pp. 29–31 and 60.

536 MoMA Crawford. Lauste "Questionary [sic] and Answering of Mr. Eugene Lauste, Regarding the 'Invention' of Mr. Woodville Latham, the Eidoloscope" c. 1927–1928.

537 EHS. Testimony in Patent Interference no. 18,461, 15 December 1897.

mended an intermittent movement which was tried and did not work. Presumably this was for the camera since the first projector, built in December 1894, apparently ran continuously and would not have needed the intermittent movement. Lauste credited Dickson with recommending adding a roller to the film path of the camera in order to keep the film engaged with several of the sprockets and not tearing the film by lifting off too quickly.[538] Beyond these two specific recommendations, the testimony of all the participants regarding Dickson's relations with the Lathams is cloudy. When Dickson testified in 1911 for the Patents Company in their suit against the Independent Motion Picture Co., the one occasion when he told his story under oath, he tried very hard to put the best face on the affair. He claimed he resisted pressure from the Lathams to become more involved; that he studiously avoided looking at their plans or the machines they worked on and never gave them information which would compromise his relations with Edison. By 1932 he was still trying to put a positive spin on this affair. At that time he told Earl Theisen that he was spying on the Lathams: "My only connection with the Lathams was to try to find out what they were doing – Mr. Edison only laughed when I told him what they were doing as 'we had patents' – my espionage (of which I wasn't particularly proud) was misconstrued ...".[539] For their part, all of the Lathams expressed disappointment in discovering that Dickson had nothing to offer after promising to help them.

These were after the fact pronouncements. In the fall of 1894 Dickson's relations with the Lathams were still good and they continued to be good through most of the winter. He regarded them as interesting friends, he was curious about the potential of projecting images and he was tempted by the prospect of getting in on the ground floor of a promising and potentially lucrative new business. He was at a crossroads in his career. For the first time he could enjoy a certain amount of public recognition. The articles that he had written with his sister were now being compiled into a biography of Edison which was being published in time for the Christmas market. Their article about the Kinetoscope had appeared in *Century Magazine*, one of the leading monthly magazines and his name had appeared in national magazines in connection with Edison's Kinetoscope. He was playing host to a procession of popular entertainers and celebrities who traveled to Orange to appear in Kinetoscope films. Despite this new-found celebrity these were troubling months. Although he had one a partial victory in the contretemps over his copyright, his relations with William Gilmore were rocky. Though he persisted in claiming that he was the "... chief of the electro-mining ... department",[540] he had no duties connected with ore separation and was no longer on the pay roll as an experimenter and he found this difficult to accept.

Adding to his distress, in early September Dickson was summoned to appear in court. Judge DePue charged a grand jury in Newark with investigating the staging of the Corbett boxing match as a possible violation of law. The court issued a summons for Edison and Dickson

538 Lauste testimony, Equity 5/167, 7 April 1911.

539 Academy Library, Theisen Collection. Dickson to Theisen, 4 July 1932.

540 Antonia Dickson, "Wonders of the Kinetoscope" in *Leslie's Monthly*, February 1895.

to appear and they faced possible charges. Dickson was easy to find but the *New York Morning Advertiser* reported that a sheriff's constable was searching for Edison – who was out of sight at Ogden. They reported that a constable was posted outside Edison's home in Llewellyn Park.

At the time that he received the summons Dickson was involved in filming several prize fights for Raff & Gammon. The Corbett fight seemed to stimulate an interest in boxing that was both serious and light hearted. All but one were comedy routines featuring mismatched pairs of vaudeville performers in mock battles, but one was a real match. A month after filming Corbett, Dickson and Heise filmed a five round match between Eugene Hornbacker and a challenger named Murphy. Shortly after this Dickson registered a protest about the boxing films which elicited a note from Edison which advised him that he had to do as instructed by Gilmore: "We are compelled to take Boxing Matches for Raff & Gammon or Maguire & Baucus either in long or short films, therefor when Gilmore requests you to take films of this character please do so. All that we have to do is that Latham's order shall be filled first ...".

Although neither he nor Edison were charged, Dickson appeared in court in late November and ultimately the Grand Jury apparently decided that it was not a "real" boxing match. The case may have caused Edison to have second thoughts about staging another match. On 19 December 1894 *The Newark Evening News* reported that Edison was now opposed to filming boxing matches and had canceled plans for a championship match between Corbett and challenger Bob Fitzsimmons to be staged in Mexico. Later in the month the *New York Herald* reported that the Kinetoscope could not be used for the bout because of technical problems. There was concern that the machine might jam, which could allow the more tired fighter to recuperate and the Kinetoscope could not film the three minute round required by the Marquis of Queensbury rules. The ban on filmed prize fights was not absolute and the favorable court decision may have eased their concerns. Early in 1895 Dickson filmed a five round bout between Billy Edwards and an unknown opponent and there is no indication that either he or Edison objected to this bout.[541]

But Dickson's rocky relations with Gilmore continued and Edison joined the mix. On 5 February 1895 Edison sent Raff & Gammon a testy letter objecting to the Dickson's booklet on the Kinetoscope:

"I object to the little book gotten out by Dickson. The part about Dickson being a co-inventor in the Magnetic Separator etc, is incorrect, as there is no co-inventor in the Ogden business with Dickson or anybody else. I have given Dickson full credit for his labors in my manuscript letter, and I object to lugging in outside things in a Kinetoscope book. Mr. Dickson will get full credit for what he has done without trying to ram it down peoples' throats, I have seen him and he will see you. I am not especially stuck on having my own photograph in the book. It looks too much like conceitedness [sic] and self-glorification on my part, and the public never takes kindly to a man who is always pushing his personality forward. Its the thing they

541 EHS; Musser, Op. Cit., pp. 121–132 and 172–173; NMAH Hendricks. *Newark Daily Advertiser*, 11 September 1894; "Hunting for Edison" in *New York Morning Advertiser* 14 September 1894; Edison to Dickson, 15 October 1894; *Newark Evening News*, 20 November and 19 December 1894; *Orange Chronicle*, 1 December 1894. The Glenroy Brothers, a vaudeville act, were filmed 13 and 22 September, and 6 October 1894; Walton & Slavin, another comedy act was filmed on 6 October 1894; the five round bout between Hornbacker and Murphy was filmed 2 October, 1894; and Billy Edwards and his unidentified opponent in January or February 1895. The Billy Edwards bout was filmed for Maguire & Baucus, the others were for Raff & Gammon.

want to know about and not the man for whom they do not care a D—. ... Please say what you will do."[542]

This letter is rather remarkable considering that Edison had seen the Dickson's articles in *Cassier's*, *Century*, a recent one by Antonia Dickson in *Leslie's* and the compilation of the Dickson's articles which were published in book form a few months earlier and were still in bookstores. Since praise for the "Wizard" was a common theme running through all of these articles, they hardly struck the modest note that Edison's letter called for.

Edison's letter looks like it was written in response to an objection made to him by William Gilmore who continued to be irritated by Dickson's free-wheeling style. Gilmore also expressed his displeasure with Dickson's activities to Raff & Gammon. Late in February they wrote Gilmore assuring him that Dickson had visited their office to discuss arrangements for taking films and paying people who appeared in them. They assured Gilmore that they were not discussing separate business arrangements with Dickson and that they would deal with Gilmore or Edison on such matters. In fact, the arrangements for publishing the booklet were apparently made without consulting Edison and Dickson was negotiating with Raff & Gammon to sell copies of his Edison photos.[543]

This atmosphere of tension and change influenced Dickson as he considered how to respond to the Latham's efforts to involve him in their scheme.

The Lathams' workshop was operational in late November or very early December and after it opened Dickson was a frequent visitor. He often went to New York in the evening after work to stop by the workshop or to visit Woodville Latham in his rooms in the Hotel Bartholdi at 23rd and Broadway. As Woodville Latham put it: "... it was Mr. Dickson's habit to come over to the shop at 35 Frankfort street from his home in Orange, NJ, one night in every week professedly to direct Eugene Lauste, the one mechanic in my employ, in his work ...".[544] Frankfort Street was apparently convenient to the ferry from New Jersey. There was frequent service on the Orange Branch of the Erie Railway to the ferry terminal and regular ferries to Chambers Street or 23rd Street in Manhattan. The last train to Orange arrived shortly after midnight so it was possible for Dickson to go to New York after work, visit and return the same evening.[545]

Dickson characterized these visits as purely social and claimed that he scrupulously avoided examining machines or drawings, but it is hard to imagine that he remained aloof from a project he was curious about in a field so familiar to him. The Lathams seem to have counted on this and during the closing months of 1894 they maneuvered to involve Dickson in their project as much as possible. It was no coincidence that Dickson found it easy to visit their workshop because they seem to have picked a location that was convenient for him. While Dickson may not have intended to discuss the project when he visited Woodville Latham, he doubtless found it difficult to avoid the subject. Latham said it was

542 EHS. Edison to Raff & Gammon, 5 February 1895.

543 EHS. Raff & Gammon to Gilmore, 28 February 1895.

544 NARA. Patent Interference no. 18,461, December 1897.

545 Orange (NJ) Library. Ad for Erie Railway, Orange Branch in *Orange Journal*, 14 December 1889. Though this was an earlier schedule, the service in 1894 was probably about the same.

Patent Interference 18,461 and Equity 5/167

The Patent Office declared interference 18,461 because they received almost simultaneous applications for projectors from the Lathams, Herman Casler, Thomas Armat and Edward Amet. Armat succeeded in getting Amet's claim dismissed on a technicality, but the decision as to which was the earliest claim hinged primarily on the question of who had made drawings of their proposal and revealed them to others so questions of when drawings were made, by whom they were made and who saw them loomed high in the testimony. This influence the testimony of the Lathams in the case and affected the way witnesses like Eugene Lauste were questioned. The Lathams, of course, wanted to establish that they made drawings and showed them to Dickson, Lauste and others. Since there were no dated copies of these drawings that survived, the testimony of others became important. Dickson was not called in this case because he worked for Casler's company, but was involved with rival inventions by Edison and the Lathams. Lauste worked also worked for Biograph and, though he had worked for Latham, he was brought to testify by Biograph as a hostile witness. Equity 5/167, Motion Picture Patents Co. v. Independent Motion Picture Co. was a lawsuit in which the Patents Co. accused Carl Laemmle's Imp Company with infringing their patents, particularly the Latham's patent which was controlled by the Patents Co.

546 NARA. Patent Interference no. 18,461, December 1897.

547 It is not clear what Woodville Latham's ailment was. Terry Ramsaye said he had heart trouble (Op. Cit., pp. 121–122) but there are hints that he a drinking problem. He left West Virginia University under a cloud having been accused of drinking too much, being irascible and using profanity. Although he has been regarded by Ramsaye and others as an ailing old man, in 1894 he was 57 years old. His heart cannot have been too badly damaged because he lived at least 17 more years and was able to testify in 1911 in Equity 5/167.

548 NARA. Patent Interference no. 18,461. In March 1899 Woodville Latham was called again to rebut Lauste's 1897 testimony and at that time he accused Lauste of lying and perjury.

a regular topic. "During such visits there was a discussion between us as to the merits of his suggestion and the merits of mine. ...".[546] It was a game of wits.

Woodville Latham's hotel room was the nerve center of their operation. He was the guiding force behind the project but for the most part he was a commander in absentia. Because of health problems he rarely went to the workshop. The three Lathams apparently shared the room but during the fall Gray was absent most of the time. He was in Boston exhibiting the Corbett fight until late December. It was Otway who directed the day-to-day operations at Frankfort Street, apparently discussing the day's work with his father when he returned in the evening.[547]

Although the Lathams were pursuing Dickson they claimed, in their testimony for Patent Interference 18,461, that they already had a plan for the projector before they approached him. Woodville Latham said he sketched a plan in September, before the project started and that he showed his drawings to the boys, to Dickson and to Lauste. Otway said that he discussed his father's ideas with Dickson who said projection was possible but that Woodville's plan would not work. In his testimony in Equity 5/167 in 1911, Dickson said that he knew of such drawings but refused to look at them. Testifying in both cases, Lauste said that he was not given any sketches but worked from a description of the device that Woodville wanted made and that he made his own drawings.[548]

If the Lathams had a plan in mind, it was apparently a fluid one and Dickson's participation was part of it. Even though they downplayed his importance in their 1897 testimony and said that very early on they decided he had little technical information to contribute, their actions show that they felt that Dickson was important to the success of the project. While their interest might have been limited to the value his participation had in the eyes of potential investors, it is hard to imagine that they did not covet his knowledge and experience. Through the winter and into the spring of 1895 they continued their efforts to involve him in their company. In February or March, after the camera was tested, they offered Dickson one quarter of the stock in the Lambda Company (most of which was held by the Lathams). On the surface this was a very generous offer because it had a face value of $125,000.00. While the stock would not have traded at that value at the time it was offered, it is easy to see why Dickson was tempted by the offer. More about this later

So, in mid-winter, 1894–1895, Dickson was still a *very* interested observer and the relations between Dickson and the Lathams had not deteriorated. During December 1894 the prototype projector which used Edison's 35mm film was completed and just before Christmas Lauste started work on a second projector that would use film a bit wider. The final version of the camera and projector would have an image one and a half inches wide by three-quarters of an inch high with four sprockets on each side. With sprokets the resulting film was about two inches wide. Soon after they started on the new projector the Lathams decided to postpone it and make the camera first. Their decision was apparently influenced by the opinion of a new machinist, Emil W. Kleinert, another former Edison employee. Kleinert, who had worked on the Kinetoscope at the Phonograph Works, was hired by the Kinetoscope Exhibition Company to handle technical matters. He had been with Gray at the exhibit in Boston and came to New York at Christmas time. Kleinert apparently thought it would take too long to make the projector and because the Lathams felt the camera was more important they decided to leave the projector unfinished. Kleinert's opinion probably counted for something because, even though he was Lauste's helper, he was not a journeyman machinist. At the Phono Works he worked on repairing the perforating machine in 1893 and in August 1894 William Gilmore asked him to compute the price to be charged for the version of the special Kinetoscope enlarged for the boxing matches.[549]

Kleinert's arrival worried Dickson. Woodville Latham said Dickson "... exhibited a morbid dread of having Mr. Edison learn of what he was doing ...". He said that Dickson told him he might have to stay away because he could trust Lauste, but not Kleinert. Despite his concern, Dickson continued to take evening trips from Orange to Manhattan. Lauste was also bothered by Kleinert but probably because he threatened Lauste's position as principal machinist. As the new year began, the atmosphere in the Lathams' workshop was becoming more tense.

Work on the camera started about Christmas of 1894 and it moved

549 EHS. Vouchers, 29 May 1893; Gilmore to Phono Works, 7 August 1894.

briskly along. By 12 February 1895 the camera was nearly complete and the Lathams placed an order with Eastman Kodak for a dozen rolls of Trausk film, two inches wide by twenty-five feet long.[550] The film arrived a couple of days later but they waited another two weeks before testing the camera. The film was unperforated so they made a perforator and they also needed a cover for the camera. With the film perforated and a cover in place, the camera was tested about midnight on the night of 26 February 1895. Otway and Lauste loaded the camera in a dark-room, then persuaded Dickson to operate the camera and develop the film. After examining it for quality, Dickson tore off a short strip and wrote a brief note which was delivered to the ailing Woodville Latham's hotel room sometime in the pre-dawn: "To my friend Mr. Woodville Latham. Compliments of W.K.L. Dickson. 26–27 February 1895." In retrospect, Dickson regretted doing this. In his 1911 testimony he said: "... I found, however, that it had been settled to photograph the filament of an incandescent lamp and someone present suggested swinging same during the exposure. I was asked to turn the handle, I stupidly did, and further adding to my stupidity by not being able to see through their purpose, developed for them a short piece of the exposed film ... tearing off a piece of about six inches long ...". Dickson added that the camera ran about half the speed of Edison's, i.e. about twenty frames per second. The picture was, he said, sharply focused and clearly defined with only a slight halation caused by the intensity of the light bulb.[551]

The most serious problem they confronted in completing the camera was finding an intermittent movement that could stand the strain of high speed operation. Dickson's failed recommendation of a watch movement was intended to solve this problem and it seems to have been the first that they tried. It was not strong enough to stand-up to rapid motion and broke. They ordered a Geneva movement from the Boston Gear Works but it did not fit the camera so they used it to draw a pattern that would fit and it was made in a machine shop in New York. This movement worked and was in the camera that Dickson tested. A few days later they tried the camera at a more rapid speed using an electric motor and a tooth on the gear broke. After repairing the movement, the film path in the camera was further modified by adding the roller that Dickson recommended to the upper sprocket wheel to ease tension by keeping more of the film's sprocket holes engaged with the teeth of the sprockets. After this they were ready to make their first film, a four round boxing match between "Young Griffo" (Albert Griffiths), an Australian "ex-feather" and Charles Barnet of the Fourth Ward. It was filmed 4 May 1895 on rooftop of Madison Square Garden with W.K.L. Dickson and Otway Latham operating the camera.[552]

Except for going to view the projection of the Griffo-Barnet film, this was Dickson's last involvement with the Lathams' enterprise.[553]

Because of his conflicting emotions, Dickson found it difficult to explain why he decided not to join the Lathams in their projection scheme. In his 1911 testimony he confirmed that he was tempted by their proposal. "... it was my intention with Mr. Edison's approval, to

---

550 Patent Interference 18,641. Woodville Latham placed in evidence the bill from Eastman Kodak with dates ordered and shipped.

551 Latham testimony in Patent Interference 18,641 and Dickson's in Equity 5/167.

552 Patent Intereference 18,641. Latham submitted an invoice for the intermittent movement from Boston Gear Works, dated 7 January 1895, sold to E.W. Klienert; bills from J.B. Colt & Co. for projection lamps dated 18 December 1894, 14 January 1895 and 1 February 1895; and a bill for 12 rolls of Trausk film, 2 in. by 25 ft. dated 18 February 1895.

553 The projector, named the Panoptikon, premiered 20 May 1895 at 153 Broadway.

go into or participate in the exhibition business, Edison manufacturing, Latham to have the right. This ... could not be granted, owing to a contract Mr. Edison had made with Messrs. Raff & Gammon; after that I was quite undecided what to do. I did not enter into any agreement with the Lathams." When questioned as to why he decided against joining the Lathams Dickson responded: "... I soon became disgusted with their business methods... Had they behaved as gentlemen I most likely should have thrown myself heart and soul into the work ...".[554] When asked what he meant by this, he confirmed that he objected to their personal morals as well as their business practices. "My idea that morals and business should go hand in hand decided me, and as these gentlemen were not leading the sort of life that I was brought up to believe in, it made me feel that the less I had to do with them, the better." This seems to refer to the Latham boys' reputation as Gay Nineties playboys. Believing all of the Lathams were dead, he did not want to be specific and he was not asked to be. He was less specific about their business methods but said that he felt their effort to give him stock was done "... with the distinct ... object of compromising me".[555]

The offer of one quarter share in the Lambda Company caused Dickson to think more seriously about his several-month-long flirtation with the Lathams. The offer was apparently made soon after the successful camera test and the timing fits the Lathams' understanding of their relationship with Dickson. As Woodville put it: "My sons and I were under promise to him that if the machinery which he claimed to be able to have constructed at once without experimentation should prove to be efficient we would give to him ... one fourth of the stock of the company which we expected to form ...".[556] It is not clear exactly how the Lathams made this offer, but Dickson was cautious about responding and asked his friend and attorney Edmund Congar Brown to advise him. A meeting was set up in Brown's office with Mr. & Mrs. Dickson: Otway Latham and John Murray Mitchell attended. Mitchell was apparently a legal adviser to the Lathams. At Brown's recommendation the $125,000 worth of shares were to be held by Brown while Dickson decided what he wanted to do. The stock was not transferred to Dickson, but put in Brown's name and Dickson had the option of accepting it.

Dickson said that he understood that if he accepted the stock he would sever his relations with Edison and at this point, c. March 1895, he was giving this serious consideration. It was a big decision because he had built his career on his association with Edison. When he examined the situation a year later, he realized that the Lathams were using this as a final lever. In 1911 he spoke of it as an effort to force him to leave Edison. "... The Lathams' object, however, was to try and force the stock on me, for me to accept same during my sojourn with Edison, presumably to compromise me and force me to join them as quickly as possible ... before knowing if the business were good or bad."[557]

As it turned out, the Lathams' tactic was successful. A few weeks after this Dickson was no long an employee of Thomas Edison.

554 Equity 5/167, 11 April 1911.

555 Ibid. Otway Latham died in August 1906 in Manhattan from complications following an operation for a duodenal ulcer. Gray Latham died in March 1907 from injuries received in a fall from a trolley car in Manhattan. Woodville Latham was not dead. Shortly after Dickson's testimony he was found selling books in Harlem and testified in Equity 5/167.

556 Patent Interference 18,461.

557 Ibid.

Matters came to a head on Tuesday, 2 April 1895. William Gilmore accused Dickson of disloyalty and of having a dishonorable relationship with the Lathams. Dickson and Gilmore met with Edison and Dickson demanded that Edison make a choice between Gilmore and himself. Edison refused to discharge Gilmore and Dickson lost his temper and resigned. As Dickson described the confrontation in 1911:

"... That person [Gilmore] had the pleasure of being confronted with Mr. Edison by me and asked to repeat the remarks he made to me. Mr. Edison's remark was, 'I don't believe a d___ word of it.' I then insisted on Mr. Edison making his choice between the aforementioned person and myself, but either owing to Mr. Edison having contracted with this person, allotting to him full power or whatever it was, and the decision not being sufficiently whole-hearted, I lost my temper and resigned on the spot. ..."[558]

and putting a slightly more positive spin on it to Will Day in 1933?

"How can I put it – Why did I leave Edison?

"Difficult to word in your book [on cinema history] & have the facts credited 'where there is smoke there is fire' will be said.

"Having a large interest in movie work as a compensation for my labours – I was making money & was anxious to avoid competition – so my investigations were *interpreted* as *Disloyalty* & *Edison who knew what I was doing believed* & gave me *no support* which caused me to see Red -& so resigned on the spot – it seemed too cruelly unjust after what I had done & sticking to him since 1881.

"The next day at his home 'Glenmont' I called to have it out – & was ordered back to my duties – which I refused – ...:[559]

This brief confrontation not only ended Dickson's twelve year association with Edison, it was a watershed that divided his career – and life. Bitterness and regret stayed with Dickson for the rest of his life and he could hardly mention Gilmore's name. He demonized him forever after as his "rival" and "arch-enemy". A proud man whose pride was severely injured, in later life Dickson wrote letter after letter trying to get Edison to recognize him as a friend again. Edison stubbornly refused. While it was not so traumatic for Edison, the confrontation apparently left him with an some scars. Even though he eventually softened and payed Dickson a monthly pension, he continued to call him a double crosser. The pension was a reward for his testimony on Edison's behalf and for continually taking Edison's side in the debates about the invention of cinema which engaged film historians during the 1920s and 1930s. But Edison refused to answer Dickson's letters forcing Dickson to communicate through associates on Edison's staff like William Meadowcroft. The depth of Edison's feelings are reflected in comments he wrote in 1921 when he reviewed passages in Terry Ramsaye's text describing the Lathams' experiments. Edison annotated the passage describing Dickson's filming of the swinging lamp: "You see the Double X with Dickson here". Later he annotated a passage about growing discord between Dickson and Latham with: "Dickson

558 Ibid.

559 BiFi, Fonds Will Day. Dickson to Day, undated document, "Extra notes for Mr. W.E.L. Days Consideration in *conjunction with* his book " probably written in 1933.

quit me D X", a phrase that could be interpreted as indicating that he regarded Dickson's resignation as a double cross. Interestingly, Edison's resentment is much stronger against Dickson than against the Lathams.

Edison's animosity towards Dickson was honored by Edison's associates. Despite his obvious qualifications, Dickson was never enrolled as a member of the Edison Pioneers.

Dickson said that after the confrontation he cleared his things out immediately, implying that 2 April was his last day with Edison. In reality, he seems to have stayed on until Saturday, 20 April. Raff & Gammon mentioned this date as his final day in a letter they wrote to Dickson on 29 April 1895 and articles reporting his resignation did not appear in the local papers until the end of the month. It was mentioned in the *Orange Chronicle* on 27 April and in the *East Orange Gazette* on 2 May 1895.

This momentous change in Dickson's career calls for a final look at what he called his "Edisonian work" but before reviewing the Edison-Dickson years, we should wrap-up his involvement with the Latham family.

Dickson and the Lathams

After resigning from Edison's employ, Dickson had to give serious thought to his relations with the Lathams. The $125,000 worth of stock in the Lambda Company was still in the hands of his lawyer pending his decision. Though he did not sever relations immediately, sometime during April or early May he made up his mind and decided against joining them. Although he seems to have continued to visit the workshop, the comments he made in 1911 show that he was increasingly uncomfortable with the Lathams. Their attempts to manipulate him put him in the untenable position that he feared and tried to avoid. But he decided to take a little more time before instructing Mr. Brown to return the stock. He ended his association with them in May or June, about the time that the projector was finished and after Gray, Otway and Lauste had learned to operate the camera.

Dickson's involvement with the Lathams lasted through the planing and building of their camera and projector. It ended when they were ready to launch public exhibitions. This might lend credence to the assumption that both devices were invented by Dickson. But if he was the inventor, after 2 April he was free to claim them as his own. He didn't and even though he could have claimed them in his court testimony or his correspondence with film historians, he never did. Instead, he stuck to his story that he did not involve himself and never examined their machines before the swinging lamp projection. His variation on this story was the claim that he was conducting unappreciated industrial espionage. Dickson preferred to tie his reputation to Edison and he did not want to also attach himself to the Lathams.

If he was not *the* inventor, it is hard to accept his explanation that he was an innocent bystander. He spent too much time with them even though he was well aware that it jeopardized his relatively secure position with Edison. Since none of the others who were directly involved in the Lathams' project said Dickson worked on it, we are left with the slimmest of evidence and no proof of what he did. By mutual agreement he contributed one thing that did not work – the clock intermittent movement – and one that did – an additional roller to prevent tearing the film. He also operated the camera and developed the film for one test and helped shoot their first film.

There are particulars of the Lathams' project which might well have been the result of Dickson's advice or example. Film and optics were Dickson specialties and while he understood mechanics, he was accustomed to working with skilled machinists who knew how to solve problems. Lauste was the mechanic on the Latham project and Dickson had confidence in him so Dickson's contribution to the Lathams was on the photographic side: lenses, film and intermittence. There is little information about the lenses used in the Lathams' camera and projector so we can only assume that Dickson gave them some advice about them.

The Lathams were not well schooled in photography and Dickson had first hand experience with film and the companies manufacturing it. It would have been natural for the Lathams to turn to Dickson for advice about film and if he would not give them direct advice, they were capable of worming it out of him. Deciding which film to use was crucial to the design of the camera because the width, strength and sensitivity of the film determined the design of the transport mechanism. After his frustrating experience with miniature images, Dickson was convinced that larger film produced sharper images and reduced the impact of flaws. Dickson's opinion may have influenced the Lathams' decision to use film that was wider than Edison's. Theirs would be about the same height as Edison's and like Edison's, it would be advanced by sprockets and the film would have four perforations on each side of the frame to engage with the sprockets. As a bonus, changes in the format of the film and the design of the camera might avoid conflict with Edison's pending camera patent. Some of these decisions could have been made by observing the workings of the Kinetoscope and the Lathams had ready access to the machines exhibiting their boxing matches, but Dickson knew the "why" of the design.

It seems quite possible that it was Dickson who advised the Lathams to use off-the-shelf Eastman film in contrast to the custom-made product he had gotten from Eastman prior to 1893 and the special order film Edison was buying from Blair Camera Co. in 1894. If this is the case, his modified attitude reflected an important change in the photographic materials that were available at the end of 1894. Eastman had made progress in solving the problems that plagued them in the early 1890s and Blair was making a consistently acceptable product as well. The availability of film that was strong, relatively free of defects and sensitive enough to take instantaneous images made it much, much easier for a new group of speculators to build and market motion picture devices. The improvements that had been made in film for moving image work had apparently filtered over to the still photographic field and Dickson seems to have found regular Eastman film quite acceptable as 1894 came to an end.

The Lathams' scheme for production was a "system" for taking and projecting movies and their camera and projector were separate devices. While it is normal today to separate the camera from projection, the most widely admired pioneer film system, the Lumières' Cinématographe combined taking and projecting in one machine. Although the early versions of the Kinetograph were planned as combination cameras and projectors, Dickson – and Edison – had decided that there had to be two machines. In his experience, the different rate of shrinking between negative (camera film) and positive (projection film) increased the chance of tearing or otherwise damaging the film as it passed over the sprockets. The Lathams were following Dickson's lead and even though the Lumières' light-weight and flexible Cinématographe was more sensational than the Lathams' Pantoptikon, in the long run, the two machine system would dominate the commercial film industry.

In addition to the camera and projector the Lathams needed a perforating device, a printing machine to make positives from the camera negatives as well as a darkroom for developing the film. While the need for these additional elements might seem self-evident, their plan echoed the system that Dickson designed for Edison. The Lathams probably saw the darkrooms and printing machines in West Orange, but Dickson's experience in designing and operating these essential support devices would have been very helpful and Dickson may have felt he could help since Edison had not applied for a patent on them.

It is very hard to judge Dickson's influence on the mechanical work that Lauste and Kleinert were doing. During his visits to the workshop he discussed things with Lauste. Since Lauste was more comfortable in his native language, their discussions were often in French. This annoyed Otway Latham who could not understand what they were saying and he suspected that they were keeping things from him. They were asked to speak English so Otway could be sure that he was in on what was being talked about. Dickson may have been passing on confidential information to Lauste, but Lauste had his own skills to contribute. As we have seen, skilled machinists such as the Ott brothers were key aids in completing the Kinetoscope and Kinetograph. Their knowledge and ability were essential to solving specific problems of design. Lauste's (and, perhaps Kleinert's) contributions are not obvious, but they were important, nonetheless. The one mechanical recommendation that Dickson made, using a clock movement to provide intermittence was a failure. But Lauste and Kleinert were able to solve the problem. Ultimately they chose the Geneva movement – which is a clock movement. The Geneva movement was also used in Edison's camera.

Dickson's contribution to the Lathams camera and projector will remain an unresolved question, but it is well to remember that by late 1894 it was possible to produce moving image cameras and projectors without having Dickson at hand. What was needed was somebody with imagination who understood the basic principles and a well equipped machine shop staffed with experienced machinists. After the introduction of the Kinetoscope interested innovators in North America and Europe went to work almost immediately and several of them were successful – and in a surprisingly short time. Several of them were working in parallel with the Lathams and a brief summary of some of the more successful efforts is useful to put the work of the Lathams in perspective.

Other moving image experimenters

Charles Chinnock was no fly-by-night experimenter. He was well known to Edison who had hired him in the 1880s as superintendent of the Pearl Street electrical station and as manager of the Edison United Manufacturing Co. For several years he was a trustee of the Edison Electric Illuminating Co. of New York City. In 1892 Dickson's testimony was influential in a favorable decision for Edison in a patent interference case in which Chinnock's patent was one of those involved.

The Holland Brothers' Kinetoscope parlor opened in mid-April 1894, and by mid-summer two people were working on competing peep show devices: Herman Casler and Charles Chinnock. Casler's inspiration came from Dickson and Harry Marvin who discussed the possibilities of a thumb book in the late spring or early summer. Charles Chinnock, who visited the Hollands' parlor, said he wanted to make a similar device. He started with a camera and made sketches for it during June or July, about the same time as the Dickson-Marvin discussion. By early October he had arranged with Frank D. Maltby to have the camera built in Maltby's machine shop in Columbia Heights, New York. They also built a prototype Kinetoscope and they claimed that to test the camera a boxing match was filmed on a rooftop in late November or early December 1894. They claimed that they began making films in January 1895 and had taken a number of them before a Kinetoscope parlor was opened in late spring or early summer. One of the dancers who was filmed for Chinnock's Kinetoscope was a very young Ruth Dennis (later St. Dennis).[560]

Chinnock was not the only American inspired by the Kinetoscope. When the Kinetoscope opened in Washington DC in early October a young stenographer for the U.S. Life Saving Service, C. Francis Jenkins, was one of the early customers. Jenkins was an ambitious young inventor who toyed with a variety of things in his spare time, among them the phonograph and motion photography. Through his interest in the phonograph he had made a connection with the Columbia Phonograph Co. which was based in Washington. Columbia Phonograph had the concession for the Kinetoscope in Washington and Atlantic City, New Jersey and they were unhappy because they could not get enough Kinetoscopes to satisfy their patrons. E.F. Murphy, who was in charge of their Kinetoscope concession knew that Jenkins had experimented with motion photography and asked him if he could

560 NMAH Hendricks. Testimony by Charles Chinnock, 9 May 1911 and Frank D. Maltby, 23 May 1911 in Equity 5/167, Patents Co. v. Imp. For a more complete description of Charles Chinnock's camera and Kinetoscope see: Gordon Hendricks, *The Kinetoscope*, Appendix D, pp. 161–169. Ruth St. Dennis described being filmed on a roof in Brooklyn in a letter to George Pratt of George Eastman House, 18 February 1959.

make a version of Edison's machine. With backing from Columbia Phonograph, it took Jenkins a little over a month to build it and it was ready for exhibit in time for the opening of the third annual Pure Food Exposition at Convention Hall, Washington, DC on 14 November 1894. Although it was based on Edison's Kinetoscope and used Edison films, it was not an exact copy. Jenkins tried, unsuccessfully to produce intermittence with a pulsating light and had better success with an arrangement of revolving light bulbs. Jenkins was enrolled in the Bliss School of Electricity and it was Prof. Louis D. Bliss who suggested the light bulb arrangement.[561]

Jenkins applied for a patent for his Kinetoscope on 24 November 1894 and in December he applied for a patent for a "Kinetographic Camera" which had four lenses and which could also project films. As the winter progressed he was working on a projector but was having problems with it. By this time, Bliss had introduced Jenkins to Thomas Armat, a fellow student who was also interested in reproducing movement. Armat was the son of a prosperous Virginia farmer who came to Washington to join his cousin's real estate firm. Like Jenkins he had seen the Kinetoscope at Columbia Phonograph's parlor on Pennsylvania Avenue. The two young inventors decided to join forces and by April their revised version of the Phantoscope projector was taking shape. Like the Lathams, they had problems with intermittence but by August these were being resolved and they scheduled a debut for their projector at the Cotton States Exposition which opened in Atlanta at the end of September.[562]

Things did not go well in Atlanta. They had competition. Raff & Gammon's agent, Henry A. Tabb had a large concession of Kinetoscopes at the fair and Gray Latham was exhibiting the Eidoloscope in downtown Atlanta. The public was reluctant to go into the darkened area where the Phantoscope was showing Edison films. To lure them in they finally resorted to admitting the public without charge, asking them to pay if they felt the show was worth it. They had problems with the film catching and tearing and worked late into the night repairing damaged sprocket holes and torn films. The final blow came when a fire which destroyed an adjoining exhibit severely damaged the Phantoscope exhibit area, including at least one of their projectors. Jenkins had left the day before the fire to attend his brother's wedding in Richmond, Indiana. Armat was suspicious that Jenkins, who continued his relations with Murphy and Columbia Phonograph, was planning an independent business deal. The partners had a bitter argument, dissolved their agreement and never said a civil word to each other again. Armat made some modifications in the projector and in December he persuaded Frank Gammon to come to Washington for a demonstration. Raff & Gammon, in turn, got Gilmore to agree to a trial and Edison, reluctantly, agreed to manufacture Armat's version of the Phantoscope as the Edison Vitascope and it had it's premiere at Koster & Bial's Music Hall, 23 April 1896. Jenkins sold rights to his version of the Phantoscope to Columbian Phonograph Co. and American

561 Franklin Institute, C. Francis Jenkins Collection; NMAH Hendricks; Academy of Motion Picture Arts & Sciences Library, Earl Theisen Collection. Jenkins Kinetoscope was reported in the *Washington Star*, 15 November 1894.

562 Franklin Inst.; NARA, Patent Interference 18,461 & Equity 5/167.

Graphophone Co. who manufactured and sold the projector to independent exhibitors, often in small towns and rural areas.

The enmity between Jenkins and Armat makes it difficult to determine which was the creative mind and contributed most to the Phantoscope. Armat accused Jenkins of carelessness, inaccuracy and bluff. Jenkins said that Armat had little understanding of machines and that he contributed only the money necessary to pay for the development of the Phantoscope. Like Edison, Jenkins was skilled at self-promotion and although he was something of a gadfly inventor, he was very prolific and registered hundreds of patents during his lifetime for devices ranging from automobiles to airplanes to photography and television. Armat was more conservative and business-like and despite coming from a prosperous family he was not idle. He had studied mechanics and worked in a machine shop and held a number of patents. Emil Wellauer, the machinist who worked on their devices at John Schultzbach's machine shop characterized the difference between the two men, saying that Jenkins worked hastily because he was impatient and in a hurry while Armat insisted on neat, careful work. While they each denied that the other had creative skills, in fact, after they separated they continued to make important contributions to the development of cinema.[563]

The experience of Jenkins and Armat parallels that of the Lathams. They shared certain assets: curiosity, ability to draw on their own experience and synthesize it with information available to them, and enough financial resources to take their experiments through to a conclusion. Like the Lathams and Charles Chinnock they relied on the mechanical experience of professional machinists. Jenkins and Armat used the machine shop owned by John Schultzbach and most of their work was done by Emil Wellauer, one of Schultzbach's machinists.

The Kinetoscope was not exhibited in Europe until the fall of 1894 but once it arrived it stimulated a flurry of activity. Maguire & Baucus' London parlor opened at 70 Oxford St. on 17 October 1894 and their parlor in Paris opened a few weeks later. Within weeks a number of skilled innovators were at work on similar devices, some newly inspired by Edison's device, others perfecting machines they had worked on before.

In the fall of 1894 two businessmen approached a London instrument maker, Robert Paul and asked him to make copies of Edison's Kinetoscope for them. George Georgiades and George Tragides (sometimes spelled Tragidis, Tragedis or Trajedis) traveled to the United States during the summer of 1894, saw the Kinetoscope and purchased one or more of the machines from Norman Raff.[564] They shipped them to London and opened a Kinetoscope parlor on Old Broad Street in London. Business was good, but Kinetoscopes were hard to come by and the two Greek businessmen wanted to expand their operation. At first Paul was reluctant, but on learning that Edison had not patented the Kinetoscope in England he felt that he could proceed. By the end of the year he had succeeded in making several copies and he was so

563 Ibid.

564 Baker Library, Raff & Gammon. The Kinetoscope Company account with Holland Brothers, New York shows a payment of $497.50 from George Tragides on 14 September 1894, "paid to N.C. Raff.

impressed with their commercial potential that he decided to exhibit Kinetoscopes himself. Since the only source of films was Edison and he was mounting competition to Edison's business, he needed to make his own so he needed a camera. Having little experience with photography, Paul joined with Birt Acres, an experienced photographer who he met through a friend, Henry Short (who also introduced Paul to Georgiades and Tragides). It did not take them long to produce a camera. They began work on it in February, 1895 and Acres took their first picture a few weeks later in late March.[565]

Paul and Acres soon parted company and the question of who was responsible for Paul's camera remains in dispute. In July the two parted company in an acrimonious disagreement reminiscent of Armat and Jenkins and the conflict over their contributions is unresolved. Birt Acres claimed that he had already made the camera before he worked with Paul and Paul said that Acres contributed little to the camera. As is the case with the other squabbling pioneers of cinema, both Paul and Acres went on to make important contributions to the development of cinema. At the end of May, Paul opened an exhibit of his Kinetoscopes at Earl's Court with the first English produced films and in 1896 he introduced his own projector, the Theatrograph. He continued to produce films and is widely credited with being the father of British film production. Acres continued to make films, introduced his own version of a projector, the Kineopticon, and even went into the manufacture of film stock.[566]

Tradition has it that after seeing the Kinetoscope in Paris, Antoine Lumière, the scion of the photographic firm of Antoine Lumière & ses Fils, returned to Lyon where he showed a strip of Edison's film to his sons Louis and Auguste. He urged them to design a machine that could project moving images on a screen. They set to work on it and produced the Cinematograph, the light-weight, flexible combination camera and projector which quickly outstripped Edison's peep show Kinetoscope and introduced moving pictures to thousands around the globe. Recent scholarship has revised this simple version of the story. Early cinema scholars Marta Braun and Laurent Mannoni have pointed out that about the time that the Kinetoscope was first shown in Paris, the Lumières were contacted by George Demenÿ who offered the Lumières his Phonoscope. Demenÿ had been Marey's assistant and the Chef du laboratoire for his Physiological Station, but had recently left Marey to set up his own studio. In the early 1890s, working independently under Marey, he introduced his Phonoscope, a system for recording human speech in order to analyze it and he then experimented with his system as a means of teaching speech to deaf people. In 1893 Demenÿ made modifications to his camera, among them an eccentric intermittent movement that was used later by a number designers of motion picture devices. After receiving Demenÿ's invitation, Louis Lumère visited Demenÿ and though he did not take on the Phonoscope, his examination of the machine may have influenced the design of the Cinematograph.[567]

565 NMAH Hendricks; BiFi, Fonds Will Day; John Barnes, *The Beginnings of the Cinema in England*, [Vol. 1], pp. 12–19; Ramsaye, *Million*, p. 138; Herbert & McKernan, eds., *Who's Who of Victorian Cinema*, pp. 12–13, 56–57, 107–108; *Proceedings of the British Kinematograph Society, No. 38*, pp. 2–3. Paper delivered by Robert W. Paul, 3 February 1936; *Journal of the S.M.P.E.*, November 1936, Robert W. Paul, "Kinematic Experiences". It is quite possible that Georgiades and Tragides bought Kinetoscopes from the Holland Brothers. In 1893 the Hollands had found a profitable market for phonographs in England and were probably willing to sell if they could sell them for more than the $200 that Edison was charging for the standard machines. At the end of August 1894, when Col. Gouraud cancelled his order for 100 machines for the European market, William Gilmore reported stories of offers ranging from $240 to $500 being made by interested parties.

566 Ibid.

567 Marta Braun, Op. Cit., p. 183; Mannoni, Campagnoni, Robinson, Op. Cit., pp. 387–390; *Bulletin de Société Française de Photographie*, December 1891; October 1893; *Anthony's Photographic Bulletin*, 26

It is not clear whether the Lumières had a chance to examine a Kinetoscope to inspect its mechanism, but they would not have had to. Edison's quest for publicity had produced a number of articles about the Kinetoscope and some had technical descriptions and detailed illustrations (see illustration on page 227). Edison's patent, issued in 1893, was also available, though that was filed before the 35mm version of the Kinetoscope was made.[568] The point is that there was a great deal of information available to Lumières as well as to others trying to produce screen machines. August and Louis Lumière filed for a patent on 13 February 1895, the first of a number of patents they applied for in various countries to cover the original machine and modifications that they made. On 22 March 1895 they gave the first private demonstration for the Société pour l'Encourgement de l'Industrie Nationale and in June they filmed members of the Union Nationale des Sociétés Photographique departing from an excursion boat at Lyon. It was another six months before the first public exhibition, but the delay seems to have been caused by commercial rather than technical considerations. The famous debut of the Cinématographe took place in the Salon Indien of the Grand Café in Paris, 28 December 1895, a date frequently cited as the beginning of modern motion pictures.

There were, of course, many others working on cameras and projectors. George Demenÿ began working on a large format camera which was marketed through photo and optical instrument merchant Léon Gaumont. Parisian Henri Joly patented a camera in August which he sold to Charles Pathé, who had discovered a growing market for Edison's phonographs and Kinetoscopes. In Germany, Max Skladanowsky was working on his Bioskop projector and exhibited films in Pankow, a suburb of Berlin in July 1895 and at Berlin's prestigious Wintergarten in November 1895. During 1894 and 1895 a number of patents for moving image devices were registered by individuals who never made it to the list of contenders for primacy in the invention of cinema.[569]

This very brief summary of the transformation of cinema during 1894 and 1895 is intended to illustrate the simultaneous nature of the efforts of the major figures and to show that by championing individual contributions historians of past generations greatly distorted reality. By 1894 all of the elements needed to create modern motion pictures were in place and with the right combination of imagination, mechanical skill and resources, numbers of people were able to create cameras and/or projectors.

To emphasize and further illustrate this point, let's look at what was happening during the months after September, 1894 when Raff & Gammon and Maguire & Baucus began introducing a large (but not large enough) number of Kinetoscopes in more locations in Europe and North America. [Some of the dates shown are not fully documented claims, but the dates are close enough to gauge what was going on.]

•**October 1894.** In New York City, the Lathams discussed a proposal to make a projector with W.K.L. Dickson and Charles Chin-

---

November 1892. Demenÿ's camera took up to twenty-four images, two by three inches in size. For viewing they were arranged around disk and viewed by illumination.

568 In particular, the article in *Scientific American*, 20 May 1893, after the demonstration at the Brooklyn Institute of Arts and Sciences and one in *La Nature* in the fall of 1894 which had detailed illustrations.

569 Among those that I know of are: British Patent 25,100, Anderton, 7 December 1894; British no. 182, Wray, 3 January 1895; U.S. no. 540,545, Robert D. Gray, New York City, Camera, 9 March 1895; U.S. no. 546,093, Owen E. Eames, Boson, Mas., Camera-Lantern, 25 March 1895; British no. 9881, Justice, May 5, 1895; U.S. no. 560,367, A.N. Petit, 19 May 1895; U.S. No. 560,424, A. N. Petit, Camera, 16 July 1895; British, no. 12,486, European Blair Co. & Thomas Blair, Camera, 27 June 1895 U.S. no. 546,439, O.A. Eames, chrono-photographic apparatus, 10 September 1895; U.S. no. 547,066, William C. Farnum, motion viewing device, 1 October 1895. Most of these were cases cited by patent examiners or lawyers in the various lawsuits and patent interferences.

nock worked on a version of the Kinetoscope. After seeing the Kinetoscope at a parlor in Washington, DC, C. Francis Jenkins began
working on his own version. In Syracuse, NY Herman Casler was
completing the design of the Mutoscope. Maguire & Baucus opened
the first Kinetoscope parlor in London. An article describing and
illustrating the mechanism of Edison's Kinetoscope appeared in *La
Nature*.

•**November 1894.** The Lathams hired Eugene Lauste and found
a location for a workshop; Chinnock was working on his camera;
Herman Casler applied for a patent for the Mutoscope and Jenkins'
Phantoscope, his version of the Kinetoscope, was exhibited at the Pure
Food Exposition in Washington, DC. In London, Robert Paul was
asked to produce copies of the Kinetoscope for a London exhibitor. A
Kinetoscope parlor opened in Paris and in Lyon, France, Antoine
Lumière suggested that his sons make a machine to project Edison-type
films. The article from *La Nature* which described and illustrated
Edison's Kinetoscope was published in English in *The Literary Digest*
(see page 227).

•**December 1894.** The Lathams built a prototype projector designed to use Edison films; Charles Chinnock completed a camera and
made test films; Herman Casler began work on a camera; Robert Paul
constructed about six clones of Edison's Kinetoscope and the Lumières
began work on a combination camera and projector. In Germany, Max
Skladanowsky worked on a projector and a film copying machine.

•**January 1895.** The Lathams were working on their camera;
Chinnock began shooting films; Herman Casler was working on the
Mutograph camera; Robert Paul asked Birt Acres to help him construct
a camera and the Lumières were working on their camera-projector.
An article describing Georges Demeny's camera appeared in *Photographic
Times*, it was a translation of an article that appeared in *La Nature* in
September 1894.

•**February 1895.** Cameras were completed by the Lathams,
Casler, Lumières, and Robert Paul & Birt Acres. Most were tested and
the Lumières applied for a patent in France.

•**March 1895.** Casler made the first tests with the Mutograph
camera. The Lumières gave the first private demonstration of the
Cinematograph presenting a film of workers leaving their factory in
Lyon. Paul and Acres made a printing machine, perforator and a
processing plant and Birt Acres shot their first films. In Washington,
DC, C. Francis Jenkins and Thomas Armat signed an agreement to
work on a projector to show Edison films. An entry in John Ott's work
book indicates that he worked on a projector for Edison between March
and June, 1895.

•**April 1895.** Thomas Edison turned down Robert Paul's offer to
sell him films; the Lathams began work on their projector for wider
film and Jenkins and Armat made their first unsuccessful test of the
Phantoscope projector.

•**May 1895.** The Lathams filmed a boxing match between Young

Griffo and Charles Barnet and began public exhibition of the film in New York City at 156 Broadway. Charles Chinnock formed the North American Kinetoscope Company and began exhibiting films in Brooklyn. Chinnock claimed that in May 1895 he sold two cameras to J.E. Hough for use in England and France. Birt Acres applied for a patent for a Kinetic Camera and filmed the running of the Derby.

•June 1895. The Lathams' Eidoloscope opened in Coney Island, New York; the first test was made with Casler's Mutograph camera, a sparring match between Casler and Harry Marvin (probably filmed by W.K.L. Dickson). The Lumières filmed delegates from the Union Nationale des Sociétés Photographique leaving an excursion boat in Lyon, France and projected it for them the next day. Birt Acres filmed ceremonies at the opening of the Kiel Canal in Germany. Armat and Jenkins eliminated the shutter and experimented with an intermittent movement for their projector.

•July 1895. The Lumières demonstrated the Cinématographe in the reception rooms of *Revue Générale des Sciences* and placed an order for construction of twenty-five Cinématographes with Jules Carpentier of the Ruhmkorff works in Paris. Edison was working on a "universal machine", a combination camera and projector.

•August 1895. Armat and Jenkins solved problems with the intermittent movement for their Phantoscope projector, applied for a patent and arranged to project Edison films at the Cotton States Exposition in Atlanta, Georgia. In Canastota, New York, the first film was shot with Casler's Mutograph camera, *Sparring Contest at Canastota* between Professor Al Leonard and Bert Hosley. In France, Georges Demenÿ and Henry Joly patented cameras.

•September 1895. At the Cotton States Exhibition in Atlanta, Georgia, Armat and Jenkins projected Edison films with their Phantoscope projector and there was a large exhibit of Edison's Kinetoscope. In downtown Atlanta, Gray Latham projected films with the Eidoloscope. In Canastota, New York, Elias B. Koopman, Harry Marvin, Herman Casler and W.K.L. Dickson established an informal partnership to pool their patents and business interests which they called K.M.C.D.

•October 1895. The Lumières discussed proposals to market the Cinématographe. A disagreement between C. Francis Jenkins and Thomas Armat ended their partnership. Jenkins projected movies with the Phantoscope projector at his cousin's jewelry store in Richmond, Indiana. The Lumières' Cinématographe was discribed in an article in *La Nature*. Raff & Gammon urged Edison to hasten the completion of a screen machine and thanked Edison for improving the magnification of the Kinetograph.

•November 1895. Herman Casler experimented projecting with the Mutograph camera. Max Skladanowsky's Bioskop opened at the Wintergarten in Berlin. Jules Carpentier delivered the first of his Cinématographes to the Lumières. The Lumières had problems with the film bought from European Blair and began negotiations with

Victor Planchon, Boulogne-sur-Mer to develop a method of making film. They might set up a manufacturing company for Planchon if he was successful. The Lumières reported that De Bedts, who represented European Blair was attracting attention with his chronos camera-projector. C. Francis Jenkins patented his own version of the Phantoscope.

•**December 1895.** C. Francis Jenkins gave a talk and projected moving pictures at the Franklin Institute in Philadelphia, Pennsylvania. Thomas Armat demonstrated his version of the Phantoscope to Frank Gammon and opened negotiations that led to an agreement with Edison to market it as the Vitascope. The American Mutoscope Company was organized to market Casler's Mutoscope and other devices patented by the K.M.C.D. group. Jules Carpentier completed a number of Cinématographes and the first public exhibit of the Lumières' machine took place in the Salon Indien of the Café de la Pais in Paris. Among the early spectators were Léon Gaumont and Georges Méliès.

This sketch of the status of moving images in 1894–1895 is intended to illustrate that even though W.K.L. Dickson's advice and counsel might have helped the Lathams, it was not absolutely essential to the success of their efforts. There was enough information available and skilled mechanics at hand to assist clever inventive minds so that projectors and cameras could be assembled and put to work. If devices appeared more rapidly after the fall of 1894, it was not just because information and models were available. By this time, the manufacture of celluloid film had advanced to the point where a quality product was available for use in motion picture work. Blair Camera Company had been selling to Edison for more than a year and their increasingly independent European affiliate, European Blair made the film available in Europe. By the end of 1894 Blair was pre-cutting the film to the Edison-Dickson specification of 1 9/16th inches wide (though they did not perforate the film). By this time Eastman had solved most of its problems with celluloid and emulsion. The Lathams, Chinnock and Casler bought Eastman roll film; Robert Paul and the Lumières bought pre-cut film from European Blair. Edison had no patent restricting the use of film 1 916th inches wide, nor having four perforations per frame, so Paul and a number of others adopted the format that Dickson had devised for Edison.

During 1896, Edison found that his film and rival films that fit his camera, were in use around the globe. A global industry was being launched, based on the format that Dickson devised at the end of 1891.

Edison and Dickson

"'Edison a genius'? You ask – His genius *principally* could be found by his uncanny discoveries of what was wanted to commercialize same for the benefit of the world's industries ...".[570] (W.K.L. Dickson to Earl Theisen, 7 January 1933)

"... I don't even go to cinemas, it's too depressing heartbreaking to go unrecognized in the art, yet it was my work which was as commercialized

[570] Academy Library, Theisen Collection.

by me, adopted in every detail by the whole million making world – ah me –".[571] (W.K.L. Dickson to Merritt Crawford, 16 November 1932)

So what was Dickson's role in Edison's inventions and how did he feel about his achievements? Where do the Kinetograph and Kinetoscope fit in the beginning of cinema?

Dickson's abrupt departure from Edison's Laboratory in April, 1895 ended an eventful twelve year association. Although bitterness, remorse and resentment followed Dickson's heated departure, the previous years had been cordial and productive. Their partnership produced the Kinetograph and Kinetoscope and even though these were only two of many patents that Edison claimed, it was the motion picture and phonograph business that sustained Edison from the 1890s into the twentieth century and, as Al Tate noted, they were the basis of the fortune that Edison left to his heirs.

The Kinetoscope was the first successful commercial moving image machine, but its importance has been debated and it has been regarded by some as a transitional step or as a forerunner of the real thing – the argument being that movies were created when pictures were projected onto screens. This view dominated the recent celebration of the Centennial of the motion pictures. Europeans almost unanimously accepted 1896 as the anniversary year and very few Americans championed Edison's work. 14 April 1994 passed with very little recognition that it marked a century of public viewing of movies in the United States.

Dickson's reputation suffered a similar fate. As the complaint he made to Merritt Crawford (quoted above) indicates, Dickson found obscurity painful and frustrating. His anguish was eased when he received belated recognition from the Society of Motion Picture Engineers who made him an honorary member, but this came only after he complained because the Society had recognized others including his friend Eugene Lauste and had not approached him.[572] Film historians have recognized Dickson as an important pioneer but not many of them are clear about what his contribution was and very few lay persons would recognize his name.

A number of historians have downplayed Edison's role in the invention of the Kinetoscope and Kinetograph. Foremost among them was Gordon Hendricks who argued that Edison exaggerated his own role and failed to credit Dickson with the major role in the invention. Hendricks' book, *The Edison Motion Picture Myth*, published in the late 1950s, had a powerful influence on two generations of historians. But Hendricks was not the first to belittle Edison's role. Earlier historians, many of them championing one or more of the pioneer inventors of cameras and projection systems, discounted Edison's contribution because projection was such a significant improvement over the brief, small image presented in the Kinetoscope. Some champions of the Lumières' Cinématographe put forth this argument, but they were by no means the only ones. The ruthless way in which Edison pursued competitors during the years when his company dominated the Ameri-

571 MoMA Crawford.

572 Dickson was notified by the Society of Motion Picture Engineers that the had been made an honorary member on 17 October 1933, two years before his death on 28 September 1935.

can motion picture industry gave Edison a negative reputation and made it easy to assume that he was the bad boy – the dark figure – of the American motion picture industry.

Truth is, of course, never as simple as this and the dark figures are never as black as some might view them. Hence this detailed examination of the Dickson-Edison years. But so much detail requires a summary in order to clarify matters.

Dickson was reluctant to claim publicly that he was the inventor of either the Kinetoscope or the Kinetograph. He frequently expressed his loyalty to Edison and consistently said Edison deserved recognition as the inventor of motion pictures. Though he never presented himself to the general public as the primary inventor, privately he occasionally made the claim to trusted friends. In his correspondence with Will Day he made the following interesting claim. "Had friend Day met me even as late as the Old Biograph days he would have, I feel sure diagnosed the case of who actually produced The First & Only Standardized and Commercialized the Complete Moving picture machine as adopted by Edison and the world – which was created as you now know irrefutably by me for all to enjoy."[573] In his testimony in December 1897, Woodville Latham said that during their early discussions Dickson said that he had invented the Kinetograph and Edison had not given him credit for his work. When asked about this in 1911, Dickson denied making any such statement, calling it "... a spiteful dab ... I hardly think even if I had been the inventor, so-called, would it have been politic to have made such a statement to utter strangers."[574]

Dickson seems to have been of two minds in considering his role vis-à-vis Edison. He knew that if he promoted Edison's role, he was also promoting himself and he was aware that Edison's reputation enhanced his own reputation. He also understood that he had been Edison's employee and as such, Edison had the right to claim his work as his own. This was a situation that Dickson was familiar with because he operated his own laboratory with a staff of specialists working under him. But he was a proud person and he was probably genuinely unhappy that during his lifetime he was left off the roster of claimants to the title of "Father of Film".

For his part, Edison was perfectly happy to have others make the claim that he invented movies and he stayed out of the arguments that historians seemed to enjoy. He preferred to press his case in courts of law where the stakes were for profit rather than glory. Glory was a common enough commodity in Edison's life, but throughout his career he was frustrated because as he churned out invention after invention he had to share the anticipated riches with investors and competing inventors as well as the lawyers who profited by the inevitable court cases that grew out of patent and commercial conflicts. His suits over the motion picture patents were not the first he engaged in, but because he was striving to keep economic control over his moving image patents, he pursued them more doggedly than earlier cases.

There is justification for Dickson's desire for recognition and a

573 BiFi Fonds Will Day. Dickson to Day, undated, probably 1933.

574 EHS & NMAH, Hendricks. Woodville Latham, Patent Interference 18,461, December 1897; W.K.L. Dickson, Equity 5/167, April 1911.

share of Edison's honors. He was the person directly responsible for developing the Kinetoscope and Kinetograph as well as the system for making the films that made Edison's invention work. He was given the project at its conception and he stayed with it until it was completed and continued with it as it became a commercial reality. But Dickson did not work alone. Edison's method of invention was a forerunner of the team systems popular today and the Kinetos, both scope and graph, were produced by teaming a variety of talents. From the beginning Dickson had a mechanic assigned to work with him and two of them spent enough time on the Kinetos to qualify as assistants. Charles Brown worked daily with Dickson from the fall of 1888 until January 1891 followed by William Heise, Dickson's right hand from the fall of 1891 through 1895 when Dickson resigned. Brown worked part-time on the Kineto, spending most of the rest of his time on ore milling, but Heise worked on the Kineto for almost 100 per cent of his time. Dickson also had the services of Edison's staff: mechanics, electricians, carpenters, pattern makers, blacksmiths and laborers who were assigned as required, sometimes working only an hour or two, but occasionally putting-in days and even weeks on the project. These part-time contributors brought invaluable skill and experience to the project and were particularly helpful in solving mechanical and electrical problems. The Ott brothers, John and Fred, made particular contributions and were called into service during critical stages of the project. Fred Ott worked on the final phase of the cylinder project and assisted in the transition to the strip design. John Ott supervised all of the precision mechanical work. He played a significant role in the early cylinder experiments and supervised construction of the final versions of the Kinetograph and Kinetoscope. Machinist Hugo Kayser helped solve problems with the intermittent movement on the strip Kinetograph. While most of this mechanical work was done at Dickson's request, he cannot be credited with exclusive responsibility for the mechanical design of either the camera or the peep show machine.

While Dickson had important support from mechanical specialists, there was no one to help him with the crucial photographic elements: film, optics, exposure and lighting. He was the only one on the staff capable of understanding and solving the stream of problems that were confronted on an almost daily basis and it is here that Dickson's contribution is clear. He was knowledgeable in electricity and mechanics, but there were others on the staff with equal or greater knowledge, so he can only be credited with contributing to the mechanical and electrical design, but the photographic elements are clearly his.

The elements that can be credited to Dickson

First of all, the selection and improvement of photographic materials. Even though Dickson would like to have some credit for helping George Eastman bring celluloid roll film to the market, there is no credible evidence that he visited Rochester in 1888 when Eastman and Henry Reichenbach were developing the chemistry and a method of producing Eastman's roll film. But he was one of the first customers to use Eastman's revolutionary product and his persistent efforts to improve the toughness of the base and the speed of the emulsions made an important contribution to improving the quality of Eastman's product and, apparently, Blair's as well. Although there is no evidence that he visited Rochester in 1888, he was there very soon after Eastman announced that celluloid rolls would be available and his detailed descriptions and drawings of Eastman's manufacturing process indicates that his visits involved more than just discussions in the front offices. While Dickson could be sharply caustic in his critical comments, Eastman apparently respected him because through the most crucial stages of the Kineto experiments Eastman supplied Dickson with the best photographic material available. Dickson and Eastman both benefitted by their exchanges. In 1896, when Eastman decided to enter the "Cine" film market, they produced a special film whose specifications were based on the specifications that Dickson had been insisting on four and five years earlier.

Even though Dickson's experiments with traditional photo materials for use with cylinders were unsuccessful, the tests helped him establish criteria that were not only useful in completing the design of the Kinetograph and Kinetoscope, but set standards adopted by the commercial industry. In his first Caveat, written in October 1888, Edison said that a minimum of eight frames per second was necessary to create the illusion of motion but that he expected that twenty-five would be enough to give acceptable results. Dickson's tests led them to increase the number to forty in order to avoid the flicker effect. Although the commercial industry chose to use sixteen frames per second as a standard during the silent era, this was a decision driven more by economics than by issues of quality. Film was priced by the foot and there was more running time at sixteen frames per second than at thirty or forty. Complaints about flicker plagued the commercial industry for years and though very few have advocated going as high as forty frames per second, it has been known that projection at faster speeds improves the picture image. When sound was introduced, the speed was increased to twenty-four frames per second, close to Edison's initial recommendation.

Dickson's most lasting contribution was the film format that came to be known as 35mm which he settled on in late 1891 while struggling to solve problems of film damage and poor registration. He increased the image to one inch, decided on a landscape format, moved it to run vertically in the camera. driven by two sprocket wheels that engaged four perforations on each side of the frame. The format dictated the final design of the Kinetograph and Kinetoscope and then, because it was not covered by Edison's patents, was quickly adopted by much of the rest of the film industry. It is still in regular use in film theaters throughout the world, more than one hundred years after it was introduced. The adaptation of the format to still photography came later, just before World War I, and though the orientation of the film and the number of sprocket holes per frame are different, the size and shape of the sprocket holes are similar to Dickson's original ones.[575]

When designing the format for the Kinetograph, Dickson chose the landscape rather than a portrait format, with the horizontal side slightly larger than the vertical: one inch wide by three-quarters of an inch high. While this format was probably based on his experience as a still photographer, it set the standard used for cameras and projectors, projection screens in theaters and, because of persistent use by the motion picture industry, the ratio was also chosen by television manufacturers and later by computer manufacturers. Although there have been numerous variations, the format has continued in use since the 1890s.

The camera required a special lens, one that could record objects at a specified distance with enough flexibility to keep the subject being filmed from going in and out of focus while moving about in the camera range. It took him several months of negotiations to get an acceptable one. He also selected the lens for the Kinetoscope, but this was of less critical design.

The Kinetograph and Kinetoscope were elements in a system and Dickson also pioneered the design of the parts of the system that supported them: a pedal operated device for preparing the rolls of film for photography by trimming and perforating them; developing and printing equipment; and a studio designed to photograph subjects with an optimum amount of light.

Dickson also pioneered film production and he is one of the few pioneers who used the equipment he designed. In establishing film production for Edison he anticipated production techniques that would be used by the commercial industry in future years. Filmmaking was done in a studio in a strictly controlled environment. Dickson played the role of the producer-director. He planned and rehearsed the shot, instructed the camera operator on what he wanted and supervised the take.

So what of Edison? With Dickson and the lab staff working day-by-day and Edison increasingly absorbed by the never successful ore milling project in Northern New Jersey, what does he deserve credit for?

It should be remembered that it was Edison who initiated the project and formulated the first phases of the work. There is evidence that during 1888 and the first half of 1889 Edison may have worked with John Ott on the mechanism of an early version of the cylinder machine. By the summer of 1889 his attention was increasingly absorbed by ore milling, but he continued to monitor progress of the Kineto experiments. When he was at the lab, regular rounds to review projects were part of his daily routine and when he was away, as he was increasingly after June, 1891, he received written reports from Dickson and other project heads. He was kept up-to-date on the Kineto project and was never out of touch with what was happening. Edison made or approved all the crucial decisions related to the design and construction

575 Newhall, Op. Cit., pp. 220–221. Beaumont Newhall credits Leica with introducing the first 35mm single lens camera with design by Oskar Barnack.

of both the Kinetograph and Kinetoscope, ultimately giving his OK to changes like the increase in the size of the image, the use of celluloid rolls, the shift from cylinder to strips, etc. It was Edison who decided that the films would be viewed in a peep show device and not projected and he made the final decision about when they would be exhibited for the first time and how they would be marketed. It was Edison who approved William Heise spending most of his time on the project and beginning in 1891 he gave Dickson an increasing amount of time on the project. Most importantly, through all of the vagaries of experimentation, he made funds available to keep the project going – this despite what must have been moments of serious disappointment and his continuing cash flow problems.

The Kinetograph and Kinetoscope were the most successful innovation conceived and created in Edison's state of the art laboratory in Orange, NJ, a facility that Edison conceived as a design and research center with "... facilities incomparably superior to any other for rapid & cheap development of an invention, & working it up into commercial shape".[576] Most of the other devices produced there were begun before moving there, or were of relatively obscure success.

There is some justification for the criticism that the Kinetoscope was an inferior beginning for motion pictures. The miniature image it showed and the awkward position that the viewer had to assume virtually ensured that its commercial life would be short – and it was. It was introduced in April 1894 and after the initial profitable spree in the fall of 1894 the market began to decline. By the time Dickson left, the Kinetophone was being prepared in order to shore up declining sales – even though the phonograph cylinder could not synchronize with the image being viewed. The Kinetophone was a commercial failure and by the end of 1895 Edison was experimenting with a projector and Raff & Gammon were negotiating with Thomas Armat to demonstrate his projector to Edison. During 1896 the Kinetoscope business came to a virtual end, eclipsed by the more spectacular images that were being projected in an ever increasing number of venues.

If the Kinetoscope had only limited success, it did provide Edison with profit at a crucial point in his business life. It helped him weather the recession of 1894 and the virtual collapse of the phonograph business. It bridged him through to a period of recovery and helped him readjust the phonograph business.

Although the Kinetoscope was soon consigned to the backwaters of history, the Kinetograph proved to be the prototype of modern cameras. It used the system common to all subsequent cameras: a single strip of 35mm film, moved intermittently past the exposure area then taken up on a reel, removed from the camera, developed in a darkroom and printed on a separate machine for subsequent exhibition on another separate machine. Films taken by the Edison-Dickson system can be used on modern equipment and several dozen films taken by Dickson during 1893, 1894 and 1895 are available for viewing today. As Dickson put it, it was "The First & Only Standardized and Commercialized the

576 EHS, lab notebook N-87-11-15, Edison's lab book, November 1887 – September 1888 pp. 671–680.

Complete Moving picture machine as adopted by Edison and the world – which was created as you now know irrefutably by me for all to enjoy".[577]

577 BiFi Fonds Will Day. Dickson to Day, undated, probably written in 1933.

Chapter 24

Between Careers. Publishing and New Opportunities

"Mr. Dickson to leave the laboratory

"W.K.L. Dickson has resigned his position of electrical engineer at the laboratory of Thomas A. Edison in order to go into business for himself, his company being the Electric Light and Power Co., lately incorporated in the State of New Jersey with Llewellyn H. Johnson as President; W.K.L. Dickson as Electrical Engineer; H.C. Douglas as Secretary. Mr. Dickson has made many friends in Orange and all join in good wishes for his success in his new field."[578] (*Orange Chronicle*, 27 April 1895)

"... About that time however, I met my old friend of early Edisononian days, Mr. H.N. Marvin, and being thoroughly disgusted with the business methods of the Lathams, after taking the Griffo-Barnet fight I threw up both the matters and joined Mr. Marvin in a new moving photographic venture ...".[579] (W.K.L. Dickson, testimony in Equity 5/167, 11 April 1911)

His dalliance with the Lathams caused Mr. Dickson to consider leaving Edison and launch a new career, but a dramatic confrontation was not what he had in mind. Edison's intransigency was a blow to his ego – a serious blow – and the abruptness of the confrontation added to the shock. As a result, the memory of the affair festered, refusing to fade away. He took his time deciding on his next move and it was the end of the year before he took on regular work. He was not destitute, nor was he without prospects – or resources. His lawyer, Edmund Congar Brown was still holding the shares in the Lambda company that the Lathams had offered him and he was in touch his friends Marvin and Casler who were still mulling what to do with their Mutoscope. In the interim, Dickson told the *Orange Chronicle* that he had formed a new business, the Electric Light and Power Company in partnership with Llewellyn H. Johnson.

Loose ends

Although Dickson said that he left work immediately on resigning, Dickson's relations with Edison were not severed completely on 2 April.

578 NMAH Hendricks.
579 EHS.

Apparently there were loose ends to take care of. The *Chronicle's* report appeared in the 27 April edition and the note from Raff & Gammon to Dickson, written on 29 April, mentioned that he was leaving as of 20 April and they indicated that he was still making films. They mentioned that he had been unable to film Capt. Ross because of poor weather.

Dickson said that he met with Edison once or twice after the confrontation and that Edison asked him to return to work, but he refused to return unless Edison fired Gilmore which Edison would not do. When he finally left, he seems to have cleaned out his work areas taking his notebooks, some photos and strips of film with him. In later years he claimed that Gilmore destroyed these documents but the only evidence supporting this accusation is the existence of only one of his note books among Edison's papers and documents. It is more likely that Dickson removed them. His animosity towards Gilmore was more intense than Gilmore's dislike of Dickson. And documents were not all that he had. In early May the lab asked him to turn-in his key to the gate and return the Remington Typewriter that Tate had loaned the Dicksons – probably to help prepare their articles for *Cassier's*.

Although it is doubtful that he destroyed Dickson's notebooks, Gilmore was not finished with him. In May he asked Dyer & Driscoll if they could press for assignment of Dickson's photographic copy-rights. He was told that the exchange of notes the previous summer seemed to confirm that Edison had consented to let Dickson keep those copyrights as his own. "The question as to whether or not the negatives are the property of Mr. Edison depends upon what the understanding was between Mr. Edison and Mr. Dickson, but the fact that Mr. Dickson executed the assignment of the Kinetoscope copyrights and refused to assign the others on the ground that the pictures were his property, and your acquiescence, indicates that there was an under-standing that they belonged to Mr. Dickson."[580] The negatives re-mained with Brady's photo shop in Orange and Dickson was preparing an inventory in order to sell them through Raff & Gammon. The Kinetoscope had opened a promising new market for Edisonia!

At the end of May, the lab compiled a list of payments made to Dickson that they felt he should repay. These were mainly those made to him and to his wife while he was recuperating in Florida. The total was $596.53. However, there is no record that they billed Dickson for the sum. It is possible that Edison, who had paid the money to Dickson out of concern for his health, intervened feeling that Gilmore had done enough. This was the final interaction between Edison and Dickson, at least the last until several years had passed. In November Edison told attorney Frederick Fish that "... Mr. Dickson has not been in my employ for some time and we are not the best of friends. I would prefer that you communicate with him direct ..." at his home.[581]

580 EHS. Dyer & Driscoll to Gilmore, 13 May 1895.

581 EHS. Edison to F.P. Fish, 1 November 1895.

Interim matters

The Electric Light and Power Company, formed at the time Dickson left Edison, was organized with the intention of marketing a mining lamp that he had designed. His partner Llewellyn H. Johnson, whom Dickson called "the financier", was a dealer in bicycles and cycling accessories and apparently they had plans related to bicycles as well. The previous August, Dickson applied for a patent for "Lantern for Bicycle-Riders" with one half assigned to Llewellyn H. Johnson, Orange. The patent was awarded 28 May 1895.[582] The business never developed because the lamps depended on light weight batteries. Dickson hoped to get the batteries from the Chloride Accumulator Company but they could not make batteries that delivered enough power and were too heavy. The company, which was never incorporated, was allowed to die a slow, quiet death.

While this is a brief interlude in Dickson's career, it demonstrates his roving mind and diverse interests. Having spent much of his career with Edison studying mines and minerals, Dickson was aware of the need for improved – and safer – lamps for individual use by the miners and he knew that there was a market for them. The bicycle may have been a secondary thought, but the bicycle craze was sweeping the country and it was very possible that a light weight and relatively inexpensive lamp that was easy to use would be popular and profitable. But his ideas were tabled and Mr. Dickson never became a tycoon of the battery-operated lamp market

Writing and publishing

Cultural activities were of central importance to the Dicksons and the early 1890s were a particularly rich period for them. Antonia continued to perform and lecture. Laurie was a member of the committee that organized the Hayden Orchestra in 1893 and he was active in its violin section. In June he was a member of a string quartet.[583] Their journalistic activities were flourishing and the public's interest in the Kinetoscope opened new opportunities. The final installment of the biography of Edison appeared in the December 1893 issue of *Cassier's Magazine* and preparations to publishing it in book form were already underway. The October installment had a description of Laurie's photographic activities which included brief descriptions of the Kinetoscope and Kinetograph. Antonia's description of the Black Maria was replete with dramatic adjectives such as "weird", "Stygian", "somber" and "portentous".

This text was the useful framework for a series of pieces in which the Dicksons recorded the history, present condition and future prospects of the Kineto.

The first appeared in the June, 1894 issue of *Century Magazine*. In the fall the Dicksons expanded their article into a booklet, *History of the Kinetograph, Kinetoscope and Kineto-Phonograph* which was printed privately in 1895. The article for *Century* was published with minor changes in the December, 1894 issue of *Cassier's*. The Dicksons also used the article from *Century* for the expanded description of the Kineto in the book version of *Life and Inventions of Thomas A. Edison* which was published in November. In February 1895 Antonia was the author of

582 NARA. U.S. Patent no. 539,799, applied 4 August 1894, awarded 28 May 1895.

583 EHS & NMAH Hendricks. The *East Orange Gazette*, 9 May 1895 reported that Dickson, L. St. Clair Colby, Thomas B. Criss and George Dixon were on the committee for the orchestra. On 26 April 1927, George Dixon, The Union Club, New York City, wrote Edison asking confirmation that he had seen one of the earliest strips of film which Dickson had shown him. It was an image of Sandow (filmed in March 1894).

an article "Wonders of the Kinetoscope" which appeared in *Leslie's Monthly*.

Laurie's wife also contributed to the burst of literary activity – but she did not write about her husband's work. Her article appeared in March, 1895 in *Leslie's Weekly* and it described meeting Anton Rubinstein during their honeymoon.

This flurry of activity served both Dicksons well. The article in *Century Magazine* stimulated other articles. Notably, it was the basis of an article in the June 1894 issue of *The Electrical World* which in turn was excerpted in the 21 July 1894 issue of *The Literary Digest*. The author apparently interviewed Dickson and credited him with a major contribution to Edison's latest wonder. *Cassier's* and *The Electrical World* were professional publications and these articles corroborated Dickson's credentials in the engineering and electrical communities where professional training and status was becoming increasingly important.

Century and *Leslie's* were popular magazines that could be found in the parlors of thousands of American homes. *Century* was the most serious of the two, with *Leslie's* taking a more popular approach. *Century* competed with *Harper's* and *Atlantic Monthly* and each month it covered a variety of topics with articles on politics, science, art, literature, travel, nature, etc. by prominent specialists. Some of the best known names from the literary world contributed poetry and fiction. People who received the June 1894 issue could read field notes by John Burroughs; an article on Tissot's biblical illustrations by Theodore Stanton; a letter from Robert Todd Lincoln commenting on the spoils system in the consular service (the President's son, a former ambassador to England, favored a civil service system); and Chapters XX and XXI (the final chapters) of Mark Twain's new novel *Pudd'nhead Wilson* in the pre-publication serialization. (The hard cover edition was published later in 1894.) Subscribers and regular readers of issues published in 1894 could read Nicholas Murray Butler on reforming secondary education; a commentary on the Serbian poet Zmai Iovan Iovanovich written by Nikola Tesla who also provided his translations of several of Iovanovich's poems; a commentary on Franz Schubert by Antonin Dvorak; the publication of letters by Edgar Allen Poe and Edwin Booth; and poems by a variety of authors, among them James Whitcomb Riley and Thomas Bailey Aldrich.[584] The Dicksons were in heady company!

Although the description of the Kineto in *Cassier's* provided the framework for their subsequent pieces, the Dicksons made an effort to give every article unique character. Consequently each has information of interest and together, they make up the earliest historical writing on the modern motion picture. The article in *Century* has a valuable summary of the stages of the experiment and Edison's endorsement is his acknowledgment of Dickson's contribution. It is likely that Dickson wrote it, but it was published as written by Edison in his best, formal handwriting. The description of work on the invention in *History of the Kinetograph, Kinetoscope and Kineto-Phonograph* is from the *Century* article but with a notable addition: they added the claim that Dickson projected

584 *The Century Magazine*, Vol. XLVIII, New Series Vol. XXVI, May–October 1894 (The Century Co., New York & T. Fisher Unwin, London). *Pudd'nhead Wilson* was published serially in *Century* during the first half of 1894 and appeared in book form in November 1894.

synchronized sound for Edison when he returned from the Paris Exposition. This is the first appearance of this controversial claim. Dickson also introduced recognition of the contributions of lenses by Bausch & Lomb and Gundlach. "... the opticians spared no skill or trouble in carrying out our specification". Since this was intended as a souvenir most of the text was devoted to a description of the films that patrons could see – or had seen – on the Kinetoscope. Illustrations from the films could be used to remember the experience or to show to others.

All of the articles were well illustrated, with strips from a number of productions that would not survive otherwise and there were drawings that show production techniques. The cover of *History of the Kinetograph, Kinetoscope and Kineto-Phonograph* (see page 341) is an outstanding example of Dickson's artistic technique and the several scenes from his various productions are commentary about the films he felt were important and his interpretation of them. The booklet also contains interesting examples of his still photographs.

In their articles the Dicksons expressed a firm belief in the potential of the moving image as historical record and as a source of entertainment and enlightenment. The *Century* article ended on this optimistic note:

"... No scene, however animated and extensive, but will eventually be within reproductive power. Martial evolutions, naval exercises, processions, and countless kindred exhibitions will be recorded for the leisurely gratification of those who are debarred from attendance, or who desire to recall them. The invalid, the isolated country recluse, and the harassed business man can indulge in needed recreation, without undue expenditure, without fear of weather, and without the sacrifice of health or important engagements. Not only our own resources but those of the entire world will be at our command. The advantages to students and historians will be immeasurable. Instead of dry and misleading accounts, tinged with the exaggerations of the chroniclers' minds, our archives will be enriched by the vitalized pictures of great national scenes ...".[585]

The *History of the Kinetograph, Kinetoscope and Kineto-Phonograph* was a personal undertaking apparently initiated by Dickson. Neither Edison nor Gilmore was involved with it. Dickson met with Albert Bunn, a printer, on 5 September 1894 and Bunn agreed to produce 10,000 copies of a thirty-two page booklet at a cost of $325.00.[586] In December Raff & Gammon signed a contract to help the project and distribute the brochure. It is possible, but not certain, that they had been involved earlier since Dickson's agreement with Bunn was made a couple of weeks after Raff & Gammon received their concession and just four days after they began doing business as the Kinetoscope Company–although this may only be a coincidence. In the agreement, signed 15 December 1894, Raff & Gammon agreed to pay expenses up to $350.00 and the 10,000 copies were to be delivered to them. One half of the receipts were to reimburse Raff & Gammon and the other half would be split. Dickson retained copyrights as well as the text and photo plates. Raff & Gammon had the right to publish future editions.[587]

585 Ibid.

586 Dickson probably knew Bunn from his contacts with *Cassier's*. Bunn's business office was in the World Building where *Cassier's* had its office. In November Dickson paid $10.00 to Bunn.

587 NMAH Hendricks. City Court of New York, Albert Bunn v. The Kinetoscope Co., Abstract of Correspondence, Memoranda &C., Between Parties.

The Dicksons were still working on the text in November. This is indicated by illustrations and mentions of film productions made in November.[588] Between September and December, the Dicksons' text grew longer and an abundant number of illustrations had been chosen. Instead of 32 pages, it was now 55 pages and Bunn's bill was increasing. This caused problems. Raff & Gammon paid the $350 they agreed on, but Bunn wanted an additional $608.40 and sent them a bill in that amount on 15 March 1895. He received an additional $200 the next day, but then sued for the balance. The case was decided in July, 1896 with a judgement against The Kinetoscope Company. Sometime after the first of the year the booklet went into distribution and Raff and Gammon continued to distribute it for some months, changing the cover after they began distributing Edison's Vitascope projector. The new version was renamed *History of the Photographic, Scientific Experiments and Developments Leading to the Perfection of The Vitascope.*[589]

The life and inventions of Edison

Plans to publish the Dicksons' articles about Edison as a book were made before the series finished its run. The Dicksons probably worked on the book during 1893 and the first part of 1894. Published at the beginning of November 1894 for the Christmas market, it appeared simultaneously in New York and London. The New York publisher was T.Y. Crowell and the British version was by Chatto and Windus. The *Orange Chronicle* was pleased to promote local talent, touting it as the "... gift book of the season". *Cassier's* offered it to its readers at $4.50 in quatro cloth, gilt top and boxed. They declared that "This magnificent volume makes one of the handsomest gift books of the year". After Christmas *Cassier's* offered it in combination with a subscription to the magazine for $7.50.[590]

In book form the fourteen monthly articles became twenty-four chapters – with a fanciful tribute to Edison added. It predicted that the new century would open an era of physical and spiritual well being thanks to Edison who "... has done more than any other to neutralize the gross fixity of matter, to extend the limited range of the senses, and to furnish a plastic basis for the incoming spiritual forces, 'the greatest genius of this or any other age' ...". The book was 362 pages long and used much of the original text with minor alterations. The most significant change was an expanded description of the "... latest marvels of the laboratory", the Kinetoscope and Kineto-phonograph. The revised text incorporated most of the text from the *Century* article including the text of Edison's preface with its recognition of Dickson's contribution. Cassier liked the revised version so well it appeared in the December 1894 issue of *Cassier's Monthly.*[591]

It was generously illustrated. In all there were more than one hundred and fifty illustrations, many of them by Dickson. These were supplemented with drawings by Bauhan, Outcault and Meeker. There were also photographs by photographer-school teacher James Ricalton taken while he was searching for bamboo in India and south Asia. The

[588] Charles Musser, *Edison Motion Pictures* ..., pp. 156–157, 159–160 and 163. Among the productions are Opium Den, Row in a Chinese Laundry, Milk White Flag and Fire Rescue, all of which were made in November. Musser was unable to provide exact dates but his estimates are based on thorough research.

[589] NMAH Hendricks. The renaming occurred following the first showing of Edison's Vitascope in April 1896.

[590] NMAH Hendricks. *Orange Chronicle,* 22 November 1894; *Cassier's Magazine,* November 1894 and February 1895. The combination with subscription was offered for several months during 1895.

[591] "Edison's Kineto-Phonograph" by Antonia and W.K.L. Dickson, *Cassier's Monthly,* Vol. XII, No. 37, December 1894, pp. 145–156.

section on the Kineto used a variety of photos. Meeker's drawing of
Heise filming a scene in the Black Maria was the only illustration from
Century that appeared in the book. Strips of frames were reproduced as
examples of various productions and to show that action changed from
frame to frame. Sixty-four frames of Fred Ott sneezing were spread
across two pages; thirty-two frames of Carmencita's dance filled another; and there was a similar selection of frames from Annabelle's
Serpentine Dance and Caicido on the slack wire. A strip from "Monkey
Shines" illustrated the early stage of the experiments. These same
illustrations were used for the December 1894 issue of *Cassier's*.

London's *The Christian World* (1 November 1894) gave the Dicksons a favorable review, but not all the notices were positive. Silvanus
P. Thompson writing in the British journal *The Electrician* savaged the
book. Thompson was a defender of British science with no great love
for Edison. In his lengthy review (three pages) he called the narrative
naive and said it was of little scientific value. "The authors are so lost
in the worship of their hero that they lose all sense of proportion and
perspective." He singled out a number of inventions which he felt were
inferior or useless and criticized the Dicksons for treating them as
important works. Thompson was particularly critical of the failure to
recognize the work of others that anticipated or improved on Edison's
work. He named a number that were ignored, specifically mentioning
Tainter and the Bells in his comments on the phonograph and Joseph
Swan in his comments on electric lighting. Antonia's prose drew scorn:
"... a tiresome series of discourses ... overflowing with references to
Assyria and Babylon, Sparta and Hymettus, Shakespeare, Milton and
Spenser, all fired off like fourth-of-July fireworks to dazzle the reader."
He put down the Kinetoscope as a toy that was little different from
earlier devices. "... At the present moment his [Edison's] fame, in public
estimation, rests upon two toys, the phonograph and the Kinetoscope,
one purely mechanical, the other optical and photographic." Though
he found the book filled with "... amusing blunders and juvenile
outbursts ...", he had kind words for "... Mr. Dickson's photography ..."
which he found "... distinctly above average".[592]

Antonia and Lucie on their own

In her article, "Wonders of the Kinetoscope" in the February issue of
Leslie's Monthly Antonia occasionally lapsed into illusion and metaphor,
but for the most part her writing style was more reserved. This may
reflect an editor's effort to give it quality by changing the content and
the tone of the article. Though it used information from the earlier
accounts, it was not a reiteration of its predecessors. It opened with a
capsule history of photography and an explanation of persistence of
vision. It traced photography back to the sixteenth century when
Giambattista della Porta experimented and wrote about camera obscura
and it credited Joseph Priestly with achieving "the first sun print";
Daguerre and Niépce with launching photography and, as in the
previous articles, Maddox was credited with opening the way to motion

592 *The Electrician*, 14
December 1894, pp.
185–187.

photography by improving film speed. Without crediting anyone with establishing an understanding of persistence of vision she tried to demonstrate the phenomenon and gave the Zoetrope as an example. Since Dickson was almost certainly the source of her information, her article is an interesting summary of his understanding of the antecedents of his own work.

The article is also notable because Edison's name rarely appears. He is mentioned only four times. One is in a photo caption and another is limited to a mention of "Edison's laboratory". Significantly, she did not credit Edison with originating the experiments. *Leslie's* readers probably understood that she was describing Edison's machines but her passage describing the development of the Kineto devices gave responsibility to her brother:

"... the working out of the problem being intrusted to Mr. W.K.L. Dickson, electrical engineer and chief of the electro-mining and photo-kinetographic departments, Edison Laboratory... The final outcome of these experiments was the adoption of a band of highly sensitive film, especially prepared. An ingenious mechanical device holds the film rigidly in place, while a shutter in the apparatus opens and allows a beam of light to enter. ...The effects produced, though more diminutive than when projected on a screen, are essentially realistic. ... The Kinetoscope was complete; the visual impressions were as perfect as the imitative faculties of man could make them ..."[593]

She concluded with the quotation from Edison that linked Dickson with Muybridge, Marey and Edison, himself.

Lucie's article, "A Reminiscence of Anton Rubinstein", also in *Leslie's Weekly*, appeared in March 1895. The noted pianist-composer died the previous November, so Lucie's account of meeting him during their honeymoon tour of Europe was a timely memorial.

Mrs. Dickson's writing echoed Antonia's flamboyant prose and mythic metaphors – perhaps an indication of editorial contributions by her sister-in-law. There were suggestions of mystery and doom, a fatalism that also appears in Antonia's writing. Sorcery, magic, madness, demons and portents of death pervade both women's writing, a gloom that seems a common thread between the two women dominant in Laurie's private life. Lucie and Antonia were apparently good friends, sharing a bond that joined the three into a family. Whatever the relationship between the two women was, in retrospect the pessimistic foreboding that affected their prose was a portent. The health problems which Antonia had suffered from in the past were destined to become more serious.

A moment of fame

Dickson's reputation was spreading beyond the community that surrounded the laboratory and this may have annoyed Gilmore – and Edison.. The Dicksons had appended a favorable review the Kinetoscope and their article in *Century* to the text of the brochure. The author, W.E. Woodbury, the Editor of the *American Annual of Photography* was very complimentary. He called the Kinetoscope the "... photo-

593 EHS. *Leslie's Monthly*, February 1895, p. 248.

graphic discovery of the year" and said "... Edison conceived the idea
the working out of the arrangements was intrusted to Mr. W.K.L.
Dickson, a clever young engineer. There are few who really can imagine
the thousands of difficulties that required to be overcome before such
an apparatus could be made to work satisfactorily ...". He gave a capsule
biographical sketch of Dickson, quoted Edison's introduction to the
Century Magazine article, praised the Dicksons' biography and concluded with hopes that moving pictures might be made in color saying
that though it seemed doubtful, "We have, fortunately, men – clever
men – among us who are ever trying to invent and to improve. Men
who devote their lives to the advancement of photography with but
little reward, for who ever heard of a photographic inventor growing
rich by his labors? But they work on, satisfied with their efforts to
benefit their fellow creatures and the fascination that always exists in
experimental work."[594]

Soon after this was published, the Annual's parent magazine,
Photographic Times featured Dickson again in an article in their January
1895 issue. It mentioned the Dicksons' articles in *Century* and *Cassier's*
and summarized the history of the invention, again giving Dickson
credit for "... working out the necessary details ...". They commented
that "... the whole world is talking about this invention, and marveling
thereat ...".[595]

While Dickson's name was not on everyone's tongue, he was
becoming known to a growing circle of national figures who would
prove useful in the future. He was becoming known to the technical
specialists who were interested in moving images, engineers, electricians and photographers. Through his work in the Black Maria he was
meeting show people, athletes, promoters and theatrical entrepreneurs.
His writing and photographic materials brought him in contact with
other writers, editors and publishers. He would soon put these contacts
to good use.

KMCD

Despite Laurie's being unemployed, the family was ready to enjoy a
summer of relaxation and leisure. At the beginning of May Lucie went
to Petersburg, Virginia to spend three weeks with her brother, Col.
Alexander W. Archer and other members of her family. In July the three
Dicksons went to Geneva, New York for a vacation in upstate New
York's Finger Lakes. It was a time for pleasure mixed with a little
business.

A few days after Lucie left for Virginia, Dickson met with his friend
and some-time associate Herman Casler who came from Syracuse to
New York City with the apparent intent of discussing the Mutoscope.
If Casler's testimony in the various patent interferences and lawsuits is
accurate, the Mutoscope had been completed and the camera was
almost ready. It was several weeks since Casler tested the movement of
film through the camera's mechanism using strips of paper and they
were now ready to try it with film. Casler's record of this meeting said

594 Dicksons, Op.
Cit., pp. 54–55. In the
edition of the
Dicksons' book in the
collection of the
Museum of Modern
Art which is
annotated by W.K.L.
Dickson, he
underlined the phrase
with but little reward.

595 NMAH
Hendricks.
Photographic Times,
January 1895, pp.
22–26.

Chapter 24 Between Careers. Publishing and New Opportunities

399

nothing about what they discussed, but it seems probable that he wanted Dickson's advice about film and filmmaking. Dickson's experience with Eastman and Blair film and his months of producing film would have been important to making the Mutoscope a commercial reality.[596] It is also possible that they discussed the potential for marketing the Mutoscope.

First motion picture projection

The Griffo-Barnet film which opened 20 May 1895 at 153 Broadway, New York City, was the first motion picture projected for the public. Eugene Lauste, who projected the film, said that it was a large hall and during the rehearsal prior to the opening they had trouble getting enough light on the screen and had to modify the shutter but even after the modifications the picture was apparently dark.

The Lathams did not advertise their program so it was publicized by several newspaper articles commenting on the novelty of their projector.

Casler's trip was well timed. It was a month after Dickson's sudden resignation from Edison's lab and the time was right for Dickson to consider what the future held. He had not yet severed relations with the Lathams but he was increasingly disenchanted with them. The night before meeting Casler he had been on the roof of Madison Square Garden helping the Lathams make their first film, the boxing match between Albert Griffiths, known as Young Griffo, and Charles Barnet. According to Woodville Latham, Dickson attended the film's premier on 20 May and came to several subsequent performances. But Dickson said that the filmmaking ended his relationship with the Lathams.[597] The Griffo-Barnet match was the first film projected for the public and Dickson was probably interested in the public's reaction as well as the quality of the projection.

Although he was leaning in their direction, it was several more weeks before he cast his lot with Marvin, Casler and Koopman. In the meantime he planned to have a relaxed summer in the family's favorite vacation place, upstate New York – where the spas, healthful waters, lakes and woods were conveniently near Syracuse where Casler was finishing his camera and Harry Marvin was organizing his business affairs.

The film-test of the camera was delayed until mid-June, several weeks after Casler's trip to New York. The subject was familiar, a boxing match, but not a match between professionals. Instead the antagonists were the men shepherding the project, Herman Casler and Harry Marvin. A crude stage was constructed, probably on the grounds of Charles Lipe's machine shop. The match had comic qualities. Marvin was a large, imposing man who stood well over six feet while the diminutive Casler was about a foot shorter. Casler took off his suit coat for the match but Marvin kept his hat and suit-coat on. Although Dickson does not seem to have been in Syracuse for the filming, he may have provided the inspiration. Their bout was similar to Dickson's film

596 NMAH Hendricks. Mrs. Dickson's trip to Petersburg was reported in the *Orange Chronicle*, 4 May 1895. Herman Casler's visit on 5 May 1895 is recorded in a notebook which his son Roger made available to Gordon Hendricks.

597 NARA. Woodville Latham's testimony in Patent Interference no. 18,461, December 1897.

of a comic bout between Charles Walton and John C. Slavin, an excerpt from Rice's Broadway show, *1492*, which relied on extreme differences in height and build for comic effect.

At the time of Casler's visit with Dickson the plans to market the Mutoscope were beginning to gel. Casler had worked as a machinist and draftsman at his cousin's machine shop in Syracuse but in 1895 he started working for Harry Marvin. Marvin had set up an operation in Lipe's shop to manufacture the mining drill he patented in 1887. In March 1895, Charles Lipe died and in June Marvin decided to move his shop to Canastota, New York, a small industrial town twenty miles east of Syracuse. Marvin had married Oramella Tackabury, the daughter of a Canastota banker and after her father died, the Marvins moved into "The Evergreen", the Tackabury's impressive Victorian house on Canastota's main street. Although it was small, Canastota was well located. Near Syracuse, it was on the Erie Canal and the New York Central Railroad, the main shipping routes through New York state. In June

Herman Casler taken c. 1895, about the time he worked on the Mutoscope. [NMAH.]

Marvin negotiated for a former match factory near the canal on the east side of town. By the end of July equipment had been purchased or moved from Syracuse and they were ready to start operations.[598] A part of the shop was set aside for the Mutoscope operation. Casler relocated to Canastota to manage the works and the Mutoscope operation.

In late July, about the time that machine works opened, the vacationing W.K.L. Dickson came to Canastota to visit the Marvins. He returned several more times as summer turned to fall.[599]

On 5 August a four round boxing match between Prof. Al Leonard and his pupil Bert Hosley was filmed with the Mutograph. This was still a test it but is counted as the first production of the not yet created American Mutoscope Company. The Leonard-Hosley match was filmed in Canastota on an improvised stage constructed outside the James Mahan Machine Shop near the center of town. The *Canastota Bee* reported that it was photographed by H.J. Dobson of Syracuse. Historian Gordon Hendricks argued that H.J. Dobson was a pseudonym for W.K.L. Dickson, used to disguise Dickson's involvement. Hendricks searched for Dobson's name in city directories for Syracuse and could not find him and this, coupled with Dickson's experience in filming led Hendricks to conclude that Dickson was secretly involved. Although

598 NMAH Hendricks & Hendricks, *Beginnings of the Biograph*, NY, The Beginnings of the American Film, 1964, reprinted in *Origins of the American Film*, NY, Arno Press & The New York Times, 1972, pp. 6–7 & 16–18. Marvin also had financial backing from businessmen in Canastota. John Pross, a machinist who worked with Casler in Lipe's shop testified in Patent Interference No. 18,461 that Charles Lipe died in March 1895.

599 NMAH Hendricks. *Canastota Bee*, 20 July 1895.

there is no proof, Hendricks' assumption may have validity. The match was staged very much like the bouts filmed in the Black Maria. The backdrop was a black cloth, the boxers were in light clothing and the floor of the stage-ring was white. Two posts on either side define the limits of the area that could be filmed and ropes were strung in the front and back to simulate a boxing ring. These efforts to enhance the contrast and sharpen the action are things that Dickson would have done if he set up the filming – which might be the case.

This test seems to have been regarded as a success because there is no record of any other filming done during the summer. It was a time for leisure. The Dicksons were taking the waters in Geneva and relaxing in the Adirondacks. The *Orange Chronicle* reported that Dickson shot two deer on "a jacking expedition". In late August Harry Marvin's wife was vacationing at Lewis Point.

This summer idyl of leisure and socializing combined with a little bit of business solidified the informal relationship that had existed between Koopman, Marvin, Casler and Dickson. It led to a business understanding which they called KMCD – after the first letters of their family names. Sunday, 22 September is the symbolic date for the beginning of this affiliation. Dickson was in Canastota visiting the Marvins and Caslers and Elias B. Koopman joined them. After lunch the group posed for G.D. Dunn, a local photographer and the picture has become the identifying icon for their partnership. The picture seems to celebrate a significant moment in their lives but it also symbolizes an important moment in the development of the American film industry. They may not have been aware at the time, but they were about to launch the most influential of the early American film companies, The American Mutoscope and Biograph Company – later, just The Biograph Company.

According to Dickson, KMCD was an informal affiliation without signed documents and it continued as a separate understanding after the company was formed.[600] Despite their unofficial relationship the partners seem to have agreed on a course of action which they pursued in the weeks following the photo session. Koopman and Marvin who were experienced in business apparently spent the months of October, November and December negotiating for capital to launch the Mutoscope. Dickson and Casler, the principal technicians, spent the next several months brainstorming, experimenting and designing. Dickson spent much of October and November in Canastota working with Casler – and Marvin. They modified the camera in order to experiment with projection and they tried projecting from Mutoscope drums. Several variations of the Mutoscope were designed and over the next few years a number of these were patented. Very few papers from this period survive, but two, dated 3 December 1895, have sketches and descriptions in Dickson's hand showing revolving colored disks which could be used for single or stereo projection.[601] Neither of these experiments were carried to completion, but it indicates the broad approach that Dickson and his associates were taking.

600 EHS. Dickson, testimony in 1911 in Equity 5/167. At that time Dickson said that the informal agreement still existed.

601 Gordon Hendricks acquired copies of these from Harry Swanker of Canastota who apparently got them from a former employee of Herman Casler.

By the summer of 1895 work on the Mutograph camera moved from Syracuse to nearby Canastota, NY where Harry Marvin was setting-up a machine shop. On 5 August a movie subject intended for possible release was taken. Boxing was still the favored film subject and the participants were Prof. Al Leonard and his pupil Bert Hosley, both from Syracuse. The four rounds were filmed outside the James Mahan Machine Shop. If Dickson did not do the filming his advice is evident. The stage and set-up closely resembles the boxing matches he filmed for Edison. [MoMA.]

Casler and Dickson probably enjoyed this period of creativity. Experimentation and innovation were their favorite games. In fact, all of the members of KMCD were fascinated by gadgets, novelties and innovations – preferably useful, but impractical ones could also stimulate them. Their shared interest in detective cameras, portable lanterns, mining drills, cigar lighters – and moving images – had brought them together and it sustained their comradeship for the next few years. Dickson and Casler were the most experienced experimenters and they the took the lead during the closing months of 1895, but Marvin and Koopman were also creative and experienced in the design of new and novel devices. During the next few years they also contributed to the stable of machines designed by the KMCD. Since Koopman had been marketing novelties through his Magic Introduction Company, he was able to advise his colleagues on the market potential of a device.

There was a purpose to this flurry of speculative innovation. The KMCD had limited capital and needed to raise funds to launch the Mutoscope. The patent for the Mutoscope was issued in November and, importantly, there was no indication of conflict with Edison's Kinetoscope patent.[602] It had a number of features that made it a more attractive machine than the Kinetoscope. It was a simple but sturdy device. Operated by a crank. it could be viewed with natural light or illuminated by a bulb or oil lamp. The version as patented was portable but a more substantial iron version was available for use in parlors, railroad stations, retail shops, hotels and other places of public gathering. The larger machine could be operated with a coin and it was heavy enough that it was difficult to move. The Kinetoscope had a smaller image and it was motor driven, housed in a bulky cabinet and was

602 NARA. U.S. Patent No. 549,309, Mutoscope, was approved 5 November 1895. The application for patent had been filed 21 November 1894.

On 22 September 1895 G.D. Dunn, a local photographer in Canastota took several photos to commemorate an agreement establishing the KMCD group, an alliance of Elias B. Koopman, Harry Marvin, Herman Casler and W.K.L. Dickson. The group posed for the photo above (left to right, Marvin, Dickson, Casler & Koopman) and Dunn took a less formal picture (below) of (left to right) Dickson, Casler, Koopman and a woman, probably Mrs. Marvin on the lawn of Evergreen House, the Marvins' imposing home in Canastota. [NMAH & Canal Town Museum.]

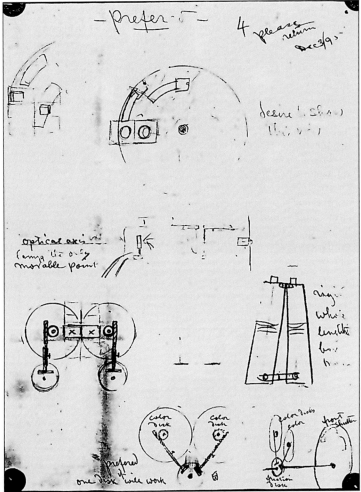

During the fall and winter of 1895 the KMCD group worked on ideas with potential for their proposed enterprise. These sketches of a system of disks to provide color effects was among the ideas that did not work out. Though the handwriting is not Dickson's it is the sort of innovation that appealed to him and may well reflect his input. This drawing came from a former Marvin-Casler employee, Harry Swanker. [NMAH.]

dependent upon expensive, untrustworthy batteries. These were advantages that potential investors might appreciate, but KMCD offered other assets. Their innovative machine came with quartet of inventors with proven creativity who were not resting on their current accomplishments, indicating that they not only had their eyes on the future but were working to anticipate potential competition from similar devices. Each member of KMCD had something positive to offer a potential investor. Koopman had commercial experience and a couple of patents to his credit. Marvin's mining drill had a solid reputation and was well enough received by the mining industry that he now had his own manufacturing firm. Casler was credited with developing the Mutoscope and the Mutograph camera and was working on improvements. But their most valuable asset was W.K.L. Dickson whose reputation was at its peak. He offered potential investors more than the promise of new creativity. He had first-hand knowledge of Edison's equipment and could create devices that would not infringe Edison's patents. Of almost equal importance at a time when it was becoming clear that the public had an appetite for a variety of new and novel images to view, he was the one person with experience making films that appealed to potential customers.

This proved to be an effective formula. Three months after the gathering on the Marvin's lawn, a major new entertainment company was created. It had solid financial backing and a conservative, but effective marketing plan. Although the partners may not have anticipated it, their creation, the American Mutoscope Company, was destined to be the most influential pioneer American film company. The foundation for the company's future success was laid by W.K.L. Dickson.

Part V

1896–1903
Biographing: Filming in the States and Abroad

Chapter 25

The Age of Movement.
A New Enterprise

"What is the Mutoscope? A Mirror of Life, reproducing the *Events* of the *Year*, the *Doings* of *Yesterday* & *To-Day, Moving*, Living *History*, For the *Present* and the *Future*."[603] (Brochure, "The Age of Movement" London, The International Mutoscope Syndicate, [1901])

"There are fifteen or twenty motion picture machines in England, but an American form of the machine – the Biograph – leads them all. I have seen seven types of these machines, all told, and the Biograph is the best of the lot as regards absence of vibration and clearness of definition. They have some of the best pictures too."[604] (*New York Telegraph Mercury*, 1 June 1897)

O ne of the persistent mysteries of W.K.L. Dickson's life is the question of how well off he was. Leaving Edison's laboratory was a wrenching experience, but Dickson was not thrown into a state of poverty – or despair. After resigning he remained unemployed from April until the end of 1895, but neither he nor his family suffered. In fact they spent an enviable summer visiting relatives and traveling about upstate New York taking the waters, hunting and visiting friends. It is clear that he had the economic resources to survive comfortably, if not luxuriously. He had extra income during 1894 from commissions on the profits of the Kinetoscope and the films he produced. This was in addition to income from the occasional sale of photographs and his literary efforts. He also had a portfolio of investments, but not all of them were doing well. His stock in Edison's mining company was not productive and its future was grim. He returned the shares in the Lambda Company that the Lathams had given him – a provident decision because their business was in trouble. He had stock in Raff & Gammon's Kinetoscope Company which had been doing well, but the Kinetoscope business was also faltering – and about to suffer a fatal blow from Edison and from Dickson and his associates. While most of the stocks that he held were of dubious value, he was about to acquire a new block which would make him a wealthy man – at least on paper. The partners in KMCD were about to receive blocks of stock in their new company in exchange for rights to the patents they owned.

603 Academy of Motion Picture Arts & Science Library.

604 *The American Biograph*, p. 1. Reproduced in Kemp Niver, *Biograph Bulletins, 1896–1908*, p. 26 (Los Angeles, Locare Research Group, 1971)

The new company, American Mutoscope Company, became a reality during the Christmas holidays. The papers organizing the company were signed on 27 December; it was incorporated on 30 December 1895 and operations began in January 1896. It had substantial backing from investors apparently serious about setting up a firm to compete with Edison's Kinetoscope. The Mutoscope company began with approved capital of $2,000,000 divided into 20,000 shares of $100 each. Funds to start the business came from a chattel mortgage of $200,000 from the New York Security and Trust Co. The major investors had backgrounds in banking, railroads, coal mining, publishing and retail. The company's president was George R. Blanchard, a Commissioner of the Joint Traffic Association with previous connections to the Baltimore & Ohio and the Erie Railroads. Harry Marvin was second Vice President and Koopman was General Manager. Dickson and Casler were "Technicians to ..." the company. Each of the members of KMCD received stock in the company in exchange for the North American rights to their moving image patents. Each of them were members of the company's board of directors. A Bradstreet report made in September, 1897 said: "All identified with the enterprise are considered shrewd and capable, and the prospects of a larger growth, to their business is considered very flattering. Locally they have no trouble in getting what credit they require, and pay promptly".[605]

The purpose of the new company was the "Manufacture and sale of photographic, mutographic and mutoscopic implements and appliances, implements and apparatus in any manner connected therewith, or for projecting the same, and the using the same for exhibition or other purposes, and the selling or leasing or otherwise disposing the same, or the right to use the same". As the company's name indicates, the focus was on the Mutoscope and moving pictures that could be watched on the Mutoscope. Koopman and Marvin had, apparently, convinced the railroad men, bankers and merchants that Mutoscopes had a wider variety of possibilities than the Kinetoscope. They would be placed in railroad stations, hotels, stores, cafes – anywhere that the public might have to kill a few moments of time and welcome a nickle's worth of diversion. Koopman believed that the Mutoscope would be a unique and valuable tool for salesmen to use to illustrate concepts that were difficult to describe in words.

Dickson returned to New York in December and in January he joined Marvin and Koopman in the company's newly established New York office. Casler remained in Canastota at the Marvin Electric Rock Drill Works which manufactured Mutoscopes, several Mutograph cameras and other equipment needed for operations. Their rented space was in the Roosevelt Building –also called the Hackert-Carhart Building – at 841 Broadway in New York City. This was the same building where Koopman's Magic Introduction Company was located.

Producing movies for the Mutoscopes was Dickson's responsibility. It took him several months to get everything in place but this seems to have been considered in their planning. They needed a studio, a

605 EHS. The American Mutoscope Company was incorporated under the laws of the state of New Jersey. The Bradstreet report is among Edison's papers and apparently was supplied him at his request.

The roof-top studio at 841 Broadway was probably photographed soon after completion in the spring of 1896. Dickson (2nd from right) is standing with Harry Marvin (right) and two unidentified men, presumably investors in the American Mutoscope Co. (one of them might be George R. Blanchard who was President of the company). Although similar to the Black Maria, there are significant innovations. It could be moved but the pivot was limited to the area of regular mid-day sun, the camera is in a movable house which was not fixed in place and the frame in back of the stage allowed the background to be changed. There was no black tunnel to absorb unwanted light. [LC.]

laboratory for developing and printing the films and facilities for mounting the prints on the Mutoscope reels. Staff to man the facilities had to be hired and trained. Remembering the problems that Edison had supplying enough machines and films to meet demand, Dickson apparently convinced his partners and their investors that they should have a generous reserve of film subjects available so that they could provide a variety of programs when they introduced Mutoscopes to the public. Film production began in late spring or early summer and Dickson had shot more than seventy-five films by fall when the first subjects were projected for to the public.

The new studio was built on the roof of 841 Broadway. It was an open air studio with no structure covering it. The Black Maria was his model, but Dickson had learned a thing or two during two years of film production so it was not a duplicate. Like the Maria, the new studio could be moved to take advantage of sunlight, but only in a semi-circle. The area on the roof was limited and the Maria had been rarely, if ever turned in full circle. The stage was mounted on a sturdy frame of steel girders which fanned-out from the pivot. Wheels and iron rails allowed the whole structure to be moved as needed. The camera was housed in a corrugated shed which provided darkness and protected the camera from weather. The shed was on tracks connected to the stage so it could be move closer or farther away as needed. The stage was a bare floor mounted on iron beams which gave it stability while allowing it to be moved. It was bare and uncovered, but an open framework which extended from either side across the back made it possible to put up a variety of backdrops and scenic flats. The stage was larger than the shooting area in the Black Maria and there were no crude railings to define the limits of the camera range. Perhaps Dickson had more confidence in his ability to control the action of his players and he had found other ways to keep the action in camera range. (A rectangular rug is a common prop on many productions and it seemed to be placed to define the critical area for action.) The most significant change from the Black Maria was the absence of a "black tunnel" behind the stage. Eastman's film had apparently improved significantly and the open design seemingly gave enough light on sunny days.

The Mutoscope Company's choice of the Roosevelt Building set a trend for the emerging American film industry. The Roosevelt Building was on Broadway between 13th and 14th Streets, immediately south of Union Square. In the 1890s this was still the heart of New York's theater district even though it was already moving up Broadway towards Times Square – which was still known as Long Acre Square (the New York Times did not move there until after 1900).[606] Union Square proved to be an ideal location for film production during the 1890s and the decade from 1900–1910. It was convenient to the props, costumes, players and supporting equipment essential for staged productions. Although the Mutoscope company moved to a building on nearby 14th Street after the turn of the century, the Mutoscope Company and it's successors, the American Mutoscope & Biograph Co. and the Biograph Co. remained in the area for the next seventeen years. In 1913 the company finally moved to a larger, more elaborate studio in the Bronx, but by that time the company's period of artistic dominance had come to an end.

Facilities: making the works work

A studio was only one part of the preparations for making and showing films. Staff had to be hired and trained and the working models that Casler designed had to be refined so they could be manufactured and serviced efficiently. The Mutoscope company acquired a building at 1013 Grand Street in Hoboken, New Jersey as their technical facility – the equivalent to Edison's Phonograph Works. They planned to locate developing, printing and the assembly of Mutoscope reels there. While they negotiated for this property and built the roof-top studio, they used working space adjacent to their office on the sixth floor of 841 Broadway. It was utilitarian but it made a useful prototype for the more elaborate production facilities in the works. The Mutograph camera was installed and Dickson set up a darkroom and printing facilities.

Dickson was used to having capable assistants and his production method depended on support by associates who understood the processes and had skills that could complement his own. Over the next several months the Mutoscope Company assembled a staff of capable workers who made it possible for them to expand operations and gave them the flexibility necessary to meet unanticipated challenges. The

606 *The Encyclopedia of New York City*, pp. 846–847 & 1185. Adolph Ochs acquired control of the *Times* in August, 1896 and moved the newspaper into a new building at what is now Times Square shortly after 1900. The opening of the subway station and nearby Grand Central Station greatly enhanced the importance of the area. By 1914 it was the focal point of theatrical life and the new film companies being formed in the period from 1910–1912 often established themselves in the Times Square area, though a number remained in the Union Square area until after World War I.

company's ultimate success depended on its ability to set trends and adapt to changes in a very fluid and competitive market. The ground work for their success was laid during the first months of operation.

Dickson's first requirement was an assistant and he found an outstanding one almost immediately. Johann Gottlob Wilhelm Bitzer, who was studying electricity at Cooper Union, had been hired by Koopman to work at his Magic Introduction Company. In March, 1895 Bitzer was transferred to the American Mutoscope Company where he became Dickson's trainee-assistant. It was the beginning of a long and productive career for Billy Bitzer who gained renown as D.W. Griffith's cameraman. For the next year Billy Bitzer (Gottlob Wilhelm became "G.W." and Johann disappeared from his name.) was Dickson's most important assistant. During this period he operated the camera for more than one hundred films. These were the first of more than 1800 films that he would shoot during a very productive career.

Billy Bitzer was born on 21 April 1872 into a working class family in Roxbury, Massachusetts. In his youth he showed skill at drawing which his father encouraged by sending him to drawing classes. Later he apprenticed in a metal engraving and design shop and he worked briefly for the Gorham silver company in Providence, Rhode Island. He quit Gorham and came to New York to take electrical courses at Cooper Union. A friend and fellow student, Fred Loring, worked at the Magic Introduction Co. and recommended that he apply there. According to Bitzer, Loring also worked briefly for the American Mutoscope Co. and induced Koopman to transfer Bitzer to the Mutoscope company. After Loring quit to try his luck as an electrical engineer for mining companies in the west Bitzer stayed on.

Bitzer's first job for the Mutoscope company was electrical work with motors and preparing Mutoscopes. Bitzer described it to Terry Ramsaye:

"E.B. Koopman hired me. H.N. Marvin was around the partitioned off office space. The floor was quite empty a little work shop had been partitioned off and also a film developing room and an adjoining film printing room. The big bulky Mutoscope camera was also there and several home made looking cabinets with Mutoscope reels in them and the turning mechanism to flip the pictures. Dickson had made some pictures. The work was chiefly ironing out the flaws in the camera testing motor speed changing storage batteries and what I liked best of all developing and printing the films. I had ruined many a table top with developer stains with the little camera I owned. (There was no drug store Kodak finishing done then) also I spent considerable money on buying developers, etc. Now I had big tanks full to play with. I liked the work immensely (one secret of success like your job.) ...".[607]

607 GU Ramsaye Collection. Bitzer to Ramsaye, 21 August 1940. Bitzer had written to Ramsaye earlier in August, 1940 and Ramsaye asked him some detailed questions about his early experiences at the Biograph Co.

Getting the Mutoscope in shape for manufacture was a priority. Casler designed a working model but now it had to be produced in quantity – and with quality. Before this could happen there were problems to solve. The machines would be made in Canastota, but the rolls of pictures would be made at the plant in Hoboken and there were important details to work out before manufacture could begin. Printing

A table top version of the Mutoscope open to show the reel and its very simple mechanism. When the crank was turned the reel revolved and a wooden lever at the top held the images back so they could be viewed one at a time. [EHS.]

pictures for the Mutoscope was a slow, tedious process. It took more than thirty minutes to print a film that ran one minute. In the darkroom, the person operating the printing machine had to check the alignment of each frame and the exposure took about one second (the camera usually exposed thirty frames in one second). The prints for the Mutoscope were made on long rolls of bromide paper which was ridged enough to avoid curl and stay flat as image after image flipped past the observer's eyes. A minute of viewing consisted of more than 1900 individual images and each frame was separated by blank space which provided the area to mount the prints onto the hub of the reel. To assemble the roll, the long strips of prints had to be cut apart and kept in sequence, then they were mounted onto the hub with the blank space hidden inside the hub. Each image had to be secure enough that they would not slip or wobble because if they slipped during printing or wobbled on the reel the viewing experience would be unacceptable. In the early stages Dickson's crew resorted to some ingenious improvisation:

"... Loring and myself were trying to dope out some way of assembling easily the mutoscope pictures which when put together resembled stacks of playing cards stood on end and mounted in a circle upon a wooden spool. We had trouble getting the last bunch in evenly. Casler had forced the sample reels in by hand at Canastota but a more mechanical way was necessary. We wore elastic arm bands to keep the shirt sleeves at desired cuff length in those days. A round rubber, covered with cotton or silk webbing was one type, by punching round holes through the cards opening the sleeve rubber and inserting it through these holes and then closing the band again we could stretch the circle over the wooden core spool. ..."[608]

According to Bitzer, the flanges to hold the Mutoscope images steady were designed by Joseph Mason who had a machine shop in New

608 GU Ramsaye Collection. Bitzer to Terry Ramsaye, [26] August 1940.

609 NARA and
NMAH Hendricks.
The assets at 101
Beekman St. were
sold at sheriff's sale in
June or July 1896 and
despite Woodville
Latham's resistance,
their patents were
acquired by the E. &
H.T. Anthony
Company. After the
sheriff's sale, Raff &
Gammon bought the
Beekman Street
property with the
intent of starting their
own film production
organization. Their
plans never worked
out. The Lathams
wanted to continue in
the business but were
never again involved
in production or
distribution. During
1896 and 1897 they
testified in the various
patent challenges that
arose as several
projectors were
patented and their
testimony is an
important part of the
historical record of
the period. Both of
the Latham boys died
unexpectedly and
tragically. Otway
Latham died on 10
August 1906 of
peritonitis and heart
failure. Gray Latham
died on 3 April 1907
from injuries caused
by a fall off a crowded
trolley car a few days
earlier. Completing
the tragic demise of
the Latham family,
Otway's former wife,
Natalie Dole Latham
a socialite and painter,
committed suicide in
Paris on 7 March
1907, a month before
Gray's death.
Woodville Latham
survived his boys and
died naturally in
November 1911 a few
months after
testifying in Equity
5/167, Patents Co. v.
Imp.

York. Mason was persuaded to sell his interest in his shop and join the Mutoscope company as a machinist-technician. Dickson gave him training as a camera operator and he proved to be a versatile Jack of all trades. Mason stayed with the Mutoscope company into the early 1900s and later he was one of the technicians who worked on the Prisma color process.

There is no record of all the employees hired during the beginning months of the Mutoscope company but one that is known stands out, Dickson's friend Eugene Lauste. Lauste continued to work for the Lathams through 1895 but he quit after the Latham's lost control of their business. During 1895 the Lathams moved to a studio and technical facility at 101 Beekman St. in Manhattan. Despite occasional successful exhibits, their projections were never very successful and they continued to operate on a tight margin. Early in 1896 the Lambda company was reorganized as the Eidoloscope Company with the prestigious photograph concern, E. & H.T. Anthony Co. as principal investor. Even with new backing they continued to have financial problems. These were aggravated by a dispute between the company and the Lathams. The investors wanted the Lathams' patents assigned to the company and Woodville refused. As a result, Grey and Otway were forced out of managerial positions. It was at this point that Lauste went to Dickson looking for a new position. Dickson told him to talk to Koopman who hired him as a machinist, electrician and equipment operator. Lauste was now an experienced film veteran. He had built a number of cameras and projectors for the Lathams; developed and printed films and operated the cameras during film shoots. His most significant contribution was the modification of one of their cameras to increase the amount of film that could be shot. The capacity was increased to almost ten minutes of exposure – about the capacity of most 35mm cameras used during subsequent years. Lauste and Grey Latham used two modified cameras to film a bull fight in Mexico City. The resulting film ran nearly twenty minutes – one of the longest films shown during the first days of film exhibition.[609] Lauste remained with the Mutoscope company for the next five years and he worked with Dickson for most of the next decade.

In 1908 when D.W. Griffith directed his first film for the Biograph Company, the successor to the Mutoscope Company, his cameraman was Arthur Marvin, the brother of Harry Marvin. Arthur Marvin and Bitzer were the anchors of the company's staff of capable camera operators and when Griffith began directing they each had more than ten years experience filming all kinds of subjects in all kinds of places. While there is no record confirming that Arthur was one of Dickson's students, Arthur's career extends back to 1897 and he may well have started under Dickson. If not, he benefitted from the training and work practices that Dickson established for the Mutoscope company. The objective was to hire capable people, train them and make them capable of working together following established production patterns and procedures. As we will see, Dickson's prototype worked very well.

The Mutoscope was conceived as a convenient method of illustrating various concepts and actions and the intent was to market it as a business tool. This film of an engine pump was one of the earliest productions (number 6 in the company's production log) and was, in all likelihood, intended to be shown to potential investors and used to demonstrate the Mutoscope as a commercial instrument. [LC.]

Biographing

Several months passed before all the pieces were in place and film production could begin. A few tests were made with the Mutograph, but during the year following the sparring match between Casler and Marvin, surprisingly few films seem to have been shot. The bout between Professor Leonard and Bert Hosley was logged as the first production of the Mutoscope company – actually, the first four productions since it seems to have been four rounds. The fifth and sixth productions were tests probably made to demonstrate the Mutoscope's use as a sales tool. Number five was "Threshing Machine" and six was "Engine and Pump". These seem to have been made in Canastota or in the work rooms on the sixth floor of at 841 Broadway. Some of the tests did not make it into the company's production book. In his autobiography Bitzer described some of the early attempts to show the sales potential of the Mutoscope:

"The first pictures we took were of loom-weaving materials which the traveling salesman could use to show merchants what they were buying. We also photographed very large machines, whose working parts could be demonstrated by this method better than they could by chart. All the salesman needed was to carry a lightweight box with a cord to hook into an electric plug. Inside the box was a series of postcard size flip pictures, which could be stopped at any point for discussion or inspection, and were a great boon to sales."[610]

Bitzer's several accounts of these early days at the Mutoscope headquarters demonstrate the company's focus on service for business, but while they were preparing for production the situation changed.

610 Bitzer, Op. Cit., p. 9.

Among the projects that never got beyond a test was an attempt to convert a Mutoscope into a projector. It was apparently devised by Dickson since the photo has annotations in his hand. The Mutoscope images were to be projected onto a glass screen for viewing. [NMAH.]

When the days warmed and the sun became brighter, improving conditions for filming, the company faced unanticipated competition. Reports of the debuts of moving picture projectors were appearing in newspapers, journals and the entertainment press. As it became clear that projection was capturing the public's interest, the attractiveness of peep show machines began to fade.

The Lumières' Cinématographe opened at the Salon Indien of the Grand Café on 28 December 1895, the day after the Mutoscope Company was organized. That same December Thomas Armat bought a railroad ticket so Frank Gammon could come to Washington, DC for a demonstration of Armat's Phantoscope projector. By the 28th Raff & Gammon were negotiating an agreement with Armat and making plans to show the Phantoscope to Edison and Gilmore. In January Raff & Gammon told Dickson that they were restructuring the company because of the declining Kinetoscope business. That same month Robert Paul demonstrated his Theatrograph projector at the Royal Photographic Society and in February it was used to show films at the Olympia Theatre in London. By March Birt Acres' Kineopticon was also playing in London.

Films were projected in New York the next month and by 23 April when Armat's Phantoscope opened at Koster & Bial's Music Hall as Edison' Vitascope, several other projecting machines were waiting in the wings. In the months after the Vitascope premiered at Koster & Bial's one projection machine after another opened at theaters in New York City. April was the end of the theater season and attendance at the not yet air-conditioned theaters in mid-town Manhattan usually slacked-off during the summer, but the novelty of film projections seems to have enlivened the summer of 1896.

This eruption of interest was not lost on Dickson and his associates. They had experimented with projection and had some ideas but it suddenly became important to give projection more serious attention. Bitzer described the activities in New York:

"... The early attention was all centered upon Mutoscopes. We had made some experiments towards projecting pictures, by throwing two arc lights on the mutoscope reel and projecting this reflected light through a lense

[sic] upon the screen. When Edisons [sic] Vitascope came out at Koster and Bial's Music Hall we removed some interferences from the inside of our camera and progected [sic] an arc light into a mirror at right angles upon a positive film that we made and the brilliancy as compared to Mutoscope reflected light was so startling with this wide film that Casler at Canastota was informed and began furiously building the mechanism for a projected [sic] ...".[611]

The earlier experiments with projection were very limited and there is no evidence of a serious effort to build a projector before the spring of 1896. As late as November, 1895, while Dickson and Casler were experimenting on various designs for the Mutoscope, the only experiments with projection were the modifications made to the Mutoscope machines and the Mutograph camera. In testimony for Patent Interference 18,461, Casler said that in November the camera was modified by adding pegs to change the movement of the film and a mirror was set at an angle to pass light through the lens. Since this patent hearing was intended to settle conflicting claims about who projected movement first, Casler would have tried to put a best foot forward. Ultimately the Patent Office ruled in Armat's favor because he had patented a machine designed specifically for projection while both the Lathams and Casler had used a camera which was modified for projection.

The test using the Mutograph as a projector is reminiscent of Dickson's attempt to modify the Kinetoscope for the Lathams a year earlier. Even late in his life Dickson was convinced that the design of a projector was based on the camera and almost all of the experiments with projection that he made involved using a camera – back as far as his projection for Edison in 1889. He insisted that Edison had no need of turning to Armat for a working projector. The following quotation from a letter written to Earl Theisen while Dickson was working on his paper for the SMPE typifies his feeling about the ease of designing a projector:

"En passant, I never quite understood Mr Edisons [sic] necessity to use the Armat patents as we had all that we needed in the Kinetograph taking & projecting machine.

"The Kinetograph had a Geneva Stop motion which I always came back to – the film I settled to the size & picture of today with 4 holes (*slightly* smaller than now) & sprocket wheel to match these perforations ... & owing to the slight film shrinkage after Developement [sic] I used a different sprocket wheel a shade smaller to fit – for projection ...".[612]

As Bitzer reported, the success of the Vitascope at Koster & Bial's started a flurry of activity and some weeks later Canastota had a projector ready. Sometime during the summer it was installed on the sixth floor of 841 Broadway and demonstrations for the proprietors of New York theaters began .[613]

The Biograph, the chosen name for the projector, was an awkward, bulky and noisy machine, but as Bitzer indicates, the image it produced was more impressive than any of its competitors. Bitzer's comment indicates that he and his associates were surprised by the results of the

611 GU Ramsaye. Bitzer to Ramsaye, August 1940.

612 Academy Library, Dickson to Theisen, 26 October 1932.

613 GU Ramsaye. Bitzer to Ramsaye, August 1940.

The Biograph was universally regarded as the most outstanding projector of its day but it was huge and so complicated to operate that the company had to supply operators trained to handle it. [NMAH.]

test and were encouraged to shift emphasis from peep show to projector.

Dickson was probably not as startled as the others. He had first hand experience with the problems with miniaturization and was a consistent advocate of increasing the size of the image. The Biograph was designed to use film the same size as the negatives produced by the Mutograph camera, i.e. 2 and 23/32 inches wide by 2 inches high. It was several times larger than the image that Dickson devised for Edison and which was now the size adopted by Lumière, Paul and a growing number of competitors. (The Edison "standard" was 1 inch wide by ¾ inches high.) The larger format of the Mutoscope-Biograph allowed more light to reach the unexposed film in the camera which improved registration, i.e. made each image sharper. More light reached the screen during projection and a much larger image could be projected. Larger sizes, and a brighter, sharper image gave the Biograph a distinct advantage over competitors. The quality was also improved because the images were steadied by filming and projecting at thirty or more frames per second – the rate Dickson had favored with the Kinetograph. Following the Lumières' lead, many Europeans, and some Americans, were electing to film at about fifteen or sixteen frames per second. Because film was priced by the foot this made their films less costly, but the trade-off was an increase in flicker – one of the most frequent complaints of silent film patrons. Being projected at the same speed as exposure, the Biograph's picture was steadier and had less flicker – hence, was more realistic. Even though the Mutoscope company was late into the market, they arrived with a superior product and quickly secured a solid place for themselves.

While the image was an improvement, the Biograph was far from perfect. The projector was very noisy and very difficult to operate. Bitzer called it a thrashing machine and he compared it to a coffin (because of its size). He said that operating the projector was like running a trolley car. The camera was also immense, complicated and awkward. These negative factors were the consequence of using larger film, running at comparatively rapid speeds and using a mechanism designed to avoid conflict with Edison's patents. It took a large case to house a large mechanism to handle large film. The size and weight were increased even more by a heavy and bulky motor needed to drive the mechanism and provide the precision that a well regulated motor afforded. Since motors vibrated, an iron base was added to reduce the effect.

The effort to evade Edison's patents – as well as those of the Lumières, Lathams, Armat, Paul and Acres – made the design complicated so both the camera and projector were difficult to operate. The sprockets which guided the movement of film through the Kinetograph and Kinetoscope were deliberately avoided in the Mutograph and Biograph. The film was advanced by friction and a beater cam movement. Registration was uneven in the camera (i.e. the space between each frame was not the same) but this was compensated for by making one perforation on each side of the film at the time of exposure. The two perforations were used to register the film during printing. This assured that the frames would be properly aligned during printing. Because the prints had no perforations, the operator of the projector had to constantly adjust the film to keep it in frame.[614]

The Biograph projectors and the films produced for them were not sold or leased. Because the projector was unwieldy and complicated but capable of producing an outstanding, even dramatic spectacle, the company decided they would not emulate Edison's practice of marketing machines and films through agents. Instead, they offered individual exhibitors an entertainment package: projector (or Mutoscope), an operator (or maintenance person) and a program of films which would change regularly. This was similar to the way the Lumières marketed their Cinématographe in 1896. The Lumières sent a camera operator into the field with arrangements to show the films he shot along with others in their repertoire at various venues around the world. But the plan for the Biograph was more focused. The projector was particularly effective in a large auditorium so they concentrated on theaters in urban areas that catered to middle-class, family audiences. While this was a restricted approach, it was where the most reliable and monied audience could be found. The plan for the Mutoscope was similar, but less tailored to a specific audience.

This scheme seems to have evolved over the summer while work on the Biograph progressed. During that summer of 1896 various projectors were being featured in New York and audiences responded

614 Bitzer, *Billy Bitzer, His Story*, pp. 13–20.

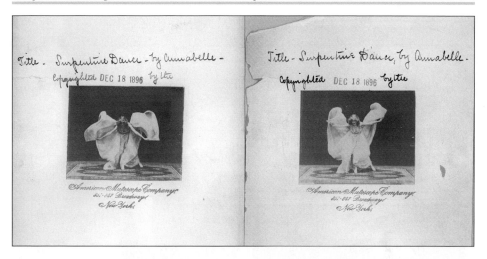

well to them. After opening in late April, the Armat-Edison Vitascope continued its run at Koster & Bial's Music Hall. It opened in Boston and Philadelphia in May; by August it had been seen by audiences in New Orleans, Los Angeles and Canada. The Lathams' projector, improved with a new intermittent movement and re-dubbed the Eidoloscope by its new proprietors, opened at Hammerstein's Olympia Music Hall in May where it remained for eight weeks. The Lumières' Cinématographe opened at B.F. Keith's New Union Square Theater at the end of June. The Lumières sent Felix Mesguich as their operator-representative and the arrangements were made by W.B. Hurd, Lumières' representative in the U.S. The Cinématographe was in Philadelphia in July and New Haven in August. In August Birt Acres' Kineopticon opened at Tony Pastor's theater in New York. It was presented under the auspices of A. Curtis Bond. By this time a number of C. Francis Jenkins' Phantoscopes had been sold to entrepreneurs in smaller American cities.

Sometime during the summer the Mutoscope company reached an agreement to include Biograph projections as an "act" in a variety show which was being produced by Charles B. Jefferson, son of the storied actor Joseph Jefferson. The show, which featured one of Dickson's favorites, Eugen Sandow, was scheduled to open at the beginning of September when the new theater season began. There would be trial runs of one week in Pittsburgh, Philadelphia and Brooklyn and then an opening in New York. Although this agreement was signed during the summer, the negotiations may have started earlier. Sandow was one of the first persons filmed in the new rooftop studio.

The beginning of production in the new facilities revisited familiar territory. Five of the first six films made on the roof of 841 Broadway featured Annabelle, the dancer, and Sandow – at least as they were recorded in the company's meticulously maintained log of productions. Although no date was recorded, these were probably shot on one or two

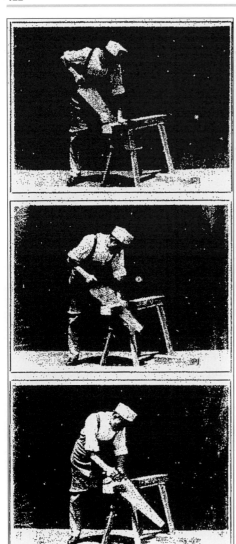

Annabelle and Sandow were popular and they repeated their popular performances for the Mutoscope company which were among the first films projected. But more prosaic subjects such as Saw-ing Wood were made. The com-pany's rooftop studio is easily identified by the carpet which ap-pears in many productions. It was decorative and defined the area where action could be filmed. The photo of Sandow is from a com-pany publicity brochure, The Age of Movement *issued c. 1901. [LC, AMPAS & MoMA.]*

sunny days in May or June 1896. Annabelle performed three dances and was costumed differently in each: "Skirt Dance", "Tambourine Dance" and "Serpentine Dance". Sandow, dressed in briefs, flexed muscles in films annotated as "Sandow (no sun)" and "Sandow (sun)". "Annabelle Skirt Dance" was entered in the log book after the two Sandow films which could indicate that these might have been filmed on the same day.[615] They were probably intended for Mutoscope showing since they were two of the most popular Kinetoscope subjects. Re-filming them gave the company a competitive product and allowed Dickson a chance to evaluate the new facility by comparing it with his

A scene from one of two films of Union Square that were the first shot outside the studio. The company's office was in a building on Broadway just below 14th Street which is the corner shown in this film. The camera was either in a window on a lower floor or on a canopy over an entrance. Elevating the camera allowed a more panoramic view of the area including the sharp turn of the trolley at the left of the frame. Keith's Union Square Theater where the Biograph was programmed for several years was just around the corner, off screen to the right. [LC.]

earlier work. These subjects proved durable enough because the two Sandow subjects and the "Serpentine Dance" (retitled as "Butterfly Dance") were still offered to customers in a catalog published in 1902.

Sandow and Annabelle were filmed for public entertainment, but the company had not given-up on tapping more than the amusement market. A more prosaic film subject was sandwiched in the middle of the Annabelle-Sandow titles. "Sawing Wood" was clearly intended to demonstrate that the Mutoscope could be used to show activities that were difficult to describe in words.[616]

If the log is chronologically accurate, these were not the first films made in New York city. Two films of Union Square precede the studio made titles and they give the clearest hint that production did not begin until the spring or early summer of 1896. The leaves on the trees in the square are well developed as they would have been in mid-May or June, so it is reasonable to assume that production began about that time. Dickson filmed the square from an overhead angle – probably from an overhang over a doorway or a second or third story window on the building next door to the building where the Mutoscope Co. had its office. This created a more interesting perspective, a bird's eye view that allowed the viewer to see more of the area. The camera was positioned so the corner of Fourteenth Street and Broadway was in the foreground. The activity of pedestrians, trolleys and other vehicles at the intersection gave the film motion and was the primary visual interest while the square and the taller buildings on the north side form a more stationary backdrop. One of these films remained in the company's repertoire.

616 Ibid.

The 1902 catalog pointed out that film No. 8, "Union Square" showed old style trolley cars rounding "Deadman's Curve".

That the first productions recorded in New York were outdoor scenes shows that Dickson and his partners had suddenly altered their production plans. Like the Kinetograph, the Mutoscope camera was designed for the controlled environment of a studio where the subjects could be brought to the camera. Like its cousin, the size and weight of the Mutograph made it difficult to work in the open. By the time production began, the public's taste was changing. When the Vitascope opened at Koster & Bial's it was Robert Paul's film of waves breaking on the shore at Dover that most attracted the interest of the audience. The familiar Black Maria films "Umbrella Dance", "The Barber Shop", "Burlesque Boxing", "The Bar-room", etc., drew less attention. The press agreed. In their review of the opening the *New York Times* discussed Paul's film: "... but it was the waves tumbling in on a beach and about a stone pier that caused the spectators to cheer and to marvel most of all. Big rollers broke on the beach foam flew high, and the weakened waters poured far up the beach. Then great combers arose and pushed each other shoreward, one mounting above the other, until they seemed to fall with mighty force and all together on the shifty sand, whose yellow, receding motion could be plainly seen ...".[617] The film received similar attention from the *New York Journal* and the *New York Herald*. Dickson was aware of this. If he was not in the opening night audience, he attended soon after. He had made most of the films on the program and he would have been particularly struck by the response since he was about to launch competing fare.

Although Paul's film held New York's attention for a while, it was the Lumières who were popularizing this new genre on an international scale. Their cameramen traveled about Europe filming street scenes, tourist attractions and public events. These were shown to audiences in the many places they visited. The Cinématographe made its New York debut at Keith's Union Square Theater in June. Keith's was just around the corner from the Mutoscope offices so it was easy for Dickson and his associates to check the competition. If they were at the opening they would have seen "... Life Scenes, such as: – 'The Arrival of the Fast Express', 'A Morning Dip in the Surf', 'The Old Gardener and the Naughty Boy'. 'London Street Arabs Dancing and Singing.' 'Parade of the 6th French Infantry' ...", Etc. Once again, the papers reacted favorably. On 6 July *The Dramatic Chronicle* commented that "... Nothing more realistic or thrilling than the 'Charge of the 7th Cuirassiers' has been seen on a local stage in many a month. It never fails to arouse ...". Although the Vitascope and Cinématographe were appearing during the slack summer theater season, they proved very popular. *The Dramatic Chronicle* said that the Cinématographe would continue at Keith's through the summer with a regular change of films including views taken in New York.[618]

By mid-summer it was evident that regardless of how bulky it was,

617 NMAH Hendricks. *New York Times*, 26 April 1896.

618 NMAH Hendricks. *New York Herald*, 28 June 1896 & *New York Dramatic Chronicle*, 6 July 1896.

the Mutograph would have to film outside the studio if it was to meet its competition.

Dickson's first venture away from the Union Square area was to film a bicycle parade on the Boulevard (upper Broadway) – a particularly popular public event during the bicycle-crazed 1890s. During the summer of 1896 an exhibition of bicycles at Madison Square Garden attracted huge crowds.[619] The two films he made showed a variety of street activity. In addition to the bicyclists, there are trolleys, carriages, pedestrians and onlookers. As in the films of Union Square, Dickson had the camera elevated above the heads of the onlookers and positioned so that the parading vehicles passed the camera at a diagonal from the left side. A treed boulevard in the middle background set off the action in the foreground.

In July he left the city to make a dozen films in Atlantic City and five films of the Pennsylvania Railroad line between New York City and Philadelphia. Since railroads were the most efficient and fastest way for vacationers and weekenders from New York and Philadelphia to get to Atlantic City, this series seems intended as promotional matter for the railroad, albeit a very soft-sell form of advertising. It may well have been made at the request – or commission – of the Pennsylvania Railroad. It will be remembered that Koopman regarded the Mutoscope primarily as a tool for advertising with entertainment taking a secondary role. The solid financial backing that KMCD received shows that he was successful using that approach. Railroads were well represented on the board of the Mutoscope company and the railroad men had probably invested because they found the prospect of using the Mutoscope as a promotional tool attractive. Films with a common theme and an evident promotional purpose were frequently produced by the Mutoscope Company, indicating that advertising and promotion were foremost in the minds of Dickson's associates during and after the summer of 1896.

These films did not make it into the company's long-term repertoire and it seems probable that they were primarily used for Mutoscope showing, probably strategically placed in railroad stations, hotels, bars and other places where the railroad's potential customers had a minute or two to while away. There is no record confirming that the railroad bought Mutoscopes for this purpose, but because Atlantic City is a summer resort, there would have been little value in showing the films after the end of August.

Among the Atlantic City films was a sea scene – waves breaking on the beach. The three surviving frames from this film are rather tame, apparently less dramatic than Robert Paul's film, but probably lively enough to satisfy early audiences who were fascinated by moving water. Over the next months Dickson continued to supply images of water in motion for the company's programs. The films of bathers are rather predictable, set up much like post cards, but moving post cards would have been a genuine novelty. One of these, Boys Bathing at Atlantic City shows a group playing leap frog and is somewhat reminiscent of

619 *The Encyclopedia of New York City* (New Haven & London, Yale University Press, 1995), 107. The entry by Trudy E. Bell says that 120,000 people attended the exhibition "... including a number of the city's most socially prominent residents."

early films that the Lumières made at the shore. In keeping with the underlying theme of transport, there are a pictures of trolleys discharging passengers and horse-drawn busses leaving the railroad depot. To tie the train trip to fun at the beach, Dickson made two films from the front of a trolley as it traveled through town. Three of the films on the Pennsylvania Railroad were filmed with the camera on a car at the front of the moving train, allowing the viewers a view of the scenery along the line that they would not have in a passenger car. These are among the first "phantom rides", a very popular genre during the first decade of film viewing. Dickson believed that movies should record movement, so putting the camera in a moving vehicle was an obvious way to animate static objects like buildings, trees and geography. At the end of the 19th century, trains moved faster than any other mode of transport so the films shot from the front of a train produced a unique sensation of movement. Audiences were thrilled, so Dickson and his associates at the Mutoscope Company continued to produce them and over the years Dickson made several remarkable examples of the genre which became something of a signature for the Mutoscope Company.

While in Atlantic City, Dickson made two films that do not fit the travel package. Monkey's Feast is a crude film which is disturbing by modern standards. It featured two monkeys who were eating bananas. It was shot in a semi-close up with a white cloth casually draped behind them to provide contrast. The monkeys were restrictively chained so they wouldn't – couldn't – move out of frame. Although it would offend today's audiences, it apparently amused Dickson and did not offend his contemporaries. It was still available in the Company's 1902, catalog. In a more acceptable vein, Dickson shot the Atlantic City Fire Department throwing a stream of water to demonstrate a pumper in action.[620] Fortunately fire departments proved more saleable than monkeys as this was the first of a steady stream of fire department films made by Dickson, his disciples and almost every other pioneer film producer. Early film enthusiasts were as fascinated with firemen in action as they were with trains and water. (It will be remembered that Dickson had made a "Fire Rescue Scene" in the Black Maria.) Come to think of it, the interest in fire fighting has never quite abated – nor has our less passionate, but still persistent interest in our simian cousins.

In August Dickson joined his wife and sister who were vacationing in Saratoga Springs, New York. Antonia had gone there at the end of May. In July she was injured in a fall from a bicycle and spent part of the time in bed. Before leaving for Saratoga Springs, Dickson made several films at the New York studio. Annabelle returned to perform a charming flag dance, holding a small flag in her right hand and appropriately attired in red and white stripes. Sandow again demonstrated his chest expansion and Dickson recorded a brief moment from the sensational Broadway drama *Trilby*. The excerpt from *Trilby* continues the recording of New York theater which Dickson had begun for Edison, but *Trilby* is certainly better known and better remembered than the several plays filmed in the Black Maria. *Trilby*, which opened in New

620 MoMA and Copyright deposits at the Library of Congress. Gordon Hendricks dates "Fire Engine at Work" as taken before 18 July 1896 from an article in *Atlantic City Daily-Union* of 18 July which reported that "Agent Stewart of the American Ball Nozzle Company gave an exhibition of the possibilities of the patent ball nozzle this morning at North Carolina Ave. with the view of having it introduced into the fire department in this city. A States engine was used to force the water and was run at its highest speed ... The test was witnessed by Chief Whippey, ex-chief Lackey, Lewis Evans and other prominent members of the fire department. The exhibition was photographed for a Kinetoscope by the Edison company and will be reproduced in the Boardwalk in a few days." Hendricks points out that no such film was shown on Edison's Kinetoscope so he assumed, quite reasonably, that this was the filming by the Mutoscope Co. The comment that it would be shown soon on the Boardwalk is the only indication that these films might have been exhibited during the summer of 1896, though Atlantic City audiences might not have seen the fire department since the company's records say the film was only 8 feet long, too short to make a complete Mutoscope roll.

Dances continued as popular fare with theater audiences and fans of the Mutoscope. Annabelle was filmed several times with different costumes and new choreography such as this Flag Dance. The brief scene from Trilby continued the recording of moments from popular theater that started at the Edison company. These images were sent by the company to register copyright for the films. [LC.]

York in 1895, was based on George du Maurier's 1894 novel of the same name. Drawn from his experiences as a student in Paris it was a story of innocence, bohemian life in Paris and mesmeric dominance. The story captured the public's fancy and its anti-hero, Svengali became a popular characterization of domination and bewitchment. Svengali does not appear in Dickson's less-than-a minute long episode from the play and there is only a hint of the erotic overtones of the original. Instead, the innocent heroine, Trilby O'Ferrall was filmed carrying on an animated conversation with her student friend "Little Billee" (though he looks more like a business man than a student). The actress who played Trilby was, apparently, Virginia Harned who was perform-

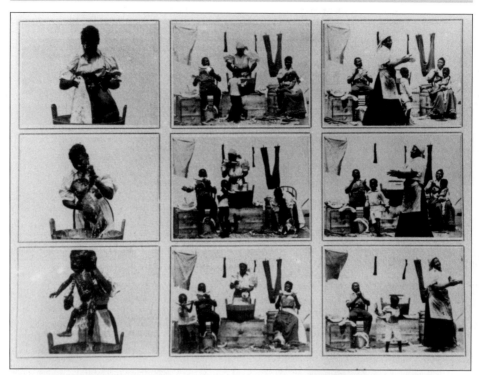

The first films featuring African Americans displayed common stereotypes. The film on the left, A Hard Wash *was one of the company's most popular and frequently shown titles – no matter how hard she scrubbed, the baby remained black. In the center is* Watermelon Feast *and* Dancing Darkies *is on the right (only the young boy dances). The featured group may have been a family appearing at a local theater. [Musser.]*

ing the role in the stage production. The actor playing Little Billee is unidentified, but may be either Burr McIntosh or Leo Ditrichstein who were supporting her in the production which featured Wilton Lackaye as Svengali. Although they were appropriately costumed as they might have been on stage, the only props were the table that she sits on and a chair that Billee occupied. Like most of these early staged productions, it was shot against a black backdrop similar to the dark area behind the stage in the Black Maria. The only other decoration was the oriental rug which defined the area of camera exposure (and was more pleasant to look at than the wooden rails that were so evident in the Black Maria films). [621]

The next three films listed in the registry, "A Hard Wash", "Watermelon Feast" and "Dancing Darkies" were made with a group, possibly a family, of African Americans. The best known and most notorious title is "A Hard Wash" which shows a African American woman scrubbing a naked black child in a wash tub. The woman and child were very black and a white cloth back drop, substituted for the black one used previously, intensified the contrast. A lather of white

[621] MoMA, Biograph photo book; *The Oxford Companion to English Literature* and Daniel Blum, *A Pictorial History of the American Theatre* (New York, Greenburg Publisher, 1950).

Dickson's mixed heritage included strong ties to Virginia where his mother was born. He and his sisters lived in Petersburg for a few years. His wife Lucie Archer was from there and her family had lived through the Civil War. When they married the reforms of emancipation and reconstruction were being reversed and racism and Jim Crow were on the rise. This undated picture of the Archer family was taken at Lucie's brother Col. Alexander Archer's home in Richmond. Lucie is front left, next to her is Adele Archer Small, Adele's daughter (also named Adele) and her brother, Col. Archer. The others are unidentified. Their maid was included with the family, but in uniform and in the background. The photograph was given to Gordon Hendricks by Allene Archer. [NMAH.]

suds vigorously applied, was particularly visible against the child's black skin. This sharp contrast of blacks and whites was not lost on audiences who supposedly assumed that the mother was trying to scrub away blackness. Though offensive today, "A Hard Wash" proved to be one of the company's most popular early productions. It was among the first films shown when the Biograph projection programs opened in theater after theater in the U.S. and abroad. In testimony to the impact the film had, Edison made a version of this film, "A Morning Bath" the following October. Edison's film was almost identical in staging and content and was made within a few days of the first projection of Dickson's film.

"Watermelon Feast" was described in the company's catalog as "A family of darkies revelling [sic] in a feast of the favorite fruit of their race". The catalog described "Dancing Darkies" inaccurately as "A company of little darkies showing off their paces to the music of a banjo". No banjo is evident in the surviving frames of the film and only one young boy danced.

The watermelon stereotype was so well established that it is hardly surprising to see it acted out early in the Mutoscope company's production schedule. Edison made a watermelon film about a month later – late August or early September 1896 – although it was staged differently from Dickson's.[622] Although Dickson's films exploited popular stereotypes and pandered to the prejudices of the dominant middle class white audience, they are not stridently racial. The performers were dressed to emphasize the class and racial differences and a centrally placed wash tub and cloths hanging on the line emphasized that this was a view of life at the back of the house. In spite of this, the performers seem to be enjoying what they are doing and there is an air of dignity in the staging that moderates the blatant racial tone. As noted earlier, Dickson's American roots were in Virginia where racial separation and segregation were the norm and the N___ word came easily from his lips. It is not likely that he was a rabid segregationist however. Instead, he probably had a very paternalistic attitude towards Blacks, regarding them as a race apart that was useful but inferior. A picture of his wife's family, taken at the home of her brother Alex Archer in Richmond, Virginia shows Lucie, her brother, his wife, daughter and two other family members with a Black servant standing dutifully in the background. A servant, but close enough to the Archers to be included in a family photo.

"Watermelon Feast" and "Dancing Darkies" were the first productions that seem "original", i.e. staged for filming rather than adapted from an existing performance such as the scene from"Trilby", Annabelle's dance repertoire or Sandow's sundry poses. Although the African American group may have been performing at one of New York's entertainment sites, the filming has a unique quality that is not theatrical. A few of these staged-for-film productions had been made for Edison, but Dickson seems to have been reluctant to test his own imagination. Most of his original sketches were light hearted treatments of real situations that were familiar to him and his co-workers: a blacksmith and his helpers sharing a bottle or a group of men in a barber shop. His next attempt at an original sketch was made soon after "A Hard Wash." In "Stable on Fire" men led horses to safety and pulled a wagon out of a smoke-filled stable door. It was reminiscent of "Fire Rescue" made earlier for Edison. Both films were meant to simulate a real, life-threatening situation as closely as possible and the intent was documentary rather than fictional. He had little hope of carting the bulky Mutograph to a real fire, and though staged, Dickson tried very hard to create a realistic situation and a realistic look – in effect a pre-cursor to neo-realism. "Stable on Fire" shot outdoors in what appears to be real stable yard had a more realistic look than "Fire

622 Musser, *Edison Motion Pictures, 1890–1900*, pp. 233 & 250. Musser credits James White with producing both of Edison's films for Raff & Gammon.

Rescue" which was filmed on the stage of the Black Maria. The men leading the horses out of the burning stable were dressed naturally and moved quickly as they would in an emergency. The company's 1902 catalog called it "Very realistic". It would not deceive a modern audience, but the viewers in 1896 who were experiencing filmed action for the first time probably found the film exciting and realistic since they were closer to the action than most of them would have been if they were at a real fire.

Although Dickson seemed reluctant to stage fiction, he was quite comfortable with staging or emulating real life situations. As we have seen, he planned and rehearsed the action and was not shy about asking anyone, even the eminent and powerful, to move in a certain way to a certain place at a certain time. He had only a limited amount of film to work with and a camera that was immobile once put in place, so it made sense to have the most control possible over the subject being filmed. It produced an image which was more pleasing to the audience and easier to understand.

Staging reality is generally frowned on today, but it was not unusual in the beginning years of film production and the public rarely objected to the practice. Although photographers had been documenting historical events and famous personalities since the 1850s, in the 1890s, most of the illustrations in books, magazines and newspapers were provided by artists working from photographs, written notes or quickly drawn sketches. Until the 1880s, photo emulsions were too slow for instantaneous photography and even with the introduction of roll film and improved emulsions, professional cameras were still large and unwieldy so portraits and pictures taken in the wake of an event were more common than on-the-spot coverage of breaking stories. The introduction of the half-tone process in the 1890s made it easier to print photos in newspapers and magazines, but journalistic photography was still in the developmental stage when Dickson began making films and the notion that illustrations should be authentic, accurate and unstaged was still a promise rather than reality.

"Stable on Fire" was filmed at Buzzard's Bay, Massachusetts, probably in late August 1896.[623] On 29 August, the *Orange Journal* reported that Dickson had visited "his friend" Joseph Jefferson at his estate in Buzzard's Bay, so Dickson seems to have gone to Buzzard's Bay after a very brief mid-August vacation in Saratoga Springs. If Dickson had met the prominent American actor, it was probably through Joseph Jefferson's son, Charles B. Jefferson. Charles Jefferson was producing Sandow's "Olympia" which was scheduled to open in two weeks with films by the Mutoscope company as a part of the bill. Joseph Jefferson was a genuine legend of the American stage and his most legendary role was as Rip Van Winkle. He had been appearing in the role since 1865 when he commissioned Dion Boucicault to create a play from Washington Irving's popular story. The play opened in London and during the ensuing thirty years he played the role in theaters throughout Europe and North America. Dickson, assisted by

623 Biograph catalog, 1902, p. 148.

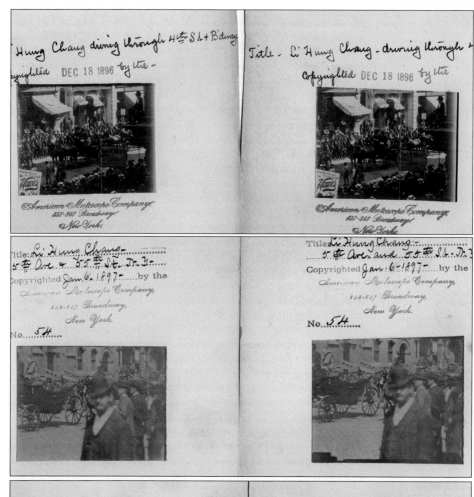

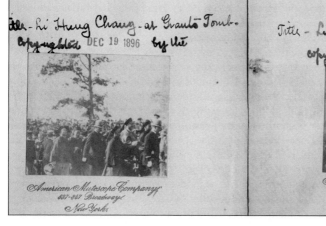

Facing page: *The visit of the Chinese diplomat and general Li Hung Chang was the first public event filmed by the Mutoscope company. There was general excitement at the visit of a prominent Asian. Dickson made three films during the three day visit. On the top is Chang's carriage passing 4th and Broadway after his arrival; in the center, on 5th Avenue near 55th Street on the second day; and at Grant's Tomb on the final day of his visit (bottom). The final film is significant because, as indicated in the two images following his approach to the nearly completed monument. This was accomplished despite the weight and bulk of the Mutoscope camera. [LC.]*

624 *Webster's Biographical Dictionary*; *Reader's Encyclopedia of American Literature*; MoMA; Hendricks, *Beginnings of the Biograph*, p. 27. The titles of the eight films vary slightly but as listed in the company's photo book, they are: "Rip Meeting the Dwarf", "Rip's Toast", "Exit of Rip and the Dwarf", "Rip Passing Over the Mountain", "Rip's Toast to Hudson and Crew", "Rip's Twenty Years Sleep", "Awakening of Rip" and "Rip Leaving Sleepy Hollow". According to the production log, a secondary negative, combining all of the scenes was made in 1897.

Billy Bitzer, filmed Jefferson in eight abbreviated scenes from the play. A large rock on Jefferson's estate in Buzzard's Bay was a convenient substitute for the Catskills and the outdoor setting and Dickson's placement of the camera gave his audience a new view of the traditional stage vehicle. Although the scenes were only excerpts from the drama, Dickson's camera brought the spectator closer to the action and the rocks and trees in the background gave the scenes a sense of reality not possible on stage. All of the scenes were filmed at the same rock, but the camera was moved so that each scene had a different background. For "Rip's Toast" the camera moved in for a ¾ shot which gave the audience an unusually clear view of Jefferson's face and gestures.

This was the most ambitious project the Mutoscope company had undertaken. The eight scenes were brief but they encapsulated as much of the original as possible in the thirty to forty second-long exposures allowed by the Mutograph camera.[624] It was the first multi-scene film production and earliest attempt to recreate a longer, well known literary work. Previously Dickson had filmed scenes from several plays for Edison, but each was a separate act and there was no attempt to emulate the complete play. In these eight films Rip (Joseph Jefferson) meets the Dwarf, they open a keg, drink together and Rip toasts Henry Hudson and his crew, falls asleep for twenty years, awakens with a long, white beard and goes back to his home. All in less than five minutes running time. Each scene could be shown as a separate element and the company seemed unwilling to try and present the complete production in its theatrical projections. It may have been offered in a succession of Mutoscopes, but there is no account of a showing of the complete set in a theater during 1896 and 1897. Instead, individual scenes were shown from time to time, the most frequently shown being "Rip's Toast".

After filming "Rip Van Winkle" Dickson returned to New York City to film Li Hung-Chang, a Chinese diplomat-general who came to the U.S. after attending the coronation of Tsar Nicholas. The visit of a prominent government official from China stirred a great deal of public interest. He arrived from Europe on 29 August aboard the "St. Louis" and was escorted to the Waldorf Hotel by a troupe of U.S. Cavalry. The next day he met with President Grover Cleveland at the Whitney residence and on the third day he visited Grant's Tomb (which was nearly complete but not yet dedicated). Dickson filmed him on each of the three days.

These were the first "news" films made for the company and they were to be part of the program for Sandow's *Olympia*. It was a chance to test how well the awkward Mutograph camera could perform. There was no chance to rehearse these takes, but Dickson, or his associates, were able to arrange advantageous filming locations. This was crucial to success since proper placement of the camera determined how well the shots would come out. On the 29th he was at an elevated location at 4th and Broadway which allowed him to record a clear overhead shot of Li Hung-Chang's procession as it moved diagonally from right to left across the frame. The camera was too far from the procession to get a close view of the visiting dignitary, but it was a clear view of the action. On the 30th he was across the street from the Whitney residence and Li Hung-Chang's carriage was filmed at an angle from street level. Even though they were apparently restrained from blocking the view, the crowd pressed into the frame. This was disadvantageous, but when the carriages moved away from the house, he got a good view of the occupants – but too far away for untrained eyes to see President Cleveland or Li Hung-Chang clearly. The next day, at Grant's tomb, Dickson achieved the seemingly impossible! He panned the camera from a view of the crowd to a clear shot of the dignitaries walking down wooden steps which had apparently been constructed at the uncompleted monument. There is no record of how the pan was done. According to Bitzer, the camera was very difficult to move. It is possible that the camera was mounted on a vehicle which could be moved smoothly.[625] These films were presented to Li Hung-Chang by Harry Marvin before he returned to China. Marvin also presented him with a table-top version of the Mutoscope.[626]

The three films of Li Hung-Chang brought the number of films in the company's library to fifty-five, a respectable backlog to support the public programs that would start soon, but production continued. They apparently had a commission from the New York Central Railroad who wanted a set of films similar to the one made for the Pennsylvania Railroad. The NY Central's line ran up the Hudson River valley to Albany then across New York state to Buffalo and Niagara Falls. The Falls were one of the most popular tourist attractions in North America and a favorite destination for honeymooners. The railroad promoted itself as the best and fastest route to Niagara. Their crack express train, the Empire State Express was touted to be the fastest train in the world, running at sixty miles per hour across upper New York state. Dickson was on the road for much of September filming the falls and the railroad. In the process he made a couple of side trips which may have included a visit to Pittsburgh in preparation for the opening of Sandow's *Olympia*.

The first of these films were made at West Point where he photographed cadets of the Military Academy in parade drill and cavalry action. Military and naval activities were as popular as moving water and fire departmens and these were the first of many military actions that Dickson would film over the next few years. The most interesting of the four is a cavalry troupe charging directly towards the camera. It emulated a film which Dickson had probably seen and admired at Keith's Union Square. Shot by an unknown Lumière camera operator, it showed a large troupe of French Cuirassiers charging directly at the camera. Dickson's West Point film was staged in much the same way, but because the troup of cadets was smaller than the troup of Cuirassiers the visual impact of Dickson's film was not as startling as the Lumière film – even though Dickson ratcheted the excitement up by having horses charge close to the camera, passing it on both sides. Audience

625 MoMA, Biograph photo book. Only three stills from this film survive but they show distinctly different scenes that could only be recorded as the camera was moved. These are not enough to determine how successful the pan was (i.e. how free from jerkiness or bumping), but as we will see, there are other films where the camera is panned, so we can only assume that it was successful.

626 Hendricks, *Beginnings of ...*, pp. 44–45. Hendricks quoted an article, "The Wonders of Photography" in The *Canastota Bee*, 3 October 1896 which told of the presentation to Li Hung-Chang. In 1901, one of the company's photographers, Raymond Ackerman filmed Li Hung-Chang in Beijing viewing the scene at Grants Tomb on a table top Mutoscope ("Li Hung Chang and Suite: Presentation of Parlor Mutoscope").

reactions to the Lumière films were very positive so Dickson would continue to atempt to match or exceed the standards set by his best known competitor. The reaction of the public to the Lumière film is demonstrated by the following description from *The Evening Times* (Providence) made after the Cinématographe opened at Keith's Opera House in that Rhode Island city on 7 September:

"... The enthusiasm gradually increases in volume as each succeeding picture is shown, until it culminates in an uproar when the mad, dashing charge of the Seventh Cavalry [Cuirassiers] is displayed. Then the spectators cheer and shout themselves hoarse, so realistic is the reproduction by the Lumières' Cinématographe.

"The bugle call advance is heard, the clanking of sabers rings out through the theatre and the ceaseless pattering of horses' hoofs, all add to one of the most exciting scenes ever displayed. Mr. Keith has surely never had a more popular playhouse ...".[627]

A dozen titles were made at Niagara Falls but there is no record of exactly when they were photographed. The entries in the production log seem to indicate that they were made immediately after the West Point films but this is not necessarily the case. Dickson's activities during the first half of September were not documented so we can only guess the sequence of production. He filmed William McKinley in Canton, Ohio on 17 or 18 September, and the *Canastota Bee* reported on 20 September that he and Koopman had visited Harry Marvin at his home in Canastota and that Koopman stayed for several days. The *Bee* later reported that Dickson filmed the Empire State Express Palatine, NY, near Canastota, at 12:13 p.m. on 30 October. An article in *Phonoscope*, based on an article in the *Albany Argus*, reported that it took ten days to plan and complete filming on the New York Central so it seems probable that Dickson was in Canastota during the last ten days of September.[628]

Regardless of when he was at the Falls, Dickson was only one of a procession of filmmakers traveling to Niagara. An Edison crew was there the previous June and Alexandre Promio, the cameraman sent by Lumières to make American scenes, visited the Falls shortly after he arrived in early September. Since this was very close to the time that Dickson was there, it is interesting to speculate on the possibility that they might have met.[629] Dickson made six films of the Falls themselves, one of the rapids above the falls and five films of the gorge and rapids below the falls. This gave the Mutoscope company a stock of rapidly rushing water to satisfy audiences reveling in images of rapid water movement. Two of the films of the Canadian Falls were made from Table Rock which was below the Falls on the Canadian side and these allowed audiences to see water rushing over the brink, hurtling past the camera and creating an impressive amount of spray. Films of the American Falls were made from Luna and Goat Islands located at the top of the falls. These emphasized the cascade over the precipice. There were two panoramas, one taken from a car on the Michigan Central Railroad, the other using an unidentified panning device placed oppo-

627 University of Iowa Library, Keith-Albee Collection.

628 NMAH, Hendricks; *Phonoscope*, 15 December 1896.

629 Musser, *Edison Motion Pictures ...*, pp. 208–210; Musser, *The Emergence of Cinema*, p. 143; Herbert & McKernan, *Who's Who of Victorian Cinema*, pp. 114–115. Musser credits supervision of the Edison film to James White and camera operation to William Heise. White may have supervised these films, but according to his testimony in Equity 6928, Edison v. Amer. Mutoscope, 9 February 1900, White was employed by Raff & Gammon until October 1896 when he left to join Edison. Since Raff & Gammon would have commissioned the Niagara Falls films, it is possible that they sent White to supervise production.

The Empire State Express *was one of the most sensational and popular of the company's films. By carefully positioning the camera close to the tracks and near a curve, the train grew in size, curved towards the audience then suddenly disappeared. First-time movie viewers were startled by the effect, especially those in the front rows. [LC.]*

site the American Falls – the second time that Dickson got the immobile Mutograph to move. Two of the films in the Gorge were panoramas. One shot from the Erie Railway above the gorge, the other from a trolley running along the edge of the river. Several of these films became staples for the company's early programming and at least three of them remained in the catalog through 1902.

Filming the New York Central Railroad required careful planning and several days of tests before Dickson found the results satisfactory. Five films made at Palatine, New York made it into the company's log, but apparently there were rejects that did not. One that survived the cut, "The Empire State Express", became one of the best known, most popular – and most sensational – of the early railroad films. Ten days seems a long time to prepare for the final take and Dickson may not have worked on it *all* that time. The problem seems to have been timing. Dickson was going for an effect – visual impact combining drama and surprise. To achieve this the Express would have to be in the frame from the beginning through to the end of the shot. Although Palatine was chosen because the trains slowed their run in order to take water from troughs along the edge of the track, they were still moving at high speed, so placing the camera in the right location and starting at the exact moment to complete the run was crucial to the effect. In the version of "The Empire State Express" that was accepted, the tracks curve from the right center of the frame around to the lower left hand corner. The left side of the frame is a pastoral scene with a farm and woods in the background. A crew is working on the tracks with the train visible as a small dot and puff of smoke on the tracks at the horizon. The train enlarges as it approaches the camera, the crew moves off, away from the track, and the train fills the frame, moving off screen on the left side. The shot ends as the last car passes. The visual impact was enhanced by placing camera very close to where the engine would pass. One set of tracks separates the camera from the train.

Dickson's visits to Keith's Union Square may have influenced the making of "Empire State Express". He had probably seen one of the best known Lumière productions, "L'arrivée d'un Train en Gare", a film often credited with causing viewers to scream, faint and duck for fear of being hit by an oncoming locomotive. In "Empire State Express" Dickson tried to intensify the threat – and succeeded. In retrospect, the earlier film is not very menacing – although it may have startled first time viewers. It was shot on the platform of a railroad station with a number of people awaiting the arrival. The train pulls into the station and slows to a stop. In contrast, Dickson filmed the Express is in open country and the track crew had to get out of the way as the train passed at high speed. There was nothing to indicate that it would stop or even slow down. Placing his camera close to the tracks emphasized the speed, nearness and size of the locomotive. The threat was intensified by enlarging the train from a small dot to full screen size, an effect similar to the threat created by the approach of the horses in the assault by the Cuirassiers.[630] The Mutoscope company would brag that this was "The greatest train view ever taken" in its 1902 catalog.

Party politics: Biographing the candidate

In mid-September, before filming the Empire State Express, Dickson was in Canton, Ohio to film presidential candidate William McKinley. Arrangements for this engagement were probably made through the candidate's brother Abner McKinley, a New York lawyer who owned stock in the Mutoscope company. The five films that resulted were publicity for McKinley's campaign and were probably produced with the blessing of the Republican Party's campaign committee. Four recorded a campaign parade on the afternoon of September 18, 1896 and the fifth was shot on the lawn of McKinley's home on North Market Street, a short distance from downtown Canton.

The 1896 presidential campaign was quite different from today's media marathons. The glib, William Jennings Bryan was pitted against the taciturn, stay-at-home William McKinley. The country was just emerging from the depression of 1893–1894 and economic issues were of primary concern to the voters. Bryan campaigned for labor and free silver. He opened his campaign with one of the most famous speeches in American political history, his ringing condemnation of the gold standard: "You shall not press down upon the brow of labor this crown of thorn. You shall not crucify mankind upon a cross of gold".[631] McKinley was widely believed to be the choice of monied interests – the hand picked candidate of political boss Mark Hanna and a consortium of business leaders. Bryan, a former Congressman from Nebraska, traded on his growing reputation as an orator and styled himself as a champion of the common man. He toured the country speaking at

630 These descriptions are based on viewing copies of the films at the Library of Congress. Only a few early reviews mention people screaming and fainting. Most discuss the realism of the situation

631 John Bartlett's *Familiar Quotations*, 11th edn. (Boston, Little Brown & Co., 1938) pp. 752–753.

438 The Man Who Made Movies

whistle stops and public events. In contrast, by his own choice and tradition, McKinley stayed at home. He recognized that he could not compete with Bryan on the speaker's platform. The Republicans flooded the electorate with campaign literature which stressed McKinley's wholesome family, his service to community and the nation with particular emphasis on his record in the Civil War (he retired with the rank of Major), membership in Congress where he served from 1876 until 1891 and Governorship in Ohio (1891–1895). His name was associated with high protective tariffs (he sponsored the McKinley Tariff Act of 1890) and with retaining gold to back the currency. This was translated in the campaign as "Sound Money" and clubs bearing that name were formed throughout the country.[632]

Instead of taking McKinley to the people, the Republicans brought the people to McKinley. Trainloads of supporters were brought to Canton. The railroad companies, who were ardent supporters of McKinley's business friendly campaign, offered reduced fares to the groups – the *Cleveland Plain Dealer* commented that the trip to Canton "was cheaper than staying at home".[633] The groups detrained in Canton and paraded to the McKinley house to greet the candidate. McKinley would come out of the house and meet the delegates, usually giving a small speech and shaking the hands of many of the delegates. He was usually well coached by his assistant, Joseph Smith, who gathered information about the delegations including the names of important members. They were flattered when the candidate greeted them by name. This began during the summer with a few scattered groups and the pace increased as fall drew near. 18 September was a high point in this front porch campaign. Groups supporting McKinley converged on Canton from Pittsburgh, Cleveland, Youngstown, Wheeling, Toledo, Columbus, Cincinnati, and even from Chicago. More than 50,000 supporters were expected and the number that arrived may have exceeded that figure – the *Canton Repository* bragged that the crowd numbered more than 60,000. As the delegations arrived they trouped to McKinley's house where the candidate greeted them from a platform that was built at the edge of the street. It was a busy day for the candidate and for the people of Canton.[634]

Canton was a moderate sized industrial town of about 30,000, located in northeastern Ohio, south and a just a bit east of Akron and Cleveland. It had grown impressively during the last half of the 19th century but it had never enjoyed the spotlight as much as it did during the last decade of the 19th century. In addition to the presidential candidate, it was the home town of Norman Raff of Raff & Gammon. The Raff family was as well established in Canton's social, economic and political life as were the McKinleys and the two families mixed professionally and socially. Norman's father, George W. Raff was a lawyer, banker, judge and a prominent member of the local Democratic party. His law office was downtown, not far from the McKinley building where William had his law office. George Raff established the Central Savings Bank in 1887 with Norman's older brother Edward as

632 Margaret Leech [Margaret Leech Pulitzer], *In the Days of McKinley*, (New York, Harper & Brothers, 1959), pp. 66–96. H. Wayne Morgan, *William McKinley and His America* (Syracuse, Syracuse University Press, 1963), pp. 209–248.

633 Leech, Op. Cit., p. 88.

634 *Canton Repository*, 15–19 September 1896; Leech, Op. Cit., pp. 87–88.

Parade at Canton, O. Showing Major McKinley in Carriage *was one of five films made on 18 September 1896 the busiest day of McKinley's successful presidential campaign. They inaugurated the use of moving images in political campaigns. McKinley, a former Congressman and Governor of Ohio, was a Major because of his service in the Civil War. [LC.]*

635 John Danner, ed., *Old Landmarks of Canton and Stark County, Ohio, Vol II.* (Logansport, Indiana, B.F. Bowen, 1904); Edward Thornton Heald, *The Stark County Story, Vol. II. The McKinley Era, 1875–1901.* (Canton, The Stark County Historical Society, 1950); *Canton City Directory, 1893–94; Canton Official City Directory, 1895 & 1896–1897.* (Akron, Burch Directory, 1895); *Canton Repository*, September 17, 1896. The *Repository* reported on 2 January 1898 that Canton's population had reached 40,000 and that between 1850 and 1890, it grew from 12,258 to 26,189, reaching 32,176 in 1892. Today Canton is best known as the home of the Professional Football Hall of Fame.

Cashier. In the early 1890s William McKinley was a member of the bank's Board of Directors. On the eve of Dickson's visit Edward Raff, his wife and Mr. and Mrs. McKinley were among the friends attending a dinner party given by Mr. and Mrs. Shields. Robert Shields was an officer of the Central Savings Bank.[635]

Historian Gordon Hendricks believed that before Bitzer and Dickson arrived in Canton they were in Pittsburgh for the opening of Sandow's *Olympia* at the Alvin Theater on the 14th. It was a reasonable assumption, but there is nothing to confirm it. Hendricks found no mention of Dickson in the Pittsburgh papers and though Bitzer described filming McKinley in his biography he said nothing about being in Pittsburgh. Dickson's major concern was film production and he was only marginally involved with setting-up and operating the projector. But, he was the company's principal technician and it is logical that he would be on site to make certain that the first public showing went well. Once the projections had started and no serious problems were confronted he, and Bitzer, would have been free to take the short train trip from Pittsburgh to Canton.

On the afternoon of 18 September Dickson and Bitzer filmed four units in the McKinley-Hobart campaign parade: McKinley and Party in a Carriage; the Americus Club; the Sound Money Club and Elkins'

Cadets. The Americus Club came from Pittsburgh, arriving by train at 11:45 Friday morning. The 350 members wore white hats, sported "elegant badges" and carried red, white and blue umbrellas which they maneuvered about as they marched. The Sound Money Club of Canton also carried umbrellas and had banners with pictures of McKinley and mottoes supporting him. The Elkins Cadets were from Wheeling, West Virginia. They wore white duck trousers with a West Point styled jacket and each of the 100 cadets carried a spear with a yellow streamer. The unit was preceded by their drum corps "... with a colored lad as drum major".[636]

A brass band led the parade followed by the carriage carrying McKinley, Governor Asa Bushnell of Ohio, Senator John Thurston of Nebraska and County Chairman Jolin Thomas. Seven carriages with other dignitaries followed; among them Senator Shelby Cullom of Illinois, Congressman J.T. McCleary of Minnesota, Governor Daniel Hastings of Pennsylvania and sundry state and local officials and party organizers. Senator Thurston had been chairman of the Republican convention that nominated McKinley and he was one of a battery of dignitaries scheduled to speak at a McKinley rally later that afternoon in a tent on North Washington Street, a few blocks from the McKinley residence.[637]

For unexplained reasons Americus Club was filmed on a downtown street but the rest the parade was shot on a residential street, possibly North Market Street at a location near the McKinley house. This leads to speculation that Dickson may have been able to mount his camera on the platform McKinley used to address visiting delegations. The camera set-up was the same for the three parade shots. The camera was raised above the heads of the crowd and directed so the units approached at an angle. The diagonal movement and overhead view kept the subject on camera longer and gave the audience an unobstructed image. Dickson got a particularly good shot of the opening of the parade, capturing the band that led McKinley's carriage and then got a clear shot of the candidate in the back of the carriage on the side near the camera. This shot was remarkable because the surviving four frames indicate that the shot ended with a pan to focus on McKinley as he rode by. In this last frame McKinley can be seen very clearly and the house in the background appears to be McKinley's. The house is not in the earlier frames, nor in the other two films shot at this location.[638]

Before filming the parade, Dickson made one of the most important of his company's early films; one that drew audiences to their programs as they introduced the Biograph. It was campaign propaganda which purported to show McKinley receiving notification that he was the Republican Party's presidential candidate. It was shot on the lawn of McKinley's home and the action was staged quite convincingly.

Although the exact date and time that the film was made is still open to question, there is enough information that it is possible to assume that it was made in the late morning on September 18th.

636 *Canton Repository*, 17 & 18 September 1896. The paper published a special edition on 18 September.
637 Ibid.
638 MoMA Biograph Photos & LC Copyright Deposits. Still frames are the only surviving material on these films. My identification of the McKinley house is tentative, based on a comparison of the right corner of the house in the McKinley in carriage scene with the house in the background of McKinley at Home, the porch and windows are similar in the two shots. Taking most of the parade scenes from a location near McKinley's house would have been much more convenient.

McKinley at Home, Canton, Ohio. *Filming the presidential candidate was an early coup for the Mutoscope company. Arrangements were probably made by the candidate's brother, Abner McKinley who held stock in the company. This placid scene belies the frantic activity going on off camera as 50,000 supporters arrived and paraded past the McKinley's house. The candidate's wife, an invalid, is seated on the porch. McKinley's aide is not identified though Bitzer, who operated the camera, identified him at a later date as George B. Cortelyou. But Cortelyou may not have been associated with McKinley this early. The company recycled this film for the next year or two, changing the name to suit the occasion.* [LC.]

Because McKinley was kept busy greeting the visiting delegations, it would have been easier to make the film a day or two earlier or later, but there is no evidence that Dickson was in Canton earlier and he was in Canastota early the following week. According to the *Canton Repository* the weather on the 18th was clear and sunny, ideal for the events – and for filming. It rained on Saturday and there may have been showers on Thursday, so Friday was the best of the three days. The surviving copy of the film confirms that it was made under ideal sunny conditions. Billy Bitzer said the film was shot in late morning just before lunch when "... the sun shone brightly, making it ideal for photographic purposes".[639] Since the parade started at 1:30 pm, with McKinley in the first unit, the filming was apparently squeezed in around 11:00 a.m.[640] If this is the case, the placid image that Dickson captured belied the crowds and charged atmosphere that gripped Canton that morning.

The trains began arriving early on Friday and each one carried 100 or more supporters. Organized groups paraded to the McKinley home to greet the candidate and hear a few words from him. The *Canton Repository* described the scene:

"Major McKinley was in great demand almost from the time the first delegation arrived in the city Friday morning. Many thousands of people surrounded the McKinley residence in North Market street, and sent up cheer after cheer for the Major. Many delegations, headed by bands stopped to serenade the Major, but the Columbiana county [Ohio] delegation, one of the largest of those in the city insisted upon a speech. Major McKinley was conducted to the stand erected in the front yard, and addressed the delegation. As the Major concluded his talk to the Columbiana people, the immense Pittsburgh delegation ... arrived ... They cheered and cheered the Major who also addressed them. As the Major concluded he was informed that the Columbus people, with Governor Bushnell and Judge Shauck, were at that moment awaiting their turn ... McKinley addressed the Columbus people and was accorded liberal applause. Other delegations asked for speeches but as it was nearing the time for the grand parade Major McKinley bowed the acknowledgments to the admirers before him."[641]

Dickson prepared the shot very carefully. The camera was on a corner of the lawn directed so that the house filled the left side of the frame with a stand of trees as background on the right side. The porch of the house was the prominent feature and the steps leading to the front walk were visible at the left edge. Shadows from trees filled the foreground, but the center of the frame was bathed in sunlight. As the film began, McKinley and an unidentified man walked down the steps and strolled to the center of the frame into the pool of sunlight. The man handed a paper to McKinley who read it, then the pair resumed the stroll, walking towards the camera and moving off frame on the right side. During the action McKinley, dressed in suit with a frock coat, carried a hat in his left hand but put it on while reading the paper. The unidentified man was also dressed in a suit but wore his hat through all of the action. The intent was to show the candidate as a serious, involved professional man who was also a home body. The atmosphere was calm, with no hint of the cheering, noisy delegates flooding the city. It was very carefully timed and was probably rehearsed before the take – with the other man doing the walk through. As in most of Dickson's films, the action begins before the camera starts. McKinley and his assistant

639 Bitzer, Op. Cit., p. 12.

640 There was no report of the filming in the *Canton Repository* and Bitzer did not date his account, but the films of the parade make it clear that Dickson was in Canton on Friday, September 18th.

641 *Canton Repository*, Special Edition, 18 September 1896.

descend the steps, walk to the center of the frame, do the bit with the letter, then walk off, leaving the frame as the scene ends.

Billy Bitzer, who operated the camera during the shoot, pointed out that McKinley's wife, Ida, an invalid who was confined to a wheel chair, was seated in a rocking chair on the porch during the filming and she is visible, though not prominent. Bitzer said the man accompanying McKinley was his secretary George B. Cortelyou, but this is unlikely, since he was not in that position in 1896.[642] It seems more likely that it was Joseph Smith who was assisting McKinley at that time.

Despite the candidate's busy schedule, the filming was another of Dickson's special occasions. They were invited to lunch. Bitzer described the post screening:

"We were invited inside the house for luncheon, where once more Mrs. McKinley presided. She chatted a bit, but not much. I myself had little or nothing to say, as I was merely the man who assisted Mr. Dickson, to whom I looked for instructions. Many took him for my father, especially since I had grown the mustache, emphasizing (I hoped) a resemblance. He was a magnificent dashing figure of a man, with an eye for the ladies and a manner I admired and hoped someday to achieve."[643]

Dickson's staging of this scene suited the image that the Republicans were trying to create for McKinley. A professional man, dignified and capable, with roots in the American middle class where home and family were an important. While business and finance were important to the Republican cause, they played no role in Dickson's political vignette.

It was raining on Saturday morning so Dickson and Bitzer apparently moved on to Canastota and the filming of the New York Central's Empire State Express. When that was completed they returned to New York where he made one more film to complete the campaign documents – a film of the United States flag fluttering against a dark background. With almost a hundred films ready, it was time for the show to begin.

642 Ibid.
643 Bitzer, Op. Cit.

Chapter 26

The Playful Specter of the Night. The Biograph on Screen

"No ghost can startle after this, no Frankenstein pursue us, for we have seen the instrument of the day become the playful specter of the night."[644] (Cincinnati *Enquirer*, November 1897)

"What the invention of the alphabet has done in the preservation of the facts of history, the Biograph and kindred inventions promise to do in the restoration of historical atmosphere. The future student of this age will have at his command the moving and glowing simulacra of its vital forces. ... He will see his forbears at work and at play, and there will smile out of the canvas the faces that march in processions which have marched into history."[645] (*New York Mail and Express*, 25 September 1897)

The critical reaction to Biograph was almost unanimously positive and it was widely regarded as the most successful of the early projection machines. The company documented its introduction in a scrapbook filled with an impressive collection of positive news articles. The *Cincinnati Enquirer* (2 November 1896) called it "The Marvel of Science"; the *Baltimore Sun* (3 November 1896) said it was "... a genuine surprise ..." and J.E. Dennis of the *New Haven Paladium* (16 November 1896) said that "... the biograph is so far superior to the cinematographe as the latter is to the vitascope ...".[646] The positive reactions continued as the company expanded exhibition in cities across the country.

But, surprisingly, when it opened in Pittsburgh the response was rather bland. With little advance notice, the one week run at the Alvin Theater began on Monday, 14 September 1896 as part of *Olympia*, a variety show built around Eugen Sandow. The Biograph's program consisted of several films from the company's library, among them "Sandow", "Trilby and Little Billee", "Li Hung Chang", "Stable on Fire" and one of the Joseph Jefferson Rip Van Winkle subjects, probably "Rip's Toast." Without advance publicity, the first mention of the new picture machine came the day after the opening and the reactions were favorable but not overly enthusiastic. The *Pittsburgh Press* said the

644 Niver, *Biograph Bulletins, 1896–1908.* "Biograph, The Marvel of Science" *Cincinnati Enquirer*, 2 November 1896.

645 *The American Biograph*, pp. 1 & 3. Reproduced in Kemp Niver, *Biograph Bulletins, 1896–1908*, p. 26 (Los Angeles, Locare Research Group, 1971)

646 Ibid.

Biograph was well received and the *Chronicle Telegraph* called it the best machine seen so far. The most extensive comment was in the *Pittsburgh Post* which reported that the "Biographe" was a surprise at the end of the program and commented that the picture was twice as large as other machines "... and the impression is clear-cut and distinct. The Biograph may have been a bit upstaged by the show at the Bijou where Edison's sensational film "The Kiss" was running on the Vitascope program. Even though the image was inferior, the public's interest was aroused by the closer than life view of John Rice and May Irwin reenacting their on stage kiss from the show "Widow Jones". Two days after the Biograph's opening, the *Pittsburgh Press* reported "... the other evening ... the audience relapsed into one of those decidedly quiet spells which usually follow a great surprise, when suddenly there came ... a boyish voice loud and shrill from the gallery through the stillness: 'I'll tell yer mother on yer!' just as Irwin and Rice were in the middle of the kiss, and the laugh that followed fairly shook the building ...".[647]

Sandow's company moved to Philadelphia the following week for another one week run at Gilmore's Auditorium. This time there was advance notice of the film program with the *Philadelphia Times* and the *Philadelphia Bulletin* reporting that three scenes from Rip Van Winkle would be shown as well as Li Hung Chang at Grant's Tomb.[648] The reviews following the opening were also positive but not sensational. The pre-Manhattan run ended with a week at the Columbia Theater in Brooklyn. Although the bill was covered by the local press there was little attention to Biograph's part of the program.

Sandow's *Olympia* was in trouble. On Tuesday, 6 October, the day after it opened Manhattan, the New York *Herald* reported that it would close at the end of the week.[649] The Mutoscope company must have sensed that the show had problems – which may account for lack of advance publicity during the show's tour. At any rate, they were prepared for the cancellation. Arrangements for a more spectacular "debut" were already in the works when Sandow's show opened at the Grand Opera House, 23rd Street and 8th Avenue, in Manhattan.

The Biograph found a new venue. They moved from *Olympia* the play to "Olympia" the theater. It was to be a feature of a variety program in the Music Hall at Oscar Hammerstein's Olympia Theater, a two-house theater on Broadway between 44th and 45th Streets in the heart of what is now Times Square.[650] The Biograph was on the concluding half of the program.. It opened on 12 October, the Monday after the close of Sandow's show. There was a press preview on Sunday the 11th and Monday's show was for an invitation only audience. The four weeks with Sandow were quickly forgotten and ever after the Mutoscope company claimed that the 12 October program was their premiere showing – with good reason. The new program was a resounding success.

It was the opening on 12 October that established the Biograph as a leader in increasingly competitive moving picture business and almost immediately it was declared to be the standard against which other

647 NMAH Hendricks

648 NMAH Hendricks; Hendricks *Beginnings* ..., pp. 43–44.

649 *Ibid.*

650 If it seems there were too many "Olympias" about in 1896, it should be remembered that it was the year that the Olympic Games were revived in Athens.

systems were judged. The audience at the invitational screening was
made up of politicians and railroaders. Members of the Republican
National Committee occupied flag draped boxes. Other prominent
Republicans, members of the Sound Money League and officials of the
New York Central Railroad filled the orchestra. The audience in the
rest of the theater shared these partisan interests and they were treated
to a program designed to satisfy their enthusiasms. The show opened
with six acts of vaudeville and after an intermission, the Biograph led
off the second part of the program which concluded with additional
vaudeville acts. There were nine films on the Biograph's portion:
"Stable on Fire" "Niagara Upper Rapids", "Trilby and Little Billee",
Joseph Jefferson in the "Toast Scene from Rip Van Winkle", "A Hard
Wash", "Niagara, American Falls from Goat Island", "Empire State
Express, 60 Miles an Hour", "McKinley and Hobart Parade at Canton,
O." and "Maj. McKinley at Home". As an unannounced bonus, McKin-
ley was followed by the film of the American flag.

The hall was filled and as the program progressed the atmosphere
became electric. They were warmed up by a roller skating act, an
equilibrist, a ventriloquist and a couple of comedians. A feature of the
vaudeville program was "The Great Amann", a European impersonator
brought to the States from London's Empire theater. He stirred the
politicians with impressions of New York's Republican mayor William
L. Strong and William Jennings Bryan. Bryan drew hisses from the
audience but when he shifted to William McKinley the hisses changed
to enthusiastic applause.[651] After the intermission, the climax of Biograph's program stirred these zealots to an uproar. The railroaders
cheered "Empire State Express" and it had to be run three times before
they were satisfied. "During the last view the audience actually shrieked
with enthusiasm."[652] The McKinley-Hobart parade was received with
a storm of applause and it was followed with the feature of the evening,
"McKinley at Home". The excitement was described in the *New York
Daily Advertiser*:

"The presidential candidate came down from the porch of his house
accompanied by his Secretary. The latter handed the Major a telegram. Mr.
McKinley adjusted his eyeglasses, smiles gladly as if it brought him good
news, removed his hat, stroked his forehead for a moment and then walked
majestically down the lawn with full face toward the audience.

"The effect was so realistic that the house roared with one voice 'Speech!
Speech!' Then the absurdity of the demand came back in a moment and a
roar of good humored laughter went up. ... the audience contented itself
with yelling 'Three cheers for McKinley and Hobart.' They were given with
a vim such as the halls of Olympia have never heard before.

"It was a great night for McKinley and Hobart and sound money and also
for Hammerstein's Olympia."

At the conclusion the audience rose to their feet waving American
flags and continued cheering for several minutes.[653]

651 NMAH
Hendricks. Program,
Hammerstein's
Olympia, 12 October
1896. Dickson later
filmed Amann for the
British Mutoscope
Co.

652 NMAH
Hendricks; *The New
York Advertiser*, 15
October 1896.

653 *Ibid.* Hendricks
received his copy of
the *NY Daily
Advertiser* article from
Herman Casler's son
Harry Casler.
Dramatic Mirror
reported the flag
waving and the length
of the response.

"Incidents in Major McKinley's Daily Life in Canton, Ohio" appeared in the New York Herald *on 12 October 1896 with illustrations taken from the film which premiered at Hammerstein's Olympia Theater that day. Providing illustrations for newspapers and journals was a regular business for the Mutoscope company. Interestingly, these drawings reverse the images from the film indicating that the artist worked from a reversed copy. [NMAH.]*

While the film of Major McKinley did not swing the election for him, it had a positive effect on the faithful Republicans who were at the core of the campaign – and it must have given them a real boost. It remained on the program at Hammerstein's through most of October, then moved to Koster & Bial's as the month ended. Several other Republican and Sound Money groups attended showings during October. Audiences continued to cheer and occasionally shout "Speech! Speech!" There were reports of an occasional hiss from a Bryan enthusiast, but most of the audiences were dedicated McKinley supporters. Since the pre-election showings were almost all in New York City, not enough uncommitted voters saw the film to affect the outcome of the election.[654]

Films weren't the only campaign material the Mutoscope company produced. The day of the opening at Hammerstein's, an article in the *New York Herald*, "Incidents in Major McKinley's Daily Life in Canton, Ohio" was illustrated by four pictures showing McKinley on the lawn outside his house. They were credited: "made from instantaneous photographs".[655] The pictures were supplied by the Mutoscope Company which inaugurated a service adapted from Dickson's practice of supplying photographs to the press and other interested parties. The company changed emphasis and primarily sold pictures made from newsworthy subjects that they filmed. This evolved into a journalistic service which did not necessarily promote the company or their films – though they asked for and received credit and certainly did not object to some publicity. Some of the pictures were copied from film frames but others were still photographs made at the time of the filming. Dickson usually took a still camera with him, especially when the subjects had news potential and this became a company practice as they expanded production and added new camera teams. For the next few years the sale of news pictures was an active business.

654 Niver, Op. Cit., pp. 12–15. All of the newspaper clippings prior to election day, 3 November 1896 were from New York newspapers except a 2 November 1896 clipping from the *Baltimore News* reporting the opening of the Biograph at Ford's Theater in Baltimore on Monday, 1 November, the day before the election. The paper reported that the film showed "... McKinley receiving a hopeful message from Maryland headquarters ..."

655 NMAH Hendricks.

Show business

The Biograph was a late entrant in the projection race. The introduction of the Edison-Armat Vitascope in April, 1896 roused the public's interest and during the summer of 1896 motion picture devices were introduced at several leading variety halls in New York City. Summer was a slack season for theaters and when the new theater season opened in September the competition heated up. By the time the Biograph came to Manhattan, audiences had been exposed to a bewildering selection of "scope" and "graph" machines, all claiming to be the newest and best available. At the beginning of October the Vitascope was featured at several of Proctor's houses in New York and Raff & Gammon were scrambling to supply machines and films to concessionaires in other locales. The Lumières' Cinématographe was being shown at Keith Albee theaters in New York, Boston, Providence and Philadelphia as well as a number of other locations around the U.S. By October Robert Paul's Theatrograph and Birt Acres' Kineoptikon had come to America from England. The Columbia Phonograph Company of Washington, DC was manufacturing C. Francis Jenkins' version of the Phantoscope and selling them to eager entrepreneurs throughout the U.S. – much to the annoyance of Raff & Gammon's customers who were grousing about the unexpected competition.[656]

The competition was so stiff that the E. & H.T. Anthony & Co. who purchased rights to the Eidoloscope from the Lathams was having trouble booking it. They sold the Latham's production studio in New York City to Raff & Gammon who hoped to use it for film production – a wish that was never fulfilled. Raff & Gammon's problems increased. In addition to the unexpected competition, they had to deal with testy concessionaires complaining about the lack of new film subjects, problems with torn, damaged or defective films and difficulties finding adequate electric current at projection sites. At the end of October Edison announced that his own version of the Vitascope would be sold directly to interested parties, effectively ending the exclusive market that Raff & Gammon enjoyed. Edison also lured one of their best technicians, James White to take charge of film production. In January Raff & Gammon filed suit against the United States Phonograph Co., Newark, NJ, for marketing a machine almost identical to the Vitascope.[657] Although Raff & Gammon remained in business for another year, their domination of the American market was at an end.

The Mutoscope company entered this highly competitive market with one advantage: a better and larger picture. At 2¾ inches wide by 2 inches high, the Biograph's image was four or more times larger than any competing image. This made it possible to fill a large screen – the screen in Hammerstein's Music Hall was said to almost fill the proscenium. When properly projected it was also less susceptible to flicker, the most common complaint about competing systems. The Lumières successfully reduced the speed of the Cinématographe to 15 or 16 frames per second and, with the exception of Edison, most new filmmakers followed their lead. When projected at that speed, the flicker

656 Ibid.

657 NMAH
Hendricks,
Phonoscope,
January–February,
1897.

could be irritating but there were practical reasons for slower exposure speed. Film was expensive and since it was priced by the foot, less footage was used at slower speeds. Exhibitors were particularly worried about cost so they accepted increased flicker as a pragmatic trade-off. Through the closing years of the 19th century the Mutoscope company and Edison continued to expose film at almost double the rate of other filmmakers. The speed of the Mutograph camera could be adjusted, but the company standardized exposure rates at 30 frames per second to relieve their projectionists from having to change the rate of projection for each film. Occasionally a film would be taken at a slower or faster rate and shown at 30 fps for special effect.[658]

There was a down side. Like the Mutograph camera, the Biograph was difficult to operate. Without sprockets to guide and steady the image, the projectionist had to watch the screen all the time, adjusting the image to keep it in frame. It was a job for a specialist.

To offset the projection problems and take advantage of their edge in image quality, the Mutoscope company formulated a business plan that was somewhat different from their competition. They combined projector, operator and a changing program of films and unlike the Lumières who were marketing the Cinématographe very widely, the Mutoscope company customized their entertainment package to suit large theaters in large cities. The Biograph program was available as though it were another vaudeville act, albeit different from standard variety fare, and it was tailored to houses that presented "high class" variety acts to middle-class family audiences. So, while most of their competitors were selling projectors and films at best available prices, the Biograph projectors and films remained property of the company.[659]

This was a revision of their initial intent. The company had been set up to market the peep show Mutoscope as a business tool and entertainment device. But the growing interest in projection forced them to revise their plans and by the fall of 1896 the Biograph had replaced the Mutoscope as their primary focus. But the Mutoscope was not put into limbo. Up in Canastota, Herman Casler was busy producing Mutoscopes which were still available to amusement sites as well as for advertising and promotional use. Territorial rights for Mutoscopes could be had for a license fee of $100. Machines and image reels were rented, not sold and the company asked for a percentage of the local company's stock as well as a percentage of the daily take. Licensees were expected to start with fifty-two machines, each with a reel of images. New subjects could be rented or, for a fee, old subjects could be swapped for different ones through an exchange service that the company set up.[660]

Because of its large and steady image, films projected by the Biograph had exceptional impact. Ironically, this came about by accident rather than from intent to outdo rivals. As noted earlier, the projector was an after-thought and while Dickson and Casler may have suspected that it had great potential, that would not have been fully

658 GU Ramsaye. Bitzer to Ramsaye, c. 1940.

659 NMAH Hendricks. The exceptions to this were occasional exhibits with touring programs, including some open air projections but these were still done by a crew furnished by the company.

660 Ibid. *The Biograph and Mutoscope Up to Date*, Vol. 1, No. 1, October 1897.

determined until after the prototype was finished. Projections in the company's offices gave Dickson and his associates an inkling of the projectors' potential, but the full impact would not have been apparent until it was on screen in a theater filled with people.

We can only speculate about Dickson's reaction to the Hammerstein premiere. If he was in the audience, as he probably was, Dickson would have been pleased but it must have been a revelation as well. If he needed confirmation that properly staged images could profoundly affect spectators, he had it. Furthermore, it was apparent that it was possible to create an interaction between the audience and the images on the screen. He staged each film as carefully as possible, but could only guess at their effect in a darkened theater. The intense response to "Empire State Express" and the McKinley films went beyond wonder at a novelty. The audience's reaction to the images was emotional and an indication that individual viewers were responding in a very personal way. But there was also a group response and it was more intense than the usual reaction of an audience. Instead of applause there were cheers, cries of "Speech! Speech!" and the embarrassed laughter that followed the realization that this was an absurd reaction. Crowd intensity of this sort is more common at sporting events or political rallies than in theaters. And it is often produced by manipulating and deliberately organizing stimulus that will stir the crowd. The interaction between the public and the screen at Hammerstein's is one of the earliest occurrences of "cinema" experience, something that scholars have struggled to define ever since. Dickson would continue to search for ways of engaging his viewers as intensely as possible.

Of course, the Hammerstein premiere was something of a political rally, so an intense response from McKinley's supporters could be expected, but subsequent newspaper accounts show that Republicans and Sound Money advocates were not the only ones that responded strongly to Biograph's films. On 15 October, the *New York Telegram* complained: "When you can throw the picture of an express train on a screen in such a realistic way that persons who see it scramble to get out of its way and faint from fright it's about time to stop. ... It makes even an unimaginative person kind of shiver and wish he could get off to one side, but women – it scares them to death. ... the next thing you'll hear they've brought suit against Mr. Hammerstein for damages to their nerves."[661]

"Empire State Express"quickly became the company's biggest hit and viewers often demanded that it be run again and again. Although there were no confirmed faintings, spectators close to the screen were startled and the numerous accounts of audiences reacting to the film indicate that this was often a mixture of fear, relief and amusement.[662] Dickson's practice of filming action that started before the shot and continued after the end of the take was particularly successful in this film. A description of the effect by a writer for *Phonoscope* magazine is typical:

661 Niver, Op. Cit.

662 Stephen Bottomore "The Panicking Audience?: early cinema and the 'train effect'", *Historical Journal of Film, Radio and Television,* Vol. 19, No. 2, 1999, pp. 177–216.

Who fainted?

One of the most persistent stories about the introduction of movies is that people screamed, ducked under seats and even fainted as trains or other threatening objects seemed to rush towards the audience. These accounts appear in early news stories, reminiscences of film pioneers and early historical accounts. The *N.Y. Telegram* reported on 15 October 1896, that two women had fainted on seeing the Empire State Express on a "'Picture Projecting' Devices" [*Phonoscope*, April 1897, p. 10] and on the 17th the *NY Mail and Express* said that they had nearly fainted. Similar reports came after showings of the Lumières' films of trains arriving in stations. While some film historians have questioned the truth of these journalistic accounts – and there is reason to suspect journalists of exaggeration – there is little doubt that scenes of trains, rushing water and charging cavalry had a dramatic affect on audiences who were not accustomed to them.

Dickson had taken care to film "Empire State Express" with the camera positioned so that the engine and the cars following it would be close and completely fill the screen. Also, following his custom, the action began before the camera started and continued after the camera stopped rolling. This heightened the effect.

A number of contemporary scholars have re-examined this phenomena and concluded that although incidents of fainting may have been exaggerated, the train films had a very genuine impact on early film viewers. Historian Stephen Bottomore has synthesized and summarized this scholarship in his article "The Panicking Audience?: early cinema and the 'train effect' [*Historical Journal of Film, Radio and Television,* Vol. 19, No. 2, 1999, pp. 177–216].

"... The view of the Empire State Express was even more thrilling. At first there was only the long line of the railroad coming straight down the picture, and curving off to one side at the front. Some section hands were at work on the track. There was a spot in the distance with a fine line of smoke streaming away from it. It grew with every second until it was a throbbing engine pounding its way right toward the audience. People held their breath as the train swept toward them, and it seemed an actual escape when it swung off on the curve and out of sight."

The author shrewdly speculated that the motion picture "... promises to hold the public mind in wonder and amazement longer than any invention of the century".[663]

The McKinley films may not have swayed the election, but it pleased the party faithful including the candidate himself. The night of the election, at the invitation of the *New York World*, the McKinley films and a selection of others were projected on the walls of the Pulitzer Building, the paper's office at Broadway and 32nd Street. They were a feature in an elaborate show the paper dubbed "colored fire and light" which was intended to pass the election results on to a large number of people in the New York area. Different colored lights shown from the top of the Pulitzer and other tall buildings in Manhattan and New Jersey signaled whether McKinley or Bryan were ahead. In addition to the film, slides showing the returns were also projected on the Pulitzer building. The show was a success and the *Journal* credited the Biograph with amusing the large crowd and arousing "... a great deal of patriotic

663 "'Picture Projecting' Devices." *Phonoscope,* April 1897, p. 10.

*The Biograph, as the projector was called, was a formidable beast and a specialist was needed to make
it operate. But when it functioned properly it furnished the most spectacular show available during
cinema's early years. This illustration appeared in* Scientific American, *Vol. LXXVI, No. 16, 17
April 1897, p. 248. [NMAH.]*

enthusiasm".[664] The show was free and it was the first look at the
sensational attraction for the general public. *The Phonoscope,* a new
journal for phonographs and film which began publishing that November, boasted that this was the first election in which science aided the
candidates. It cited the McKinley film and said that Bryan had made
recordings to communicate with his supporters. They speculated per-
ceptively about the potential of the media. "Who knows but that all
future electioneering campaigns will be carried on entirely mechani-
cally ..." although they also predicted "... that we shall be able to buy
catching speeches, with the accompanying paraphernalia, by the yard.
Qui vivra verra."[665] Our interest in keeping campaign speeches for
future reference has waned, but the enthusiasm for visual reporting has
not.

The popularity of "Empire State Express" and the McKinley film
continued and lasted a surprisingly long time. As McKinley's political
career evolved, the Mutoscope company changed the title of the film,
but not the content. Before the election it was usually called "McKinley
Receiving Telegram Announcing his Nomination"; after the election
but before his inaugural, it became "McKinley at Home" and after the
inauguration it was simplified to "President McKinley". "Empire State
Express" was also subject to variations. Baltimore audiences were told
they were seeing the Baltimore and Ohio's Royal Blue Express. They
also understood that they were seeing a Baltimore delegation parading
in Canton even though none was filmed there.[666] We don't know who
made these changes, but there since there were no titles attached to the
head of the films, titles could be changed just by preparing a new slide
and apparently the Mutoscope company, or its clients, believed in

664 Niver, Op. Cit.
New York Journal, 5
November 1896.

665 *The Phonoscope, A
Monthly Journal
Devoted to Scientific and
Amusement Inventions
Appertaining to Sound
and Sight,* Vol. 1, No.
1, November 1896.
Published by The
Phonoscope
Publishing Co., New
York. An article,
"Screen Machine
Politics".

666 Niver, Op. Cit.
Baltimore American, 3
November 1896.

getting their audiences more involved by seeming to offer films made locally.

On screen

The company's decision to keep control over presentations of the Biograph programs was a pragmatic one. The projector was very difficult to operate and not the sort of machine that could be entrusted to novices. The projector was huge, awkward, complicated – and noisy. Bitzer had become experienced running the projector in the company's headquarters and, with no one else willing, operated it at the press screening and premier. The projector was set up in a box in the balcony and curtained off to hide it from view. The films were spliced together in a long roll and as there were no titles on the film, individual film titles were lettered on glass slides and projected between each film. To keep the frames in alignment he had to watch the screen all the time and make adjustments when it moved out of frame. While monitoring the screen, he also had keep an eye on the lamp to prevent overheating. Bitzer's vivid description of the press screening describes the problems that the operator faced:

"When the press screening started, the first thing that struck me was that I had the picture a little high on the screen. I had the coffin very slightly tipped forward, with a piece of wood under it. I was afraid to tip it further, lest its vibration topple it over into the orchestra seats below. There wasn't much space for bracing it anyway. I had the little magic lantern (stereopticon) which projected the title slides placed in front of the projector lower down at the side. On the floor there were also a couple of large, bulky rheostats, to control the flow of electric current, with their wires lying about. I had glass slides in my jacket pocket and had to keep shifting them from my right pocket to my left, as the shown slides were pretty hot. An electric switch was also on the floor, because I had no place to put it without mutilating the booth. I had hung some maroon-colored drapes on either side of the railing in front of the booth to prevent the balcony occupants on either side from peeking in. In addition, there were a couple of fire pails filled with sand, the box I brought the film down in, a stack of tools and a wood saw!

"The *modus operandi* was this: the full reel film was evenly adjusted upon the large upper brass pulley, its diameter being about ten inches with its eight or ten pictures across its diameter. After adjusting the reel upon the pulley, I kept it covered with a couple of damp towels, since it was not advisable to thread the machine completely until you were about ready to run. There was a long stretch between the reel and where it came to the first set of pulleys, and if left too long in the air, the film would curl up like a hose. Just before the finish of the vaudeville act on stage, ahead of the Biograph, I threaded the film over the wooden pulleys, clamped the webbed driving-belt as the film made the long lower loop, two feet long, leading it over another series of rollers, and gripping it on to the take-up pulley. Then I threw on the main switch, turned on a smaller switch, and put the first slide into position. It was the American Biograph trademark, a spreading eagle. The show was finally under way.

"In the Biograph lamp, which was also a 35-amp Colt hand-feed lamp with gimping down to the front lamp I put on the next slide, then stepped back up to the big upright coffin. There was a single step up into this booth, which raised the rear chairs higher. I gingerly started the large motor controller, my left hand reaching up to help guide the film. When it got up to speed, my right hand quickly clutched the rod that controlled the picture on the screen. The beater cam movement, which pulled the picture down into position, was uneven and could gain or lose in the aperture frame. The lever which operated a friction drive disk controlled this; when I put my foot down and pushed, the pedal would open the light gate.

"I had hung a mirror in a wooden frame on the front drape, at an angle which enabled me to intermittently observe how the film was feeding. If it tried to creep toward the edge of the feeder pulley, I would give it a push back with my forehead or nose. I straightened it out enough to finish the first one-minute picture, all the while keeping my eyes pretty well glued to the screen, otherwise the picture would have started riding up and down. There was a slack leader between pictures, and bank! off went the motor control.

"With a jump at the big reel on top, I had to stop its momentum when the reel was full, as the film piled on the take-up reel, I slapped a monkey wrench onto one of its spokes to help it hold the film as the diameter increased. Then I pulled the next slide out of my pocket and went down to the lantern, which rested on a board with on end on a chair and the other on the balcony rail."[667]

Bitzer's description makes this seem an ad hoc performance but this was, after all, a professional performance in a prominent house in the center of America's theatrical world, so every attempt would have been made to make it impressive. It must have been carefully rehearsed before hand and the four weeks on the road would have worked some of the kinks out. Bitzer and the other projectionists that the company was hiring were carefully tutored to avoid embarrassing errors

Creating a spectacle required coordination with the staff of the theaters where the Biograph played. Although the film was silent, the presentation to the public was not. The Music Hall's orchestra, directed by Theodore Johns, provided musical accompaniment and appropriate sound effects which dramatized some of the images. Rushing and splashing water made Niagara Falls more realistic and train whistles and the increasing roar of a locomotive enhanced the Empire State Express. All of the films were shot in black and white since color film was not available yet. Nevertheless, some of the Edison films shown at the premier of the Vitascope were hand colored and though there is no record that any hand colored films were on the Hammerstein program, the Mutoscope company probably had some films colored in order to match their competition.[668] There is no record when hand colored films were first available for Biograph films.

The Biograph was an instant hit and the premiere at the Music Hall was the beginning of a run in New York theaters that lasted for more than a decade. After a two week run at Hammerstein's the Biograph moved to Koster & Bial's and remained there from 26 October until 18 January 1897 when it began an extended run at Keith's Union Square. By early 1897 New Yorkers were becoming used to moving images and the novelty factor had begun to fade. Both the Vitascope and Cinéma-

667 Bitzer, Op. Cit., pp. 14–17.

668 . An article in *Phonoscope*, May 1897 described sound effects used at the Palace Theater in London in some detail. Press reviews of the 12 October premiere indicate that similar sound effects were used. The review of the premier of the Vitascope at Koster & Bial's in the *New York Times*, 26 April 1896 mentioned color, music and indicated that there were sound effects. Although the Lumières were among the photographers working on color processes, none were available in 1896 and 1897.

tographe were having trouble finding bookings in New York theaters. The move of the Biograph from Koster & Bial's to Keith's was occasioned by the ending of an earlier contract that Keith's had with the Lumières. It had been signed in the fall of 1896 in anticipation of a long engagement but the agreement fell through and at the end of December Keith's made the switch to the American Mutoscope Company. The Mutoscope company's films would be featured on programs at Keith-Albee owned theaters in New York, Boston, Philadelphia, Providence and Hartford. This gave the Biograph a presence in popular, family-oriented theaters in three of the country's largest cities. Except for brief interruptions, the company's films remained on the program of Keith's theaters well into the next century.

As new projectors came from Canastota and new operators were trained, the Biograph opened in other cities. At least two machines and operators traveled with road shows. One was with W.S. Cleveland's Greater-Massive Minstrels show which played Baltimore at the beginning of November. (It was here that the "Empire State Express" became the Royal Blue.) Not surprisingly in an era when racial humor was commonplace and African Americans were confronting increasing prejudice, "Hard Wash", the film of a Black woman scrubbing a Black baby, was on the program with the performers in black face. It was not, however, the hit of the show. At Christmas time, Cleveland's Minstrels played Keith's Opera House in Providence, Rhode Island with the Biograph on the program (and the Empire State Express was once again a New York Central train). Another projector traveled with Palmer Cox's "Brownies" which played at the Columbia Theater in Chicago in mid-November, moving to St. Louis for Thanksgiving week and Kansas City in early December. By the end of 1896 the Biograph had also played in Pittsburgh, Rochester, Baltimore and Atlanta.[669] New projectors and new operators brought Biograph's films to an ever increasing audience.

Diversifying the program

As exhibition expanded, Dickson continued to add to the production library and for the first time shot films at a site where the Biograph was about to open. J.E. Dennis, a reporter for the *New Haven Paladium*, stimulated local interest with his article that raved about seeing the Biograph at Koster & Bial's (see page 444). Dennis had been "Attracted by the highly flamed descriptions printed in the New York papers ..." and he patriotically rejoiced that an American had made a projector superior to the French competitor. He praised the quality of the projection, but was even more impressed by the beauty and interest of the subjects shown – especially because they were American. He urged one of the local theaters to book it.[670] The Biograph opened at Poli's Wonderland Theater in New Haven on 30 November.

This may have been a publicity ploy. The Biograph seems to have been already booked for the Wonderland with urging from Sylvester Z.

669 *Phonoscope*, December, 1896; Musser, *Emergence...*, p. 155.

670 Niver, Op. Cit. *New Haven Paladium*, 16 November 1896. J.E. Dennis' article was "I have seen the biograph".

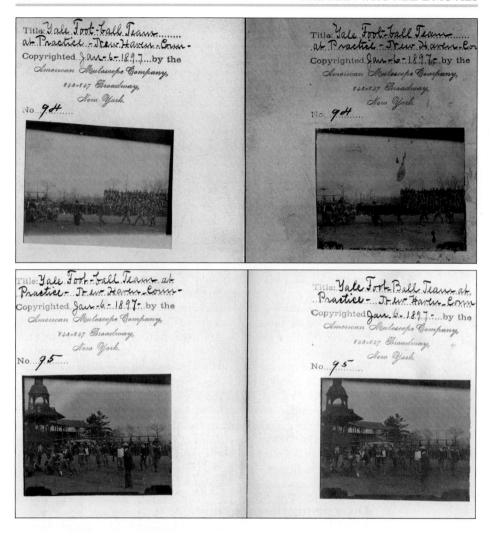

Poli to make films of local interest. On 17 November, the day after
Dennis' article appeared, Dickson was in New Haven with a full
schedule of filmmaking. In the morning he filmed Engine Number 2
of the New Haven fire department coming out of the doors of the
firehouse and racing down Artizan Street. At noon, borrowing a scene
from the Lumières, he captured employees of the Winchester Repeating
Arms Company emerging from the factory's main gate on their way to
lunch. After lunch the camera was in front of the Wonderland Theater
where he filmed the New Haven Police arresting a man. This was
another of Dickson's staged events: the man being arrested was Joe Poli,
S.Z. Poli's brother, and the marquee of the theater was conveniently
prominent in the background. An attempt to film employees leaving
the L. Candee rubber shop was cancelled because it was too dark and

As bookings for the Biograph increased, the company co-operated with theater owners to provide fare with a local touch. At the urging of Sylvester Z. Poli owner of Poli's Wonderland Theater in New Haven, Connecticut, Dickson made several films locally. The Arrest (right) was staged outside Poli's with Joe Poli as the culprit arrested. The Yale football team (left) was filmed as were workers leaving the Winchester Arms factory at noon (above). Locals gathered to see themselves or friends and neighbors on screen. (LC)

No. 9';
Title *An Arrest.*

overcast, but the next day, the 18th, he filmed the Yale University football team at practice. The New Haven Evening Register covered Dickson's activities in detail and commented that Joe's friends would laugh when they saw the action on the screen at the Wonderland. They also predicted that the faces of hundreds of Winchester Arms employees would be recognizable on the Wonderland's screen.[671] Mr. Poli must have been delighted with the package of local film and the publicity it generated!

Twelve days after Dickson's visit, the Biograph opened at Poli's. It was greeted by large, spirited crowds – and the flood of articles in the local press continued. The program for the first week was a repeat of the Music Hall program: Trilby, Niagara Falls, Joseph Jefferson doing Rip's toast, McKinley and Empire State Express, etc. What worked in New York worked in New Haven – the audience was enthusiastic The scenes taken in New Haven were shown during the second week of the run. Today's sports fans would find them confusing, but the papers were particularly taken with the views of the Yale football team.[672]

Technical innovations

Taking the large, unwieldy Mutograph camera into the field required imagination and innovation. We have seen that Dickson found ways of making the seemingly immobile camera move by putting it on moving vehicles. Trains and streetcars were preferred because the movement was smooth, whereas horse drawn carts and carriages were jerky and roadways were uneven.

Filming during cold weather created different problems. Emile Lauste who accompanied Dickson to New Haven in late December 1896 said that in order to film outdoors during the winter Dickson put an oil lamp on the mechanical side of the camera's interior in order to keep the bearings in the motor from freezing. The lamp had a red glass chimney, apparently to prevent spoilage of the film. This would have been a risky business because the film being used was nitro-cellulose which is very flammable.

Apparently the lamp was used at other times of the year. Bitzer mentions having a warming device in the camera to prevent static build-up. He said that an air pump was added to the camera in order to keep the film flat in the gate during exposure and a blower to expel the small chips made as the film was perforated after exposure. It didn't eliminate all of them. I was told by John Hiller who was inventorying the Smithsonian's film equipment collection, that he found such chips in their Biograph camera.

The impact of these home town subjects was not lost on Dickson and his associates. He was back in New Haven on 21 December with the very young Emile Lauste, Eugene Lauste's son, as his assistant. He made several rather conventional films, including horse drawn sleighs, children playing in the snow and a sack race featuring some local boys – more familiar faces for the Wonderland's screen. But he made two

671 NMAH Hendricks & Musser, *Emergence ...*, p. 155. All this activity was reported in *New Haven Evening Register*, 17 and 18 November 1896. The AMB Co. *Picture Catalog*, p. 75 said the football game was a practice between "... the first and second elevens."

672 Ibid.

films which were quite unusual. A stage was constructed near the Wonderland in order to make two short comedies: "The Prodigal's Return, 3 A.M." and "Why Papa Can't Sleep". "The Prodigal's Return" showed the trouble that greeted a well lubricated husband returning after a night on the town. In "Why Papa Can't Sleep" a couple's sleep was interrupted by their baby's persistent crying with papa bearing the brunt of parental duties. These are unusual because they were made away from the studio in New York and because they are the first Biograph comedies to use theatrical scenery and props.

Productions in the New York studio were almost always filmed against a plain background, usually a black cloth, white if the costumes and/or complections were dark. Props were kept to an absolute minimum and the patterned carpet in the center of the stage usually defined the focal area where the action should take place. This schema had worked well in the Black Maria and it was adapted for the roof top studio. It was originally devised to improve contrast but keeping distracting elements to a minimum also kept the viewer's attention focused on the performance. The dark background particularly suited the confines of the Kinetoscope or the Mutoscope, but when the films where projected larger than life at Hammerstein's, Koster & Bial's – or the Wonderland – they probably seemed unnecessarily stark. This may have prompted S.Z. Poli to recommend the tests and he was willing to provided scenery, props and players to make the point. In both films a fireplace, potted plants and an elaborately painted wall provide a background and each film had appropriate furniture for the performers to work with. Made just before Christmas, the films were on the screen at the Wonderland before New Years. They were shown in a Biograph programs in other cities, but, according to Charles Musser, Poli retained rights for exhibition in Connecticut.[673]

The two comedies made in New Haven did not trigger an immediate change in production methods at the New York studio. Films of magicians, acrobats, dancers and other performers were still filmed against plain backgrounds with a minimum number of props, suitable to the action being filmed. Some simple comedy scenes were staged in a similar manner and films of animals, children and children with animals were added to the repertoire. The first films with sets and props were made about February, 1897. There were three versions of "Sausage Machine", a vaudeville routine about the "Catchem and Stuffem's Sausage Factory" where dogs and cats were dumped into a machine that spewed out links of sausage. About the same time two comedies about errant husbands were also done with sets and props. "The Pretty Typewriter, or Caught in the Act" showed a wife walking into an office and catching her husband kissing his typist. Two versions of "Waiting for Hubby" reprised "The Prodigal's Return" by showing the wife greeting her besotted husband (made, perhaps, to show in other parts of Connecticut).[674]

Comedy sketches such as these are the most puzzling and paradoxical products of early cinema. They were necessary to give movie

673 Musser, *Emergence...*, pp. 155–157. The exhibition was described by the *New Haven Evening Register*, 29 December 1896.

674 The three "Sausage Machine" films (nos. 132, 133 and 135), "The Pretty Typewriter" (no. 134) and the two "Waiting for Hubby" films (Nos. 138 and 139) were entered in the production log just before the films of McKinley's inauguration (nos. 142–153) which were made 4 March 1897, so it appears that they were made in February since the entries seem to have been made as the films were developed and approved.

programs balance by amusing the audience but the examples that survive – and quite a lot of them do – are cheaply made and amateurish. It is difficult to appreciate that shoddy, slipshod productions such as these were the seed of the future industry. Nevertheless, this is the case. There is a direct line from the comedies staged on the roof of 841 Broadway in 1896 and 1897 to the creative work of D.W. Griffith. The career of Dickson's assistant, Billy Bitzer spans those years and continued more than a decade beyond that.

Although comedy sketches were necessary and something that the audiences of the day apparently craved, very few early filmmakers had the experience or skill to venture into the world of visual fiction. The obvious exception was Georges Méliès, but he was one of the few professional entertainers who became a film producer – and he was exceptionally gifted. The quartet who founded the American Mutoscope Company were also gifted, but in different ways. None of them had the skills, experience or instincts necessary to produce original and artistic comedies or dramas. At the beginning they relied on existing talent and were able to lure skilled performers like Sandow, Joseph Jefferson, Annabelle and Little Egypt to appear before the camera. While movies were still a novelty, they or their managers were willing to appear on film because of the publicity it generated or the experience of appearing in a new, exciting form of entertainment. But this could not last forever and it was not long before producers had to pay for talent.

The Mutoscope company was close to the resources they needed to make comedies. Their office and studio was convenient to the theater district and companies that made or rented costumes, sets, props and other accoutrements were not far away and unemployed (and hopefully experienced) actors, writers and directors were around. But it cost money to hire professionals and rent or make sets, costumes and props so it took a while before the production budgets allowed for more than a minimum of decoration. Bitzer said that rather than hire actors "... we would just take anyone handy".[675] He also described putting sets together from minimal material. He said they had a couple of Japanese screens and would improvise to put the set together. "The interior ... is a cheap wooden door, the transom above it is brown wrapping paper tacked to the framework. It has a scroll design marked upon it[,] why I don't [sic] know. 'I was responsible for it.' The window is also paper with a cross frame painted upon it with black marking ink. Flanked on the upper sides, are some folding screens, and tacked length wise below the screens, some striped awning canvas ...". A potted palm added to the set would indicate prosperity and two of them, wealth.[676]

Although he had designed the roof top studio, Dickson was apparently uncomfortable directing these early comedies and he may have willingly surrendered the directorial chore to others. He is conspicuously absent from a photograph of film production on the roof which was published in an article about the Mutoscope company that appeared in the 17 April 1897 edition of *Scientific American*. Although he is the

675 Bitzer, Op. Cit., p. 28.

676 GU Ramsaye, Bitzer to Ramsaye, 26 August 1940. Bitzer, Op. Cit., p. 28.

No. 132
Title *Sausage Machine.*

Length *160 ft*

Most of the scenes filmed in the rooftop studio were comedies or other light hearted stuff. They were not always suitable for today's taste. Sausage Factory *in which dogs and cats were stuffed into a machine and came out as links was very popular. Dickson only directed a few such comedies. Dickson is not in the photo illustrating "Movable Stage for Photographing Scenes With the Mutographe [sic]" which appeared in the 17 April 1897 issue of* Scientific American. *The film being made is* Love's Young Dream, *a comedy about the problems a young suitor has with his beloved's father. That's the father coming through the door. [Musser & LC.]*

apparent model for the drawing of the camera operator filming the Pennsylvania Limited which appeared on the cover, the person in the director's chair on the stage is definitely *not* WKLD. He is a large man, built very much like Harry Marvin (though it could be Harry Marvin's equally large brother Arthur Marvin who was working for the company as a camera operator). This photo was not staged, but was taken during the actual filming of one of their productions, "Love's Young Dream". There is a copy of "Love's Young Dream" in the Library of Congress' Paper Print Collection and it is possible to match the action in the still with the action that takes place in the film, so the photograph is a convincing indication that Dickson was not the sole director of these early comedies.[677]

During 1897 the company hired two people who claim to have directed the company's early productions, Lee Dougherty and Wallace McCutcheon. Dougherty came to New York from Boston where he had been exhibiting films on a variety program at the Boston Museum. McCutcheon was the manager of a theater in Brooklyn. They both had stage experience. Although it is not certain when they started, it is possible that one or both had initial training from Dickson or someone trained by Dickson. Dougherty stayed with the company until 1916. Although McCutcheon had a brief spell working for Edison from 1905–1907, he rejoined the company again and remained through the company's salad years. He is sometimes confused with his son, actor Wallace McCutcheon, Jr. who also worked for Biograph. Together, this pair oversaw the company's productions for the next decade and although it is not possible to determine the extent to which Dickson trained them, it is clear that he established a successful pattern of production that sustained the company through the transition from short variety and news productions to one reel comedies and dramas that were perfected by D.W. Griffith.

There are a couple of early comedies that seem to have Dickson's touch. In "The Theatre Hat" (production no. 159) members of the audience strain to see the action on stage which is obstructed by several very large lady's hats. The camera was place behind a double row of theater seats and placed low enough that the performer could only be seen when jumping in the air. At the end of the film a man uses a telescope to try and see around the ladies. A sequel, "Theatre Hats Off" (production no. 197) was made a few weeks later showing an audience able to see the entire show. The set-up was the same, but the camera was raised above the bare heads of the audience, allowing a very clear view, from the waist up, of a woman dancing. Although they were not made at the same time, the company apparently paired them and they were listed as companions in the company's 1902 catalog. "A Pillow Fight" was made at about the same time as "The Theatre Hat". Four school age girls were sleeping in two beds. One of the girls wakes and attacks the pair in the other bed with a pillow and a fight ensues which culminates as two of the pillows burst and feathers shower over the set. This was the most popular of the company's early comedies and was

677 *Scientific American*, 17 April 1897, Cover and p. 249. A copy of "Love's Young Dream" is in the Paper Print Collection at the Library of Congress and the action of the film matches the action on stage in the photo in *Scientific American*.

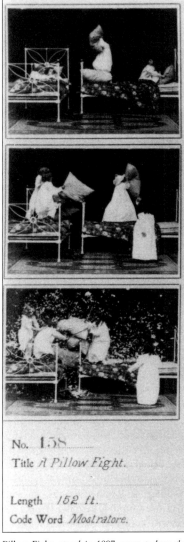

Pillow Fight, *staged in 1897, seems to have the Dickson touch. It was carefully staged so the pillow came apart just in time to end in a cloud of feathers. It proved very popular with audiences at home and abroad. After running normally it was often reversed, delighting spectators as the flying feathers filled the girl's pillow case. [Musser.]*

featured on their programs for many months – and copied by rival companies. Audiences were delighted when the picture was run backward and the feathers returned to the pillows and the girls settled back in their beds. The 1902 catalog called this "The most famous children's picture ever made."[678]

Ceremonial politics: McKinley again

According to Bitzer the Republicans were so pleased with the films of McKinley's campaign that he and Dickson were given special privileges for filming the new president's inauguration. They received an invitation and on inauguration day, 4 March 1897, were given a choice camera location at the corner of 15th Street and Pennsylvania Avenue. Their camera was mounted in rear of a police van which could be turned to capture both the procession from the White House to the Capitol and the parade back following the swearing in ceremony. Although March weather in Washington is often unreliable, the day was clear and ideal for filming.[679] The classically-columned Treasury building on 15th Street provided a suitably official background for the procession to the Capitol. McKinley's carriage was escorted to the Capitol by Troop "A" from Cleveland and the elegantly uniformed cavalry were filmed coming down 15th Street and turning onto Pennsylvania Avenue. McKinley, accompanied by outgoing President Cleveland was in a carriage that followed. McKinley was on the side nearest the camera and could be clearly seen in the film that Dickson made as the carriage turned onto Pennsylvania Avenue. After the inauguration ceremony,

678 LC Paper Print Collection; Niver Collection, American Mutoscope & Biograph Co., *Picture Catalog*, pp. 11 & 214/
679 Bitzer, Op. Cit., pp. 12–13.

the camera was turned to look down Pennsylvania Avenue and several parade units were filmed from that location. The Post Office building was prominent in the background for these films. It was still under construction, but its tower and massive facade are clearly visible. The Capitol building was visible at the end of Pennsylvania Avenue, giving the scene's location clear identity.

There was, apparently, no attempt to film the swearing-in ceremony at the Capitol and this put them somewhat behind the competition. The inauguration of the new president was one of the first major news events to occur in America since the advent of moving images and Dickson's was one of four crews in the Capitol. Edison, Lumière and a new firm, International Film Company, recorded both the swearing-in ceremony and the parades to and from the Capitol. A surviving frame from the Edison film of the swearing-in ceremony was made by a camera mounted on an elevated platform erected at a distance from the principals.[680] This allowed a wide view of the crowd and dignitaries surrounding the new President, but the camera was so far away that it was difficult to make out McKinley, and, of course, without sound, little could have been made of McKinley's speech. Dickson may have felt that it was such a poor camera position that it was not worth the effort to move the bulky camera there.

Edison's crew was headed by James White who had recently left Raff & Gammon to take charge of production. William Heise, Dickson's former assistant, was on camera. It is not certain who operated the Lumière camera but it may have been the well-regarded Felix Mesguich. The International Film Company was organized by another former Raff and Gammon technician, Charles H. Webster along with Edmund Kuhn and one or both of them may have been in Washington.[681]

To film the parades, White and Heise placed the Edison camera on an elevated platform on Pennsylvania Avenue not far from where Dickson was. Their overhead angle gave them a clear shot of the units parading by and they claimed an advantage in filming McKinley's carriage because one of the horses pulling the carriage fell just in front of their camera. Dickson was closer to the action and, being at a corner where the units turned was able to keep them in the frame longer and allowed viewers a changing perspective.

This cycle of films was made complete by a pair of films reputedly showing the train that brought McKinley to Washington for the inauguration. They were filmed a la "Empire State Express". The set-up was almost identical down to the group of workmen repairing the tracks.[682]

Although he may not really have been given an advantage in filming the inauguration, Dickson was ahead on the social front. After the parade Dickson and Bitzer were invited to the nearby Ebbett House for one of the inaugural dinners. The always modish Mr. Dickson had brought an appropriate dress suit and he loaned a shirt and tie to Billy Bitzer. Bitzer was nervous about attending: "I was young and bashful and green in social graces ... On entering the dining room we found the

680 The frame is reproduced in Musser, *Edison Motion Pictures, 1890–1900*, p. 277.

681 MoMA, Biograph Picture Book; Musser, *Emergence...*, pp. 166–167; *Edison Motion Pictures ...*, pp. 276–284; Michelle Auber & Jean-Claude Seguin, *La Production Cinématographique des Frères Lumière*, pp. 103–104. ([Paris], Bibliothèque du Film, Editions Mémoires de cinéma, 1996)

682 MoMA, Biograph Picture Book; Dickson actually made three films of Pennsylvania Railroad trains at the same location which is identified as Washington, D. C. in the Production log. The work crew appears in the two identified as McKinley's train and since the camera set-up is the same for both films, it seems likely that two trains were filmed.

table beautifully set with silver and shining glass. The fern decorations and the clean white linen made me wish my sister Anna was there to see it. I got through the evening somehow or other."[683] In its early days, film production was both an adventure and an occasion. It must have been fun!

Shortly after returning to New York, Dickson began preparations for a new venture. He was going back to England.

683 MoMA, Biograph Picture Book & Bitzer, Op. Cit., pp. 12–13. They took nine films in all.

Chapter 27

Home Again

"It is no exaggeration to say that nothing the way of a spectacle has ever captured the British heart so completely as this ingenious idea of a New York inventor. The living scenes were placed before the English public two months ago in the Palace Theatre, and such was the astonishment and admiration that it was impossible to get standing room after the story became noised about. Only twice in the history of the theatre has the manager been called before the curtain. Manager Martin came forward in response to a vociferous encore after the Empire State Express had dashed down to the footlights with such realistic force that the people in the front rows shrank back and held their breath." (*Phonoscope*, May 1897, p. 5)

"Mr. W.K-L. Dickson, the Inventor of the Kinetoscope and the principal expert of the American Mutoscope Company, which owns and operates the Biograph, is in Hartford for the purpose of obtaining pictures of life in Hartford to be shown throughout the country. The photographic apparatus employed by Mr. Dickson ... is an elaborate machine mounted on a wagon and operated by an electric storage battery. Several hours were consumed this morning in charging the battery at one of the electric light stations and this afternoon the first attempts to photograph Jumbo [a horseless fire engine] will be made in Charter Oak Avenue.

"Tomorrow noon the workmen at the Pope factory on Capital Avenue are to be photographed when they come out for dinner. This will be a very valuable picture as will numerous other views that are to be made here. Much depends upon the presence of sunlight and the attainment of all the elemental conditions for a perfect picture. Mr. Dickson will remain here several days. (An article: 'Biographing' Jumbo; Moving Pictures of Scenes in Hartford" in *The Hartford Times*, 8 April 1897, p. 1.)[684]

Dickson, his wife Lucie and sister Antonia sailed for London on 12 May 1897. They were members of a large party which included Eugene Lauste and two operators. Elias B. Koopman may also have been a passenger, though it is possible he was already in England and Dickson was joining him there.[685] The American Mutoscope Company was expanding their horizons and England was their immediate objective.

The European premiere of the Biograph had taken place at London's Palace Theatre of Varieties two months earlier and it was an instant success. The Palace was London's most prestigious variety stage

684 Natural History Museum of Los Angeles County, Dickson Collection, from Connecticut State Library Microfilm 10019.

685 MoMA Crawford and Hendricks, *Myth*, p. 157. Reported by *The Orange Chronicle* 15 May 1897 and Crawford's interview with Eugene Lauste who said the two operators were Gibbons and Coward. It is unclear whether Koopman was along or was already in England.

and though other theaters were showing movies, the Palace had resisted. Koopman went to London in January, 1897 and returned with an agreement which gave the Palace an exclusive exhibition for one month at £200 per week with an option for renewal. Although Koopman may have sought the Palace out, it is possible that the theater's management saw the positive reviews for the New York programs and encouraged Koopman to make the trip. The agreement gave the Palace exclusive exhibition privileges for London and the Biograph's films proved so popular that for the next four years, it was the only place in England's leading city where the Biograph and its films could be seen. But plans were in the works to extend showings to other cities. In April, prior to Dickson's departure, they signed agreements with the theatrical companies of Moss & Thornton and Stoll. Moss & Thornton had theaters in Edinburgh, Glasgow, West Hartlepool, Liverpool, Newcastle-upon-Tyne, Sheffield, South Shields and Birmingham. Stoll's were located in Cardiff, Hanley, Leeds, Leicester, Liverpool, Newport, Nottingham and Swansea.

The premier at the Palace took place on March 18, 1897 before an invited audience which saw a selection of proven winners: "Trilby", "Washing the Baby", a scene from Rip Van Winkle (probably "Rip's Toast"), views of Niagara Falls and "McKinley at Home." The program was enriched by shots of McKinley's inauguration which were taken only two weeks earlier and the London papers took note of the timeliness of the presentation. *The Illustrated Sporting and Dramatic News* commented that: "... it says much for the enterprise of the management to have them brought from America in such a short time ...".[686] Interestingly, the Biograph replaced a series of "Living Pictures" (Tableau Vivant) which the Palace had been presenting.[687]

The American subjects were well received, but to keep the program palatable they needed films made in England and this was Dickson's mandate. His immediate purpose was to film events scheduled during Queen Victoria's Diamond Jubilee which was to be celebrated during the last weeks of June 1897. But the company had other reasons for sending Dickson to Europe.

Patent matters

A legal battle with Thomas Edison was on the horizon and the Mutoscope company apparently felt that Dickson's presence would complicate matters.

Film historian and publicist Terry Ramsaye is the source of the speculation that the Mutoscope company wanted Dickson – and Eugene Lauste – out of the country because their presence would irritate Edison – and Gilmore – during the impending legal conflict. Ramsaye's journalistic writing style and the absence of any footnotes or other documentation has led to scepticism about his accounts, but in this case there is reason to take him seriously. Ramsaye's source was, in all probability, Harry Marvin and it would have been Marvin, the executive running the New York office, who engineered the move.

686 Richard Brown and Barry Anthony, *A Victorian Film Enterprise* (Trowbridge, England, Flicks Books, 1999)

687 NMAH Hendricks, *London Topical Times* quoted in *The Biograph and Mutoscope Up to Date*, Vol. 1, No. 1, October 1897, p. 4. Their reviewer was especially taken with "The Prodigal's Return", particularly when it was run backwards.

Patent lawsuits

Motion picture historians have tended to regard the "Patent Wars" as a matter unique to the early film industry in the U.S., but this is not the case. Suits over patents were almost inevitable in the American patent system. Very few inventions are created in a vacuum and it has been common to have similar inventions registered simultaneously. Edison was continually in court with lawsuits involving the electric light, generating systems, the phonograph and many other of his inventions. His patent activities and subsequent legal battles were almost a full time activity for his patent attorneys, Dyer & Driscoll.

The suit between the American Mutoscope Co. and Edison lasted ten years, but it was not the only case protracted by legal postponements, appeals of decisions and other delays. In a related field, the contention between Eastman and Rev. Hannibal Goodwin over the invention of flexible celluloid lasted from 1887 until 1914. It took years for Hannibal Goodwin to obtain a patent for his process of making celluloid (May 1887 to September 1898). A lawsuit charging Eastman with infringing the Goodwin patent lasted from January 1903 until August 1913. By this time the good Reverend had died and the patent was owned by Ansco, a successor company to E. & H. Anthony and Scovill & Adams. Eastman lost and had to pay dearly, but Ansco only enjoyed a year of exclusivity before Goodwin's patent ran out [Breyer, Op. Cit., pp. 55, 191–105; 386–389].

Edison has born the blame for the protracted lawsuits that plagued the film industry during the early years and it is true that his company initiated most of the court cases. But the legal wrangling actually began in the U.S. Patent Office during 1896 with Edison as only one of several parties involved. Applications for motion picture devices flooded into the Patent Office and a number of them were so similar that "interferences" were declared to sort out conflicting claims. On 27 February 1897 the Patent Office notified Edison's attorneys, Dyer and Driscoll and E. Marble & Sons, attorneys for Herman Casler that there was a interference between their applications for a camera patent. This was the opening chapter in the dispute between the two companies, but it was not the first case of conflicting claims for motion picture devices – most, but not all, for projectors. Casler was already involved in two other "interferences", the most complicated one for conflicting claims for projectors with applications from Casler, Thomas Armat, the Lathams (whose patent was owned by E. & H.T. Anthony & Co.) and Edward Amet.[688] Not surprisingly, decisions by the Patent Office frequently did not settle matters and many of these disputes spilled over into the courts.

Casler's application for a patent for the Mutograph was made the previous February (1896), well after Edison's but Edison had allowed his application to languish. After filing it in August 1891, hoping to extend the period that he might have exclusivity, Edison deliberately delayed completion.[689] The normal time for completing application was three years and in October, 1895 the Patent Office notified him

688 NARA, Patent Interference 18,461. Edward Amet was, as noted earlier, late in filing his brief and Thomas Armat succeeded in getting his application dismissed from the claim. The interference was initiated in January 1897 and testimony, rebuttal and appeals continued until February 1900 when a decision awarding priority to Thomas Armat was made. The testimony in this case is particularly valuable for historians because many of the principle figures involved in the development of these three devices testified under oath. The conspicuous exception is W.K.L. Dickson who was not asked to testify even though he was associated with both the Latham and Casler machines.

689 NMAH Hendricks. On 1 December 1892, Dyer & Seely responded to Edison's query about the delaying the Kinetograph application: Dyer and Seely replied to Edison that "... we can let it 'soak' until 20 May 1894".

that his application was rejected because no action had been taken. This stimulated Edison. He appealed the rejection and revised his application so extensively that the patent examiner, Mr. Fullwood, complained that Edison was not only using delaying tactics but had, in effect, submitted a new set of specifications. But Edison and Frank Dyer pressed their case and John Seymour, the Commissioner of Patents accepted their appeal and allowed them to proceed. Fullwood had already cited Le Prince's patent as basis for rejecting several of Edison's claims and the lawyers for the Mutoscope company apparently felt that this and the differences in design between the Mutograph and the Kinetograph, gave them a substantial case for contesting Edison's application. It will be remembered that in the Kinetograph the film was guided through the lens by a set of sprockets but the Mutograph advanced the film by friction – a difference in design that was almost certainly made on Dickson's advice.

The differences between the two cameras and the existence of earlier inventions cited by the Examiners gave the Mutoscope company confidence that they could contest with Edison. Their persistent efforts to block Edison's attempts to create monopoly were as important a factor in prolonging the dispute as were Edison's stubborn attempts to sue all competitors.

The lawsuit did not begin immediately. After a flurry of revisions and some apparent pulling of strings, Edison received a patent for the Kinetograph on 31 August 1897. The following December he began the series of lawsuits that initiated the "patent wars." An ad placed by the Edison Manufacturing Co. in the November–December 1897 issue of *Phonogram*, warned: "We are protected by broad U.S. patents and **all films of other make are infringements**. ... The public is warned not to purchase any but genuine Edison films, as we intend to enforce our rights". On 7 December 1897 Edison filed suit in the Circuit Court of Southern New York against Charles H. Webster and International Film Co., the first of 23 suits charging infringement of his patents that were filed between that time and 15 September 1901. In January 1898 he filed suit against Siegmund Lubin and Edward H. Amet.[690] Edison waited until 13 May 1898 to file suit against the American Mutoscope Company, and the suit added B.F. Keith as a partner.

Since Dickson had been in Europe for a year when the suit was actually filed, it is unlikely that it was a primary reason for his trip. Nevertheless, it was convenient to have him out of the way since neither the Mutoscope company nor Edison wanted him to testify and except for the two written documents described below, his voice is conspicuously absent from any of the patent cases prior to the settlement in 1908 that ended the dispute.[691] The reason for this is obvious: neither side could predict how Dickson might testify under oath and both were concerned that he might compromise their case. He was a proud person who was particularly proud of his creative experiments and he longed for more recognition. Edison did not want him clouding the claim that he invented the Kinetoscope and Kinetograph. The Mutoscope com-

690 GU, Ramsaye Collection.

691 The Mutoscope company was not masking Dickson's presence in Europe. On 15 December 1897, Woodville Latham's attorney, Mr. Bowen commented that Dickson and Eugene Lauste were not available because they were in Europe and could not testify in Patent Interference No. 18,461, Latham v. Casler v. Armat. The Mutoscope company's lawyer, Mr. Marble commented that there were provisions for taking testimony of persons abroad and that there was no reason why their testimony could not be taken. (NARA)

pany, which had gone to lengths to establish Casler as the inventor of the Mutoscope, Mutograph and Biograph, knew that Dickson would not degrade Edison's accomplishments and might reveal too much about his own role in Casler's patents.

So Dickson made only the two official statements. The one was for the Casler-Edison Patent Interference; the other in response to questions raised in a lawsuit filed by Thomas Armat against the Mutoscope Company.

The statement for the Casler-Edison case was made May 4, 1896, a week before he sailed for England. It was a sworn statement affirming that before 14 April 1894 (the date the Holland Brother's Kinetoscope parlor opened) he had made films for Raff & Gammon and delivered films and exhibition machines to 1155 Broadway, New York City. He further affirmed that he had operated a camera similar to the one pictured in Edison's patent application in a studio he had designed and that a number of people had witnessed the camera in operation. This testimony was made for Casler's case in the Patent Interference over cameras and it was intended to support Casler's attempt to have Edison's application rejected by showing that Edison's camera had been in use while he was delaying the completion of the application. Dickson's statement is useful because it confirmed that he made the final preparations and supervised the installation of the Kinetoscopes for the opening.

In March and April 1901, Dickson responded to a series of questions about the design of the Kinetoscope and Kinetograph. These came from Parker W. Page an attorney representing the Mutoscope company. Page's first questions were sent to London by Harry Marvin in a letter to Koopman. After Dickson responded, Page then sent a second set of questions directly to Dickson. Dickson confirmed that in the design of the Kinetoscope and Kinetograph it was understood that to achieve the effect of reproducing motion it was necessary for the film to be stopped for a period. Dickson said that before the Kinetoscope was designed, he had projected images which were stopped for nine-tenths of the time and in motion one-tenth of the time while the film advanced. He also said that in the Kinetoscope the film did not stop so intermittence was achieved by using a shutter that he designed. Although Dickson's answers were not notarized, Page had them entered into the court records.

For those of us trying to reconstruct the work of Dickson and his associates, it is regrettable that these are the only statements he made during the many hours of testimony recorded in these cases. The testimony by others in these cases is an invaluable window on the beginning of cinema in America.

The European market

Keeping him out of sight during the legal engagements was a secondary reason for sending Dickson overseas. There was, in fact, a more urgent one. The engagement at the Palace opened a rich and potential new market and was the opening wedge in expanding the company's business to the European continent. It is not clear that a plan was in place when Dickson departed, but within weeks of his arrival a new company, the Mutoscope and Biograph Syndicate Ltd., was organized with Koopman as General Manager and Dickson as the principal technical officer, a position similar to the one he held with the American company. Although he seemingly was not involved in negotiating the financing of the new company and was never prominent in managing the firm, the role he played was crucial to organizing the new business because he was ideally equipped to ensure success – and attract investors. Although he had been in the United States for 18 years, he had English citizenship and had lived in France, Germany and England when he was growing up. His knowledge of the continent was solid because he traveled with his family to a number of other countries in Europe. Importantly, he was fluent in English, French and German, languages that would be key to the success of their plans. And, of course, his technical know-how was vital. He had proven that he could create the tools of production, make films of quality and train the staff to maintain a high standard of production. He may have lacked experience in money matters, but Koopman could handle that and Dickson's proven ability to create a product the public wanted was important to attracting the financing needed for the European operation. In short, he was the company's most attractive asset.

Dickson's achievements during the sixteen months since the American Mutoscope Company had been formed were quite remarkable and certainly must have impressed potential investors. He designed a film studio, created the facilities to develop and print films, established a production system, supervised the production of more than 200 films that met the demands of projection and peep show and trained a rapidly growing staff to a degree of competence where production could be maintained and quality sustained after he left.

His filmmaking skills were particularly important for the new enterprise. During 1896 the public was attracted by new machines – novel projection systems – but by 1897 images were more important than systems. The audience came once to experience a system, they returned to see new pictures – and pictures were Dickson's forte. His reputation was solid and his pictures were widely imitated. It was an era of imitation and there were no training courses or text books to learn from, so successful films begat other films. In the search for public favor it was natural that Dickson and his contemporaries would study and learn from competitors. In Dickson's case, he often sought to create a variation or improvement on models he admired. If audiences were intrigued by trains arriving in stations, they would thrill to a speeding Empire State Express and if they liked that, then Edison's similar film of the Black Diamond Express might also be popular. If audiences liked waves breaking in Dover, then they might also enjoy the turbulent rapids below Niagara Falls – or carefully shot scenes of the Falls themselves. Dickson was very much a part of this inter-active process and not only did he learn and interpret the work of others, he taught his assistants techniques which would produce films of quality.

The students he trained are his legacy, and because it has scarcely been recognized, Dickson's service as a teacher of film technique deserves greater consideration. Nothing demonstrated the caliber of his instruction better than the consistent quality of the American Mutoscope Company's productions after he left for England – or that at the Edison company earlier. There was no vacuum, no visible decline in the quality or quantity of production after he sailed for England. In fact, it is difficult to determine which were the final films that he made before he left.[692] After his departure the pace of production was brisk both for Biograph projection and viewing on Mutoscopes. At the end of the summer an anonymous Mutograph cameraman produced a film that was one of the most widely praised and imitated films of the period – "The Haverstraw Tunnel". With the camera mounted at the front of a train, the film took viewers on a thrilling ride along the edge of the Hudson River north of New York City. Audiences cheered at the effect created as scenery raced by and the train plunged into the tunnel, emerging on the other side after a brief period of darkness. The reaction of *The Sketch* when the film opened in London is typical:

"Every week new and representative scenes are added to the collection which the American Biograph Company exhibits at the Palace Theatre. Of these, the palm must be awarded to the panoramic view of the tunnel, which was very weird. The spectator was not an outsider, watching from safety the rushing of the cars, but a passenger on a phantom train that whirled him through space at the rate of nearly a mile a minute. There was no smoke, no glimpse of shuddering frame or crushing wheels, nothing to indicate motion save that shining vista that was eaten up irresistibly, rapidly, and the disappearing panorama of banks and hedges. The train was invisible, and yet the landscape swept by remorselessly, and far away the bright day became a spot of darkness. That was the mouth of the tunnel, and towards it the spectator was hurled as if a fate was behind him. The spot of darkness became a canopy of gloom. The darkness closed around, and the spectator was being flung through that cavern with the demoniac energy behind him. The shadows, the rush of the invisible force, and the uncertainty of the issue made one instinctively hold one's breath, as when on the edge of a crisis that might become a catastrophe. But the daylight shone ahead, and again the spectator was being swept through the fields.[693]

Although Dickson did not supervise "The Haverstraw Tunnel", it was made in Dicksonian style. Scenery, however interesting and beautiful, did not move, so when it was the focus, then the camera had to be on something that moved. It was done to good effect several times during the summer of 1896 and "Haverstraw Tunnel" gave it a new dimension. The *Boston Transcript* described the experience as "... subjective rather than objective. He is not simply sitting still and looking at figures or objects in motion. He enters, or seems to enter, into that motion ...". This comment would have pleased Dickson. Action drawing the spectator into motion being filmed was the essence of Dickson's filmmaking style. "Haverstraw Tunnel"[694] created a demand for "Phan-

692 Dickson probably supervised the filming of the parade for the dedication of Grant's Tomb on 27 April 1897 (nos. 185–195) and it is possible that he shot "Ring Around a Rosie" (no. 221) and "See Saw" (No. 222), which were made at Harry Marvin's home in Canastota, NY with his children as featured players. This may well have been a final gathering of the KMCD group before Dickson departed.

693 *The Sketch*, No. 250, Vol. XX, Nov. 10, 1897

694 *Boston Transcript*, 8 October 1897, an article "Excursions While You Wait." In Niver, Op. Cit., pp. 30–31.

Dickson pioneered the genre that became known as "phantom rides", filming action from the front of a moving vehicle – especially trains. This dramatic publicity photo showing Billy Bitzer on the front of a locomotive was taken in October 1897 to publicize films made for Boston's Keith's theater. It was taken in the railroad yard of the New York, New Haven & Hartford, RR in Dedham, Massachusetts. The engineer leaning out of the cab is George C. Dustin and Wallace McCutcheon was supervising the filmmaking. Only the lens mounting of the huge camera can be clearly seen in this picture. While Bitzer appears as a daredevil, it is unlikely that he rode the cowcatcher very often as it was more comfortable – and safer – to be on a flat car at the front of the engine. (NMAH)

tom Rides" and Dickson and many others continued to arouse audiences with trips filmed on trains running through scenery in North America and Europe.

The Kings, the Queens, the Lords, the Earls

On arriving in England, Dickson's immediate goal was to film Queen Victoria's Diamond Jubilee which was scheduled to take place in June. The celebration of the sixty years on the throne promised to be one of the most newsworthy events of the year. Victoria had been reclusive through much of her reign, but she had been seen in public more in recent years and in 1897 her popularity was at a peek. The parades and ceremonies surrounding the celebration promised the pomp, pageantry and spectacle that the British excelled at. As Dickson and his entourage sailed for Europe, the Mutoscope company bragged that the films would be rushed to America so that Biograph's audiences could be among the first to enjoy the ceremonies. For many, it would be their first opportunity to see the colorful military units in motion rather than

In Dickson's Hand: "Kodak picture / I took at Aldershot Showing Roped off enclosure or stand given me by Duke of Connaught Queen's & Roayl carriages adjoining. Another photographer with large plates ordinary camera next to us by our permission."

/ From Mrs. Smith, 7/57./

Dickson said this was a "Kodak" of his filming Queen Victoria's Jubilee activities at the military center at Aldershot, England, 1 July 1897. The typewritten notes are by Gordon Hendricks. [NMAH.]

in still photographs, drawings or paintings.[695] The company explained the schedule to *Phonoscope:* "One day after the last picture is taken ... the films will be ready for transportation. It will take full seven days from London to New York, including the time for unpacking and developing the negatives. In two days more they will be distributed through the points nearest New York, and then on through the West as fast as steam can carry them ...".[696]

As a warm-up for the main even, Dickson's crew filmed two famous horse races. On 2 June the finish of the English Derby was filmed at the track in Epsom and on the eighteenth they were at Ascot for the race for the Gold Cup. Before he left for England, Dickson may have prepared for this by filming several races at the Gravesend track in Brooklyn. At Ascot he was able to film the arrival and departure of Edward, the Prince of Wales. The heir to the throne was an avid fan of the "sport of kings".[697]

Although Edison had chosen not to film the Jubilee, a host of others were intent on recording the event and the jockeying for choice camera positions was intense. Film historian John Barnes has identified at least eighteen companies and more than twenty cameras ready to film the Royal Procession on 22 June.[698] Barnes was unable to identify the location of Dickson's camera, but it was probably a reasonably good

695 The Lumières; Robert Paul, Birt Acres and others had filmed military units and royal events previously and these films had been shown in the U.S., but the Jubilee was the most exciting event involving the British monarchy. See *La Production cinématographique des Frères Lumière*, pp. 288–290 and John Barnes, *The Beginnings of the Cinema in England[, 1896]*, pp. 204–219 (London, David & Charles and New York, Barnes and Noble Books, 1976).

696 *Phonoscope*, May, 1897, p. 5. The lead article entitled "Royal Parade Here".

697 The English races were: "Finish of the English Derby of 1897" (No. 23E); "Arrival of H. R. H. The Prince of Wales at Ascot" (No. 24E); "Departure of H. R. H. The Prince of Wales from Ascot" and "The Race for the Ascot Gold Cup (No. 26E); the American films: "Six Furlong Handicap" (No. 209), "Going to the Post" (No. 210), "Finish of the Brooklyn Handicap" (No. 211) and "Hurdle Race" (No. 212) were apparently filmed very close to the time that he left the U.S.

698 Barnes, Op. Cit., pp. 178–199. Barnes devoted a full chapter of his history of British cinema in 1897 to the filming of the Jubilee.

Members of the Royal family pictured in Afternoon Tea in the Gardens of Clarence House, among them the future Kings Edward VII and George V. The royal family were very co-operative with the infant film industry and this film was made in July 1897 at their request. [Anthony.]

one. Koopman had made some very advantageous connections and Dickson's personable demeanor and experience in negotiating with celebrities seemed to put them in an unusually favorable status for newcomers from a foreign land. Dickson had probably not lost his English accent and it is reasonable to assume that it was an accent that would identify him as a member of the educated class. We know that following the Jubilee Procession, the company enjoyed a remarkably close relationship with the extended royal family. This is evidenced by an annotation that Dickson made on the back of a "Kodak picture" of his camera set-up for taking the military review at Aldershot on 1 July. It was a "... roped off enclosure or stand given me by Duke of Connaught[;] Queen's & Royal carriages adjoining".[699] The Duke was the Queen's third son and one of her favorites, so the company's connections appear to have been unusually solid.

Dickson arrived in England with a new version of the Mutograph camera. It was slightly smaller than the first version, but to accommodate the large film it still had to be substantially larger and less flexible than the cameras of competitors. The new camera, dubbed "Camera B" by Herman Casler, could be mounted on a tripod with telescoping legs which allowed it to be raised to about six feet. When the tripod was fully extended the operator had to stand on a ladder, a box or some other object that would raise him to the level of the camera (see illustration on page 474). The wooden camera case was still a formidable piece of furniture – Dickson spoke of using it as a dining table. Casler had been able to reduce the size by mounting the motor and the box holding unexposed film on the outside of the case and putting the lens in an

699 NMAH
Hendricks.

adjustable bellows at the front of the camera. Pictures of the camera taken in 1897 indicate that the motor could be attached separately. Bitzer said the motor for "Camera A" weighed more than two hundred pounds. While this appears to be smaller, it would still have been very heavy, but being able to mount the motor separately would have made set-up easier – though it was still a formidable task.

The new camera seems to have had a couple of features that made it more flexible. The exterior film box would have made it possible to use larger rolls of film, and the bellows would have made it easier to adjust and change the lens.[700]

The Jubilee Procession was first of a series of filming events involving the Royal family. Four days after the Procession, on 26 June, Dickson's crew was at Spithead, the channel between Portsmouth and the Isle of Wight, to film the Diamond Jubilee Naval Review. On 1 July they filmed the Diamond Jubilee Review at the military base in Aldershot, not too far from Windsor. Members of the Royal family, including the Prince of Wales, seem to have been intrigued by this novel way of communicating with the public and gave permission to take several quite personal films of the family. Historians Richard Brown and Barry Anthony speculate that they felt that it was a way of becoming accessible to their public while remaining aloof and mystical – visible and seemingly real and at the same time distant and enigmatic . Sometime in late June or early July Dickson filmed the Prince of Wales leaving Marlborough House en route to St. James Palace. He was uniformed as a Field Marshall of the British army and accompanied by a troupe of Horse Guards.

More remarkably, the family allowed Dickson to stage two films purported to show family social affairs, "Afternoon Tea in the Gardens of Clarence House" and "The Clarence House Lawn Party". Participants in the "Afternoon Tea ..." were Victoria's son Prince Albert (The Duke of Saxe-Coburg-Gotha and Duke of Endinburgh) and his wife; the Queen's second daughter, Alice (Grand Duchess of Hess) and her husband the Grand Duke of Hess; Prince Edward's son George (the Duke of York and future King George V) as well as Prince Charles of Denmark (Prince Edward's wife was the daughter of Prince Christian of Denmark) and the Hereditary Prince of Saxe-Coburg (Queen Victoria's consort, Prince Albert was the Prince of Saxe-Coburg). Viewers watching "... Lawn Party" saw the Prince of Wales, his brother and sister-in-law, the Duke and Duchess of York, Prince George of Greece and others. In a comment made to Will Day, Dickson confirmed that he staged the tea party: "... I also interviewed the Duke of Edinborough [sic] in a sham tea party – the Duchess of Teck [sic] pouring T. receiving our present King Geo & others – insisting that her parrot should be in evidence".[701] This is confirmed by a frame from the film reproduced in *The Era*, 24 July 1897 (see photo on page 475). The tables are set up in full sun, on the lawn of Clarence House and most of the participants are arranged around the back of the table, facing the camera with Prince Alfred seated prominently on the right side of the frame.

700 The illustrations for the article about the American Mutoscope Co. in *Scientific American*, 17 April 1897, show Dickson and Casler with Camera A. This drawing was probably made from a photograph taken while filming on the Pennsylvania Railroad in November 1896 or March 1897. The company documented all of their equipment by taking detailed photographs and a number of these survive. There are copies in the Gordon Hendricks Collection at the Smithsonian and I found others at the Canal Town Museum in Canastota, New York. The photographs are very useful in identifying how the camera worked and was operated.

701 BiFi, Fonds Will Day, Dickson to Will Day, 17 February1933.

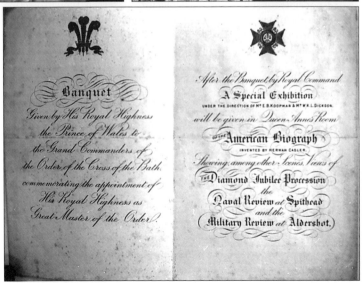

The Biograph's films of the Diamond Jubilee were presented at an invitational screening in St. James Palace, 21 July 1897. Dickson's wife Lucie (left) and sister Antonia (right) may have purchased these elegant gowns for the occasion. The portraits were taken by Lafayette, a London photographer. [NMAH.]

There is one chair on camera side of the table, but it is on the left of the frame. To add a more humane touch, one of the royal dogs lounges in front of the tea tables with an infant, the child of Princess Alice, playing with it. Everybody is formally dressed and all of the men but one are wearing top hats. Although filmed on the lawn, a leafy backdrop of trees provides a contrast which focuses attention on the group at the table. It is a typical Dickson set-up and its casual formality is reminiscent of his film of William McKinley.

The Prince of Wales was pleased and invited Dickson and Koopman to prepare a command performance of the Biograph at St. James Palace on 21 July 1897. Films of the Jubilee celebrations and others were to be shown in Queen Anne's Room following a Banquet given by the Prince for the Grand Commanders of the Order of the Cross of the Bath commemorating the appointment of the Prince as Great Master of the Order.

While it was a signal honor and quite unique, it posed some serious logistical problems. The films that Dickson had taken so far were sent to the United States for developing and printing. They had two weeks to get ready for the projection, not enough time for all the films to make the round trip. Koopman arranged to take over the offices of European Blair Company in Cecil Court, off Charing Cross Road, a few blocks north of Trafalgar Square. Eugene Lauste told Merritt Crawford that he was given the job of fitting out a laboratory with developing tanks and large drying reels. He claims to have done the job in four days and then worked days and nights developing and printing films. Lauste was also responsible for setting-up the projector and screen, then projecting the film. Koopman and Dickson were credited with directing the program and were presented with gold stick-pins by the Prince. Portraits of Dickson's wife Lucie and sister Antonia in particularly elegant dress lead me to speculate that they may have attended (see page 477). As an added bonus, the Prince was so pleased with the program that he allowed Dickson to film him again the next day.[702]

The Mutoscope and Biograph Syndicate Ltd.

The Royal Command Performance coincided with the announcement of a new company, The Mutoscope and Biograph Syndicate, Ltd. The British branch of the American company was begun with nominal capital of £60,000, divided into £1 shares. The company purchased rights to patents owned by Casler, Marvin, Koopman and Dickson for £39,000; £13,000 to be paid in cash installments which were to be completed by 1 April 1898, and 26,000 full-paid shares. This gave the company rights to the Mutograph camera; the Biograph projector and Mutoscope machines, as well as versions of the machines that the KMCD group had patented in the U.S. and England. They also obtained rights to various "mutoscopic views" (i.e. films and Mutoscope reels) and the papers establishing the company gave them title to one Biograph projector and six Mutoscopes. This arrangement seems to

702 NMAH Lauste Collection and MoMA Crawford; Anthony & Brown, Op. Cit., pp. 57–59. Eugene Lauste's description of the screening is from an undated interview by Merritt Crawford which was probably conducted about 1928.

have been a bit loose, since the camera that Dickson was operating was not transferred to the new company and there must have been more than one projector in England. One was in permanent use at the Palace and the company had already begun touring at variety halls outside London.[703]

The new company was not a wholly owned subsidiary of the American parent. Instead, Koopman followed the same tactic in England that he used in the United States. He approached potential investors with a business plan and was able to convince men of substance that there was a solid commercial future for projected motion pictures and peep show machines. The substantial reputation that the Biograph had earned in the U.S. and now at the Palace in London put him in a much better position than he had been in the fall of 1895 when he approached American investors. But there was no assurance that the public would continue to be entranced by cinema and Koopman's achievement in creating two well financed companies under such tenuous circumstances is quite remarkable.

The key to Koopman's success seems to have been an emphasis on the usefulness of films in other fields besides entertainment, particularly in advertising. The glowing reports from journalists, theatrical people and the public's enthusiasm for the Biograph's programs are the most memorable aspect of this period, but they were not necessarily attractive to the investors during the 1890s. Serious investors often considered show business to be very risky, largely because the popularity of performers and shows could change unpredictably. Koopman had been able to attract investors to the Mutoscope by emphasizing its use as an advertising and instructional device and he continued to emphasize the promotional use of both the Biograph and the Mutoscope. The programs at Keith's and the Palace continued to mix pure entertainment with soft-sell advertisements such as Empire State Express.

By the time Koopman began negotiating with British businessmen, the American company had also established itself as form of visual journalism. The public was attracted by the possibility of seeing presidential candidates, events like the dedication of Grant's Tomb and other newsworthy activities. Print journalists were not put off by this new way to see the news. The American company had worked with Joseph Pulitzer's *New York World* and in 1898, during the Spanish-American War, they worked with William Randolph Hearst's *New York Journal*. We have seen that the company was making and selling photographs to newspapers and magazines. It is not surprising, then, that two prominent publishers, Newnes & Hudson and Sir Cyril Arthur Pearson were investors in the British company. Sir George Newnes was publisher of *The Strand Magazine* and *Country Life* (which was edited by Edward Hudson); Pearson published *Pearson's Magazine*.[704]

Although the Biograph dominated the company's activities in the fall of 1896, the Mutoscope continued to be a parallel enterprise. In fact, Koopman seems to have made the Mutoscope a major element in this British campaign. This was probably because the nature of the Biograph

703 Letter from Richard Brown, 8 April 1997. For a more detailed discussion of the business arrangements establishing the company and its operation after it began, see Richard Brown & Barry Anthony, *A Victorian Film Enterprise, The History of the British Mutoscope and Biograph Company, 1897–1915.* Richard Brown gives a thorough, well-written account of the company's business activities.

704 Brown & Anthony, Op. Cit., pp. 124–126.

projector and the company's insistence on keeping the projection of films in their own hands, limited the scope of the projection business. The Biograph was established at a half dozen theaters owned by Keith-Albee, and was touring to other American cities, but it was by no means flooding the country. In England, the Palace had exclusive rights to the Biograph in London and two or three touring companies were being organized, so it would be available, but in limited doses. In the summer of 1897, there were no ambitious plans to build hundreds of projectors, instead, they had their eye on lucrative markets in Paris, Berlin, Amsterdam and other major European cities. With their reputation for quality, they could demand higher fees than their competitors. The number of theaters able to pay this premium rate was limited and Koopman and his associates recognized this. So the business plan was to use the Biograph to provide a steady, predictable income and the Mutoscope to reach a larger, more varied market.

It is not known if this was the approach that Koopman used with potential British investors, but it seems probable that he stressed the Mutoscope's potential as an advertising device and as a diversion in hotels, railroad stations, stores and other public places. He may also have raised the potential of parlor machines for home use, but it is unlikely that emphasized use in amusement parlors. Coin-operated entertainment devices were relatively new and the parlors that had opened still had a degree of respectability, but they were already attracting the attention of conservative moralists concerned that the young and the innocent would be led astray in them. While the moral reformers were often guilty of exaggeration and worst case speculation, the American company had already discovered the market for racy peep show subjects and was ready to exploit it. Three films of "Little Egypt" with her belly exposed were made early in 1897 and as Dickson was preparing to depart, the roof top studio was kept busy turning out "Bag Punching by Sadie Leonard" two films of her boxing with a man (and apparently decking him); a "French Acrobatic Dance"; "Kicking Willie's Hat" (girls high kicking with an ample display of petticoats); "Girl's Boarding School" (three young ladies in nightgowns cavorting); "A Dressing Room Scene" (show girls changing), etc. The appeal of such stuff was probably not mentioned in Koopman's negotiations, but the potential was probably understood by the parties involved.

In retrospect, the emphasis on the Mutoscope may seem misplaced, but it should be remembered that, attractive and dynamic as the theatrical film industry is, it has always been only one of the uses to which moving images have been put. In these formative years of the film business, speculators were open to a variety of avenues and it was not at all certain that its future lay in the theatrical world. Edison's skepticism about the future of the industry was shared by others and this cautious approach was probably the proper one to use with potential investors. And it seems to have worked, because Koopman was able to put together a solidly financed company and one that could continue to expand.

Among the films made for showing in Paris were two films of a charge by two regiments of Cuirassiers. Dickson was familiar with the Lumières' films of the same subject and tried to improve and add excitement by having the cavalry charge directly at the camera and pass it on both sides. The photo on top is from the beginning of Charge of the French Cuirassiers – Paris and on the bottom is the end of Cuirassiers Charging a Field Battery – Paris. Although they are different films, both ended with the cavalry overrunning the camera, and in this case, the battery of artillery. The impact of the subject converging on the viewers then suddenly disappearing was sensational.
[NMAH & BiFi Meusy.]

On the Continent

A few weeks after the formation of the new company Dickson, with camera in tow, journeyed to Paris, Budapest and Berlin. The Biograph made its premier on the Continent in Paris on 16 September at the Casino de Paris and this was probably the occasion for his visit and the immediate reason for making films. Although the exact dates of his trip are not known, he probably arrived a few days before the premier. He shot a half dozen films in several locations in and about the city. Five days later, on September 21, 1897, he was in Budapest to film a meeting between Kaiser Wilhelm II of Germany and Emperor Franz Joseph of Austria-Hungary. He went on to Berlin after that.

The visit to Paris gave him the opportunity to emulate, and perhaps improve on a Lumière film that he admired, the assault of the Cuirassiers. He made the obligatory shots of Place de l'Opéra and Place de la Concorde, but these were the only films made in the heart of the city. Strangely, he did not film the Eiffel Tower, or, if he did, the film did not come out. His eye was on the French army and the military was featured in four of the six films made in the French capital. At the École Gymnastique in Joinville he filmed two military exercises, a mock assault on a wall in which a battalion of soldiers scaled a wall forty feet high and a second of a troupe passing through a gate. The First Regiment of Cuirassiers charged his camera at the Château de Bagatelle, near the Bois de Boulogne and he repeated the exercise by filming the 27th Dragoons in a similar attack. In both cases he asked the assaulting cavalry to approach from a distance, riding at high speed towards the camera with horsemen passing it on both sides. In their publicity for the charge of the Cuirassiers, the Mutoscope company claimed several of the horses fell. H.L. Adam, writing in *The Royal Magazine* in 1901, said that Dickson caused the collision when he unexpectedly signaled for them to turn. The charge of the Dragoons, filmed at Camp de Satory, was made distinctive by staging a mock battle. Cannons from the 11th Artillery Regiment were set in the foreground firing at the charging Dragoons who then over-ran them. Once again the speeding horsemen were directed to pass closely on both sides the camera.[705]

This emphasis on the military was a response to an evident preference for military subjects by audiences in London and New York. Dickson had probably observed this at theaters where his films and those of his competitors were showing. There were no audience surveys in the 1890s, but in their April 1897 issue, *Phonoscope*, used audience reactions to various types of films to measure their popularity. They reported that serpentine dances and high kicking got moderate applause but there was a good deal more for military scenes, particularly marching scenes that seemed to head into audience, but none of these received an encore. It was scenes of the surf breaking on piers at Manhattan Beach and the Empire State Express that drew requests for encores.[706]

Apparently aware of this taste for the martial, Dickson had spent a deal of time filming military units. Before leaving the U.S. he had made more than a dozen films at military bases, among them West Point, Governor's Island, New York and Fort Ethan Allen in Vermont. During his British summer he made two trips to Aldershot, one for the Jubilee and the second to film Hiram Maxim firing his rapid-fire gun, a forerunner of the modern machine gun. Although he filmed parades, bayonet exercises, wall-scaling and other military drills, it was the cavalry charge that gave audiences a particular rush, and he worked

705 There are copies of several of these films in the collection of the Nederlands Filmmuseum. H.L. Adam's article, "Round the World for the Biograph" in *The Royal Magazine*, April 1901, pp. 120–128 is quoted in Brown and Anthony, Op. Cit.

706 "'Picture Projecting Devices", *Phonoscope*, April 1897, p. 10.

At the end of summer in 1897 Dickson was in Budapest and Berlin taking films suitable for new venues for the Biograph. In Budapest he filmed Emperor Franz Josef who was meeting Kaiser Wilhelm of Germany and in Berlin another military parade was filmed. [NMAH.]

carefully at perfecting the technique. By the time he arrived in Paris he was ready give audiences a new thrill by applying the close-to-the-subject technique that was so successful in "Empire State Express".

He was not done with the cavalry. In Budapest he filmed a unit of Austrian Hussars in a similar charge. The Hussars wore plumed shakos and had fur lined coats draped over one shoulder. This contrasted nicely with the blue uniforms and silver helmets worn by the French unit –

Europeans had much neater uniforms than the rather drab and utilitarian American troops.

But his objective in Budapest was filming the two Emperors, Wilhelm of Germany and Franz Joseph of Austria-Hungary. He was able to make two films of them together, one of them at the dedication of the Republican Museum in Budapest. He also filmed Franz Joseph laying the cornerstone of a new barracks in Budapest. There are no surviving copies of these films and I have seen no still images from them, but the American company's 1902 catalog said that the film at the dedication had "Admirable portraits of both Emperors ... as they enter their carriages and are driven away. The other film recorded "...the elaborate pageantry of the occasion".[707]

There was considerable interest in two other pictures made in or near Budapest. "A Camp of Zingaree Gypsies" was taken on what appears to be a country road and there was a great deal of activity in a rather crowded scene. *The Sketch* was cynically intrigued by the other, a film of a construction site in Budapest which showed women working along side men. "... how curious are some of the customs of the Austro-Hungarian people, ... groups of women, all of whom are engaged in erecting a house, bricklaying, mixing cement, ascending ladders, attending to carts, &c. All these artisans are women, but they go about their work with apparently far more zest than the average British workman, whose ineptitude has almost passed into a proverb". The article told of the British Mutoscope Company's intent to present copies of their pictures to the British Museum.[708] Pictures of "Home Life of a Hungarian Family" and "Hungarian Women Plucking Geese" showed other aspects of life in a part of Europe that was less familiar to many Western Europeans and Americans.

There is less information about Dickson's trip to Berlin, but among the films made there were a military parade (page 483) "Changing Guard" in Berlin and "A Children's Carnival in Germany".

A growing business

Although Dickson may not have been actively involved in the company's business dealings, his trips were often preliminary to the expansion of the company's activities into the places he visited. This happened often enough that it seems unlikely that they were not part of a preconceived plan. During 1898 and 1899 the company established affiliated, but independently financed companies in France, Germany, Austria-Hungary, the Netherlands, Italy, Belgium, South Africa and India. With the exception of Belgium, South Africa and India, Dickson made films in all of these countries prior to the establishing of the off-shoot companies. (He was in South Africa during the Boer War, but this was after the South African company was established.) Since England, Germany and France were Western Europe's largest and most populous countries, they were the primary objectives in this campaign of expansion. The company was oriented towards Northern and West-

707 *Picture Catalog*, 1902, p. 101.

708 *The Sketch*, No. 250, Vol. XX, 10 November 1897.

ern Europe, so the populous countries of Italy and Austria-Hungary took a secondary role, perhaps reflecting common prejudices of the day. Immigrants from Italy and Eastern European countries were crowding into tenements in American cities, feeding the widespread racial and class stereotypes of the period. The Austro-Hungarian empire straddled the area between Eastern and Western Europe and included a large Slavic population which still seemed foreign to Western Europeans. Another populous Mediterranean country, Spain, was not on the company's list and the short, but dramatic war between the U.S. and Spain in 1898 probably contributed to its omission.

Because they were home to the most influential entertainment centers, England, France and Germany were logical targets. In 1898 London with a population of 4,500,000 had 24 theaters seating 30,852; Paris with a population of 2,500,000, had 16 theaters seating 24,000; Berlin, with a population of 2,000,000 had 12 theaters seating 14,400 and New York, with a population of 1,800,000 had 18 theaters seating 27,450.[709] With the Biograph playing at prestigious venues in New York and London, the company had its eye on Paris and Berlin as the summer of 1897 came to an end. They followed the scheme that worked in England and the U.S.: a contract with a major theater in the city, followed by a new commercial enterprise to manage affairs in the country. We have seen that in Paris the theater was the Casino de Paris. In Berlin it was the famous Wintergarten and the Biograph opened there on 15 August 1897, a few weeks before opening at Casino de Paris. So by September 1897, the company had established itself in prestigious variety houses in the most important entertainment centers of the day. And these were not brief engagements. In each city the Biograph remained a featured and well regarded entertainment until well after the turn of the new century.

These engagements and the new affiliated companies meshed well with the company's plan to also program shorter engagements of the Biograph in other entertainment venues and market the Mutoscope through regional sub-contracts.

The French company, The Biograph and Mutoscope Company for France is a good example of how this worked. A key figure in the French company was Eugene Lauste, Dickson's longtime friend.[710] The Parisian-born Lauste was sent to Paris in September 1897 to set up and operate the Biograph at the Casino de Paris. According to Lauste, he was dispatched to France suddenly and unexpectedly. He had been with the Mutoscope Company for about a year, having joined it in the spring or summer of 1896 after leaving the Lathams' Lambda Company when the new owners took over. Dickson, who helped him get the job with the Lathams, sent him to Koopman who hired him as a technician-projectionist[711] Lauste operated the Biograph at the Poli Theater in New Haven and came to England with Dickson in May 1897.

In addition to setting-up technical facilities at the company's London office and operating the projector at St. James Palace, Lauste had been operating the Biograph at places outside London. In July he ran

709 These figures were published by *The Sketch*, 23 March 1898, p. 372. To complete their table: St. Petersburg with a population of 1,000,000 had 7 theaters seating 10,500; Amsterdam was 500,000 with 4 theaters seating 4,800; Brussels was 500,000 with 3 theaters seating 4,500; Rome was 500,000 with 6 theaters seating 12,000 and Copenhagen was 400,000 with 4 theaters seating 4,800.

710 MoMA Crawford and NMAH Smithsonian, Lauste Collection. Lauste left a valuable record of his activities, documenting his activities with newspaper clippings, correspondence and photographs. These have survived in the Merritt Crawford collection at the Museum of Modern and the Eugene Lauste Collection at the National Museum of American History of the Smithsonian Institution.

711 MoMA Crawford, Statements made in response to Terry Ramsaye's *A Million and One Nights*. A copy was given to Jean A. LeRoy with permission to publish it. Probably made in 1927 or 1928.

the projector at the Winter Gardens in the popular seaside resort of Blackpool and in August he was in Newport in South Wales. When he got the call to go to Paris he was at the People's Palace in Bristol. A letter of recommendation from the theater's assistant manager, Charles Gascoigne, dated 10 September 1897, confirms that Lauste had less than a week to prepare for his trip to Paris.

The Casino de Paris was a well-thought-of center of social gathering and entertainment. It was a café-music hall and not arranged like variety theaters in America and England. There were conventional theater seats near the stage and behind them was an area with small tables where customers could have drinks and watch the show. The floor was long and flat and it was surrounded by galleries on several levels, some with enough drapery and potted vegetation to discretely conceal the occupants. It was a congenial atmosphere that encouraged Parisians to meet and socialize while being entertained. The Biograph could not be set up in a balcony as it had been in New York and London, so a booth was built in the center of the floor. It was covered with heavy, dark draperies and surrounded with potted plants. It looked not unlike a catafalque. The programs presented at Casino de Paris were similar to, but not identical with, the mixed variety shows at Keith's Union Square and the Palace Theatre of Varieties. On 16 September, when the Biograph made its debut, it shared the bill with a ballet-pantomime in three tableaux by Jacques Lemair and Rossi set to the music of Henri José. The Biograph was the second part of the program and the presentation consisted of ten films drawn from tested "classics" like "A Hard Wash", and "A Pillow Fight" and more timely productions such as scenes from Queen Victoria's Jubilee and "A Military Review at Aldershot". To stimulate the audience, they were shown "A Cavalry Charge" (probably one filmed at Ft. Ethan Allen) and two of Dickson's railroad films: "The Pennsylvania Limited Express" and one identified as "Le Train-éclair (110 kilomètres à l'heure")" which may have been "Empire State Express".[712]

As in New York, theaters in Paris were often closed during summer, and if this was not the reopening for the Casino, it was very early in the fall-winter season. The program was well received and the press reviews were very favorable (though it was not unusual for theaters to pay reviewers to write favorable reviews). *La Semaine parisienne* called it an enormous success and reported that audiences gave "profuse hurrahs" for "The Pillow Fight", "Pussy's Bath" and "Hard Wash". As in New York and London, this was the beginning of an extended run. The Casino's managers, Louis Borney and Armand Desprez kept the Biograph until mid-June and in mid July it moved to the Théâtre Marigny which was open during the summer. In October of 1898 it moved to Folies-Bergère where it continued as a regular feature until 1902.

Booking the Biograph for the program at Casino de Paris was an act of some daring. Enthusiasm for cinema was at a very low ebb during the second half of 1897. The novelty of the Lumières' Cinématographe had already begun to fade when Parisians – and many others – were

712 Jean-Jacques Meusy "Paris-Palaces ou le temps des cinénas (1894–1918) (Paris CNRS Éditions, 1995), p. 62.

713 Jean-Jacques
Meusy and Paul
Spehr "Les débuts en
France de l'American
Mutoscope and
Biograph Company
(Paris, *Histoire
Economie et Société, No.
4*, 1997), pp. 671–708
also published as
"L'Esordio in Francia
dell'American
Mutoscope and
Biograph
Company/The
Beginnings of the
American Mutoscope
and Biograph Co. in
France" (Gemona,
Italy, *Griffithiana*, N.
62/63, May 1998, pp.
128–169. Motion
picture film was
highly flammable. It
was made on a
cellulose nitrate base,
a chemical formula
closely related to
TNT. It could ignite
at relatively low
temperatures and
when burning it
produced its own
oxygen so it was
difficult to put it out.
"Nitrate" film was
used until c. 1950
when manufacturers,
led by Kodak, began
using a flame resistant
tri-acetate base.

The Biograph premiered at the Casino de Paris in Paris, a popular gathering spot. The theatre presented a variety show and had rows of seats near the stage and tables in the back where the public could enjoy drinks and socialize. The projector was housed in the catafalque like structure in the center. Eugene Lauste, who supervised the projections, is standing by the velvet draped booth. (NMAH)

stunned by the disastrous fire at the Charity Bazaar on 4 May 1897 when 128 people, many members of French nobility, died in a fire which was blamed on ignited motion picture film.[713] The emphatically favorable reception that the Biograph received in New York and London may have emboldened Borney and Desprez to take a chance on a cinema novelty.

The successful run at Casino de Paris encouraged the company to open business offices in Paris. The Biograph and Mutoscope Company

A French poster for Pillow Fight *at the Casino de Paris.*
[From the collection of M. Gianati, courtesy of Jean-Jacques Meusy.]

for France was incorporated on 6 June 1898 with a nominal capital of
£100,000. Most of the investors were British, among them publishing
magnate Sir George Newnes and two members of Parliament, John
Scott Montague and William Kenyon Harvey. There were only two
French names on the Board of Directors, Alfred D.M. Messéar, 33 Quai
Voltaire and Charles Berthier, 62 Ave. du Bois de Boulogne. An office
was at opened at 29 rue Tronchet (8/9 arrondisment) with Julian W.
Orde as manager. In October 1901 it moved to 33 rue Joubert (9 arr.).[714]
In order to maintain a fresh supply of French subjects, a studio was built
in the Paris suburb of Courbevoie. The exact date of the opening is
unknown, but the studio was in operation by May 1899. It had an
outdoor stage; a storage shed for costumes and props; rooms for
developing and printing film; facilities for inspecting film and assembling mutoscope rolls; and a work shop for repairing and maintaining
equipment. The operation was supervised by Eugene Lauste. For the
next two years the studio was very busy. By November 1902 they had
recorded at least 377 titles in their production log book.[715] Most of these
films were for French audiences, but the listing of 42 titles made in
France in the catalog published by the American company in 1902
shows that selected titles were seen in the U.S. and Europe.

As in England, the screenings at Casino de Paris, Théâtre Marigny
and Folies-Bergère provided the company with both publicity and an
established income, but their business plans relied strongly on developing the Mutoscope business and production of reels for Mutoscopes
was an important part of the work done in Courbevoie.

714 Brown &
Anthony, Op. Cit., p.
141.

715 The production
log for the French
company does not
survive, but these
numbers come from
French productions
included in the
American company's
1902 catalog.
Productions at
Courbevoie received
numbers beginning at
5000 and higher.
Since a production
numbered 5377 is in
the 1902 catalog there
must have been at
least that many films
produced in France.

The Mutoscope business

Since the American and British Mutoscope companies anticipated profits from marketing the Mutoscope, during 1897 and 1898 they put a major effort into developing this side of their business. In the U.S. and England they fostered the formation of territorial Mutoscope companies, i.e. companies that had exclusive concessions, usually within a defined geographic area. The American company's plan was described in a publicity publication:

"In the introduction of the Mutoscope to the public outside of the City of New York, it is proposed to employ the services of local parties to whom exclusive rights will be given for certain territory on county or state lines as may be agreed upon in each case, this to secure the location of machines in the most desirable places and provide for their proper maintenance and the changing of views in the machines."[716]

The machines were offered on lease and the owners of the property where the machine were placed were entitled to a percentage of the take, usually about 15 per cent. The cost of a license was fairly high. Licensees were required to take a certain number of machines and pay $100 per machine for the lease. The required number of machines was rather large, too. A company prospectus published in 1898 anticipated that sub-companies would take about 500 machines. In addition, the American company demanded a percentage of the local company's stock.

It took a while for the Mutoscope plans to develop because of the quantity of machines that had to be manufactured. The machines were made at the Marvin Electric Rock Drill Company in Canastota. The company was formed independently and was not a subsidiary of the American Mutoscope Company, but since Harry Marvin was the company's Second Vice President and Herman Casler, who supervised the plant, was one of the company's "Technicians", the distinction was rather irrelevant. Casler was quite busy during 1896 and 1897 since in addition to producing several hundred Mutoscopes, he made several new versions of the Mutograph as well as enough Biograph projectors to service the growing number of projection sites in the U.S., England and the Continent.

Since Casler was struggling to supply the needs of the American company, the British company negotiated an agreement with Léon Gaumont to manufacture Mutoscopes for the European market. The negotiations with Gaumont apparently began when he sought a concession for the Mutoscope and Biograph in France. While this did not come about, at the end of 1897, Koopman and Gaumont were in correspondence about producing the machines at his plant in Paris. By February 1898 Gaumont sent Koopman prototype models of the European machines which he had made based on the American design. He made modifications in the exterior which make the European machines distinctly different from the American version. During 1898 the British and French companies contracted with Gaumont to make 2000 Mutoscopes.[717]

716 NMAH Hendricks, *The Biograph and Mutoscope Up to Date*, Vol. 1, No. 1, October 1897, p. 2. (New York, American Mutoscope Co.)

717 BiFI, [Fonds Léon Gaumont]. The British company ordered two lots of 500 each but not for completed devices. Parts were also ordered from the firm of Marshall in Manchester and the machines were assembled in London. The French company ordered 1000 machines. I am indebted to Jean-Jacques Meusy for supplying this information.

Both the British and American companies promoted the Mutoscope through brochures and other advertising devices and though the peep show machines had a lower profile than the projector, they sustained business for several years and the companies continued to produce titles for both entertainment and advertising.[718]

But Mr. Dickson was not in the business of marketing Mutoscopes. He was occupied with supplying films – a rich variety of films. By the spring of 1898 the British company was completing construction of an outdoor studio and making ready to film stage personalities, scenes from theatrical productions, comedies and films for the Mutoscope. In the meantime Mr. D. and the company's camera roved about England.

[718] The Mutoscope was a very durable machine. Operable machines were still in use in amusement parlors as late as the 1960s and a company that had rights to produce Mutoscope rolls was still in existence in the 1970s. The Newark Museum purchased reels from the company for an exhibit in 1976, though the films available, excerpts from Chaplin films, were not from this early period.

Chapter 28

The Pope and the Mutoscopes

719 "The Man Who Took the Pictures" in *Phonoscope*, December 1898, p. 14. The article incorrectly credited Dickson with operating the camera during a recent boxing match between Corbett and Fitzsimmons in Carson City, Nev.

720 Brown & Anthony, Op. Cit., p. 191.

721 Brown & Anthony, Op. Cit., pp. 249–254. There is no surviving production log for the British company, but film and theater historian Barry Anthony prepared a list of productions using the surviving programs from the Palace and augmenting it with other sources as he found them. Since not all the programs survive and not all of the productions would have been shown at the Palace, it is not exhaustive but it is the best record we have of the films produced by the British company and it was enormously helpful in preparing this book.

"The propriety and good taste of this sort of portraiture [of the Pope Leo XIII] is already arousing a storm of discussion among churchmen."

"There is no gainsaying the fact that the representation of His Holiness in his daily walks and drives has robbed him of something of his grandeur and dignity. The great churchman becomes simply an infirm old man, sustained by a lot of exceedingly gross, worldly and commonplace looking attendants.

"It is to be hoped that the papal benediction conferred upon Mr. W. Kennedy-Laurie Dickson also carries with it absolution for his share in the prize-fight portraiture."[719]

"I found the Pope a most lovable man, and owe much to his kindness. He took a great interest in the pictures, and on one occasion, having received some prints from London, I showed them to him. He was delighted, and exclaimed 'Wonderful! Wonderful! See me blessing!' – referring to the one representing him giving the Apostolic blessing and turning to Mons. della Volpe, he added, 'How splendid you look!' All the time he held my hand, which he pressed affectionately."[720] (W.K.L. Dickson to H.L. Adam, *The Royal Magazine*, April 1901, pp. 120–128.)

In June of 1898 Dickson was in Rome. He had been there several weeks negotiating with officials at the Vatican to film Pope Leo XIII. Persuading the Pope to appear before the cameras was a major coup for the Mutoscope companies and it proved to be the crowning achievement of Dickson's career as a filmmaker. While he was away, the company apparently completed construction of an outdoor studio and was ready to begin filming stage personalities, scenes from theatrical productions and comedy films.

During the months following his foray into France, Germany and Austria-Hungary, the pace of film production was leisurely. In the eight month period from October 1897 through the end of May 1898, less than three dozen new productions appeared on screen at the Palace, but several of them were noteworthy.[721]

Twenty-first of October was Trafalgar Day and crowds gathered in Trafalgar Square to view the decorations adorning the famous monument to Admiral Nelson. Dickson and his crew filmed the crowd at one o'clock; developed and printed the film that afternoon and had it on the screen at the Palace that evening.[722] This is the first reported instance of same day presentation and it set a precedence for the future. The company liked to characterize their major exhibition programs as a form of journalism so newsworthy events were given special attention and presented to the public as soon as possible. There were several other "same day" presentations. The Grenadier Guards returned from the Sudan where they had fought in the battle of Omdurman (2 September 1898) which secured the Sudan for the British Empire. Dickson filmed them marching from Waterloo Station to the Wellington Barracks on 6 October 1898. Two weeks later, on 27 October, he filmed their commanding officer, General Sir Herbert Kitchener, known at the time as the Sirdar (Commander in Chief of the Egyptian Army). Kitchener was filmed at Calais embarking for Dover and then at his reception by the Mayor of Dover. On 20 April 1899 the Marriage of the Earl of Crewe and Lady Peggy Primrose was filmed as the couple left the West door of Westminster Abbey. Among the dignitaries caught on film were the Prince of Wales and the Duke of Cambridge. According to a report in *The Music Hall and Theatre Review* (21 April 1899) the customary awning was not put up in order to facilitate the filming. The best known and most publicized same-day filming was the Grand National Steeplechase, 24 March 1899. The race was at 3:35 pm in Liverpool and with police and railway cooperation, the film was shown at the Palace at 11:10 that evening.[723] More about that later.

While the practice of rapidly developing and printing topical subjects was not exclusive to the Mutoscope company, it is the sort of thing that appealed to Dickson. His pride in accomplishment, flair for the dramatic and strong sense of competition made him particularly suited to this type of filming.

All of the films made during the months before filming the Pope were actualities, i.e. films of real people, places or things; and they were usually made in clusters with several films shot at the same place, usually of the same general subject or theme. In October or November he was in Aldershot again satisfying the seemingly insatiable interest in military activities. Although there is no record that he was ever in the military, Dickson seems to have enjoyed being around military people and he was usually able to establish a rapport, particularly with the officers in charge. This proved to be a valuable asset when he was in South Africa filming activities during the Boer War.

Films of training activities such as bayonet drills and calisthenics seem rather perfunctory, but three made at this time are interesting. Following his practice of staging action, he recreated camp activities of the fabled Gordon Highlanders. The setting was a group of tents and the soldiers were shown marching into camp, at leisure with the obligatory bagpipes and Highland Fling and responding to an alarm. In the latter, a messenger comes into an almost deserted camp, the bugler sounds the alarm, the troops emerge from their tents, fall into formation and march off, presumably to a mock battle which was not shown. The

722 Niver, *Biograph Bulletins*, p;. 35–36. Reported by the *Daily Graphic* [London] 28 October 1897 and *Morning Advertiser*, London, 27 October 1897.

723 Brown & Anthony, Op. Cit., p. 126 and pp. 249–264.

films are unusual because they are like shots made for editing into a story. While Dickson never assembled them together – that was the job of the person planning the programs – it is clear that he conceived of the potential to arrange them into a sort of story and, in fact, the three films appeared together on the program of the Palace on 13 December 1897. But Dickson's artifice did not satisfy a reviewer for *The Playgoer* who complained that the series "... lacked spontaneity, having too evidently been 'set up', if I many use the expression in connection with an animated photograph."[724]

Dickson was back in Aldershot in mid-February and he stayed at the Royal Hotel, apparently spending a couple of days making more films.[725] On this occasion he returned to filming cavalry in action and captured an unexpected incident that became something of a sensation. While jumping over an obstacle, one of the riders was thrown over the horse's head, fell to the ground and the horse landed on top of him. The film ended with soldiers running to carry the injured rider away. It was claimed that he was seriously injured and the film was dubbed "A Terrible Spill". It figured prominently in the company's subsequent presentations. They also filmed a balloon ascent which may have been made with Dickson's camera on board taking a panorama of the military base.

Before his return to Aldershot, Dickson and his crew made a series of films along the route of the London and North Western Railway. The excursion was probably commissioned by the railroad and seems to have had a dual purpose. Like the railroad subjects made in the U.S. for New York Central and Pennsylvania railroads, it promoted travel, but one film was apparently made for evidence in a law suit. This interesting bit of information comes from the memoirs of Emile Lauste, the son of Eugene Lauste. Dickson was training Emile to be a camera assistant – the beginning of an important career as a cinematographer. In reminiscences written in 1935, Emile wrote:

"Crewe. 6 March / Here we took photographs of how a man using a long-arm could couple and uncouple wagons on the L.N.W. Railway without danger of accident to himself if he used the long-arm as instructed. This picture was taken to make a mutoscope reel to show Judge and Jury, I believe in defense of a law suit on behalf of someone who had met with an accident. This I think was the first time Moving pictures were made for use in a Law Court."[726]

A letter from Dickson to Emile's father, written on February 4, 1898 from the Crewe Arms Hotel, Crewe, England makes Emile's dating of 6 March 1899 seem incorrect, but that said, his account is an interesting glimpse of the way Dickson's crew worked. Emile, who was eighteen and only recently arrived in England, made this interesting description of his initiation into the world of the itinerant cameraman:

"... I was stopping at the leading hotel, in Crewe (Cheshire) having some important work to do on the L.N.W.Rly in the shape of Panoramas from a train, etc., etc. It was here one evening that a rollicking good dinner had been prepared, a few speeches were said, and glasses clinked, a glass the

724 Ibid, p. 195. *The Playgoer*, 9 March 1898, p. 5.

725 MoMA Crawford. Dickson wrote a letter to Eugene Lauste on 18 February 1898 on stationary of the Royal Hotel, Aldershot.

726 Southeast Film and Video Archive, Brighton, England; Emile Lauste Collection.

shape I had often seen, but, its use or contents were to me yet to be unfathomed. This came about quickly, a few gulps and with twinkling eyes, a throbbing breast which was getting nicely warmed. I said, 'Gentlemen, this is the best Cider I have ever drunk'. The roar of laughter that went up put me ill at ease, for here I had either said something out of place or else blundered. The reader can best imagine my feeling when they replied, 'Why – Boy, this is not Cider, but the best Champagne in the Hotel!!'.

"The same evening – while sitting around the good old English open fire, quietly smoking, I was asked what I would care to drink. I mentioned black coffee. 'Coffee?? Did you say coffee?' 'Yes sir, I did' – 'Now look here young man if you drink coffee at this time of night, you won't be able to sleep'. 'Oh, I think I will', was my joyful answer. 'Well, look here, we will order you coffee only on one condition, that is you must be asleep within ten minutes after you have drunk it.' I undertook to be asleep as per instructions. I evidently kept my promise for these good gentlemen had all retired to bed without awaking me, the night porter waking me at 2 a.m. said 'Don't you think sir that you would like to go to bed?' Its rather late.' Exit me."[727]

The commission from the London & Northwestern Railway was probably influenced by the sensational reaction of London audiences to the American company's "Haverstraw Tunnel" film which opened at the Palace in late October. The London papers gave it rave reviews and favorable comments from ten British journals were pasted in the American company's scrapbook. The *Sun* called it "Mr. Morton's Marvel", *Travel Life* said it was "... simply colossal; it is no longer a spectacle, but an experience ..." and the *Court Circular* said it was "... the most remarkable film ever exhibited in England".[728] It quickly became the company's number one hit and established the phantom ride as a genre that would endure for at least the next decade – and reoccur from time to time in sensation-bound formats like Cinerama and Imax.

We have noted that Dickson did not make "Haverstraw Tunnel" and it is possible that he was jealous of its popularity and was anxious to see if he could match or better it. But rather than produce a succession of phantom rides, several different approaches were tried, with very interesting results.

One, "Conway Castle – Panoramic View of Conway on the L. & N.W. Railways" was shot with the camera on a car at the front of a moving engine, a true phantom ride. The castle and village of Conway are on Conway Bay on the north coast of Wales and the castle, built in the thirteenth century, is a well-preserved, classic example of fortress architecture. As the film opens, the castle is in middle distance at left center, mountains and a village are in view and a broad expanse of sky fills half the film. The castle looms larger as the train approaches on the S-shaped tracks; the castle disappears as it passes some impressively heavy stone walls, the track curves again revealing the walls of the town and an arched gate through which the train runs; it goes under several arches, through a culvert and the scene ends as the train is about to emerge in open country. The scenery and mediaeval architecture give this phantom journey a quite different feel from its American cousin. Dickson probably scouted the route before choosing it because the

727 Ibid. Also from Emile Lauste's 1935 draft memoire.

728 Niver, Op. Cit., pp. 35–36. The *Sun*, 28 October 1897; *Travel Life*. 30 October 1897; *Court Circular*, 27 October 1897.

several curves give the viewer an ever changing perspective. While it did not displace "Haverstraw Tunnel" it proved especially popular in England and was well received in the United States.[729]

A few miles west of Conway the railroad crossed the Menai Strait which separates the North Wales mainland from the island of Anglesey. The bridge across the straight was designed and built by Thomas Telford early in the 19th century and was the first important modern suspension bridge. Dickson filmed the "Irish Mail" as it crossed the bridge. The set-up was reminiscent of "Empire State Express". The camera was stationary and mounted on an elevation which allowed a view of the bridge's impressive stonework and the two sets of tracks carrying the trains to the bridge. The tracks curved, allowing a good view of the "Irish Mail" which was approaching the bridge as the film opened. After it was past, a work crew crossed the tracks, then a second train emerged from the bridge and curved past the camera to close the film, giving the audience two trains and a work crew for their money. The effect was more benign than "Empire State Express". The camera was farther away from the track, the first train moved away from the audience, offering no threat to those seated near the screen.[730]

The "Irish Mail", one of the L & NW's featured trains, was the focal point of this excursion and it figured prominently in the most visually interesting and brilliantly devised film in this series, "Irish Mail – L. & N.W. Railway – Taking Up Water at Full Speed" (also called "The Jennie Deans – Bushey"). The railroad yard at Bushey, just outside London, had several sets of tracks. This allowed the placing of the camera on one train and filming the "Irish Mail" as the two trains ran in parallel at a relatively fast speed. The "Irish Mail", drawn by an engine named the Jennie Deans, scooped water from troughs placed alongside the track. In the course of the filming the two trains pass a third one on a separate track. As the film ends, the camera train slows, allowing all the cars of the "Irish Mail" to pass the camera. The timing of the shot is quite amazing and the viewing effect is altogether different from any of the other railroad films.

Trains were not the only modes of transport presented on screen. No one in England is very far from the waves that they ruled, so nautical matters were important to British audiences. After completing the rail series, Dickson and his crew went to the south coast where he filmed Nelson's Flagship, Victory. In Portsmouth he made two films of the crew of HMS Seaflower showing them in General Quarters and aloft in the rigging furling the sails. At about the same time Dickson embarked on another of the venturous escapades that were becoming a characteristic of his production method. The result was another sensation for Biograph audiences. The operators of two tug boats were paid £5 each to go to sea in a heavy surf. Following the same pattern he used for the "Jennie Deans" film, he lashed the camera and operator – and, presumably, himself – to the deck of one tug and filmed the other as it maneuvered in the heavy seas. His assistants needed stout hearts and steady nerves. As H.L. Adam described it, it was done "... for an 'effect'.

729 There is a hand colored copy preserved in the collection of Nederlands Filmmuseum, Amsterdam.

730 The film was titled: "Menai Bridge: The Irish Day Mail from Euston Entering the Tubular Bridge Over the Menai Strait." There is a copy of the film in the Shultze Collection at the National Film and Television Archive, British Film Institute, London.

... The whole thing was so 'lively' that the hardy skipper agreed that there 'wasn't no fun in it', and hinted that the £5 each hardly 'met the case'. But £10 each did." In the blurb for the film in their 1902 catalog the American company bragged that "Many spectators who have viewed this picture on the Biograph have insisted that they have experienced the pangs of seasickness. ...", and they called it "One of the biggest hits of the Biograph".[731] Never one to waste a filming opportunity, Dickson also filmed three men in a small boat being towed through the heavy seas by a tug, presumably the same one.

A few weeks later, on 6 April 1898, Dickson was in Worthing, a coastal town south of London. He stayed three days making a series of films recording the launching of a rescue boat by the English Coast Guard. Richard Brown describes this series as a subject of particular interest to Victorian audiences because the rescue service of fire depart- ments and coast guardsmen were important to them. Brown observes that Dickson created a series of films showing the complete work cycle of the life saving station in separate films which comprise a complete story – an antecedent of James Williamson's *Fire!* and Edwin S. Porter's *Life of an American Fireman*. The films show the coast guardsmen at leisure in the station ("Idle Hours of the English Coast Guards"); taking the rescue boat out of the station with horses pulling it to the seaside; the launch (two films titled "Launch of the Worthing Life Boat"); the boat's return showing a man being resuscitated on the beach ("Return") and the boat being paraded through town with spectators watching. An additional scene showed a young girl seated in the bow of a boat with a cat and a large St. Bernard dog – a representation of Victorian tranquility and family life, a sentimental icon that was particularly favored by Dickson. Children and animals figured in several films made before he left New York. Brown astutely credits Dickson with making this scene to be included with the rest to relate the work of the rescuers to everyday family life. The kitten and St. Bernard also appear in the scene of the coast guardsmen at leisure which would seem to support Brown's conclusion.

Film production was becoming more complex and sophisticated. This is the second occasion when several related scenes with common narrative elements were taken, the earlier one being the three films of the Gordon Highlanders made at Aldershot the previous fall. The thirty seconds of exposure that comprised the normal "take" was too short a time for some subjects, so Dickson was moving towards longer, more structured coverage. However, the Mutoscope company had commit- ted to a pattern of exhibition that discouraged producing longer, more integrated films. The design of the Mutoscope, a circle of images mounted on a revolving drum, limited the length of viewing time and made it necessary to keep each film about the same length – and in 1898, production for the Mutoscope was receiving particular emphasis. And while it would be possible to present longer films at the Palace and other projection venues, the short films that comprised the Biograph pro- grams suited the over-all variety format that the theaters were offering.

731 Brown & Anthony, Op. Cit., p. 252. H.L. Adam, "Round the World for the Biograph" in *The Royal Magazine*, April 1901, p. 122. AMB, *Picture Catalog*, p. 196. There is a copy of the film in the Nederlands Filmmuseum.

Furthermore, with their large library of subjects to choose from, they could mix and match films, presenting some new subjects, repeating favorites and occasionally slipping in one taken much earlier.

Although Dickson played a crucial role in supplying a generous number of lively and exciting audience pleasers, he apparently had little or nothing to do with planning the way they would be presented on screen. The Worthing life guards were on the bill at the Palace the week of 5 September 1898 and only two scenes were shown: "Launch of the Worthing Life Boat" and "Return". They shared the screen with three scenes of events taken during the Bastille Day celebration in Paris the previous 14 July; with "Elephants at the London Zoo"; with "He and She" a comedy featuring popular comedians Frank Wood and Miss Roma in a quarrel between an elderly husband and his young wife; and a film showing Sir George Newnes, the prominent publisher who was a director of the Mutoscope company, saying farewell to an Antarctic expedition. The program ended with a diving scene taken near Cleveland, Ohio which was shown normally, then repeated in reverse, so the diver popped out of the water, sailed backwards through the air and landed on the platform – an effect that had delighted audiences at the Palace and elsewhere from the beginning of the company's exhibition programs.

Ironically, the Mutoscope company was in a better position to produce longer films than most American and British film producers. By supplying projector, operator and films to their clients they maintained complete control over their product. Most of their competitors sold films to exhibitors and thus lost control over how, when and where they were shown. So in most cases, it was the exhibitors who arranged the films into a program. But the Mutoscope companies had some say in the way their program was presented – though it was necessary to plan this in cooperation with the management of the theaters where the film was shown. At the Palace the usual program consisted of fifteen to twenty films spliced together and it lasted about twenty to thirty minutes. The process of assembling a group of films for projection had its own problems and in this, the company also had an advantage. Joining one film to another was a risky business, but since the Biograph program was always spliced together the process had become routine. Splicing offered a challenge for those using the 35mm format. The joins had to be carefully made because they would pull apart if not properly glued or if a fragment of film protruded from the join, the film might catch on the sprockets or gate causing a break or tear. If the film rode off the sprockets holes would be punched in the image area of the film until the projector was stopped. Since the film in the Biograph did not advance over sprockets, this was not a problem. Dickson had been splicing film since he received short pieces from Eastman in 1889, so he undoubtedly trained the company's technicians in the most effective way to assemble the projection reels.

The programs assembled for the Biograph involved a rude, but basic form of editing: selecting a proper scene, then joining it to another.

In the process, attention had to be given to the relationship of the scene to the ones preceding and following. So they had the capability and experience to make longer films with integrated themes, but chose not to. In retrospect, this seems strange. We are so accustomed to edited theatrical and documentary movies that it seems an obvious and normal practice but this was not the case at the end of the nineteenth century.

Given his skill in photography, experience in film production, venturesome spirit and talent in science and the arts, Dickson seems an obvious candidate to have experimented with more complicated presentations, but he never moved beyond producing short films. The Gordon Highlander and Worthing life saving series show that he had the impulse to create longer, more complicated works, but he never did. This can be accounted for in part by the company's emphasis on short films for the Mutoscope and their variety programs. But other factors must have come into play. Despite mingling with famous people, leading an adventurous life and enjoying a degree of public recognition, Dickson was not altogether happy with his situation and his frustration came out one of his letters to Eugene Lauste:

"... I do not want articles written about me. It's all the same to me. I have been fleeced so often that I am going to drop animated photography as quickly as possible.

"Hoping that in a few years we will be back in New York in a little shop."[732]

He wrote this letter from London's Hotel Cecil where he had been living in transitory comfort since arriving in London. The recently built Hotel Cecil which styled itself as "The most Fashionable and Popular Hotel in Europe ..." was conveniently located on the Strand, not far from Trafalgar Square and within walking distance of the company's headquarters. *The Sketch* was impressed by the Cecil's modern sanitary facilities and called it "... a monument of architectural construction and supreme comfort".[733] Antonia and Lucie were with him but their situation was impermanent. There is evidence that they expected to return to the U.S., but for the time being their plans were indefinite. Their furniture was in storage and a tenant occupied their house in Orange, so despite mingling with royalty and having bottles of champagne at the best hotels, Dickson's life was unsettled. The correspondence with Eugene Lauste added to his discomfort. Lauste was going to New York to testify in the patent interference between Casler, Latham and Armat. He would be quizzed about his work on the Lathams' Eidoloscope and had written to Dickson for advice. This was an unpleasant reminder of Dickson's own involvement with the Lathams, the confrontation with his nemesis William Gilmore, and the unhappy end to his association with Edison. Dickson had not been called to New York which may have annoyed him because it deprived him of the opportunity to put himself into the consideration as a pioneer of projection.

The reference to a "little shop" in New York is a reminder that Dickson's first love was experimentation and invention and no matter

732 MoMA Crawford. Dickson to Lauste, 26 January 1898.

733 Ad for the Hotel Cecil in *The Sketch*, Christmas Number, 1897; and an article about the Hotel Cecil in *The Sketch*, 21 June 1899, p. 387.

how successful he was as a film producer, he thought of himself as an engineer first, and a filmmaker second. It would be another four years before he opened his "little shop", an experimental lab and machine shop a la Edison, but his mention of it shows that he had already discussed it with Lauste. The shop interested him more than creating new forms of visual experience, but for the moment the shop had to wait. There were films to make and new adventures in store.

"How I Biographed the Pope"[734]

W.K.-L Dickson regarded "Biographing" the Pope as one of his most important accomplishments, a viewpoint shared by his compatriots in both the American and British Mutoscope companies. The films were touted as one of the most important achievements of the infant industry and the company's publicity stressed the difficulties involved in negotiating permission to make the film. Dickson called the negotiations "arduous". The Pope's poor health and the political situation in Italy made the negotiations difficult. Pope Leo XIII was eighty-eight years old and had suffered ill health throughout his Papacy. Years earlier, while he was Bishop of Perugia, he had contracted typhoid fever and now he suffered from rheumatism which made it difficult for him to walk. Recent reports of new illnesses added to concerns that he was feeble and could not survive much longer, a concern which persisted from his elevation to the Papacy in 1878. Ironically, despite the concerns about his health, he held the office longer than any of his predecessors. The political situation was complicated by an unresolved dispute with the government of Italy which annexed the Papal States during the reign of his predecessor, Pope Pius IX. Pius refused to recognize the annexation and this stance was continued by Leo. Although Leo had a reputation for improving relations with other governments, he refused to improve relations with the Italian government and he was sometimes called the "Prisoner of the Vatican" because he rarely, if ever left the premises.[735]

Dickson claimed that he spent four months negotiating with officials at the Vatican and implied he was in Rome the entire time. While this seems to be another of his dramatic exaggerations, it did take a long time to obtain the necessary permissions. The publicity releases of the British and American companies also said that it took four months to complete the arrangements, and if the report of R.H. Meer in *Pearson's Magazine* (February 1899) is accurate, they may have begun as much as a year before the filming.[736] Although he was not in Italy for four months, Dickson had a lengthy visit lasting from six to eight weeks. It is possible to confirm that he was there for almost all of June and part of May. At the beginning of April he was filming in Worthing so it is doubtful that he was in Rome before mid-April.[737] But two or two and a half months is an extraordinary amount of time to devote to one film project and it symbolizes how important the films of the Pope were to the British and American companies.

Dickson was in Rome as the representative of the British company,

734 GU Ramsaye. In a letter to J.I. Crabtree, Society of Motion Picture Engineers, 16 January 1932, Dickson claimed that an article by him, "How I Biographed the Pope", was published in "all U.S.A. papers." No copies of such an article have been found, but the Mutoscope company frequently used the term "Biographed" or "Biographing" to characterize the process of filming a person or an event.

735 "The Daily Life of the Pope" by Mary Spencer Warren in *Pearson's Magazine*, Vol. XI, July–December 1898, p. 386.

736 BiFi, fonds Will Day. "The Wonders of the Biograph" by R.H. Meer, *Pearson's Magazine*. 7:38, February 1899.

737 Brown & Anthony, Op. Cit., pp. 253–254. On 9 April 1898 the *Worthing Intelligencer* reported that he was filming there.

but the project seems to have been a joint venture between the American and British companies and it may have been initiated in America where Catholic communities were an important potential constituency. There was a significant potential audience of Catholic faithful in England, but at the time of the filming relations between Protestants and Catholics were very poor. Accusations that the Catholic church was exerting too much influence on the established Anglican church were exacerbated in September 1896 when the Pope issued an encyclical denying the validity of holy orders in the Church of England. This stimulated anti-Catholic prejudice and made the marketing of films of the Pope a rather chancy proposition.[738]

Before approaching the Vatican the two companies sought support from prominent Catholic prelates. Dickson arrived in Rome with documents endorsing the project from a number of prominent church leaders, among them the Archbishop of Ireland, Monsignor Martinelli and America's foremost church leader, James Cardinal Gibbons.[739] In Rome he negotiated with Count Soderini, Monsignor della Volpe, and Count Camillo Pecci, the Pope's nephew.[740] There are no accounts of the specifics of these negotiations, but according to Dickson there were two arguments that finally won the day. First was the possibility that the pictures might persuade the public that the Pope was not an infirm invalid and secondly, that through the films the Pope could extend his blessing to the faithful around the world. The latter was particularly effective because only visitors to Rome could receive his blessing since he rarely left the Vatican.

It is possible that the Pope may have been Dickson's ally. Although he was conservative on some issues, Leo XIII was very sympathetic to scientific progress and his interest was motivated by a wish to find improved means to deliver the church's message. The motion picture, the child of science, fitted nicely into both categories and this may have appealed to the Pope, who was apparently swayed by the possibility of extending his blessing to untold numbers of Catholics around the globe. It is probably not co-incidental that Leo was also the first Pope whose voice was captured by the phonograph.

Although the negotiations with the Vatican were prolonged, they were not so intense that they prevented Dickson and his assistant Emile Lauste from filming other activities. They had taken up temporary residence at the Hotel Marini, via del Tritone, apparently rather close to the Trevi fountain. Emile mentions that in return for contributing a coin to the fountain, he was in Rome nine years later – and was cordially greeted by the manager of the Marini who remembered their earlier stay. From their base in Rome they took side trips to Orvieto, Pompeii, Florence and Venice. In keeping with the churchly nature of their visit, they filmed several ceremonial processions, usually by members of religious orders: in Orvieto it was the Corpus Domini procession, filmed in the Plaza outside the famous Cathedral; in front of the duomo in Florence, a funeral procession of the ominously dark hooded Brothers of the Misericordia carrying a draped coffin; in Venice, a procession

738 *Ibid.*, pp. 60–61 and footnote p. 72.

739 *The British Journal of Photography*, Supplement, 8 February 1899, p. 15.

740 Pope Leo XIII was born Vincenzo Gioacchino Pecci, 2 March 1810 in Carpineto Romano, Papal States and died on 20 July 1903 in Rome. He was head of the Roman Catholic Church from 1878–1903.

While in Italy, conducting prolonged negotiations to film the Pope Leo XIII, Dickson and his assistant, Emile Lauste, made several trips to supplement the films of the Pope with other religious subjects. This group portrait of Armenian monks was made after filming their procession at their monastery on the island of St. Lazar in the Lagoon near Venice. The Abbot-Archbishop is in the center. [NMAH.]

of Capuchin Monks; and on the island of St. Lazar in the lagoon near the Lido, a procession of Armenian Monks, among them the Abbot-Archbishop. In the Vatican, he captured a parade of five units of the military guard: a detachment of the Noble Guards, a Palatine Guard of Honor, the Swiss Guards, Gendarmes and a fire brigade.

The two films in Venice and the parade at the Vatican were staged for the camera, so it was possible to plan and rehearse the action to allow the audience a view of the full procession with an opportunity to see some of the members of the procession in close proximity. The staging of the parade in the Vatican was quite remarkable, an outstanding example of Dickson's ability to compress visual information and create interest and clarity. In a film running about one minute the five units approached the camera from the rear of the frame, moving in an "S" pattern which kept them on camera longer and showed them from several angles. The camera was elevated to give perspective and maximum viewing of each unit, but close enough that faces of participants were clearly distinguishable as they passed off camera. The films in Orvieto and Florence were less satisfactory because they were public events. Since he had limited control over the action, the camera was placed further from the groups. However, he did manage to capture the

Feeding pigeons in St. Mark's square was one of several obligatory tourist subjects filmed while in Venice. Dickson figures prominently in the film but this may have been because of necessity rather than ego. The young girl in the film was easily distracted and inclined to wander off camera, but Dickson was able to control her – after a fashion. The girl and the woman acting as her mother or guardian are unidentified. [Antony.]

Brothers of the Misericordia approaching the camera up a rise and the casket and their dark robes, masked faces and tall, pointed head pieces created a disturbingly ominous, klan-like quality.[741]

Although creating a library of religious subjects was the main object of Dickson's trip, there was time for other subjects. In late May, with Emile in tow, Dickson was in Naples where they apparently found little or nothing of religious interest, but in near-by Pompeii they filmed a group of costumed folk dancers in the ancient Forum performing what the company called a Neopolitan dance.[742] Interestingly no films of the famous ruins made their way to the screen at the Palace. In fact, despite the abundance of ancient ruins, works of art, fountains, spectacular buildings, picturesque villages and lovely scenery, no films of touristic interest were on the screen at the Palace. We can only speculate why, but the reason may have been the abundance of competing still photographs and the comparative difficulty of making films which Dickson and his associates would find acceptable. To film buildings, scenery or works of art, Dickson's camera had to move and the rough, often narrow cobblestone streets made the smooth, well timed images that he favored hard to come by.

The one exception was Venice which seemed to inspire him. In addition to the two religious subjects already mentioned, Dickson chartered the Clairssa, "the fastest yacht in Venetian waters", mounted the camera in the bow and took panoramas of the Grand Canal and the Doge's Palace.[743] In addition, two films of human interest were shot: a

741 "Famous Procession of the Corpus Domini" copy in the Library of Congress Paper Print Collection (LC) and the Nederlands Filmmuseum (NFM); "Funeral Procession of the Misericordia" also in LC and NFM; "Procession of Capuchin Monks, Rome [sic]" also LC and NFM; "Procession of Armenian Monks, Including the Abbot-Archbishop, St. Lazar, Venice" also LC and NFM; and "The Vatican Military Guard, Consisting of a Detachment of Noble Guards, Commanded by Count Pecci, Followed by a Palatine Guard of Honor, Swiss Guard, Gendarmes, and Fire Brigade" also in LC and NFM.

742 No copy of this film survives but a frame was reproduced in an unidentified publication and a copy is in the Merritt Crawford Collection at MoMA. Gordon Hendricks had it examined by specialists who identified the men's costume as Sicilian and the dance as a Tarantella.

743 Niver, Op. Cit., p. 43. An article "The Biograph in Venice" in *Mail & Express*, 1 April 1899. The article said the film of the Doge's Palace had a stereoscopic effect.

group of boys swimming in a canal and a scene of feeding the pigeons in Piazza di San Marco.[744]

"Feeding Pigeons ..." is significant because it is the only commercial film in which Dickson appears in his own production. It was staged as a family scene with Dickson and an unidentified woman helping a little girl, a toddler, feed the pigeons. A vendor with a tray of seed stands by. It was warm day and the trio was appropriately attired in white. The always elegant Mr. Dickson wore a suit, tie and a smartly visored white cap. The woman had an elaborately flowered hat which obscured her face. Her dress had full sleeves, a large yoke collar with a flower decorating the bosom. The little girl wore a knee length dress and a large white hat. The film opened with Dickson buying a cone of feed from the vendor, then helping the little girl. She became distracted and when she wandered out of the frame she had to be brought back but she wandered off camera again, giving the film an amusingly candid quality.

This unusual glimpse of Dickson at work and play raises more questions about him than it answers. Who is this woman? Is she related? Where did the little girl come from? Historians Barry Anthony and Richard Brown speculate that the woman was Dickson's wife Lucie, but it is very hard to confirm this because her face is obscured by her hat. Dickson had a still from the film in his own collection and a close examination shows that although her features were obscured, the woman had a rather square jaw with prominent cheek bones. A portrait of Lucie taken in London about this time shows a woman of rather delicate features (see page 477). There is a possibility that it was Antonia. She was larger and more heavily-set than Lucie.

Of course, the woman and the girl may have been tourists or local residents commandeered for the filming. In fact, this would be the normal assumption, but the mysterious presence of a similar little girl in two other photos taken about the same time clouds the issue. A girl of similar age and dressed in much the same style appears in a photo taken in Rome during Dickson's visit. The photo is in the collection at the Edison Historic Site and it shows Dickson with a group of Italian military and workmen at the launching of a hot air balloon. Dickson is standing on the right side next to a priest and Emile Lauste is seated on the ground in front of him. It is an all male group except for a young girl, three or four years old, standing in the center of the assembly. She is dressed in white with a large, frilly white hat which stands out in contrast the dark uniforms of the large unit militia who fill the center of the picture. She is so reminiscent of the girl in Venice that it is quite startling. However, little girls from proper families were often dressed in this style, so it is possible it was pure coincidence. However, ... a similarly dressed little girl appears in another photo from Dickson's personal collection. This one was taken at St. Malo near Dickson's birthplace in Brittany. It is a picture of a fortress near the old walled city and there, seated on the rocks is a girl about three or four, dressed in white, with a large white hat. The photo is undated, but on his way back

744 The films are: "Panoramic View of the Grand Canal – Venice" (NFTVA & Nederlands); "Panorama of the Grand Canal: Passing the Fish Market 6 o'clock in the Morning" (NFTVA & Nederlands); "Panorama of the Grand Canal: Passing the Vegetable Market"; "Panoramic View of Venice – The Prisons, Palace of Doges, and the Royal Palaces" (Nederlands); "Boys Bathing, Venice" (NFTVA) and "Feeding Pigeons at St. Mark's Square, Venice" (NFTVA and Nederlands).

to England from Rome, Dickson stopped in Paris and made several films. It is seems a very possible occasion for a side trip to Brittany where he took a number of photos of places familiar to him from his youth. Was this little girl along with him? Who else was along? What was her relationship to Mr. Dickson? This is an unsolved mystery and the only clue is that in his correspondence Dickson mentions visits by nieces. But they seem to be from Lucie's family since neither W.K.L. nor Antonia had children and Dickson's other sister, Eva had three sons and no daughters.[745]

The negotiations to film the Pope seem to have been completed early in June and the filming apparently extended over several weeks – long enough for some of the early films to have been shipped to London and returned in time for the Pope to see himself on film.[746] The logistics were complex and it undoubtedly took days to agree on which activities should be filmed and to select appropriate locations. It was important to have a variety of visually interesting locations – but not so interesting that they would distract viewers from the Pope. Dickson needed a

745 Dickson may have had nieces in England as there were members of the family in the U.K.

746 Brown & Anthony, Op. Cit., p. 191. Dickson's account of showing films to the Pope was quoted by H.L Adam in his article "Round the World for the Biograph" *The Royal Magazine*, April 1901, pp. 120–128. It is quoted at the head of this chapter.

Left: *While in Rome Dickson apparently attempted to film the city from a balloon. Here he is posed with a military group before departure. He is standing to the right of center next to a priest. Emile Lauste is seated just below him and in the center is a young girl whose presence is unexplained.*
Right: *A very similar young girl also appears in a photo of the fortress at St. Malo, near Dickson's childhood home. Dickson stopped in Paris after finishing a second set of films of the Pope and may have taken this picture on a side trip to Brittany. [EHS & NMAH.]*

maximum amount of light for proper exposure so most of the scenes were taken in the Vatican Garden. An examination of the films makes it clear that each shot was carefully staged with nothing left to chance. Before the camera was loaded, the action was discussed, plotted out, timed and rehearsed. Six locations were chosen and there were six to eight separate takes which ultimately resulted in eight separate films, though only five were commonly shown to the public.

To make these arrangements, Dickson worked closely with Monsignor della Volpe and the Pope's nephew, Count Camillo Pecci. Not only were they principals in the negotiations, they also figured prominently in most of the scenes. As major domo, Monsignor della Volpe made preparations for the Pope's activities and assisted him in moving to appropriate locations. Count Pecci commanded the detachment of Noble Guards who frequently accompanied the Pope as he moved about. By the time the filming began, Dickson was well acquainted with them and used them to control the action and maintain the timing of the takes. This could be done inconspicuously because their normal activities included supervising the ritual. The cordial relations Dickson established with the two Vatican officials made it possible to carefully rehearse and time each take without requiring the Pope's presence until the camera was loaded and ready to go.

Although most of the films were taken in the Vatican gardens, two were taken in a well lighted corridor inside the Vatican complex. This was unusual since despite regular improvements, film emulsions still required a great deal of light for satisfactory exposure and most interiors had to be lit artificially. However, at the time of the summer Solstice,

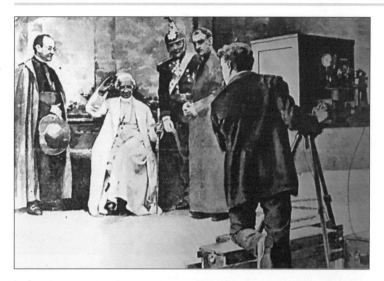

Rome enjoys quite brilliant sunshine and it was apparently enough to make an "interior" feasible. In one of the two shots taken in the "Upper Loggia" the Pope, carried in a Sedan chair by four attendants, is clearly visible as he approaches the camera. The long hallway was flooded with light which streamed through arches on the left side of the frame. A second shot was apparently made in the same corridor but with the camera moved to show the Pope being carried in the opposite direction. The light now streamed in from the right side and the camera was set up near that side to take advantage of the light flooding the center of the corridor.

There was no attempt to show services or liturgy. The purpose was to illustrate the Pontiff's daily activities. In each of the films the Pope wore the white surplice that marked his office and this focused attention on him because it contrasted nicely with the uniformly dark attire worn by the clergy, guards and attending dignitaries. In all but two of the pictures the Pope was conducted to a location where he could face the camera and extend his blessing and he took advantage of every opportunity he was given. Dickson told Eugene Lauste that while his son Emile was operating the camera he was blessed fourteen times. Off camera, Dickson received the Pope's blessing while kneeling on top of a platform made by assembling battery boxes. "One of the most insecure perches incident to [my] Biograph experience ...", Dickson said laughing.[747]

Rapport with the Vatican staff was essential to the success of the project and the sessions appear to have gone smoothly and amicably. None of the shots appear "posed" and the officials went through their activities comfortably and unselfconsciously. Dickson seems to have established a particularly amicable relationship with Monsignor Della Volpe who was responsible for maintaining ceremonious dignity. He fulfilled his duties with a curious mixture of formality and informality.

747 MoMA Crawford. Dickson the Lauste, 25 January 1930 and Lillian Joy, Op. Cit.

This drawing of Dickson operating a camera while filming Pope Leo XIII (left) was widely used for publicity and has been reproduced frequently. It was made from a photo and accurately reproduces one of the scenes, Pope Leo Blessing in the Garden (right). Attending the Pope are his major domo, Monsignor Della Volpe (at left) and Count Pecci, the Pope's nephew (with helmet) and an unidentified priest.

In several films he can be seen looking at, and even addressing Dickson to see how things are going – often with a very pleasant smile. This is evident in the film showing the Pope passing through the garden in his carriage. After the carriage paused and the Pope gave his blessing Monsignor Della Volpe turned to the camera and smiled as if to say "that's a take". He gave a similar smile at the end of one of two films showing the Pope giving a blessing from his chair.

It was not unusual for the public to show their curiosity about the camera during these early years of filmmaking, particularly when they were being filmed. Curious glances, waves, smiles and even unheard comments give a charmingly candid and human quality to early documentary footage, but it is startling to find on-camera reactions in such dignified surroundings. But even the Pope took part in the interplay with the camera. In most of the shots he faced the camera and looked directly at it as he blessed it. His on-camera demeanor was natural and unforced although his infirmities and the hindrance of age was evident when he moved about. His easy eye contact with the camera and frequent smiles indicate that he was enjoying the experience. This is most evident in a film that showed the Pope and Count Pecci walking past kneeling guards. As the pair were about to walk off camera the Pope paused, turned, pointed in the direction of the camera and said something to his nephew with a wry smile, then turned again to end the film by walking out of the frame. It is a unexpected moment because the Pope's walk was staged in the presence of a stiffly formal line of helmeted guards holding lances and kneeling on one knee while saluting as he Pope passed.

Dickson probably fostered these brief moments of relaxed intimacy as a way of humanizing the Pope and relieving the inherent tediousness of the ceremonious formality that characterized the Pope's activities. Similar moments appear in several films and they add a candid quality that makes them more palatable. The careful staging of each shot is evidence that before the camera was loaded there were discussions, rehearsals and walk-throughs to establish timing, composition and proper staging.

Although there are no details of the filming, some incidents described by Dickson flesh-out the picture. He told Will Day that before the filming started he warned the Pope that the mechanism of the camera was very noisy and sometimes startled people. The Pope laughed and responded "Never mind, so they are not Cannons". According to Dickson this was a reference to artillery fire he had heard as a child during the Napoleonic era. Although the weather was hot Dickson persuaded the Pope not to shade himself with his umbrella and, in order to get a clear shot of the Pope giving blessing from his carriage, he persuaded them to leave the top down even though the Pope usually rode with the canopy up. He had an interesting off-camera encounter with the Pope which intrigued Will Day who wrote it up for his unpublished history of the screen.

"... Towards the latter part of Dickson's visit to the Vatican, he was wandering in the beautiful gardens and enjoying the special privilege accorded to him, when he was met by his Holiness Pope Leo XIII, who stopped in his walk and facing Dickson said, 'My son we have been much together of late, and now I would like to know what religion you profess.' Dickson was taken aback, as he hoped that such a question would never be put to him, more especially as he dare not acknowledge he was a protestant, and neither could he say he was of the same faith as the Pope. Something seemed to prompt him in the predicament he found himself, and he answered: 'Your Holiness, my religion is to do the best I can in all things' to which the Pope replied, 'A good religion, keep it sacred'. After saying which His Holiness gave Dickson his blessing. Dickson thinking the incident closed, and was congratulating himself on the manner in which he dealt with a rather unpleasant situation, when, after walking silently along together, the Pope being engrossed in deep thought, turned once more to Dickson, and shaking his finger he said, 'But my son, that was a very diplomatic answer'. In grateful acknowledgement of His Holiness and his kindly forbearance, Dickson kissed the ring on the Pope's outstretched hand, and so the incident closed."[748]

The number of films that resulted from the session is subject to interpretation. In his filmography of British productions, Anthony Anderson lists six titles. In his article "The Wonders of the Biograph", R.H. Mere (1899) said there were five titles. In December 1898 the American Mutoscope Company deposited eight separate Mutoscope rolls as evidence for the copyright deposit of "Pope Leo XIII".[749] To add to the confusion the Mutoscope companies titled the films several ways to suit the changing circumstances of exhibition, a practice that started as soon as the company began exhibiting the films.[750]

The eight Mutoscope rolls that were deposited at the Library of Congress in 1898 are earliest surviving copies and they offer the best evidence of what was filmed and how the company planned to exhibit them. There were seven different camera set-ups: two in the upper loggia and five in the Vatican garden. There is evidence that Dickson had a camera capable of exposing a longer roll of film, perhaps a new one recently built by Casler. At least two of the surviving Mutoscope rolls are so closely related that they seem to be a single take that was cut in half to supply the two rolls. The roll showing the Pope leaving his

748 BiFi Fonds Will Day. Copyright W.E.L.Day F.R.P.S., F.R.S.A., August 1935. The account is based on Day's correspondence with Dickson.

749 Brown & Anthony, Op. Cit., pp. 255–256; John Barnes, Op. Cit., Vol. 3, pp. 158–159 & footnote 58, p. 236; Library of Congress, Paper Print Collection.

750 The American Mutoscope Company copyrighted frames from these films in November and December 1898 and they registered a confusing mix of tites: "Pope Leo XIII, No. 31–58 (28 November 1898; 69155-69180); "No. 57–82 (28 November 1898; 73533–73558) No. 100–107 [the Mutoscope rolls](15December 1898; 73559–73566); "Pope Leo XIII and Count Pecci, no. 1 (22 November 1898; 68157); "Pope Leo XIII Approaching Garden Seat (7 November 1898; 65480); "Pope Leo XIII Attended by Guard" (7 November 1898; 65484); "Pope Leo [XIII] Blessing in the Garden" (7 November 1898; 65482); "Pope Leo XIII Giving Blessing From Chair" (7 November 1898; 65479); "Pope Leo XIII in Carriage" (7 November 1898; 65485); "Pope Leo XIII in Carriage, no. 1" (22 November 1898; 68154); "Pope Leo in Chair, no. 1" (22 November 1898; 68156); "Pope Leo XIII in Sedan Chair,

carriage and walking to a seat in the garden ends as he arrives at the seat and the roll showing him giving blessing from the seat in the garden begins as he is sitting down. Since they were shot from the same camera position and the principals are in the same positions it looks like it was a single take. There are two scenes of the Pope seated in his chair giving blessings. In the first he walks to the chair, sits down and gives blessing. The second shows him already seated; he gives a blessing then gets up and walks off screen – a mirror image of the first one. Again the camera position is the same and the principals are also the same. While the camera was moved for the two shots in the upper loggia, the shots are clearly related and it is easy to imagine that both shots were made on a single roll of film.

The speculation that Dickson had a camera with a larger capacity is supported by the company's claim that a film of a hotel fire in Paris was the longest film that the company had made to date, 610 feet. This film was made during a stop-over in Paris when Dickson returned to London after filming the Pope.[751]

Dickson returned from the Vatican with an ensemble of films tailored to the company's rather schizophrenic exhibition practice. Each film could be viewed separately, even be divided into two parts, but they could also be assembled into a longer program. The framework for the longer program was loose enough that the programmer could use as many as seemed suitable and arrange them in various ways. The two films shot in the upper loggia could be paired together. They showed the Pope being carried through the hall in different directions and were sometimes identified as going to and from the Sistine Chapel. A scene showing the Pope leaving his carriage, walking to a bench in the garden then sitting down and giving his blessing could be broken into separate parts – and was for Mutoscope showing. This scene could be linked to another scene of the Pope giving blessing from his carriage. That scene ended with the carriage leaving the frame on the right side which matched the direction of the carriage in the scene at the bench. (A close examination shows the two carriages were different, but viewers would probably not notice the difference because only a portion of the carriage can be seen in the second film.) The carriage scene could also be linked to the scene of the Pope walking in the garden, since both were clearly taken there. The scene with the Pope walking in the garden could also be linked to the scene of the Pope giving blessing from his chair because the presence of uniformed guards gives them a sense of unity. The scene of the Pope giving blessing from his chair is the most formally staged and was suitable to conclude the program – though it could also be an introduction. If it was cut in the middle it could be shown with the Pope walking on screen and giving his blessing or giving his blessing then walking off screen.

While the structural framework was loose, it demonstrates once again that Dickson's vision very often went beyond the individual film to a larger concept. The series of scenes from Rip Van Winkle made at the beginning of production for the Mutoscope was an earlier example

no. 1" (22 November 1898; 68151); "Pope Leo XIII in Vatican Garden, no. 1" (22 November 1898; 68151); "Pope Leo XIII Passing Through Upper Loggia, no. 1" (22 November 1898; 68153); "Pope Leo XIII Preparing to Give Blessing From Chair" (7 November 1898; 65478); "Pope Leo XIII Seated in Garden" (7 November 1898; 65481); "Pope Leo *(contd.)* XIII Walking at Twilight, no. 1." (22 November 1898; 68155); "Pope Leo [XIII] Walking in the Garden" (7 November 1898; 65483).

751 Niver, Op. Cit., p. 42. An article "The Biograph on Brooklyn Bridge", [New York] *Mail and Express*, March 11, 1899. At 780 feet, the film made on the Brooklyn Bridge became the company's longest film, passing the record made by the Paris hotel fire film.

and a case could be made that the excerpts from Broadway shows made in the Black Maria were even earlier examples of grouping individual films into units. And, as a reminder, a number of similar groupings were made for the Mutoscope and Biograph: the scenes in Canton that complement the film of McKinley on his lawn, the three related films of the Gordon Highlanders, the scenes along the Northwest Railway which showed scenes along the route between London and the Welsh coast, and the series filmed in Worthing just before leaving for Rome. Although Dickson was flirting with story telling through film editing – the joining of several independently made shots into an integrated whole – the distribution pattern of the Mutoscope companies discouraged showing of long films. A mixture of these short, Mutoscope-length films did well in theaters where they were projected, so the company was reluctant to experiment with longer, single-themed presentations. With these limitations in mind, Dickson's attempts at more complicated, longer compilations were cautiously structured for flexible use.

One of the films that Dickson made in the Vatican is unique because it has two separate but related scenes on a single reel. It is the film of the Pope walking in the garden. It opens with the Pope and Count Pecci strolling down a path past a line of guards, kneeling and saluting. The pair strolls past the guards and out of the frame; then there is a cut and the Pope emerges from a doorway, still accompanied by Count Pecci, and walks past a similar group of kneeling guards. The two camera set-ups are different. In the opening shot the Pope and his nephew walk from the upper left side of the frame at a diagonal that takes them off screen at the lower right corner. In the second take they enter from the right side and walk almost directly across the frame leaving on the left side. The two shots are tied together by the participants, the Pope, Count Pecci and the kneeling uniformed guards. The action is logical because in the second shot the Pope enters from the same side that he left in the previous shot. While this is close to an edited cut, it was apparently done on one piece of film rather than by splicing two pieces of film together. In other words, the camera was stopped, moved to the second location and shooting was resumed with the same piece of film. Although it was not edited in a cutting room, it was an innovation that anticipated the structure of modern movies.

At the end of June (or the beginning of July) Dickson returned to London with a stop in Paris. Before leaving Italy he apparently made a stop in Gressanay, in Northern Italy, where he filmed Queen Margharita of Italy at her country residence. In Paris he made the film of the Hotel fire mentioned above "Hotel on Fire (Rescue Work by Paris Pompiers)"; "101st Regiment, French Infantry – Paris" (in heavy marching order) and "The Zola-Rochefort Duel, Paris". The latter being a re-enactment of a well-publicized duel between the well known author and the statesman, Henri Rochefort filmed allegedly on the grounds where the duel had taken place. Three films were also made during the Bastille Day celebrations on 14 July: "President Faure Arriving at the Grand Stand, Escorted by Cuirasseurs", "St. Cyr Mili-

En route home from Rome Dickson stopped in Paris and made A Hotel Fire in Paris, and Rescue by Parisian Pompiers *a more elaborate, and longer variation of the ever-popular fire engine and rescue subject.* [NMAH.]

tary School Passing in Review" and "4th Brigade Chasseurs Passing the President at the Charge." It is not clear whether Dickson remained in Paris to make these films or went to London after the earlier filming and returned for the Bastille Day filming. If he remained in Paris, then another camera operator filmed Queen Victoria at Aldershot on 7 July 1898 and a film made at Boulter's Lock on 10 July.

752 The popularity of railroad films created a similar problem for the pioneers and a case could be made that Porter's "Great Train Robbery" was an elaboration of the many train films he and his cohorts made. In this film Dickson may have benefitted from a training exercise staged by a Parisian fire unit or, perhaps, an amusement park spectacle similar to the "Fighting the Flames" act at Coney Island's Dreamland which was filmed by Billy Bitzer for the American Mutoscope & Biograph Co. in 1904.

Although the film of the hotel fire in Paris was publicized as documentation of a real event, it was either a staged enactment or an exercise by a Parisian fire company. As such, it was the third and most elaborate fire-rescue film that Dickson produced. It was a much more complicated production than the simple fire dramas he staged for Edison and the American Mutoscope Company and a major step in the development of story film. With the staging fleshed out, it clearly anticipated Edwin S. Porter's more famous "Life of an American Fireman" (1902) and James Williamson's "Fire!" (1901). Dickson and other pioneers were having trouble satisfying the public's apparently insatiable appetite for views of fire apparatus and rescues so it is not surprising that firemen played such a key role in creation of filmed drama. Creating novelties that did not revisit familiar territory challenged Dickson and others. The Parisian film was filmed from a single camera position and it lacked the staged scenes and dash from the fire station to the burning building that made Porter's film a landmark, but the arrival of the firemen and the rescue of a woman from an upper story window created a drama that excited Dickson's international audience.[752]

Early in June the British company created the Biograph and Mutoscope Company for France, Ltd. and though the company later opened a studio outside Paris, at the time of Dickson's visit there were no production facilities in France. So these films provided local fare for the new company. The Biograph program was so popular that when the Casino de Paris closed for the summer the management moved the Biograph to Théâtre Marigny where it played during the summer, then moved to Folies Bergère in September.[753] The stop-over gave Dickson a chance to meet with Eugene Lauste who had recently returned from New York where he testified in the patent interference between Casler, Armat and the Lathams.[754] It was during this stopover that Dickson may have visited his former home in Brittany with the mysterious young girl (see pages 504–505).

By mid-July the films of the Pope were in London but they were not shown publicly until December and only on rare occasions after that. The company publicized them vigorously stressing their uniqueness, the difficulties in completing the negotiations and the high cost of the undertaking, but screenings were so few and far between that a list of known projections that I prepared is surprisingly brief.

My list: December 1898, Washington, DC for Mons. Martinelli for his approval; 14 December 1898, Carnegie Hall, New York City; 18 December 1898, Archbishop's Palace London for Cardinal Vaughn and other officials; Carroll Hall, Washington, DC, 30 November 1898; Courbevoie, France, 26 May 1899 for invited guests of the French company; Galerie Georges Petit, Paris, 25 January 1900 for two weeks; Salle de la Société Industrielle, Lille, France; Grand-Théâtre Hippodrome, Roubaix, France, 28 & 29 March 1900; Salle de la Société Industrielle, Lille, France, 17–25 November 1900; Grand-Théâtre Hippodrome, Roubaix, 30 November – 2 December 900; Salle des Concerts, Cambrai, France, 4 & 5 December 1900; Palais de Glace, Lyon, France, 20 December 1900; Round Room, Rotunda Concert Hall, Dublin, Ireland, December 1900 & January 1901; Free Trade Hall, Manchester, 25 December 1901; and Pavilion Gardens, Kingstown (now Dùn Laoghaire), Ireland, July 1903.

Richard Brown and Barry Anthony made a similar observation in their book about the British company. Strange as scarcity of exhibitions may seem, the explanation is clear enough. The films could not be shown in variety theaters and before they could be projected in other venues the arrangements had to be cleared with appropriate members of the Catholic hierarchy. During the negotiations, the church officials had insisted that the films be shown in proper context and stipulated that the Pope should not appear on a program with frivolous entertainments such as dancers, jugglers and mimes. As Dickson explained it to H.L. Adam: "... none of the views may be shown in a place of secular amusement, nor without the authority of the church".[755] This restriction seems onerous, but it was accepted because it fit with the company's end of the century marketing plan which emphasized an expansion of the Mutoscope business. They anticipated that by leasing Mutoscopes to church organizations, images of the Pope would find their way into the thousands of Catholic parishes spread across the globe. Further negotiations would not be necessary since the church could control exhibition. This was not only a potentially lucrative new

753 Meusy & Spehr, Op. Cit., pp 135–151. The Biograph & Mutoscope Company for France, Ltd. was established 9 June 1898. The Biograph opened at Folies Bergère 4 October 1898 and remained there with only minor interruptions until 1902.

754 MoMA Lauste & *The Phonoscope*, June 1898, p. 8. Lauste sailed from New York on 7 May 1898 aboard the SS "La Bourgogne". On 4 July 1898 the SS "La Bourgogne" was sunk in a collision with British sailing ship Cromartyshire off Nova Scotia. 549 persons lost their lives including Mr. and Mrs. Anthony Pollock. Mr. Pollock was a senior partner in the firm Pollock & Mauro, attorneys for the American Graphophone Co. and Columbia Phonograph Co. who owned the patent for C. Francis Jenkins' version of the Phantoscope.

755 Brown & Anthony, p. 192 & pp. 211–212, Footnote 20. H. L Adam, "Round the World for the Biograph" *The Royal Magazine*, April 1901, p. 122. Dickson's statement is confirmed by an article in the Dublin *Evening Telegraph* , 27 July 1903 "[i]n accordance with a pledge given to the Vatican authorities, these views are reserved by the British Mutoscope and Biograph Co., Limited, for occasions in keeping with the dignity of the subject,

market, but one which added much needed prestige at a time when rumbles of moral indignation were being heard in the vicinity of Mutoscope machines offering views of "seminary" girls preparing for bed, show girls changing costume, "Little Egypt" gyrating her lower anatomy and similar provocative subjects.[756]

Rare as they were, the public screenings were usually prestigious affairs. The first one took place in Carnegie Hall, 14 December 1898 with Archbishop Corrigan and other dignitaries in attendance. Prior to the showing the arrangements were confirmed by Monsignor Martinelli at a private screening in Washington, DC The films of the Pope were augmented with a selection of films which included some of the religious groups filmed during Dickson's Italian sojourn and a selection of "safe" subjects, among them three phantom train rides, The Haverstraw Tunnel, Conway Castle and the Che Tor Tunnel in England. The films were accompanied by organ music performed by A.E. Johnson. The most elaborate and, perhaps, the most successful program was at Galerie Georges Petit, 8, rue de Sèze in Paris where the films were shown continuously for two weeks beginning 25 January 1900. The art gallery was turned into an exhibition hall for a multi-media event. The program opened with tableaux illustrating famous religious paintings: The Adoration by Alinari; Christ Removed from the Cross by Filippo Lippi; The Annunciation by Murillo; Jesus at the Mount of Olives by Perugini and Christ in Glory by Carravaggio. This was followed by films of Rome (including some films made after Dickson's visit). The films of the Pope were preceded by a photographed portrait of the Pope and the program concluded with a Tableau of The Assumption after Murillo. There was musical accompaniment by Eugene Gigout, organist of Saint-Augustin, and the Chanteurs de Saint-Gervais under the direction of Vincent d'Indy. The hall seated 300 and it was estimated that 20,000 people saw the show including many notables and persons prominent in Parisian society. "The performance was continuous and all day long until late into night a line of fashionable equipages lined all the streets approaching the salle Petit." For the showing there were two Biograph projectors. The installation and film showing was supervised by Eugene Lauste.[757]

There was an interesting epilog to the involvement of Pope Leo XIII with what the critic Robert Grau was to call "The Theatre of Science". In June 1899, *The British Journal of Photography* published a poem in praise of photography that the Pope had written in Latin. Although it concerns photography in general, one can well imagine that his experiences before the Mutograph influenced it:

"Ars photographica,
Expressa Solis siculo
Nitens imago, quam bene
Frontis decus, vim luminum
Refers, et ovis gratiam!
O mira virtus ingeni!
Novumque monstrum! Imaginem

and offers of large sums from theatre managers have been refused for the use of these pictures." Brown & Anthony credit Robert Monks for supplying this reference.

756 There is nothing specific, but there is ample evidence that the company expected growth and profit in the Mutoscope market at the end of the 1890s and the dearth of programs projecting the films of the Pope during these years indicates that the films were being marketed on Mutoscopes. That the American company registered copyright for its Mutoscopes is the most specific indication of the importance of that market.

757 NMAH Lauste. It is unclear from the program if the "tableaux" of the paintings were pictorial reproductions or tableaux vivant. The description of the program is an English translation from an uncredited newspaper article.

Natura Apelles amulus
Non pulchriorem pingeret."[758]

On stage

In July the Mutoscope and Biograph Syndicate celebrated its first anniversary. Dickson had been filming in Europe for more than a year and so far the output consisted almost exclusively of actualities – i.e. films of real persons, places or things. This was about to change. Early in September of 1898 the audience at the Palace was treated to "He and She", a film about a husband and wife contretemps, which revisited the problems confronting a husband who returns home at a very late hour and finds an angry wife in waiting. It featured the popular English comedy team of Frank M. Wood and Miss Roma T. Roma recreating an on-stage routine familiar to veteran theater goers. It was one of the first comedies produced by the British company and it filled a notable void. Previously the comedy diversions shown on the Biograph programs and the more racy fare for the Mutoscope had been produced by the American company. Now British audiences could see British made variety fare.

Construction of an outdoor production stage was begun while Dickson was in Italy and it was apparently ready for use soon after he returned. It was presumably built to specifications Dickson prepared before his departure. By this time Dickson was a veteran of studio design. This was his fourth purpose-built photo studio and the third designed specifically for film production. Although no pictures or drawings survive, it was certainly patterned after the New York studio and probably very like a studio built the following year for the French company's production facility at Courbevoie (see photo). Adequate sunlight was still the crucial factor in filming and all of Dickson's studios were positioned to illuminated the stage with mid-day sun coming over the camera and into the faces of subjects being filmed. As in New York, the stage could be moved to capture optimum illumination but, if it was like the French studio, it did not have an elaborate iron framework that supported the New York studio. Instead, the stage could be moved on railroad tracks set in a semi-circular arc. At the French studio the camera was housed in a free standing shed that could be turned or moved closer to the stage as required. This design was simpler, less costly and more flexible than the New York studio.[759]

The British studio was located near the Thames and not far from the Hotel Cecil where Dickson and some of the other Mutoscope company officials stayed while in London. A contemporary article indicates that there were nearby facilities to store scenery and props as well as dressing rooms for performers.[760] During the summer months a half dozen film were apparently made at the new studio. The subjects were very similar to early productions at the New York studio. "A Good Story", a visualization of a popular painting of two clergymen amusing themselves after a hearty meal, was a remake of a film made previously in New York. "He and She" was preceded on film by "The Prodigal's

758 *The British Journal of Photography*, [30 June 1899], p. 406.

759 The sturdy iron framework that supported the New York studio may have been necessary to stabilize the structure. It was on the roof of a multi-storied building and therefore was subject to occasional high winds. This would have been less of a consideration for a studio built at ground level.

760 Brown and Anthony, Op. Cit., pp. 64 &73, Nt.71. Roderick Grey, "The Art of the Camera" *The Royal Magazine*, February 1899, p. 300. The exact location is uncertain, but I think it was located at the rear of the Tivoli Theatre in the Strand and was probably on the roof or in the garden of a building overlooking Embankment Gardens, adjacent to Adelphi Arches and just below Adelphi Terrace.

The studio at the French company's production facility in Courbevoie outside Paris was probably very similar to the earlier on built at Thames-side in London and is another refinement of Dickson's studio design. The stage is on a simple semi-circular track for positioning in maximum sun. The camera shed (left) is also movable. [NMAH.]

Return" and "Waiting for Hubby" but the British version was performed by veterans who added a twist – the errant husband made peace by surprising his wife with an unexpected gift. Films of mischievous children were audience pleasers – "The Pillow Fight" had proved a perennial favorite and the British company produced a variation: "Burglars in the Pantry" in which the children were caught smearing jam on themselves rather than pelting each other with pillows.

One of the more enterprising – and sensational – of the early British productions was "Duel to the Death". It reproduced a scene from Benjamin Landeck and Arthur Shirley's play "Women and Wine" in which two women removed their ball gowns and clad in shirt waists and petticoats, attacked each other with large knives. This juicy and provocative scene was performed by Edith Blanche and Beatrice Homer from the original production. This too, had a precedent in an earlier American production, "An Affair of Honor" in which two women (fully clothed) fought a duel to the death with swords. "Duel to the Death" was a prelude to a more ambitious – and less risque – production, "Fencing Contest From the Play 'The Three Musketeers'", which featured a popular matinee idol, Lewis Waller, as D'Artagnan with Messrs. Esmond and Loraine in support. It was the first film recording a prominent English actor and since it was made just before the play opened it not only provided a glimpse of exciting dramatic action, it served as an advertisement for the new play.[761]

The most interesting and creative variation on earlier productions was "Facial Expressions -The Fatal Letter" in which the rapidly changing expressions of comedian Ben Nathan were filmed in close-up as he read a letter telling of the death of an aunt. His mood shifted as he learned of criticism that he was a spendthrift and ultimately found that

761 Ibid., pp. 226–227. The play opened at the Metropole Theatre, Camberwell, 12 September 1898 and at the Globe in the West End on 22 October 1898 to warm reviews.

Facial Expressions – The Fatal Letter *featured Ben Nathan, a popular comedian from the London stage. The tight close-up allowed him to transmit changed emotions as he learns of his prospects following the death of a wealthy but critical aunt. [Anthony.]*

he inherited £5000. Three films made earlier in the U.S. bear a resemblance to this one: "The Oration" "Showing the efforts of a speaker to make himself heard by the people in the rear of a large hall;" "His First Smoke" "a study of the joys and sorrows of a young man's first taste of the weed;" and "The Miser" A "... misguided creature ... counting his hoard of gold coins and apparently [hearing] someone approaching".[762] "Facial Expressions ..." is perhaps more effective because the camera was brought a bit closer to show Nathan from the waist up while the three American films showed most of the body. Ben Nathan was a popular comedian who also acted as booking agent for the British Mutoscope company through his firm Nathan and Somers of Covent Garden.[763]

One other film from these early productions deserves mention because it is an early version of a joke that was repeated in productions by other pioneer filmmakers. "He Kissed the Wrong Girl" began with a lover's tiff on a park bench. The angry girl stalked off and the boy turned to kiss her only to discover an old maid seated in her place. Film historians will recognize the joke from "What Happened in the Tunnel" (Edison 1903) where Edwin S. Porter modified the joke by having the girl change places with her black-faced maid in the darkness of a railroad tunnel.[764]

Most of the productions that are mentioned here were shown at the Palace but a number of others were made for exhibition on Mutoscopes. "He Kissed the Wrong Girl" was one that probably went to a roll of Mutoscope cards rather than the transparent film used in the Biograph. This would certainly be the case for "Why Marie Blew

762 The descriptions are from the 1902 *Picture Catalog* published by American Mutoscope & Biograph Co., pp. 11 & 237.

763 Brown & Anthony, Op. Cit., pp. 53 & 255.

764 There are two other American versions of this substitution joke in which African-Americans are involved: "A Kiss in the Dark" American Mutoscope & Biograph Co., filmed 30 December 1903 and "The Mis-Directed Kiss" made by AMB 4 January 1904. Charles Musser (*Before the Nickelodeon*, pp. 261–262) mentions Ferdinand Zecca's "Flirt en chemin de fer (1901) and Lubin's "Love in a Railroad Train" as predecessors of Porter's film and credits the joke to antecedents in comic drawings.

Stage productions in London provided the British company with regular fare. Here leading man Lewis Waller is featured as D'Artagnan in Fencing Contest from the Play 'The Three Musketeers'. [Anthony]

Out the Light" which showed Marie undressing for bed and "Wicked Willie" which displayed a schoolboy's curiosity about an apparently nude lady. We know more about the films shown at the Palace and other prominent exhibition halls because the press frequently commented on the more popular subjects. Films made for Mutoscope showing were generally ignored by the press unless, like "Marie ..." and "... Willie", they attracted the ire of moralists and politicians.

Although British-made films were welcomed at the Palace and other places where the Biograph projected films, entertainment subjects were selected carefully and the programs continued to be predominantly composed of actuality productions. Brown and Anthony point out that Charles Morton, the manager of the Palace, and others programming variety theaters had to be very careful in scheduling performances because presentation of staged productions in variety halls was forbidden by an Act of Parliament designed to protect theaters presenting plays. Apparently images projected by the Biograph fell outside this restriction and allowed additional leeway in programming.[765]

As was the case at the New York studio, Dickson seems to have taken a limited role in filming at the London studio. His task was to film in the field and once the studio was functioning, he was apparently called on only for special occasions. But he undoubtedly oversaw the initial productions and his handiwork is evident in several of these introductory films. Placing the camera closer to Ben Nathan in "Facial Expressions" is typical of Dickson's work. It not only made Nathan's facial expressions more visible, it brought him closer to the viewers, giving the film audience an intimate perspective that was not possible

765 Brown & Anthony, Op. Cit., pp. 220–221.

in an on-stage situation. The staging of "The Fencing Contest from the Play 'The Three Musketeers'" is typical of Dickson's attempts to clarify a complex visual. There were eight men in the scene, four dueling pairs, aligned so that their sides were towards the camera which was raised slightly above their heads, allowing a view of all four pairs. Lewis Waller and his opponent were nearest the camera but all of the pairs could be seen. There was no attempt to duplicate stage scenery, instead the engagement was filmed against a plain, light colored backdrop which did not divert attention from the fencers as a scenic backdrop would have.

In early September Dickson and Emile Lauste packed their bags for a trip to Amsterdam. The news event of the fall was the coronation of the young Dutch sovereign, Queen Wilhelmina. It was an opportunity to provide audiences at the Palace – and elsewhere – with lively images of newsworthy and up-to-date fare.

Chapter 29

The News in a Pictorial Way

"In building up our business we were of the opinion at first that what the public would desire would be a series of finished and artistic pictures representing a scene or event of historic interest or artistic value. At first we followed such a course, but we soon found that the public demanded of us the prompt and reliable service of the daily newspaper rather than the artistic or aesthetic finish of the weekly or monthly magazine. That is to say, the public has expected us to gather the news in a pictorial way and disseminate it at once ...". (Harry N. Marvin, 23 July 1901)[766]

"The place of the special descriptive correspondent, and even of the special artist, seems likely to be filled by scientific photography. One is led to this conclusion by the rapidity with which important events can now be reproduced in living pictures. A case in point is the launch of the Oceanic at Belfast on Saturday. On Monday night the scene was reproduced in London ... at the Palace Theatre and at the Royal. ... we have after the launch the rush of the crowd from the great wave of spray which was sent up by the backwash as the great ship nestled on the water. No pen and no pencil could so graphically reproduce the scene. Instead of buying a penny paper to read about the great function we shall in future go to a music-hall to see it enacted with mechanical and mobile accuracy." (*Sheffield Telegraph* (England) [January] 1899)[767]

By the fall of 1898 gathering "... the news in a pictorial way" had become increasingly important for the Mutoscope companies and the particular responsibility of W.K-L. Dickson. (He had begun inserting a hyphen between Kennedy and Laurie.) The September trip to Amsterdam to record the coronation of young Queen Wilhelmina of the Netherlands was followed by a succession of other news gathering efforts.

Princess Wilhelmina had succeeded to the throne in 1890 when her father, King William III, died, but she was ten at the time so her mother, Queen Emma served as regent. Wilhelmina turned eighteen on 31 August 1898 and the coronation took place in Amsterdam's Nieuwe Kerk the following week on 6 September. As an indication of the increasingly sophisticated approach to filming such ceremonial occasions two cameras were used. This is a first time use of multiple cameras and one of the cameras seems to have been designed to use a longer load of film. The procession to the church was filmed from two

766 EHS, Harry N. Marvin, testimony in Equity No. 6928, Edison v. American Mutoscope Co., 23 July 1901.

767 Niver, Op. Cit., p. 43.

different locations and the two strips were joined together to produce
a film that ran almost two minutes, more than double the usual scene
on the Biograph's programs. The cameras were expensive – costing
about $600 – so committing two of them to a project was a measure of
its importance. In addition to the procession to the church, the arrival
and departure from the church were also filmed and after the ceremony
the newly crowned Queen and her mother were filmed greeting an
enthusiastic crowd from a balcony at the Royal Palace. To add a touch
of pomp and color, a guard of honor dressed in uniforms of the Dutch
Army dating from the middle ages to the present was also filmed:
"There are quaint halberdiers with steel casques and spears; companies
armed with arquebuses, etc.; finally the up-to-date soldiers of Her
Majesty's army".[768]

The film of Queen Wilhelmina greeting the crowd from the
balcony of the Royal Palace featured another deviation from routine. It
was shot from a location above the crowd, near the same level as the
balcony. After establishing the crowd and the Queen's response to it,
the camera was moved to position the Queen closer to the center of the
frame. The move was smooth which was quite a feat considering the
heft of the camera! There is no clue as to how this was done.

After the ceremony, it was inevitable that windmills, wooden shoes
and quaint costumes would be filmed, but making distinctive images
presented a challenge. A clutch of windmills were found in the Zaan
district, not far from Amsterdam. As in Venice, mobility was achieved
by mounting the camera on a boat and positioning it very low to make
the windmills seem lofty and dominant. By chance or pre-arrangement
most of their vanes were turning and the naturally flat terrain made
them stand out dramatically against the sky. An interesting church in
the background gave variety to the scene. Once again, careful planning
resulted in a natural, visually interesting scene. Wooden shoes were
provided by a troop of costumed children on Marken, an island in the
Markermeer north of Amsterdam – not far from Zaan. The children
were filmed in four separate shots, apparently taken with a single roll
of film. The first shot showed five costumed girls watching a boat
loaded with children being poled into the frame by one of the boys. As
the boat left the frame the camera panned to reveal an old boat, the rest
of the house in the background and some laundry on a line. In the
second shot the boat with the children aboard was in the foreground
close enough that the faces of the children could be clearly seen. They
smiled and waved at the camera as the boat moved off frame. The third
shot was similar, but in the fourth the camera was raised well above the
heads of the children to capture them forming two circles and dancing
in a ring. Some adults in traditional dress watch them and all this
complicated staging took place in the span of a minute and a half.

The album of Dutch subjects was completed with films of a
procession of carriages decorated with flowers taken in Haarlem, bathers and promenading vacationers at the North Sea resort of Scheven-
ingen, two shots of Dutch fishing vessels and an unusual comic film in

768 AMB *Picture
Catalogue*, 1902, p. 102.

which two carts pulled by dogs and filled with costumed passengers tried to cross a rude bridge across a canal. The first cart made it but the dog pulling the second one faltered, the cart tipped, spilling the occupants into the canal. Perhaps it was planned, but more likely it was an accident. Some windmills in the background indicate that it was shot while filming in Zaan.

Although the coronation films and some of the others found their way into the company's international venues, this very "Dutch" and touristic package was primarily shown to audiences at the Circus O Carre Theater in Amsterdam where the Biograph was playing.

The coronation films were showing in London in the week of 17 October but may have opened earlier.[769] By now the company was aware that the audiences at the Palace welcomed and even expected prompt, up-to-date presentation of newsworthy events. A week earlier, on 6 October they were treated to a same-day showing of the celebratory parade of the Grenadier Guards who returned from the Sudan after defeating the Mahdist forces of Abd Allah. It was a highly popular victory because it secured control of the Nile river for British dominated Egypt and extended the British colonies in Africa from the Mediterranean to the Cape of Good Hope. The afternoon parade from Waterloo to the Wellington Barracks drew a huge crowd. That evening Charles Morton, manager of the Palace invited reporters to the theater where the film was shown to an astonished audience. The cheering began as soon as a slide announced "See the conquering heroes come! Welcome Home!". The orchestra accompanied the film with the Grenadier's march and the *Daily Chronicle* reported that the cheering in the theater seemed more vigorous than it had been on the streets.[770]

This coup was followed three weeks later by films of the return of Major General Sir Herbert Kitchener, the commander at Omdurman and popularly known as the Sirdar. His reception in Dover took place about four in the afternoon and it was on screen at the Palace that evening. It became available on Mutoscopes the same week.[771]

The rush to cover newsworthy stories was spurred-on by competition from other British companies. Robert Paul filmed the parade of the Grenadier Guards and Kitchener's return. The Coronation of Wilhelmina was filmed by Warwick Trading Company. Both companies filmed in the so-called Edison standard format (35mm) and exposed at c. 15 frames per second, so their films lacked the spectacular quality of the Biograph's projection, but their cameras were smaller and more portable than the Mutograph so they had greater flexibility. While neither company had as prestigious and visible London situation as the Palace, their strong position in an expanding film market gave them much more flexibility in both projecting under their own auspices and making the films available to others. The Mutoscope company was restricted by contract to the Palace as their only venue in London, a situation that the British company was beginning to regret.

It will be remembered that Robert Paul was the British pioneer who built a version of Edison's Kinetoscope in 1894. He had been

769 The set of surviving programs from the Palace is incomplete, so it is possible they were shown earlier

770 Brown & Anthony, Op. Cit., pp. 197–198. *Daily Chronicle*, 7 October 1898.

771 Ibid., pp. 136. British Mutoscope and Biograph Prospectus.

A publicity photo of Dickson and associates filming somewhere in rural France, possibly in December 1898 when President Faure was filmed hunting pheasants. Dickson is seated in the center and the gentleman seated next to him is probably Julian Orde, head of the Biograph and Mutoscope Company for France. The two men standing on the left are unidentified but Eugene Lauste is behind Dickson, next to the center camera and his son Emile Lauste, Dickson's assistant, is on the other side. Emile is holding a still camera to show that taking still photos was an important aspect of their assignment. The box under the camera on the left is the battery that powered the camera. [NMAH Lauste.]

involved in the production and distribution of films as well as the manufacture and sale of motion picture equipment since that time. The Warwick Trading Company was a London based firm that also traced it's origins to the Kinetoscope. It evolved from Maguire & Baucus, Edison's former European distributor. Edison ended their exclusive contract in November of 1896 when he began selling films directly. Maguire & Baucus responded by expanding their business to handle films produced by other companies, notably Lumière films perforated to fit Edison standard machines. In 1897 M&B sent Charles Urban to London and soon promoted him to manager. The company's name was changed to Warwick Trading Company (after the street where their office was located). By this time Warwick was distributing the films of Georges Méliès, G.A. Smith, R.W. Paul, Riley Brothers, Prestwich and some others. Early in 1898 they expanded further by going into film production. In May they filmed Gladstone's funeral (an event the Mutoscope company missed, apparently because Dickson was in Rome). Charles Urban was an aggressive manager and Warwick was soon the Biograph's principal competitor – though the two companies occasionally cooperated on projects.

In December Dickson returned to France to film President Faure shooting pheasants. While this was not breaking news, it proved to be very timely because Faure died suddenly the following February. Since the film is among the many that have not survived this would only be a footnote in Dickson's career, but a photo of Dickson's crew in the field, apparently taken at this time, gives a tantalizing view of filmmaking at the end of the 19th century. The bare trees in the background indicate that it was taken in late fall or early winter which would correspond with the time that President Faure was filmed. Considering the obvious rural setting, how well dressed they are! This may have been in deference to meeting the President of the Republic, but filming was always an occasion for Dickson and his crew – even in the French countryside. This was apparently the lunch break as next to Dickson is a small table with several bottles on it. Dickson is conspicuous in the center seated in front of one of two Mutograph cameras. Eugene Lauste is behind him on the left of the camera and Emile Lauste is to the right of the camera. The three men on the left of the photograph are unidentified, but the man seated to Dickson's left is probably Julian W. Orde who was head of the Biograph and Mutoscope Company for France. The gentleman with the white beard is very similar to a man appearing in a photo of the staff of the studio in Courbevoie which leads to the assumption that this is a company photograph. To the right is a small, picturesque donkey-drawn wagon which was probably transport for Dickson and his guests. A larger wagon for the equipment completes the scene. Dickson is wearing a fur trimmed top coat and an elegant top hat. The coat was apparently a recent purchase and it figured in several photos taken about this time. Everyone looks very serious, except Mr. Dickson who looks blase, though his pose recalls that of Edison in his well-known "Napoleon of Invention" picture [see p. 68].

The presence of two cameras is most interesting; an indication that production facilities were expanding. The French studio was not yet opened, but in December, 1898, it was probably in the planning stages. When it opened in Courbevoie, near Paris, the following spring it was equipped with at least two cameras like the ones in this photo.[772] Emile Lauste (standing to right of the camera in the center) is holding a Kodak still camera, evidently a demonstration of the importance of coordinated still photographs. This is one of the earliest photographs showing the carts used to carry the camera and crew and while the donkey cart is not very elegant, its quite fetching!

The following January there was another race-to-the-screen. The White Star Line's *Oceanic* was to be launched at Harland and Wolff's shipyard in Belfast, Northern Ireland on the 14th. The launching came at a time when national pride in steel ships was peaking and the *Oceanic* was the largest passenger liner yet built. Charles Urban had obtained exclusive rights to film the launch for Warwick, but the Mutoscope company managed to negotiate rights to join the filming and on 11

772 This photograph and the photographs of the cameras at the Courbevoie studio are in the Eugene Lauste Collection, NMAH.

January Dickson and Emile Lauste took the ferry from Fleetwood to Belfast.[773] In a draft of his reminiscences, Emil Lauste recounted how the filming almost turned into a disaster:

"... I nearly miss the Launch of s/s 'Oceanic'

"In the early days, great secrecy was kept as to the nature of how our camera worked, for the film was perforated as it stopped at each exposure. In fact, while photographing – it was no uncommon thing for bystanders to grumble as the fast ejected perforations & stampings fell down their neck. In those good old days our type of camera, in which the film travelled at the rate of 1,800 (revolutions/pictures) per minute (30 pictures per second) often caused static discharges to take place, so causing what is known as lightening marks – to avoid this to a minimum, the negative film was passed over jets of cooled steam, overnight – doing this in one's bedroom gave rise to all sorts of risks. The day for the launching the Oceanic had arrived in Jan. 1899 – I had my camera set ready when lo the film was stuck together – there was no time to loose [sic]. I jumped in a cab & hastened to the hotel to load my magazine again – with unsteamed film – but no darkroom was handy. Time pressed – a good thought, the Hotel safe, yes I could have use of it, as I entered the safe the man kept near to open the massive door – should I lack air – but the loading was soon finished as I came out I trimmed the end of my film which dropped on the floor. A gentleman whose name is now a household word in the cinematograph industry [Charles Urban?] at once picked it up, not believing that our film was not perforated before-hand. I hope he was satisfied for he seemed to still entertain a doubt. Back to my camera – and a few minutes later the largest vessel in the world (in 1899) was gracefully gliding into the water – which rose above the jetty where onlookers were situated wetting their feet, their scramble away from the barrier & the great liner coming to a standstill, was all faithfully recorded, whereas an hour before it stood the good chance of not being recorded. Peculiar as it may seem, I never saw that Ocean monster till June 1913 in Southampton – 14 years later, now a moderate vessel compared to her giant sisters."[774]

The companies filming the event were afraid that the steamship company's usual black and red colors would provide poor contrast should the January weather prove dismal and drear so the ship's owners were persuaded to paint the liner white especially for the launching. The films were rushed back to London but the trip took seventeen hours so the films were not shown until two days after the launch. Warwick's films were shown at six theaters, and while Dickson's film was only on screen at the Palace the audiences who saw it must have been thrilled.[775] The Biograph's large format and Dickson's careful placement of the camera captured the immensity of the ship as it slid past the camera. The movement of the ship and the resulting water turbulence creates a startling effect – and the film, which survives, remains impressive to this day.[776]

Mr. D and Emile remained in Ireland after the launch. They filmed Irish farmers, pigs on a farm, a phantom ride on a tramway and the home of Pres. McKinley's ancestors in Conagher. This was more down-home program fare, but satisfying the continuing craving for water scenes became an adventure. To capture the impressive surf near

773 John Barnes, Op. Cit., Vol. 5. *1899*, pp. 138–39.

774 SEFVA Emile Lauste Collection. Lauste draft Reminisce, 1913. The gentleman referred to was probably Charles Urban.

775 John Barnes, Op. Cit.. Vol. 4, pp. 138–139 & 162–163. Barnes credits Urban with negotiating the agreement to paint the vessel and says that the resulting publicity was probably worth the £600 cost.

776 An article in *The Sketch*, January 18, 1899, p. 492, said the *Oceanic* was the largest and heaviest ship ever made. 705 ½ ft. long compared with the Great Eastern's 631 ft. It weighed 17,000 gross tons and the propeller was 21 ft. in diameter. It took twenty two months to build at a projected cost of nearly £1,000,000, would carry 1499 passengers and a crew of 395. A copy of the film is preserved by the Museum of Modern Art.

the "Giant's Causeway", they spent several days at a nearby cave and, for the first time I am aware of, used artificial light on a field trip. This otherwise ordinary excursion turned into a life-threatening venture – at least as Emile Lauste saw it:

"A very effective picture was secured of the mighty waves rolling and dashing themselves into the mouth of the Port Coon Cave which lies on the road to the Causeway.

"These were secured with some risk to life and apparatus as the ingress to the cave was situated in a rather risky position, namely by working at the extreme base of the cliff and jumping from stone to stone in between each shower of spray from the fast incoming waves, untill [sic] the mouth of the cave was reached. Here it was a wave was misjudged as to how far it would go. Mr Dickson – a guide and myself were taken off our feet by the force of water and only a stroke of luck saved us from being sucked under to probably a watery grave. But we were all very thankful of having got out of the predicament by a good ducking in icy water which drenched us to the skin. This proving too risky, a picture was secured from a safer distance of the waves splashing against the mouth of the cave.

"A side entrance permitted, at a certain tide, to enter the cave. Once inside there was plenty of room to take shelter, but neverless [sic] the awful sensation of waves in all their fury, hurling themselves against the mouth, entirely shutting out the day – by a solid wall of sea water was to put it mildly awe inspiring and at first rather unnerving.

"The taking of our heavy camera – batteries, tripod, cable etc from the hill some 180 ft above the sea level inside of Port Coon cave was no light task. Foothold was scarce where weight was concerned and damp and wet not adding to the comfort of the burly men engaged to carry them down. Eventually the apparatus was safely landed – set up and as is usual when the camera is ready the sea abates, so daily journeys were made till the storm raged as when we first visited the cave. This duly repeated itself and a good picture was secured.

"I already mentioned that the sea when dashing against the mouth completely cut out the light as from a photographic point we could not record the incoming waters, a set of specially designed continuous magnesium lamps were brought into use, so that the daylight was excluded from the cave a fairly successful picture was made of the action of the water splashing and foaming within, thus making an unbroken record.

"These lamps worked continuously for 1 minute, emitting great [actinic] power.

"It has to be recorded that the complete apparatus remained in the cold damp cave for 3 days and 2 nights.

"The mutograph losing all its beautiful polish and metal rusting and corroding."[777]

The public's enthusiasm for timely coverage encouraged a particularly daring and very newsworthy same-day expedition. The Grand National Steeple Chase was to be run at a track in Liverpool in early March. The race was scheduled for 3:30 in the afternoon and it was determined that it was possible to film the race and get it on screen at the Palace that night. The London and Northwest Railway provided a baggage car and agreed to delay the departure of the 4:05 express to London for up to

777 SEFVA Emile Lauste Collection. Draft reminiscences, 1913.

ten minutes while the film was brought to the station for the non-stop run to London. Prior to the race the baggage car, which was rented, was modified by partitioning it and installing developing tanks, drying reels and holding vessels for the chemicals. The plan was to film the race, rush the film to the train, develop it during the run to London, then print it at Great Windmill Street and rush it to the Palace. The manager of the racecourse, Mr. Gladstone gave them a choice filming location; they booked the fastest horse in Liverpool for the run to the railroad station and arranged with Chief Inspector Cross of the Liverpool police to clear the way. The camera was set up about ten in the morning at a location near the finish line and about one hundred and fifty yards from the water jump. Dickson had at least two assistants for the filming, Emil Lauste and George W. Jones. Jones' account of the race was published in *Photography*, Vol. 11, No. 546, 27 April 1899, p. 284.[778]

There was a dramatic hitch. Just before the race was run Mr. Gladstone informed them that it would be delayed for twenty-five minutes which would make it impossible to make the train. They pleaded with Gladstone who discussed the situation with the jockeys who agreed to speed-up their preparations. The horses were on the track at three thirty, the race started at three thirty-five. Jones was operating the camera and as soon as the race finished he pulled the film case from the camera and he, Emile and Dickson raced across the track to the waiting wagon. The five mile run to the station started at 3:45 and each stage of the run was timed by the participants. They arrived at seven minutes past four, delaying the train by only two minutes. The film was developed on the train which arrived at London's Euston Station at eight fifteen, five minutes early. The audience at the Palace saw the finish of the race at eleven ten that night.[779]

Emil Lauste gave this account of the filming in his 'Reminiscences':

"Head Office decided to take pictures of the Grand National at Liverpool and show it the same night at the Palace Theatre, it being intended to develop the negative on the train on the way back to London, so they wrote me to arrange to return on Thursday so as to assist them in both taking and developing the pictures, arrangements being made for another operator to take my place where I happened to be showing at the time – 'The Public Hall, Worcester'.

"A London & North Western Luggage Coach was hired – it was attached to the train at Euston. The dim lights overhead in the coach were covered with red fabric, the doors where light might come in were covered with black paper, while on the floor laid large trays for developing and fixing and part washing. With the swaying of the train I feared several of us unwillingly put our feet in the baths – fortunately the film was not in at the time. The idea was for us to accommodate ourselves to this novel darkroom so as to be sure of what to expect when on our return journey.

"The pictures were taken – a rush made for the train at Aintree, and when the train started – non-stop to London – we knew no inquisitive person would open the coach doors to see what was inside and so probably spoil the day's work. The work proceeded very well. The films were left on the frames to dry – the doors being opened to allow air to enter – but when we reached Euston the films were still tacky – so had to get into a hansom –

778 The text is reproduced in John Barnes, *The Beginnings...*, Vol. 4, 1899, pp. 139–142.

779 Barnes, Op. Cit., pp. 139–142. This is from Jones' account.

the quickest means of transport in those days – and hold the frames so that they would not either touch us or the body of the hansom. On reaching the Works everybody was on the alert having expected us to have the films dry ready to print, but as they were still tacky they were drummed to finish the drying – this caused some delay – then prints were made. But the time was getting on – it was feared we would miss the Show. However it was arranged to throw a slide and tell the audience that the Biograph would show pictures of the Grand National after the last act. This saved the situation. The films were duly shown – though a bit late – to a rapturous audience – as this was the first time such a distant event was shown in so short a time."[780]

The daring and imaginative filming of the Grand National captured the public's fancy. The sprint from the track to the Palace was as dramatic as the horse race – Jones said that spectators at Euston Station in London were placing bets on the success of the run and time of arrival. The generous swath of publicity was welcomed by the railroad, the race track and the Mutoscope company and the coverage in popular dailies and the professional press encouraged the company to continue treating late night audiences at the Palace with timely features. The day after the Grand National the late audience at the Palace saw not only the Grand National but coverage of the eight-oar race between Oxford and Cambridge which Dickson's crew had filmed at Putney that afternoon. On 20 April the patrons enjoyed a view of the Prince of Wales emerging from Westminster Abbey after attending the wedding of Lady Peggy Primrose to the Earl of Crewe that afternoon. Queen Victoria's arrival at South Kensington to lay the cornerstone of the Victoria and Albert Museum was filmed and shown on 17 May 1899.

These events were primarily of interest to British viewers, but in late May Dickson made a film that struck a cord in the U.S. The American Lines steamship *Paris* was abandoned after it went aground on one of the Manacles, a cluster of rocks off the Cornish coast that were an infamous maritime hazzard. Dickson and his crew left for Cornwall as soon as the news reached London and although it was claimed that they arrived the next day they arrived too late to film the evacuation of the ship's 386 passengers and crew of 372. But Dickson filmed a panoramic view of tugs from the Hamburg and Copenhagen Salvage Co. straining to pull the ship off the rocks with the Paris aiding the effort by reversing its engine. The scene played well and he was proud enough of the image that he kept a glass plate negative of one of the still photographs for his personal collection. The Manacles' reputation as a nautical graveyard was well earned. Some fifty ships had gone aground on there in the preceding thirty years. The *Paris* had a reputation of its own. It had made the news in 1890, when 1050 people, passengers and crew, were stranded at sea for a period of time before the ship finally made port at Queenstown.[781]

Although he missed the evacuation of the *Paris*, Dickson was able to film a rescue at sea while he was at the Manacles. A four masted sailing vessel, the *Mohegan*, had sunk after going on the rocks and he filmed the life saving crew from Porthoustock launching their craft and rescuing seamen clutching the rigging. Dickson chartered a boat and

780 SEFVA Emile Lauste Collection. Lauste's recollection is from notes he wrote 26 March 1901. Jones said that a furniture van was hired to take the reels of film to Great Windmill Street and drawings made from sketches by Dickson for *The Golden Penny*, 6 May 1899, p. 391 show this van. The drawings are reproduced in Barnes, Op. Cit., pp. 140–141.

781 "The 'Paris' Aground on the Manacles." and "The Manacles are Merciless" in *The Sketch*, 31 May 1899, pp. 228, 532 with a photo by J.C. Burrow, Camborne, Cornwall. Gordon Hendricks acquired Dickson's negative of the *Paris*.

Pictorial news

Here are some events filmed in 1899 by British Mutoscope Co. that may have been shown to audiences on the day the were filmed or within a day or two of filming:

- The Launch of the Oceanic; 14 January 1899
- Grand Military Steeple Chase at Sandown, 3 March 1899
- Landing of Lord Chas. Beresford from S.S. "St. Louis", at Southampton, 8 March 1899, on His Return from His Mission to China
- Departure From Folkestone of the Queen, 11 March 1899
- The Lincoln Handicap, Doncaster, South Yorkshire, 21 March 1899
- Grand National Steeplechase, Liverpool, 24 March 1899
- Crews Leaving the Water/Oxford and Cambridge University Boat Race, 25 March 1899
- Oxford and Cambridge Boat Race, 25 March 1899
- The Marriage of the Earl of Crewe and Lady "Peggy" Primrose at Westminster Abbey, 20 April 1899
- Reception of the Duchess of York at Tenby, 9 May 1899
- Her Majesty the Queen Arriving at South Kensington on the Occasion of the Laying of the Foundation Stone of the Victoria and Albert Museum, 17 May 1899
- The Wrecks of the "Paris" and "Mohegan", Cornwall, 22 May 1899
- Their Royal Highnesses, The Duke and Duchess of Connaught Opening the Article Club Insdustrial Exhibition, Crystal Palace, 30 May 1899
- The Derby, Epsom, 31 May 1899
- Members Enclosure, Epsom, 31 May 1899
- The Right Hon. Cecil Rhodes and Lord Kitchener After Receiving the Degree of D.C.L. at Oxford, 21 June 1899
- The Prince of Wales at the Aldershot Review, 26 June 1899
- Her Majesty, Queen Victoria, Reviewing the Horse Artillery, Windsor, 1 July 1899
- Henley Regatta, 7 July 1899
- Stage Coaches Leaving the Hotel Victoria, Annual Parade of the Coaching Club, 8 July 1899
- Australian Cricket Test Match, Manchester, 17–19 July 1899
- International Collegiate Games, London, 22 July 1899
- Church Parade, Hyde Park, London, July 1899
- Coach Meet and Polo, Hurlingham, July 1899
- Embarkation of the "Fighting Fifth" for Natal, Southampton, 18 September 1899
- Four Scenes from "King John" featuring Mr. Beerbohm Tree., 18 September 1899
- General Buller Leaving the Carlton Club, London, and Embarking for South Africa at Southampton, 14 October 1899
- Lord Wolseley, Southampton, 20 October 1899
- Gordon Highlanders on Board Transport, Liverpool, 9 November 1899
- Her Majesty Queen Victoria reviewing troops, Windsor, 11 November 1899
- Lord Roberts Embarking on the "Dunottar Castle" for South Africa, Southampton, 23 December 1899

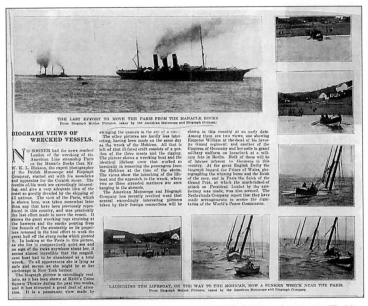

THE LAST EFFORT TO MOVE THE PARIS FROM THE MANACLE ROCKS.
From Biograph Motion Pictures, taken by the American Mutoscope and Biograph Company.

BIOGRAPH VIEWS OF
WRECKED VESSELS.

NO SOONER had the news reached London of the wrecking of the American Line steamship Paris on the Manacle Rocks than Mr. W. K. L. Dickson, the expert photographer of the British Mutoscope and Biograph Company, started out with his associates and apparatus for the Cornish shore. The results of his work are exceedingly interesting, and give a very adequate idea of the coast so greatly dreaded by the shipping of all nations. The view of the Paris, which is shown here, was taken somewhat later than any that have been previously reproduced in this country, and was practically the last effort made to move the vessel. It shows the great wrecking tugs straining at the hawsers and the smoke pouring from the funnels of the steamship as its propellers reversed in the final effort to work the great hull off the sharp rocks which pierced it. In looking at the Paris in this picture, as she lies in comparatively quiet sea and no sign of the rocks anywhere about her, it seems almost incredible that the magnificent boat had to be abandoned as a total wreck. To all appearances she is lying as safe and secure as she might be at her anchorage in New York harbor.

The biograph picture is exceedingly realistic, as it has been shown at Keith's Union Square Theatre during the past two weeks, and it has attracted a great deal of attention. It is a panoramic view made by swinging the camera in the arc of a circle. The other pictures are hardly less interesting, having been made on the same day as the wreck of the Mohican. All that is left of that ill-fated craft consists of a portion of the three masts and the rigging. The picture shows a wrecking boat and the identical lifeboat crew that worked so heroically in removing the passengers from the Mohican at the time of the storm. The views show the launching of the lifeboat and the approach to the wreck, where two or three stranded mariners are seen hanging in the shrouds.

The American Mutoscope and Biograph Company has recently received word that several exceedingly interesting pictures taken by their foreign connections will be shown in this country at an early date. Among them are two views, one showing Emperor William at the head of his favorite Guard regiment, and another of the Empress of Germany and her suite in grand military uniform on horseback at a military fete in Berlin. Both of these will be of intense interest to Germans in this country. At the great English Derby the biograph bagged the Prince of Wales, photographing the winning horse and the finish of the race, and in Paris the finish of the Grand Prix, at which the much-talked-of attack on President Loubet by the aristocracy was made, was also secured. The Netherlands Company report that they have made arrangements to secure the dignitaries of the World's Peace Commission.

LAUNCHING THE LIFEBOAT, ON THE WAY TO THE MOHICAN, NOW A SUNKEN WRECK NEAR THE PARIS.
From Biograph Motion Pictures, taken by the American Mutoscope and Biograph Company.

Providing timely coverage of current events was a major activity for the Biograph companies. The New York Mail, *3 June 1899, found the activity of filming news as newsworthy as the images of the efforts to pull the shipwrecked liner Paris off the Manacle Rocks near the Cornish coast and the efforts to save the crew of th Mohigan which was also wrecked while Dickson was filming there.*
[NHMLA Guisling Scrapbook.]

filmed the launch and rescue with the camera mounted on deck. All that survives of the filming are six photographs printed in the New York *Mail and Express* but they show quite graphic scenes. There are three pictures of the *Mohegan* and one of them shows people standing on part of the deck that is still above water. In the other two the deck is no longer visible and only the masts are out of the water.

The films were rushed to the U.S. and they were on screen at Keith's Union Square within two to three weeks. An accompanying press release stimulated several stories featuring Dickson's work, The most extensive article was "Biograph Views of Wrecked Vessels" that appeared in *The Mail and Express* 24 June 1899:

"No sooner had the news reached London of the wrecking of the American Line steamship Paris on the Manacle Rocks than Mr. W.K.L. Dickson, the expert photographer of the British Mutoscope Company, started out with his associates and apparatus for the Cornish shore. The results of his work are exceedingly interesting, and give a very adequate idea of the coast so greatly dreaded by the shipping of all nations. The view of the Paris, was taken somewhat later than any that have been previously reproduced in this country, and was practically the last effort made to move the vessel. It shows the great wrecking tugs straining at the hawsers and the smoke pouring from the funnels of the steamship as its propellers reversed in the final effort to work the great hull off the sharp rocks which pierced it. In looking at the Paris as she lies in comparatively quiet sea and no sign of the rocks anywhere about her, it seems almost incredible that the magnificent boat had to be abandoned as a total wreck. To all appearances she is lying as safe and secure as she might be at her anchorage in New York harbor.

"The biograph picture is exceedingly realistic, and has attracted a great deal of attention. It is a panoramic view made by swinging the camera in an arc of a circle.

"The other pictures are hardly less interesting, having been made on the same day as the wreck of the Mohican [sic]. All that is left of that ill-fated craft consists of a portion of the three masts and the rigging. The picture shows a wrecking boat and the identical lifeboat crew that worked so heroically in removing the passengers from the Mohican [sic] at the time of the storm. The views show the launching of the life-boat and the approach to the wreck, where two or three stranded mariners are seen hanging in the shrouds."[782]

Fame and prosperity?

The popularity of the Biograph reached a peak in 1899. It remained a feature at the Palace and attracted crowds at other sites whenever it was on the program. The public's taste for cinematic entertainment and the unique form of visual news that the company offered seemed insatiable. The steady stream of publicity that the British and American companies dispensed enhanced their reputation and Dickson's exploits were often featured in their propaganda. His penchant for the dramatic and will-ingness to take difficult, sometimes life-threatening chances made savory copy and his activities had particular appeal for those Victorians who relished the adventuresome tales spun by Ouida, Rudyard Kipling and Sir H. Rider Haggard. Although he had achieved a degree of recognition through his work with Edison and the publications that he and Antonia generated, his work as a filmmaker added a new dimension. Persuading the Pope to appear on film was almost enough to ensure him public esteem. The Pope's reluctance to leave the Vatican and the rumors of his ill health made the films especially welcome and the feat was widely recognized as a coup that was only possible because of the patience and persistence that Dickson exhibited. In fact, the act of persuasion was almost as important as the resulting images. Subsequent stories of Dickson's activities were often prefaced with a reminder that it was he who convinced the Pope to appear on film. By 1899 Dickson was as well known as anyone working in the motion picture field – excepting, of course, Edison and the Lumières whose ubiquity made some think they personally made the films that bore their names.[783] With the Papal story as a base, stories of rushing to London with the Grand National film and dashing to Cornwall to film the *Paris* pro-moted the American and British companies and gave Dickson a cachet that few in the profession could match. While it would be an exaggera-tion to call him a celebrity, he was certainly prominent and at this point better known for film production than for his work with Edison – which was never mentioned in the companies' feeds to the press.

At this stage of his career Dickson seemed quite willing, perhaps even eager to gain public recognition. He had worked in relative anonymity for Edison and despite the Mutoscope companies' wish to

782 NHMLC Van Guisling Scrapbook. In *Leslie's Weekly*, 27 July 1899 and *The Mail and Express*, 24 June 1899 and *Phonoscope*, April 1899, p. 10. This version is taken from *Phonoscope* which appeared some months later but is a reprint of the 24 June article.

783 Yes, the list could include Georges Méliès, but at this time he was just beginning to capture the public's fancy.

avoid rousing Edison's litigious wrath, now he had the opportunity to step out of the shadow. Edison was a master at self-promotion – perhaps one of the all-time champions – and Dickson had ample opportunity to watch the wizard in action. And Dickson had all the instincts to practice what he had observed. He was flamboyant, daring, confident, courageous and uninhibited; also cunning, a bit ruthless and quite willing to advance himself. Furthermore, he was not made of bluff and bluster. While he was prone to exaggeration in some of his boasting, he had long since proven that he was willing to do what he claimed he could do and capable of doing what many were unwilling to do. He was an advertising man's dream!

It is difficult to pass judgment on the value he had added to the Mutoscope companies. They traded on his exploits, but their cautious approach to Edison kept his name from being used prominently in their business information. He was a founder of the American company and a member of its board but the KMCD group operated as an equal partnership and as the company grew they continued to share responsibility. Though Dickson (and the others) continued to work on new inventions and submit patents, credit for the the invention of the Mutoscope, the Mutograph camera and the Biograph projector went to Casler. In the printed programs that accompanied projections "Invented by Herman Casler" always followed mention of the Biograph.

Although the Biograph was established as a standard setter in projection, it was the quality of the films Dickson was producing that attracted customers both new and old. As the months went by, Dickson had more than proved his worth.

Dickson must have been aware of his importance to the growth of the Mutoscope companies but he seems not to have pressed for a prominent role in either company. The ties of friendship among the KMCD group and their understanding of the complementary skills that each possessed were strong enough that Dickson did not feel it necessary to press an advantage. After all, he was gaining recognition for his work and he and his associates were making money – probably well beyond their expectations. By 1899 Dickson was prosperous, if not wealthy. He held more than 2000 shares in the American company which had a face value of $100 each and while they may never have been traded at full value ($202,000), they were trading relatively well in 1899. When the British company reorganized in 1900 as the British Mutoscope & Biograph Co, Ltd, Dickson had 28,500 shares at £1 each (a face value of £28,500). He also held 2000 shares of the Austrian & Hungarian Mutoscope & Biograph Co. and his wife Lucie had 1000 shares as well (face values not known). He undoubtedly had stock in other branches of the company such as the French, Italian, Dutch, German and Belgian organizations as well as local Mutoscope companies being formed in England and the U.S.[784]

784 Brown & Anthony, Op. Cit., pp. 121 & 139.

He was also paid a generous salary and living expenses both in London and on the road. While there are no firm figures as to Dickson's salary it was probably equivalent to what Koopman was paid as General

By the end of the 19th Century Dickson enjoyed both prosperity and a degree of celebrity. He sported a silk top hat and fur trimmed coat when he posed for this photo with Etienne Jules Marey at Marey's Physiological Station in 1898 or 1899. [NMAH Lauste.]

Manager, £1000 a year – at a time that £250 to £350 was considered a living wage.[785] Since coming to England Dickson and family had stayed at the fashionable Hotel Cecil on the Strand in London, almost certainly paid for by the company. As Emile Lauste's diaries indicate, Dickson also enjoyed a generous expense account on the road, staying in good hotels and enjoying the best in food and wine. As if this were not enough, Dickson received several dividends during 1899. The British company paid a 25 per cent dividend and he received checks from the American company in the amount of $1161.89 on 26 April and $1500 on 22 May.

    Dickson displayed his newfound fortune with the purchase of a stylish bearskin coat and top hat – seen here in a photograph taken

785 *Ibid*, p. 118. Koopman also received 10 per cent commission on net annual profits. It is not clear that Dickson received similar payments but it is quite possible. Brown reports that Koopman was paid £2252 commission between March 1900 and February 1902. Since much of these profits resulted from the films Dickson produced in South Africa it would seem likely he received something similar.

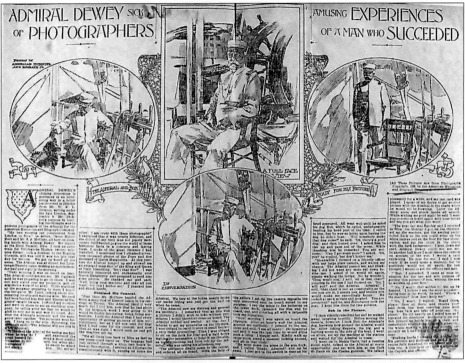

Admiral Dewey, America's hero of Manila Bay was one of the celebrities that Dickson persuaded to pose for his still and motion cameras. He caught up with the Admiral in harbor at Villefranche while he was en route home to a triumphal reception for his victory in Manila during the Spanish American War. The New York Herald found Dickson's story and pictures worth featuring. Pictorial journalism was just reaching the point where photographs could be used to illustrate articles but, like these, many of Dickson's photos were turned into drawings for publication. [NHMLA Guisling Scrapbook.]

786 NMAH Lauste; Kelly's London Directory, 1901; SEFTA, Emile Lauste collection. The photograph with Marey was probably taken during the winter of 1898–1899 as Dickson was in South Africa the following year. The Dicksons' move to Hillmarton Rd. may have been caused by his assignment in South Africa as the company might not have paid for the rooms at the hotel after he left. The earliest confirmation that they were there is an entry in Emile Lauste's diary for 1900, Sept. 28, 1900, which mentioned visiting Mrs. Dickson at 7 Hillmarton Rd.

during a visit to Étienne-Jules Marey at his Physiological Station. Increased prosperity may have encouraged the Dickson family to put an end to living out of suitcases and put down roots in England. Sometime during 1899, possibly after Dickson left for South Africa, Mrs. Dickson and Antonia moved to a house at 7 Hillmarton Road, in Islington, a residence belonging to an artist, Samuel John Hodson, R.W.S., possibly a friend of the Dicksons or of Dickson's father.[786]

As the British company grew and prospered their capabilities for producing film expanded. By 1899 Dickson had trained a number of crews to produce films. Independent crews were working in England, France and Germany. This makes it more difficult to identify which films Dickson himself produced as the quality of some of these productions was very high. In June Emile Lauste was back in Holland filming in Schweringen, Haarlem, Naardam and Amsterdam. His diary mentions receiving some Guilders from Dickson, but doesn't mention him otherwise – though he described problems encountered when moving the heavy camera equipment from Amsterdam to Haarlem in a none too efficient early motor truck. Although Dickson was not

Sir Herbert Beerbohm Tree as King John in The Last Moments of King John of England in the Orchard of Swinstead Abbey. *[Anthony.]*

mentioned in that account, it seems likely that he was in Holland because the main purpose of the trip was to record the arrival of delegates to the peace conference in Haarlem on 4 June 1899. Emile had handled solo assignments well on an earlier trip to the U.S., but he was not ready to negotiate prime camera locations with international diplomats.[787]

"Historical facts in a concrete and lasting form"

Dickson was in France again in August. This time at the request of the American company. Admiral Dewey and his entourage were visiting ports in the Mediterranean en route to the U.S. from the Pacific. After his spectacular victory over the Spanish fleet in Manila Bay, Dewey had become an American idol and the American Mutoscope Company wanted films to celebrate the hero's return. He was scheduled make port in Villefranche on the French Riviera and to catch him there Dickson traveled from London to Nice. When the film was ready to ship to the U.S. Dickson wrote a letter describing the filming in some detail. The letter was given to the *New York Herald* who featured it in their 24 September edition. The article, entited "Admiral Dewey Sick of Photographers; Amusing Experiences of a Man Who Succeeded", was illustrated with drawings made from still photos taken by Dickson. It is the most detailed self description of his work thus far and though

[787] The film of the delegates, *Aankomst de Vredesconferentie te Haarlem, 4 Juni 1899* survives at the Nederlands Filmmuseum. On his trip to the U.S. in March, 1899. Emile Lauste filmed scenes at sea aboard the S.S. St. Louis; the dedication of the Grant monument in Philadelphia and athletic scenes at Yale University in New Haven. He went to the U.S. with Koopman in order to film the dedication of the Grant monument. The American company was apparently short handed at the time.

he would soon be sending regular diary entries from South Africa, this one is unique so the complete text is reproduced here:

"Admiral Dewey's obliging disposition is portrayed in an interesting way in a letter just received in this city from Mr. W.K.L. Dickson, writing under the date London, 3 September. Mr. Dickson's purpose in visiting the Olympia was to procure photographs of the Admiral for the American Mutoscope and Biograph Company.

"'My two sleeping car companions from London to Nice', he writes, 'were Robert Barr and Mr. S.S. McClure, all bent on shaking hands with Admiral Dewey. We stayed at the Hotel Termini, Nice. I took an early train for Villefranche Harbor, twenty minutes distant, took a rowboat to the flagship Olympia, and was told it was too late that day for visitors. We got on board all the same. The Admiral was at dinner, but Lieutenant Brumby came, making an appointment for half-past eight in the morning.

"'Next morning I was on board on time. The Admiral could not see me. Mr. Caldwell said he was preparing to go on shore. I was not very elated over my prospects, and all arguments were of no avail. While standing at the gangway preparing to leave I heard the navigator, Mr. Laird, talking about illuminating the ship and wanting wire. My card had been handed him first and 'Electrical Engineer' caught his eye. I offered my services and went on shore to see an electrical company, he calling after me that he would be glad to help me in any way he could. Just then the Admiral's secretary and the navigator came together. The secretary went below. I hung on to the ship. Returning, the secretary said: "The Admiral will see you in a few minutes.'

"'I thanked the Admiral for seeing me just when he was so b[usy] and expressed the great honor I felt [and] received a most cordial invitation to come aboard, but when photographing [was mentioned] he swore he would not allow [any to be] taken. 'No, not another! I am crazy with these photographers!' I explained that it was totally different, and the object of my visit was not purely mercenary, but I wanted to give the world at large historical facts in a concrete and lasting form. I spoke of the great distance I had travelled [sic]. I mentioned how I obtained seventeen thousand photos of the Pope and five thousand of Queen Margherita. At this juncture the Admiral jumped up and showed me an enlarged snap shot of the King and Queen of Italy, remarking, 'Isn't that fine?' I was naturally interested and enthusiastic over Queen Margherita and promised to send him some photos. He thanked me and said, 'Well, bring your machine and take all you want: but don't bother me.' I thanked him and shook hands.

"'Obtained His Consent

"'Just then Mr. McClure handed the Admiral a snap shot of himself taken in his carriage in Trieste. The Admiral liked it very much, but I told him now that he had given in, the biograph work I was going to do would be doubly interesting, being living portraiture. I told the Admiral that I had every opportunity of getting pictures of him surreptitiously, but [how] I did not care for that kind I had come for his comment, and now that all was right I would rush on and get the machine set up.

"'We all three tore back to Nice as fast as our horse could carry us. The baggage had just arrived through a hitch two hours before at Nice station. I arrived at Villefranche simultaneously with it, passing en route the Admiral. We tore at the boxes nearly broke our backs lifting and just got the half when he came.

"'The Admiral saw my distress and greeted me smilingly. I remarked that as this was a picture I didn't wish to talk without permission I would therefore come on board. The Admiral nodded and smiled. All that day I labored to get my apparatus on the Olympia. I was obliged to carry it over in small boats – a very risky proceeding. Then I was obliged to sit on deck for four and a half hours waiting for permission to hoist it up the side, as no instructions had been left by the Admiral, who was taking his afternoon nap.

"'The navigator finally came to the rescue and ordered all on board. With the help of the sailors I set up the camera opposite the only uncovered spot on board suited to my purpose. I ran the wires to the batteries on the lower deck, threaded the film and focused, and, and [sic] covering all with a tarpaulin, took my departure.

"'Next morning I was again on board the Olympia. After an hour's wait the Admiral greeting me cordially. I pointed to the machine and said, 'I am all ready'. He demurred and said it was the last time he would allow such a thing. I simply said, 'Kindly walk up those steps, stand a moment looking around and sit in that chair'.

"'He went down the steps in the gun deck and I called 'Ready, Admiral!' And up he came. I just got to the switch in time as his head appeared. All went well untill [sic] he spied his dog Bob, which he called, unfortunately bending his head part of the time. I called to him, but he was so intent upon having the dog he didn't hear. 'Will somebody make that dog come?' he said. 'Oh, there's a good dog'. and then leaned over. I asked him to rise up and pass out of the scene. While thanking him he remarked 'You are welcome.' 'Can I get some more?' I asked. 'Oh yes!' he replied, 'but don't bother me'.

"'Meanwhile I focused on a friendly officer with my large plate camera, and waited my chance. The Admiral passed me and thinking I did not want any more sat down beside me. I asked if he would sit again, simply walking the bridge. No, he wouldn't. 'Then won't you', I said, 'sit in that chair?' Pointing to the one I had focused on. 'No, I will not!' said the Admiral. 'Admiral', I said, 'that chair is just as comfortable as the one you are in, I assure you, and besides you would make me exceedingly happy'. He looked at me a minute and laughed. 'You are persistent!' said he, and deliberately took the seat. I kept him there for two pictures.

Bob in the picture

"'I then silently raised my hat and he walked away, laughing heartily. Before moving the camera, however, I took Bob the Admiral's dog, knowing how pleased the Admiral would be. After taking Sagasta, the pig, and a bathing scene at the side of the "a" boat. I went on shore, set up the machine at the station and waited for the Admiral to come.

"'I went on to Monte Carlo, had a rousing social night, talked to the admiral at every opportunity, and sat with him at the Café de Paris on the Casino grounds. We talked pleasantly for a while, and my last card was played. I spoke of my desire to get another picture with the Admiral in the shade where he would not be frowning. Later the Admiral arose and shook hands all around. While wishing me good night he said 'I want you to come on board again with your things and see you get what you want'.

"'The next day was Sunday and I returned to Nice. On Monday I got on the Olympia, set up the machine, got the awning partly rolled back so the sun could shine on the white canvas laid on the floor for face illumination, and put the chair in the shade with the dark background. I sent down my card. Admiral Dewey could not see me. In another half hour I must move the camera on account of the sun. I wrote a card explaining. He sent for me. I said I was ready if he could spare a moment, but he positively would not sit again. He had thought I meant to get the officers and men.

"'But', I remarked. 'I came at your invitation for the one and sole purpose of getting this picture of you, without the sun to wrinkle up your face'.

"'No, I won't! that settles it.' but up he jumped. 'I believe I am the most accomodating [sic] man in the world'. he said. 'Where is the machine? Now, don't keep me'.

"'No, I won't', I replied. 'Stand there please: then sit there, and receive your mail from that man carrying your mail bag, lean back and take off your cap. Go, please.' He did exactly as I asked him as I repeated the directions. Incidentally his dog Bob jumped up beside him in a chair, and immediately received the Admiral's attention, the whole making a very good picture, especially as I had brought the camera very near'.

"'Shaking hands I thanked the Admiral for his patience and kindness and said I would return fully rewarded for my efforts and my long trip. A little later on I took a picture of the Captain and officers.'"[788]

Dickson's account illustrates, once again, his ability to establish a companionable working relationship with his subjects even trouble-some ones. As in his account of working with the Pope, he seemed to savor the challenge of convincing a reticent or contrary subject to perform for the camera. His mixture of good natured interplay, a confident display of authoritative knowledge and bossiness – brassy, but carefully applied, was effective. And, as always, any difficulties were ofset by making it an occasion that called for socializing when the camera stopped. The evening in Monte Carlo with Admiral Dewey may have matched a luncheon with Major and Mrs. McKinley or a stroll through the Vatican gardens with Pope Leo.

A striking aspect of this account is the cooperative involvement of Robert Barr and S. S. McClure. Dickson was in distinguished company. Like Dickson, Robert Barr was a Scot with international roots. Born in Scotland, he was raised in Canada and had worked in the U.S., notably for the *Detroit Free Press*. After establishing his reputation as a short story writer (with the pseudonym Luke Sharp), he moved to England where he established *The Idler*, an independent illustrated literary magazine which published contributions by Sir Athur Conan Doyle and Rudyard Kipling. Irish born, American educated Samuel Sidney McClure had pioneered the syndication of newspapers. *McClure's Magazine*, which he founded in 1893, was emerging as the most influential periodical in the U.S. Over the next few year he would publish articles by John Phillips, Lincoln Steffens and Ida Tarbell that exposed economic and social ills and give the term "muckrakers" an unexpected place of honor in the world of journalism. The presence of Barr and McClure makes this a major story and takes it out of the category of news gathering or capturing just another story of a new celebrity. The cooperation of major figures in the publishing world belies the common assumption that moving pictures were a rival to the printed word and that serious

788 LACMNH Van Guisling Scrapbook. *New York Herald*, 24 September 1899.

literary figures regarded the "flickers" as culturally inferior and a potential menace to the written word. In fact, as we have seen, the
Mutoscope companies in England and the U.S. were closely tied to the
publishing world. There is no information about the preliminary arrangements for the trip to Villefranche, but Dickson may have known
McClure who had previously been associated with *Century Magazine*,
publisher of his account of his experiences with Edison. *Idler* was
published by Chatto and Windus who published the British edition of
the Dicksons' biography of Edison. It is also possible that Sir Cyril
Arthur Pearson or Sir George Newnes, publishers on the board of the
British company, played a role. At the end of the 19th century the
Mutoscope companies' connections with the press worked at the highest level.

Interestingly, Dickson did not mention an assistant helping him
with this filming and if he handled it all himself, it was quite unusual.
Since at least four hands were usually needed to handle the bulk and
complexity of the Mutograph it seems unlikely that he was by himself.
McClure and Barr might have helped with the set-up (Dickson implies
they helped unload the shipment), but they were executives not jour-
neymen. It seems more likely that Dickson did not choose to mention
having assistants – despite usually crediting his assistants.

Shakespeare on film

Within a month of his return to London another memorable and
newsworthy commission came his way. Herbert Beerbohm Tree, one
of England's most prominent actors was about to open at Her Majesty's
Theater in Shakespeare's *King John* and arrangements were made to film
him and members of his company in scenes from the much anticipated
production. This was the second of three productions of Shakespeare
plays that Beerbohm Tree produced. The first, *Julius Caesar*, drew
unusually large crowds and it was expected that *King John* would
maintain the surprisingly popular revival. Surprising because although
Shakespeare was univerally revered, his plays were not always successful in performance.[789] *King John* opened on Wednesday, 20 September
1899, and the filming took place a day or two before (perhaps earlier
than that as he exact date is uncertain). Four scenes were filmed: "The
Battlefield Near Angiers", with Beerbohm Tree as King John; Franklyn
McLeay as Hubert de Burgh and Percy Sefton as Arthur of Brittany;
"The French King's Tent" with Julia Neilson as The Lady Constance,
Arthur's mother; Gerald Lawrence as the Dauphin; William Mollison
as King Philip of France and Louis Calvert as Cardinal Pandulph; "The
Last Moments of King John of England in the Orchard of Swinstead
Abby" with Beerbohm Tree as King John; and "The Little Prince Henry
is Accepted by the Barons as John's Successor and Faulconbridge
Prophesies a Glorious Future for England" with Dora Senior as Prince
Henry and F.M. Paget as Robert Bigot. The filming took place at the
Mutoscope company's outdoor stage on the embankment very near the
Hotel Cecil, Dickson's home away from home in London.

789 Brown &
Anthony, Op. Cit.,
pp. 228–229. Barry
Anthony comments
that the success of
Julius Caesar and two
other Shakespeare
plays, which drew
some 600,000 people,
proved that the
widely held belief that
Shakespeare's plays
were box office
poison to be false.

This was by far the most ambitious dramatic production staged by the British company. It involved a large cast, scenery (provided by the theater) and suitable costumes for the period (also from the theater). The scenery, designed for the larger stage at Her Majesty's Theater, had to be adapted for the company's smaller one. The support facilities near the studio were very limited so for regular productions costume changes and make-up were done in the Hotel Cecil or some other nearby location. Recognizing this, the cast of *King John*, including Beerbohm Tree, changed and did their make-up at the theater. When appropriately transformed to figures from the era of the Magna Carta, they were then transported in wagons to the Hotel Cecil. It was, apparently, quite a sight! H. Chance Newton, writing in the urbane, cynical prose expected by readers of *The Sketch*, described the expedition as a "trying ordeal":

"... [the] writer called upon Mr. Beerbohm Tree ... found that popular actor-manager and his numerous adherents just passing through a most trying ordeal. In other words, Mr. Tree and the whole strength of his company were being 'biographed' wholesale, retail, and certainly for exportation, by that shrewd firm which supplies Animated Photographs to this or that amusement resort throughout the United Queendom.. It was truly a very quaint experience to see this extensive company ... who will to-night (Wednesday) ... present... 'King John' ... Hurrying off clothed in more or less 'complete steel' – and in perfect make-up – to the vicinity of the Hôtel Cecil, to be snapshotted, as it were, for pictures to be presently shown in all sorts of places in Europe, but especially at the Palace Theatre, London. For the going and coming and the to-ing and fro-ing of the latest King John and his vast retinue a new and picturesque awning had been prepared outside Her Majesty's Theatre and several 'Black Marias' had been chartered for the carrying of the company ... There was also something of humour in the sight of ... hurrying back with the dark-blue-armoured King John Tree at their head, newly escaped from the clutches (and the 'Kodaks') of the Animated Photographers.

"... the production, which, whatever its other merits may prove to be, will to-night assuredly be hailed as one of the grandest examples of *mise-en-scène* ever witnessed even at this theatre ...".[790]

Of course, this production recalls the earlier filming of another theatrical legend, Joseph Jefferson, in scenes from *Rip Van Winkle*. The two film series come closest to fulfilling Edison's persistent prophecy that the camera would capture and preserve legendary performers in great roles. Sadly, Dickson's camera was only capable of recording brief segments; a minute or less of each scene and without sound – a major deficiency in the case of Shakespeare. The brevity of the scenes and the misconception that early film was awkward and primitive have kept these scenes recording 19th century theater from being studied by modern scholars of the theater – although this is changing as a new generation of researchers are revising our view of the early cinema and taking a fresh look at popular theater.[791]

For audiences (and Mutoscope viewers) watching *Rip* and *King John* the brevity of the scenes was a minor problem. There was no attempt to recreate the continuity of the original and viewers did not

790 "'King John', at Her Majesty's" by H. Chance Newton in *The Sketch*, 20 September 1899, pp. 388 & 389. On 27 September 1899, p. 413, *The Sketch* published four photographs of he play provided by British Mutoscope and Biograph Co., Ltd.

791 Film historian Luke McKernan has given particular attention to these films through articles and presentations of the surviving copies.

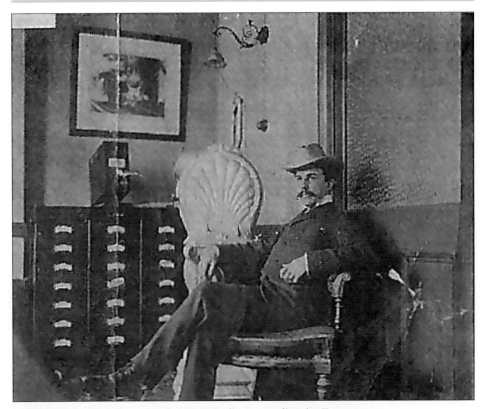

Mr. Dickson photographed in the London office at the height of his career as a filmmaker. Two versions of the Mutoscope are pictured, an iron clad model is next to him and a hand-cranked parlor version is on the shelf. [LC.]

expect to see the original. These were samples, intended to give theater goers and Mutoscope viewers enough of a taste of the original to whet their curiosity and, perhaps, lure them to the theater. There was a bonus, however. Once again, Dickson's camera was closer to the action than all but the very best theater seats, so the samples had an immediacy not possible in most theater situations. Perhaps this was what gave them special appeal.

King John, and to a lesser extent, *Rip Van Winkle,* were advertisements; a means of calling attention to and promoting Beerbohm Tree and his production. But, like Dickson's railroad films, the primary object was to entertain and luring customers (and creating new admirers) was an important, but secondary objective.[792] Interestingly, in the case of *King John*, the advertising value was as much in the making as the showing. The newspaper articles, photos and coverage by journals like *The Sketch* may have lured as many or more people to Her Majesty's Theater as the images on screen at the Palace. The publicity generated by the almost simultaneous showing at the variety theater was also valuable – as was the announcement that the films were being shipped

792 *Rip Van Winkle* was not, strictly speaking, an ad for the play, nor was it a promotion for Joseph Jefferson who was already legendary. It was, however, a promotion for Sandow's *Olympia* which was directed by Joseph Jefferson's son, Charles B. Jefferson.

immediately to Paris, Berlin, Brussels, Amsterdam, Milan and Vienna. The company's promotion of the event was not limited to the theatrical presentations. It was announced that *King John* would be shown widely in England on Mutoscopes. This came at a time when the company was promoting the Mutoscopes heavily and encountering increasing criticism of the racy content of some Mutoscope releases. W.T. Smedley, the Chairman of the British company, tried to assure the press that *King John* on Mutoscope was an indication that the taste of the Mutoscope audience was improving.[793]

The notion of presenting Shakespeare without words is admittedly strange, but it bothered audiences less at the time the films were made than it does today. Although some contemporary critics found fault with watching *King John* in pantomime, audiences seemingly accepted the scenes – as later audiences accepted versions of Shakespeare produced by Vitagraph, Thanhouser, Kalem, Selig, Metro, Fox and others (including Biograph). It is said that audiences of the period were more familiar with many of the plays. *King John* is not one of the more familiar ones but the British knew King John as the monarch whose reign brought forth the Magna Carta (though Shakespeare neglected to include that in his play).

Directing *King John* must have been a collaborative effort. Beerbohm Tree had already staged it for performance and would have been unwilling to have major changes made since the film was supposed to represent what was on stage at Her Majesty's Theatre. But he would have had to rely on Dickson's experience with staging works for the camera; particularly crucial matters such as arranging the scene so the action was clear to the audience and timing the shot so the desired action was shown. Unlike the filming of Admiral Dewey, we have no clues as to how well Dickson and Beerbohm Tree got along. Other than the characterization of the filming as a "trying ordeal" in *The Sketch* (which seems more journalistic hyperbole than accurate reporting) there is nothing to indicate that the filming did not go smoothly. Dickson was well versed in dealing with theatrical people and his habit of turning the task into a social event had produced lasting relations with people as diverse as Annabelle, Sandow and Joseph Jefferson. There is no indication that Dickson and Beerbohm Tree developed a long-term relationship, but the four scenes were completed in a single day. (The filming was probably done during mid-day when the sun was most advantageous.) With several sets to change (three of the four scenes were in different locales); probable walk-throughs before filming and different players from scene to scene, the logistics were fairly complicated.

793 Brown & Anthony, Op. Cit., pp. 228–229. Barry Anthony quotes an article "'King John' in the Mutoscope. A Glimpse at Mr. Tree for Penny." in *The Westminster Gazette*, 21 September 1899.

The four episodes fit with Dickson's very cautious move towards producing longer, more complicated films. In this case, two of the scenes, "The Battlefield Near Angiers" and "The French King's Tent" are unrelated scenes, but the last two, "The Last Moments of King John …" and "The Little Prince Henry is Accepted … as … Successor …" are related and could be played together. Nevertheless, there is no indication that he thought to join them as a single piece. It is another case where the instinct was there, but the obstacles discouraging longer productions were so entrenched that he could not take the final step. Perhaps some of those obstacles were in his own mind?

Two days after the opening of *King John* the *The British Journal of Photography* published an article reporting that the previous Saturday cameramen at Southampton had filmed the embarkation of troops sailing for South Africa. They speculated "... that, if war does unfortunately come about in South Africa, enterprising cinematographers and photographers will not be far off ...". Mr. Dickson was about to pack his bags for his most memorable adventure.

Chapter 30

The Road to Ladysmith: The Biograph Goes to War

"I note that the biograph has gone to the war, and, if anything in the way of a battle piece is possible, Mr. Dickson, the gentleman in charge, is just the man to secure it. As money is no object with a Company such as this, and the technician mentioned is a man full of resources, the British public will, no doubt, through the medium of the instrument at the Palace Theatre, be treated to some most interesting episodes. ... but, when it comes to the actual fight, then the distance dictated by prudence, if not insisted on by the general in command, will preclude anything like a near enough approach to the scene to get a presentable picture except by long-focus lenses ... for with ordinary lenses the photograph will only be a microscopical reproduction of the scene. I have often witnessed military manoeuvres and sham fights, and should have liked to portray what the eye sees, but the camera of ordinary make, with lenses of moderate length of focus, is quite unequal to the task. Mr. Dickson may be equipped differently to what I suppose for his biograph camera and so upset my conclusions. Any way, I know he has with him cameras other than the biograph, so perhaps he may obtain some good set scenes as well as animated."[794] G.R. Baker, *The British Journal of Photography*.

"... the author of "The Biograph in Battle" may fairly claim to have broken entirely virgin soil. We are all familiar with the Biograph, and we have all read largely about the war, but the story of the combination of the two is a thing absolutely new in the annals of war or science. ..." (Prefatory note to *The Biograph in Battle*)

T he fighting in South Africa followed an ultimatum from the Boers against further reinforcement of the British forces in their territories, the South African Republic and the Orange Free State. Their ultimatum was issued on 11 October 1899 and on 14 October W.K.L. Dickson, accompanied by his assistants William Cox and John Seward, sailed for Cape Town aboard the S.S. Dunottar Castle. It was the beginning of Dickson's most remarkable – and best documented – experience as a filmmaker. He was in South Africa from 30 October 1899 until 18 July 1900 filming what was expected to be the final stages of the British campaign to restrain the Boers who proved to be surprisingly resourceful despite their relatively smaller numbers. He

794 In "Lantern Memos" *The Lantern Record*, Monthly Supplement to *The British Journal of Photography*, 3 November 1899

Dickson sailed for South Africa on the Dunottar Castle, the same ship carrying General Sir Redvers Buller to take command of the British forces. Dickson managed to position himself prominently so that he not only appeared in the British Mutoscope's film of Buller boarding the ship (shown here) but on the film made by the competing Warwick company. [Anthony.]

was one of a new breed of war correspondents, reporters with movie cameras. He was about to record an event that was at once the climax of Britain's imperial glory and, in retrospect, an augury of its impending decline.

The impressive list of passengers aboard the Dunottar Castle is a clear indication that the ultimatum was no surprise. At the head of the list was General Sir Redvers Buller, the newly appointed commander of the British military in South Africa. The General was accompanied by his staff and more than a dozen war correspondents representing several of Great Britain's leading journals. A number of these reporters had gained prominence covering the frontier engagements in India and the campaign in the Sudan. Among them was a youthful Winston Churchill who had been engaged by the *Morning Post* to cover the fighting. Although he was just turning 25, the well-born and socially prominent Churchill had gained a following for his reports on his experiences as a junior officer in India and the Sudan and as a private citizen visiting pre-revolutionary Cuba.[795]

Friction between the British and the original Dutch colonists dated back to the Napoleonic era when the British protected the water routes to their Asian interests by taking control of the strategic Cape of Good Hope. Serious trouble developed when foreign speculators began flooding to the territories following the discovery of rich deposits of gold and diamonds in the Dutch controlled areas. The potential for conflict was further escalated by Cecil Rhodes' ambitious plans to extend British influence from the Cape to Cairo. By September 1899 the preparations for warfare were well underway with enthusiastic support from the many British who firmly believed that it was their

795 In addition to his reports to the newspapers, Churchill authored several books which were well received by the British critics and the public.

Before sailing, Dickson, always dapper and suitably attired, posed in field dress purchased for his African adventure. In the field he dressed more practically, but with a military-styled uniform fashioned on those worn by British officers. This portrait was used as the frontispiece for his book Biograph in Battle. [Author's copy.]

country's function to spread the benefits of modern life to the less privileged abroad.

The departure of the Dunottar Castle was an occasion for patriotic celebration and a huge crowd filled the dock area in Southampton to cheer the General and his staff when they arrived by train from London's Waterloo station. The Lord Mayor of Southampton led the ceremonies and the cameras of the Mutoscope company and the Warwick Trading Co. were prominent while recording the scene. In a fit of playfulness, Dickson managed to positioned himself so that he was clearly visible in Warwick's film of General Buller at the ship's gangplank – as well as Biograph's own film. The band played *God Save the Queen* and as the ship sailed the crowd spontaneously sang *Rule Britannia, Auld Lang Syne* and *He's a Jolly Good Fellow*.[796]

796 "Good-Bye to the General" by George Griffith, *The Illustrated War News,* 21 October 1899, pp. 10–11. Warwick's film showing Dickson is either *"General Buller Embarking on the 'Dunottar Castle' at Southhampton"* or *"Passengers Boarding the "Dunottar Castle."* General Buller and his staff wore civilian clothes because the *Dunottar Castle* was a scheduled passenger liner rather than a military ship.

With ample warning of the impending conflict, the British company had prepared well for Dickson's departure. The recent war with Spain had given the American company increased business at a time when interest in the Biograph seemed to be flagging and the British company looked for a similar response. The American company sent their most experienced cameramen, Billy Bitzer and Arthur Marvin, to Florida and Cuba immediately after the news that an explosion had sunk the Battleship Maine. Bitzer achieved something of a coup by filming the wreckage of the Maine before the conflict broke out and that picture and scenes of military preparations in Florida were received enthusiastically. The American company made it a policy to provide their public with authentic war pictures at a time when competitors were offering re-enactments of combat filmed in the fields of New Jersey and their genuine pictures of the war brought the company timely new engagements.[797] With this in mind, the American company dispatched Raymond Ackerman to the Philippines to film the American efforts to suppress the anti-American rebellion that followed the swift and relatively easy victory over the Spanish.

The British company had good reason to believe that despite the expense, sending a crew to South Africa would be a sound investment and the American company which was apparently eager to have more war films gave them support. One of Dickson's assistants, John Seward, was an American, quite possibly furnished by the American company.[798]

As we have seen, the business had evolved into a fledgling news service, albeit one that dealt in supplementary material rather than hard news. Photos taken by Biograph crews appeared in publications on both sides of the Atlantic, among them *Pearson's Magazine* and *Royal Magazine* (both published by board member Sir Cyril Arthur Pearson) and *The Strand* (published by Sir George Newnes, another board member). *Frank Leslie's Weekly*, one of the most popular American magazines, frequently used pictures supplied by the American company.[799] When he boarded the Dunottar Castle Dickson's baggage included still cameras, a sketch pad, a notebook, some pencils, the Mutograph camera and a supply of film. The theaters and other locations showing films would also have photos and drawings of things that could not be filmed and still pictures, drawings and a written record of his activities would be available to press.

The well-placed members of the company's board were undoubtedly helpful in making arrangements with businessmen and politicians who could open doors, provide access to military activities, ease transport and facilitate shipments. Because of their reputation for timely exhibition the company was concerned that the films would be received promptly. Travel from South Africa involved a sea voyage of almost two weeks from Cape Town and an even longer one from Port Elizabeth, East London and Durban which were east of Cape Town. Transport from the combat zone to the nearest port would add to the time lag. A meeting with the proprietor of the Castle line which served South Africa, Sir Donald Currie, resulted in an agreement to expedite the company's shipments. The Castle lines gave a similar concession to the Warwick company a few weeks later. Throughout his stay Dickson made a point of maintaining a friendly relationship with the representatives of the shipping company and if his diary can believed, he received excellent service from them.

The most important contact made before Dickson's departure was with Cecil Rhodes, the most potent figure in South Africa and much of the rest of British Africa. In addition to creating Rhodesia he was a former governor of the British South African colonies and his extensive business interests included the world's largest and richest gold and diamond mines. These were mostly in the Boer territories and the

797 Musser, *The Emergence ...*, pp. 244–247; Bitzer, *Billy Bitzer ...*, pp. 33–44. The explosion on the "Maine" occurred on 15 February 1898, Bitzer said he sailed from New York on the *Seguranca* and arrived in Havana on 19 February 1898. When war was declared on 25 April 1898 Bitzer was ordered back to Cuba.

798 John Seward seems to have been a former neighbor of Dickson's from Orange, NJ. A Mrs. John L. Stewart was Dickson's guest when he filmed Bucking Bronchos on 16 October 1894. The *Orange Journal*, 18 October 1894 reported that she lived on Main Street. Dickson referred to Seward as his friend (Dickson, *Biograph in ...* pp. 63–65) and William Cox referred to him as the son of Dickson's friend (National Army Museum, Cox diaries, 29 December 1899, 8209-33-4).

799 NMHLA, Van Guisling scrapbook. Among the illustrated articles in the scrapbook are: *Leslie's Weekly*, 27 July 1899, "Photographing a Rescue at Sea" Mohegan off the Manacles", *Leslie's Weekly*, 5 August 1899 published "Queen Victoria's Latest Picture" and *Leslie's Weekly*, 26 August 1899, has photos surreptitiously taken of Dreyfus in prison at Rennes which also appeared in *The Sketch*, 16 August 1899 and *NY Journal*, 14 August 1899.

influx of foreign workers at his mines was the immediate cause of the crisis. If Dickson can be believed, Rhodes hoped to publicize South Africa and encourage potential immigrants through films shot by the Biograph company. It is possible that this was discussed in May when Rhodes was filmed riding on horseback in Hyde Park or in June when he was filmed with Sir Herbert Kitchener and the Duke and Duchess of York outside the Sheldonian Theatre in Oxford after Rhodes received the Degree of D.C.L.[800] There is no indication of formal negotiations but when he sailed Dickson carried a letter to Rhodes and expected support from him while in South Africa. Rhodes' brother, a Major in the army, was aboard the Dunottar, but he offered little encouragement and this was particularly true after the news was received that Rhodes was under siege at his Diamond mine near Kimberly. In spite of this discouragement, Dickson paid a visit to Rhode's home outside Cape Town shortly after his arrival hoping to meet some of Rhodes' staff. They were not there, but Dickson had a luncheon meeting with Rhodes after the siege of Kimberly was broken.

There were restrictions on the amount of equipment that could be taken on the Dunottar so cameras, film and batteries had priority. Tents, a cape cart, a pair of horses, cooking utensils, canned food and other necessaries for survival in the field were purchased after their arrival. It was important to Dickson that he be suitably attired so he and his two associates were outfitted with khaki field uniforms intended to blend with those worn by the troops. Dickson also had a dress version of the uniform and posed wearing it for the frontispiece in *The Biograph in Battle* (page 545). Dapper as ever, he appears as the exemplar of a colonial officer. He sported a well trimmed beard, a splendid mustache and carried a riding crop. A stylish hat similar to that worn by Anzac forces in World Wars I and II created the finishing touch. The hat and dress togs were rarely used in the field, instead he and his assistants wore the lighter khakis and the topee used by the colonial militia.

There are a number of photographs showing the Mutograph camera in the field and it appears to be a modified version of the "B" model, a slightly (but not too much) smaller version of camera that Dickson brought to England in 1897. It was probably capable of using longer loads of film than the earlier versions – films running longer than thirty seconds had been made during the weeks prior to sailing for South Africa. A bicycle wheel attached to the tripod appears in a number of photos and drawings and this seems to have been used to drive a suction pump that flattened the film against the aperture plate during exposure. One of the assistants rotated the wheel by hand during the filming.[801] The tripod was also modified. A hand crank at the point where the camera is mounted was new and this probably made it easier to adjust the level and may have been used to pan the camera. Prior to departure Dickson purchased a telephoto lens from J.H. Dallmeyer, Ltd. in hopes that it would be useful in filming action from a distance. He was disappointed in the results and rarely used it.

These modifications may have improved image quality but they

800 *The Biograph in Battle*, p. 7, Gutsche, Op. Cit., p. 44; Brown & Anthony, Op. Cit., pp. 265–266. The film in Oxford was made on 21 June 1899. Although Rhodes never invested in Biograph's South African company, Dickson was entertained by Rhodes at his estate and the cordial reception he received indicates that Rhodes was interested in his activities.

801 Billy Bitzer mentioned such a modification in an interview for the Society of Operating Cameramen. (Billy Bitzer, *The Biograph Camera*, Society of Operating Cameramen, 6 September 1939. The interview is on the SOC Website: www.soc.org/so02022.html) Dickson may have played a role in designing this device. He had been tinkering with vacuums and on October 17, 1899, three days after he sailed, he submitted specifications for an improved vacuum pump to the British Patent Office. It was for use in producing incandescent lamp bulbs or "... to produce a vacuum for any other purpose." The patent was accepted 16 December 1899, while he was in South Africa.

Dickson took a modified version of the company's camera "B" to South Africa. It was slightly smaller than the original but still formidable. The tripod weighed about 100 pounds. The newest modification was a bicycle wheel attachment, apparently used to provide a steady stream of air against the film to hold it rigid in the gate during exposure. This photo, taken in Canastota, NY, shows a version similar, but slightly different than Dickson's. This one mounts the motor outside the case and the surviving photos indicated that Dickson's had the motor inside the case. [Canal Town.]

did little to reduce the camera's impracticality. The weight restricted mobility and it was not only difficult to move around, it could not easily be disguised and it was often an unwelcome guest since it was such an obvious a target. But it's massive size made it a handy dining table or desk.[802]

This was a liability that Dickson confronted from the day he took it out of the studio so compensating for the camera's immobility was a continuing challenge. Doubtless there were times when he envied the smaller 35mm machines used by others (though most were not *that* small), but the clarity of the image the Mutograph produced made its liabilities bearable.

Anticipating harsh conditions at the front, Dickson brought an additional assistant and hired a native to tend the horses, do chores, watch the camp and help move and set up the camera. The two assistants had complementary skills. William Cox, the Englishman, was a skilled and innovative mechanic who was beginning an association with Dickson that lasted several years. John Seward, Dickson's American friend, was capable of handling the camera and able to provide sketches to supplement those that Dickson drew to illustrate their activities. The Cape cart, which was purchased in Durban, not only provided transport but served as an auxiliary stand for the Mutograph. In the field the camera was usually mounted on its tripod, but by keeping it on the ready in the Cape cart it was less conspicuous while still available for the unexpected.

The Mutograph had another serious liability: the electric motor

[802] *The Biograph in Battle* & National Army Museum, Cox letters. Dickson mentions using it for dining and William Cox told his wife he was writing his letter to her on the camera, 11 November 1899 (National Army Museum, 8209-33-3). I am indebted to Stephen Bottomore for generously sharing his notes on Cox's diaries, which consist mostly of his letters to his wife. Cox's correspondence is a valuable supplement to Dickson's diary.

which drove the camera was powered by batteries whose size and weight further complicated operations. According to Joseph Mason the motor was a ¼ hp that required four boxes of batteries weighing 1200 lbs.[803] In Europe a supply of charged batteries could be kept near at hand, but they were not readily available at the front. How Dickson solved this problem is a mystery. Presumably he brought a supply and the company shipped replacements but although his diary notes briefly mention using batteries they provide no clue as to how a supply of fresh batteries was maintained. Strangely, the surviving photos and drawings of the camera in the field provide no clues because they do not show the batteries.

The liabilities of the Mutograph became more onerous as the weeks went by. This was a problem the American cameramen who operated in Cuba in 1898 faced and it was shared by cameramen dispatched to the Philippines and China in 1899 and1900 so designing a camera for field work was a priority for Herman Casler. The obvious first step was removing the weight of the motor and the batteries. In March 1900, after the relief of Ladysmith Dickson cabled the London office that a portable camera was "indispensable". The new hand-operated camera from America was supposed to arrive from London in April but there is no indication he received it so it seems likely that Dickson spent the entire time in South Africa dealing with the liabilities of the "Bio", as the camera was now called.[804]

Reporting the war

The 11 November edition of *Pearson's Illustrated War News*, had an article, "On Board the 'Dunottar Castle; Jottings by Mr. Dickson of the British Mutoscope and Biograph Company". It was a new publication and the introduction explained that the article was the "gist of a private letter sent ... to his manager in London, Mr. Smedley ...". It went on to say they arranged "... to pick out the cream of anything that comes over ...".[805] This was the first publication of his diary. The second selection , which appeared 2 December 1899, said that the account of his activities would appear only in *Illustrated War News*.[806] They were published irregularly for the next six months with the last appearing in the 26 May 1900 edition. With only minor alterations, the text is the same as *The Biograph in Battle* but only the early entries of that account appeared in *The Illustrated War News*.[807]

Dickson considered the articles important and tried to find time each day to record activities. His texts were included with the periodic shipments of films and still photos sent to the London office. Providing London with fresh film in a timely manner was a top priority and there was no regular mail in the combat area so one of the crew carried the bundle to Durban by train, delivered it to the Castle Line and returned with supplies.

Pearson's had an exclusive right to publish the diary in England, but the film company retained rights to use the text in connection with exhibiting the films. In celebration of the Biograph's third anniversary,

803 GU Library, Ramsaye. Mason to Glenn Mathews, 2[1] November 1937.

804 Dickson, *Biograph in Battle*, p. 186, entry written 7 April 1900 in hospital in Durban. Cox, Op. Cit., 17 March 1900. (8209-22–9).

805 *Pearson's Illustrated War News*, p. 10.

806 Op. Cit. The brief delay in announcing that the diary notes would be published exclusively in *Pearson's Illustrated War News* might indicate that the decision was made after publishing the first excerpt as extracts from a letter. By early December Dickson and Cox knew that they were to be published in a Pearson's weekly. In a letter written on December 4, 1899 Cox told his wife to look for them. Interestingly, the notes published 11 November cover the trip from Southampton to Madeira which were not in *The Biograph in Battle*. They recounted rough weather and accompanying seasickness of the first few days and the reluctance of Gen. Buller to consent to being photographed.

807 The last account published in *Illustrated War News* described activities at Christmas 1899 and New Year 1900.

on 19 March, 1900 the audience at the Palace was given a souvenir brochure, *The War by Biograph*. It was replete with Dickson's photographs from South Africa and activities at home taken by other staff photographers. These were accompanied by carefully edited excerpts from Dickson's diary. Stills that represented films being presented by Biograph or Mutoscope were indicated by an asterisk. They bragged that the films were being seen "... by millions of spectators throughout the world".[808]

The Biograph company sold copies of the photographs to other journals, but ironically, although the word "illustrated" figured prominently in the name of Pearson's wartime journal and the articles were well illustrated there no photographs. Instead, the illustrations were engravings, many made from photographs. Dickson's diary entries were usually accompanied by three or four engravings, usually made from photos that Dickson provided. While this was not an unusual practice, it seems strange since the technology for printing photos with text had improved and competitive journals like *Black and White* were filled with dozens of photographs of military activities (hardly any from Biograph). In retrospect, Pearson's publication has a very dated look. Realistic drawings adapted from photos taken at the front were mixed with artists' impressions which were fancy rather than reality. The cover page of *The Illustrated War News* invariably featured a dramatic drawing, often with lurid, jingoistic overtones.

This holdover of militant romanticism blunted the sincere effort by Dickson – and his company – to record and present a realistic picture of the war. Dickson and his associates were very aware that they were creating a unique and valuable cultural artifact. Once the bragging about the size and scope of their audience was over, the introduction to *The War by Biograph* went on to say "This marks an epoch in the history of photography, and the Biograph's special correspondent now takes his place alongside those of the representatives of the press."[809]

This was, of course, not the first time that the reality of war was recorded on camera. In fact, camera images existed for most of the major conflicts of the last half of the nineteenth century. Roger Fenton's pictures of the Crimean War (1854) and Brady's record of the America Civil War (1861–1865) set a very high standard and from that time on courageous photographers attempted to record military activities. The bulky equipment and the lack of high speed emulsions made it impossible – or very, very risky – to film during combat, but they recorded scenes of camp life, important persons, battlefield damage and casualties. This gave non-combatants a new perspective on the realities of wartime and the historical potential of such images was not lost on pioneers in the movie industry. Artist-correspondent Frederic Villiers claimed that as early as 1897 he filmed scenes during the Greco-Turkish "Thirty Day's" conflict, though they were seen by few, if any viewers. Villiers also attempted to film at Omdurman in 1898 and a wealthy Englishman from near Brighton, John Bennett-Stanford, made a film at Omdurman in 1898.[810] The American company sent Billy Bitzer and

808 Op. Cit. p. [3], Introduction.

809 Ibid.

810 Barnes, Op. Cit. *Vol 3, 1898*, pp. 61–63 and Herbert & McKernan, *Who's Who...*, pp. 22–23 & 147. Stephen Bottomore believes that Villiers attempted to film the Greco-Turkish engagement and failed.

The Churchill film company?

The notion of using film to report and record the war apparently occurred to a number of people not already in the film business. The most interesting of these was young Winston Churchill. Churchill persuaded [Murray] Guthrie, a relative by marriage, to finance his scheme but at the last minute Churchill abandoned the scheme after learning that an "American" company (presumably, the Biograph Company) was sending a camera to South Africa. On 12 October, two days before sailing for South Africa he wrote Guthrie that "I have no doubt that, barring accidents, I can obtain some very strange pictures". But he gave up the scheme because he feared "all the theaters will be pledged to the American company".

Churchill and Dickson were together on the Dunottar Castle for two weeks and this may have been when Churchill decided that his scheme would not succeed.

Although there is no indication that there was anything more than a casual relationship between Dickson and Churchill their paths crossed several times and they had interesting commonalities: American-born mothers; aristocratic lineage (though Churchill's blood was more evidently blue) and an instinct for self-promotion. Churchill was quite young, a few weeks shy of his twenty-fifth birthday when the two were on the Dunottar, while at thirty-nine Dickson was in full maturity. Despite his youth Churchill had already made a reputation for himself that was based on more than his distinguished lineage. His reports of rebellion in Cuba, action on the frontier of India, and the battle of Omdurman in the Sudan had been published London's *Daily Telegraph* and *Morning Post*; he had combined these into two books; written a short story and a novel (published while he was in South Africa) and run, unsuccessfully, for Parliament. He was clearly a young man on the rise.

811 According to Thelma Gutsche, *The History and Social Significance of Motion Pictures in South Africa, 1895–1940* (Cape Town, Howard Timmins, 1972), pp. 45–48, Hyman brought his Empire vaudeville company, including a exhibition of motion pictures, to the Good Hope Hall in Cape Town 16 October 1899. He saw them off to England, and began filming after that. An illustration on p. 38 in Gutsche's book shows him posed with a camera which she identifies as a "... remarkably compact 'Bio-Kam'..." The Biokam was a combination camera, printer and projector produced for the amateur market and advertised extensively by Warwick in late 1899. See Barnes, Op. Cit., 1899, pp. 170–172. It exposed film 17.5mm wide (35mm split in half) and reportedly could be used for still as well as motion photography.

Arthur Marvin to Cuba and Edison contracted with William Paley to film in Cuba that same year.

A small army of reporters covered the Boer war and Dickson was one of the many photographers at the front. There were dozens of still photographers, some from major news services, some free lancers working on their own. In addition to Dickson's crew, there were at least a half dozen cinema cameramen in South Africa during the hostilities. Robert Paul sent two cameras (but, apparently, no cameraman) to South Africa, one was given to Colonel Walter Beevor of the Scots Guards the other was given to Sidney Melsom, an enlistee in the C.I.V., the civilian volunteer unit from London which sailed for South Africa in January 1900. Col. Beevor was able to take several films, some of which were shown at London's Alhambra Theatre. Charles Urban's Warwick Trading Company, which was aggressively filming actualities, had several cameramen in the field at various times. Edgar M. Hyman of the Empire Palace Theatre of Varieties in Johannesburg filmed some early military activities, at first in and around Cape Town and later at the front.[811] At the end of November John Bennett-Stanford arrived in South Africa with an apparent commission from Warwick. He made several films near the front and may have been forced to retire because of wounds. In December Urban dispatched his leading cameraman,

THE GENERAL TRIED TO SHOVE THE CAPTAIN IN THE WAY.

General Buller proved as reluctant to be filmed as Admiral Dewey but eventually he relented. In this snap Buller (center rear) is pushing Captain Rigby of the Dunottar Castle out of the way. [Author's copy, The Biograph in Battle, p. 16.]

Joseph Rosenthal to cover the war; perhaps as a replacement for Bennett-Stanford. Like Dickson, Rosenthal remained in South Africa until after the surrender of Pretoria, and his exploits and accomplishments closely parallel Dickson's.

Warwick's cameramen had several advantages. They were familiar with the country. Hyman was a resident, Bennett-Stanford apparently had business interests there and Rosenthal had filmed there the previous spring. Selling cameras was a major business for Warwick so Urban supplied his operators with lighter, more flexible cameras. Because they used the standard 35mm format and were hand cranked and were not hindered by batteries and motors, Rosenthal could move about the war zone more freely. He was also able to develop sample frames using his tent as a darkroom so he had a more accurate idea of his results than Dickson whose exposed film was sent to London for processing.[812] As mentioned, Urban also arranged with Castle Lines to expedite shipments from South Africa.

It might appear that Warwick and Biograph were bitter rivals but the competition was not as intense as might be supposed. For most of the campaign the Warwick cameras were primarily in the Orange Free State and the Bio crew was in Natal covering the efforts to relieve Ladysmith.[813] Warwick's primary business was selling films and equipment to exhibitors in a widely diverse market while the Biograph company continued its policy of limited screenings for the middle-class with the Mutoscope catering to the general audience. Although there was competition at theaters in central London, the loyal clientele that frequented the Palace dulled the impact of the "rivalry". In reality the two companies provided British audiences with complementary visual records of the war.

Biographing

"... the crew and stokers of the *Dunottar Castle* gave three hearty cheers, the cinematograph buzzed loudly, forty cameras clicked, the guard presented arms ..." (Winston Churchill describing the ceremonies welcoming Gen. Sir Redvers Buller to Cape Town)[814]

The Dunottar Castle arrived in Cape Town the night of 30 October 1899 too late to dock. Dickson and his assistants were up at 5:30 the next morning preparing to film the ceremonies welcoming Gen. Buller. They had been at sea for two weeks, with a single refueling stop in Madeira so they were delighted to be on land again. There were preparations to complete, necessities to buy and contacts to be made before leaving for the front. Dickson spent the rest of his first day in Cape Town at the office of the Castle Line and trying in vain to contact Cecil Rhodes who was still surrounded by the Boers at his mine in Kimberly.

Fifteen days on the Dunottar gave Dickson an opportunity to make himself known to key members of the officer corps. The mammoth Mutograph and ever present snap-shot cameras made him a particularly conspicuous passenger. General Buller proved to be as reluctant a photo subject as Admiral Dewey. He was particularly loath to "pose" but using a combination of persistence, humor and good natured flattery, Dickson persuaded him to allow photos of daily activities. His crew took part in and filmed ship-board activities such as the hijinks accompanying the crossing of the equator and recreational competitions, some of which Dickson helped organize. Later, prior to going to the front General Buller gave him a letter of support for his filming activities. He arrived with valuable connections, but this only partially smoothed his way.

They were in Cape Town for several days taking some local pictures and assessing the situation. Other than brief messages from passing ships they had been out of contact with any source of news while at sea and it took a few days to sort out the conflicting reports about the military situation – which proved to be very discouraging. It

812 Stephen Bottomore, "Joseph Rosenthal: The Most Glorious Profession", *Sight and Sound*, Vol. 52, No. 4., Autumn 1988, pp. 260–263.

813 *Ibid.* Rosenthal said, in *Bioscope*, 1908, that when he arrived in South Africa he went to Natal and was there for the battle of Spion Kop which Dickson covered, but none of the surviving records list films that he might have taken there.

814 Gutsche, Op. Cit., p. 42. The quote is from Churchill's book *From London to Ladysmith*.

had been assumed that Gen. Buller would proceed to the Orange Free State, one of the two independent Boer states. But while the Dunottar was en route, the Boers had launched a military incursion into British Natal and isolated the Gordon Highlanders and other British units in the town of Ladysmith. The beleaguered forces had enough provisions to last several weeks, but the situation seemed desperate. After some consideration Buller decided that relief of the garrison at Ladysmith was a priority and decided to go on to Durban, the principal port in Natal. Dickson followed his lead. On 5 November when the Dunottar left Cape Town to continue on to Port Elizabeth and Durban, Dickson, Cox and Seward were aboard.

Going to Durban by boat was a last minute decision made because the Boers had severed railroad connections to Durban. Before sailing they purchased the Cape cart, but had no time to buy mules or horses. Horses were a valuable war-time commodity, but with the aid of Captain Rigby of the Dunottar, they purchased a pair of sturdy greys from a dealer Rigby knew in Port Elizabeth. In Port Elizabeth Captain Rigby also helped get the first package of film, snaps and diary notes on the Tintagel Castle for its return trip to England. The package contained films and snaps taken on the Dunottar, the welcoming ceremonies in Cape Town, a prison ship stationed off Simonstown near Cape Town and some scenics made near Cape Town. The Tintagel Castle had transported two hundred refugees to Port Elizabeth which presented the first opportunity to record the impact of the war. Dickson was particularly taken with the plight of a black woman and a baby: "She has her eyes closed and looks the picture of misery. From another group we pick out a baby playing with its toes on its mother's lap, while all stand around, indifferent and worn."[815]

By the time they arrived in Durban their load of cargo had grown impressively. The Dunottar had to unload outside the entrance to the harbor so Dickson engaged a tug and two lighters to transport their gear to shore . The horses, Cape cart and baggage were hoisted from the ship to the lighters and though the sea was relatively calm, the water at the harbor entrance was rough enough to raise memories of the sea sickness that had plagued Dickson during the first days of the trip.

Establishing proper liaisons remained a priority. Dickson had secured introductions from Captain Rigby to friends in the harbor whose support over the next few weeks proved invaluable. The railroad was the only link to the front. Dickson sought-out David Hunter, General Manager of the Natal Government Railway and established a valuable friendship. He received permission for free use of the trains as long as it did not interfere with the military.[816]

The scene in Durban was one of disorder and chaos. The city was filled with refugees and there were disturbing (but baseless) rumors that the Boers were going to attack. A fierce dust storm and heavy rains added to the confusion but through it all Dickson maintained a full schedule of photography. Ship after ship arrived loaded with British troops who were filmed parading through town to board trains to the

815 *The War by Biograph*, p. 13.

816 *The Biograph in Battle*, pp. 32–33 & 37–38 and *The War by Biograph*, 10 February 1900, p. 10. Dickson also paid a visit to the home of "the Hon. Mr. Jameson" outside Durban (pp. 44–45). It is not clear if this was a relative of Sir Leander Starr Jameson, Rhodes friend and the leader of the infamous Jameson raid.

K.-L. Dickson.   Native.   Jno. Seward.   Wm. Cox.

OUR CAMP.

"Our Camp" shows the Biograph crew in the field. Dickson is on the horse to the left and John Seward on the other. William Cox is by the tent with the nameless native helper standing by the Cape cart. The two horses, though feisty, were essential to their success. [Author's copy, The Biograph in Battle,

front. The trains brought back the sick and wounded who were filmed as they were put on a hospital ship. Pictures were also taken of an armored train returning from the front and marines from the man-o'-war *H.M.S. Terrible* who brought their large naval cannons ashore and hauled them through town en route to the front. When the cameras were quiet they arranged storage for the baggage they could not take to the front, prepared the horses and the cart for the trip and dealt with mundane matters like buying camping gear, cooking utensils and eatables.

The horses required particular attention. They were lively, hard to control and difficult to hitch-up. They were inclined to rear-up and liked to nip at each other. Dickson displayed a hitherto un-demonstrated skill in handling horse flesh. On one occasion when Cox was struggling with them Dickson took a whip to them with such vigor that it had to be replaced. To control the nipping they a put a nose bar between them and began a routine of running them in a circle each morning to tire them.

There was time for a little sightseeing. They enjoyed the surroundings but Dickson's descriptions of their experiences show that he shared the jingoistic prejudices prevalent in Victorian society. He was enchanted with the scenery from the verandah of a home he visited but was unprepared for a visit to a "Hindoo" temple. Taking his boots off was humiliating, the bottles on the sanctuary looked as if they contained beer or wine and he said the statues were "... grotesquely hideous ...".[817]

His descriptions of the natives, though not unusual for the period, are grating to modern ears. Although he occasionally referred to natives as

817 *Biograph in Battle,* pp. 45–46.

"black", he used the "N" word freely and on one occasion described a
street of "... Zulus, Kaffirs, Arabs, &c. ... [as like] a swarm of black
cockroaches, rudely surprised during a feast".[818] The native hired to do
errands and guard the camera who remained with them through the
fall is mentioned in the dairy entries, but without any personalizing
description. It is clear he was regarded – and treated – as an inferior.
Dickson's ability to get along with blue collar workers did not cross
racial lines.

Dickson's attitude towards Blacks was undoubtedly influenced by
his mother and his experiences in Virginia, but it was tempered somewhat by romantic impressions drawn from reading H. Rider Haggard.
There are several references to Haggard in *The Biograph in Battle* and
these leave the impression that Dickson read his books on South Africa
in preparation for his trip. The strength and speed of a rickshaw runner
particularly impressed him:

"... Never shall I forget that 'run' to my dying day. We were off like a shot,
swiftly and silently – a horse could not have gone any faster. With perspi-
ration rising and falling in perfect rhythm with the felt-like patter of his
feet, he sped along encouraged by voice and an occasional peep at a
half-crown, at which he covetously took time to give a sideway glance, thus
affording me an opportunity to get a glimpse of his fine and noble features.
He was a veritable Umslopogas. This, of course, vividly recalls Rider
Haggard's masterly description of the death-ride of Umslopogas for the
White Queen ...".[819]

To the front

They left for the combat zone on 20 November. The first stop was
Pietermaritzburg, the capital of Natal, about 75 miles inland from
Durban. Like Durban, Pietermaritzburg was overcrowded and their
first night was spent sleeping "... on sofas in a miserable parlour of a
tenth-rate despicable inn. What a night!".[820] Boer raiding parties were
disrupting the rail line and the next station, Estcourt, was cut off. They
set up their tent in a field near the railroad station and remained for a
week. They left for Estcourt on the 27th but fears that the line would
be cut by the Boers forced them to stop the at the Mooi River station
for another uncomfortable night at a local inn. They got to Estcourt the
next day and to Frere the day after. This put them about seven or eight
miles from the Boer lines and within sound of the guns at Ladysmith.

By this time Dickson had the letter from General Buller allowing
him to accompany troops in the field, with freedom to film anything
of interest – or so he hoped. The War Office's regulations covering
correspondents "at the Seat of War" were quite specific, but they were
for newspapermen and Dickson did not see himself as a newspaperman.
War correspondents were licenced by the Commander in Chief and
could only write for the paper specified in the licence. English, French
& German were the only languages allowed; they could not use ciphers;
and preference was given to former military personnel. It was necessary
to get permission in writing from a staff officer empowered to issue
passes for each separate visit to an outpost. The staff officer was charged

818 Ibid., pp. 39.
Although the word
"Kaffir" (Arabic for
infidel) is regarded as
unacceptable today in
South Africa, it was
commonly used at
the time.

819 Ibid., p. 41.

820 Ibid., p. 49.

to review all copy and acted as press censor. Undesirables could be ordered out of the war zone and although violators of the regulations could be court martialed, it was rarely done.[821] Despite his strong press connections Dickson was not accredited to a specific newspaper, and though he had his letter from Gen. Buller, the Commander-in-Chief, he did not have a formal licence. Either through ignorance, guile or stubbornness, he chose not to honor the specifics of these regulations – particularly the requirement that he get specific permission to be at an outpost.

He seems to have ignored the censors, too. The diary notes, films and stills were carried by courier and mailed directly to London and there is no indication that he ever submitted them for review. Since the films and photos were not developed it would have been impossible for military censors to review them and if they tried, exposure to light would have destroyed them. While he was not really reporting on the progress of the war, other journalists were sending back similar personal impressions of day-to-day activities and observations of the general scene .

It did not take long for him to run afoul of officials who did not share his free-wheeling attitude. One in particular was an unnamed officer on General Buller's staff whose concerns about Dickson started on the Dunottar Castle where the officer tried to prevent Dickson from meeting with General Buller. In Pietermaritzburg he tried to prevent Dickson from meeting with General Buller to get the promised letter of permission. Dickson, of course, met with the General anyway which doubtless aggravated the situation. By 7 December, when Dickson wrote about the incidents, the situation had deteriorated further. The officer remained nameless – Dickson named those he liked, but not those who were out of favor – and, despite a moment of triumph, Dickson was forced to act pragmatically.

"... it is amazing to relate that so virulent was this official's objection to yielding to even General Buller's permit for my accompanying the army, that he issued an order that I should draw no rations for myself, men, or horses, knowing that this would in all probability prevent my proceeding with the army. But it didn't, though he also ordered that we should be thrown out of camp if we persisted in following. The upshot of the whole is that two hours after hearing of this inexplicable order I pulled up pegs and marched forward. We were stopped at Estcourt, and while I was foraging for food was handed a note reading, 'Tell Mr. Dickson I expressly forbid his going on. Send him back with his men. (Signed) _____', ... I only laughed to myself, still feeling secure with the General's permit. My papers were overhauled, some surprise evinced during the examination, and then a muttered apology ...".[822]

The unnamed officer's dislike seemed to Dickson a personal matter, but the officer was following regulations – rules that Dickson chose to ignore. After encountering other officers who demanded to see his "pass between stations" Dickson decided to attach himself to the brigade of naval gunners from H.M.S. Terrible. Dickson had met the unit's officers, Commander Limpus and Captain Jones, when he filmed them

821 The regulations were published in *The Sketch*, 18 October 1899, pp. 562 & 564.

822 *Ibid.*, pp. 64–65.

in Durban and they met again on the train to the front. They were cordial and much less conscious of War Office regulations so although Dickson and his crew ranged about the combat zone and filmed various military units, the naval brigade remained their home throughout their tour in Natal.

Before setting-up housekeeping with the naval brigade, they took a number of more graphic subjects of activities near the front and packed them off to London. The flood of soldiers passing through Durban had reached Frere and Dickson marveled at the seemingly endless crowd of tents and soldiers. He persuaded the station master to allow the filming of a panorama of the sight from a moving railroad car. With the Mutograph mounted in the Cape cart they road out to photograph two obstructions blocking the railroad: a railroad bridge near Frere that the Boers had blown-up and an armored train derailed by the Boers in an earlier attack.

The derailed train was a major story. One of the passengers on the train was Winston Churchill and his adventure during the derailing is one of the more remarkable chapters in his remarkable career. When the Dunottar reached Cape Town Churchill did not wait for General Buller to decide where he was going but left immediately for Natal and got to Durban before the Boers cut the line. He was on the way to the front on the armored train when the Boers attacked. Two cars and one of the two engines derailed, but one engine and two cars were still on the tracks. The newspapers reported that Churchill took charge, rallied the troops on the train to uncouple the usable cars, and helped many of the survivors to board them. A number of soldiers escaped but Churchill was taken prisoner and held by the Boers at a prison in Pretoria. The papers relished the story and liked it even more when he subsequently escaped and made his way across country, mostly on foot, to Lourenço Marques (now Maputo) in Portuguese Mozambique. In early 1900 he was back at the front.[823]

When the Bio crew arrived at the site two weeks later, the Boers were not in the area and Churchill was imprisoned in Pretoria. The wreckage had not been cleared and there were still some bodies that had not been removed from the train. They took still photographs of the train, shell holes and some graves nearby, but did not film the train. Apparently the terrain made it too difficult to set up the Mutograph and Dickson did not like moving images of images that did not move. In such cases he would have put the camera on something that allowed it to move, the Cape cart in this case. He opted not to, probably because the camera would bounce too much to get a steady image.

On 7 December Dickson took the first of several iconic views of the military in a battle stance. He found a squad posted with rifles at the ready behind an embankment near the top of a hill. Dickson set up at the side of the unit in a position that showed the commander, Captain Bartram, and a flag man standing behind them. He was filmed flagging a message from Colonel Kitchener ordering another picket station to send out a patrol. The picture that resulted is one of the most frequently

823 Gilbert, Op. Cit. and Roy Jenkins, *Churchill, A Biography* (NY, Farrar, Straus & Geroux, 2001); Churchill's version of this is recorded in *From London to Ladysmith*; see: Winston S. Churchill, *Frontiers and Wars, His Four Early Books Covering His Life as Soldier and War Correspondent*, Edited into one volume (New York, Harcourt Brace & World, Inc., 1962), pp. 376–388.

RIFLE HILL SIGNAL STATION.

"Rifle Hill Signal Station Near Frere". Although this photo and the film taken at the same time were not taken during combat, the image was convincing to viewers. It was taken near Frere on 7 December 1899. The officer in the center is Captain Bartram and the signal flag is sending the message: "Have your picket under arms and send out patrol. [Col.] Kitchener, 7 December." [The Biograph in Battle, p. 63.]

reproduced images to come from the war – and one that pleased Dickson. "This is a splendid scene, and one of which we are very proud, for we nearly killed ourselves and our horses in our endeavour to get planted in time."[824]

While this, and most other pictures, were made at a safe distance from the front lines, they gave viewers at home a more realistic impression of war-time activities than was otherwise available.

Camping with the naval brigade gave Dickson an advantage over the licensed correspondents. They were forced to stay in Frere, several miles behind the main military encampments. On 10 December, when the naval gunners were ordered to relocate, the Biograph crew followed along. The change of location began during the cover of night. They were up at 2:30 and the move started at 3:30. The Cape cart fell in behind the twenty-eight bullocks teams that were hauling the two largest naval guns, the 4.7s. As they passed the picket lines the Biograph crew were challenged by a Colonel Reeves:

"... 'Hello, you there, Cape Cart! How did you get there? You must fall out. Who are you?' I replied: 'I am the representative of the Mutoscope and Biograph Company. Commander Limpus and Captain Jones know all about it'. 'Well, I must see about that', and off he rode with the escort, of which he had charge ...".

The officer did not order them to the rear and Dickson was pleased that he was with the naval unit: "... I thanked my stars that I had broken rules, taken the bull by the horns, and was acting to suit myself".[825]

824 *The Biograph in Battle*, pp. 62–63.
825 *The Biograph in Battle*, pp. 68–69.

Brave Lads!
The Battle of Colenso

"... Most people in England – I among them – thought that the Boer ultimatum was an act of despair, that the Dutch would make one fight for their honour, and, once defeated, would accept the inevitable. All I have heard and whatever I have seen out here contradict these false ideas ...". (Winston Churchill, *London to Ladysmith*)[826]

The battle of Colenso opened General Sir Redvers Buller's drive to relieve the siege at Ladysmith. It was a failure and a major embarrassment. The British did not break through to Ladysmith and they suffered significant casualties while inflicting only minor damage on the Boers.

By mid-December of 1899 the British force in Natal had increased to about 30,000 men and outnumbered the Boers by three, four or, perhaps, five to one.[827] The British had no accurate information about the size of the Boer forces in Natal so the estimates varied and the reporters and military speculated wildly. Later estimates place the size of the Boer military, commanded by a very young General Louis Botha, at about 4,500 men.[828] While greatly outnumbered, they had the advantage of familiarity with the terrain and more than that, they were motivated by patriotism and disciplined by pietistic Calvinism. They were equipped with new, very accurate Mauser rifles and were reputed to be excellent marksmen. They also had a small amount of artillery and a few Maxim guns, Hiram Maxim's rapid firing prototype of the machine gun. Importantly, they used a recently developed smokeless powder. Without the tell-tale drift of white powder characteristic of most 19th century battles, the British had difficulty pin-pointing their positions.

To reach Ladysmith, the British had to cross the Tugela River and Colenso was one of the crossing points. An undestroyed bridge at Colenso was the bait that attracted the British to the site. But because he was suspicious that the bridge was mined, Buller planned to ford the river rather than take it by frontal assault. But the site favored the Boers. The river was bounded by craggy bluffs, mountains and steep sided hills which the locals called kopjes. To confound the British, Botha built a series of false emplacements on the heights above the north side of the river creating the impression that his forces were dug-in there. In reality, the main body of his army was below, concealed in trenches that covered approaches to the river.

The situation was described in a dispatch to *The Times*:

"On Tuesday, 12 December, the first move was made. At dawn General Barton's brigade, with the two large and six small naval guns, marched out and occupied a position about three miles from Colenso. The position chosen was a stony kopje directly in front of the draw village of Colenso, just to the east of the railway line. From this kopje the country slopes gradually down to the river, and is absolutely open except for a few small dongas intersecting it. The river cannot be seen from the kopje for the reason that it has high, steep banks, and that along them here is a good deal of brushwood. The road bridge, however, which till yesterday stood intact, can easily be seen ...".[829]

826 Churchill, Op. Cit., pp. 176–177

827 *The Times* 17 January 1900, p. 4 "The Battle of Colenso."

828 Pakenham, Op. Cit., p. 231. Louis Botha was thirty-seven and had just replaced an ailing General Piet Joubert.

829 *The Times* (London), January 17, 1900, p. 4 "The Battle of Colenso"

AFTER GETTING OUR PICTURES WE RETURN TO CHIEVELEY.

Here Dickson is posed with the Biograph camera while filming the naval gun battery firing. After his frustrating efforts to film army units, Dickson stayed with the battery of long range naval guns from H.M.S. Terrible who were stationed well behind the front. [Author's copy: The Biograph in Battle, p. 71.]

The heights where the naval guns were placed was soon renamed Naval Gun Hill. It had a commanding view of the town and the potential battlefield and on the morning of 13 December the gunners began firing preliminary salvos intended to feel-out the Boers. This gave Dickson an opportunity to film the guns in action with relative safety. The following morning the crew had to make a quick trip back to Chieveley to replenish their nearly exhausted supply of food. They were delayed because the supplies had not arrived and they had to wait for the train from Frere. They dashed back, arriving in time to film General Buller who was using the heights as his headquarters. As the situation was calm, Dickson also took a pre-battle panorama of the site. He was several thousand yards from the river and might have gotten a better view with the telescopic lens but he opted not to use it since he was not sure how well it would function. After the shot he had the camera dismounted and moved to a sheltered position.[830]

The battle began the next morning, 15 December. The Biograph crew was rousted out of bed at 2:30 and the naval guns began firing at 4:00 a.m. Dickson was effusive in praise of the gunner's accuracy. "... our infantry slowly advanced under cover of the naval guns, which kept up a steady action, bowling over the fortifications and shelters on the opposite side of the river".[831] Apparently he was unaware – or chose to ignore – that the guns were firing at the dummy positions on the upper hillsides. During the firing they tried to film the explosion of the shells on the other side of the river using the telephoto lens but gave it up because the haze and distance from the site made it difficult to focus properly. The noise of the cannons firing was tremendous. "My companions used cotton-wool in their ears to prevent the tremendous concussion but as I wished to hear which way the shells were coming

830 *The Biograph in Battle*, pp. 72–74.
831 *The Biograph in Battle*, pp. 76–77.

I preferred to drop the jaw at the word 'Fire', a trick I learned at Sandy Hook, U.S., ... which answered the purpose very well ...".[832]

There were three places where the river could be forded and Buller's plan was to send sorties towards each of them. Things went badly from the beginning. They had a general idea where the fords were, but their maps were inaccurate so the unit commanders had to rely on local natives to direct them. The left wing of the assault was led by Major General Fitzroy Hart. He was a traditionalist and arrayed his troops, the Irish Brigade, in close order as if they were on parade at Aldershot. They marched towards the presumed location of the ford into a loop of the river where the well concealed Boer trenches were on both sides and ahead of them. When the Boers opened fire there was confusion and chaos. On the other flank Colonel C.J. Long moved his field artillery too close to the river and within range of the Boer rifles. The guns were soon silent and instead of fording the river, Buller was worrying about how to rescue Hart and recover Long's guns which were now in the open surrounded by dead horses. It was only 8:00 a.m. and Buller was forced to call off the assault.[833]

Dickson and crew watched the battle from Naval Gun Hill with the Mutograph set-up inconspicuously in the back of the Cape cart. They were well out of rifle range, but the hill was struck by some Boer artillery shells. One hit a Red Cross unit very close to where Dickson was – close enough that Dickson thought that the camera could have been damaged had they not moved it for a possible shot. They abandoned attempts to film and began helping the wounded move over the hill to the hospital. The firing stopped about 3:00 p.m. and in the evening Dickson took a walk to see some of the battlefield and visit the hospitals. Among the dying he found the doctor who had inoculated him against typhoid on the Dunottar. "How painfully near home this brings us". he wrote.[834]

Exhausted and thirsty, they slept that night in a temporarily abandoned native kraal.

The next day they ventured down to the river in search of a place to bathe. Water was generally in short supply, a situation aggravated by a run of especially hot days. They had not bathed for several days and a truce allowing the removal of the wounded and burial of the dead made it safer to approach the river. When they neared the bridge in Colenso they were startled to see a Boer officer riding towards them. They were apprehensive at first, but he proved to be friendly, talkative and unwilling to leave them until they left the area – Dickson's German made communications easier. While talking they wandered onto the battlefield into a gruesome area where a number of bodies lay unattended, beginning to deteriorate under a very scorching sun. "... it is the most harrowing thing I ever witnessed." They took a photo of a Red Cross burial party working in the area.

As they wandered and talked, they discussed the possibility of filming the Boer side. The officer, Commander Van Niekerk, said he was familiar with the Biograph, having seen it in Johannesburg, and

832 *The Biograph in Battle*, pp. 74–75. Dickson had filmed a disappearing coastal defense cannon at Sandy Hook, New Jersey for the American company.

833 Pakenham, Op. Cit., pp. 234–247.

834 *Biograph in Battle*, pp. 77–80.

said he would discuss it with the General. Unfortunately nothing came of this interesting prospect and the Biograph remained on the British side.

They returned by a circuitous route and found a place to bathe. It felt uncommonly good on a very hot and harrowing summer day.

Surrounded by the dead, the dying and the wounded, they had to confront the moral issues raised by photographing the dead and dying. William Cox discussed this in a letter to his wife:

"Oh how awful war is. Men strong and well a few hours since are now rotting in the sun. Others now returning alive but mortally wounded. ... Here are men dying all around without any visible sympathy or special friend who could convey a message home to wife or mother. Yet how natural it seems that it should be so for in less than an hour I (who acknowledge myself too sensitive) am walking about taking Photographs without inquiring the nature of the case or really studying the wounded man's like or dislike to his surroundings."[835]

Regrouping for Spion Kop

On 17 December Buller's army pulled back from Colenso but the naval guns moved only a short distance to a camp outside Chieveley, about three miles from Colenso. On the 19th, with General Buller watching, the gunners fired at the bridge in Colenso, destroying it.

The day before the destruction of the bridge, Dickson and Seward went to Durban to send film and notes to London, pay bills and restock their supplies. It was an all night trip. They arrived in the morning and luxuriated at breakfast "... served *on a table!* Nothing canned, and fresh bread and butter."[836] They were quizzed by people from the town eager to get first hand information about the battle. During the return trip that evening they heard angry criticism of the British tactics from local colonials who were angry because they were not given the chance to fight the Boers.

The sense of disillusionment expressed by the Natal colonials was shared back home. The set-back at Colenso came on the heels of a series of discouraging reports from the campaign at the Modder River. The early optimism that the war would be quickly settled was fading. The War Office in London shared the dissatisfaction with General Buller and on 19 December it was announced that Lord Roberts, known affectionately to the British public as "the Bobs", would replace Buller as commander in South Africa. Buller would remain in command of the forces in Natal. Lord Kitchener, "the Sirdar", would be Roberts' Chief of Staff.[837]

Although the Mutograph camera recorded little or nothing during the heated fighting on 15 December, the package sent to London on the 18th had a number of films and stills with vivid images of action at and near the front. In addition to the naval guns firing and Rifle Hill signal station, there were a number of scenes of infantry squads in battle readiness. Most of these were probably taken during field exercises, but

835 National Army Museum, Cox diaries, 8209-33-4.

836 *Biograph in Battle*, p. 86.

837 Pakenham, Op. Cit., pp. 252–254. Buller had sent two cables reporting on the battle. The first was moderate in tone, "I regret to report serious reverse." The second was more emotional and in it he recommended abandoning Ladysmith. This was unacceptable to the government and reinforced the decision to replace him. Lord Roberts' affectionate nickname, "The Bobs" was based on a popular ballad in which Rudyard Kipling called him "Little Bobs".".

* ADVANCING IN EXTENDED ORDER.

"Advancing in Extended Order". Although he was unable to take the cameras close to combat, several shots simulating action were sent home and they reflect Dickson's interpretation of the action he was experiencing. This picture was published in The War by Biograph, *a publicity brochure distributed by the Mutoscope company. [Bottomore.]*

they were more realistic than the actions being staged in the fields of Southern England and Northern New Jersey.

The next major battle in the relief of Ladysmith took place at Spion Kop in late January. In the interim the two armies felt each other out with scouting forays and occasional skirmishes. The naval gunners stayed at their forward position through the Christmas holidays and the early days of 1900. Although closer to Chieveley, the guns were near enough to Colenso that they could shell the Boer positions. Dickson was firm in his decision to stay with the naval unit. The guns were within range of Boer artillery which fired on them occasionally, but Dickson felt the risk was worth it.

"... we are still keeping to the front so as to miss nothing and always be able to see every move of the enemy. This is a privilege which no other civilian seems to have cared to attain. Occasionally we are visited by correspondents and others when our cannons roar. But to me the charm of it all is in being on the spot where I can look down and across to their lines and see a sudden dash of horsemen from behind a clump of trees, making rapidly for another, to be instantly fired into by our boys, always with telling result, never failing to dislodge the enemy from their covert. Our guns may truly be said to be *the* life of this campaign; and to the guns I stick ! straying around whenever I wish, to get a picture of anything interesting that may be recurring. On returning we are always sure of a kindly welcome ...".[838]

By this time the Biograph crew had become something of a fixture and there were fewer questions about their presence. Dickson's efforts to cultivate useful officers paid off and several of them were cooperative. Colonel Lord Dundonald, the commander of Buller's cavalry was exceptionally helpful. Dundonald was a Scotsman with an interest in

838 *The Biograph in Battle,* pp. 87–88.

A RECONNOITRE IN FORCE.

"Lord Dundonald and Major Mackenzie Leading A Reconnaisance Near Spion Kop". This picture of Lord Dundonald leading his South African Light Horse Infantry on a reconnoiter was another effort to produce a convincing image of the war. Dundonald, who took a liking to his fellow Scot and treated Dickson with favor, let Dickson know in advance that they were headed to the field which gave Dickson time to set up in time to take this shot. [Author's copy The Biograph in Battle, p. 97.]

invention and at 47 he was just a few years older than Dickson. He seemed to find that a Kennedy-Laurie with a connection to the best known inventor of the era a person of unusual interest.[839] On several occasions he alerted Dickson of an impending sortie and though Dickson often had to rush to set up the camera, he got several choice bits of action. It was Dundonald who provided Dickson with one of his most compelling action shots.

"Through Lord Dundonald I am informed of a sortie, and we get away, cutting across country, meeting the party, who point to the kopje, and we turn our cart containing the machine on to the spot, they very kindly keeping away from the machine, so that considering the rush, I feel that we have a good and valuable picture. They ride up sharply, dismount, horses are led back, and the men advance to the edge of the kopje. Not finding the enemy they mount and gallop to the next, and so on until they meet them and drive them off. I need not add that this was a *tour de force*, and that in spite of the fact that our horses were only half hitched up, and that we had to drive at a gallop across country to intercept the horsemen, it may be dubbed a 'winner'." [840]

There was less danger to the Biograph crew during this lull which made it easier to take this kind of action film.

In spite of three days of rain, a hiatus for Christmas and New Years was a chance to relax and pay attention to matters other than the military. But there were unexpected problems with some of the local

839 *Pearson's Illustrated War News,* 10 March 1900, p. 16.

840 *The War by Biograph,* p. 26

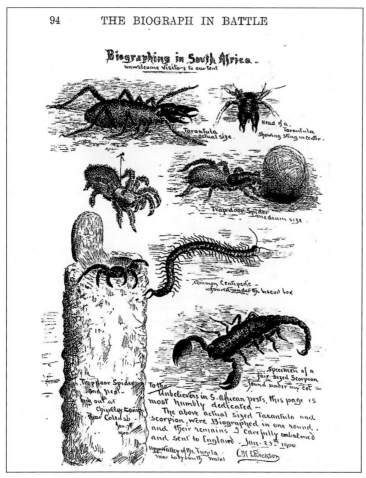

94   THE BIOGRAPH IN BATTLE

"Biographing in South Africa; unwelcome visitors to our tent". Dickson and his companions were fascinated by the variety of creatures that invaded their campsite. He made this composite drawing of some of them. [Author's copy The Biograph in Battle, *p. 94.]*

inhabitants. On Christmas eve while Dickson was writing his notes he was interrupted by the appearance of a tarantula above his head. He swatted it with his notebook, but it was found alive, captured and put in a bottle. The Bio crew (as they now called themselves) soon added a pair of scorpions to the haul and the amused naval brigade began presenting contributions to the menagerie. By the end of the week they had "... four huge tarantulas, fourteen scorpions, three centipedes, two snakes (black, flat-headed and poisonous), no end of curious bugs, insects and worms; three chameleons, a pet kitten, a puppy dog, and a huge trap-door spider".[841] One of the snakes lived in their tent for three days before they captured it. Dickson and Cox were fond of pets so they kept the kitten and puppy.

The collection fascinated Dickson. He drew pictures of them and

841 *The Biograph in Battle*, p. 100.

proposed a film of the tarantulas and scorpions fighting each other – which was made after the weather cleared.

Not all their holiday activities were so perverse. Dickson arranged and filmed a symbolic tug-of-war between members of the Naval Brigade with one side being John Bull and the other Oom Paul Kruger. John Bull triumphed of course. When plum-puddings, chocolate and other good things were distributed to the troops, the Bio crew were invited to dine with Commander Limpus and Captain Jones. Their festivities concluded with toasts to wives and sweethearts.

Insects and other "unwelcome visitors" were not the only disagreeable aspects to life at the front. The army was operating in a highland area where the days were often brutally hot and the nights were often very cold. There had been little rain during December so searching for water to drink and bathe in became routine. They were particularly concerned about their horses who lacked water and had little growth to forage on. Their own diet was very limited. They lived out of cans, eating bully beef, figs and drinking coffee with occasional gifts of bread from the naval group. They worked long hours and their sleep was frequently interrupted. They learned to sleep through the firing of the big cannons. "... we hear them, for of course each shot nearly shakes us out of our cots, but we are asleep again before the next one is fired. I never could have believed this possible had I not tested it personally".[842]

The Bio crew got along remarkably well considering that they shared a single tent and were together day after day, week after week. Cox's letters to "Fan", his wife, show a warm affection for Dickson and in several he mentioned how well they got along. To his wife he was "Will", but Dickson called him "Coxy" though Cox referred to Dickson as Mr. D. Since John Seward left no record of his experiences, we know less about his relations with his tent mates, but both Cox and Dickson referred to him as Dickson's friend.

When not capturing unwelcome guests – or struggling with other problems of survival – they spent evenings writing or talking. Dickson worked on his notebook every evening while Cox wrote regularly to his wife. Their discussions included speculation about future plans. Cox's wife was told that they might go to Italy, India or Australia after South Africa. Cox shared Mr. D's interest in experimentation and things to work on at some future time seems to have been a popular topic because a couple of projects were started shortly after they returned to England. This camaraderie survived the tribulations of their tour. In his final letter to his wife, written shortly before returning to England Cox described "Mr. D ... singing at the top of his voice and dancing around saying something to 'Coxy' my pet name (by the way) 'Coxy's writing to his wifey oh'. And so we go along working happily together making the time seem very much shorter to me than your [sic]."[843]

Shared hardships may have solidified their friendship. The day after Christmas the weather turned on them. The prolonged period of drought was ended by a mixture of dust storms and intense rain which

842 *The Biograph in Battle*, p. 104.

843 National Army Museum, William Cox Diaries, 8209-33–13, Bloemfontein Hotel, Bloemfontein, May 27, 1900.

forced them to improve the drainage around their tent and seek protection for their horses. The continuing rain ushered in a new problem
– illness. Cox and Seward caught an unidentified ailment that was
passing through the camps. Their malady, possibly flue, was short lived
but as they were recovering Dickson came down with it. Contagions
were plaguing the military camps and the increasingly damp living
conditions, lack of clean water and very limited diet boded ill for the
future. The well being of the horses was a particular concern because
the loss of even one of them would force them back to Durban. The
drought limited grazing and the army had priority for other fodder. The
military also had priority for veterinary service.

Unabated fury
Spion Kop

An order to move came on January ninth and the next morning the
crew was on the road with the Naval Brigade. It was an eventful trip.
The army was moving west to approach Ladysmith from a different
flank and the trek took several days. They were fortunate to find a place
to cross the Tugela River where it was undefended, but the process of
crossing was slow and difficult, impeded by high water and muddy
banks.

Dickson was still recovering from illness and had to force himself
to be active but he claimed the activity speeded his recovery. At the river
he volunteered to test crossing of a very fragile bridge and they made it
across just as night fell. It was raining heavily and they found shelter
nearby in a mud hut. They were soon asleep but in the middle of the
night they heard noises and discovered that stragglers were looting their
cart. They lost all their food and water and other goods were scattered
about. Dickson decided they had to return to Durban to re-supply.
Seward and Dickson rode the horses to Frere and took the train to
Durban, leaving Cox at the hut with the cart and the camera which "...
had not struck the looters' fancy ...". The trip to Durban and back was
arduous and done in haste. They were exhausted when they returned
but revived a bit because Cox welcomed them with stew made from a
chicken he had come upon. They finally found the Naval Brigade atop
a new hill, Mount Alice. Captain Jones was sure that Dickson would
be thrilled with the beautiful view – and he was.[844]

"Never shall I forget my first impressions of this beautiful panorama. I
could not tear myself away. Hour after hour I sat and gazed unappeased.
Far down the valley the silver Tugela wound, linking the hills and mountain, until lost on the right and left of our encampment; range after range
of mountains passing beyond my vision until lost in the exquisitely tinted
sunset clouds. The twilight falls and is succeeded by a full moon, imparting
an indescribable sense of peace and beauty. What a contrast to what it may
be to-morrow in the din of battle and crash of guns. Now there is nothing
to be heard but the distant mellow cooing of the South African Dove calling
to its mate."[845]

Spion Kop (Lookout Hill) had earned a place in Boer history as the

844 *The Biograph in
Battle*, pp. 116–122.
This was January
10–11, 1900.

845 Ibid., p. 122.

spot where the voortrekkers first looked out on the promised land of north Natal. Now the mountain would enter British military history.[846] The location was about a dozen miles west of Ladysmith where the beleaguered forces were nearing the end of their supplies. Part of the British military had crossed the Tugela but the heights of Spion Kop dominated the north side of the river, and presented a formidable obstacle. Beyond the mountain a relatively level stretch of land extends on to Ladysmith. Buller felt that a direct assault was hazardous so the bulk of his forces were deployed to the left to assault the heights from the flank. A frontal attack would be launched after the flanking movement engaged the Boer positions on the heights. It was a risky plan because the assault groups were several miles apart and coordination was difficult in those pre-wireless days when signal flags, lanterns and messengers were the principal means of communication.

The battle started well enough but quickly turned sour. The flanking forces, under the command of General Woodgate reached the top of Spion Kop at dawn on 24 January. Attacking in a fog, they drove off a small group of Boers and dug trenches to defend their foothold. The fog lifted about 8:00 a.m. and the British discovered that in the interim the Boers had rushed sharpshooters to two nearby elevated positions which gave them an excellent field of fire on the very shallow British trench line. The Boers' artillery also opened fire and the British artillery was reluctant to fire because they were miles away and were not sure if they would be firing on Boers or their own troops. A bloody fire fight ensued and the British found themselves pinned down with General Woodgate and most of his command staff as early casualties. A junior officer, Colonel Thorneycroft, found himself unexpectedly in command and he struggled to rally the beleaguered British forces. Relief was slow to come. It arrived at the end of the afternoon and by that time the remnants were decimated, exhausted and in the process of withdrawing. The counter-thrust reached the top in the dark and uncertain about the forces facing them decided to pull back. Ironically, the Boer forces also pulled back. A long line of tired, bedraggled soldiers and Red Cross wagons filled with the wounded streamed across a temporary bridge built over the Tugela. It was another demoralizing set-back.[847]

The Biograph crew remained with the Naval Brigade whose long range guns were set up on Mount Alice overlooking the battle area from the south side of the Tugela. Mount Alice offered a splendid view of the area, but it was too far from the combat zone to take anything other than scenic views. They were more than two miles from Spion Kop and even farther from Three Tree Hill where General Woodgate's assault on the flank began. Before the battle Dickson scouted to find a closer location. He hoped to cross the Tugela near Three Tree Hill and film the engagement on the left flank but the camera's bulk made it difficult to move through open country and he was not willing to risk losing it while fording the river. They returned to Mount Alice and watched the intense combat on Spion Kop from the distance. Except for additions

846 Parkenham, *The Boer War*, p. 293.

847 Ibid., pp. 297–322.

"Battle of Spion Kop – Ambulance Corps Crossing the Tugela River". This image was taken the morning after the unsuccessful effort to take Spion Kop. It is one of his most compelling photos – and films. It shows troops and ambulance wagons straggling back from the front over a pontoon bridge on the Tugela River. Spion Kop can be seen on the horizon. [Author's copy The Biograph in Battle, *p. 129.]*

to the gallery of films showing the naval guns in action there was little else to photograph .

But they had not been idle. Impressed by the scenery Dickson made sketches and did some painting during the days before the battle. The geology of the region revived his interest in minerals and, joined by John Seward, he searched for gemstones and evidence of iron ore.

Although they took very few pictures during the intense fighting, the following day, the 25th, Dickson moved the camera to a position overlooking the temporary bridge where the retreating army was crossing the Tugela. A series of very fine military views were taken from this site:

"We were not long in following with our Cape cart, and after several hours' severe work for horse and man succeeded in getting a good picture of the Ambulance Corps crossing the Tugela River over a hurriedly spanned pontoon bridge. In the immediate foreground may be seen trenches filled with our men to guard against any sudden attack should the wounded be fired on by the enemy. A little below the Tugela wends its way through great boulders and a rocky bed, over which our sick and wounded must be driven as they make their way down the opposite side across the pontoon bridge and up the embankment where we now are, the worse cases being carried by innumerable volunteer stretcher-bearers, mostly coolies.

"On the other side, as far as the eye can reach the Red Cross ambulances are seen waiting their turn to make their perilous descent, nearly all of them having been previously emptied of their worst cases of wounded for fear of an upset, the patients being carried over and replaced after arriving at the other side, when comparatively on safe ground. The picture has an additional value that in the background is part of the battlefield where Warren's men fought so gallantly as they advanced towards and up Spion Kop to the right. We had no end of difficulties in reaching our goal. Just as we were rounding a corner of the last camp in our valley a messenger from the Provost Marshal overtook us to inquire into my papers, and twenty minutes of valuable time had to be sacrificed in order to prove that General Buller's permission covered our movements.

"Another six miles and we found ourselves in a bog hole, from which we extricated ourselves creditably without harm to cart or horses. On the next rise were *cortèges* of stretcher-bearers extending over a distance of three or four miles ...

"... Half an hour later, just as we were descending the last long hill to the distant Tugela below, two officers rode up rapidly and stopping us, did their kindly best to dissuade us from going any further. All were ordered out of the valley, they said, as the Boers were momentarily expected to shell and cut the British forces off. Our Cape cart being so conspicuous, we should be a certain mark for the enemy. In addition to this, the officers pointed out a stream of artillery crossing the road and rapidly getting into position to meet the attack in the event of the Boers showing fight. This was my chance, I thought, and thanking the officers for their consideration, I drove on right into the midst of the field. We passed the artillery, who by that time were in position, their horses in the rear. Seeing no immediate signs of an attack, we drove a little further on and crossed a deep ravine, which was a herculean task for the horses inasmuch as we had to wait until a lot of artillery ammunition had passed through.

"The liveliest scene awaited us on the bank of the river. Everybody was cross–no wonder, and so was I when told I couldn't take the picture. After I had consigned that particular officer to a warm place I proceeded with my work, then drove back to the artillery. I waited until the light grew too weak for photographing, then regretfully gave it up. As it was, however, the Boers did not attack the transports, but continued firing higher up, no shells reaching us. We had taken our lives in our hands hoping to get a biographic record from the flank, a feat which would have been comparatively safe had we been dealing with civilised [sic] war tactics; but it is impossible to trust to these treacherous Boers, who would relish shooting at a nice little side-show like our Cape cart."[848]

The optimistic tone prevalent in the early diary notes became tempered after Spion Kop, which mirrored the sagging morale of Buller's forces. Dickson reported that "... there seemed to be a general feeling abroad that our men were being uselessly sacrificed in thousands without bringing us any nearer to Ladysmith". He complained that the government was unwilling to purchase the more efficient Maxim-Nordenfeldt rapid firing guns that the Boers were using so effectively.[849]

Their malaise was aggravated by personal discomfort. Dickson reported a sleepless night in which he was annoyed by a snoring companion and the rattling of a large beetle in a tin box. The beetle escaped and a mid-night search of the tent ensued. After that his sleep was interrupted by an annoying flapping of the tent cover. They had not fully recovered from their recent illnesses and several days of rain brought added discouragement.

848 *The Biograph in Battle*, pp. 130–133.
849 Ibid., pp. 134–135.

"We Must Grin and Bear It"

Immediately after the engagement at Spion Kop the bulk of the British army pulled back to Frere. Buller began to feel out the Boer defenses and he revised his plan. He replaced the full-force frontal assault with a more gradual and paced attack. Since time was running out for Ladysmith, the frustration following Spion Kop was accompanied by a sense of urgency. Buller moved the bulk of his forces back to the Colenso area and began an attack on hills commanding the river east of the town. The campaign began on 12 February with a drive to seize three hills held by the Boers on the south side of the Tugela. They were in British hands by the 18th and the Boers withdrew to the line of steep hills on the north side. The next day the British occupied Colenso and they crossed the river the following day. A pontoon bridge was set up and a drive to take the hills was launched. Six days later they drove the Boers off the heights and on the last day of February the Boers began a withdrawal, leaving the road to Ladysmith open. The siege was lifted on 1 March and Buller made an official entry 3 March.[850]

This was a particularly trying period for the Bio crew. When the army withdrew to Frere, they remained near the front with the Naval Brigade but found very little to photograph. The limitations that the camera placed on their activities were more and more evident. One or two more films of the artillery in action seems to have been the extent of their "Biographing." Dickson did some sketching, including a scenic panorama which he included as a fold-out in his book, and they again explored for minerals. The terrain made it difficult to move about with the camera in the Cape cart. The hills were steep and covered with large boulders and deep ravines. As if these weren't problems enough, the ailments that troubled Cox and Seward suddenly changed into an incapacitating fever, afflicting them simultaneously. Before he realized how sick they were, Dickson had one of his more harrowing experiences:

"One of my companions is down with some kind of fever, and cannot move hand or foot, so we are shorthanded. If we could only get to sleep at night I think we should all feel better; but what with the bellowing cattle and talkative Kaffirs, the occasional visits from our horses who try to enter the tent, and the sudden and violent showers of rain, our cup of misery is full. By noon we managed to get off and down the hillside with our paraphernalia, but it was impossible to go any further down the precipitous road leading to the lower valley by any ordinary methods of locomotion. After an hour's hard work we succeeded in tying up the wheels, and slid down the most incredibly rough and steep decent. On our return we may be able to hire a team of oxen to pull us back. My companions insisted on going with me, so anxious were they to see the battle a little nearer, and I gave in, much against my better judgement. We arrived without accident at the foot of the mountain, but there my companions caved in. I thought at first it might be sunstroke, owing to the burning heat, and after unhitching the horses I made the boys as comfortable as possible under the cart, after which I managed to make some tea, which partially revived them. Shells were bursting all around us, and thinking that in this case certainly the better part of valour was prudence, I made my preparations to get away under shelter

850 Pakenham, pp. 360–373.

of the base of the hill. Hitching up, I drove on, skirting the hills as closely as possible so as to keep out of the enemy's sight. I left the sickest man resting in a donga in charge of the Cape cart, while I went on with the other to find a spot for the camera."

"We gradually pushed our way along the hill and riverside, to emerge finally on the plain, crawling on hands and knees and taking advantage of every large boulder, until we reached the Boers' deadly fire. Just in front of us our artillery were receiving shell after shell, but not a movement did they make.

"While I was intently watching our men a soldier, standing at my side, jumped behind my boulder shouting, 'Look out, here she comes'. Just then I heard the six-inch Boer guns roar, but having previously timed the landing of the shells, I knew I had two or three seconds' time to get a snap – which I did, then dived behind the rock followed by a sound so terrible that it is enough to make one's blood curdle – the bursting of a six-inch melinite shell at close range. The moment I heard the explosion I was up and snapped it. This I repeated several times ' then, as the shells were bursting within two hundred yards of our rock and things were getting altogether too hot to be pleasant, I crawled back – not, however , before I had snapped the position I was in, for the sake of the unbeliever.

"Getting back to a safer position, we watched the valiant attack of our men as they gradually pushed on. Had we had a light camera these movements could have been secured, and many others of an invaluable nature, but the enormous bulk of our apparatus which had to be dragged about in a Cape cart with two horses prevented our getting to the spot. The difficulties were aggravated by the absence of roads, while the huge gullies we had to cross and the enormous boulders we had to get over made the enterprise almost impracticable. We really risked our lives to secure the views, but finding it impossible to drag our machine into position, we returned to where we had left our horses and sick man. They had vanished ...".[851]

Dickson found Seward two hours later and he was delirious. Cox was not much better. Getting them to proper medical care proved almost as harrowing as escaping the barrage. The next day Dickson hired a team of a dozen oxen to help pull the cart with the sick men up the steepest grades. The Naval gun crew helped him organize and store his equipment, then Dickson loaded Cox and Seward in the Cape cart and started an all night journey across open country to the station at Frere. It was an arduous trip but they caught the train and it was another twelve hours before they reached Durban. Immediately on arrival they rushed to the Durban Sanatorium where the staff confirmed that Seward had enteric fever (probably typhoid) – Cox received the same diagnosis a few days later.[852] Exhausted, Dickson took to bed and enjoyed a sound night's sleep undisturbed by chatter, bellowing cattle or visiting horses – and he was not awakened by cannon fire.

Before leaving the front he arranged to be notified if there would be something worth "biographing" so he felt he could indulge himself by taking a much needed break. He stayed at the sanatorium for several days. It was on a height overlooking the bay and he enjoyed the view – which he compared to Naples – and he had high praise for the care given by the nuns who were from Brittany, the home of his youth. Since

851 *The Biograph in Battle*, pp. 143–147.

852 Enteric fever is the term used by Dickson but it was probably typhoid fever, a sickness that was a serious problem during the war in South Africa.

it was clear that it would be a while before Cox and Seward could rejoin him, he hired a former sailor to help with the cameras.[853]

After ten days in Durban, Dickson returned to the front accompanied by his new assistant. We can assume he indeed received notice of Biograph-worthy activity because his return coincided with the beginning of the final phase of the campaign to take the hills on the north bank of the Tugela which blocked the route to Ladysmith. He reached the railway station at Frere on 22 February after an overnight trip from Durban and, on learning that the train was going through to Colenso, decided to continue on. The town was firmly in British hands and combat had now moved north of the river. On the day of his arrival the pontoon bridge was put in place and Buller's forces were moving across the Tugela to launch the attack on the fortified hills commanding the north side.

Remnants of the recent combat made Colenso an unsavory place. The fields were strewn with bits of shrapnel, unexploded shells and other debris. The carcasses of the artillery horses killed the previous December had not been removed so the air was filled with the stench of dead animals. Before retreating the Boers left a dead horse in the railway station and decorated the walls with anti-British graffiti. Dickson took snaps of the carcasses of the horses. On the brighter side, Dickson was pleased to see soldiers reading an account of his activities published that day in the *Natal Witness*. More than a hundred copies of the paper were scattered about.

His filming schedule was circumscribed during the following week but he took a number of "snaps", giving particular attention to the sick and wounded and the care they were receiving. He visited the hospital tents where he combined photo shoots with an effort to cheer and encourage the patients. After a particularly bloody assault on one of the hills there was a truce to allow the removal of the wounded which made it safe to film the Red Cross carts carrying the wounded. He was impressed by the spirit shown by the soldiers:

"I am lost in admiration over the stoical manner in which our men suffer and joke over it all. To-day I photographed the men as they were being carried from the Red Cross waggons to the trains at Colenso. Before they were lifted out I went from waggon to waggon telling them about the Biograph, and how their friends at home would see them, and that they must put the best foot forward. Although suffering severely they were cheery, and amused themselves chaffing with each other. The stretcher-bearers fell in with my idea and gave me every assistance, and soon a lot of them on stretchers, carried on each other's backs, &c., were ready to march past the machine ...".[854]

Although he felt an obligation to write encouragingly for families and friends who might read his notes, he seems to have been genuinely moved by the spirit shown by the "Tommies." The recent illness of his companions probably reinforced his sympathy.

Even though he was a non-combatant and was usually a mile or two from the front, he was not immune from life-threatening experi-

853 There is no mention of the name of this temporary assistant in the diaries and his service seems to have been limited to the three week period of the final relief of Ladysmith.

854 *The Biograph in Battle*, pp. 157–158. This took place on 26 February 1900.

ences. As he was returning from filming the Red Cross wagons, the Boer artillery spotted the Cape cart and began firing at it. After one shell landed about twenty feet from him, Dickson "whipped up and tore pell-mell". In order to make a more difficult target, he drove the horses in a zig-zag path. It was a close call, but they escaped unscathed. Dickson's account of this experience is surprisingly modest considering that he and his assistant were in grave peril.

The new assistant was a mixed blessing. He had serious shortcomings which Dickson bore good naturedly. The man was terrified of horses "... and whenever mine plunged and reared, pawing the ground, or fighting with each other, he fled for his life, assisting me at such times by doing all or a large percentage of the swearing, meanwhile running round and round the brutes at a safe distance, while I, being so convulsed with laughter at his antics, was hardly able to keep the animals in check ...".[855] Nor was care of horse flesh the only problem raised by the newcomer. He was plagued by attacks of sciatica during which he "kept the atmosphere all around him blue". Dickson found these antics, as well as his attempts to peddle a stock of paper and writing materials to the sailors in the Naval brigade, amusing.[856]

The hiatus of filming was about to end. On March 1st word came that the Boers were withdrawing and the way to Ladysmith was open. This was the opportunity he had been waiting for and Dickson was determined to reach the town that day. They left early and traveled light. To facilitate their trip the tent, camera tripod and most of their supplies were left with the Naval Brigade. They crossed the pontoon bridge and pressed on as best they could through lines of troops in file. It was another long, strenuous journey, but with determination and pluck they reached town just after dark. En route they survived officers questioning their credentials, a detour around a difficult river crossing, heavy rainfall and a near plunge down a steep drop-off. It was already dark when they reached Ladysmith and they hit something while feeling the way into town. Dickson and his assistant were thrown to the ground. They were stunned, but cart and horses were OK and they were able to continue, finally finding rooms at a hotel near the railway station. They arrived ahead of the main body of Buller's forces and were among the first civilians to reach Ladysmith.

The town had been under siege for five months and was in desperate condition. Dickson characterized their hotel as a "wretched place." Foul odors seemed everywhere and they feared that they would succumb to the fevers afflicting the city. The supply wagons had not reached town so the only food available was what they had brought in the cart – some biscuits and the water in their bottle. The garrison had been killing horses for food and the animals that survived were half-starved. Dickson hired natives to collect grass to feed their own tired and hungry team. Later he felt it difficult not to associate the town with dead things.[857]

Buller visited the town the next day and made an official entry on the following day, 3 March. Dickson spent 2 March visiting the Gordon

855 Ibid., pp. 161–162.

856 Ibid., p. 162.

857 Ibid., pp. 161–169 & 178.

THE RELIEVING FORCE PASSING THROUGH LADYSMITH.

"The Relieving Force Passing Through Ladysmith". During the ceremonies marking the relief of Ladysmith Dickson found himself standing next to Winston Churchill and took this "snap". Churchill (on the left with feather in cap) was a military officer but was covering the war as a correspondent and had already gained prominence through his writing and his adventurous exploits in South Africa. [Author's copy The Biograph in Battle, p. 175.]

Highlanders who had been in Ladysmith since the siege began. He found a number of friends from his filming of the Gordons at Aldershot in 1897. Their commander, Colonel Scott gave him a tour of the trenches built to help them survive during the frequent bombardments.

Dickson credited Colonel Scott with finding choice positions for Buller's ceremonial entry the following day. The Gordon Highlanders were "Biographed" as they marched to greet General Buller; there were "snaps" of General White, the commander of the garrison at Ladysmith, and despite having to face the sun, the camera filmed Buller leading the march of his troops into town. There was a ceremony with speeches and a good deal of cheering, especially when wagons loaded with food arrived. During the parade Dickson found himself standing next to Winston Churchill and took a snap of Churchill watching the ceremonies. Churchill's capture and subsequent escape had given him a special caché. By coincidence, while Ladysmith was being freed, his mother, Lady Randolph Churchill, arrived at Durban aboard The Maine, a hospital ship she funded through American donations.[858]

Dickson and his assistant stayed in Ladysmith for another week, departing for Durban on 8 March traveling to Colenso by cart. They found the trains jammed with troops being sent back but Dickson was able to get passage to Durban for himself. His new assistant stayed in Colenso to arrange transport for the Cape cart and horses. In Durban he began preparations to go on to Cape Town but had to interrupt his work and "... temporarily to retire from public life". The fever had caught-up with him. He put his diary aside while he recovered.[859]

[858] Pakenham, Op. Cit., p. 364. By co-incidence, Churchill's younger brother, Lieutenant John Churchill, who had just come to South Africa, was slightly wounded during the fighting that preceded the relief of Ladysmith. Winston Churchill had reinstated his commission as an officer and was nominally assigned to the Cape Town volunteer unit. It was not unusual for officers to act as correspondents and, in fact, the regulations governing correspondents gave precedence to officer-correspondent.

[859] *The Biograph in Battle*, pp. 181–186. The entries recounting these events were written in mid-April.

Chapter 31

To Pretoria and Beyond: The Heart of the Biographer at Rest

"It is known all over the world that we are here and we dare not give up for reputations sake hard as it goes sometimes, when bread is not seen for many weeks and the water so dirty and scarce. But for my dear wife I would not wish to hurry, it is an experience of a life time and who will not envy me the trip when I return to tell of all I have seen and learned." (William Cox to his wife, Fan, 7 April 1900)[860]

"Many new Scientific weapons made their first appearance on the battlefields of South Africa, but none of them was more deadly than the Biograph, which, in the able hands of Mr. Kennedy-Laurie Dickson, the pioneer of all animated photography, did great photographic execution on the field. Side by side with the 4.7 guns to Ladysmith, and then following Lord Roberts through Bloemfontein and Kroonstadt to Pretoria, where he took a fine picture of the raising of the flag, Mr. Dickson saw most of the war, and his book, which is to appear shortly, will be a valuable contribution to the literature of the war. (*Black and White*, 5 January 1901)[861]

By mid-April the Biograph crew had fully recovered and was ready to shift operations from Durban to Cape Town. After the relief of Ladysmith the military campaign shifted to the Orange Free State. The Boers had withdrawn from Natal and the main body of Buller's forces followed them to join the British military already operating there. Capetown was now the focal point for the military. The "Bobs" – Lord Roberts – had replaced Buller as commanding officer and was leading what was expected to be the conclusion of the campaign.

Dickson and his companions had lingered a bit in Durban for a much needed rest. Dickson had not been as ill as his associates – or so his physician told him – and he recovered fairly rapidly. They needed and deserved a break and apparently the military situation did not demand immediate attention – or so it seemed – and Cox's letters to his wife suggested, their stay was as much rest as recuperation.

They hoped to return to the front with a new, more serviceable

860 National Army Museum, Cox diaries, 8909-33-11.

861 British Library, Newspaper Collection. *Black and White, Vol. XXI, No. 518*, 5 January 1901, pp. 12–13.

To resolve the difficulties encountered with their huge cameras, Herman Casler worked to reduce the size. This smaller, hand cranked version of the Biograph camera is in the Will Day Collection at the Cinémathèque Française. Though Dickson pleaded for such a smaller camera, it is not certain he received it. [Photo by the author, courtesy of Laurent Mannoni, Cinémathèque Francaise.]

camera. As soon as he arrived in Durban, and before entering the hospital, Dickson cabled London asking them to ship the more portable machine that London had a promised them. The limitations of the Mutograph had been apparent for some time but the experiences of recent weeks made it clear that it was a liability rather than a mere nuisance. London assured them that the new camera would be shipped and though they hoped to have it before leaving Durban, it not arrived when they boarded the Dunottar Castle to return to Cape Town.[862]

A smaller camera had been in the works for some time – probably dating back to the struggles that Billy Bitzer and Arthur Marvin en-countered in 1898 while attempting to film the war in Cuba. Casler had been working on the lighter machine but the redesign was tricky business. Replacing the heavy electric motor with manual operation was the most obvious and immediately effective modification. Without the motor there was no need for batteries and less need for the heavy steel plate that reduced vibration. This would reduce the weight and some of the bulk, but the mechanism to move the large format film through the camera required a large housing. The case could be made smaller by feeding the film from outside the camera, but the two boxes or drums were necessary to feed and take-up the film would be large. They were committed to the large film format because it still gave them an advantage over their competitors. Furthermore, audiences liked longer films so the size of the film rolls kept increasing.

By the beginning of May they were in Cape Town and stayed for several days taking care of necessary business. They had left the network of supporters in Durban who eased transport, facilitated shipments and

[862] Cox mentioned the new hand operated camera in a letter to his wife 17 March 1900 (Op. Cit., 8209-33-9) and Dickson said they were still waiting for it in his diary entry for 7 April 1900 (Op. Cit., p. 186).

made it possible to move about relatively freely. Before embarking for the combat zone Dickson needed to make new contacts and reaffirm old ones. With Lord Roberts in command his letter from Gen. Buller carried less weight. Roberts and his staff were at the front so he sent them letters and wires soliciting support. He had another potentially influential contact. The siege at Kimberly was over and Cecil Rhodes was back in Cape Town. On 10 May Dickson had lunch with Rhodes at Rondebush, his palatial estate near the city. Among the guests were Rhodes' close associate Dr. L.S. Jameson, and Lady Edward Cecil, the daughter-in-law of the Prime Minister, Robert Cecil, the Marquess of Salisbury. Violet Cecil often acted as Rhodes' hostess and was very close to Sir Alfred Milner, the High Commissioner for South Africa. There is no record of the luncheon discussion, but it would have been difficult to avoid the topic of life under siege. Rhodes had been trapped in Kimberly, Jameson had been in Ladysmith and Lady Cecil's husband was among the British military still beleaguered in Mafeking. Dickson took "snaps" in the house and toured the gardens and zoo. After lunch Rhodes gave him a letter to General Lord Kitchener, Lord Roberts' Chief of Staff who was a former classmate of Rhodes. It asked that Dickson be given "every assistance". Rhodes also gave him a letter of introduction to the manager of his mine at Kimberly, a welcome opportunity for a former ore milling specialist.[863] It was a profitable afternoon

Dickson had less success making arrangements to use the railroad. A single-track, narrow-gauge line running several hundred miles connected Cape Town with the Orange Free State, where it branched out to destinations in the Free State and Transvaal. It was strained to capacity and was vulnerable to assault by marauding Boer guerillas. Masses of troops were moving to and from the front accompanied by carloads of food, munitions, horses, medical supplies and all the other materiel to maintain an army that now numbered some 60,000 men.[864] The Cape cart had to be loaded on a flatcar and the horses needed shelter and these were facilities in short supply. Delays and sudden interruptions of service severely hampered the crew during the rest of their tour.

This was one of several factors that forced Dickson to adjust the way he was operating. The military campaign was now quite different and the enthusiasm that buoyed the early weeks of the war was now on the wane.

With the British forces unified and operating in Boer territory their overwhelming numerical superiority made it almost impossible for the Boers to sustain the spirited resistance that had stymied the campaign for such a long time. On 13 March, while the Bio crew was in Durban, Lord Roberts occupied Bloemfontein, the capital of the Orange Free State. He had encountered surprisingly little resistance but still he paused for several weeks to consolidate and build-up his forces. When the British formally annexed the territory at the end of May he was ready to launch a campaign to seize Johannesburg and Pretoria, the capital of Transvaal. By this time the Boer army was badly decimated

863 *The Biograph in Battle*, pp. 193–197; Cox diaries, 8209-33-13.

864 Pakenham, Op. Cit., p. 401.

and although they destroyed bridges, burned buildings and tried to defend some of the river crossings, they kept falling back. Once on the move, Roberts advanced with surprising speed. To compensate, the Boers changed tactics and began operating in small, mobile units carrying out guerrilla raids behind the lines.

At home, despite the recent successes, disillusionment with the war continued. The enthusiasm which greeted the parades of troops marching off to what was expected to be a short, glorious campaign had faded. The seemingly endless sieges at Ladysmith, Kimberly and Maefeking and discouraging setbacks at Colenso and Spion Kop in Natal and Magersfontein in the north took their toll. Stories of privation, disease, casualty lists and pictures of dead and wounded brought the reality of war home, further diminishing the early optimism.[865] This shift in attitude was reflected in changes made to the journal that published Dickson's diary. His last contribution appeared in May and this coincided with a significant change of name: *The Illustrated War News* became *The Illustrated Weekly News*. The number of stories about the war declined while articles about non-war topics increased. (The following September the publication changed completely. "News" disappeared from the banner and it became *The Curiosity Shop* which featured stories, fashion news, recipes and similar light fare replacing coverage of people, places and events.)

It is not clear when audiences at the Palace stopped cheering, but by spring the Biograph's owners sensed a change. London sent word that they were anxious to have film of the ceremonies annexing the Orange Free State to the Empire and when Dickson left for the front on 18 May this seems to have been his immediate priority. If enthusiasm for the military was lessening, the appeal of Empire was still strong and a scene showing the Union Jack being raised in Boer territory could rouse audiences from their lethargy. If accompanied by appropriately patriotic music it would symbolize an end to the campaign and lend a welcome sense of finality.

After the fall of Ladysmith, the Bio crew did little filming in the combat area, but this may not have been for lack of intent. In one of his letters home Cox told his wife that they hoped to follow the army to Pretoria and after that go to Mafeking, the rather remote outpost on the border of Bechuanaland (Botswana) where the British forces led by Col. R.S.S. Baden-Powell were still under siege. Because Mafeking was relieved on 17 May, the day before Dickson left for Bloemfontein, that plan never came to fruition.[866]

Whether because of his illness, the changing nature of the war or knowledge that they were not being published on a regular basis, Dickson's diary entries changed. He stopped writing each day and sometimes the events of several days – even a week – were merged into a single entry, often with rather sketchy detail. Crucial pieces of information were left out. There is no mention of when, or even if, the new camera was received but mention that they continued to eat on it indicates that if they had a more flexible instrument, it was still pretty

865 Historian Richard Brown describes the effect this change of attitude had on the British movie industry in "War on the Home Front: The Anglo-Boer War and the Growth of Rental in Britain. An Economic Perspective". In *Film History*, Vol. 16, No. 1, 2004, pp. 28–36. Brown sees the shift happening during the summer of 1900, but evidence of it appears earlier.

866 Cox diaries, 8209-33–13. Written 27 May 1900 from the Bloemfontein Hotel, Bloemfontein and they had apparently not yet received word that Mafeking had been relieved. Col. Baden-Powell is best remembered as the founder of the Boy Scout movement in 1908.

"Annexation Ceremonies at Bloemfontein, 28 May 1900". After recovering from illness, Dickson arrived in Bloemfontein in time to film the annexation ceremonies.
[Author's copy The Biograph in Battle, *p. 211.]*

large. Also, since there is no further reference to John Seward it seems possible, but not certain, that he returned home after recovering from his illness.

Dickson and Cox traveled separately to the front. Cox had to remain in Cape Town to arrange transport for the Cape cart and horses. Dickson went ahead and near Bloemfontein on 24 May he filmed General Kelly-Kenny reviewing troops. Anxious to speed things up, Dickson wired Lord Kitchener for help – with some apparent success. Cox, the horses and the Cape cart arrived in time to set the Biograph up in Bloemfontein's market square for the formal annexation ceremonies on 28 May. Dickson was happy with the film and in a characteristically patriotic manner, declared that the ceremony was "glorious". "... Thanks to the Biograph, which faithfully recorded this magnificent scene, the people of the world who were not as fortunate as those present will see what it saw, and doubtless sing 'God save the Queen'."[867] Not everybody shared his enthusiasm, however. Dickson credited the authorities with thwarting a protest planned by the Anti-Imperialist Society.

Several films were made in Bloemfontein, among them Boer prisoners exercising and troops leaving for the font. If Dickson's diary is accurate, except for a film of a traction engine taken in Cape Town, these were the first taken since leaving Ladysmith in early March.

The day after the annexation ceremonies they left for the front. The immediate objective was Kroonstadt, a town on the main rail line to Johannesburg where Lord Roberts had his temporary headquarters. It was another arduous, frustrating trip. It started badly and continued

867 *The Biograph in Battle*, p. 208. The world was not as enthusiastic as Mr. Dickson. His films were often booed when shown in France.

in fits and starts as they struggled to catch-up with the rapidly advancing British army. Rail service was irregular because the Boers had destroyed most of the bridges at the river crossings. In Natal the naval brigade had provided a reliable home base, and the sailors were companions who shared rations, watched their tents and equipment, eased travel and offered a place to camp while moving about the combat zone. After the relief of Ladysmith, the H.M.S. Terrible, with guns and gunners aboard, sailed for China to support the campaign of the western concession states to put down the so-called Boxer Rebellion. The Bio crew had not found a substitute. With the sailors gone they were on their own and a bit adrift.

The departure from Bloemfontein was delayed while they arranged a flatcar for the Cape cart. Dickson was very anxious to press on and became quite annoyed: "... the assistant transport agent acted against Lord Kitchener's orders and caused me endless worry and serious delay, and nearly wrecked my highest ambition, namely, to get to Pretoria in time for the entrance of the troops. I interviewed every one from the Governor-General to the brakesman of the trucks, and finally succeeded in engaging and paying for two trucks ...".[868]

After spending an uncomfortable night on the flatcar they arrived in Kroonstadt very early the next morning. They took advantage of a brief delay in Kroonstadt to take snaps of temporary hospitals and some Boers waiting to surrender. But the rail lines were congested and their problems continued. The next day they were forced to take the cart and horses off the train and proceed over rough terrain and poor roads. They encountered sandy areas where the traction was so poor that they had to push the cart. To help their progress Dickson purchased a veldt pony to help their team through difficult terrain. They slept in the open and suffered through very cold nights.

Roberts entered and formally took Pretoria on the afternoon of 5 June. On the morning of the 4th the Bio crew was several miles out, trying to arrange rail transport. In fear that he would not reach Pretoria in time to film what was assumed to be the climax of the campaign, Dickson mounted an all out push to get to the railroad in time to reach the city ahead of Lord Roberts. Although he claimed he arrived in time, he apparently failed. As Dickson told the story:

"... we were struck with a horrible fear lest we should fail to follow in to Pretoria in time for the entry of the troops, news having just come that Lord Roberts had already pushed on. This failure, in the face of our bitter experiences, would be more than I could bear, therefore at noon we hastened to get away and reached the railroad, which was only about fifteen miles from Pretoria. We whipped up violently all the way, two men inside the cart, my servant *à la postillon* on the little horse. We followed in after Lord Roberts, biographing him and his Staff on the outskirts of the town, and later on the flag from a fine position in the window.

"Had the raising of the flag been done in the middle of the Square, then the surrounding crowd as well as the flag could have been photographed; but as it was raised several hundred feet high on the peak of the Rathhouse, the unfurling of the flag alone is shown on the Biograph.

868 *The Biograph in Battle*, p. 213. Dickson said he had three telegrams from Kitchener that he be given rail transport for the Cape cart and horses.

"Thus was the principal aim of our Enterprise accomplished, and the heart of the Biographer was at rest."[869]

The South African historian Thelma Gutsche has convincingly established that Dickson did not film the original flag raising. The ceremony was filmed by Edgar Hyman for Warwick and his film shows a flag that was considerably smaller than the one in Dickson's film. Lord Roberts had a small Union Jack that his wife had made for him which he used for such occasions. Dickson restaged the flag raising using a larger, more impressive flag to create a more stirring effect. He filmed a relatively close view from an upper story window – possibly using his telescopic lens. His location and, possibly, the heretofore unused telescopic lens provided an effectively close view while masking the absence of troops in formation in the area below. South Africans who viewed the two films a few weeks after the ceremony quickly noticed the difference and controversy ensued. While this manipulation of history is (and was) a widely condemned practice, not all of the people viewing the results found fault with it.[870] Thelma Gutsche quoted a letter in the press of the time from a W. Wolfram, Warwick's agent, who sarcastically sought to counterbalance favorable reaction to the Biograph film:

"... It is to be regretted that Lord Roberts insisted upon hoisting a mere pocket-handkerchief in every town he captured (the identical flag that Lady Roberts made), thus depriving historical events of all impressiveness. The 'Yanks' are indeed smart people. Whereas the British operator present at the hoisting ceremony was content to photograph the actual occurrence and thus produce a picture lacking impressiveness (though genuine), the enterprising 'Yank' had a large Union Jack hoisted a few days after the event for the purpose of photographing it; and, as the public of Durban and probably Mr. Wilkes had the pleasure of seeing a magnificent picture of the hoisting of the Union Jack at Pretoria a few weeks ago, they will admit the smartness of the 'Yank'; and the taste of Mr. Wilkes for a pretty picture rather than a true one, must have been amply satisfied. The company I represent, 'The Warwick Trading Company of London', refuse absolutely to accept and develop any film not a genuine reproduction of passing events. ... W. Wolfram."[871]

Despite arriving late, Dickson was not one to allow a set-back to become a failure. Lord Roberts' handkerchief flag probably did not suit his sense of the dramatic and since he preferred to control the scene he was filming he might well have restaged the flag raising even if he had arrived on time. A dramatic shot of the flag raising was, after all, "the principal aim of [the] enterprise".

But the enterprise was not quite finished. The Boers had one more battle left in them – though it seems to have been a diversionary move to keep the British busy while President Kruger fled the country and their forces regrouped as guerilla bands. A few days after the occupation of Pretoria, Botha made a stand at Diamond Hill, about a dozen miles east of Pretoria. The Bio crew rose early and rushed to the site, hoping to capture some of the action. After locating Lord Roberts they moved cautiously forward getting close enough to see rifle fire, but fearing that his white horses and the Cape cart were too conspicuous Dickson chose

869 *The Biograph in Battle*, p. 237.

870 This discrepancy raises questions about the accuracy of Dickson's daily record, but a careful reading of the passage quoted above shows that while he implied that he filmed the ceremony, he did not say that he had. Instead he claimed he filmed the flag "later on" after filming Lord Roberts with his staff. Admittedly this is a fine point but it shows that Dickson's pride would not allow him to admit mistakes or failure, a trait shown previously in his contretemps with Edison and the Lathams. The *Biograph in Battle* has to be read carefully, but knowing Dickson's inclination to exaggerate and mislead I find it remarkably free of self serving excess.

871 12 Thelma Gutsche, *The History and Social Significance of Motion Pictures in South Africa, 1895–1940* (Cape Town, Howard Timmins, 1972), p. 45. Wolfram's letter appeared in the *Natal Mercury*, 19 November 1900.

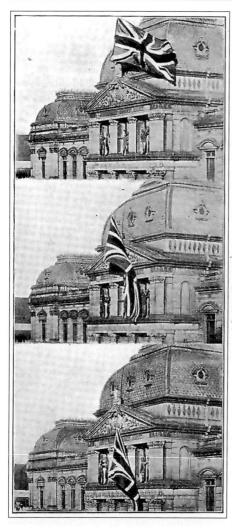

"Raising the Flag at Pretoria...". Dickson's crew apparently arrived too late to capture the flag raising at Pretoria but Dickson arranged to film it anyway. The flag he used was larger (and more dramatic) than the one used in the actual ceremony. By taking it from an upper story window he embellished the scene and masked the absence of ceremony below. [Author's copy The Biograph in Battle, *p. 241.]*

not to move closer. "... had I had a pot of khaki paint I think I should have painted the beasts".[872]

Although they did not film the action, they became involved in negotiations to end the fighting. The confrontation lasted a couple of days so they settled in at a small inn which was owned by Eli Marks, a Russian Jew who had become a millionaire through dealing in whiskey, mining and real estate. Marks had been politically prominent in Transvaal and it was he, apparently, who got Dickson indirectly involved in the effort of several Boers to negotiate with Botha. Dickson filmed the group boarding a stage to cross the lines and meet with Botha. When they returned the next day, one of the negotiators, Dr. William C. Sholtz, borrowed one of Dickson's horses and rode it to Roberts' headquarters where he reported on the negotiations. After his discus-

872 *The Biograph in* Battle, pp. 243–244.

"My Cape cart requisitioned by Lord Roberts for peace negotiations with Louis Botha, driven by the military secretary, Captain Waterfield, to the Boer lines". Dickson was proud that his cart was used for negotiating peace with Gen. Botha and optimistic that this would end the conflict though his hopes proved futile. [The Biograph in Battle, p. 283.]

sion with Roberts, Sholtz asked to borrow the Cape cart for a further visit to Botha's headquarters. This was necessary because the other negotiators had returned to Pretoria in the stage. Dickson photographed the cart driving off flying a white flag of truce and with Sholtz and Captain Waterfield of Roberts' staff aboard. The negotiations failed but Dickson kept the white flag and before returning home he persuaded Lord Roberts and members of his staff to autograph his souvenir. Among the names on the flag were Lord Roberts, Gen Baden-Powell and Neville Chamberlain who was private secretary to Lord Roberts.

Dickson used his introduction from Rhodes and his contact with Lord Kitchener to establish a cordial relationship with Lord Roberts and the command staff. "The Bobs" proved to be a more willing subject than General Buller or Admiral Dewey and this generated a flurry of activity. The result was an album full of snaps and several carefully staged films of the General, his staff and a number of other prominent officers. These were carefully composed shots which benefitted from appropriate surroundings and brilliant mid-day sunlight. They lent a positive note to the coverage of the end of the campaign and provided British audiences with a set of films that were sure to please. Roberts

was persuaded to pose in typical activities: examining a map with much
of his staff surrounding him; walking towards the camera with General
Baden-Powell (intended to show him greeting Baden-Powell on his
return from Maefeking); and on his horse with a hat that Dickson
persuaded him to put on because it was more impressive and photo-
genic. The highlight of the set was a film showing Roberts walking out
the door of his headquarters, greeting his Indian guard and receiving a
dispatch from Colonel Sir Henry Rawlinson, a staff officer. The staging
was reminiscent of the film of William McKinley that launched the
Biograph and like that carefully choreographed scene, it created a stir
when shown in London.

Cox and Dickson lingered for a while in Pretoria in hopes of
filming an official end to the campaign. They found space in one of the
city's best inns, the Transvaal Hotel which was also hosting Winston
Churchill and his cousin the Duke of Marlborough. It was a comforting
change from cold nights spent sleeping in the open. They were impressed by the city and the surrounding country but found it seriously
impacted by post-battle turmoil. It was crowded, suffering from food
shortages, affected by rampant inflation and nervously alert for hostile
intruders. They took snaps of President Kruger's residence and the
gymnasium where Churchill had been prisoner and made an excursion
to visit some nearby caves which Dickson found less impressive than
those he found near Natural Bridge in Virginia. He admired the jewelry
worn by a group of natives they encountered near the caves and he
bought some to take back to his wife and sister.

After Lord Roberts told them he was pessimistic about prospects
for a peace settlement because Botha was regrouping and would probably continue the campaign as a guerilla Dickson began considering a
return to London. The Cape cart, horses, saddles and tents were sold
on 17 June but he lingered a while in hopes that the situation might
change. Dickson, the ore specialist, also wanted to take advantage of
Cecil Rhodes offer to tour gold and diamond mines. Johannesburg, the
center of the gold-rich Rand, was nearby so Dickson and Cox went
there on the 27th. They spent several days touring mines and the
facilities where the gold was processed. They also filmed a native war
dance. Most of the labor at the mines was done by natives and the
arrangements for the filming were made by the manager of the Ferari
Mine. Dickson was very impressed by the dance and the musical
accompaniment but had difficulty filming it. The three hundred dancers raised so much dust that they had to do a second take at a less dusty
location. The size of the group made it difficult to find a camera position
to "secure the best portion of this unique dance." The experience caused
Dickson to once again recall Rider Haggard whose descriptions of
native life in Africa strongly influenced him.[873]

They lingered in Johannesburg continuing to hope for an end to
the war but a letter from Colonel Rawlinson advising them that it would
be months before any settlement would take place convinced them to
leave for Cape Town. It was a slow journey, highlighted by a side trip

873 *The Biograph in
Battle*, pp. 267–273.
Although this was
one of several places
where Dickson
mentions contact
with natives, they
clearly play a
secondary role in his
narrative. This is very
much in keeping with
the attitude prevalent
among the white
colonists both British
and Boer. The war
was fought as though
the native population
did not exist.

to Kimberly and a tour of the diamond mines. Dickson's final diary entries describe improvements made in processing diamonds.

They arrived in Cape Town about 10 July and sent wires to the home office for approval to return, then wired their families that they were on the way. On the 18th they sailed on the Carisbrooke Castle and were in Southampton near the end of the month. The date is not certain because the narrative ended with the departure from Cape Town.

"It is with the deepest feeling of gratitude that I now watch the receding shores of South Africa, and know that I am on my way home after a ten months' fever-heat of excitement, toil and peril.

"These war experiences have been of a most complex nature, but I am conscious of one supreme impression deepening as my mind reviews the whole bewildering throng. It is my admiration of the British soldiery and commanders together with a prophetic sense of their ability to maintain the high standard of an advanced civilisation [sic], which they have so signally evinced, as well in peace as in war."[874]

Historical facts in a concrete and lasting way

South Africa proved to be a watershed in Dickson's career. He was at the pinnacle of his career and had become one of the most prominent and respected persons working in film but he was considering a change. As he put it, his war-time experiences were complex and, as such, they deserve appraisal.

Although he was energetic, brave, imaginative and productive, there were limits to what he could and did achieve. He was never able to film actual combat; he filmed only the British military and never made a serious effort to film Boer combat units; and his choice of subject matter was clearly propagandistic, designed to reinforce the pro-British and pro-Empire tastes of his audience. This bias was evident in the diary entries that he sent home. His work is open to criticism because many of the scenes he photographed were carefully staged and not records of spontaneous action. Such criticism is legitimate and needs to be put into perspective.

It is quite true that he was not able to get near enough to the front to film combat at close range but this was not because he was unwilling to take risks. On more than one occasion he had to take evasive action to avoid cannon fire and if he had had a small, portable camera it seems quite likely he would have ventured into the front lines or as near to them as possible. But it is not certain that the military would have allowed him there. The regulations governing correspondents severely restricted their activities. By attaching himself to the naval gun battery he was actually able to stay closer to the front than most correspondents. The regulations required journalists to stay well back of the combat zone and only allowed them on the field after the fighting ended.

Dickson came to South Africa with a charge to provide filmed subjects that would engage, entertain and stimulate the company's audiences. While the company presented their films internationally, his

874 *The Biograph in Battle*, p. 296.

primary audience was British. When he left in October 1899, Britain
was bubbling over with patriotism and basking in the glory of empire.
The press, eager to satisfy, supplied the public with jingoistic prose and
anti-Boer diatribes; cartoonists had a hey-day depicting Boers as inhuman and caricaturing Oom Paul Kruger as a beast. Dickson absorbed
the nationalistic fervor and applied it to his choice of film subjects as
well as in his recorded notes. There is every indication this was done
with great sincerity even though his cosmopolitan, international up-
bringing might well have tempered his patriotism. Though he had only
been back in England for a short time, his commitment to his British
heritage was very strong and very genuine.

Anti-Boer partisanship was especially strong in the British military,
particularly among the officer corps. This was, in part, a consequence
of the evolving state of modern warfare. The tradition that war was a
contest between gentlemen who fought according to accepted or, at
least understood, practices was changing as new and more deadly
technology was introduced. But many British officers still marched
onto the battlefield in close formation following tactics traceable to
classical times. For very sound reasons the out-manned Boers abandoned these time-honored practices. Stealth and surprise gave them
advantages they could not enjoy in open conflict so they disguised their
locations, hid behind rocks and camouflaged their trenches. Their
up-to-date Mauser rifles and rapid-fire Maxim guns proved to be great
equalizers. Officers trained in traditional methods found these practices
"primitive", "savage" and "uncivilized". They regarded the Boers as
unpredictable, unreliable and capable of inhuman – or, at the very least,
ungentlemanly – actions. Dickson would have heard such talk during
the idle hours at the front and it reinforced his chauvinistic, anti-Boer
prejudices and made him very cautious about dealing with them. He
was nervous that his crew might be the victim of ambush and was
surprised to find that the Boer officer he met after the battle of Colenso
was not a fiend, but he did not followed up on the offer to cross the
lines and film the other side. A pity. He could easily have put on his
American hat and films of the Boers would have been a rich addition
to the record he was creating. But he was unable to assume the role of
an unbiased reporter.

His contemporaries rarely, if ever, criticized Dickson for staging
an event even though there were debates about the ethics of recreations.
More than one film showing evidence of staging was praised for its
naturalness. This had been true of the McKinley film and his film of
Lord Roberts receiving a dispatch drew lavish praise for its realism. In
January 1901, *Black and White*, a lavishly illustrated popular magazine,
published twenty-four frames from the film of Roberts receiving the
document, calling it a "... splendid series of photographs which ... mark
the beginning of a new era in illustrated journalism; for never before
has any paper been able to reproduce a series of pictures showing the
Commander-in-Chief of the British Army engaged in the actual conduct of a big campaign". They singled Dickson out as "... the pioneer

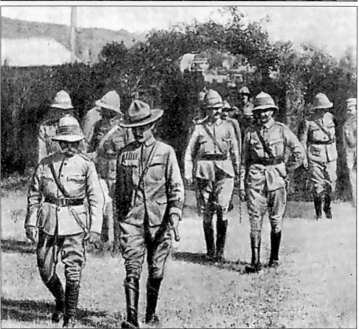

"Lord Roberts and staff" (above) and "Baden-Powell is here at last" (below). Lord Roberts proved more amenable to photography than Admiral Dewey or Gen. Buller so though he had few pictures of combat, Dickson ended his tour in South Africa with a series of well received images of the leaders of what was hoped to be the end of the campaign. Lord Roberts was posed with his staff and greeting Baden-Powell (founder of the Boy Scout movement) who had been under siege for some time.
[Author's copy The Biograph in Battle, *pp. 245 & 287.]*

"Lord Roberts at His Headquarters Receiving a Despatch from the Front/Earl Roberts". The British illustrated magazine Black and White *hailed these pictures as "... the beginning of a new era in illustrated journalism ...". [Author's copy* The Biograph in Battle, *p. 253.]*

of all animated photography ..." and they recommended that the films be "... placed in the national treasure house, that in after years our sons and grandsons may be able to see "bobs" working under the shadow of the Union Jack at Pretoria. The value of such a picture to posterity can be easily estimated when we consider how very much we should appreciate a series of pictures, such as these, of the Hon. Duke after Waterloo."[875]

Dickson would probably have been surprised that he might be criticized for manipulating "reality" because he almost certainly felt that by presenting a clearly photographed, well staged scene he was making reality more real. The criticisms made by his contemporaries were primarily directed at boxing matches with unknown stand-ins and the mock battles staged by competitors unwilling or unable to send cameras to Cuba or South Africa. The product he sent home was so evidently superior to those crude efforts that comparison was irrelevant. He was filming real military units, at real locations and his staging was based on observations of real military activity. He modified reality by adding

875 British Library, Newspaper Collection, *Black and White, Vol. XXI, No. 518*, Saturday, 5 January 1901, pp. 12–13.

The British illustrated journal Black and White *paid tribute to the images that Dickson sent home by publishing this picture of a naval gun and the Biograph camera with the caption "Two Fearful Weapons". [LC.]*

proper camera set-up and making sure that what was caught on film was intelligible to spectators. His objective was a sequence of action that was realistic, natural and logically complete. He was also looking for drama that could excite the emotions. A case in point was the substitution of a larger flag to dramatize the taking of Pretoria, a film that has parallels in the World War II film and photo of raising the flag on Iwo Jima. Even though the iconic photo was made when a second, larger flag was put up, it has remained a popular symbol of heroism. Although the film is not seen much today, it was very popular in 1945 and Joe Rosenthal, who took the still photo, is remembered for capturing one of the most memorable records of the war.[876]

Even though Dickson staged scenes and was not able to film close combat, he presented his viewers with a record that was much closer to the reality of the war than non-combatants were accustomed to. Wrecked trains and bridges, troops moving to the front, fields filled with tents, messages sent by flag, cavalry on reconnaissance missions, Red Cross wagons returning from the front filled with the wounded, prisoners of war sullenly awaiting their fate; these were realities of warfare and the stuff that soldiers at the front experienced. In their way these images were as significant as firing cannons, exploding shells, cavalry charges and riflemen with bayonets at the ready. Since the nature of war was changing Dickson and his fellow cameramen were also creating an important record of the transition. At Governor's Island, Aldershot and the military fields near Paris he had filmed scenes that would have been familiar to the veterans of Waterloo, but scattered among them were images of change: a new, more powerful disappear-

[876] Although the Associated Press photographer Joe Rosenthal does not seem related to Joseph Rosenthal who was filming in South Africa for Warwick, the coincidence of their names is intriguing.

ing coastal defense gun filmed at Sandy Hook, New York; Hiram Maxim demonstrating his rapid-firing gun at Aldershot and the test of a motorized tractor hauling at Cape Town. These and other films of technical innovations are a record of a military in transition; omens of change that would be all too evident in another fifteen years.

The Boer War has been overshadowed by the major conflicts of the twentieth century but Dickson, his crew, and the other pioneer news cameramen working in South Africa, Cuba, the Philippines and China were genuine pioneers who created a record of the realities of war unlike anything seen before. Their work would ultimately displace the fanciful, sometimes lurid and often misleading art work that most of the public was exposed to in the popular press. Dickson was well aware that he was creating a new kind of historical document and he used this as a persuasive argument to convince prominent persons to pose for him. Admiral Dewey was a case in point: "I explained that it was totally different, and the object of my visit was not purely merce-nary, but I wanted to give the world at large historical facts in a concrete and lasting way".[877] The significance of these "living pictures" of historical events was not lost on others. On February 3, 1900, *Black and White* published four photos of the Battle of Colenso taken by a "Naval Officer." One showed one of the naval canons and the Biograph camera mounted on its tripod standing by themselves in a flat, almost desolate area . The caption read: "Two Fearful Weapons".[878]

At home

While the Biograph crew was in Cape Town preparing to return, the Chairman of the British Mutoscope & Biograph Co., Ltd., Mr. William T. Smedley, presented his report on the state of the company to the Ordinary General Meeting. He reported that the previous year had been good and he was optimistic about the future. They had a profit of £28,451 for the year ending 28 February and from that, shareholders received dividends totaling £12,500. Although he recognized that "the novelty of the machines was over" he felt that the public's interest in films was still high. He was troubled by the restrictive clause in the agreement with the Palace Theatre which prohibited showings an any other theater in London. "... we know perfectly well that if we were free we could get half-a-dozen (or even more) engagements in London and the neighbourhood ...". He expected to off-set this liability with profits from Mutoscope machines and a number of other products in an expanding portfolio: an automatic banjo, a duplicating machine, some-thing called the "pianotist" and a line of battery operated lamps mar-keted under the name "Ever Ready". In fact, they were quite busy diversifying their business. They branched into publishing by selling copies of the *War by Biograph* and a new monthly, *Play Pictorial* was in the planning stages. A new, up-to-date studio had opened in a building on Regent Street. It was one of the first to use artificial lights to reduce the dependency on bright sunlight, making it usable any time of the day. Harold Baker, a prominent photographer from Birmingham, had

877 LACMNH, Van Guisling Scrapbook, *New York Herald*, 24 September 1899.

878 *Black and White*, 3 February 1900, p. 186. Although *Black and White* published many photos from South Africa, this was one of the first showing Biograph activities.

been hired to do "ordinary photography" and they expected to do a brisk business making films for members of the public who wanted a filmed record of themselves and their families.[879]

In his careful analysis of the management of the British Mutoscope & Biograph Co. in *A Victorian Enterprise*, Richard Brown is very critical of Smedley's optimistic assessment. He felt that the company was over extended and on the verge of serious difficulties. They were over optimistic about the future of the Mutoscope and, in Brown's opinion it was a mistake to diversify their product line rather than concentrate on film production and exhibition which were their strong suits. Brown points out that the Mutoscope business was in trouble in 1900 and had not gained the wide-spread acceptance that the company hoped for. Although several different versions had been announced, only the coin operated machines had been distributed. An advertising version that was portable and could be viewed by several people was in the works and they were experimenting on versions for educational and home use, but none of these were ready in the summer of 1900. The plans to have machines in hotels, shops, pubs, railroad stations and other places where they would be available to a broad social spectrum had not panned out and most of the machines were in amusement parlors where the patrons were more interested in glimpses of ladies underwear than current events. Mutoscopes were not reaching the middle-class family audience and were generating increased unfavorable judgments from social critics. This may be the problem that Smedley was referring to in this rather awkwardly phrased comment: "... Our difficulty is this : We have no easy channel such as a newspaper for circulating our moving photographs amongst the public. We have to introduce other methods, and those methods are not so easy to find, for the Mutoscopes must be easily accessible, and be under the control of the public ...".[880]

In retrospect the company's expectations for the Mutoscope appear unreasonable, but they did not seem so at the time. The Mutoscope had been the original darling of the KMCD group and though the success of the Biograph had diverted attention from it, they continued to expect that the peep show machine would find its niche. They were not alone. Many of the investors in the American and British companies had been attracted by the potential of a device that was not tied to an entertainment venue. Coin operated machines offering candy, gum and other consumables were becoming commonplace. They collected coins day and night without an attendant and required only minimum attention. The possibility of having machines with news and entertainment on every corner and then expanding the market by providing new tools for advertising and education continued to be seductive. Although the peep show business evolved into disrepute, for a while the machines played a significant role in developing the business. In Germany Hartwig and Vogel, candy merchants from Dresden, invested in Edison's Kinetoscope as a supplement to their automated candy machines. They later (1906) took control of the Deutsche Mutoskop & Biograph Co.[881] Although Charles Pathé is known for production and distribution of

[879] NHMLA, Van Guisling, A.2925 – 68. Report of the Ordinary General Meeting, British Mutoscope & Biograph Co., Ltd., Monday, 9 July 1900.

[880] Ibid.

[881] Richard Abel, ed. *Encyclopedia of Early Cinema* (London and New York, Routledge, 2005), p. 181. An entry prepared by Joseph Garncarz.

35mm films, he began as a distributor of Edison's phonographs and versions of the Kinetoscope. Although the Mutoscope's days were numbered, in 1900 it was still a very important part of the evolving movie market.

While Dickson was away, production of films for both the Biograph and Mutoscope went on apace. In fact, it was because the company had a staff capable of sustaining production that they had felt free to let Dickson go to South Africa for an indefinite stay. But as the new century evolved, so did the film business – and Mr. Dickson's career.

Part VI

1903–1935
After the Movies:
A Laboratory and a Search for
a Place in Posterity

Chapter 32

The Hope to See a Bright Future: The W.K-L. Dickson Laboratory

"... I have been fleeced so often that I am going to drop animated photography as quickly as possible ...".[882] (W.K.L. Dickson to Eugene Lauste, 26 January 1898)

"... he ask me if I am willing to work with him as he intend to open in London, a laboratory for research work, where him and I, we could developed some new inventions of his or mine, and we could make plenty money. (this was in 1901) my reply was that I accept his proposition. Few days later I went to London to meet him at the hotel Cecil to discuss our terms which was not very satisfactory to me, but with the hope to see a bright future later on, we made an agreement between us, and then he took me to the place which has in view at 64 Strand. He rent the place composed of 3 floors, and then we went to buy some machinery, and when everything was set up I began to work ...".[883] (Eugene Lauste to Merritt Crawford, 10 February 1930)

Following his return from South Africa W.K.L. Dickson's life changed. Changed rather dramatically. He retired from public life and except for some forays of letter writing to newspapers and journals, seemed quite content to stay out of the limelight. This, after several years as a public figure during which he seemed to seek – and gain – the spotlight. He abandoned filmmaking and opened a laboratory. This might appear to be a step backwards, but if there was ever a time when inventors were public heros it was the end of the 19th and beginning of the 20th centuries. This was the era of Bell, Tesla, Curie, Roentgen, Marconi, the Wrights, Westinghouse, to name just a few. Edison, Dickson's tutor and model, was a master at keeping the spotlight turned on him and that the proud and self-confident Mr. Dickson would emulate his former chief would have seemed natural, but this was not the case. The pride and self-confidence were still there, but this did not translate into a drive to advertise and promote his experimentation. If there were press releases, public demonstrations or invitations

882 MoMA Crawford.

883 MoMA Crawford. Lauste document written for Crawford, 10 February 1930.

to journalists to view his latest, the record of them has disappeared. It was as if Dickson the self promoter suddenly became Dickson the reserved, dignified scientist, content to stay in the shadows.

This rather abrupt change brings to mind the bitter comment he made to Eugene Lauste about dropping animated photography (see above). At the time this seemed to be a momentary expression of frustration. All the more so since it was followed by a burst of productivity that produced his best known work: filming the Pope and the Boer War. But despite his success and the renown that came with it, Dickson bore a resentment that his contribution to creating the Kinetoscope had never received recognition. He was bitter and carried the resentment through the rest of his life.

Invention was his first love and there is little doubt that Dickson was happy to step away from the camera and return to the trial and error world of experimentation. But the change in his life was not exclusively for his personal interests. On his return to England he found that his family needed him.

Antonia and Lucie

We have seen or heard little about Antonia and Lucie since they arrived in England. They lingered in the background while he roamed through England, filmed celebrities and traveled to France, German, Austria, Italy and other locales. They seem to have been at the Royal Command Performance for the Prince of Wales in July of 1897 but the record of other activities is sparse. During these years they shared his quarters at the Hotel Cecil and while the Cecil offered first class amenities, the impermanence of the situation must have been hard on both women. The company presumably paid Dickson's living expenses but may have been unwilling to pay for the women's stay during his indefinite stint in South Africa. At any rate, sometime in 1899 or 1900 Lucie and Antonia moved to 7 Hillmarton Road in Holloway/Islington (London). Evidently this was a rental facility because according to *Kelly's London Directory* for 1901 it was owned by Samuel John Hodson, artist – a profession that raises the possibility that he had been an associate of James Dickson or was a family friend.

Lucie and Antonia stayed at Hodson's residence for some time, but when Laurie returned from South Africa he maintained quarters at the Cecil. Although this seems a peculiar arrangement, it appears to have been a matter of convenience rather than an indication of marital troubles. The hotel was centrally located, convenient to theaters, shops, restaurants and other attractions and it offered luxuries that Dickson enjoyed, enhanced by the special treatment due a resident of several years standing. It was also an easy walk to the Mutoscope company facilities on Great Windmill Street not far from Piccadilly Circus. Dickson was so attached to the area that he chose a location near the hotel for his laboratory.

If this was an unconventional arrangement, the Dicksons were an unconventional couple. Lucie was older by a dozen years, they were childless and from the beginning of their marriage they had shared their life with Antonia. Laurie was at the prime of life – in his early 40s, while Lucie, now approaching mid-50s, could have been considered past her prime. It was a situation with potential for problems but there is no indication of trouble and no sign that Laurie was involved in extramarital affairs – with either sex. Although he had ample opportunity to rove, as a true Victorian, Dickson kept his sex life quite private and hence an unknown quantity. The several affectionate references to his wife and sister in the text of *The Biograph in Battle* indicate that he was a conventionally faithful husband. The book was dedicated "To My Wife and Sister" which this additional tribute: "These pages are lovingly dedicated in gratitude for their sustaining encouragement throughout the anxious hours of the South African Campaign".

The bond that held the family together was their dedication to the arts – to music, literature, language, drawing and painting. But the active cultural life they pursued in Virginia and New Jersey became less possible in England because Antonia's health, which may have always been fragile, deteriorated rather rapidly. She was diagnosed with tumors about the time Dickson left for South Africa. Treatments were not successful and sometime in 1903 she moved to a home care facility and she died there on 29 August 1903.[884]

His sister's illness and death had a profound affect on Dickson and probably influenced his decision to change careers. They had been life-long companions and if, as seems likely, he returned to England to find her struggling with cancer it may have caused him to reconsider the direction of his life. While this might seem a melodramatic interpretation, it is the most reasonable explanation for the dramatic change his life took after returning from the war. It was in the midst of Antonia's illness that Dickson planned and opened his new laboratory.

Making plans

It would seem natural that Dickson would model his laboratory after the one he worked in for almost a decade. He was nearby when Edison planned and laid out his new laboratory in Orange so he was familiar with the facilities needed to support research and innovation. But Edison's was not his only model; he also borrowed from Marvin and Casler, his friends and associates. The Marvin & Casler Company, an independent business, was established to develop and produce equipment for the American Mutoscope Company at the time the latter was established. The Marvin & Casler Company added research and experimentation to the already existing machine shop facilities at the Marvin Electric Rock Drill Company in Canastota, NY. It was nominally independent of the Mutoscope company, but since Marvin was a vice president and manager of the Mutoscope company and Casler was a director and a principal technician, there was no problem in directing business to Canastota. The Marvin & Casler Co. was kept busy making Mutoscopes, a few Biographs, an occasional Mutograph camera and designing new versions.

[884] Death Certificate, Gen. Register Office; St. Catherine's House. Antonia Isabella Eugenie Dickson died at 20 Brompton Square. She had been at the nursing home operated by Mrs. Lucy Catherine Jervis, 27 Brompton Square. The cause of death was certified by A.E. Stevens, MD. as "Multiple malignant tumours 4 years exhaustion."

In October 1900 the KMCD group posed for a photo during a visit to the French company's facilities in Courbevoie. They are lounging on the edge stage of the outdoor studio. Left to right: Koopman, Casler, Marvin and Dickson. [NMAH.]

If Dickson hoped to link his lab with the British company, he may have been encouraged by Marvin and Casler and it is even possible they suggested the tie-in. There was a reunion of the KMCD in London in October 1900. Marvin and Casler arrived on the 3rd and stayed until the 20th. The purpose of their visit is not recorded, but the group's interest extended beyond the film business so they may have discussed a European market for a coin-operated embossing machine Marvin and Casler were manufacturing in Canastota. The quartet spent some time together and it was an opportunity to discuss old and new affairs – a photo of the group posing casually in front of the studio stage in Courbevoie was taken during this visit. Dickson would have been interested in an update on the lawsuit with Edison since much of the testimony and Marvin's abortive attempt to buy Edison's film business happened while Dickson was out of touch in South Africa.[885]

The British company did not have an entity equivalent to Marvin & Casler and if, as Chairman Smedley indicated in his report to the General Meeting, the company intended to diversify its product line, then a research and development center with a well equipped machine shop would have been very desirable. They had access to Casler's work, but upstate New York was hardly convenient to London. Although there is no confirming documentation, Dickson's laboratory seems intended to fill this void.

While this is speculation and this is a period of his life clouded by uncertainty, there are circumstances that support the speculation that the lab began with a link to the British Mutoscope Company.

Of particular importance is the uncertainty about when, or even

885 NARA Equity 6928, Edison v. Amer. Muto. Edison sued 3 May 1898; Marvin presented Amer. Muto's case 12 August 1898; Frank Dyer presented Edison's case on 12 and 21 September 1898. Marvin and Casler presented depositions in November 1899; Edison and several associates presented depositions in January, February and March 1900. In April 1900 Marvin made a bid to buy Edison's business and the offer was apparently accepted. Marvin put down $2500 on 12 April but the day before the first payment of $300,000 was due the lending bank failed and the deal fell through. At the time of the Marvin-Casler visit there had been no decision but the court decided in Edison's favor 15 July 1901. The Mutoscope company appealed and won a decision in the U.S. Circuit Court on 10 March 1902. Edison revised his patent and re-opened the suit which dragged on until a compromise was reached in 1907.

if, Dickson severed his relation with British Mutoscope – there is no surviving letter of resignation and I have found no announcement to the press. It is also unclear exactly when the plans for the lab were formulated or when it opened, but the opening seems to overlap his work for British Mutoscope. Eugene Lauste told Merritt Crawford that Dickson was talking about his lab as early as 1901 and that the location may have been chosen that early, but Lauste's accounts are of questionable accuracy. In 1933 Dickson gave Will Day a confusingly cryptic account: "1901 On return [from the Boer War] continued as Technical adviser to the British Muto Bio Co – Took up private[886] Laboratory work- & so on to the present day [1933] in Research Work".[887] Perhaps he meant that he continued as the "Technical advisor" after the lab was opened but the statement is vague enough to leave the issue in doubt.

British and American patent records offer evidence of a link between the laboratory and the Mutoscope company. While the lab was in the planning and set-up phase, Dickson, Koopman, Cox, Joe Mason and at least two soon-to-be associates, were applying for patents, and several were seemingly related to company business. Koopman applied for "Viewing living pictures: &c." on 13 May 1901 and Dickson applied for "Voltaic cells"on 25 May 1901. But there were others such as stamps for marking papers (Koopman, January 1901) and mantles for gas lamps, (Dickson, March, April & May 1901) that were not remotely related to film.[888]

Koopman seems the most obvious champion of the Mutoscope and, like as not, he also championed the diversification of their product. He came to KMCD from the variety business and it was he, along with Harry Marvin, who persuaded investors in the U.S. and Britain that the Mutoscope had great potential for advertising, education and other non-entertainment purposes. The success the Biograph enjoyed in America's theaters was a surprise and it gave the company the opportunity to expand into the international market, but Koopman seems to have been skeptical about long-term investment in entertainment. Hence the continuing effort to broaden the market for the Mutoscope and the search for other products to merchandise. His pessimism about the future of the Biograph was apparently shared by other investors – and by his partners in KMCD, including Mr. D. But, as Richard Brown has pointed out, diversification was a misdirection which, coupled with unrealistic financing, led to a rapid decline in the British company's fortunes after the turn of the century. The decline came so soon after the lab began operation that Dickson's link with the British company became less and less important – and seemingly faded away.

The failure of the Mutoscope company would not have been apparent at the time Dickson was launching his lab, but Koopman's patents for things unrelated to the company show that, like Dickson, he felt it wise to have an alternative livelihood. His patent for an internal combustion engine in November 1900 (co-patented with H.D. Wood) does not conform to the other products the Mutoscope company was handling. As the decade went on Koopman continued to patent objects

886 He filmed Queen Victoria's funeral on 1 & 2 February 1901 and presented a Mutoscope to the Duke and Duchess of York on 16 March 1901. He was also prominently mentioned in several articles about the company's activities. *The Biograph in Battle* was published in January, 1901.
887 BiFi, Fonds Will Day, Dickson to Day, undated 1933: "Brief outline of work with Edison & after".
888 These and other references to British patent references come from *Illustrated Official Journal (Patents) Index*, the annual official publication of British patents.

as various as methods of electric welding (1910), cutlery (1910) and transformers (1911). After resigning from the Mutoscope company in June 1903, Koopman remained in London and operated a general merchandising business a few blocks up the Strand from Dickson.[889]

An end to Biographing?

When Cox and Mr. D. returned to England during the summer of 1900 the lab was just a dream and the company was a functioning reality. Despite the gathering of some clouds, the nightly audiences at the Palace were being treated to changing fare and the company's films were showing at various sites in England and abroad. Although the company regretted the agreement that restricted showings in London to the Palace, it would be two more years before the agreement was terminated. Until the end of 1902, when the Palace concluded the agreement, the film production continued a vigorous pace. But by 1900 competition was more brisk and as a steady diet of comedies, fantasies and an occasional melodrama became available, the public's enthusiasm for news faded. As the quality of other projection systems improved, venues like the Palace became reluctant to pay a premium for the large scale projections that were the company's stock in trade. During 1903 the American company began producing and releasing films in the standard format Edison introduced, 35mm. The British company was unable to make the transition.

When Dickson left for South Africa the company had several well trained, skilled teams making films. By the time of his return the quality of their productions was such that it is difficult to identify films that Dickson made.[890] We know that in the fall of 1900 he was in France to film the arrival at Marseilles of Oom Paul Kruger, the former South African President, and his reception in Paris. This is the first filming activity that can be confirrned.[891] By this time Dickson's services seem to have been reserved for filming events of state and some other premium activities, while others handled more routine subjects. But there were plenty of state occasions where his services were necessary. Queen Victoria died in January 1901 and Dickson called Emile Lauste away from Leeds where he had been operating the Biograph. Emile met him at East Cowes on the Isle of Wight, near Osborne where the Queen had died. They filmed the assembled dignitaries, including her grandson Kaiser Wilhelm, as well as the progress to London and then on to Windsor.

The following March Dickson was sent to film the departure of the Duke and Duchess of Cornwall (later King George V) who departed on the Yacht Ophir for a state visit to Australia. Before the departure Dickson presented a custom made Mutoscope along with reels of images of the family so the royal couple could view their children while away from home. As was often the case, this involved a bit of adventure. As described by Mr. D.:

" ... The Ophir – through my connections *I* arranged with Edward Prince of Wales during Queen Victorias reign – or rather with his equerry to

889 *The Post Office London Directory*, (Kelly's Directories, [High Holborn, W.] and Brown & Anthony, *Victorian Enterprise*, p. 169 & Note 41, p. 185. Richard Brown speculates that Dickson resigned from the company at the same time, but there is no evidence confirming this.

890 About the time that Dickson returned, the program at the Palace included charming images of the royal children, Prince Edward (later King Edward VIII and then the Duke of Windsor) and Prince George (later King George VI and the father of Queen Elizabeth II), that were filmed by Joe Mason. Audiences also saw the German Battleship Odin with all guns firing, a stunning film made by an uncredited cameraman with the German company.

891 SEFVA Emile Lauste. In his diary Emile Lauste says Dickson left for Marseille on 3 October 1900 and returned from France on 20 October 1900.

arrange a permit to take a Bio of all going aboard the Ophir – promising (agreed by Koop. & board) *to present the duke & Dutchess [sic] of York mutos – which I did* – think 3 mutos with previous Royalty Reels which I had personally taken.

"This extra 'Going on Board the Ophir' I got our British Bio co. To make a reel & *express letter post* to Aden (I think the port was) – I remember so well working all night at Cecil Court Darkrooms to be on time – Koop told me it had been received.

"I also rem. getting as close to the then Prince Edward later King Edward the 7th –

"After taking the 'Going on Board' picture I followed the party on board & went to Lord Curzons Cabin awaiting him as had certain duties to carry out – Though a cold austere man he … was very congratulatory as what I had done – after a hand shake – I dashed out through the door & bumped into our beloved [crossed out: stout] Prince of Wales (Edward) coming thro the passage Naturally I was horrified – my apologies were greeted with a forgiving Roar of laughter & a bang on my shoulder – Curzon who saw it all nearly fainted – …".

"… which pictures *I* took & installed on the Ophir – & was personally thanked by both the Duke of York & his father King Edward ."[892]

While this is the last documented filming, there were a stream of royal occasions during the following months and it is hard to imagine that he could resist filming the Coronation of King Edward in August, 1902. It also seems quite possible that he would have wanted to film ceremonies recognizing Generals Buller, Roberts, Baden-Powell and other figures that he filmed previously in South Africa. H. M. S. Terrible returned from the far east in October, 1902 and it would have been fitting to greet his friends and camp-mates with the Biograph's camera.

But by the end of 1902 the laboratory was functioning and with his career change no longer a dream Mr. D. would have had less time for Biographing.

On the Strand

Number 64 Strand was a three story building not far from Trafalgar Square and, as noted, not far from Hotel Cecil. It was also close to the site of the former studio of the Mutoscope company.[893] Dickson apparently occupied the top two floors and may have shared part of the first with Crabb & Parry, tailors. The lab was a formidable investment. In addition to an expensive rental in central London, he had to purchase precision machine tools, equip a chemical laboratory, buy supplies, furnish an office and hire staff. There is not a clue as to how he accomplished this, but he chose a very good time to launch the project. He was at the peak of his career and would have been an attractive risk for investors, though this seems to have been a private business. He was modestly famous, had friends in high places and a resume that included a dozen years with Edison (he claimed 15 years). But he probably did not need investors. He was prosperous enough to have covered most, if not all the necessary funds. He held large blocks of stock in the

892 BiFi Fonds Will Day. Dickson to Day, 17 February 1933. Edward would actually have been King, though the coronation had not taken place. The Mutoscope reel showing the boarding and departure was delivered to the Duke and Duchess in Malta, not Aden. Dickson does not seem to have been involved in the second delivery or the filming which the company did in Malta.
893 SEFVA Emile Lauste. An entry in Emile Lauste's diary says that the outdoor studio burned 17 November 1900.

The staff at 4 Denman Street, Dickson's second laboratory, taken in 1908 shortly after moving there. Dickson is standing, almost hidden, in the doorway and Eugene Lauste is on the right. It is possible that the man on the left is Jules H. Corthésy and the man next to him might be William Cox. The photo was sent to Edison by Dickson. [EHS.]

American and British Mutoscope companies and at least one of the subsidiary companies. His portfolio may also have included stock in some of Edison's ventures (though the stock he received for Edison's ore separation had little or no value in 1901).[894] By 1907 he had disposed of his stock in the American and British companies, so it seems likely that they were used to supported the new venture.

Although the opening date is uncertain, a patent filed by Dickson and Cox in August 1902 listed 64 Strand as their address.[895] It is possible that the period during 1901 when he did not apply for any patents might coincide with time spent planning and equipping the lab and a spurt of patent applications filed in the spring of 1902 could indicate that operations had commenced.

Regardless of when the lab was launched, Dickson's scheme for the future was already in development soon after his return from South

894 NMAH Hendricks. At the time he held 2020 shares in the American company with a face value of $100 a share and he had similar holdings in the British company as well as 2000 shares in the Austrian company. His wife Lucie also had 1000 shares in the Austrian company (per Brown & Anthony, Op. Cit., p. 139). While there is no record of it, it is possible that investors in the British company helped establish the lab, though it seems to have been a private company rather than a corporation.

895 British Library. British patent no. 17,393, William Kennedy-Laurie Dickson & W. Cox, both of 64 Strand, City of Westminster, Engineers, Barometers &c., 7 August 1902.

Africa. He assembled a staff of trusted friends and associates, people with complementary skills who had the ability and desire to experiment on their own. He had discussed experimentation with Eugene Lauste and William Cox and they were among the first to sign on. Lauste brought skill as a machinist and electrician and had unfulfilled ambitions as an inventor. Cox was something of a Jack of all trades with similar aspirations. They were friends, confidants and hard workers.

Ultimately he employed six to eight people and because he generously credited his associates' work, it is possible to get a idea of the kind of staff that he had. A photo taken soon after the lab moved to Denman Street in 1908 shows eight people (including Dickson), which was probably the complete staff. Dickson is almost hidden in the doorway, there is a clerk, a young man, probably the shop boy, and five serious looking men, certainly researchers, machinists and/or chemists – though one is probably the manager. The names of a number of those who worked for him over the years can be identified. They include the aforementioned Eugene Lauste and William Cox and Giuseppi A Guccotti, machinist-experimenter; Jules H. Corthésy, an experimenter with a specialty in turbines, his son Jules H. Corthésy, Jr., Edward Detmold, an office manager at Denman Street; Miss Powell, cashier at Denman Street and William George Stevens Tyacke, Engineer. Dickson also put Emile Lauste to work for brief periods when he was between film jobs.

Although Elias B. Koopman was never on staff, there is reason to believe that he and some of Dickson's other associates at the Mutoscope company made use of the lab, at least in the beginning year or two – and perhaps later. Koopman's diverse business activities, long friendship and shared interest in innovation are reason enough to associate him with the lab. Throughout his tenure with the Mutoscope company Koopman tried to improve the equipment and supported experiments by others to upgrade product and protect the company from competition by anticipating rival patents. Dickson's lab would have been a very convenient place to conduct his own experiments – or pay for the research of others. Although he is usually thought of as the business side of the KMCD group, Koopman had patents in his name for coin operating mechanisms (1898), "Exhibiting pictures" (1898) and "Viewing apparatuses" (1898 and 1902).

The British company encouraged experiments by staff members – and others. The U.S. patent of George Royle, West Kensington, and W.R. Wynne, Kensington for an "Optical toy" (1901) was assigned to Koopman on behalf of the company. Dickson's U.S. and British patents for "Consecutive view apparatuses (1897, 1898, 1899, 1900), "Exhibiting pictures" (1902), coin operating devices (1902), "Stereoscopic cameras" (1902) and "Taking views" (1902) were assigned to the company as were several patents of Joe Mason. Mason had patents for coin operating devices (1898, 1899), "Consecutive view apparatus" (1899), "Exhibiting pictures" (1899), Mutoscope (1902), "Chromographic cameras" (1903) and "Cinematographs" (1904).

Joseph Mason

Joe Mason was one of American Mutoscope Company's earliest employ-ees. His machine shop was doing such good work for the company that early in 1896 he was persuaded to work for them full time. He was an inventive mechanic and he became an expert cameraman-producer. He joined the English company in 1897 and seems to have supervised film production during Dickson's South African venture. He remained with the British company until 1904 when he apparently returned to the United States. He was with the American Mutoscope & Biograph Com-pany in 1908. At that time Henry Marvin asked him to shoot a film using a model of the Le Prince camera that Herman Casler had built. The company wanted to use it in their lawsuit with the Edison Company. The film was shot using the large format film made by Kodak and used in the company's big camera. Mason then solved the problem of printing it on 35mm film.

Joe Mason was versatile and creative and, like Koopman, he may have found Dickson's lab a useful place to experiment both for the Mutoscope company and for himself. He was another Jack-of-all-trades, capable of resolving sundry problems and filling unexpected voids. While employed by the Mutoscope companies he assigned a half dozen patents for equipment to the company which was the most by an employee who was not a company officer. Mason shared the KMCD's enthusiasm for diverse experimentation and it is possible that he joined the lab staff for a time before he returned to the U.S. In addition to the patents assigned to the company there are more than dozen patents which were registered in the name of "J. Mason", between 1902 and 1905. Although it's a common name, there are four patents for cinema devices (not assigned to the Mutoscope company) which seem to belong to Joseph Mason. But the other "J Mason" patents are for mélange of devices and it is difficult to guess which might be credited to him. But, given his skill and interest he may have been responsible for one or more of the chandeliers, cigar cases, window curtain poles, flower pots, manhole covers, and buttons patented by "J. Mason".[896] But there are a passel of J. Masons in England and else-where, so we can only speculate that our Joseph Mason bettered Edwardian culture by designing an improved folding bicycle, fog signal or cigar case at Mr. Dickson's laboratory.

On the other hand, Mr. D. left a substantial record of his efforts. During his lifetime he registered 129 American and British patents. About 100 of these were for work done in his own laboratory. The range is extensive, diverse, eclectic and, at first glance, unsystematic – the embodiment of a roving and restive mind. As an example: during 1902 he filed patents for machine tools, motor road vehicles, mercurial barometers, rotary steam motors and "tuning musical instruments"; there was a "device for exhibiting pictures" as well as two stereo photo devices, one for motion photography and the other designed for pano-ramas; to top things off, he revisited his "Edisonian" days with a patent for ore separation. Similar hodgepodges continued through the lab's

[896] Joseph Mason had three British patents: for a Mutoscope (no. 14,602, 30 June 1902, assigned to the British company), a "Cinematograph camera" (no. 26,479, 4 December 1903) and for "Cinematographs" (no. 11,821, 24 May 1904) and a U.S. patent for "Apparatus for displaying a series of photographs or pictures for producing an animated effect" (no. 779,954, 10 January 1905, assigned to the American company)

pre-World War period. While client orders may account for some of the miscellany, his personal interests (and the those of his associates) seem to have prevailed over logical order. This impression is confirmed by Eugene Lauste who told Merritt Crawford that he found Dickson impractical: "... he always like to start something but no patience to see it finished, that he want to go on something else".[897]

Lauste's impression of Dickson as an impractical dreamer may be a bit harsh. He was able to remain in central London for more than a decade and keep his lab operating through the remainder of his active working life. And despite the apparent disorder, there were interests that kept recurring with with some apparent system. He remained at 64 Strand until the beginning of 1908 then moved to 4 Denman Street, just around the corner from Piccadilly Circus (and a couple of blocks from the former Mutoscope company facilities). He left the center of London in April 1914, moving to an industrial complex a couple of blocks south of the Thames at Point Pleasant, Wandsworth. (The Point Pleasant lab was closed in 1921, but through the rest of his life he listed a lab at his various home addresses and as late as 1933 he was using letterhead stationary "From the Laboratory of W. Kennedy Laurie Dickson, A.M.I.E.E. – F.R.G.S" [Associate Member of the Institution of Electrical Engineers. & Fellow of the Royal Geographic Society], with an address, Waverley Terrace, [St. Saviour], Jersey, C.I. [Channel Islands] which was not his home.)

Four of Dickson's patents from 1902 were shared with co-workers, one with William Cox (mercurial barometers); one with Eugene Lauste (coin freed [operated] machines); and two with machinist Giuseppi Guccotti (machine tools and steam motors).[898] This was in contrast with Edison's practice of keeping all patents for himself and seems to reflect a resentment that Edison did not give him more official recognition. It once again demonstrates his sense of collaboration and the value he placed on the work of skilled associates. He not only shared patents, he let some employees use the lab for their own projects and did not insist on sharing the application or assignment of rights to him.

Despite the motley assortment and apparent clutter indicated by his patents, it is possible to identify a half dozen areas of interest and activity. His experience with Edison was a foundation and he added subjects that were timely or of particular personal interest:

Lighting:: Dickson's professional career began at the time that Edison was creating systems that made electric lighting practical and he always considered himself an electrical engineer. It was the profession he listed on his letterhead. Even after he moved on to ore milling and the Kineto, he stayed in touch with Edison's efforts to improve lighting. He had one patent for an electric lamp (1908) and another for an arc lamp (1911), but most of his lighting patents were for improvements to switches, fuses, sockets and current controllers. There were two patents for insulating wires which might relate to his 1885 experiments with gum balata. Several patents for magnets and batteries also relate to his previous experience. Magnetism was a crucial element of ore sepa-

[897] MoMA Crawford. Lauste to Crawford, 10 February 1930.

[898] The co-patents indicate that he had staff working with him in the new facility. The patents for machine tools and motors are further evidence that the lab was being set up and equipped in the late winter or early spring of 1902. These were practical innovations essential to the functioning of a research facility. The term "coin freed" was a rather standard term used for mechanisms that caused machines to operate after a coin was inserted. This was probably for the Mutoscope Company. Coin mechanisms for the Mutoscopes had to allow the machine to start and stop it after the roll of images ran through one cycle. The number of patents for "coin freed" mechanism by Mutoscope company staff and others reflects problems the coin machine industry had in getting the devices to function effectively.

ration and his film production depended on batteries. These projects lacked drama, but they continued throughout the time the lab functioned and may have produced necessary income.

Ironically, though electricity was Dickson's major interest, his first patents for lighting were for gas mantles and lamps (five patents in 1901).[899]

The most ambitious undertaking was a new turbine. This evolved from experiments begun by Jules H. Corthésy and when the lab moved to Point Pleasant it became the lab's principal activity. Since this evolved into a business venture we will return to it later.

Automobiles: Automobiles were low on Edison's priority list but, not surprisingly, Dickson and most of his associates were apparently fascinated by them. When the lab opened, automobiles powered by steam, electricity and internal combustion were appearing on streets after years on the drawing boards. They were stilll a plaything of the well-to-do, but their potential was recognized by a host of dabblers, many obscure, but some who were soon international hallmarks: Opel, Olds, Rolls & Royce, Benz, Peugeot. Dickson, Koopman, Cox and Mason all tried their hands at auto design and Herman Casler joined them. But even though he patented "Motor road vehicles" in 1902, no "Dicksonmobiles" have become collector's items. Despite this ambitious opening, most of his subsequent patents addressed bits rather than a complete machine and several tried to resolve problems plaguing existing vehicles. As such, they are an interesting commentary on the beginning of automobiling. There were two patents for engines (1901 and 1904) and speed indicators (1908 & 1909); one each for "speed gears" (1909), electric brakes (1903), repairing tires (1907), valves for pneumatic tires (1912), road repairing machinery (1906) and a mechanism for preventing road dust (1908). Patents by his associates were primarily directed to engines and transmissions: E. B. Koopman & H. D. Wood, Internal combustion engines (1900); Koopman and Joe Mason, a carbureting apparatus (1904) W. Cox & others, Motor gear cases (1900); and J. H. Corthésy, two patents for Gearing means (both 1909). Cox also had a patent for Pneumatic tyres (1904). Herman Casler patented a variable-speed power-transmission (1908). There was also a project that did not result in a patent. In 1906 Emile Lauste spent two weeks working temporarily in the lab turning cams for "an experimental front driven motor car".[900] While none of these innovations proved revolutionary, the number and chronological spread indicates that they had modest success in what was becoming an increasingly competitive field.

Communications: Edison's earliest successes as an inventor were with the telegraph and its cousin the telephone. Although Dickson was never directly involved with Edison's efforts to improve these technologies, he was certainly aware of what was going on. His own experiments to improve the telephone started relatively late, with an application for "Telegram & telephone apparatus" in 1907. This was followed by eight patents registered between 1910 and 1914. In related fields, there was

899 His experiments with gas may have been done in conjunction with William Cox. Six patents for meters and coin control devices for gas were issued to W. Cox between 1901 and 1910. The first were issued very close to Dickson's patents for gas lamps and mantles. Since W. Cox is a common name, I was unable to confirm which, if any, were patented to Dickson's associate.

900 SEFVA, Emile Lauste. Emile was working while awaiting a new job at the Deutsche Bioscope in Berlin.

a patent for a typewriter in 1907 and a rather surprising late patent for microphones registered in 1920 when he was sixty – an indication that even as he approached retirement he kept up with the times.

Music: In a sixteen month period between September, 1902 and the end of December 1903 Dickson filed five patents for musical instruments. Since these were mostly for mechanical instruments, they were probably intended to augment the Mutoscope company's expanding product line.[901] The Mutoscope company had created a separate company named "Pianotist" to market their coin operated automatic piano and were also offering an automatic banjo complete with an assortment of recorded banjo music. In 1901 the Pianotist company reported a profit of £7500 and there was optimism about its future.[902] Dickson's interests in novelty and innovation seems to have overcome whatever reservations his classical training and experience as a performer might have given him. Whatever his attitude was, there were no additional patents after 1903, though he did register one of his designs in the U.S.[903] This might indicate that he felt he could profit from one of his earlier designs by registering a version in the U.S. The last of his British patents coincides with the time when the British Mutoscope company's business began to decline, which would seem to confirm that his interest was stimulated more by commerce than by art.

Amusements and advertising: In April 1907 the *British Journal of Photography* announced that a new company, Illusiograph, Ltd., had been formed: "To acquire from W.K.L. Dickson the benefit of certain inventions relating to illusory entertainments, to adopt an agreement with the said vendor, and to carry on the business of providers of public entertainments, organisers of exhobitions [sic] and lectures in connection with animated photography or otherwise, dealers in lanterns, lamps, and philosophical instruments, etc."[904] It was not a very big operation. It was funded at a modest £600 in one shilling shares, which were not offered to the public. This is the only record of the company's existence, but it shows that Dickson had not abandoned the entertainment world altogether. A couple of interesting projects seem to be related to the Illusiograph. At the end of 1904 Dickson patented "Revolving rooms", a loop-the-loop type ride. Eugene Lauste worked on this contrivance as well as a mobile lunch wagon, both of which seem destined for fairs, carnivals or touring shows. About the time that mention of the Illusiograph appeared, Dickson and Lauste registered a pair of patents for something called "Entertainment-means." Dickson also began patenting several advertising devices, variously called "displays", "boards", "signs" and just "advertising". A dozen such patents were registered between 1907 and 1911. There were also patents for printing and punching tickets, cash trays and a counting apparatus. Together, these patents would almost have equipped a touring show.

Film & photography: While Mr. D. did not have a large number of patents for films and photographs, the ones he registered reveal the aspects of the industry that particularly concerned him as he ended his involvement with production. Before severing ties with the Mutoscope

901 British Library. British Patents 19,912, William Kennedy-Laurie Dickson, Tuning musical instruments, 11 September 1902; 23,565, William Kennedy-Laurie Dickson, Musical instruments, 28 October 1902; 23,853, William Kennedy-Laurie Dickson, Musical instruments, 31 October 1902; 15,817, William Kennedy-Laurie Dickson, Musical instruments, 17 July 1903; 28,183, William Kennedy-Laurie Dickson, Musical instruments, 22 December 1903. I do not have copies of these patents and have never examined them.

902 Brown & Anthony, Op. Cit., p. 159.

903 U.S. patent no. 835,604, Automatic musical instrument, 13 November 1906. Filed 20 August 1903. Probably British no. 15,817, William Kennedy-Laurie Dickson, Musical instruments, 17 July 1903. I don't have a copy of no. 15,817, but the closeness of the application dates seems to tie them together.

904 *British Journal of Photography*, Vol. LIV., No. 2451, p. 320.

Dickson (left) and Elias B. Koopman posed with a Mutoscope machine in this stereo photo. From his Edison days Dickson was interested in producing stereo images and this seems to be a test made of a potential system. Although staged to look like it was the company's office, the background seems improvised as it would have been if taken in a studio. [NMAH.]

company, Dickson worked on devices that would improve and expand the company's production and exhibition programs. At the time the American company was formed he was working on a machine to project from Mutoscope reels and he made sketches for a method of adding color to projected images. The latter was never patented, but the Mutoscope projector was . He had been interested in stereoscopic images from his pre-cinema days. In his earlier articles he mentioned stereo images as a possible format for the Kinetoscope and a few weeks before he left for South Africa he patented a method for taking and viewing stereoscopic moving images. As the photo (above) shows, a working model was developed, though, like the projecting Mutoscope, there is no record that it was offered to the public.[905]

As the British company's fortunes began their decline Dickson's patent activity for the company also declined. His last camera patent was filed 19 May 1903, near the time of the company's termination. His interest in cinema was not over but, interestingly, there were no patents for cameras or viewing machines. In 1906 celluloid attracted his attention and one of the two patents he filed was for "Non-Inflammable films". The celluloid used in photography was a nitrate compound that was a cousin of TNT. It was notoriously unstable and had a low ignition temperature. Once aflame, it created its own oxygen so it burned rapidly and was almost impossible to extinguish. Concern about film's flammable nature was aroused by the notorious fire at the Charity Bazaar in Paris in May of 1897 and increased steadily during the first decade of the 1900s as more and more storefronts were converted to makeshift theaters.[906] Reports about fires were fodder for the popular press. Dickson's attempt to resolve a problem that was disturbing exhibitors caught the attention of the *The Kinematograph and Lantern Weekly*. They tested samples which Mr. D. brought them and reported that it refused to burn when a match was applied. "It is as tough as ordinary celluloid

905 The American company did issue some still photos for stereopticons, a few examples are in the collection of the Library of Congress.

906 Ramsaye, Million p. 354.

film, rather more brittle, a little thicker in substance than the ususal material used for kinematograph pictures." The added thickness was a difficulty since it made it less suitable for tight wind and therefore more bulky and less practical for regular production. There was no discussion of the chemical make-up, but the article commented that bromide silver permeated the base so the image was recorded throughout the film rather than just on the surface. [907] Although Dickson was not a chemist by trade, he learned photography when every photographer's darkroom was a chemical lab and he claimed that he spent time with Eastman's chemists. Dickson's non-flammable film did not alter the film market, but it is a reminder of the important contribution he made to the format and quality of cine film. (It was another forty years before a practical "safety" film became available.) In 1909 Eastman announced a non-flammable film and, though it did not catch-on, the Motion Picture Patents Company briefly released their films on Eastman's new base. [908]

Dickson's next venture into film was also directed towards system rather than production or exhibition. In 1910 he patented an "improved" method of developing motion picture film and other "multi-picture photographic film". It was an attempt to design a developing tank that was compact but capable of accommodating a long strip of sprocketed film. The film was wound over a set of pins in a tray that was a little wider than 35mm film. After the film was in place, the tray could be immersed in a tank with developer, fixer or washer. The fluid would come in through holes, then drain out after the proper immersion time. This seems to have been an attempt to make it easier to handle the longer reels of film that had become standard for the theatrical industry. The reels were now about 1000 feet long which made it difficult to feed them through developing machines in a consistent exposure to the chemicals. Dickson was aware of the problem, but this solution was not widely adopted.

Talking pictures

The most substantial contribution to film technology coming from the laboratory was made by Eugene Lauste rather than Dickson. Lauste experimented on a method to record sound on motion picture film in the lab and though he was unable to market it, he succeeded in both recording and reproducing sound and matching images in a system that anticipated the sound-on-film systems introduced a generation later. [909]

He had experimented briefly while working for the French Mutoscope company but set it aside while Dickson's lab was being organized (he claimed that Dickson kept him too busy to work on it) but revived the idea and approached Dickson about the project.

"... I thought if I could interest him to develop what I had in my mind for so many years, he would probably invest some money with some of his friends (this was in 1904). So I went to his office to bring this matter up to him and the great future of it if we succeed. Well he said Lauste, you know I had done it when I was with Edison, with the Kinetoscope and not sound

907 Op. Cit., 19 September 1907, p. 325.

908 The announcement appeared in *The Nickelodeon* in July 1909. The film was apparently abandoned because of problems with brittleness and shrinkage that made it difficult to use. Also, the base seems to have had some nitrocellulose in it, the flammable material in Eastman's regular film, so it would not have been entirely flame resistant.

909 MoMA Crawford. Lauste traced his interest in sound back to 1888 when he found an article in *Scientific American* describing Alexander Graham Bell's experiments with the Photophone in the library at Edison's lab. His idea of capturing – and possibly reproducing – sound waves photographically lay dormant for years while he changed jobs, endured periods of unemployment and moved from New Jersey to England and then to France.

After leaving Dickson's lab Eugene Lauste set up facilities at his home in Brixton in South London. Here he is testing his method for recording sound on film. Lauste is supervising and his son Emile is operating the camera. The woman being filmed may be Emile's wife Bessie. [NMAH.]

photographed on film on the side I see what I can do. For months he try to interest some friends on this matter without any results ..."[910]

Dickson's comment that he'd already done that, is rather typical. He had never admitted that, despite any early success he might have had, the Kinetophone was not a success. It was one thing to simulate synchronization in a lab and another to make it work in a commercial setting. But for the rest of his life Dickson insisted he was the first to tie sound to film so if he tried to raise funds for Lauste, he may not have given him his best effort. In the end Lauste felt that Dickson let him down and blamed him for his inability to get adequate financing for the project. But Lauste often blamed others for his own failures and Dickson actually provided generous support. He not only allowed Lauste to use the lab's facilities, he let him live there.

Lauste claimed he experimented intermittently in the workshop at Courbevoie but was able to devote more time to the project after Dickson's lab was regularized. The early results were not satisfactory, but by 1905 he had built a recording device using a light grate to capture sound. It was crude but successful enough that Dickson agreed to look for funding, but with little success. With Dickson's fund raising efforts floundering, Lauste turned to Robert Haines, an Australian client of Dickson's. Haines came to London from Melbourne seeking help in solving problems with a large format, two lens projector he had designed. It was an awkward contraption and Dickson and Lauste were hard-pressed to make it work properly.[911] While working on Haines' projector Lauste cautiously told him of his experiments with sound. Haines was enthusiastic and told Lauste that he could revolutionize the movie business. He urged him to take out a patent and funded the

910 Ibid., Lauste to Crawford, 10 February 1930.

911 *British Journal of Photography*, 1907. Robert Thorne Haines registered two patents: No. 4,168. Improvements in lens mechanism for cinematograph apparatus and No. 25,074. Improvements in and relating to cinematographs.

912 NMAH Lauste. British patent no. 18,057. Robert Thorne Haines, Scientific Expert, of 26 Osnaburgh St., Regents Park, London, John St. Vincent Pletts, Electrical Engineer, of "Ivanhoe", Clarence Road, Teddington, Middlesex and Eugene Augustin Lauste, Electrical Engineer, of 64, Strand, London, A New or Improved Method of and Means for Simultaneously Recording and Reproducing Movements and Sounds.

913 Allan Osborne, an Australian film historian tells me that Lauste's account of Robert Haines is harsh and untrue. Haines had a number of film patents and made significant contributions to Australian cinema. Mr. Osborne has not published his research and does not want to pass on information he has not published. But it is true that Lauste often exaggerated the behavior of others and it is peculiar that he was unable to discern that he was sharing his patent. On Lauste's behalf, his English was always deficient and that may have made it difficult to understand details.

914 Although Lauste was three years older, Dickson often treated him as if he were a rather naive, inexperienced younger brother – at least that is the tone of the surviving

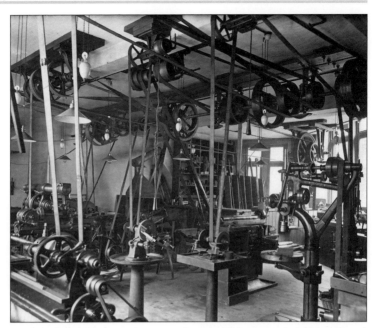

The work shop in Dickson's Denham Street laboratory. Model making and other fabricating work provided an income to support Dickson's less profitable experiments. [EHS.]

experiments for a while, but, according to Lauste, he overspent his available funds and returned to Australia before the system was ready. Before leaving, he helped Lauste patent his device, but Lauste was surprised to find that his patent was shared with Haines and John St. Vincent Pletts, a British electrical engineer who helped Haines fill-in technical details.[912] Lauste never saw Haines again and had no relations with Mr. Pletts, so his patent was seriously compromised and he felt that he had been tricked[913].

Problems of this sort plagued Lauste throughout his life. He never learned to communicate well in English and his language problems were compounded by an inability to understand and get along well with others – he lost his job with Edison because he ran afoul of John Ott.[914]

Early in 1908 Dickson's lab moved to a larger building on Denman Street near Piccadilly Circus (between Shaftsbury Avenue and Regent Street, not far from the former Mutoscope company office on Great Windmill Street). Once again, Lauste helped outfit it with new equipment "... as [Dickson] expected some important inventions to be developed and manufactured". There was no room for Lauste to live in the new lab, so he sold a boarding house he owned to pay for a house with a large yard and barn in Brixton. Some of the money was used to buy equipment and convert the barn into a laboratory. He remained with Dickson until early in 1909. His tenure ended when he had an argument with Dickson's manager. Dickson had left for an extended visit in the U.S., leaving Lauste in charge of the machine shop. A recently hired Edward Detmold managed the business during his absence. Lauste and Detmold could not get along – Lauste felt that Detmold was trying to take the business away from Dickson. After a heated argument in which Lauste called Detmold a "Dam fool" Detmold sent him a letter of dismissal. Though Dickson and Lauste remained friends, this ended the business relations between them.

Working independently, Lauste struggled to keep in operation. He continued his experiments and filed new patents for improvements he made to his system. He received backing from a couple of speculators, but none that sustained his business. He closed the lab in 1916, sold most of his equipment and moved to the U.S. with no better success. Efforts to interest movie moguls like Carl Laemmle and William Fox came to naught and for a while he was nearly destitute. In the 1920s film historian-journalist Merritt Crawford took up Lauste's case and after the success of the Vitaphone, Crawford persuaded Bell Laboratories to buy Lauste's patents and his collection of experimental devices and restore them. Bell later gave the collection to the Smithsonian. Although he was in poor health, Lauste was able to live in comfort in his final years. He died on 27 June 1935, a few months before his friend, Mr. D.

Lauste's career is a footnote in most film histories and his achievements are clouded by doubt and controversy: what did he contribute to Lathams' Eidoloscope? If he was able to record sound on film and synchronize it, what good was it if it was never shown publicly? By most standards Lauste would be regarded as a failure or, at best, an also ran. He falls into that category of experimenters who work before their time and his failures can be attributed to personal shortcomings and his inability to communicate and relate with investors. But he also had remarkably bad luck: a pair of wealthy investors who promised support were early casualties in the European war and Ernst Ruhmer, a German experimenter who aided him in the search for an improved means of recording sound and playing it back, died before their plans could develop. He worked before modern microphones and amplifiers were perfected so it was difficult to make a clear recording and play it back so it could be heard. To his credit, he was among the first to record sound on film, though the variable density sound track took up half of the 35mm strip. It was primitive but very early. The purchase of his patents by Bell labs during the peak of the early interest in sound is an indication of the value of his contribution.

A poetic temperament

"Dickson – Was with me as an Experimenter for several years he is a pretty good Experimenter & found him honest & reliable – He has a poetic temperament, & all that implies in Commercial affairs ...".[915] (Edison to Augustus D. Ledoux, 30 July 1914)

At the end of December 1912 Dickson started a new business concern. The Dickson Corthésy Steam Turbine Developments Co., was registered to fund the development of a turbine designed by Jules Hippolyte

correspondence. His letters to Lauste are full of brotherly advice and cautions about how he should behave.

915 EHS Edison to Augustus D. Ledoux, Corn Exchange Bank Building, 15 William St., New York, Agent for the Pyrites Company, Ltd., London. Ledoux had written for a reference for Dickson and this is Edison's draft reply.

Dickson sent this photo to Edison along with his pictures of his laboratory (page 602). The device is unidentified but it is probably the Dickson-Corthésy Turbine. Dickson tried unsuccessfully to get Edison to invest in his turbine. [EHS.]

916 I reached this conclusion by comparing three photographs, one taken at the studio in Courbevoie c. 1899, one taken of Dickson and a Biograph crew in the field in France c. 1899 (see page 522); and one of Dickson's lab on Denman Street (see page 602). A white bearded man appears in each and though there is no identification and no positive match, it seems quite possible that it is the same person. I was led to this speculation by Corthésy's early film related patents.

917 It is listed in *Illustrated Official Journal (Patents Index),* the annual compilation of patents for 1930–1931 but the volume does not give the exact date the patent was filed. This J.H. Corthésy might be the son. Several earlier patents were filed by J.H. Corthésy and J.H. Corthésy, Jr.

918 BiFi, Fonds Will Day. Dickson to Day 12 March 1933.

919 Jules Hippolyte Corthese, Sr. & Jr. filed for a Canadian patent of the turbine 6 April 1912; CA145549 was issued 28 January 1915.

Corthésy. Corthésy had been with Dickson for several years, possibly having come to London from the French Mutoscope company.[916] His familiarity with film technology is indicated by British patents in his name for a "Printing machine" (1900); a method of "Producing &c. living pictures" (1902); and for another printing machine and a cinematograph (1904). Dickson respected his capabilities and partnered with him in several projects. Corthésy patented a "Rotary engine" in 1904, the first of a series of patents for rotary engines, turbines and devices for producing and transmitting steam and petroleum. In 1910 Dickson and Corthésy filed a joint patent for "Steam &c. for motors". It was the first of several patents they filed jointly.

Dickson respected Corthésy's technical abilities enough to call the invention the Corthésy Turbine even though their joint patents indicate that they worked together to perfect it. His great hopes for the turbine led him to make it his principal business objective and although he was never able to market it, he worked with the Corthésys to improve and promote it through the final two decades of his life. His final patent was a for a turbine designed with J.H. and E.A. Corthésy.[917] As late as 1933, two years before his death, he solicited help from Will Day to sustain the project: "there's something big in this my turbine ... It would interest me incalculably if you did turn a 6½" model to prove the principle, as I have steam data for a Delaval & my other type for *comparison* as to efficiency [at] that size –".[918]

This turbine may have been one of the "important inventions" that Lauste referred to as reasons for moving to larger quarters on Denman Street. Corthésy's patent of 20 May 1911 was the basis of the business venture launched in 1912.[919] The improved turbine was a blade-less rotary affair that was reversible. It came in two versions, one operated by steam and another by internal combustion and the prospectus said it was usable both as a steam engine and an internal combustion engine. A photo (see page 613) of an unidentified device that looks somewhat like a jet engine which Dickson sent to Edison is probably the Corthésy turbine. Dickson also sent Edison a prospectus describing and illustrating the device. Its advantages were cheapness of manufacture, reversibility, quick start-up, ease of changing speed and power and freedom from internal lubrication.

The Steam Turbine Developments Co. was a modest enterprise, prospectively funded at £5,000 in £1 shares. The previous year Dickson had reorganized his business as a partnership between himself and Wm. George Stevens Tyacke, a fellow electrical engineer. Dickson, Tyacke and Corthésy held one-third interest each in Corthésy's patent. In 1914 a more ambitious organization, New Dickson Corthésy Turbines Ltd. was announced with planned capital of £100,000, 25,000 shares offered at £1 each with 75,000 shares deferred.[920] Among those holding stocks were Hanna Dickson, Spinster, 4 Denman St., 1 share, and Raynes Waite Dickson, 22 Cambridge Rd., Hove, Sussex, Gentleman, 10 shares. Hanna Dickson was his older half sister and Raynes Waite Dickson was related on his father's side.[921] The new company was intended to raise capital to finish the tests and develop facilities to manufacture both turbines and internal combustion engines.

Despite the ambitious prospectus, the financial state of the two companies was shaky and in March of 1914 the Developments Company suspended operations. This occurred a few days before the lab moved from Denman Street to Point Pleasant, Wandsworth. As soon as he was in the new shop Dickson wrote to Edison asking for a loan: "I have just moved into my new workshops, where I can complete my Steam & Petrol Turbine, the London premises being quite inadequate for the purpose – You will understand this has made a very serious inroad into my small income, & as I feel you would be willing to help me over rather a critical period, I am asking you to advance me £500 (five hundred pounds) a sum that I compute would put me over & secure me from the risk of failure ...".[922] He reported that final tests were being made and the company was in the process of being formed. He added that he planned a trip to the U.S. and would repay the loan then and show him a working model of the turbine. Edison refused the loan, using an economic depression as an excuse. A couple of months later Tyacke informed the Registrar that no meeting of the board had been held because the Development Company was formed to fund an experiment and that only £1,250 had been raised and that was all spent.[923]

The move to Point Pleasant and start-up of the new company took place in April, just a few months before the outbreak of the First World War. The subsequent shortages of materiel and restrictions on certain actions greatly curtailed Dickson's experimental and development work – a condition he shared with other research operations as indicated by a precipitous decline in the number of British patent registrations during the years 1914–1918. He was able to keep the lab operating but

920 EHS. According to the prospectus that Dickson sent to Edison, the directors were: Admiral W.H. Henderson, Chairman, 3, Onslow Houses S.W.; George Thomas Langridge, Shipbroker, 16, Great St. Helen's E.C.; Captain Charles Trevenen Holland, Lieut. R.F.A. (Retired), Mount Ephraim House, Tunbridge Wells; and A.H.K. Burt, printer, Director, Morton & Burt, Ltd., 83, Teignmouth Road, N. W. The consulting engineer was Capt. A.E. Tompkins, R.N., Retired, 57, Warwick Road, Ealing, London, W. Tompkins was a specialist on turbines and the author of "important books".

921 Public Records Office. I am indebted to Barry Anthony who passed this information on to me from records he found in the Public Records Office, London. A later document he also found lists Hanna Dickson's address as 4 New Grave St., Chester and Raynes Waite Dickson, 3 Cambridge Rd., Hove.

922 EHS Dickson to TAE 3 April 1914. The announcement of suspension of activities was made 27 March 1914 and the move to Wandsworth was registered 1 April 1914.

923 Public Records Office. W.S.G. Tyacke to Registar, 13 July 1914.

the Steam Turbine Developments Co. was dormant and was dissolved 3 January 1919, a few weeks after the end of the war.[924] The New Dickson Corthésy Turbines Ltd. never jelled and apparently suffered a similar fate. Although the turbine business was not a success, Dickson kept his lab open until early in 1921.[925]

On a letter Dickson wrote to Edison, 1 May 1921 he scratched out Point Pleasant, Wandsworth and the address "Wolsey House, Montpelier Road, Twickenham was written in hand and annotated "permanent Address": I base the assumption that the New Dickson Corthésy Turbines, Ltd. never became a functioning company on the entries for Dickson's business in *Electrical Trades Directory*. Dickson was listed regularly through the teens and the Development Company appeared in a number of listings but New Dickson Corthésy Turbines was not listed.

While the turbine business seems never to have been profitable, the lab apparently survived for a while by making models, conducting tests and doing machine work for clients. Eugene Lauste mentioned making models for clients in his correspondence with Merritt Crawford and though Dickson usually listed his profession as Electrical Engineer, from 1909–1914 he used the phrase "Inventor's model maker" in his listing in the Institution of Electrical Engineers' annual, *Electrical Trades' Directory*.[926]

Although research was greatly curtailed during World War I, Dickson told Will Day that munitions were manufactured at his facility and that he was involved in various home defense projects. He mentioned rifle range instructions (he was an expert shot), signaling and wireless operations.[927]

The faltering turbine business seems symptomatic of Dickson's venture into what Edison characterized as the "business of research". It was a valiant effort which was ultimately unsuccessful. Perhaps, as Eugene Lauste told Merritt Crawford, Dickson was more visionary than he realized and did not have the disposition to push projects to a final conclusion. But Edison may have said it best: his poetic temperament was not suited to the world of commerce.

---

924 Per Registry Office records. On 27 March 1917 a letter from W.G.S. Tyacke to the Registrar informed them that the company suspended operations in February 1914 owing to lack of funds.

925

926 Dickson was admitted as an Associate Member of the Institution of Electrical Engineers in 1909 and because he did not have a formal degree as an electrical engineer he was enormously proud of the honor. Henceforth his letterheads and business cards listed his name as William Kennedy-Laurie Dickson, A.M.I.E.E., F.R.G.S., Fellow of the Royal Geographic Society was added in 1908 and Dickson claimed it was recognition of his discovery several caves near Natural Bridge, Virginia when he lived in Petersburg– though I was assured by a representative of the Royal Geographic Society that membership is, and was not, an honor.

927 GU Ramsaye. Dickson chronology prepared for Terry Ramsaye in 1930. BiFi Fonds Will Day. Chronology prepared for Day, 1933.

Chapter 33

A Peculiar Memory for Details

"... you know I have a rather peculiar memory for details. ..." (WKLD to Wm. Meadowcroft, 1 May 1921)

"I am still on the Cinema Warpath as you will see ...; I simply cannot let up – I hate injustice ..." (WKLD to Meadowcroft, 30 November 1925)

"... If [it] meets with your approval, I will do all the hammering in of the Wedge of Actualities & endeavor to break up that old rotten log of falsities – Truth will out – which reminds me that that old rumour of my disloyalty to you crops up on occasion, & will ever hamper progress unless denied by you. As you know, after investigation, that there never was any truth in this & was but a cruel purposeful & deliberate misconstruction of facts – It certainly takes the heart right out of my work in my battles against these imposters. ..." (Dickson to Edison, 19 January 1926)

"He was disloyal. I think we better not answer. File."[928] (Edison's annotation on the above letter)

During his last years W.K.L. Dickson was frequently on the warpath and his memory for details certainly was peculiar. Sometimes it served him well – and sometimes it served him badly. In the years after the first World War, journalists, industry specialists and some historians began to revisit and write about the development of cinema. By that time the Hollywood industry was well established, dramatic film had become the norm and memories of the early years had faded. But many industry veterans were still around, some still working, so it was possible to do some valuable fact finding. Mr. D was one of the veterans, so beginning in the 1920s till his death in 1935 he was contacted by various persons – expert and otherwise – asking for his story. Almost always it was his time with Edison that interested them and he was not always happy with the way they interpreted his responses. This interaction is an interesting window on the way the story of the cinema was developed.

928 EHS.

Family matters

But before digging into the story of Mr. D. and the cineasts, we should catch-up on his personal life. Some important changes took place during the years he was in the laboratory.

We have seen that the illness and death of his sister influenced his decision "to drop animated photography". Four and a half years later, in February 1908, his wife Lucie died of cancer of the pancreas. Her illness seems to have been less prolonged than Antonia's, but it may have been equally difficult for Mr. Dickson since it coincided with the move of the lab to Denman Street. Sometime in 1907 the Dicksons moved to Brompton Square, and it was at the nursing facilities of Mrs. Lucy Catherine Jervis that Lucie Dickson died.[929]

It was, apparently, the need to settle affairs after Lucie's death that prompted Dickson's lengthy trip to the states – the one during which Eugene Lauste was forced to resign from the lab. Dickson left early in September, 1908 and did not return until early in 1909.[930] The primary reason for the trip to the States may have been to take her remains back to Virginia for burial, but the length of his stay, coming so soon after launching a new business venue, indicates that he had other important matters to deal with. His family's stay in London had a temporary quality. When they left for England in 1897 they expected to return to the U.S. and Lucie, who apparently hoped to return to the U.S., never really put down roots in England. They kept the house in Orange as a rental property and their household goods were in storage. Lucie apparently left an estate that included property in the U.S. Settling her estate, selling the house in Orange and disposing of their household goods could account for prolonging visit at time when he needed to tend to business in London.

He may also have severed his connection with the American Mutoscope & Biograph Co. (soon to become the Biograph Co.) at this time. He and Koopman had been the company's largest shareholders but sometime between 1906 and 1909 Dickson sold his 2020 shares.[931] Dickson's 700 shares in the British company may have dwindled away to nearly nothing as the company floundered and this may have motivated him to use the value of his American stock to help cover the cost of his new lab.

Although he had severed his connection with the American company, he would have been interested in the announcement in December of 1908 that the protracted lawsuit between the company and Edison was finally settled and that a new joint business venture, The Motion Picture Patents Company, had been launched. His friend Harry Marvin was Vice President and Edison's Frank Dyer was President. Dyer, who had been one of Edison's patent attorneys when Dickson was at the lab, had replaced Dickson's nemesis William Gilmore as Edison's manager. This would have been discussed during his reunion with Marvin and Casler. Their film alliance was crumbling, but the informal KMCD relationship endured.

929 General Register Office, London. Certified copy of an entry of death for Lucie Agnes Dickson. She died 11 February 1908 and Mrs. Jervis was present at her death. It was certified by W.G. Hill, M.R.C.S. The certificate indicated that at her death she had been in a state of asthenia for eighteen days. There is no record of their residence during 1904–1907; presumably they were still renting the house on Hillmarton Road, but the directories list it as owned by others.

930 MoMA Crawford. He had not returned by 14 January 1909, the day that Lauste was dismissed.

931 NMAH Gordon Hendricks & MoMA Biograph Co. Records. Dickson's name is not among a list of share holders in American Mutoscope & Biograph Co. (Renamed Biograph Co.) document 3 April 1909 but he was on a list of 1 January 1906. In 1906 Casler had 2011 shares and Marvin had 2009. Gordon Hendricks believed that in 1909, the 1010 shares held by M.J. Brown, 42 Broadway might actually have been Dickson's since Dickson's lawyer was Edmund Congar Brown. I question this as there would have been no reason to disguise his holdings.

While in America Dickson also visited his sister Eva, her husband John T. Pleasants, and their children, Robert and Duncan Struan Pleasants.[932] They lived in Baltimore where John worked for the *Baltimore Sun* as a writer and editor. Another nephew, John Laurie Pleasants had died of typhoid fever in 1904. Dickson probably visited some of Lucie's relatives as well. Two of her nieces lived in Philadelphia and other family members were in Petersburg and Richmond.

Eva was now his closest family member, even though his older half sister Hanna lived in Chester, England. His oldest half-sister, Dora seems to have disappeared, though Dickson's mention of a nephew living in Australia in the 1920s raises the possibility that Dora married and moved there. (A third sister, Linda who was two years older than W.K.L. D., presumably died young.) Laurie kept in contact with Eva, visiting her again in 1911 and 1915.

When he returned to England, it was to the home owned by the Jervises at 27 Brompton Square. It had formerly been a nursing home, but apparently Mrs. Jervis was only providing occasional nursing services and was willing to rent quarters to Dickson who lived at that address for the next five years. Brompton Square was a good address and it was convenient to the lab – though a fairly vigorous walk. The *Survey of London*, XLI, 1893, described buildings of Brompton Square as having been built between 1820 and 1826 and in 1841 were "... inhabited, mostly by families of "independent means with about two or three servants each ...". It said that "... No. 27 is noteworthy for an altered rear elevation exhibiting Gothic details of powerful ferocity, probably dating from around 1860 ...".[933]

In 1913 or 1914 Laurie moved from Brompton Square to Richmond-upon-Thames and, as so often before, the move marked a changing point in his life. Richmond was convenient to the lab in Wandsworth but the choice of Wandsworth seems to have been because it was convenient to Richmond rather than the reverse. In the spring of 1913, prior to moving the lab to Wandsworth, Dickson had married again and after the wedding they settled in Richmond. His new wife was Margaret Helen Gordon Urquhart-Mosse, a Scotswoman and the daughter of James Urquhart Mosse.[934] Unfortunately there is scant biographical information about her and some that survives is confusing. She died in 1938 and her death certificate gave her age as 56 but this may have been an error because it would have meant that she was more than twenty years younger than her husband and she does not appear to have been that much younger. The records of births at the Public Records Office in London show a Margaret Urquhart born between October and December 1871 in Newcastle upon Tyne. Urquhart is not the most common of names, so if that is the record of her birth, she would have been 66 rather than 56 years old at her death – and eleven years younger than he was. Whatever her date and place of birth, she was younger than Laurie Dickson and this was in contrast to his previous marriage where his wife was a dozen years older than he was.

They were married in Kensington where Dickson was living and

932 NMAH Hendricks. In a telephone call with Gordon Hendricks in 1963, Robert M. Pleasants said that his uncle, W.K.L.D. visited his family in Baltimore in 1909 and 1911 and that he last saw him in Petersburg, Virginia in 1913 (this was probably 1914 or 1915 when Dickson was in America again). Robert Pleasants was living in Kansas City. His mother died in 1953, one month before her 88th birthday. Duncan Struan Pleasants (named after the Duncan clan and Struan Castle) died in 1920.

933 *Survey of London*, XLI, 1893. Southern Kensington's Brompton, pp. 40–46. I examined the copy at Kensington Library.

934 The marriage was recorded in a volume dated April–June, 1913, but no exact date was given.

935 *Kelly's Directory of Richmond* for years 1914–1920. The house at 12 Peldon Avenue, Richmond has not survived. The neighborhood is not ostentatious, but it is a conveniently short walk to the shops and transportation available in central Richmond. They either shared the house with or rented it from George Cubitt Standering whose name was also listed at that address at various times. Standering may have been the owner. I have found a couple of other addresses on letters Dickson wrote during this period, 115 Oakhill Rd., [Wandsworth] London S.W. (March 1915) and The Warren, Sheen Lane, Sheen, Surrey (3 December 1916). Both of these addresses are in the general vicinity of the lab so they may have been mail drops for the lab. But, as we shall see, the Dicksons changed addresses rather frequently so these may have been temporary moves. Since the listings for Peldon Avenue continue until 1919 I assume it was their principal residence during this period.

936 *The Guardian*, 18 August 2001, an article from "Suburban Hymn" a new book about an area that attracted Sir Alexander Pope, Mick Jagger, Alfred Lord Tennyson and Peter Townsend (of The Who) who owns No. 15 which formerly belonged to Tennyson.

Margaret Helen Gordon Laurie-Dickson, W.K.L. Dickson's second wife. This is one of several portraits taken by Mr. Dickson. [NMAH Hendricks.]

he chose Richmond because they could get more commodious, but modest rental quarters.[935] Richmond was an attractive community bordering a very pleasant part of the Thames. It was a popular spot for weekend getaways and the site of several royal residences. Although their home was not as elegant as Brompton Square, Richmond was a good address, with agreeable surroundings and the Dicksons remained there for several years. In the spring of 1920 they moved across the Thames to Twickenham. The new residence was on Montpelier Row, which was then, and remains now, one of the best residential addresses in Twickenham. Simon Hoggart of *The Guardian* described Montpelier Row as "one of the finest Georgian streets in greater London".[936] It is a semi-private block of houses with the more modest homes, three story town houses, located close to Richmond Road, the main thoroughfare running from Richmond on to the commercial center of Twickenham. The houses more distant from Richmond Road were semi-detached and detached homes with gardens and quarters for servants. Among the past and future residents of Montpelier Row were Tennyson who lived there in the 1890s and Walter de la Mare who lived at South End House

Number 4 Montpelier Road taken by Gordon Hendricks in the 1950s. [NMAH Hendricks.]

for sixteen years. The Row is adjacent to Marble Hill, a splendid Palladian villa build by King George II for his mistress Henrietta Howard.

The Dicksons' new residence was one of the more modest houses located a few doors up from Richmond Road, but rather than use the street number, his new stationery listed the address as "Wolsey House, Montpelier Road, Twickenham". This move corresponds with the time that the lab in Point Pleasant was closed. It is not clear whether they rented or purchased Wolsey House, though it seems they probably purchased it.[937] Whatever their status in Wolsey House, in 1923 they purchased number 29 which is known as Montpelier House. It is one of the more imposing residences located at the end the row and they apparently bought it as an investment. It was rented to others for much of the time that they owned it. As a consequence their life was gypsy-like during the decade that followed the purchase. They moved into Montpelier House in November or December of 1923 and the following November (1924) they were in Boulogne-sur-Mer, France. A year later, in November of 1925, they were in Brighton, England and remained there until January, 1926 when they returned to Twickenham. In May 1926 they were back in Boulogne and remained there for an indeterminate time. They were in Twickenham again in October 1927, remaining there until May of 1928 when they moved to Jersey,

937 The information about this move and the several subsequent moves comes from a combination of the entries in several of *Kelly's Directories* for the London suburbs and from correspondence in the files at the Edison Historic Site. *Kelly's Directory of Richmond, 1921* lists Dickson in residence at 4 Montpelier Road which seems to indicate that the Dickson's purchased it. Helen and W.K.L. Dickson were also listed in the *Twickenham Register of Electors* for 1920 as in residence at 4 Montpelier Rd. The lab in Wandsworth was listed in *Electrical Trades Directory – 1921* but not in the 1922 edition. The directory was usually published in February and reflected the status of the previous year.

Channel Islands. They lived on Jersey until Christmas of 1933 when they returned to Montpelier House, remaining there until Dickson's death in September 1935.[938]

While in Jersey they moved three times. They stayed for a few months at St. Magliore, a townhouse in St. Aubin, a community across the bay from St. Helier, Jersey's principal city. The house is now a guest house with some pleasant rooms overlooking the bay, but in 1928 it was a private residence. In February of 1929 Mrs. Dickson purchased Ambleve, a townhouse about a block away. It also overlooked the bay and had a small shop which Laurie may have used as a laboratory-work-shop. They remained there until early in 1932 when they moved to Vermont Cottage, La Haule, St. Brelade a country community a mile or so inland from St. Aubin. For part of the time in Jersey Dickson rented space for a laboratory in St. Saviour, a suburb of St. Helier and Mrs. Dickson purchased La Cigale, a hillside residence that the Jersey-ites call a cotil. This seems to also have been an investment since there is no indication that the Dicksons ever lived there. The house overlooks the bay at the village of St. Martin and would have been a desirable vacation spot.[939]

The Dicksons never had children of their own but sometime in the 1920s, probably about 1925, they adopted a son, John Forbes Graham who became John Forbes Laurie-Dickson. His parents John and Elsie Graham were deceased. He was born May 25, 1916, so he was a long way into childhood when he became part of the Dickson family. There is no information about his parents, though from his birth date it could be romantically speculated that his father might have been a combat casualty and that the one or both of the Dicksons knew one of his parents. John was registered at Christ's Hospital school, Horsham in May of 1927 where he remained until 1 August 1928 when he transferred to the Naval branch of Victoria College, St. Helier, a private school for boys. He remained in school there through much of the family's stay in Jersey.

The Dicksons' motive for moving to Jersey may have been to be near John while he was in school or because Jersey was a piece of England that was geographically like Laurie's childhood home in Brit-tany. But the move to Jersey raises an issue that has come up before: how well off was he? Jersey is well known as a haven for wealthy Brits who find it a convenient place to shelter money. The Dicksons moved there at a time when WKL was pleading impoverishment. He had complained about how hard up he was to a number of people. He apparently laid it on heavily to his former student, Billy Bitzer, who visited him when was in London to film "Hearts of the World". "I contacted Dickson when I was in England in 1917. He was living just outside London. I telegraphed him to come to the Savoy Plaza Hotel. But went out to see him at his place instead where I discovered that he was very poor, financially. I dont [sic] think he could have afforded the trip to London."[940]

In 1924 Dickson appealed to Edison to help him "out of the woods"

938 The dates of his various moves are taken from surviving correspondence.

939 The dates and addresses are taken from Dickson's very active correspondence while in Jersey as well as the *The Jersey Directory and Express Almanac* and other resources at Lord Coutanche Library, Société Jersiaise, St. Helier, Jersey, C.I.

940 GU, Ramsaye, Bitzer to Ramsaye, 21 August 1940.

and Edison came through with an allowance of $50.00 monthly, a sort of pension that Dickson continued to receive even after Edison's death in 1931. In 1932 he made a similar – but unsuccessful – pitch to Oscar Solbert of the Eastman Kodak Company. He brazenly asked for a monthly stipend based on his interaction with Eastman in the 1880s and 90s.

The purchase of several properties and the expenses of private schools make it hard to give credence to such claims, yet there may have been some basis for them. Impoverishment can be a relative thing and in all likelihood Dickson was not as well off in the 1920s as he had been at the turn of the century. His business had not flourished and the restrictions brought on by the war had been hard on him. He had no salary or pension so he was living off his reserves and inheritances. He had long ago divested himself of the stocks he held in film companies – which had become virtually worthless anyway. It is quite possible that Montpelier House was purchased with proceeds from the sale of equipment and other assets from his lab. Both of the properties they purchased on Jersey were in Mrs. Dickson's name and may have been bought with her personal resources. So it is quite possible that they felt they were living on the edge, but from the distance that time allows us, it looks like a rather comfortable edge.

In pursuit of Mr. Edison

When he wasn't testing turbines or tending his family, two activities consumed much of Mr. D's time during his final years: striving to re-establish himself with Mr. Edison and trying to justify his role in the invention of cinema. The two were inescapably related. To ensure his own place at the birth of movies, it was necessary to protect Edison's reputation and re-establish recognition of the key role he played in Edison's achievements. He had limited success in gaining recognition and even more limited success in regaining favor with his former boss.

He had been obliged to keep a low profile and avoid contacts with Edison during his decade long affiliation with the Mutoscope companies. This was imperative during the protracted lawsuit between Edison and the American company, so Dickson must have been pleased in 1908 when the formation of the Motion Picture Patents Company ended the seemingly endless litigation. It had been a difficult time for Dickson because he regarded his experience at the lab as the highlight of his career. Like many of his former co-workers, he proudly displayed his affiliation with Edison on his business cards and stationery. The memory of his acrimonious departure rankled and, for personal as well as business reasons, he longed to get back in Edison's good graces. His contribution to the Kinetograph and Kinetoscope had become all the more important as the popularity of movies spread around the globe. It was, in short, his hope of future renown. He knew he could not, and should not, upstage Edison, but Edison's reputation and his contribution as a key assistant could earn him recognition as the brains behind the invention. As the years went by he was increasingly convinced that the Kinetoscope and Kinetograph were his creations, but he remained judiciously cautious about separating himself from Edison's reputation.

His efforts to make peace with Edison were a matter of personal pride. He blamed William Gilmore for the abrupt end to his days with Edison and as long as Gilmore was in charge of Edison's businesses Dickson knew he had very little hope for a rapprochement. The formation of the Patents Company and Gilmore's departure raised his hopes but Gilmore's replacement, Frank Dyer was familiar with the Latham affair and held an unfavorable view of Dickson's involvement. While Dyer held less animosity, he was not one who would act as a go-between in Dickson's peace-making efforts.

The Motion Picture Patents Company merged the interests – and patents – of Edison, Biograph and several other companies. It ended the litigation between Edison and Biograph, but new lawsuits were launched to squelch the rapid growth of competing companies. One of these cases gave Dickson his first opportunity to visit the lab and renew old acquaintances. In 1910 the Patents Company brought him to the U.S. to testify in their litigation against the Chicago Film Exchange.[941] The suit hinged on Edison's camera patent, with the lawyers for Chicago Film Exchange contesting Edison's claim for priority of invention. Dickson's testimony, with supporting testimony from George Eastman, was a vital element in the Patent Company's case. Edison and associates did not have to testify because the lawyers used their testimony for the suit against the American Mutoscope & Biograph Company. Dickson had not testified in those cases, so his deposition was an important addition to their case.[942] His testimony, given at the Edison laboratory on 6 and 7 May 1910, covered work on the Kinetoscope and Kinetograph from the early cylinder experiments through the change to strip film and design of the Kinetoscope. He described his own contribution and was careful to stress Edison's role as supervisor and coordinator of his work and that of his assistants.

It was fifteen years since he'd been at the lab and this gave him a chance to renew friendship with the few veterans still about – though it is not clear that he saw Edison. The most import of these renewed contacts was William Meadowcroft who had recently become Edison's assistant and confidential secretary. Dickson had known Meadowcroft since his days at Goerck Street, and though Meadowcroft worked primarily in Edison's New York City offices, their paths crossed from time-to-time. They had not been close in the old days, but after his visit their relationship grew. Through the teens and twenties Dickson and Meadowcroft exchanged Christmas greetings and Meadowcroft, who was born in Manchester, stayed with the Dicksons during a couple of trips to London. Their friendship turned out to be fortuitous. Frank Dyer resigned at the end of 1912 and Edison assumed management of his several businesses. As his personal assistant, Meadowcroft had the significant role as his gate keeper. Dickson relied on Meadowcroft to

941 NARA: In the Supreme Court of the District of Columbia, In Equity 28,605, Motion Picture Patents Co., Plaintiff vs. Chicago Film Exchange, Defendant.

942 EHS. Dickson's deposition for the Plaintiff was made before Anna R. Klehm, Notary Public with Melville Church attorney for the Plaintiff and John W. Munday and H.N. Low attorneys for the defendant present. Dickson's and Eastman's testimony in this case provide source material and quotes for earlier chapters in this account of Dickson's work.

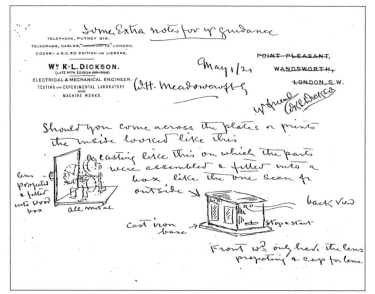

Dickson made a number of historical notes and drawings in an effort to regain favor with Edison. This drawing of the Kinetograph from a letter of 1 May 1921 is one of the few surviving images of the camera's interior. [EHS.]

pass his letters on to Edison and Meadowcroft was almost certainly instrumental in persuading Edison to give Dickson the monthly pension – which Dickson regarded as an indication that he had regained favor with Edison.

This was the second of four visits to the U.S. that Dickson made between 1908 and 1915. In 1911 he returned to testify in a lawsuit against Carl Laemmle 's Independent Motion Picture Company.[943] Late in 1914 he returned in his attempt to interest investors in his turbine company.

The trips in 1910 and 1911 were made at the request of Frank Dyer and his testimony was important to each case. The second case, a suit against the Carl Laemmle's Independent Motion Picture Company (Imp), was a thornier matter than the earlier case. It involved infringement of the Latham patent and, more specifically, the threading pattern for film that it contained – commonly called the Latham loop. The Biograph Company had bought the Latham patent and the threading pattern was important because it was the best known method to reduce tension as the film passed through the projection gate, and reduce the possibility of scratching and/or tearing the film while providing a steadier image.[944]

Before coming to testify, Dickson wrote Edison a personal letter asking if he agreed to his testimony and promising to phone him when he arrived in the U.S. When he received the letter, Edison asked Dyer "What about this" and Dyer assured him that they needed Dickson's

943 EHS. Circuit Court of the United States For the Southern District of New York, in Equity 5/167. Motion Picture Patents Co., Complainant, vs. Independent Motion Picture Company of America. Testimony by Dickson, Eugene Lauste and Woodville Latham in this case has been used extensively in earlier chapters. The senior Mr. Latham was a surprise deponent. Both of the younger Lathams had died and it was assumed that the father was also dead but he was found selling books in Harlem. Dickson testified 10, 11, 12 & 14 April 1911 in the offices of Kerr, Page, Cooper & Hayward, 149 Broadway, New York City. He was questioned by Parker W. Page, Counsel for the Patents Company and cross examined on the 14th by Richard Eyre, Counsel for the Imp Company.

944 The Latham's patent had passed through several hands. The American Mutoscope & Biograph Co. purchased it in 1908 from the Ansco Company which had acquired it when the E. & H.T. Anthony Co. merged with Scovill Adams & Co. in 1901. The Anthony Co. acquired it in 1896 when the Lathams encountered financial difficulties. The patent was valuable because it contained a pattern for threading film in a camera – the so-called "Latham Loop".

A wartime adventure

On 15 March 1915 Dickson wrote William Meadowcroft telling of his harrowing trip returning from the U.S. on the White Star steamer Lapland which sailed from New York on 20 January 1915:

"... At midnight (Thursday, 28 January) our boat was stopped by a British naval gunboat & we were made to *back full speed*, then turn & go out to sea again, just as we were entering the Irish Channel —quite an excitement –

Then we followed instead of preceding the Mine Sweepers – meanwhile a German submarine was being harassed by our gun boat – 9 hours later we got into Liverpool no going to bed that night –

I hope old friend, to see more of you next trip ..." (EHS, Dickson to Meadowcroft, 15 March 1915)

---

testimony for the suit.[945] There is no indication that Edison responded and his question shows that Edison was troubled by Dickson's testimony. As it turned out, Dickson, who testified in New York City rather than in Orange, trod a rather careful line in his testimony, stating that he was originally intrigued by Woodville Latham but became increasingly troubled by the family as their project developed. He indicated that Woodville Latham was rarely present and gave the two sons little credit for creating the Eidoloscope, reserving most of the credit for Eugene Lauste (who also testified in the case). Dickson did not claim credit for their device but his testimony does not over-ride suspicions that he made important contributions to the Latham's system.

Dickson returned to the U.S. in 1914 specifically to find funds for the Corthésy turbine and Mr. Edison was high on his list of prospects. He stayed several weeks and his schedule included a visit to the lab and a visit with his former boss, though he did not persuade Edison to invest. By this time Dickson had consolidated his relationship with Meadowcroft and on the eve of his departure he sent Meadowcroft a cordial note transmitting a letter to Edison: "Just an 'au revoir' old friend ...". His letter to Edison returned documents from the lab that were "inadvertently" kept among those assembled for the biography of Edison.

These were Dickson's last trips to the U.S. – at least, the last on record – but they were productive to the extent that he was able to reestablish contact with the lab and could depend on Meadowcroft to maintain communications. On his own Dickson would have found it difficult to reach Edison, whose attitude towards Dickson remained ambivalent. Although he accepted Dickson's communications and consented to Dickson's pension, he never forgave Dickson for double crossing him – a phrase he used repeatedly, often shortening it to "XX".

Meadowcroft smoothed the way for Dickson by receiving his letters and passing them on to Edison for comment and Edison often let Meadowcroft sign his response. For Meadowcroft, who had a strong sense of history, Dickson was a useful contact. Meadowcroft was trying to collect, organize and maintain the lab's records, many of which had

945 EHS. Dickson to Edison, 21 March 1911.

been neglected – after Edison's death he became the librarian and historian of the lab. Several times during the 'teens and twenties he probed Dickson's memory in an effort to fill gaps in the historical files. In 1913 Dickson sent a photo of the original tinfoil phonograph, some European currency signed by Edison's great grandfather; a bit later he supplied information about articles that might have stimulated Edison's first attempts to combine the phonograph with images and in 1915 Dickson found a copy of his biography of Edison to fill a void in the library. In 1921 the lab recieved a request for a photo of the original Kinetograph camera which stimulated a search for the stock of negatives taken by Dickson. They could not be found and Dickson didn't have one. He made sketches including a unique drawing of the interior of the camera. Dickson's letter included an account of his early photographic work which confirmed that there was a mix of personal and official work, apparently with Edison's consent:

"... "If I were in the States (fr. a mental picture) I could put my hands on several plates – negatives & prints.

"At the foot of the stairs leading up to the projection loft of the 1st studio (glass roof) there were pigeon holes crammed with plates (Technical – *all* of which remained in charge of Heise – I took only the personal ones. Photos of my Wife – family groups – Va. niece & such like Other plates of Mr. Edison & life records on glass were *all* at Brady's (Orange) for trade purposes – also a small box with brass handles of exteriors of machines – such as appears in print – see booklet I published at the time – exterior of camera joined up with Edisons [sic] phonograph-

"The loft also had a negative rack of machine photos ...".[946]

The issue of the missing photographs festered in Dickson's mind and he raised it again in 1926. This time his concern was aroused by Charles Edison who was looking for certain photos of his father and the family that he could not find. Dickson was so upset that he wrote letters to Charles, to Edison and Edison's wife urging an intense search for the missing negatives. After hearing nothing from them, Dickson wrote to his American lawyer, Edmund Congar Brown and an old friend, Claude Thorpe, who lived not far from the Brady studio in Orange where Dickson had placed the negatives for sale to the public (in 1892–93). Brady had apparently returned the negatives to the lab in 1920, but they seem to have vanished sometime after that. Dickson had reason to be upset because he apparently had only a few examples of the photographs that he took while working at the lab. It is unfortunate because except for ten or twelve that Gordon Hendricks got from a former neighbor in Twickenham, none of Dickson's negative originals survive and we have to rely on a few original prints and copies published in Dickson's books and articles to evaluate his work as a still photographer.[947]

These contacts encouraged Dickson to hope for rapprochement but it was an elusive goal. Edison's responses were an inconsistent mixture of cordiality, tolerance, condescension and disdain. There were occasional hints of genuine warmth, a remnant, perhaps, of the fond-

946 EHS. Dickson to Meadowcroft, 1 May 1921.

947 Quite a number of prints survive, enough to confirm the quality of Dickson's photographic work. The best set, showing the care he took in preparing prints, is in a souvenir photo album he prepared for Al Tate when Tate left the lab in 1894. Tate gave the album back to the lab.

ness Edison once felt for Dickson; a fondness that developed as Dickson matured from an inexperienced youth to a maturing experimenter. Their shared work on two of his favorites experiments, ore milling and the Kineto, could not have been easily dispelled. But sentiment aside, Edison accepted Gilmore's judgement that Dickson's frequent visits to the Latham's workshop were an unforgivable subterfuge and he refused to accept Dickson's unconvincing plea that he was just scouting in an effort to learn what the Lathams were up to. Although the Lathams had long since passed from the scene and their Eidoloscope had become a museum piece, they were the first of Edison's many competitors and he had not forgotten them. By the end of World War I, competing film companies had forced Edison to close his studio and end his motion picture business. Movies had joined the list of inventions that slipped out of his hands and made fortunes for former rivals. He had watched others enrich themselves with improvements he had made to the telegraph and telephone and he saw rivals take over the electrical industry that he pioneered. Now he was watching new competitors taking over the movie and phonograph. In spite of the popular adulation and his reputation as a master inventor, competition had been the bane of his career as an entrepreneur and he held deep resentments towards those who had thwarted him. Dickson had double crossed him and his persistent attempts to regain favor raised old scores that Edison would have preferred forgotten.[948]

Dickson never understood this and, besides, it was not in his character to apologize and beg forgiveness. In reality, Dickson could not and would not admit that his affair with the Lathams was at all questionable and he persisted in blaming Gilmore for the blow-up. As the years went by he often called Gilmore his "successor", but, as noted, Gilmore had not "succeeded" Dickson in any realistic sense of the term. Gilmore was the business manger and never an experimenter. Dickson surely knew this, so his concern was about their standing with Edison rather than their roles at the lab – a clear demonstration of the exaggerated view Dickson held of his status at the lab. While there is no question that Dickson had an important position and little question that Edison held him in high esteem, it took chutzpah to translate this into star status! His stubborn refusal to recognize that his dubious actions caused his fall from grace, turned his efforts to curry favor from Edison into a virtual obsession. It was a futile effort. Edison was equally stubborn and was not about to give him the ultimate reward that Dickson wanted so badly – public recognition of his role in creating the Kinetoscope and Kinetograph.

On the cinema warpath

The quarrel over who invented cinema went on for such a long time that its origins are lost in time. In fact, the dispute began before modern movies were seen by the public and since it was never satisfactorily resolved, it has festered through much of cinema's history. Contemporary scholars generally prefer to credit a number of pioneers for their

948 Baker Library; Ramsaye Collection & EHS. In undated comments penciled by Edison on Terry Ramsaye's manuscript for Chapter Two of the articles that led to *A Million and One Nights* Edison wrote after the text of the note that Dickson wrote to Woodville Latham following the test screening of the first test film made for the Lathams: "... you see the Double X with Dickson here" followed by a second comment: "Dickson quit me D X". In a letter to Thomas Armat, 25 May 1922, in which Edison said he would support Armat's protest to the Smithsonian about their exhibit of C. Francis Jenkin's equipment, Edison wrote: "There are lots of mistatements [sic] trying to get into the history of motion pictures, some through Dickson's double crossing me and selling me out to Latham for his own benefit."

various contributions and most of them reject the partisan, often jingoistic wrangling that prevailed through much of the 20th century. In the U.S., during the years before World War I, the dispute about priority had a distinctly legal character and was, in fact, serious business since it had to do with patents and the exclusive benefits to be gained from them. The first engagements were fought in the Patent Office where, in a system unique to the U.S., professional examiners reviewed applications for cameras, projectors, viewing machines and celluloid. Each application was checked for originality and specific claims were dismissed when covered by previous patents. Patents registered as early as the 1860s were cited as predating some aspects of the first moving image applications. In addition, challenges, called interferences, were declared when several similar applications were received simultaneously. In these cases, priority, in the form of the earliest original application, was the standard for the award.[949] The most significant of these several challenges were settled by 1898, at which time the conflict moved into the courts where it dragged-on for more than a decade as Edison and, later, the Motion Picture Patents Company used patents to challenge and subvert as many rivals as possible.

The court challenges ground to an end in the teens. The exclusive terms of patents had run out and superior apparatuses belonging to less litigious owners had become standard. By the end of the first World War audiences gathered in ever larger and more elaborate theaters to watch longer and more complex films and the pioneers had been replaced by a new generation of producers. A generation had passed since the Kinetoscope astounded viewers and the films of yesterday seemed dated and primitive. As the memory of the early days grew dim, the sparring over priority passed from lawyers to journalists and historians (though the number of academics giving serious attention to the movies remained dismally small).

Articles about the pioneers appeared occasionally in the press, often championing one or another as the first inventor. Edison's aggressive efforts to dominate the industry made him unpopular in film circles and he had relatively few champions. They were particularly scarce in the English and French journals that Dickson read, so he appointed himself defender of the faith. It was a role he savored. Dickson's campaign began early. An article, "Evolution of the Kinema" in *The Financial News* of 30 March 1914 pushed his button. It was a rather fair minded article about a number of pioneers, but the author, Frederick A. Talbot credited Robert Paul with recognizing the possibilities of projection which stimulated others, including Edison to follow suit. He called the Kinetoscope "... a dismal failure ..." which doubtless stuck in Dickson's craw. The article appeared while Dickson was moving to Wandsworth. He drafted a letter to the editor and enclosed it with his letter to Edison requesting a loan for his turbine business. He asked Edison to sign it as his own. "I think it may settle for all time the Priority of *First Projection*. I can give dates & sketches if needed, & establish without further doubt that you were the *first in the world* to project ...

949 The most important of these early challenges was Interference No. 18,461, Edward H. Amet vs. Woodville Latham vs. Herman Casler vs. Thomas Armat for a Picture Exhibiting Apparatus, i.e. projector. Testimony in this case, which was eventually settled in Armat's favor, has been cited several places in this text.

living pictures ...".[950] He commented that no one was disputing Talbot's article and that a letter from Edison in such a prestigious paper would "... come like a thunderclap over here, and will be read by the millions who are making a god of this upstart ...". Dickson's draft letter was an account of the test projection that he claimed to have made when Edison returned from the Paris Exposition in October 1889. Edison ignored the request and when Dickson raised the issue again in June, Edison told Meadowcroft that he did not care to deny newspaper accounts.

The dramatic death of William Friese-Greene in May of 1921 and the public outpouring that followed roused Dickson to action again. Friese-Greene collapsed and died in the midst of poignant plea to representatives of the British film industry to support the impoverished pioneers who had made their wealth possible. The public responded with moment of silence in cinemas, a public funeral and a subscription for his widow. It was too good a story for the press to ignore. Dickson was outraged and dashed off a letter to Edison urging him to protest:

"It seems too bad that the whole credit should be given to Friese Green [sic] as Pioneer & inventor of moving photography – He died here as you have doubtless read rather tragically & a great national funeral is to be organized – a 2 minute silence for prayer imposed, etc. etc. –

" If you chose you could have supported me in my battle over here for you as the Pioneer –

" By allowing this to take root – History will so have it for all time – & your work & my humble contribution to same – by reflection – goes untold, & will never be recognized – Surely as I have so often shown precedence for you can easily be proven.

"Mr Meadowcroft has a clever pen & could cull sufficient data & proofs of priority – the very size & shape of the picture has been standardized since 1888 – my printed records (booklet etc) showed that you were working on same in 1887 –

"How is it that Friese Green [sic]when he wrote you in 1890, (you showed me the letter) described what he was doing & you had to write that you had already secured the whole thing in 1888 – best hunt up A. O. Tates [sic] letter he wrote at yr dictation –

"Who therefore is the pioneer of practical moving photography – ...'"[951]

Once again Edison declined

The British public's interest in Friese-Greene continued through the 1920s causing Dickson to don war paint several times. In 1925 an article in the *Daily Express* about the projection of natural color films by Claude Friese-Greene identified him as the son of the inventor of cinematography. In 1928 an article in the *Daily Mail* described Dickson's demonstration test for Edison on his return but concluded with a statement that Edison's device could not be the first film device since "Mr. Friese Green [sic], the Englishman, had that distinction ...". Dickson tried vainly to get Edison to respond to both articles and he sent an anonymous letter challenging the 1925 claim and protested the second over his own signature.

950 EHS. Dickson to Edison, 3 April 1914.

951 EHS, NMAH, Hendricks.

In France it was the Lumières who set him on the warpath. In 1924, while staying in Boulogne-sur-Mer he learned of plans to erect a plaque honoring the Lumières and dashed off another letter to Edison describing his frenzied efforts:

"... [I] am having a rare good fight to knock out Lumière whom the Parisians intend to honor as the *Inventor of Cinematography* or moving pictures – so put on my war paint & went to Paris to see if I couldn't substitute Edison for Lumière [sic] as chief witness! I think I may have succeeded – but not on my Paris interviews with Gaumont & editors – all refusing to put my opposition information & French articles into print – as Gaumont & others told me the municipality intended to erect a monument or Bronze Plaque to Lumière within a short time as the Inventor of Cinematography – I showed them my much despised booklet (history of the Kinetograph etc.) – as evidence of priority in the art & after translating it, Gaumont who has always been most friendly on other matters was forced to suppress my contradiction (or real facts) owing to Gaumonts business relations with Lumière – That settled it as far as that source or sources were concerned so got a friend in Paris to take my articles around to other editors – & returned to Boulogne to await – Events knowing that time was the essence of the contract in other words I wanted to stop the *Lumière Plaque* if once erected would never be removed & the fat be in the fire *for all time* –

"I at last received a letter from my Paris friend which stated that the other Editors one & all had determined to follow the Lumière stunt [sic] – off I went again to Paris & squarely asked Gaumont if he thought it was playing the game to *cut you out of it all* – he then showed me a letter he had received fr. You wh' I read –

"If anything was to be done I saw I must work alone & get this through somehow for right sake – for old sakes although I dont [sic] suppose you care much either way –

"I had to put on my thinking cap to find some way of upsetting Lumière's film cart and did – by making friends with the proprietor editor of this big French paper, *Le Télegramme* published *here – reprinted in Paris* – Lille & other places throughout France & elsewhere –

"I sat up all night (an old trick you taught me) & wrote & made sketches – took the lot around to his offices – showed the booklet as proof – convinced him that my data was irrefutable & correct – that the true facts should be published

"I pointed out that if Lumière & others claimed priority in 1894 *you* could prove that you could through me yr chief witness & assistant at the time claim priority & completion in 1888 of the mechanism to take & project the FIRST perforated film – I pointed out that after this discovery it was easy enough for Lumière or anyone else to use the
"*Edison perforated film* –
and get the credit, as Mr. Edison would not bother to dispute the matter his friends must – the attached article is only the first to appear I expect I shall have a hot time with the opposition crowd – I enjoy a good fight when based on fact as I did on my two trips out to NY Testifying to yr rights –

"The article is pretty good & diplomatic – only sorry they emblazoned my name on headlines I was too late to stop it – its French I suppose – Hope you got my last letter re. The Brady stored plates or negatives & that you will approve of my battle royal Edison vs Lumière & the worlds host of claimants ...".[952] W.K Laurie Dickson

952 EHS. The article in *Le Télégramme*, "Comment M. W. Laurie Dickson, Collaborateur d'Edison, participa, en 1887, à l'invention du film perforé" by Jules Gallos, was published in the Pas-de-Calais and La Somme edition on 31 May 1924, and was largely a summary of the Dicksons' pamphlet for the Kinetoscope. Edison's hand written introduction was reprinted at the head and translated in the text. Dickson added three drawings of the various sizes of film and added one showing the perforated film passing over a sprocket drum. Dickson's letter to Edison was much more passionate than the article and Dickson was careful to annotate the article with apologies for the prominent placement of his own name in the headline and the body of the text.

Dickson's attempts to get Edison involved invariably came to naught. This was because Edison had his larger reputation to consider and avoided becoming involved in public squabbles about the uniqueness of his inventions. But Edison also could not forgive Dickson. So Dickson found himself campaigning on his own. He found it difficult to persuade the British public to abandon Friese-Greene or the French to modify their prideful admiration for the Lumières. He persuaded a couple of newspapers to print his claim that he projected film for Edison, notably the brief article in the *Daily Express* and the longer article in *Le Télégramme*, but these did not bring him recognition. In the long run he was his own worst enemy. Though his written articles were carefully composed, his letters were sometimes written in haste and inconsistencies in the letters and articles raised doubts about his truthfulness.

He used the Kinetoscope pamphlet as the aide memoire for his responses but, except for Edison's statement that in 1887 the thought occurred to him that it might be "... possible to devise and instrument which should do for the eye what the phonograph does for the ear ..." and the claim that he projected for Edison 1889, the pamphlet is ambiguous about the dates – and how successful the experiments were. The phases of the experiments were described but without specifics as to date and sequencing and Dickson began moving events earlier. In *Le Télégramme* Dickson said celluloid film was received from George Eastman in 1888. His letter to the *Daily Express* said that "... in the early part of 1887 & 1888 I assisted Mr. Edison in producing a perforated film – Sprocket wheel -Stop motion etc. as now in use – the first film was manufactured for Mr. Edison by Mr. Geo. Eastman ... Further – the size of each phase or picture, width of 'Film' ... was all done within these years ...".[954]

The clear implication in these letters is that all of this work was finished before 20 June 1889, the date of Friese-Greene and Evan's patent. These claims were repeated in an article that he wrote a in January 1926 intended for a radio broadcast.[955] By this time he asserted that the "Edison standard" or 35mm format and Maltese cross were used in 1888. "This doubly perforated 'film' of 1888–1889 became the world's standard both as to size of picture or phase and width of strip or band, and has been used in all countries without any alteration whatever in principle and effect down to the present."[956]

Dickson knew that Friese-Greene's patent preceded Edison's applications by two years and he should have known that it preceded the change to using strips of celluloid. He was playing fast and loose with the dating to make it appear that Edison was ahead of his competition. Ultimately, the inability of Friese-Greene to bring his experiments to commercial success has dimmed his reputation, but Dickson, who was writing at the time that Friese-Greene's reputation was at a peak, was not satisfied with that argument. This did not serve him well because these and other seemingly deliberate mis-statements have caused historians studying his work to mistrust him. So far as Dickson was

954 EHS. *Le Télégramme*, 31 May 1924 and Dickson to Editor, *Daily Express*, 2 December 1925.

955 EHS. Dickson to Edison, 19 January 1926. The broadcast was on London Wireless 2LO.

956 EHS. Dickson to Edison, 19 January 1926..

concerned, he had done the work, it was successful and by dating it early he could stress that it was accomplished early in the game.[956]

It is clear that Dickson mis-stated the facts and did it deliberately. Hardly any work was done on the Kineto before the fall of 1888 and the evolution from cylinder to strip to present-day 35mm format took place after celluloid was received in late August, 1889 and the winter of 1891–1892.

Dickson claimed "... a rather peculiar memory for details" and this is certainly true. As late as December 1933, when he was 73, he could make remarkably accurate drawings of sprocket wheels and other parts of the machines he had designed forty years earlier. While some of these were probably recreated from notebooks he had taken with him from the lab, there were other images, such as his drawing of the interior of Goerck Street testing lab (pp. 25 and 28), that must have been made from memory. But his memory could trick him. He insisted that Sacco Albanèse posed for the cylinder film known as "Monkey Shines" but Albanèse was not employed when he was experimenting with cylinders. Albanèse undoubtedly performed "monkey shines" for one or more tests, but so did Fred Ott and, apparently, several others. This confusion with names is most evident in his identification of William Heise as his assistant in 1889 at the time of the demo for Edison. The pay records show that Charles Brown was his assistant at that time and although Heise was at the lab, he did not replace Brown until the fall of 1890. Such mistakes resulted from memory lapses rather than deliberate mis-statements.

It is likely that as the years went by Dickson began to believe his own chronicles. For years his letterheads and business cards proclaimed that he was "With Edison, 1881–1897" rather than the more accurate, 1883–1895. The claim that he began with Edison in 1881 appears as early as December 1894 in a biographical blurb in *Cassier's Magazine* which was promoting his biography of Edison. At that time the use of an earlier date seems to have been deliberate, but by the 1920s and '30s he believed it as fact.

The historians

This mix of fact and fiction – truth and fabrication – characterizes the extensive correspondence that Dickson carried on with a succession of people trying to memorialize the movies. The first and most prominent of these was Terry Ramsaye whose popular history, *A Million and One Nights*, for many years the dominant history of the American film industry. Ramsaye began work on it late in 1920 when James R. Quirk, the editor-publisher of *Photoplay Magazine*, asked Ramsaye to write a series of articles on the history of the motion picture. The original twelve articles ultimately grew into thirty-six and in 1926 they were re-edited into book form and published by Simon and Schuster. Ramsaye was a newspaperman who had worked for a number of Midwestern papers. In 1915 he joined the Mutual Film Corporation and while editing *Reel Life*, their house organ, later he claimed to have promoted

[956] Gordon Hendricks, who prided himself on discovering the errors of others, listed "Fifty Representative Dickson Errors" in Appendix C of his *The Edison Motion Picture Myth*. Hendricks hoped to champion Dickson's work and dedicated the book to him, but he was dismayed to discover that Dickson "... wandered far afield from the truth" (p. 163).

Chaplin's career. While with Mutual he also edited a newsreel, *Screen Telegram* and at a later date he established a second newsreel, *Kinogram*. As a result, by the time his articles for *Photoplay* appeared he had gained a reputation as a professional and a member of the film establishment. Ramsaye's articles and the resulting book are a fascinating blend of journalistic hubris and cryptic information. He delved deeply, studying documents, court records and interviewing many surviving veterans, among them Edison and Dickson. Although he drew praise from Edison, Robert Sherwood and H.L. Mencken, serious historians have regarded his book with suspicion because of his cunning, flippant prose and the absence of footnotes. Since only fragments of his correspondence survive, the reader has to make judgements about the accuracy of his statements and sometimes must guess the source.[957]

It is not clear how extensive his correspondence with Dickson was – or when he first contacted him – but Ramsaye's account of the experiments at Edison's lab bears evidence of influence from the accounts that Dickson was dispensing in the early 1920s. Text from two letters from Dickson are quoted in the book. These were written in May of 1924 and describe the early experiments and the 1889 demonstration for Edison. The account of Dickson's later activities seems to have come from other sources. Ramsaye accepted Dickson's assertion that virtually all work on the Kinetoscope and Kinetograph was completed in 1887 and 1888 and that the Edison standard format was devised before the introduction of Eastman's celluloid in 1889. He also acknowledged Dickson's claim that he projected film for Edison on his return from the Paris Exposition in October 1889 though he speculated that the test was less successful than Dickson claimed.[958] The narrative of the Latham's venture into projection seems drawn from testimony in the patent and court cases; and though he praised the quality of the Biograph projections and emphasized the importance of the backing of the company by Wall Street investors, his account of the KMCD-Mutoscope Company is rather spare. He credited Dickson with suggesting a flip card book but credited Casler with design of the Mutoscope; remarked that Dickson's intimate familiarity with Edison's inventions guided the design of the Mutograph and Biograph; and said that sending Dickson and Lauste to Europe in 1897 got them conveniently out of the way lest their presence stir Edison's ire. Ramsaye's account seems the result of interviews with Harry Marvin and gleanings from the court cases.

The book made Ramsaye something of a celebrity – at least in cinema circles – and he relished his assumed role as a semi-official historical spokesperson for the American film industry. He also became a champion of Edison as the inventor of movies. In 1928 Ramsaye was asked to speak at a banquet for the Society of Motion Picture Engineers where he repeated his account of Dickson's demonstration. This was later published in the *SMPE Journal* as "Early History of Sound Pictures". This account came when talking pictures were revolutionizing the industry, so the claim that Dickson showed synchronized sound in

957 There is a small collection of documents, most post-*A Million and One Nights* in the Georgetown University Library; the Baker Library at Harvard has Edison's comments about chapters covering Edison and there are a number of letters at the Edison Historic Site. But the body of papers he collected while writing and other papers documenting his career as a writer and film producer have not surfaced.

958 Ramsaye, Op. Cit., pp. 54–73. In 1924 Ramsaye quizzed Edison on the correctness of Dickson's claim and got a cryptic acknowledgment from him that there were experimental projections using both a modified Kinetoscope and the Kinetograph. Edison even acknowledged that his oft quoted statement in the Mutoscope suit that "there was no screen" may have been made because he misunderstood the question.

1889 took on new importance and the debate over Edison's role gained intensity with Ramsaye in the role of spokesman for the establishment opposed by a small but vocal chorus of dissenters.

The loudest challenge came from Ramsaye's occasional adversary, Merritt Crawford. Crawford was also a journalist who had worked as a studio publicist and he had a strong interest in the history of cinema. As he told Will Day, he and Ramsaye were friends but rivals: "Ramsaye and I are both members of the Historical Committee, S.M.P.E., so you can see that while we are good friends, we are, in a sense, the attorneys for opposite sides – he taking the Edison end".[959] While gathering information on the early years Crawford found Eugene Lauste living in New Jersey in a state of near poverty. Crawford's campaign championing him as *the* pioneer of talking film bore fruit. The story of a forgotten, destitute pioneer resonated with the press and accounts appeared in newspapers in Newark, New York and Detroit and the trade journals *American Cinematographer*, *Zit's Theatrical Newspaper* as well as the British journal *Bioscope*. Crawford brought Lauste to the same meeting of the Society of Motion Picture Engineers where Ramsaye held forth on Edison's behalf. Crawford's comments denying that Edison was the father of the motion picture were reinforced by a statement from Lauste that he was present at Dickson's test demonstration and the image was so poor that Edison walked out in disgust.

This put the issue on the burner. It simmered for a year then came to a boil in the late spring of 1930 in the form of a heated exchange of letters in the *New York Sun* debating Edison's role. Crawford wrote a couple of lengthy letters contending that, although Edison had commercialized movies successfully, he had invented nothing new and had really only adapted technology that had been previously been demonstrated by others such as Muybridge, Marey and Le Prince. His argument was based on the 1902 decision by Judge Wallace in the Edison-American Mutoscope & Biograph Co. case. He received support from the respected cinema journalist Epes Winthrop Sargent. Frank Dyer was prominent among those defending Edison. The issue became so volatile and the correspondence so detailed that in July the *Sun* announced that they would not publish any more letters on the subject. This triggered an article on the dispute in *Motion Picture News*.[960]

It was in the midst of this wrangling that Crawford first contacted W.K.L. Dickson. In August of 1930 Crawford wrote on behalf of Eugene Lauste who was recovering from high blood pressure and wanted a photo of Dickson to include in a scrapbook he was preparing. In addition to this favor he asked Dickson to send him accounts of his own work. He explained that he was writing articles on film history which he planned to consolidate into a longer, more authoritative history. He sent Dickson a copy of an article he had written about Lauste, the second of a series entitled "Men in the Movie Vanguard" that he was writing for *Cinema Journal*[961].

Dickson's initial response was negative. "For the moment I do not

959 BiFi, Fonds Will Day. Crawford to Day, 18 September 1930. Like Ramsaye, Crawford had worked as a publicist for Mutual in the 'teens.

960 MoMA Crawford & GU Ramsaye. Letters by Crawford were written 10, 18 and 20 June 1930; Dyer's article defending Edison was printed after these letters and reported in the article "Did Edison Invent Pictures? Big Row Reaches Boiling Point but Cools Off" in *Motion Picture News*, 5 July 1930, pp. 22 & 24. The *News* also published a rebuttal to Dyer's letter written by Crawford but not published in the *Sun*.

961 *Cinema Journal* was a short-lived attempt at a serious journal about the industry. Crawford wrote six articles, each focusing on a pioneer: the first about Jean A. LeRoy appeared in April, 1930; the second, on Lauste in May; third, on Étienne-Jules Marey in June; fourth on William Friese-Greene in September; fifth on Georges Méliès and the sixth and final, on Louis Aimé Le Prince in December 1930.

see my way to do what you want as I had too many bitter disappoint-
ments in trying to make it clear both fr. early prints & books published
at the time that Edison & Edison alone with my help only (bien
entendu) was the pioneer in the universally used perforated film of 1888
– *as now in use* ...".[962] Dickson's negative response may have been a
response to Crawford's article about Lauste, but it is also possible that
Dickson was aware of Crawford's stance on Edison. Regardless, Dickson had second thoughts and in October he relented and said that if he
had time he would "give you what you want – especially as I note you
want *facts* ...".[963]

   In December he sent Crawford an eight page hand-written account
of his work for Edison, supplemented by two pages of drawings illustrating intermittent movements and the progressive changes in film and
image size with the concomitant evolution of perforations and sprockets. He continued to exaggerate Edison's early interest in the experiment with a claim that Edison talked about combining a Zoetrope-like
device with the phonograph as early as 1886. Even though Dickson
modified earlier claims about solving all problems in 1888 by admitting
that there was no satisfactory apparatus until 1889, he nevertheless
contended that "... 1888 was our lucky year ... [because] ... we ... proved
all the essential points ...".

   In spite of his distortions of timing, this document contains some
interesting details of the research. He credited Edison with modifying
a pre-existing telegraph paper strip perforating machine in order to
perforate the celluloid. He also said they used a Geneva stop movement
with the first sprocket wheel to provide intermittence and that this was
later replaced with an intermittent device designed by Mr. Edison. He
stressed that the final format, an image one inch by three-quarters with
four perforations on either side was quickly adopted by rivals and
became a standard that was still being used.[964]

962 MoMA
Crawford, Dickson to
Crawford, 1
September 1930.

963 Ibid. Dickson to
Crawford, 15
October 1930.

964 Ibid. Dickson to
Crawford, 1
December 1930.

965 Ibid. Dickson to
Crawford, 31
December 1930. I
have not found a copy
of Crawford's letter
of 19 December 1930
but he apparently
called Dickson's
attention to the copy
of his letter of 2
September 1889
which was
reproduced in Terry
Ramsaye's *A Million
and One Nights*.

   Crawford replied quickly with questions, most of which involved
clarification of details such as the wiring to synchronize the phonograph
for projection (which Dickson had illustrated). One of Crawford's
comments caused Dickson to modify his claim that he was experimenting with Eastman's celluloid in 1888. Crawford apparently cited the
letter from Dickson acknowledging receipt of a roll from Eastman on
2 September 1889 as evidence that he had not used Eastman's film in
1888. Dickson protested that there was something wrong with the date,
but backed off from the claim he had seen a demonstration and gotten
samples in 1888. "If I was mistaken as to delivery of some film fr.
Eastman in 1888 – well, 1889 will do just as well. Anyway Eastman must
have delivered film *early* in 1889 for us to experiment & produce the
first Kinetoscope ...". This rare modification of his story was followed
by an unusual description of problems he encountered: "... I remember
so well tearing my hair over the first samples of Eastman film which
coating would frill or peel off during developement [sic] though we
used it for our experiments ...". He added that his complaints and
exhortations led to improvements in Eastman's films.[965]

There was a hiatus in their correspondence during 1931, caused by a period of severe personal problems bedeviling Crawford – unemployment, marital troubles and accompanying economic difficulties. Early in 1932 the correspondence resumed. Dickson was pleased to receive word of favorable mention in an article by Crawford and responded warmly, praising him and sending him samples of early films.[966]

By this time Dickson had become embittered about the reaction of the press to his letters and what he viewed as misuse of the information he provided to his correspondents. He was particularly annoyed with Terry Ramsaye who had assumed a place near William Gilmore on his roster of enemies. This is a harsh judgement since much of what Dickson told Ramsaye found its way into *A Million and One Nights*. But Dickson overlooked the positive elements. He was apparently annoyed by Ramsaye's speculation that the post Paris Expo test may not have been as perfect as Dickson claimed and he was probably unhappy with Ramsaye's sympathetic treatment of the Lathams and Gilmore. Ramsaye found Woodville Latham an interesting and romantic figure and wrote sympathetically of him. He did report that Dickson became disenchanted with the Lathams and returned the stock that the Lathams offered him, but he did not mention Dickson's claim that his involvement with the Lathams was an attempt to spy on a potential competitor. Ramsaye regarded Gilmore as a no-nonsense business manager and did not cast him in the villainous persona that would have satisfied Dickson.

For a time Dickson hoped that Crawford would be the person to present the authorized Dickson version. To encourage Crawford he wrote cordial letters, made annotated drawings and sent sample strips from films in his collection (usually misdated). This came to an abrupt halt in 1933 after Dickson read a manuscript which Crawford had sent Will Day contending that Edison should not be credited as the inventor of modern cinema. In it Crawford asserted that the 1889 demo for Edison was a failure; that it was made with a cylinder device because the strip machine was just being developed; and that it was Edison's visit to Marey's lab that convinced him that they should change to a strip device. For evidence Crawford cited Eugene Lauste's account of watching the demo from a hiding place and seeing Edison walk-out in disgust because the images were blurred and the film broke. Lauste claimed that after seeing Marey's camera, Edison sent Dickson a flurry of telegrams with detailed instructions to begin a similar device using strips of film and that because this was not completed the demo must have been done with a cylinder device.

This revelation was a severe blow to Dickson. He regarded it as a "betrayal" and it soured his relations with Lauste for the remaining months of their lives. He told Day "... [it] grieves me inexpressibly ..." and he accused Lauste of defaming him in order to gain recognition for his efforts to synchronize sound and for his work on the Latham Eidoloscope.[967] "I never though that after nearly ½ a century Lauste of

966 MoMA Crawford, Dickson to Crawford, 26 January 1932.

967 BiFi Fonds Will Day. Dickson to Day, 26 April 1933. Will Day showed Dickson a manuscript from Merritt Crawford that contained the statement.

all people should be the one to vilify me in order to gain ... notoriety of being the 1st and only Talkie ...".[968]

Angry and hurt, Dickson dashed off a hasty affidavit stating his claims, had it notarized and sent it to Will Day for inclusion in the history of cinema that Day hoped to publish. It contained the ritual statements that had become part of his lexicon: he began with Edison in 1881; the demonstration film was taken by his assistant William Heise and it was an "... entirely successful exhibition of the first synchroniza-tion of phonograph and Kinetograph". It was so hastily prepared that it included a slip of the sort that made Dickson's memory so "peculiar". Here he said the demonstration took place on 6 November 1889 when he intended to say 6 October. Dickson soon regretted his haste, but not because of the apparent errors. He asked Day to repress it and not include it in his book because he felt it implied that *all* of the work was done while Edison was absent in Europe.[969]

Smoothing ruffled feathers

"... its a bit late to smooth my much ruffled feathers ..." (Dickson to Will Day, 19 May 1933)

Crawford had ruffled Dickson's feathers, but he also put Dickson in contact with people who helped smooth them: the Historical Commit-tee of the Society of Motion Picture Engineers (S.M.P.E.) and through them, Will Day, the British film historian, sometime filmmaker and collector par excellence. The Historical Committee published Dick-son's account of the Kinetograph/Kinetoscope and Glen Mathews of the Committee introduced Dickson to Will Day who proved a very companionable friend. His relationship with Day served Dickson well during his final years.

Dickson learned that Eugene Lauste, Jean LeRoy and other pio-neers were made honorary members of the Society. He complained to Crawford that he had been ignored and, characteristically, grumbled that he suspected a conspiracy with Ramsaye as the responsible party. "I have ... satisfaction in knowing that my work was accepted by the whole world – yet I am left out of the Pioneer list of your Society ... perhaps purposely by T.R.'s influence ...".[970] Crawford apparently cued the Historical Committee.

Crawford and Ramsaye were journalist-historians, but most of the members of the Historical Committee were professionals with strong technical backgrounds. The Chairman was Carl Lewis Gregory, a veteran cinematographer, director and sometime studio executive. Among the members were John I. Crabtree, a prominent research chemist for Eastman and a past president of the Society; Glenn E. Mathews who also worked for Eastman; C. Francis Jenkins the film pioneer and a founding members of the Society and Earl Theisen who was Vice-Chairman. Theisen, who had a strong interest in film history,

968 Ibid, Dickson to Day, 8 May 1933.

969 Ibid, Dickson to Day, 6 May 1934. Day's book, *25,000 Years to Trap a Shadow* was never published. It exists in manuscript form in BiFi.

970 MoMA Crawford. Dickson to Crawford, 5 November 1932.

A street photographer took this photo of Dickson in the commercial area of Twickenham on 10 October 1931. [NMAH.]

971 The members of the Historical Committee of SMPE were C.L. Gregory, Chairman; W.E. Theisen, Vice Chairman; W. Clark, O.B. Depue, N.D. Golden, C.F. Jenkins, G.E. Matthews, O. Nelson and Terry Ramsaye (*Film Daily Yearbook 1933*). Crawford, who was going through a period of personal troubles, was no longer a member. The members of the Museum Committee were W.E. Theisen, Chairman; B.P. Depue, O.B. Depue, C.L. Gregory, C.F. Jenkins, F.H. Richardson, T. Ramsaye, A. Reeves, A.F. Victor.

972 *Film Daily Yearbook*, 1933, p. 637. By 1933 Crawford was no longer a member of the Historical Committee though he apparently was on the Committee when it first contacted Dickson. The seriousness of the members' inquiries is demonstrated by the questions they raised about a claim by C. Francis Jenkins that he projected films in Richmond, Indiana in June, 1894. Jenkins had produced a newspaper article to that effect but on examination it was evident that two articles had been pasted together to appear as one. Members of the committee, led by Earl Theisen, corresponded with a number of people in Richmond and concluded that the June, 1894 projection could not be verified.

left Consolidated Film Industries, one of the most prominent film laboratories, to head a project to gather equipment, documents and other memorabilia for an S.M.P.E. collection at the Los Angeles County Museum.[971] Crawford and Ramsaye were also members despite their conflicting view about the early years. Crabtree, Matthews and Theisen took a dim view of these partisan haggles and made a serious effort to sort out fact and fiction as they interviewed one pioneer after another – though not always with success.[972]

   In December 1931, Dickson was contacted almost simultaneously by Theisen and Crabtree. Theisen wrote from Los Angeles on behalf of the Museum Committee which he chaired and Crabtree wrote from New York on behalf of the Society. Dickson sent each of them a variation on the summary of his work that he had prepared for Crawford a year earlier. Consistent with previous claims, it said that Edison proposed a moving image device in 1886, that work began in 1887 and by 1888 the essential elements had been designed. He repeated the claims that in 1888 he attended a lecture describing Eastman's celluloid, immediately went to Rochester where he met George Eastman and received samples that were used in various tests with perforated cellu-

One of the last portraits of Dickson was taken in Jersey, C.I. in 1932. [NHMLA.]

Jenkins, who played a major role in establishing SMPE, was a member of the Committee and had been instrumental in launching the project to gather historic information so it was courageous to raise questions about his claims.

973 NHMLA, Dickson Collection, Dickson to Theisen, 1 January 1932; GU Ramsaye, Dickson to Crabtree, 15 January 1932.

loid and that these were made in 1888. Dickson urged Crabtree to check his claim with George Eastman.[973]

It was Theisen who accepted this suggestion and forwarded Dickson's document to Rochester. The response he received from Eastman's Vice President Frank W. Lovejoy was provocative. Lovejoy apologized for responding, explaining that Eastman's "... health is not such that he can go into this matter very carefully", and added that: "As far as he [Eastman] can recall, the statements made to you by Mr. Dickson are correct". This proved very fortunate for Dickson because a month later Eastman was dead, having taken his own life. Consequently, even though the Committee was carefully vetting the conflicting, often contradictory claims of the pioneers, they found it difficult to challenge Dickson's assertion that he contacted Eastman and received samples of celluloid in 1888. This gave Dickson's efforts to push the dates for Edison's experiments new acceptance – though it proved temporary. In an article published in February, 1933, Theisen wrote that Dickson received film from Eastman late in 1888 and that same month Merritt Crawford told *Film Daily* that Dickson had sent him a sample of 1889–91 film which he believed to be the earliest surviving piece of celluloid.[974]

Dickson's claims so impressed folks in Rochester that Kodak executive Oscar Solbert wrote the following June asking Dickson to elaborate on them. Dickson's response is a remarkable document in which his questionable dating is counterbalanced by vivid descriptions of the manufacture of celluloid and drawings that make it clear that had been in the manufacturing area at a very early point (see illustration on page 223). This document is the most graphic evidence that Dickson's story of rushing off to Rochester, meeting with George Eastman and working with Eastman's staff to improve film stock had a factual basis.[975]

Dickson's effort to gain recognition was successful. John Crabtree forwarded Dickson's communication to the S.M.P.E. President, Alfred Goldsmith, who recommended that it be published in the *Journal* – though the formal invitation came a year later. In May, 1933 Glenn E. Matthews wrote asking Dickson to add specifics about using collodion and gelatine bromide; short and long strips of celluloid; the various image sizes; details about perforations and sprockets; the name, location and date of the camera club meeting and details of his visits to Rochester. Matthews letter arrived at an inopportune moment. The "much ruffled" Mr. Dickson was dashing off a flurry of correspondence expressing his anger and frustration over the Crawford-Lauste affair. In fact, the invitation arrived about the time that the ill-conceived affidavit regarding the "first talkie" was notarized so, not surprisingly, Dickson's initial response was coyly cautious. He reiterated his customary tale that he gave Edison full credit while keeping in the shadows but, having said that, he said he would consider it. "... I don't feel very enthusiastic as I have never been recognized by your society while the world at large since 1888 & 9 ... benefit of my work to build up colossal fortunes. So let's leave it at that for the moment."[976]

The moment was quite short. Two weeks later, on 2 June, he told Matthews that he had started writing and the text was mailed on 14 June.[977]

Since Dickson had been writing accounts of his work for years and years, he was able to compose this, the most comprehensive description of his work, in about a month – still a surprisingly short period of time. He was well prepared since, as mentioned in his letter, Matthews' inquiries were based on a reading of the Dicksons' 1894–95 booklet which Dickson had been using as a starting point for most of his subsequent accounts. His memory was further stimulated by the flurry of queries he had received in recent years. He had been busy reviewing documents, scrapbooks, souvenirs and delving into that "peculiar"

974 NHMLA, Dickson. F.W. Lovejoy to E. Theisen, 15 February 1932; Phil M. Daily, "Along the Rialto" in *Film Daily*, 17 February 1933, p. 7 and Theisen, *International Photographer*, February 1933, p. 6. This last article is mentioned in a letter that Matthews wrote to Will Day, 3 May 1933 discussing the earliest uses of celluloid in photographing motion (BiFi Fonds Will Day). Crawford did not identify the subject of the sample that Dickson sent him, but during this period Dickson sent samples from several early films to Theisen, Crawford and Will Day. They were cut from strips of Blacksmith scene (1893); Sandow (1894) and Carmencita (1894). None were made earlier than 1893.

975 NMAH Hendricks. Dickson to Solbert 10 December 1932. Oscar N. Solbert, who once planned to co-write a biography of George Eastman with Frank Lovejoy, was the first Director of the George Eastman House.

976 NMAH Hendricks & BiFi Fonds Will Day. Matthews letter was dated 4 May 1933 and the request was made on behalf of Terry Ramsaye and himself. Dickson sent Will Day a draft of his affidavit on 10 May 1933 and the signed and notarized version on 15 May 1933. He mentioned Matthews' memory. This made it possible to augment the customary litany with details seldom found in other accounts.

Glenn E. Matthews proved an astute monitor. Before contacting Dickson with the offer he sought background information about him from Will Day and Harry Marvin – and, presumably, others. After receiving Dickson's text he reviewed it thoughtfully and his judicious inquiries were calculated to identify misstatements and make the text more accurate. This was not easy. Dickson was stubbornly dogmatic and he had spun his tale so long and so often that his "peculiar" memory had transformed problematic elements into reality. And, with feathers still ruffled from the Crawford-Lauste affair, he was especially sensitive about treatment by outsiders. Soon after mailing the text, Dickson sent an emphatic request that it be published "... in toto & as signed by me and *my responsability* [sic] ... so often have I suffered from an Editor's 'Views'". He repeated this plea a few days later. Matthews assured him that they would edit it with care but made no commitment to publishing without change. In the interest of space and economy they eliminated some biographical information and the text of W.E. Woodbury's testimonial from the *American Annual of Photography, 1894*.

Dickson accepted these changes, but balked at several questions that Matthews raised about dates. Dickson agreed to change the claim that Edison proposed experiments as early as 1886 "... it was only one of my daily *talks* with Edison and nothing came out of it until the following year ... when I started some of these experiments".[978] Matthews also raised pointed questions about the dates when Dickson had contacted Eastman. Matthews and Crabtree were in a position to examine company documents and a letter that Matthews wrote to Will Day in May 1933, about the introduction and availability of celluloid, shows that Matthews had researched the subject carefully.[979] He knew that Eastman's effort to produce celluloid roll film was in the experimental stage in late 1888, that it had not advanced to the point where he was willing to make public announcements of the product until late spring – early summer of 1889 and that it was not available to consumers until the fall. Matthews pointed this out to Dickson, stressing that the demonstrations at film societies took place during the summer of 1889. Put on the defensive, Dickson responded with passion. He could not give the specific day in 1888 when he learned of Eastman's experiments, but the talk was an unscheduled one on another topic – perhaps developing photos in daylight – and only lasted ten minutes and Eastman's representative gave him a small sample when he learned that he worked for Edison. Dickson said he was in Rochester two days later, the first of a number of trips. He stressed that this was all sub rosa.[980]

In the letter cited above, Matthews told Will Day that he believed that Dickson was the first to use Eastman's film and that "... Apparently he was in touch with the Kodak Company for some months before the commercial product was first announced (June 1889)". He reviewed Dickson's letter with Crabtree and they accepted Dickson's statement and changed the final version to: "Towards the close of the year 1888

letter in a letter to Will Day dated 19 May 1933 and his reply to Matthews was written on the 20th.

977 NMAH Hendricks. Dickson to Matthews, 20 May 1933 & 2 June 1933.

978 Ibid. Dickson to Matthews, 16 August 1933 replying to Matthews letter of 7 August 1933.

979 BiFi Fonds Will Day. Matthews to Day, 3 May 1933.

980 NMAH Hendricks. Dickson to Matthews, 16 August 1933.

it was rumored that the Eastman Company was experimenting ...". They also accepted 1892 as the date that the Black Maria was built. Dickson was pleased and these statements went into the public record.[981]

Dickson's pleasure was increased in October when he received a letter informing him that he was made an honorary member of the Society of Motion Picture Engineers. By this time the feathers were considerably smoothed.

Final days

Dickson's article appeared in the December 1933 issue of the Society's *Journal*. By the time the article was published, the Dicksons had moved back to Twickenham, ending a stay of nearly five years in the Isle of Jersey. During that time he had modified his name to Laurie-Dickson, a form he used for the remaining year and a half of his life. The publication of his story of the invention concluded the stream of correspondence from journalists and would-be historians. The honor bestowed by SMPE gave him great satisfaction and he added "Hon. Me. S.M.P.E." to his letterhead. His correspondence with Earl Theisen resulted in a movement to reconstruct the Black Maria as a historical structure.[982] He returned to Twickenham in a much mellower mood. As he addressed his annual Christmas greetings, he sent a conciliatory note to Merritt Crawford:

"While sorting old letters I came across some of yours – & kept them – feeling that perhaps as time went on you would see things in their true light & so renew a friendship well begun -

"Anyway – life is too short for misunderstandings, especially in my case when but a few years are left me – so am writing to wish you well for this 1934."[983]

Dickson received a cordial response from Crawford which he forwarded to Will Day saying he was glad to receive it though he continued to blame Eugene Lauste for getting Crawford "off the track". So Dickson was at last at peace with the film community – though the controversies had not ended.

His relationship with Will Day remained amiable. Their correspondence probed matters in greater depth than any of the other correspondents He offered Day exclusive access to his material and even offered to decline the invitation from SMPE in order to give Day priority to his version of his role. But since Matthews and Theisen were helping Day collect information for his own publication, he encouraged Dickson to go ahead. The drawings that Dickson supplied for the SMPE were duplicates of ones he had prepared for Day. Dickson was sure that the book that Day planned to publish would set his story straight, but there was an unresolved problem: Day was William Friese-Greene's most vocal and persistent champion. Although they generally avoided arguments and Dickson respected Day too much to press too hard, the discord festered and occasionally emerged:

981 Ibid. Matthews to Dickson, 15 September 1933 & Dickson to Matthews, 2 October 1933.

982 AMPAS Theisen. Dickson to Theisen, 6 April 1933; Theisen to Dickson, 9 June 1933; Dickson to Theisen, 5 July 1933. In April Dickson complained that the Black Maria had been destroyed by his successor and should be rebuilt for "Historical reasons." Theisen apparently agreed because in July Dickson sent him drawings of the exterior and interior with dimensions as well as he could remember. Nothing came of this immediately, but in the 1950s the Thomas Alva Edison Foundation paid for building a reconstructed version which is now a featured attraction on the grounds of the Edison Historic Site in West Orange, New Jersey.

983 MoMA Crawford. Dickson to Crawford, January 1934.

"Since I got back home [insert: from] Jersey I have been considerably exercised in mind over your giving Friese Green [sic] the credit of being the 'Father of moving photography', which I cannot but help believe you will (I hope) take a more modified view of the case after a further study of actual facts as I have disinterestedly tried to show you that Mr. Edison, & not anyone else should be the one to be known *unreservedly* as the 'Father of Moving photography' as created by him between 1888 – 1889 in a practical camera for taking & projecting a rigidly [insert: held] perforated film which he gave to [insert: the] world from that time to this without any practical alteration – why therefore did not someone even Friese Green [sic[bring out a better machine in all these years, a simple commercial apparatus, in competition to Edisons [sic] system – why? Because they were not ready to do this – I his assistant who carried out this work for Mr Edison feel that I can verify each & every detail of this creation as fully stated elsewhere & that Friese Green [sic] did not have such an apparatus as produced in 1888 – 1889 but was able to get his patent of June 1 1889 as an *Anticipatory* patent not actually based on a Working Model – but on what he *intended* to do – Sentiment of friendship should not enter into this question – ...".[984]

984 BiFi Fonds Will Day. Dickson to Day, [no month or day] 1935.

985 BiFi Fonds Will Day. Dickson was Vice President of the Society.

986 BiFi Fonds Will Day. *Reynolds's Illustrated News*, 7 October 1934, "Shining Movie Lights Were Not All American /Protest to Premier About a Talkie"; *The Richmond and Twickenham Times* Sat., 6 October 1934 "Edison's First Talkie /Twickenham Man's Part in Far reaching Invention ' Disclosed in a Film"; *Richmond Times* 13 October 1934, "The First Film. *Reynolds's* said Will Day had written the Prime Minister protesting that the film did not mention Friese-Greene or that Dickson was English. Day apparently overlooked that Blackton was born in Sheffield, England though it credited Blackton's partners Pop Rock and Wainwright with founding Vitagraph.

But a lecture that Dickson gave shortly before moving from Jersey to Twickenham shows his respect for Day. Dickson described "The Birth of the Cinematograph" at the opening of the winter session of the Jersey Guild of Science, Arts and Crafts. His lecture, which he illustrated with slides, borrowed from Day's proposed book *25,000 Years to Trap a Shadow* by tracing the origins of the motion picture back to cave drawings and paying tribute to the pioneer work of Muybridge, Le Prince and Marey.[985]

While the queries from correspondents quieted, the controversy over origins erupted one final time. In the fall of 1934 a short film, "Cavalcade of the Movies", was shown at the Luxor theatre in Twickenham. The film, produced by film pioneer J. Stuart Blackton, included a dramatic restaging of Dickson's "first talkie" demonstration for Edison. Because it was dedicated to Edison and made no mention of Friese-Greene the film raised a heated controversy in the U.K. *Reynolds's Illustrated News*, proclaimed that "British film pioneers are indignant. An American talkie called 'Cavalcade of the Movies' takes all the credit for the motion picture. The Prime Minister has been appealed to in the hope that it may be withdrawn or amended ... With all the 'Hail, Columbia', blare of brass at its command, it claims for the United States all the stars, and all the stripes awarded to world cinematography." In addition they complained that the movie did not mention that Dickson was English. When the local papers interviewed Dickson he persisted in crediting Edison, and when asked aboutt he controversy: "'Rubbish!' was his laconic comment."[986]

This was the last time he saw his work recognized by the press.

In recent months his health had been declining and this probably caused the Dicksons to return to Twickenham. He died 28 September 1935 at his home on Montpelier Row. The cause recorded was cancer of the colon and there was no indication of the duration of the illness but, he referred to health problems in several letters written from Jersey, which indicates that his illness lingered over a fairly long period.

However, these mentions were brief and in photos taken in the early 1930s he appears spry, fit and as dapper as ever – if a bit greyer.[987]

He was buried in Twickenham Cemetery and the local papers eulogized him as a "Friend of Edison". They credited him with pioneer work on movies and the "Edison effect", a predecessor to the radio. The obit that *Variety* published would have really ruffled his feathers! They credited him with using 35mm film with four perfs per frame, but said he experimented with various bases without success until he learned that Europeans were using film made by Blair and that the experiments were started when Edison gave Dickson the viewing box and camera that he received from E.J. Marey, of Paris. The article credited Lauste with being the mechanic and stated that Lauste left Dickson to work with the Lathams because he was dissatisfied with Dickson's peep show and Dickson's experiments. It concluded: "Dickson did an immense amount of experimenting but his only creative contribution to the pictures was the kinetescope [sic] viewing device". Glenn Matthews memorial article in the *S.M.P.E. Journal* was much kinder. It used much of the material from Dickson's article and concluded: "... we have lost a distinguished colleague whose contributions to the birth of motion pictures were real and lasting".[988]

His final legacy is quite sad. He was survived by his widow, Helen and his step-son, John Forbes Laurie-Dickson and they did not fare well after his death. Helen moved into a smaller house a block from Montpelier House but she lived only three years more, dying there in August 1938. She was buried with her husband. John Forbes Laurie-Dickson had a brief career in aviation and joined the RAF after the outbreak of World War II. In the early summer of 1941 he was reported missing and presumed dead on a mission over France. His death left a void in the record. He was survived by Pauline Ruth Montieth who he married early in 1936, but the family record ends there. John would have inherited Dickson's surviving papers, photographs and drawings, but except for the small collection of glass plate negatives that Gordon Hendricks obtained from a former neighbor on Montpellier Row nothing more has turned up. It would be nice to know that some family survived to maintain his legacy.

987 LACMNH, Dickson & BiFi Fonds Will Day. Dickson mentioned being "laid up" in a letter to Earl Theisen, 28 February 1932 and again in a letter Dickson to Will Day, 5 February 1933.

988 NMAH Hendricks. *Thames Valley Times*, 2 October 1935; *The Richmond and Twickenham Times*, 5 October 1935; *Variety*, 9 October 1935; *Journal of the S.M.P.E.*, Vol. 26, No. 3, March 1936, pp. 279–281.

Chapter 34

The Grandad of Us All

In 1995 Dickson joined Mickey Mouse, Audrey Hepburn, Humphrey Bogart and other figures from the movie world who have been recognized by the U.S. Postal Service with a stamp honoring their work. His stamp was in a series honoring pioneer inventors from the 19th century: Ottomar Mergenthaler for linotype, Frederick E. Ives for the half-tone process and Eadweard Muybridge for photography. They were appropriate companions who also contributed to the revolution of communication that took place at the end of the 19th century. Although Dickson would have been delighted at the recognition, his pleasure would have been dampened by finding that the Post Office recorded his name as William Dickson, the form that he never used. It was an insignificant error but it would have loomed large in his eyes. It exemplifies the mix of information and misinformation that has surrounded his career.

Dickson was flattered but disturbed by the journalists and historians who beleaguered him during his retirement. He was happy they recognized his significance as a pioneer but he was troubled by their skepticism about his accounts. This mixture of respect and uncertainty persists today. The modest recognition he enjoyed during his life faded rather quickly and even though his name was, and is, familiar to those interested in cinema's early years, the general public knows little or nothing about his work. The scholarly community remembers him primarily for his uncredited work for Edison and his partnership with the founders of the Mutoscope company. His seminal work in establishing commercial film production has been largely overlooked and even when he is recognized as a filmmaker, more often than not it is as a "cameraman" rather than "director" or "producer", the modern terms that describe his work most accurately.

The flurry of interest in the early years that consumed so much of Mr. D's last years was short lived. Through much of the twentieth century serious scholarship was directed primarily towards narrative cinema and often with emphasis on national contributors. The films that seemed to represent cinema at its best were produced after the first World War and movies made in the decades prior to the war seemed but a quaint antecedent. The early years were often given only brief

In 1995 Dickson was honored by the U.S. Post Office with this commemorative stamp. He would have been pleased by the honor and the distinguished company but dismayed that he was called William Dickson. [U.S. Post Office.]

recognition with particular attention given to work that seemed to anticipate the more sophisticated achievements of classic cinema. Images projected on a screen were and are the accepted standard, so the early years seemed to begin with the first public exhibition of the Lumières' Cinématographe at the Salon Indien on 28 December 1895. Edison – and his assistant – seemed to be a preliminary curiosity.

The emergence of a new generation of scholars has renewed interest this early period. The emphasis on personality and nationalism that was prominent during much of the twentieth century seems less relevant and, while not a consensus, there is sentiment that cinema developed through the efforts and contributions of many individuals; that it is misleading to assign credit to a single person – or country. In this view, it was the contributions of various pioneers that created cinema and that it was international rather than national in scope.

The evidence supports this perspective. The presence of more than one name on many early patents demonstrates that no individual had a lock on the creative process. Friese-Greene worked with Mortimer Evans and before him, J.A.R. Rudge; Robert Paul turned to Birt Acres for help in designing a camera; Wordsworth Donisthorpe received assistance from W.C. Crofts; the Lathams had Eugene Lauste; C. Francis Jenkins partnered with Thomas Armat; even the renowned Étienne-Jules Marey employed Georges Demenÿ and, of course, Edison had W.K.L. Dickson – and Dickson had Charles Brown and William Heise as assistants. While the contributions of these associates varied considerably, the existence of so many secondary figures shows that the complicated mechanisms of cameras and projectors and their interaction with photo chemistry required a blend of minds and experience to create workable devices. It is no co-incidence that the most commercially successful of the earliest film companies were Edison and Lumière who had the most sophisticated technical, economic and personnel resources at their disposal.

At first glance Edison might seem to fit this pattern less comfortably than his competitors. He is often thought of as a proto-typical do-it-yourself American. He reveled in his role as "the Wizard" and the concomitant image of the self-made independent who created wonders through persistence and the sweat of his brow. But, while persistence and sweat were factors, planning, adequate staff and proper resources were essential to make his system of invention work. He relied on proper materials, up-to-date machines, and, most importantly, skilled associates who were well trained and fully informed about their specialities. By the late 19th century, when industrialization had transformed Europe and North America, it was essential to think internationally and Edison surrounded himself with talent from North America and Western Europe. There were chemists, electricians, engineers, machinists, carpenters, blacksmiths and the laborers he liked to call "muckers". The stock room was filled with necessary and exotic materials and the library was stocked with the journals and books essential to support his diverse activities. It was a cosmopolitan workplace with a cosmopolitan outlook; information and inspiration came from anywhere and everywhere. Dickson was not the only expert capable of reading technical articles in French, German or Italian.

Critics, most notably Gordon Hendricks, have charged Edison with taking credit for Dickson's work on the Kinetograph and Kinetoscope. This is misleading. Dickson was an employee and Edison not only initiated the project, he provided Dickson with resources to carry out the experiments. Dickson was responsible for the photographic aspects – that was his particular skill – but expert machinists were at hand to resolve mechanical issues. Machinists Charles Brown and William Heise were assigned to work with him; and John Ott, Edison's trusted precision specialist, and Fred Ott, John's very experienced brother, made major contributions to the project. In fact, John Ott was in charge of the construction of the commercial version of the Kinetoscope and should probably receive some credit for the final design. As for Edison, while he was not at Dickson's side day and night – he was at the ore separating plant in Ogden much of the time – he monitored the experiments and it was Dickson's responsibility to keep him abreast of progress through regular reports and occasional demonstrations.

W.K.L. Dickson fits comfortably into today's more international and cosmopolitan consideration of cinema's early years. He possessed an unusual blend of talent, skill and experience. His background was multi-national, he worked internationally and his career had cross-cultural impact. In all aspects of his work, as experimenter, planner-designer, filmmaker – and author – he benefitted from and valued the work of associates who assisted and augmented his own skills and talents.

The cooperative team work that Edison encouraged at his lab suited Dickson. He adapted it for filmmaking, used it in his business ventures and his own laboratory. His ability to work with others, train them, use their talents and launch their independent careers is one of his outstanding accomplishments.

Dickson, inventor

Although various members of Edison's staff made contributions, there are components of the Kinetograph and Kinetoscope that were clearly Dickson's domain. He contributed to the mechanics, but the extent of his involvement with them cannot be measured. The photographic elements were his responsibility and specific contribution: the film, its size, shape, durability, clarity and speed; the lenses for the camera and viewer; methods for preparing the film, then developing and duplicating it; and the studios with their essentially simple but effective systems of illumination.

What he invented for Edison was a system and Dickson borrowed elements from various sources to make it work. The negative-positive processing came from still photography; he adapted the methods used by Eastman Kodak for producing film stock as well as developing and printing film; and plans for photo studios were found in books and magazines. But these were models and they had to be modified to be effective. His modifications produced something new: a method for film production consisting of all the essential elements. It worked and it was a remarkable accomplishment. He took this system, with modifications, to the American Mutoscope Co., then replicated and refined it for the company's offshoots in England, France and Germany. There are no studies to determine how influential his methods were, but he created the first American production facilities and they dominated production in the U.S. in the pre-World War I era. His influence on European production is less direct but his studios and production teams functioned very early. The Lumières' Cinématographe, a combination camera-projector, has been revered as the originator of modern cinema, but the huge commercial industry that followed chose to use 35mm film and a separate camera and projector, the system originated by W.K.L. Dickson.[989]

Dickson's most tangible – and lasting – contribution is the film format; known today as 35mm. It was devised to increase the size of the image to a width of one inch and height of three quarters of an inch. It was steadied by perforations on each side, four for each frame. This format is still used by the theatrical motion picture industry, though digital systems are beginning to displace it in some theaters. It never occurred to Edison that it could be patented or commercially restricted (until it was too late) and the film manufacturers who adopted it, Kodak

989 The Cinématographe was a compact unit that served as camera, projector and, occasionally, as a printing machine and while it was an undeniably ingenious design that was widely admired, it never became an industry standard. By 1897 Lumière's films were being offered in Edison's format and soon after the Cinématographe faded and machines using Edison's format grew more and more common.

and Blair, had no exclusive claim to it. Without patents, the eager innovators entering the industry were free to use it and it was adopted so widely that it soon became an industry standard. The availability of films with consistent width, frame size and uniform perforations made the rapid dissemination of movies possible. People, young and old, rich and poor, literate and illiterate in villages, towns and cities throughout the world benefitted from Dickson's invention. Other formats have come and gone, but Dickson's 35mm format has survived.

The importance of this stable, uniform format cannot be exaggerated. It has been the foundation of the commercial movie industry. The phonograph and television industries, film's media cousins, have been plagued by a succession of confusing and conflicting formats that have flummoxed professionals and consumers alike. Video engineers have had to deal with more than a dozen incompatible tape formats during the past forty years and consumers have had to switch from Beta to VHS to DVD. Expensive machines have been scrapped, disks and tapes transferred from format to format. This is in sharp contrast with the consistent technology that the movie industry has enjoyed for more than a hundred years. Although sound tracks have been added, the shape of the perforations modified and the size and shape of the image changed, the width of the strip and number of perforations have remained essentially the same. A film made fifty, seventy or even a hundred years ago can be shown or reproduced with comparative ease. In fact, films that Dickson made in 1893 and 1894 have been reproduced on modern motion picture copying machines though some allowance was made for changes in the shape of the perforation and the shrinkage of the film.

Other picture machines: The Lathams' Eidoloscope

Edison and Gilmore did not believe Dickson's claim that his nocturnal visits to the Lathams were simply to monitor what a competitor was doing. So, if Edison believed that Dickson had something to do with designing the Latham's camera and projector, what are we to believe? Despite plentiful testimony and reams of documentation, the record is inconclusive and we are forced to speculate. There has been conjecture that Dickson was the primary designer and the frequency of his visits and the extent of time involved – several months – plus his familiarity with the technology would seem to support this notion.

As with the Kinetograph, Dickson may not have had to contribute much to the mechanics, but the Lathams and their assistant, Eugene Lauste would have valued Dickson's advice on other matters. His experience in selecting film and lenses, designing equipment for preparing and processing films, setting-up and staging productions and preparing film for exhibition would have been invaluable. It would have been surprising indeed if the Lathams did not turn to him for advice on these critical components.

The controversies that surrounded the Latham's camera and projector have clouded the story and remain unsettled. Both the Lathams and Dickson denied that he made any substantial contribution to either device. The truth may never be known, but the suspicion that he was more than a casual bystander persists and will persist.

Other picture machines: KMCD's Mutoscope, Mutograph and Biograph

While his controversial involvement with the Lathams ended his career at Edison's lab, it was probably Dickson's alliance with his KMCD friends that made Edison regard him as a double crosser. His involvement with Elias B. Koopman, Harry Marvin and Herman Casler dated back to 1893 when they fashioned and marketed the Photoret camera. This was a seemingly harmless beginning and Edison even gave the camera his endorsement,[990] but by 1896 the informal alliance had evolved into Edison's most challenging rival in the movie business. The American Mutoscope Company was founded on the patents the group produced, primarily those for the Mutoscope (peep show machine), Mutograph (camera) and Biograph (projector). The key patents were in Casler's name, but it was the involvement of W.K.L. Dickson that attracted serious investors. His reputation as a specialist in moving images was the company's most recognizable asset and the company's investors probably assumed that Dickson played an uncredited role.

Dickson's involvement with KMCD was quite different from his relations with the Lathams. The partnership was based on friendship and a shared enthusiasm for novelty and innovation. Movies were only one of the group's interests, but the movie machines were the most successful of their innovations. They were designed to avoid conflict with Edison's patents – almost certainly with advice from Dickson. He claimed credit for the idea behind the Mutoscope – and, implied he had much to do with its design, but willingly gave credit to Casler. Dickson respected Casler as a skilled machinist and an excellent designer, but once again, Dickson's knowledge and experience with film, lenses, exposure rates and other details related to photography would have been essential to making their devices functional. Their choice of a film that was even larger than competitors is a clue that Dickson anonymously influenced the design. The resulting reputation the Biograph gained for an image reputed to be most exciting of the Victorian era seems to justify Dickson's faith in large format film.

The W.K.L. Dickson laboratory

It would be pleasing to credit Dickson's laboratory with major achievements, but the best that can be said is that it functioned successfully for about a dozen of years. New patents were registered, but none could be described as a major innovation. Eugene Lauste's experiment with recording sound on film was innovative and promising but while Dickson supported Lauste by allowing use of the facilities, he could not raise the funds to sustain Lauste's experiments. Lauste was unable to

[990] Edison wrote a letter endorsing the Photoret on 2 January 1894. Gordon Hendricks copied Herman Casler's son, Roger Casler's copy of the letter.

maintain his efforts on his own and they came to a dead end. This may typify an inability to push projects through to completion that seems to characterize Dickson's business and managerial style.

Improving film

If the 35mm format is Dickson's most lasting contribution to cinema, improving the quality of early film deserves equal recognition. Before Eastman introduced his strips of celluloid in 1889, there was no photographic material suitable for recording more than a limited number of images of motion. Eastman's celluloid held promise but, as Dickson quickly discovered, the strips had their own limits. From 1889 until 1894 it was Dickson's effort to overcome these problems and adapt the film for rapid exposure that dominated his experiments. The problems were multiple: emulsion peeled off the base, there were cracks and tears; images were spoiled by graininess, spots and lightning bolt-like defects in the corners; some emulsions were too slow for registration. As soon as one problem was solved, another cropped up, keeping him in constant contact with Rochester.

Eastman's celluloid was designed for his point and shoot Kodak camera. It was sold pre-loaded in the camera and after exposure the customer sent the camera to Rochester for developing and printing. The camera was returned with a new load of film. The system eliminated the mysteries of photo-chemistry and put photography in the hands of the uninitiated. The film only had to be strong enough to be rolled a few inches from one exposure to another and while the exposure had to be rapid enough for a "snap shot", it was not designed to take 40 images in one second.

Pinpointing Dickson's contribution to the improving Eastman's film is difficult, but he left an ample record of his efforts. In his correspondence he hounded Eastman for film "fast" enough to take clear images and strong enough to withstand the force of stopping and starting rapidly. Words like "tough", "leathery" and "clear" and complaints about excessive grain, brittleness, peeling emulsion and frilling made his requirements clear in letter after letter. His demands were vigorous, but he had established credibility with Eastman's staff who took his demands seriously. In 1896 when Eastman began offering "Ciné" film the specifications the company announced reflected the criteria that Dickson set-out in the early '90s. Eastman built a dominant position in the photo world on a reputation for quality and reliability and there's little question that W.K.L. Dickson contributed to his success.

Dickson's involvement with celluloid had unanticipated consequences affecting still photography, film exhibition, television and computers. Although unintended, the 35mm width became a standard in still photography. Dickson did not invent the 35mm still camera, but after film manufacturers adopted Edison's gauge for "ciné" use. It was subsequently adapted for still photography.[991] The landscape image chosen by Dickson in 1891 became the standard projected image the

991 The orientation and perforations of 35mm still photo film differs from motion picture film, but the width of the film and use of perforations can be traced back to Dickson's design for Edison. Ironically, Dickson was never satisfied with 35mm and not only recommended larger formats for the Lathams and the Mutoscope Company, but seems to have abandoned film work about the time that his company changed from the large format to 35mm.

movie industry used for many years (again, with some modifications). Later it was borrowed by television for the cathode ray tube and then showed up as the screen for computers. As with Dickson's other innovations, precedent for the shape of the picture can be found in still photography, but it was the image used by Edison's films of 1893–1894 that influenced the industry that followed.

Film production

In Dickson's view, film production was a temporary activity and when the time was right he abandoned it, but the hundreds of films he produced during cinema's introductory years were enjoyed by thousands of viewers and set standards that had global impact. Given his own disregard for this secondary career, it is not surprising that there has been little recognition of his pioneer efforts, yet his credentials match or exceed those of any of his contemporaries. He established production for the two companies that dominated the early years of American film production; set up similar units in England, France and Germany and trained camera operators and production supervisors on two continents. The hundreds of films he produced in the final years of the 19th century were widely admired and frequently imitated. As the only available models, his first productions for Edison were a touchstone for those who followed. The quality of his post-Edison productions made the Biograph the most respected and popular screen presentation of its day.

The first movies were not as primitive and naive as some have assumed and they were not made for a "primitive" audience – at least, not as produced by W.K.L. Dickson. He was a skilled photographer with an artist's eye for composition, lighting and presentation. His films were made with care and discrimination. His studio, the Black Maria was designed to present a properly lighted subject, in focus and with action that was clearly visible and comprehensible. Viewers saw well known, popular personalities from the variety stage, circus and athletic worlds and, while curiosity was the initial attraction, it was content and interest rather than sensation that lured viewers back.

Enticing spectators to return became Dickson's task and he was good at it. He had experimented to reproduce movement and showing movement was basic to his filmmaking. He produced movies that moved – exemplars for the action movies that became a Hollywood staple. But action was a means rather than an end. The finished product had to have quality and interest.

Filming and post-production work required a team and Dickson trained a succession of assistants in the essentials of photography and staging productions. The ability of his assistants to work independently and produce memorable films after he moved on is evidence of his skill at identifying and training his heirs. His best known pupil, Billy Bitzer called him "my idol".[992] It would be an exaggeration to call Griffith his heir, but the man usually credited with creating modern American cinema inherited a system that had been in place for more than a decade,

992 Bitzer *Billy Bitzer, His Story*, p. 10.

and two cameramen, Bitzer and Arthur Marvin, who learned the trade in Mr. D's school.

Living, filming and writing history

The Dicksons were an energetic family with a boundless need to express themselves creatively. Music and drawing were their main outlets, but writing was also important. The Dicksons' biography of Edison was an early contribution to what has become a crowded field. It was a challenging project requiring co-ordination with Edison and his staff and after-hour work by W.K.L.D. Antonia did most of the writing while Laurie provided technical details and photographs. Their book has been overshadowed by more modern and professional historical works. Antonia's flowery prose, obscure classical metaphors and unabashedly worshipful tone make it unpalatable to modern readers, but the Dicksons' biography has an air of immediacy similar to the later memoirs of fellow workers like Francis Jehl, Frank Dyer and Al Tate.

Their account of Edison's work generated an important by-product: the dozens of photos that documented machines, research areas, experiments and people at work. Edison was photographed in the lab, at home and with his family. Dickson sought out and copied earlier photographs, among them portraits of Edison's father and mother, Edison at ages four and fourteen, his home in Milan and pages from the newspaper that Edison published and sold on the Grand Trunk Railroad. To provide the Dicksons with source material Edison's staff searched, compiled and saved an important historical record of Edison's work. The Dickson's may not have initiated the practice of record keeping that has made the lab's records so valuable, but their use of the documents emphasized their importance.

The several articles the Dicksons wrote during 1893, 1894 and 1895 are some of the earliest records of the creation and introduction of moving pictures. Mr. Dickson supplemented this by recording his activities during the Boer War, and his 1933 article for the *Journal of the S.M.P.E.* is a useful and professional summary of his work for Edison. Altogether these writings provide an invaluable record of the early years. As with other personal records, they must be studied carefully and checked against supporting documentation. Mr. D's pride, bravura and predilection to exaggerate dates sometimes obscures the valuable first-hand information that he has passed on to us.

The Biograph in Battle is an unique document detailing the early efforts to record the realities of warfare and bring them to the public. It is not the only account of early film work, but it is one of the longest and most detailed. Dickson and his associates in the Mutoscope companies understood that cinema was a new field of journalism and they were proud of their role in gathering and presenting visual news. They called it "Living history". Dickson's cameras "Biographed" the people and events that were changing and molding a new world. His still and moving images documented visiting emissaries, military leaders, royalty, presidents, ship launchings, modes of transport, sporting events,

races, armaments and new technology as well as scenes of more worka-
day interest. Dickson and his associates also knew that these images had
long term cultural value – that they were creating a record for historians.
A brochure for the British Mutoscope company declared that the
Mutoscope presented "a Mirror of Life" reproducing "the *Events* of the
Year, the *Doings* of *Yesterday* & *To-day*, *Moving*, Living *History*".[993] Dickson shared a hope expressed by Edison that the camera would produce
a record that would enlighten viewers and provide future generations
with a visual record of times gone by. Commercial success was a major
objective, but concern about how history would benefit from his work
was equally important. His faith in the long term value of moving
images has been justified.

The crown and flower of nineteenth century magic

W.K.L. Dickson's career was paradoxical. He lived during the transition
from the Victorian era to the twentieth century; from a world that
seemed sedate and conservative to the age of speed and rapid change;
from propriety and formality to liberty and informality. His role was as
a facilitator of change, but through it all he remained a Victorian
gentleman, proud of his family, his heritage and a staunch supporter of
Queen and Empire. But despite having a foot in each era he seemed
comfortable with the posture. He gave the movie industry a major
impetus, but withdrew from it as the new century dawned. He seemed
to sense that it would develop in ways foreign to his heritage. Nevertheless, he understood that moving pictures would alter the world in
unexpected ways. He was, in fact, a visionary. In words written with his
sister Antonia, they predicted an unlimited future for the Kinetograph:

"Ask ... from what conceivable phase of the future it can be debarred. In the
promotion of business interests, in the advancement of science, in the
revelation of unguessed worlds, in its educational and re-creative powers,
and in its ability to immortalize our fleeting but beloved associations, the
Kinetograph stands foremost among the creations of modern inventive
genius. It is the crown and flower of nineteenth-century magic ...".[994]

I have called him "the man who made movies" and he was, of
course, not *THE* man who made movies. He was part of a legion of
pioneers whose efforts combined to bring movies to audiences across
the globe and created what can now be regarded as the modern world's
new art form. But he stands out from that crowd. During the formative
years of the movies he influenced almost every aspect of the industry.
Few, if any, other filmmakers then, or now, designed cameras and used
them themselves; and even fewer also designed studios, laboratories,
trained operators, coaxed performances from dancers, boxers, acrobats
and actors; cajoled politicians, military figures and rulers to pose for
posterity; amused audiences with comedies and thrilled them with
speeding trains and views of popular public figures. Billy Bitzer summarized his career well: "he was the granddad of us all".[995]

993 *The Age of Movement* ([London, The International Mutoscope Syndicate, 1902?]), back cover. Fanciful names extracted from Greek and Latin were intended to impress the public and were widely used by developers of moving image systems: *bios* = life; *graphos/graphein* = to write; *skopion/skopein* = to see . The origin of "Muto" is less clear.

994 W.K.L. & A. Dickson, *History of the Kinetograph ...*, p. 52. This paragraph is the conclusion of the Dickson's pamphlet.

995 Bitzer, *Billy Bitzer, His Story*, p. 10.

Bibliography

Collections:

Academy of Motion Picture Arts & Sciences, Beverley Hills, California, Margaret Herrick Library: Earl Theisen Papers; Charles Clark Papers; Kemp Niver Papers

Adams County (Pennsylvania) Public Library, Gettysburg, Pennsylvania: Reference and general collections

British Film Institute, London, National Film & Television Archive: Shultze Collection & Biograph films preserved by Nederlands Filmmuseum

British Library, Colindale: Newspaper & Periodicals Collection

British Library, St. Pancras: Business & Intellectual Property Centre; Science & Technology

Canal Town Museum, Canastota, New York

La Cinémathèque française, La Bibliothèque du film: Fonds Will Day, La collection des appareils

Edison National Historic Site (U.S. Department of the Interior, National Park Service), West Orange, NJ: Thomas Edison Papers. Also used: Thomas Edison Papers edited by Rutgers University on microfilm and online

Franklin Institute, Philadelphia, Pennsylvania: C. Francis Jenkins Collection

General Registry Office, St. Catherine's House, London

George Eastman House, Film Archive & Library, Rochester, NY: George Eastman Papers & Eastman Kodak Corporate Records

Georgetown University Library, Lauinger Library, Washington, DC: Thomas Armat Collection, Terry Ramsaye Collection, Martin Quigley Collection.

Gettysburg College, Gettysburg, Pennsylvania, Musselman Library. Periodicals Collection.

Harvard University, Graduate School of Business, Baker Library, Historical Collections, Cambridge, Massachusetts: Raff & Gammon Collection & Terry Ramsaye Collection

Henry Ford Museum & Greenfield Village, Dearborn, Michigan; Equipment collection & library, Edison Pioneers Collection

Historic Petersburg Foundation, Inc., Petersburg, Virginia

Library of Congress, Washington, D.C.: Motion Picture, Broadcasting & Recorded Sound Division; Prints & Photographs Division; Newspaper Reading Room; Rare Book Collection; Manuscript Division

Museum of Modern Art, New York, N.Y.: Film Department, American Mutoscope & Biograph Company Collection & Merritt Crawford Papers

National Archives and Records Administration, College Park, Maryland; Washington, D.C..: New York, N.Y.: Patent Records; Federal & District Court Records

National Army Museum, Chelsea, England: William Cox Diaries

Los Angeles County Museum of Natural History, Seaver Center for Western History Research, Los Angeles, California: W.K.L. Dickson Collection; Theisen Film Frame Collection; Van Guisling Collection of American Biograph Co.; Edison Photo Collection

Orange, New Jersey, Public Library: Newspaper Collection

Public Records Office, The National Archive, Kew, England

Sears Merchandising Group, Archives, Hoffman Estates, Illinois

Service des archives du film, Centre national da la cinématographie, Bois d'Arcy, France

Smithsonian Institution; National Museum of American History, Washington, D.C.: Archives Center: Gordon Hendricks Collection

Smithsonian Institution; National Museum of American History, Washington, D.C.: Photographic History: Gordon Hendricks & Eugene Lauste Collection.

Société Jersiaise, Lord Coutanche Library, St. Helier, Jersey, C.I.

Southeast Film and Video Archive, Brighton, England: Emile Lauste Collection.

Stark County District Library, Canton, Ohio: Newspaper Collection; city directories and city histories

University of Iowa Libraries, Iowa City, Iowa, Special Collections Department: Collection of Benjamin Franklin Keith and Edward Franklin Albee

Wayne County Historical Museum, Richmond, Indiana: C. Francis Jenkins, Collection

Books and Articles by W.K.L. Dickson, Antonia Dickson and Lucie Archer Dickson

Cassier's Magazine, November, 1892, pp. 71–74, Miss A. Dickson, "Nine Hundred and Fifty Miles by Telephone" (New York & London, The Cassier Magazine Company)

Cassier's Magazine, November 1892 – December, 1894, A[ntonia] and W. K. L. Dickson, "The Life and Inventions of Edison" (New York & London, The Cassier Magazine Company)

Cassier's Magazine, December 1894, pp. 145–156. Antonia and W. K. L. Dickson, "Edison's Kineto-Phonograph" (New York & London, The Cassier Magazine Company)

The Century Illustrated Monthly Magazine, Vol. XLVIII, No. 2, June, 1894, Antonia and W. K. L. Dickson, "Edison's Invention of the Kineto-Phonograph" (New York, The Century Co., London, T. Fisher Unwin)

Dickson, Antonia & William Kennedy Laurie Dickson, *History of the Kinetograph, Kinetoscope and Kineto-Phonograph* ([New York], Albert Bunn, 1895)

Dickson, Antonia & William Kennedy Laurie Dickson, *The Life and Inventions of Thomas A. Edison* (Boston, T.Y. Crowell & Co., 1894)

Dickson, William Kennedy Laurie, *The Biograph in Battle* (London, T. Fisher Unwin, 1901)

Illustrated War News, Oct., 1899; became *Pearson's Illustrated War News*, Jan. 1900; became *The Illustrated Weekly News*, 14 April 1900; became *The Curiosity Shop*, October 1900. Searched October 1899 – October 1900.

Leslie's Monthly, February, 1895, pp. 245–251. Antonia Dickson, "Wonders of the Kinetoscope"

Leslie's Weekly, March, 1894, pp. 319–320, Mrs. W.K.L. Dickson, "A Reminiscence of Anton Rubenstein"

Phono-Cinema-Revue, No. 2, April, 1908, pp. 4–7, W.K. Laurie Dickson, "Les Origines de la Cinématographie"

Schmid, Christoph von, Lucie Agnes Archer translator, *Rosa von Tannenburg, a Tale* (New York, J. Scott, 1881)

Society of Motion Picture Engineers, *Journal of the Society of Motion Picture Engineers, December, 1933*, pp. 9–16, W.K. Laurie Dickson, "A Brief History of the Kinetograph, the Kinetoscope and the Kineto-phonograph"

The Sun (Baltimore) 20 February 1896. W.K.L. Dickson, "The Roentgen Rays. How They Are Applied in Making Shadowgraphs"

Books:

Abel, Richard, *The Ciné Goes to Town, French Cinema, 1896–1914* (Berkeley, Los Angeles, London, University of California Press, 1994)

Abel, Richard, ed., *Encyclopedia of Early Cinema* (London and New York, Routledge, 2005)

Ackerman, Carl W., *George Eastman* (Boston & New York, Houghton Mifflin, 1930)

Albera, Françoise, Marta Braun & André Gaudreault, eds, *Stop Motion, Fragmentation of Time, Exploring the Roots of Modern Visual Culture; Arrêt sur image, fragmentation du temps, Aux sources de la culture visuelle moderne* (Lausanne, Editions Payot, 2002) Papers presented at the conference of Domitor at La cinémathèque québécoise, Montreal, October, 2000.

American Mutoscope & Biograph Company, *Picture Catalog* (New York, American Mutoscope & Biograph Co., 1902)

Aubert, Michelle & Jean-Claude Seguin, dir., *La Production Cinématographique des Frères Lumière* ([Paris], Bibliothèque du Film, Editions Mémoires de cinéma, 1996)

Baldwin, Neil, *Edison, Inventing the Century* (New York, Hyperion, 1995)

John Barnes, *The Beginnings of the Cinema in England*, [Vol. 1] (London & Vancouver, David & Charles; New York, Barnes & Noble Books/Harper & Row Publishers, 1976); *Vol. 2: 1897* (Exeter, University of Exeter Press, 1996) published as *The Rise of the Cinema in Great Britain: Jubilee Year 1897* (Bishopsgate Press Ltd, 1983); *Vol. 3: 1898* (Exeter, University of Exeter Press, 1996) published as *Pioneers of the British Film 1898: The Rise of the Photoplay* (Bishopsgate Press Ltd., 1988); *Vol. 4: 1899* (Exeter, University of Exeter Press, 1996) published as *Filming the Boer War: 1899* (Bishopsgate Press Ltd., 1992); *Vol. 5: 1900* (Exeter, University of Exeter Press, 1997)

Bitzer, G. W., *Billy Bitzer, His Story* ([New York] Farrar, Straus & Giroux, 1973)

Blum, Daniel, *A Pictorial History of the American Theatre, 1900–1950* (New York, Greenberg: Publisher, 1950)

Boorstin, Daniel J., *The Americans, The National Experience* (New York, Vintage Books, 1965)

Bottomore, Stephen, *I Want to See This Annie Mattygraph, A Cartoon History of the Coming of the Movies*, ([Gemona, Italy] Le Giornate del Cinema Muto, 1995)

Braun, Marta, *Picturing Time, The Work of Étienne-Jules Marey (1830–1904)* (Chicago & London, University of Chicago Press, 1992)

Brayer, Elizabeth, *George Eastman, A Biography* (Baltimore & London, The Johns Hopkins University Press, 1996)

British Mutoscope & Biograph Co., *The War by Biograph* (London, The British Mutoscope and Biograph Co., Ltd., 1900)

Brown, Richard & Barry Anthony, *A Victorian Film Enterprise* (Trowbridge, England, Flicks Books, 1999)

Churchill, Randolph S., *Winston S. Churchill, Vol. I, Youth, 1874–1900* (Boston, Houghton Mifflin Co.; Cambridge, The Riverside Press, 1966)

Churchill, Winston S., *Frontiers and Wars, His Four Early Books Covering His Life as Soldier and War Correspondent*, Edited into one volume (New York, Harcourt Brace & World, Inc., 1962)

Churchill, Winston S., F.W. Heath, ed., *Great Destiny, Sixty Years of the Memorable Events in the Life of the Man of the Century Recounted in His Own Incomparable Words* (New York, G. P. Putnam's Sons, 1965)

Collins, Douglas, *The Story of Kodak* (New York, Harry N. Abrams Inc. 1990)

Conot, Robert, *Thomas A. Edison, A Streak of Luck* (New York, Da Capo Press, Inc., 1979)

Corey, Marie-Sophie, Jacques Malthête, Laurent Mannoni, Jean-Jacques Meusy, *Les première années de la société L. Gaumont et Cie, Correspondance commerciale de Léon Gaumont, 1895–1895* ([Paris] Association français de recherche sur l'histoire du cinéma, Bibliothèque du Film, Gaumont, 1998)

Danner, John, ed. & comp., *Old Landmarks of Canton and Stark County, Ohio* (Logansport, Indiana, B. F. Bowen, 1904)

De Lange, John, *The Anglo-Boer War 1899–1902 on Film* (Pretoria, State Archives Service, 1991) typescript unpublished

Dyer, Frank L. & Thomas Commerford Martin, *Edison: His Life and Inventions* (New York & London, Harper & Brothers, 1910)

Fielding, Raymond, ed., *A Technological History of Motion Pictures and Television* (Berkeley & Los Angeles, University of California Press, 1967)

Font-Réaulx, Dominique de, Thierry Lefebvre & Laurent Mannoni, *E. J. Marey, Actes du colloque du centenaire* (Paris, Arcadia Éditions, 2006) with DVD: *Étienne-Jules Marey, Films chronophotographiques, 1890–1904, Collection de la cinémathèque française*

Gilbert, Martin, *Churchill, A Life* (New York, Henry Holt and Company, 1991)

Ginger, Ray, *Age of Excess, The United States from 1877 to 1914* (New York, Macmillan Publishing Co., 1975 & London, Collier Macmillan Publishers, 1975)

Gutsche, Thelma, *The History and Social Significance of Motion Pictures in South Africa, 1895–1940* (Cape Town, Howard Timmins, 1972)

Heald, Edward Thornton, *The Stark County Story, Vol. II. The McKinley Era, 1875–1901.* (Canton, The Stark County Historical Society, 1950)

Hendricks, Gordon, *Eadweard Muybridge: The Father of the Motion Picture. (New York, Grossman, 1975)*

Hendricks, Gordon, *The Origins of the American Film* (New York, Arno Press & The New York Times, 1972) compiling: Gordon Hendricks, *The Edison Motion Picture Myth* (Berkeley & Los Angeles, University of California Press, 1961); Gordon Hendricks, *The Kinetoscope, America's First Commercially Successful Motion Picture Exhibitor* (New York, The Beginnings of the American Film, 1966) and Gordon Hendricks, *Beginnings of the Biograph* (New York, The Beginnings of the American Film, 1964)

Herbert, Stephen, *Industry, Liberty, and a Vision, Wordsworth Donisthorpe's Kinesigraph* (London, The Projection Box, 1998)

Herbert, Stephen *When The Movies Began, A Chronology of the World's Film Productions and Film Shows Before May, 1896* ([London] The Projection Box, 1994)

Herbert, Stephen & Luke McKernan eds., *Who's Who of Victorian Cinema, A Worldwide Survey* (London, BFI Publishing, 1996)

Holbrook, Stewart H., *The Age of the Moguls* (Garden City, N. Y., Doubleday & Company, Inc., 1954)

Israel, Paul, *Edison, A Life of Invention* (New York, Chichester, Weinheim, Brisbane, Singapore & Toronto, John Wiley & Sons, Inc., 1998)

Jehl, Francis, *Menlo Park Reminiscences, Vol. 2* (Dearborn, The Edison Institute, 1938)

Jenkins, Charles Francis, *Animated Pictures; an Exposition of the Historical Development of Chronophotography* (Washington [Press of H. L. McQueen] 1898)

Jenkins, Charles Francis, *Picture Ribbons: An Exposition of the Methods and Apparatus Employed in the Manufacture of the Picture Ribbons Used in Projecting Lanterns to Give the Appearance of Objects in Motion [by] C. Francis Jenkins* (Washington [Press of H.L. McQueen] 1897)

Jenkins, Reese V., *Images and Enterprise; Technology and the American Photographic Industry, 1839 to 1925* (Baltimore & London, The Johns Hopkins University Press, 1979; reprinted 1987)

Jenkins, Roy, *Churchill, A Biography* (New York, Farrar, Straus & Geroux, 2001)

Jones, Francis Arthur, *Thomas Alva Edison, Sixty Years of an Inventor's Life* (New York, Thomas Y. Crowell & Co., 1907)

Josephson, Matthew, *Edison: A Biography* (New York, Chichester, Brisbane, Toronto, Singapore, John Wiley & Sons, Inc., 1959) Reprinted in 1992.

Leech, Margaret [Margaret Leech Pulitzer], *In the Days of McKinley* (New York, Harper & Brothers, 1959)

Lefebvre, Thierry, Jacques Malthête & Laurent Mannoni, *Lettres d'Étienne-Jules Marey à Georges Demenÿ, 1880–1894* ([Paris] Association française de recherche l'histoire du cinéma, Bibliothèque du Film, 1999)

Mannoni, Laurent, *Étienne-Jules Marey, la mémoire de l'oeil* ([Paris] & Milan, Cinémathèque française & Edizioni Gabriele Mazzotta, 1999)

Mannoni, Laurent, Donata Pesenti Capagnoni, David Robinson, *Light and Movement* ([Gemona, Italy] Le Giornate del Cinema Muto, 1995)

Marshall, David Trumbull, *Recollections of Edison* (Boston, The Christopher Publishing House [1931])

Mathews, Nancy Mowell with Charles Musser, *Moving Pictures, American Art and Early Film, 1880–1910* (Williamstown, Mass., Williams College Museum of Art, 2005) Exhibit catalog.

Meadowcroft, William H., *The Boy's Life of Edison* (New York & London, Harper & Brothers Publishers, MCMXI)

Merritt Crawford Papers (Cinema History Microfilm Series, University Publications of America, 1986)

Meusy, Jean-Jacques, *Paris-Palaces, ou le temps des cinémas (1894–1918)* (Paris, CNRS Éditions, 1995)

Millard, Andre, *Edison and the Business of Innovation* (Baltimore & London, The Johns Hopkins University Press, 1990)

Morgan, H. Wayne, *William McKinley and His America* (Syracuse, N.Y., Syracuse University Press, 1963)

Musser, Charles, *Edison Motion Pictures, 1890–1900, An annotated Filmography* ([Washington & Gemona, Italy] Smithsonian Institution Press & Le Giornate del Cinema Muto, 1997)

Musser, Charles, *The Emergence of Cinema: The American Screen to 1907; History of the American Cinema, Vol. 1* (New York, Charles Scribner's Sons; Toronto, Collier Macmillan Canada; New York, Oxford, Singapore, Sydney, Maxwell Macmillan International, 1990)

Musser, Charles, *Thomas Edison and His Kinetographic Motion Pictures* (New

Brunswick, New Jersey, Rutgers University Press & Friends of Edison National Historic Site, 1995)

Musser, Charles, ed., *Thomas A. Edison Papers, A Guide to Motion Picture Catalogs by American Producers and Distributors, 1894–1908, A Microfilm Edition* (Frederick, Maryland, University Publications of America, 1985)

Nasaw, David, *Going Out, The Rise and Fall of Public Amusements* (Cambridge, Mass., London, England, Harvard University Press, 1993)

Newhall, Beaumont, *The History of Photography* (New York, The Museum of Modern Art, 1982; Dist. By Bulfinch Press/Little, Brown & Co.)

Niver, Kemp R., comp. & Bebe Bergsten, ed., *Biograph Bulletins 1896–1908* (Los Angeles, Locare Research Group, 1971)

Niver, Kemp R., *The First Twenty Years, A Segment of Film History* (Los Angeles, Locare Research Group, 1968)

Pakenham, Thomas, *The Boer War* (New York, Random House, 1979)

Phillips, Ray, *Edison's Kinetoscope and Its Films, A History to 1896; Contributions to the Study of Popular Culture, No. 65* (Westport, Connecticut, Greenwood Press, 1997)

Pinel, Vincent, *Louis Lumière, inventeur et cinéaste* (Paris, Éditions Nathan, 1994)

Pratt, George C., *Spellbound in Darkness, A History of the Silent Film* (Greenwich, Connecticut, New York Graphic Society Ltd., 1973

Pursell, Carroll W., Jr., ed. *Technology in America, A History of Individuals and Ideas*, 2nd ed. (Cambridge, Mass. & London, The MIT Press, 1996)

Ramsaye, Terry, *A Million and One Nights* (New York, Simon and Schuster, 1926, 3d printing, 1964)

Rawlence, Christopher, *The Missing Reel* (London & New York, Penguin Books, 1992)

Rich, Norman, *The Age of Nationalism and Reform, 1850–1890* (New York & London, W. S. Norton & Company, 1977)

Rittaud-Hutinet, Jacques, ed. with Yvelise Dentzer, Maurice Trarieux-Lumière, *Letters, Auguste and Louis Lumière* (London, Boston, Faber & Faber, 1994) Translation, Pierre Hodgson

Rossell, Deac, *Ottomar Anschütz and His Electrical Wonder* (London, The Projection Box, 1997)

Schlereth, Thomas J., *Victorian America, Transformations in Everyday Life, 1876–1915* (New York, Harper Collins Publishers, 1992)

Smith, Albert, *Two Reels and a Crank* (Garden City, N. Y., Doubleday & Co., Inc., 1952)

Svejda, George J., *The "Black Maria" Site Study, Edison National Historic Site, West Orange, New Jersey* ([Washington, DC] National Park Service, 1969)

Tate, Alfred O., *Edison's Open Door* (New York, E.P. Dutton & Co., Inc, 1938)

Thomas A. Edison Papers Microfilm, Part II (1879–1886), (Frederick, Maryland, University Publications of America, 1987) and on line, edited by Rutgers University

Reference books:

Arthur M. Schlesinger, Jr., ed., *The Almanac of American History* (New York, Barnes & Noble Books, 1993)

Savada, Elias, comp., *The American Film Institute Catalog of Motion Pictures Produced in the United States, Film Beginnings, 1893–1910* A work in progress (Metuchen, NJ & London, The Scarecrow Press, Inc., 1995)

The American Heritage Dictionary of the English Language (New York, American Heritage Publishing Co., Inc. & Houghton Mifflin Co. 1969)

Annual Report of the Commissioner of Patents. With Index of U.S. Patents. 1896–1935 (Washington, Government Printing Office)

Perkins, George, Barbara Perkins & Phillip Leininger, eds., *Benét's Reader's Encyclopedia of American Literature* (New York, Harper Collins Publishers, 1991)

British Press & Jersey Times Almanac, 1873–1879 ([St. Helier, Jersey, C.I.])

Canton City Directory, 1881–1883 (Canton, Ohio, C.C. Thompson Book and Job Printer, 1881.)

Canton City Directory, 1893–1894 (Akron, Ohio, Burch Directory)

Canton Official City Directory, 1895–1925 (Akron, Ohio, Burch Directory)

Chambers Biographical Dictionary, sixth edition (New York, Larousse Kingfisher Chambers Inc., 1997)

Directory of the City of Canton, 1886–1887 (Canton, The Canton News Co.)

Electrical Trades Directory 1900–1923 also titled: *The Electrician: Electrical Trades Directory and Handbook* (London, the Institution of Electrical Engineers & "The Electrician" Printing & Publishing Co., Ltd.)

Encyclopaedia Britannica, 2001 Standard Edison CD-ROM

Richard B. Morris, ed., *Encyclopedia of American History* (New York, Harper & Brothers Publishers, 1953)

Jackson, Kenneth T., ed., *The Encyclopedia of New York City* (New York, The New York Historical Society & New Haven & London, Yale University Press, 1995)

The Evening Post Almanac, 1929 & 1930 (St. Helier, Jersey, C.I.)

John Bartlett *Familiar Quotations*, 11the ed. (Boston, Little Brown & Co., 1938)

Film Daily Yearbook, 1933 (New York, The Film Daily)

The Illustrated Official Journal (Patents) Index, 1894–1944 (London, The Patents Office)

The Jersey Directory and Express Almanac, 1928–1930 ([St. Helier], J. T. Bigwood Ltd., State's Printers, Jersey, C.I.)

Journal of the Institution of Electrical Engineers, 1900–1920 (London, E & F. N. Spon, Ltd. & New York, Spon & Chamberlain).

Kelly's Directory of Richmond 1908–1930 & 1932 (London, Kelly's Directories)

Kelly's London Suburbs 1919–1922 & 1927 (London, Kelly's Directories)

Kelly's Post Office London Directory, 1900–1917 (London, Kelly's Directories)

Kelly's Richmond, Kew, Twickenham, Isleworth, St. Margaret's Petersham, Mortlake, Sheen & Teddington Directory, 1914–1920, (London, Kelly's Directories)

Kelly's Wandsworth, Putney, Barnes, 1920 (London, Kelly's Directories)

Larousse Illustrated International Encyclopedia and Dictionary (New York, World Publishing, 1972)

London [England] Telephone Directory, 1903–1904

Harris, William H. & Judith S. Levey, eds., *The New Columbia Encyclopedia* (New York & London, Columbia University Press, 1974)

Danner, John, ed., *Old Landmarks of Canton and Stark County, Ohio, Vol II.* . (Logansport, Indiana, B.F. Bowen, 1904)

Drabble, Margaret, ed., *The Oxford Companion to English Literature, 5th ed.* (Oxford, New York, Tokyo, Melbourne, Oxford University Press, 1985

[Voter] *Register of Parliamentary Borough of Strand, City of Westminster, 1908–1915*

Richmond & Twickenham Times, 1937 & 1938 ([Richmond upon Thames, England])

Roberts' Directory of the City of Canton, 1883–84 (Canton, The Roberts News Co, [April, 1883]

Heald, Edward T[hornton], *The Stark County Story, As Told in Radio Broadcasts and prepared as a Stark County History with bibliography and index,* 4 Vols. (Canton, Ohio, The Stark County Historical Society)

Survey of London, XLI, 1893 (London, English Heritage)

Twickenham Register of Electors for 1919 & 1920 (London Borough of Richmond upon Thames)

U.S. Patent Office Annual Report 1900–1920 ([Washington, DC] U. S. Government Printing Office)

Webster's Biographical Dictionary, 1ˢᵗ Edition (Springfield, Mass, G. & C. Merriam Co., 1963)

The Year-Book of Photography and Photographic News Almanac for 1891 & 1892 (London, Piper & Carter, 5 Furnival St. E.C.) .

Walls, Howard Lamarr, *Motion Pictures, 1894–1912 Identified from the Records of the United States Copyright Office* ([Washington, DC] Copyright Office, Library of Congress, 1953)

Periodicals and brochures:

The Age of Movement ([London, The International Mutoscope Syndicate, 1902?])

The American Journal of Photography, [1890], pp. 385–88, Robert S. Redfield, "The Photographic Society of Philadelphia" (re. Demonstration by Eastman Kodak)

Anthony's Photographic Bulletin, Vol. XIX, No. 21, 10 November 1888, pp. 641–642, "A Practical Substitute for Glass in Photograph."

The Biograph and Mutoscope Up to Date, Vol. 1, No. 1, October 1897. (New York, American Mutoscope Co.)

Black and White, 3 February 1900, p. 186 "The Battle of Colenso"; 4 August 1900, p. 198; "A Future King at Play"; 5 January 1901, pp. 12–13, "Lord Roberts at Work" ; 1 June 1901, p. 299, "The Experiences of Biograph Operators"; 9 February 1901, p. [178] "Black and White, Queen Memorial Number" (London, The Black and White Publishing Company, Limited)

Black and White Budget, 1 June 1901, pp. 297–300, Pat Brooklyn,"Biograph Operators; Some of the Risks They Run" (London, The Black and White Publishing Company, Limited)

Bohemian Magazine, September 1908, pp. 357–366, John R. Meader, "The Story of the Picture That Moves"

The British Journal of Photography, various dates, 1896–1907; 30 June 1899, p. 406, "Pope Leo XIII and Photography" (London, H. Greenwood)

The Brooklyn Daily Eagle, 14 June 1888, "Amateur Photographers. An Interesting Meeting at the Residence of George S. Wheeler." (About W.G. Levison); *Supplement, February 3, 1899*, "The Biograph in the Vatican"

California Historical Quarterly, Vol. LIV, No. 2, Summer 1975, pp. 125–138, Geoffrey Bell, "The First Picture Show"

Canton [Ohio] Repository, 1896–1898

Cassell's Family Magazine, September 1894, pp. 798–799, "Edison's Kineto-Phonograph"; July 1897, pp. 327–330, John Munro, "Living Photographs of the Queen"

Cassier's Magazine, Vol. IV, No. 22, August 1893, pp. 243–256, John Birkinbine, "From Mine to Furnace, Second Paper."; January 1894, pp. 267–271,

Edward P. Thompson, "Protection of Industrial Property."; Vol. XI, No. 5, March 1897, pp. 378–386, Nikola Tesla, "The Age of Electricity."; Vol. XIII, No. 6, April 1898, pp. 525–528, George Ethelbert Walsh, "Inventing for a Living; Vol. XIV, No. 1, May 1898, E.H. Mullin, "A Short Talk on Patents."

The Catholic World, Vol. LXVIII, January 1899, pp. 435–[442], Rev. George McDermot, C.S.P., "The Papacy in the Nineteenth Century." (With illustrations by American Mutoscope Co.)

Chambers's Journal, 1901, pp. 55–56, "Antonia Kennedy-Laurie Dickson". (London, Chambers [Publishing Co.]) (obituary tribute)

Cinema, April–December 1930, Merritt Crawford "Men in the Movie Vanguard" series, April 1930, pp. 29–31 & 61–62, "Leroy, Who Took Motion Pictures Out of the Peep-box and Put Them on the Screen"; May 1930, pp. 29–31 & 60, II. "Eugene Augustin Lauste, Father of the Sound-Film"; June 1930, pp. 28–30 & 59–60, III "Étienne-Jules Marey and Eadweard Muybridge, Inventors of Chrono-Photography, the Progenitor of the Modern Cinema"; September 1930, pp. 29–30 & 54–56, IV. "William Friese-Greene–England's Great Cinematographer"; October 1930, pp. 27–30 & 56, V. "Georges Méliès–The Jules Verne of the Cinema"; December 1930, pp. 28–31, VI "Louis Aimé Augustin Le Prince, A Mystery of the Motion Picture's Beginnings" (New York, Cinema Magazine)

Comptes Rendus, Vol. 94, Session of 5 April 1882, pp. 909–911, "Notes by M. J. Janssen on 'The Principle of a New Photographic Revolver'" (translation at EHS); Vol. 107, [1888], p. 607, M. Marey, "Physiological Technics. - Modifications of Photo-Chronography for the Analysis of Movements Executed in Place by an Animal." (English translation at EHS); Vol. 111, November 3, 1890, p. 626, M. Marey, "Physiological Technics. Photo-Chronographic Applicable to the Analysis of all Sorts of Movements." (English translation at EHS)

Cosmopolitan Magazine, April 1889, pp. 598–607. Horace Townsend, "Edison, His Work and His Work-Shop"

1895, Revue de l'association française de recherche sur l'histoire du cinéma, The Will Day Historical Collection of Cinematograph & Moving Picture Equipment ([Paris & Gemona] Bibliothèque du film, Centre national de la cinématographie & Le Giornate del Cinema Muto, October 1997)

The Electrical Engineer, [24 June 1891] p. 708, "The Edison Kinetograph"

The Electrical World, 16 June 1894, pp. 799–[801], "The Kineto-Phonograph"

Film History, Vol. 7, No. 2, Summer 1995, pp. 115–236, Deac Rossell, "A Chronology of Cinema"; Vol. 16, No. 1, 2004, pp. 28–36.Richard Brown, "War on the Home Front: The Anglo-Boer War and the Growth of Rental in Britain. An Economic Perspective." (John Libbey: UK, *Film History*)

The Guardian (Manchester), 18 August 2001 review of Simon Hoggart ,"Suburban Hymn" a new book (www.guardian.co.uk/travel/2001)

Harper's Weekly, 13 June 1891, pp. 440–441, George Parsons Lathrop, "Edison's Kinetograph"; Vol. XXXVIII, 24 March 1894, p. 280,. Barnet Phillips "The Record of a Sneeze"

International Mutoscope Syndicate, *The Age of Movement* (London, The International Mutoscope Syndicate, [1901])

Jersey Morning News, 1 November 1933, "Jersey Guild of Science Lecture, Talk on the Birth of the Cinematograph"([St. Helier, Jersey, C.I.])

The Journal of Photographic Science, Vol. 3, 1955, pp. 33–40, Beaumont Newhall, "The Photographic Inventions of George Eastman."

The Journal of the Franklin Institute, December 1888, pp. 478–482, John Carbutt, "A Perfect Substitute for Glass as a Support for Gelatine Bromide of Silver for Use in Photography" (Philadelphia, Pennsylvania, The Franklin Institute)

The Kinematograph and Lantern Weekly, September 1907, p. 325; 8 July 1909, pp. 398–399, "Who Invented the Kinematograph? Mr. Friese-Greene Chats With 'Stroller'"

Kodak Milestones (Rochester, NY, Eastman Kodak Company [1958])

Leisure Hour [London, 1891], pp. 711–712, "Notes on Current Science, Invention, and Discovery. Edison's Latest Invention: The Kinetograph."

The Literary Digest, Vol. IX, No. 12, 21 July 1894, p. 14 (344) "The Kineto-Phonograph"; Vol. X., No. 4, 24 November 1894, p. (105) 15, "Mechanism of the Kineto-Phonograph" (Translated from La Nature, 20 October 1984)

Motion Picture News, 5 July 1930, pp. 22 & 24, "Did Edison Invent Pictures? Big Row Reaches Boiling Point, but Cools Off"

The Moving Picture News, 3 December 1910, pp. 11–13 & 18, "Patents Company vs. Steiner" (testimony of William Friese-Greene); Vol. IV, No. 4, 28 January 1911, pp. 6–8, Francis Jenkins, "Trust vs. Independents"; Vol. VI, No. 7, 17 August 1912, p. 23, "When C. Francis Jenkins Invented the Moving Picture Show"

Moving Picture World, Vol. 1, No. 1, 9 March 1907, p. 4, "Edison vs. American Mutoscope and Biograph Company"; Vol. 1, No. 2, pp. 21–23, "Edison vs. Biograph" (decision from U.S. Circuit Court of Appeals); Vol. 1, No. 42, 21 December 1907, pp. 679–680, Frank L. Dyer, "Edison's Place in the Moving Picture Art."; Vol. 18, 11 October 1913, p. 143, "Goodwin vs. Eastman. T.H. Blair, a Pioneer, Throws Interesting Historic Side Lights."; Vol. 21, 8 August 1914, p. 815, "Goodwin Company Files New Suits, Declares It Is Anxious to Preserve Its Rights During the Life of Its Patent."; 15 July 1916, p. 418, "C. Francis Jenkins Tells of the First Projector, Made a Crude Machine That Was Used in 1894–Was Joined by Thomas Armat in Perfecting the Device". 26 March 1927, pp. 289–300, Charles Edward Hastings, "Cinematic Beginning"; (New York, The Chalmers Publishing Company)

Meusy, Jean-Jacques and Paul Spehr "Les débuts en France de l'American Mutoscope and Biograph Company (Paris, *Histoire Economie et Société*, No. 4, 1997), pp. 671–708 also published as "L'Esordio in Francia dell'American Mutoscope and Biograph Company/The Beginnings of the American Mutoscope and Biograph Co. in France" (Gemona, Italy, *Griffithiana*, N. 62/63, May 1998, pp. 128–169.

The National Police Gazette, Summer–Fall 1894; 22 September 1894, p. 1 "Knocked Out by Corbett"; 24 November 1894, pp. 1 & 7, "Limbs and Lenses, A Gathering of London Gaiety Girls Invade Wizard Edison's Laboratory at Orange, N.J., and Give an Exposition of Their Dances Before the Kinetoscope (New York, Police Gazette Publishing House)

La Nature, 14 December 1878, pp. 23–25, "Les Allures du Cheval, Représentées par la photographie instantanée."; No. 492, 4 November 1882, "The Projecting Praxinoscope" (English translation at EHS)

New York Herald, 28 May 1891, "Wizard Thomas Edison Weds Light to Sound"; 12 July 1903, p. 8, William J. Sparks, "Under Fire With a Moving Picture Camera, Dangers and Adventures of an Operator in the Boer War"

The Nickelodeon, Vol. II, No. 2, August 1909, pp. 43–47, Austin Sherrillo, "Important Motion Picture Patents"; Vol. II, No. 3, September 1909, pp. 77–82; Austin Sherrillo, "Important Motion Picture Patents"; Vol. II, No. 4, October 1909, Austin Sherrillo, "Important Motion Picture Patents"

The Optical Magic Lantern Journal and Photographer Enlarger, 1 April 1890, "Photoramic Camera" (about William Friese-Greene)

The Orange [NJ] Chronicle 1893

The Orange [NJ] Journal 1889–1890

Pearson's Magazine, Vol. VI, July–December 1898, pp. 386–391, Mary Spencer Warren, "The Daily Life of the Pope."; Vol. IX, Jan–June 1900, pp. 166–172, Maj. Arthur Griffiths, "A British Army Corps at the Front" (London, C. Arthur Pearson Ltd.)

Pearsons's Weekly, 1897–1899 (London, C. Arthur Pearson Ltd.)

The Penny Pictorial Magazine, 1900–1901; 17 February 1900, pp. 512–[515], Lillian Joy, Photographing the Pope. How His Holiness Pope Leo XIII. Sat for the Mutoscope. An Interview With the Photographer. Photographs by the Mutoscope and Biograph Co."

The Philadelphia Photographer [1887], pp. 328–330, Dr. F. Stolze, "Anschütz's Motion Pictures and the Stroboscopic Disk" (translation from *Photographische Wochenblatt*, 17 March 1887)

The Phonogram, a Monthly Magazine Devoted to the Science of Sound and Recording of Speech 1891–1893 ; October 1892, pp. 217–220, "The Kinetograph. A New Industry Heralded" (New York, The National Phonograph Publishing Co., Ltd.)

The Phonoscope, A Monthly Journal Devoted to Scientific and Amusement Inventions Appertaining to Sound and Sight, 1896–1900. (New York, The Phonoscope Publishing Co.)

The Photographic Journal, July 1926, pp. 359–362, Will Day, "Claims to Motion-Picture Invention; Great Britain: William Friese-Greene"

The Photographic Times, January 1895, pp. 22–26, "The Kinetograph, The Kinetoscope, and the Kinetophonograph"; May 1896, pp. 222–226, C. Francis Jenkins, "The Photoscope. A Method and Apparatus for Recording and Reproducing Action." (Extract from paper read before the Franklin Institute, 18 December 1895); Vol. XXVIII, No. 10, October 1896, pp. 449–454, C. Francis Jenkins, "The Development of Chronophotography"; Vol. XXX, No. 7, July 1898, pp. 289–297, C. Francis Jenkins, "Animated Pictures" (New York, N.Y., Photographic Times Publishing Assn.)

The Photographic Times and American Photographer, 16 August 1889, pp. 414–415, "The Eastman Transparent Flexible Film."

Photographic World, Number 75, December 1995, pp. 23–26, Colin Harding, "Celluloid and Photography, Part One, Celluloid as a Substitute for Glass; Number 76, March 1996, pp. 34–36, Colin Harding, "Celluloid and Photography, Part Two - The Development of Celluloid Rollfilm"; Number 77, June 1996, pp. 7–11, Colin Harding, "Celluloid and Photography, Part Three - The Beginnings of Cinema"

Photography (London), 24 May 1894, pp. 332–333, "Edison's Kinetograph"; 1 November 1894, pp. 696–[697];"Edison's Kinetoscope in England"; 27 February 1896, p. 143, "The Cinematographe"

Punch's Almanack for 1879, 9 December 1878. "Edison's Telephonoscope (Transmits Light as Well as Sound)" ([London, Punch Publications Ltd., 1878])

Revue générale des sciences pures et appliquées, 2 Année, No. 21, 15 November 1891, pp. 689–719, E.J. Marey, "La chronophotographie, nouvelle méthode pour analyser le mouvement dans les sciences physiques et naturelles"

Reynolds's Illustrated News, 7 October 1934, "Shining Movie Lights Were Not All American, Protest to Premier About a Talkie"

The Richmond and Twickenham Times, 6 October 1934, "Edison's First Talkie, Twickenham Man's Part in Far-reaching Invention"; 3 October 1935, "Death of Mr. W.K. Laurie-Dickson" (Richmond, Surrey, England)

Richmond Times, 13 October 1934 "The First Film, Mr. W. K. Laurie-Dickson and Rival Claims." (Richmond, Surrey, England)

Royal Magazine, April 1901, pp. 120–128, H.L. Adam's article, "Round the World for the Biograph" (London, C.A. Pearson, Ltd.)

The St. Louis and Canadian Photographer, 1893–1896; January 1893, pp. 40–41, "Films Were Faulty" (re: Eastman celluloid); pp. 63–64, "Electrical Wonders" (re. Anschütz); February 1893, p. 139, "A Clergyman is Now the Owner of the Celluloid Film Patent" (re. Hannibal Goodwin); May 1893, p. 207, "A Kodak Victory." (St. Louis, Mo., St. Louis Photographic Publishing Co.)

Scientific American, 19 October 1878, p. 241, "A Horse's Motion Scientifically Determined"; 13 September 1879, p. 161, "Rapid Photographing"; 25 June 1880, p. 353, "Muybridge's Zoogyroscope"; 9 September 1882, "The Photographing of Motion"; 29 January 1887, p. 69, Samuel P. Sadtler, "Celluloid"; 20 June 1891, p. 393. "Edison's Kinetograph and Cosmical Telephone"; 31 October 1896, pp. [330]–331, "The Kinetoscope Stereopticon." (re: C. Francis Jenkin's Phantoscope); 1 May 1897, p. 281, "A Novel Chronophotographic Camera" (re: C. Francis Jenkins); 22 May 1897, p. 327, "The Development of Kinetograph Films."; 26 June 1897, p. 405, "The Lumière Cinematograph Camera"; August 1927, Milton Wright, "Successful Inventors–VIII, They Seek More Than Money Says One of Them" (re: C. Francis Jenkins)

Scientific American Supplement, No. 158, 11 January 1879, pp. 2509–2510, "A Horse's Motion Scientifically Considered"; No. 188, 9 August 1879, p. 2991, "The Zoetrope. Action of Animals in Motion"; No. 317, 28 January 1882, pp. 5058–5059, "Mr. Muybridge's Photographs of Animals in Motion"; No. 343, 29 July 1882, pp. 5469–5470, "The Attitudes of Animals in Motion. By Mr. Muybridge."; No. 334, 27 May 1882, p. 5328, "Instantaneous Photographs."' No. 336, 10 June 1882, pp. 5351–5353, "The Photographic Gun"; No. 579, 5 February 1887, pp. 9243–8246, "E.J. Marey, "Photography of Moving Objects, and the Study of Animal Movement by Chrono-Phography."; No. 644, 5 May 1888, pp. 10291–10292, Flexible Substitutes for Photographic Plates"; No. 746, 19 April 1890, p. 11921"A Machine Camera Taking Ten Photographs a Second". (About Friese-Greene); No. 784, 10 January 1891, pp. 12532–12533, "Locomotion in Water Studied by Photography" (about E.J. Marey)

Sight and Sound, Vol. 52, No. 4., Autumn 1988, pp. 260–265. Stephen Bottomore, "Joseph Rosenthal: The Most Glorious Profession"; Vol. 59, No. 3, Summer 1990, pp. 194–197, Barry Anthony, "Shadows of Early Films"

The Sketch, a Journal of Art and Actuality, 1897–1899; 18 October 1894, pp. 562–563, "How War-Correspondents Work" 20 September 1899, pp. 388 & 389, H. Chance Newton, "'King John', at Her Majesty's"; 27 September 1899, p. 413, (photographs of "King John") (London)

Société française de photographie, *Bulletin de la Société française de photographie*, 1886, pp. 46–51, M. Balagny, "Emploi des Plaques Souples en Photographie"; 1888, pp. 303–304, M. Davanne, "L'Électro-Tachyscope de M. Ottomar Anschütz, a Lissa (Poméranie); 1889, pp. 47–48, M. Nadar, "Le Kodak, Appareil a Main"; 1890, pp. 329–332, M. Marey, "Appareil Photochronographique Applicable a l'Analyse de Toutes Sortes de Mouvements"; 1892, pp. 123–130, M. Demenÿ & M. E. Cousin, "La Chronophotographie" 1893, pp. 21–26, M. Marey, "Le Mouvement du Coeur Étudeié par la Chronophotographie; pp. 598–603, M. Marey, "Étude Chronophotographique des Différents Genres de Locomotion Ches les Animaux"; 1894, pp. 480–487, "Le Cinéto-Phonographe d'Édison"; 1895, pp. 505–517. M.A. Gay, "Le Cinématographe de MM. Auguste et Louis Lumière" (Paris, Gauthier-Villars)

Society of Motion Picture Engineers, *Journal of the Society of Motion Picture Engineers*, September, October 1919, pp. 36–49, C. Francis Jenkins, "History of the Motion Picture"; 1925, pp. 23–41*, F.H. Richardson, "What Happened in the Beginning"; January 1931, pp. 172–173, Merritt Crawford, "Some Accomplishments of Eugene Augustin Lauste–Pioneer Sound-Film Inventor"; July 1931, pp. 76–83* E. Kilburn Scott, "Career of L.A.A. LePrince"; October 1931, pp. 71–74, Merritt Crawford, "Pioneer Experiments of Eugene Lauste in Recording Sound"; March 1933, pp. 118–119*, Earl Theisen, "The History of Nitrocellulose as a Film Base"; March 1935, pp. 241–256*, Thomas Armat, "My Part in the Development of the Motion Picture Projector; December 1936, pp. 640–647, Louis Lumière, "The Lumière Cinematograph" [*page numbers from Raymond Fielding, *A Technological History of Motion Pictures and Television* (Berkeley & Los Angeles, University of California Press, 1967)

Society of Motion Picture and Television Engineers, *Journal of the Society of Motion Picture and Television Engineers, Vol. 63, 1954*, pp. 134–137. C.E. Kenneth Mees, "History of Professional Black-and-White Motion-Picture Film"; Vol. 99, No. 8, August 1990, pp. 652–661, John Belton, "The Origins of 35mm Film as a Standard"

The Sun (New York) 28 May 1891, p. [1] "The Kinetograph. Edison's Latest and Most Surprising Device. Pure Motion Recorded and Reproduced. Voice and Action Both Caught in His Compound Machine."

Thames Valley (England) Times, 2 October 1935 (W.K.L. Dickson obituary)

The Times (London), 1899–1901

Variety, 9 October 1935, "W.K. Laurie-Dickson" (obituary)

War Pictures 1900 (London, C. Arthur Pearson Ltd)

Wilson's Photographic Magazine, July 1889, p. 409, "The Development of Carbutt's Flexible Film"; 17 August 1889, p. 510, Fred K. Morrill, "Chicago Camera Club." (Re. demonstration of Eastman's celluloid); 1889, pp. 529–532, "Wednesday, 7 August 1889, Third Session (Evening) (meeting of New York photo society)

The Year-Book of Photography and Photographic News Almanac, 1891, pp. 58–59, W.K. Burton & C.F. Japan, "Eikonogen; pp. 68–69, The Eikonogen Developer"; pp. 96–97, Henri van Heurck, "Photo-Micrography in 1890"; pp. 183–184, "The Rollable Flexible Film" (Eastman celluloid); pp. 217–218, "Photographs at the Rate of One Hundred per Second"; pp. 218–220, "Anschütz Photographs the Larger Wild Beasts"; *1892*, pp. 117–118, "Dr. Marey's Chrono-Photographic Apparatus"; pp. 139–142, "The Analysis of Movement by Photography"; [1895] pp. 274–277, "Edison's Kinetoscope"

Other:

DVD: Kino Video and Museum of Modern Art in cooperation with the Library of Congress, *Edison, The Invention of the Movies*, Curators, Steven Higgins and Charles Musser, Producer, Bret Wood

Exhibit: *Étienne-Jules Marey, Le Mouvement en Lumière*. 13 January – 19 March 2000, Fondation Eléctricité de France & Cinémathèque Française, Paris, France. Curator, Laurent Mannoni

Exhibit: *Freeze Frame, Eadweard Muybridge's Photography of Motion* 7 October 2000 – 15 March 2001, Documentary Photography Gallery, National Museum of American History, Smithsonian Institution, Washington, D.C. Curator, Marta Braun.

Exhibit: Moving Pictures, American Art and Early Film, 1880–1910. Williams College Museum of Art, Williamstown, Massachusetts, 16 July 2005 – 11 December 2005. Curator, Nancy Mowell Mathews

Index

Guide for Index: assoc = associate; asst = assistant; atty = attorney; bd = board; exec = executive; secy = secretary; EGE = Edison General Electric Co; illus = illustration; mgr = manager; m pic = motion picture (films from this era were subject to frequent title changes: as a rule, the titles used are as they appear in the text); phono = phonograph; rel = relative; rep = representative; secy = secretary; SMPE = Society of Motion Picture Engineers; TAE = Thomas Alva Edison; WKLD = William Kennedy Laurie Dickson.